DATE DUE

DEMCO 128-5046

Children's Literature Review

Guide to Gale Literary Criticism Series

When you need to review criticism of literary works, these are the Gale series to use:

If the author's death date is:

You should turn to:

After Dec. 31, 1959
(or author is still living)

CONTEMPORARY LITERARY CRITICISM

for example: Jorge Luis Borges, Anthony Burgess,
William Faulkner, Mary Gordon,
Ernest Hemingway, Iris Murdoch

1900 through 1959

TWENTIETH-CENTURY LITERARY CRITICISM

for example: Willa Cather, F. Scott Fitzgerald,
Henry James, Mark Twain, Virginia Woolf

1800 through 1899

NINETEENTH-CENTURY LITERATURE CRITICISM

for example: Fyodor Dostoevsky, Nathaniel Hawthorne,
George Sand, William Wordsworth

1400 through 1799

LITERATURE CRITICISM FROM 1400 TO 1800
(excluding Shakespeare)

for example: Anne Bradstreet, Daniel Defoe,
Alexander Pope, François Rabelais,
Jonathan Swift, Phillis Wheatley

SHAKESPEAREAN CRITICISM

Shakespeare's plays and poetry

Antiquity through 1399

CLASSICAL AND MEDIEVAL LITERATURE CRITICISM

for example: Dante, Homer, Plato, Sophocles, Vergil,
the Beowulf Poet

Gale also publishes related criticism series:

CHILDREN'S LITERATURE REVIEW

This series covers authors of all eras who have written for the preschool through high school audience.

SHORT STORY CRITICISM

This series covers the major short fiction writers of all nationalities and periods of literary history.

POETRY CRITICISM

This series covers poets of all nationalities and periods of literary history.

ISSN 0362-4145

volume 27

Children's Literature Review

Excerpts from Reviews,
Criticism, and Commentary
on Books for Children
and Young People

Gerard J. Senick
Editor

Sharon R. Gunton
Associate Editor

 **Gale Research Inc.** • DETROIT • LONDON

STAFF

Gerard J. Senick, *Editor*

Sharon R. Gunton, *Associate Editor*

Jeanne A. Gough, *Permissions & Production Manager*
Linda M. Pugliese, *Production Supervisor*
Paul Lewon, Maureen A. Puhl, Camille Robinson, Jennifer VanSickle, *Editorial Associates*
Donna Craft, Brandy C. Johnson, Sheila Walencewicz, *Editorial Assistants*

Maureen Richards, *Research Supervisor*
Mary Beth McElmeel, *Editorial Associate*
Daniel J. Jankowski, Julie Karmazin, Tamara C. Nott, Julie Synkonis, *Editorial Assistants*

Sandra C. Davis, *Permissions Supervisor* (*Text*)
Maria Franklin, Josephine M. Keene, Denise M. Singleton, Kimberly F. Smilay, *Permissions Associates*
Michele M. Lonoconus, Shelly Rakcozy, Shalice Shah, *Permissions Assistants*

Margaret A. Chamberlain, *Permissions Supervisor* (*Pictures*)
Pamela A. Hayes, *Permissions Associate*
Amy Lynn Emrich, Karla Kulkis, Nancy Rattenbury, Keith Reed, *Permissions Assistants*

Mary Beth Trimper, *Production Manager*
Mary Winterhalter, *Production Assistant*

Arthur Chartow, *Art Director*
C. J. Jonik, *Keyliner*

Since this page cannot legibly accommodate all the copyright notices, the acknowledgments constitutes an extension of the copyright notice.

While every effort has been made to ensure the reliability of the information presented in this publication, Gale Research Inc. neither guarantees the accuracy of the data contained herein nor assumes any responsibility for errors, omissions, or discrepancies. Gale accepts no payment for listing; and inclusion in the publication of any organization, agency, institution, publication, service, or individual does not imply endorsement of the editors or publisher. Errors brought to the attention of the publisher and verified to the satisfaction of the publisher will be corrected in future editions.

The paper used in this publication meets the minimum requirements of American National Standard for Information Sciences—Permanence Paper for Printed Library Materials, ANSI Z39.48-1984.

Library of Congress Catalog Card Number 76-643301
ISBN 0-8103-5700-3
ISSN 0362-4145

Printed in the United States of America

Published simultaneously in the United Kingdom
by Gale Research International Limited
(An affiliated company of Gale Research Inc.)

Contents

v

Preface

Children's literature has evolved into both a respected branch of creative writing and a successful industry. Currently, books for young readers are considered the most popular segment of publishing, while criticism of juvenile literature is instrumental in recording the literary or artistic development of the creators of children's books as well as the trends and controversies that result from changing values or attitudes about young people and their literature. Designed to provide a permanent, accessible record of this ongoing scholarship, *Children's Literature Review* (*CLR*) presents parents, teachers, and librarians—those responsible for bringing children and books together—with the opportunity to make informed choices when selecting reading materials for the young. In addition, *CLR* provides researchers of children's literature with easy access to a wide variety of critical information from English-language sources in the field. Users will find balanced overviews of the careers of the authors and illustrators of the books that children and young adults are reading; these entries, which contain excerpts from published criticism in books and periodicals, assist users by sparking ideas for papers and assignments and suggesting supplementary and classroom reading. Ann L. Kalkhoff, president and editor of *Children's Book Review Service Inc.*, writes that "*CLR* has filled a gap in the field of children's books, and it is one series that will never lose its validity or importance."

Scope of the Series

Each volume of *CLR* profiles the careers of authors and illustrators of books for children from preschool through high school. Author lists in each volume reflect these elements:

- an international scope.

- approximately fifteen authors of all eras.

- a variety of genres covered by children's literature: picture books, fiction, nonfiction, poetry, folklore, and drama.

Although earlier volumes of *CLR* emphasized critical material published after 1960, successive volumes have expanded their coverage to encompass important criticism written before 1960. Since many of the authors included in *CLR* are living and continue to write, their entries are updated periodically. Future volumes will supplement the entries of selected authors covered in earlier volumes as well as include criticism on the works of authors new to the series.

Organization of This Book

An author section consists of the following elements: author heading, author portrait, author introduction, excerpts of criticism (each followed by a bibliographical citation), and illustrations, when available.

- The **author heading** consists of the author's name followed by birth and death dates. The portion of the name outside the parentheses denotes the form under which the author is most frequently published. If the majority of the author's works for children were written under a pseudonym, the pseudonym will be listed in the author heading and the real name given on the first line of the author introduction. Also located at the beginning of the introduction are any other pseudonyms used by the author in writing for children and any name variations, including transliterated forms for authors whose languages use nonroman alphabets. Uncertainty as to a birth or death date is indicated by question marks.

- An **author portrait** is included when available.

- The **author introduction** contains information designed to introduce an author to *CLR* users by presenting an overview of the author's themes and styles, occasional biographical facts that relate to the author's literary career or critical responses to the author's works, and information about major awards and prizes the author has received. Introductions also list a group of representative titles for which the author or illustrator being profiled is best known; this section, which begins with the words "major works include," follows the genre line of the introduction. Where applicable, introductions conclude with references to additional entries in biographical and critical reference series published by Gale Research Inc. These sources include past volumes of *CLR* as well as *Authors & Artists for Young Adults, Classical and Medieval Literature Criticism, Contempo-*

rary Authors, Contemporary Authors Autobiography Series, Contemporary Authors Bibliographical Series, Contemporary Literary Criticism, Dictionary of Literary Biography, Drama Criticism, Nineteenth-Century Literature Criticism, Poetry Criticism, Short Story Criticism, Something about the Author, Something about the Author Autobiography Series, Twentieth-Century Literary Criticism, and *Yesterday's Authors of Books for Children.*

• **Criticism** is located in three sections: **author's commentary** (when available), **general commentary** (when available), and **title commentary** (in which commentary on specific titles appears). Centered headings introduce each section, in which criticism is arranged chronologically. Titles by authors being profiled are highlighted in boldface type within the text for easier access by readers.

The **author's commentary** presents background material written by the author or by an interviewer. This commentary may cover a specific work or several works. Author's commentary on more than one work appears after the author introduction, while commentary on an individual book follows the title entry heading.

The **general commentary** consists of critical excerpts that consider more than one work by the author or illustrator being profiled. General commentary is preceded by the critic's name in boldface type or, in the case of unsigned criticism, by the title of the journal. Occasionally, *CLR* features entries that emphasize general criticism on the overall career of an author or illustrator. When appropriate, a selection of reviews is included to supplement the general commentary.

The **title commentary** begins with title entry headings, which precede the criticism on a title and cite publication information on the work being reviewed. Title headings list the title of the work as it appeared in its first English-language edition. The first English-language publication date of each work is listed in parentheses following the title. Differing U.S. and British titles follow the publication date within the parentheses.

Entries in each title commentary section consist of critical excerpts on the author's individual works, arranged chronologically by publication date. The entries generally contain two to six reviews per title, depending on the stature of the book and the amount of criticism it has generated. The editors select titles that reflect the entire scope of the author's literary contribution, covering each genre and subject. An effort is made to reprint criticism that represents the full range of each title's reception—from the year of its initial publication to current assessments. Thus, the reader is provided with a record of the author's critical history. Publication information (such as publisher names and book prices) and parenthetical numerical references (such as footnotes or page and line references to specific editions of works) have been deleted at the editor's discretion to provide smoother reading of the text.

• Selected excerpts are preceded by **explanatory notes,** which provide information on the critic or work of criticism to enhance the reader's understanding of the excerpt.

• A complete **bibliographical citation** designed to facilitate the location of the original book or article follows each piece of criticism.

• Numerous **illustrations** are featured in *CLR.* For entries on illustrators, an effort has been made to include illustrations that reflect the characteristics discussed in the criticism. Entries on major authors who do not illustrate their own works may also include photographs and other illustrative material pertinent to the authors' careers.

Special Features

Entries on authors who are also illustrators will occasionally feature commentary on selected works illustrated but not written by the author being profiled. These works are strongly associated with the illustrator and have received critical acclaim for their art. By including critical comment on works of this type, the editors wish to provide a more complete representation of the author's total career. Criticism on these works has been chosen to stress artistic, rather than literary, contributions. Title entry headings for works illustrated by the author being profiled are arranged chronologically within the entry by date of publication and include notes identifying the author of the illustrated work. In order to provide easier access for users, all titles illustrated by the subject of the entry will be boldfaced.

CLR also includes entries on prominent illustrators who have contributed to the field of children's literature. These entries are designed to represent the development of the illustrator as an artist rather than as a literary stylist. The illustrator's section is organized like that of an author, with two exceptions: the introduction presents an overview of the illustrator's styles and techniques rather than outlining his or her literary background, and the commentary written by the illustrator on his or her works is called "illustrator's commentary" rather than "author's commentary." Title entry headings are followed by explanatory notes identifying the author of the illustrated work. All titles of books containing illustrations by the artist being profiled as well as individual illustrations from these books are highlighted in boldface type.

Other Features

• The **acknowledgments,** which immediately follow the preface, list the sources from which material has been reprinted in the volume. It does not, however, list every book or periodical consulted for the volume.

• The **cumulative index to authors** lists all of the authors who have appeared in *CLR* with cross-references to the various literary criticism series and the biographical and autobiographical series published by Gale Research Inc. A full listing of the series titles appears on the first page of the indexes of this volume.

• The **cumulative nationality index** lists authors alphabetically under their respective nationalities. Author names are followed by the volume number(s) in which they appear. Authors who have changed citizenship or whose current citizenship is not reflected in biographical sources appear under both their original nationality and that of their current residence.

• The **cumulative title index** lists titles covered in *CLR* followed by the volume and page number where criticism begins.

A Note to the Reader

CLR is one of several critical reference sources in the Literature Criticism Series published by Gale Research Inc. When writing papers, students who quote directly from any volume in the Literature Criticism Series may use the following general forms to footnote reprinted criticism. The first example pertains to material drawn from periodicals, the second to material reprinted from books.

[1] T. S. Eliot, "John Donne," *The Nation and the Athenaeum,* 33 (9 June 1923), 321-32; excerpted and reprinted in *Literature Criticism from 1400 to 1800,* Vol. 10, ed. James E. Person, Jr. (Detroit: Gale Research, 1989), pp. 28-9.

[1] Henry Brooke, *Leslie Brooke and Johnny Crow* (Frederick Warne, 1982); excerpted and reprinted in *Children's Literature Review,* Vol. 20, ed. Gerard J. Senick (Detroit: Gale Research, 1990), p. 47.

Suggestions Are Welcome

In response to various suggestions, several features have been added to *CLR* since the series began, including author entries on retellers of traditional literature as well as those who have been the first to record oral tales and other folklore; entries on prominent illustrators featuring commentary on their styles and techniques; entries on authors whose works are considered controversial; occasional entries devoted to criticism on a single work or a series of works by a major author; sections in author introductions that list major works by the author or illustrator being profiled; explanatory notes that provide information on the critic or work of criticism to enhance the usefulness of the excerpt; more extensive illustrative material, such as holographs of manuscript pages and photographs of people and places pertinent to the authors' careers; a cumulative nationality index for easy access to authors by nationality; and occasional guest essays written specifically for *CLR* by prominent critics on subjects of their choice.

Readers who wish to suggest authors to appear in future volumes, or who have other suggestions, are cordially invited to write the editor.

Acknowledgments

The editors wish to thank the copyright holders of the excerpted included in this volume, the permissions managers of many book and magazine publishing companies for assisting us in securing reprint rights, and Anthony Bogucki for assistance with copyright research. We are also grateful to the staffs of the Detroit Public Library, the Library of Congress, the University of Detroit Library, Wayne State University Purdy/Kresge Library Complex, and the University of Michigan Libraries for making their resources available to us. Following is a list of the copyright holders who granted us permissions to reprint material in this volume of *CLR*. Every effort has been made to trace copyright, but if omissions have been made, please let us know.

COPYRIGHTED EXCERPTS IN *CLR* VOLUME 27, WERE REPRINTED FROM THE FOLLOWING PERIODICALS:

American Book Collector, v. 2, March-April, 1981. Copyright 1981 by The American Book Collector, Inc. Reprinted by permission of the publisher.—*Appraisal: Children's Science Books,* v. 4, Spring 1971; v. 5, Winter, 1972; v.9, Fall, 1976; v. 10, Spring, 1977; v. 14, Winter, 1981. Copyright © 1971, 1972, 1976, 1977, 1981 by the Children's Science Book Review Committee. All reprinted by permission of the publisher.—*The Black Scholar,* v. 12, March-April, 1981. Copyright 1981 by *The Black Scholar.* Reprinted by permission of the publisher.—*Book Week—New York Herald Tribune,* May 16, 1965. © 1965, *The Washington Post.* Reprinted with permission of the publisher.—*Book Week—The Washington Post,* May 8, 1966. © 1966, *The Washington Post.* Reprinted by permission of the publisher.—*Book Window,* v. 6, Winter, 1978 for a review of "Robber Hopsika" by E.A.A.; v. 6, Summer, 1979 for a review of "Letters from the General" by E.A.A.; v. 7, Summer, 1980 for a review of "The Little Captain and the Pirate Treasure" by E.A.A.; v. 8, Spring, 1981 for a review of "The Curse of the Werewolf" by N.N. © 1978, 1979, 1980, 1981 S.C.B.A. and contributors. All reprinted by permission of the publisher.—*Book World—The Washington Post,* May 14, 1989. © 1989, *The Washington Post.* Reprinted with permission of the publisher.—*Bookbird,* v. XII, December 15, 1975; n. 2, March 20, 1986. Both reprinted by permission of the publisher.—*Booklist,* v. 75, November 15, 1978; v. 75, February 15, 1979; v. 75, January 15, 1979; v. 76, June 15, 1980; v. 77, March 1, 1981; v. 80, March 1, 1984; v. 85, June 15, 1989; v. 86, September 15, 1989; v. 86, November 15, 1989; v. 86, May 1, 1990; v. 89, September 15, 1990;v. 87, February 15, 1991. Copyright © 1978, 1979, 1980, 1981, 1984, 1989, 1990, 1991 by the American Library Association. All reprinted by permission of the publisher.—*The Booklist,* v. 72, July 15, 1972; v. 72, February 1, 1976. Copyright © 1972, 1976 by the American Library Association. Both reprinted by permission of the publisher.—*The Booklist and Subscription Books Bulletin,* v. 63, December 15, 1966. Copyright © 1966 by the American Library Association. Reprinted by permission of the publisher.—*Books (New York),* May 6, 1962. © 1962, renewed 1990, *The Washington Post.* Reprinted with permission of the publisher.—*Books and Bookmen,* v. 23, June, 1978 for "Noah's Ark" by Lavinia Learmont. © copyright the author 1978.—*Books for Your Children,* v. 6, Winter, 1970-71. © *Books for Your Children* 1971. Reprinted by permission of the publisher.—*Books for Young People,* v. 1, June, 1987 for "From Giant Snakes to Punk Pigeons: Escapism at Its Best" by Bernie Goedhart; v. 3, February, 1989 for "Feisty Young Heroines' Offbeat Adventures" by Susan Perren. All rights reserved. Both reprinted by permission of the publisher and the respective authors.—*Books in Canada,* v. 13, December, 1984 for a review of "Lizzy's Lion" by Mary Ainslie Smith; v. 18, April, 1989 for "Wake-up Tales" by Linda Granfield. Both reprinted by permission of the respective authors.—*Bulletin of the Center for Children's Books,* May, 1964; v. 19, July-August, 1965; v. 19, October, 1965; v. 20, May, 1967; v. 21, January, 1968; v. 25, October, 1971; v. 28, March, 1975; v. 30, May, 1977; v. 31, July-August, 1978; v. 32, March, 1979; v. 32, May, 1979; v. 36, March, 1983; v. 37, June, 1984; v. 39, July-August, 1986; v. 41, February, 1988; v. 41, May, 1988; v. 43, September, 1989; v. 43, November, 1989; v. 43, December, 1989; v. 43, March, 1990; v. 44, October, 1990; v. 44, July-August, 1991. Copyright © 1964, 1965, 1967, 1968, 1971, 1975, 1977, 1978, 1979, 1983, 1984, 1986, 1988, 1989, 1990, 1991 by The University of Chicago. All reprinted by permission of The University of Chicago Press.—*Canadian Children's Literature,* n. 46, 1987; n. 54, 1989; n. 59, 1990, n. 60, 1990. Copyright © 1987, 1989, 1990 Canadian Children's Press. All reprinted by permission of the publisher.—*Chicago Sunday Tribune Magazine of Books,* November 11, 1956. Copyright 1956, renewed 1984 by Chicago Tribune./ November 3, 1957 for "The Man Who Drew Pooh" by Gwen Morgan. Renewed 1985. Reprinted by permission of the author.—*Chicago Tribune—Books,* September 5, 1954 for "The Silver Curlew" by Polly Goodwin. Copyright 1954, renewed 1982, Chicago Tribune Company. All rights reserved. Reprinted by permission of the author.—*Children's Book News,* Toronto, v. 9, June, 1986; v. 12, Winter, 1989. Both reprinted by permission of The Canadian Children's Book Centre, Toronto, Canada.—*Children's Book Review,* v. I, April, 1971; v. I, December, 1971; v. III, April, 1973; v. IV, Winter, 1974-75; v. V, Summer, 1975; v. 7, February, 1979. Copyright 1971, 1973, 1975, 1979 Children's Book Review Service Inc. All reprinted by permission of the publisher.—*Children's Literature: Annual of the Mod-*

Company. All rights reserved. Reprinted by permission of the publisher.—Swann, Thomas Burnett. From *A. A. Milne.* Twayne, 1971. Copyright 1971 by Twayne Publishers. All rights reserved, Reprinted with the permission of Twayne Publishers, Inc., a division of G. K. Hall & Co., Boston.—Swinfen, Ann. From *In Defence of Fantasy: A Study of the Genre in English and American Literature Since 1945.* Routledge & Kegan Paul, 1984. © Ann Swinfen 1984. Reprinted by permission of the publisher.—Thwaite, Ann. From *A. A. Milne: The Man Behind Winnie-the-Pooh.* Random House, 1990. Copyright © 1990 by Ann Thwaite. All rights reserved. Reprinted by permission of Random House, Inc.—Thiele, Colin. From "Notes by Colin Thiele," in *Innocence and Experience: Essays on Contemporary Australian Children's Writers.* By Walter McVitty. Thomas Nelson, 1981. Copyright © Walter McVitty 1981. Reprinted by permission of the publisher—Townsend, John Rowe. From *Written for Children: An Outline of English-Language Children's Literature.* Third revised edition. J. B. Lippincott, 1987, Penguin Books, 1987. Copyright © 1965, 1974, 1983, 1987 by John Rowe Townsend. All rights reserved. Reprinted by permission of the author.—Tucker, Nicholas. From *The Child and the Book: A Psychological and Literary Exploration.* Cambridge University Press., 1981. © Cambridge University Press 1981. Reprinted with the permission of the publisher.—Waggoner, Diana. From *The Hills of Faraway: A Guide to Fantasy.* Atheneum, 1978. Copyright © 1978 by Diana Waggoner. All rights reserved. Reprinted with the permission of Atheneum Publishers, an imprint of Macmillan Publishing Company.—Wilkin, Binnie Tate. From *Survival Themes in Fiction for Children and Young People.* The Scarecrow Press, Inc., 1978. Copyright © 1978 by Binnie Tate Wilkin. Reprinted by permission the publisher.—Wilson, A. N. From *C. S. Lewis: A Biography.* Norton, 1990. Copyright © 1990 by A. N. Wilson. All rights reserved. Reprinted by permission of W. W. Norton & Company, Inc.

PERMISSION TO REPRODUCE ILLUSTRATIONS APPEARING IN *CLR*, VOLUME 27, WAS RECEIVED FROM THE FOLLOWING SOURCES:

Illustration by Jan Brett from her *Goldilocks and the Three Bears,* retold by Jan Brett. Copyright © 1987 by Jan Brett. Reprinted by permission of G.P. Putnam's Sons./ Illustration by Marie-Louis Gay from her *Rainy Day Magic.* Albert Whitman & Company, 1989. Copyright © 1987 by Marie-Louis Gay. Reprinted by permission of the publisher./ Illustration by Ernest H. Shepard from *The House at Pooh Corner,* by A. A. Milne. E.P. Dutton, 1928. Copyright 1928 by E.P. Dutton, renewed © 1956 by A. A. Milne. Used by permission of Dutton Children's Books, a division of Penguin Books USA Inc./ Illustration by Ernest H. Shepard from *The Wind in the Willows,* by Kenneth Grahame. Copyright 1933, 1953 by Charles Scribner's Sons; renewal copyright © 1961 by Ernest H. Shepard, 1981 by Mary Eleanor Jessie Knox. Illustrations copyright © 1959 by Ernest H. Shepard. Reprinted by permission of Charles Scribner's Sons, an imprint of Macmillan Publishing Company./ Illustration by Ernest H. Shepard from his *Drawn From Memory.* J.B. Lippincott Company, 1957. Copyright © 1957 by Ernest H. Shepard. Reprinted by permission of Curtis Brown, London. In Canada by Methuen London Ltd./ Illustration by Ernest H. Shepard from his *Drawn From Life.* Methuen & Co., Ltd, 1961. Copyright © 1961 by Ernest Shepard. Reprinted by permission of Curtis Brown, London./ Illustration by Ed Young from *The Emperor and the Kite,* by Jane Yolen. The World Publishing Company, 1967. Text copyright © 1967 by Jane Yolen. Illustrations copyright © 1967 by HarperCollins Publishers, Inc. Reprinted by permission of HarperCollins Publishers, Inc./ Illustration from *Lon Po Po: A Red-Riding Hood Story From China,* translated from a collection of Chinese folk tales and illustrated by Ed Young. Philomel Books, 1989. Copyright © 1989 by Ed Young. Reprinted by permission of Philomel Books.

PHOTOGRAPHS AND ILLUSTRATIONS APPEARING IN *CLR*, VOLUME 27, WERE RECEIVED FROM THE FOLLOWING SOURCES:

Courtesy of Irving Alder: **pp. 1, 11, 21;** Courtesy of Paul Biegel: **p. 27;** Copyright by Mark Kohn: **p. 31;** Photograph by Lincoln Russell, courtesy of Jan Brett: **p. 38;** The Contemporary Forum, courtesy of Gwendolyn Brooks: **p. 44;** UPI/Bettmann Newsphotos: **p. 53;** Photograph by Bernard Bohn, courtesy of Marie-Louise Gay: **p. 75;** Photograph by David Homel, courtesy of Marie-Louis Gay: **p. 85;** © Esin Ili Gokner: **P. 90;** Photograph by Dorothy M. Kennedy, courtesy of X. J. Kennedy: **p. 96;** Ann Ahearn, Bedford Minute-Man: **p. 99;** Courtesy of the Marion E. Wade Collection, Wheaton College, Wheaton Illinois: **p. 115;** Bob O'Donnell, Lord and King Associates: **p. 121;** The Bodleian Library, Oxford: **125;** Estate of C.S. Lewis: **p. 131;** Photograph by Wolf Suschitzky: **p. 141;** Drawing by Pauline Baynes: **p. 146;** Photograph by David Godlis: **p. 152;** Photograph by Mark Gerson: **p. 158;** Reproduced by permission of Colin Thiele: **pp. 192, 204, 210.**

Children's
Literature
Review

Irving Adler

1913-

(Also writes as Robert Irving) American author of nonfiction.

Major works include *The Secret of Light* (1952), *The Elementary Mathematics of the Atom* (1965), *The Wonders of Physics* (1966), *The Environment* (1976), "The Reason Why" series (with Ruth Adler).

A distinguished and prolific author of approximately eighty-five informational books for readers in the elementary grades through high school, Adler is highly regarded for presenting complex ideas from science, mathematics, and physics in an accurate, comprehensible, and interesting fashion. Taking an interdisciplinary approach to his subjects by demonstrating how science and technology are related both to each other and to significant social problems, he explains complicated theories and ideas by applying them to familiar images of daily life, such as the microwave, the washing machine, and the yo-yo. Adler is often praised for the freshness of his approach, for his success in outlining the reasoning behind his facts as well as the fact themselves, for his thorough coverage of even the most complicated aspects of science, and for the clarity and lack of condescension of his presentation. Characteristically arranging his material historically or around a single theme, Adler writes his books in a brisk, simple style that is noted for revealing a wealth of data on both familiar and unfamiliar topics. He is also well regarded for introducing young readers to science and math by demonstrating that learning is enjoyable through his explanations and suggested experiments. "Very few writers of informational books," says critic Margaret Sherwood Libby, "are as skillful at presenting precise facts and general concepts in mathematics and the sciences in as simple and lively a fashion."

Observers often note that Adler's style and approach reflect his background as a teacher: he began instructing in mathematics while attending Columbia University and later taught for twenty years in New York City high schools and at the university level. Adler began writing for children in 1952; his first wife Ruth, a writer, illustrator, and teacher, illustrated many of his books and often served as his collaborator until her death in 1968. The Adlers's daughter Peggy also collaborates with her father and has illustrated several books both singly and with her mother, while Adler's second wife Joyce has also collaborated with her husband on juvenile nonfiction. Adler is often acknowledged for covering a wide variety of subjects in his works: in the area of science, for example, he addresses such topics as weather; color, light, and sound; electricity and electronics; the environment and natural disasters; energy; astronomy; geology; and scientific instruments and discoveries, while his mathematics books include studies of the origin of mathematics and its role in history; math sets, number sequences, and numerals;

the new math; and an explanation of how math is used in modern physics. In "The Reason Why" series, books for primary graders on which he collaborated with his first wife, Adler addresses such subjects as storms, heat, atoms, communication, and the calendar. He has also written surveys of time and its origins, studies of the five senses, and books on games, puzzles, card tricks, riddles, jokes, and brain teasers. In addition to works for children and young adults, Adler is the author of informational books for adults on mathematics and education. In 1961, Irving and Ruth Adler received an award from the New York State Association for Supervision and Curriculum Development for their contributions to children's literature; several of Adler's books have also been cited by the National Science Teacher's Association and the Children's Book Council as outstanding science books.

(See also *Something about the Author,* Vols. 1, 29; *Contemporary Authors New Revision Series,* Vol. 2; and *Contemporary Authors,* Vols. 7-8, rev. ed.)

AUTHOR'S COMMENTARY

I am going to describe briefly some of the goals that my

wife and I try to achieve when we write our books on science subjects for young people. Since we think these are desirable goals, we recommend them to anyone who would like to write science books for children.

People often ask us, "How do you pick the topics of your books?" There are many answers, but I shall mention only one of them. Sometimes we choose *a topic that we know nothing about.* An unfamiliar subject offers certain obvious advantages. First, it gives us an opportunity to learn something new, and we always enjoy learning. Second, precisely because the subject matter is new to us, we have to study, analyze, and work over it until it is simple enough for us to understand. By that time it is simple enough for anybody to understand, and we are ready to explain it to children.

Our primary goal is to present scientific ideas so simply that they can be followed and understood by an unsophisticated reader. In this respect science writing has much in common with the writing of fiction. In her article "On the Art of Fiction," Willa Cather said:

> Art, it seems to me, should simplify. That, indeed, is very nearly the whole of the higher artistic process; finding what conventions of form and what detail one can do without and yet preserve the spirit of the whole—so that all that one has suppressed and cut away is there to the reader's consciousness as much as if it were in type on the page.

The science writer, too, must decide what to leave out and what to put in. He must select and organize his material so that the essential idea is developed logically and clearly and is not obscured by unnecessary detail. Of course he must be careful not to distort an idea when he simplifies it. The key to presenting a complex idea simply and accurately is to break it up into its constituent parts and then to present the parts one at a time in the proper sequence.

Simplicity of style is especially appropriate to science writing because scientific ideas are basically simple. And scientific ideas are basically simple because nature is basically simple. For example, all the chemical complexity and variety that we find in the organic and inorganic worlds is built out of a few fundamental particles—the electron, the proton, and the neutron.

As a matter of fact, if a scientific theory about some area of study is not simple, it usually means that we don't understand that area well. As scientific study progresses, connections are found between facts that at first seemed unrelated. When the science reaches maturity with an adequate theory, all the separate pieces fit together like the parts of a jigsaw puzzle.

Therefore, a science book is more easily comprehended if it is based on the most advanced scientific ideas. For example, chemistry is difficult and confusing if it is taught as a hodgepodge of separate reactions. It becomes simple and understandable if these reactions are shown to be consequences of the properties of the atom as postulated in modern atomic theory. Thus, there is no conflict between being simple and being up to date.

Being up to date is the second goal we try to achieve in our writing. Because of the rapid pace at which science is advancing, this goal is not always easy to reach. Sometimes, what is up to date when you write a book is out of date by the time you receive galley proofs from the printer. For example, when the books *Your Eyes* and *Color in Your Life* were written, we stated correctly that there was no experimental evidence for the Helmholtz theory that there are three different kinds of cones in the retina of the eye, sensitive to red, green, and blue respectively. Since then, the experimental evidence has been produced by George Wald and Paul K. Brown. This fact will be noted in the next printing of these books.

A third goal we try to achieve is accuracy. This requires checking and rechecking all the information we get, no matter how reputable its source may be. Checking is obviously necessary when two authoritative sources give contradictory information. We have discovered that it is also necessary even when several sources agree. For example, when we were gathering information for *Insects and Plants,* we found in several reputable sources the same story of how the prickly pear cactus, which choked fields and woods in Australia for a while, was originally introduced to the island. The prickly pear is the plant on which the cochineal insect feeds, and the cochineal insect is the source of a red dye. According to the story, a governor of Australia who wanted red coats for his troops introduced the prickly pear for the culture of cochineal insects. This is a rather nice story, and we wanted to include it in our book. However, according to the Bureau of Entomology of the Australian Department of Agriculture, there is no evidence to support the story. More probable is the theory that the prickly pear was brought to Australia accidentally when used as ballast in a ship that came from Galveston.

There were several other instances, too, when we found widely accepted stories to be false. Many books have reported the occasional appearance of human beings whose eyes reflect light as a cat's eyes do. We tried to verify these stories in correspondence with Dr. Arnold J. Kroll, the scientist who has studied and photographed the tapetum, the reflecting layer in a cat's eye. Dr. Kroll assured us that, because of the structure of the human eye, these stories could not be true.

Sometimes, to get accurate information in the form in which we want to present it to children, we have to make our own independent calculations. For example, recently we were writing for *Taste, Touch and Smell* . . . a section on the threshold of taste for salt, sugar, and quinine. The threshold is the smallest concentration detectable by the sense of taste. We found the concentrations given either as moles per liter or as the ratio of the weight of the solute to the weight of the solution. To make this information more meaningful for children, we wanted to translate it into this form: the threshold of taste for salt is one salt molecule in fifteen hundred molecules of water, and so on. We made our own calculations, using the data in the books we consulted. We discovered first that different books gave different thresholds. A little more investigation revealed that the differences were the result of using different techniques for measuring the threshold. We then had to decide arbitrarily which measurements we would use in our book. We discovered next that in the thresholds listed in one table of a textbook on experimental psychology, there was an error by a factor of one million. The caption for the table read "milligrams per liter" when it should have said "micromilligrams per liter." To be absolutely sure that our own calculations were correct, we carried them out by two separate methods using different raw data and were pleased to find that the results of both methods were in agreement.

So far I have been discussing errors we have discovered in other people's books. I don't want to give the impression that we think there are no errors in our own. There have been, and there probably still are errors in some of our books.

One of the errors that crept into my book *The New Mathematics* provides a good example of how difficult it is to make a book completely free of error. In the opening paragraph of the book I intended to give the number 1.414 as an approximate value of the square root of two. I type with two fingers, however, and a slight alteration of my typing rhythm produced the number 1.141. I proofread my manuscripts several times and of course proofread the galleys and page proofs, never detecting the error. Neither did my wife, who read the manuscript, nor did the editor and the copy editor. We all looked at 1.141 and saw 1.414 as we expected to. One week after the book was published, a reader called the error to our attention. Producing accurate books is a co-operative undertaking that involves the reader as well as the author and the editor. We hope that readers who spot errors will continue to call them to our attention so that we may eliminate them in future printings of our books.

A fourth goal we try to achieve is unification. Science is increasingly subdivided into specialties. The scientist necessarily studies intensively small fragments of reality. To make the scientist's discoveries meaningful to the general reader, the writer should show how these different fragments of reality are related to each other. For this reason we seek unifying topics that cut across the boundaries between specialties. We try as far as we can within the scope of any one book to relate science to technology and to relate both to significant social problems. The book *Time in Your Life* is an example of one that is based on a unifying theme.

A fifth goal we seek is to give answers to the question, "How do we know?" It is not enough merely to present "facts" discovered by science. It is necessary to present as well the reasoning by which these "facts" have been established. In this age of atomic energy and space travel, the achievements of science and technology are as fantastic as the wildest creations of the writers of science fiction. If we merely ask children to believe the fantastic facts without explaining how we know them to be facts, we will be cultivating a gullible generation incapable of distinguishing fact from fiction. This is why my book *The Stars: Steppingstones into Space* does not merely present some facts of astronomy, with the usual devices for dramatizing them, but it also outlines the techniques and the reasoning by which these facts were established.

A sixth goal we seek is to explain unfamiliar concepts by means of familiar ideas. In my book *Dust,* for example, in order to explain why dust particles, which are denser than air, can float in the air, I had to make clear first the concept that the smaller a body is, the higher is its surface-to-volume ratio. I developed the idea without using mathematics by calling attention to a familiar experience: If you break a stone into two pieces, the volume of the stone is not changed. But the total surface of the stone is increased because two new surfaces are created at the break. If you break the stone into smaller and smaller pieces, each new break adds more surface. Finally, when the stone has been ground to a powder, it has a tremendous amount of surface, but its volume is the same as it was in the first place.

A seventh goal is best expressed negatively as a prohibition: Don't talk down to the child. Talk to him seriously about serious subjects. The stuff of science is interesting by itself; there is no need to motivate enthusiasm artificially by providing a so-called "human interest" setting. I squirm with embarrassment whenever I read a science book that begins with conversations between Ned and his uncle as they take a walk. I am sure that the child reader squirms, too, because he is not interested in Ned or his uncle or their inane conversation. He is interested in science, and he wishes they would hurry and get to it.

Our eighth goal is also best expressed negatively: Do not be hobbled by word lists. If the vocabulary of a book is restricted to words that children ordinarily use, how will they ever learn to use new words? A good book should help to expand the child's vocabulary. This does not mean that we should smother the ideas in the book with five-syllable words. As a matter of fact, both in speech and in writing we prefer a simple vocabulary. Wherever a short word will do as well as a long word, we habitually use the short word. However, if a somewhat longer word is necessary to avoid circumlocution, we use the longer word and explain its meaning. Where a technical word is appropriate in a discussion, we introduce the word, define it, give its pronunciation, and use it.

A ninth goal is to convey the idea that learning is fun. Learning is a great adventure, offering the child opportunities to experience the excitement of discovery and the pride of accomplishment. We try to infuse our writing with this spirit of adventure.

The relationship between learning and fun is two-sided. You can have fun while you learn, and conversely, you can learn while you have fun. We make frequent use of recreational activities as a teaching device. For example, we develop some solid mathematical ideas through the games and puzzles of *Magic House of Numbers.* And we introduce important ideas about reasoning and scientific method through games, jokes, and puzzles in the book *Logic for Beginners.*

A tenth goal that we try to achieve through our books is to convey to the child a sense of history. The child is a beneficiary of a great cultural heritage that has grown through thousands of years. We try to get the child to appreciate his role as a participant in a great historical process. His mission is to receive the cultural heritage from past generations and add to it before passing it on to future generations. We hope that our books help to prepare him for carrying out this mission. (pp. 524-29)

> *Irving Adler, "On Writing Science Books for Children," in* The Horn Book Magazine, *Vol. XLI, No. 5, October, 1965, pp. 524-29.*

GENERAL COMMENTARY

Margaret Sherwood Libby

Very few writers of informational books are as skillful at presenting precise facts and general concepts in mathematics and the sciences in as simple and lively a fashion as Irving Adler. In some twenty-five books, either under this name or as Robert Irving, sometimes with his wife, whose illustrations are as effective as his text, and sometimes alone, he has caught readers' interests swiftly, arranged the material historically or around some single important nugget of knowledge and imparted interestingly a great deal of knowledge. Hitherto his books have been chiefly for those over 11 but [*Rivers; The Story of a Nail; Shadows; Why? A Book of Reasons; Air;* and *Oceans*], in a series called "The Reason Why," . . . are for younger children. They are excellent.

In the book on nails we learn first of handmade ones, then of the changes in the structures of buildings when more nails became available in machine-made mass production, and finally of the mining of iron ore, coal and limestone and the making of iron, steel and steel wire for nails. As for *Shadows,* his text goes from Stevenson's famous "little shadow" to eclipses, sundials, clouds, X-rays and projected shadows, while *Rivers* not only gives the natural history of rivers including the water cycle but explains formations like pot holes, natural bridges, and water gaps. The fourth book, *Why?* is different. It touches lightly on many topics. Thirty-one questions (here called riddles to intrigue the young) are asked from "Why can a fly walk on the ceiling" to "Why do clothes get dirty," and a careful scientific explanation is given to each in reply.

The most recent two in this series, on "Air" and on "Oceans," are the most detailed. *Air* discusses the spectrum, combustion, the use of air by living things, weather, radio waves and even fallout. In *Oceans,* the life in the sea, its navigation, the formation of islands, currents and problems of pollution as well as the water cycle are treated.

> *Margaret Sherwood Libby, in a review of "Rivers" and others, in* Books (New York), *May 6, 1962, p. 10.*

Isaac Asimov

Because I believe that there is no facet of science so complicated that it cannot be made clear to a nonscientist, I have not been surprised to come across books that do an excellent job of explaining the essence of atomic physics or rocketry to eight-year-olds. Authors who can be lucid on such difficult subjects are performing vital tasks in our society.

No one expects an elementary book to teach an eight-year-

old to be an atomic physicist or to take his place at the controls at Cape Kennedy. One can expect, however, that such a book will introduce the eight-year-old, or the ten-or twelve-year-old, to a subject and point him in the right direction.

Irving and Ruth Adler serve this cause superlatively. They are making a career for themselves in writing brief books on almost every aspect of science and technology for elementary school children, and they do it so well that even this middle-aged reviewer finds himself learning things. (p. 394)

> *Isaac Asimov, "Views on Science Books," in* The Horn Book Magazine, *Vol. XL, No. 4, August, 1964, pp. 394-95.*

TITLE COMMENTARY

The Secret of Light (1952)

Supplementary reading for science students at High School level, this demands an advanced degree of interest or considerable student-teacher cooperation. As an overall introduction to theories of light, this is a well-ordered, lively and better than adequate study of the stuff of the universe. Adler presents first light's general properties,— its speed, ability to travel through a vacuum. Then—with illustration in simple lens and refraction, he ties light into our everyday living, how it works for us, the behaviour of colors, etc. The elucidation of prism and spectrum sets the stage for the wave theory, invisible light, determination of atomic structure and the periodical table of elements by means of their spectra. Structure is handled in some detail. Nuclear physics is touched on and the examination of the contributions of the Curies, Planck, Bohr, Einstein— among others—amplifies the subject matter. The end result is a stimulating glimpse of the supposition that all is energy, busy correlating with everything else. The author shares his own conception of workable theories with the reader, though his breezy presentation leaves something to be desired. The book is pithy and lively, and those already interested in the subject should find it useful reading.

> *A review of "The Secret of Light," in* Virginia Kirkus' Bookshop Service, *Vol. XX, No. 10, May 15, 1952, p. 301.*

An exciting book explaining what light is and giving many interesting facts about its behavior under different circumstances in our everyday environment. On every page are clever, amusing illustrations and diagrams, by Ida Weisburd, and many simple experiments teach the reader about electromagnetic waves. Included are details of refraction and reflection, how the world is colored, and the relationship of light to atomic energy. Especially good is the explanation of relativity. Good reading for young and old. Especially valuable for junior high school.

> *Mildred I. Ross, in a review of "The Secret of Light," in* Library Journal, *Vol. 77, No. 14, August, 1952, p. 1311.*

A brief but thorough presentation of theories of light—its

properties and how it is used by man. The material is concentrated and difficult enough so that the reader will need some previous knowledge of the subject to make the best use of the book. The illustrations give the book an appearance of being for younger readers than it actually is. However, they add considerably to the understanding of the text.

> *A review of "The Secret of Light," in* Bulletin of the Children's Book Center, *Vol. VI, No. 5, January, 1953, p. 37.*

Time in Your Life (1955)

Those who contend that teachers of young people write the best books for young people will find support in this book. Mr. Adler is evidently an excellent teacher. In his first chapter he quickly establishes rapport with the reader as he points out the significance of time. In the next five chapters he treats of time as a phase of celestial mechanics and provides the reader with several simple, related activities.

The remainder of the book is devoted to rhythm and shows that this is a property possessed by everything from a chemical to a crab. Having run the gamut of the sciences, the author fails to include the psychological aspects of timing. Perhaps he will make that the subject of another book as fascinating as this one.

> *Alfred D. Beck, "What Clocks Tick," in* The New York Times Book Review, *August 28, 1955, p. 16.*

The author deserves to be congratulated on his ingenuity in compiling a book which can perhaps be best described as a concise encyclopaedia of "rhythms in nature". Mr. Adler has combed almost all the branches of science to obtain examples of the manner in which, apparently, life is controlled by natural rhythms or cycles. Astronomical cycles, the measurement of time and the manufacture and evolution of time-keeping devices, biological rhythms— the life-cycles of plants and animals, the growth rings of woody plants, the regularity of the heart beat in mammals—as well as the "uranium clock" are all described, simply and clearly, and in a manner calculated to stimulate the reader's interest and to encourage him to search for further information. It is, however, a pity that the author has made no mention of the variations in magnetic declination and dip due to the rotation of the magnetic poles; this appears, however, to be the only omission of importance. The illustrations [by Ruth Adler] which are both amusing and instructive enhance the value of a book which deserves a place in every school library.

> *J. Brady, in a review of "Time in Your Life," in* The School Librarian and School Library Review, *Vol. 8, No. 5, July, 1957, p. 378.*

[*Time in Your Life*] could satisfy a reader up to thirteen or so. Its simple arrangement, with sections of a few paragraphs only, its anecdotes and asides, examples and analogies, put it within the grasp of readers in the middle years as well, and there is a brisk, take-it-or-leave-it attitude that

reveals the teacher, who offers facts, suggests experiments and uses underlining in an almost audible fashion:

> You live in an *ocean* of space, but you live in a *river* of time. Space surrounds you on all sides, but time flows past you in a steady stream.
>
> . . . Every moment is a new *now*. Your life is made up of a stream of *nows* arranged like beads on a string, and slipping past you in a steady flow. The future becomes the present, the present becomes the past, and the past moves on behind you never to return.

The book has a stimulating central theme which gives it a wider application than if it had been confined to time as such. From the first chapter with its emphasis on palaeontology and geology to the final chapter on sound and music, the idea of time as rhythm is kept in the foreground. The attempts of Hebrew, Roman and Gregorian scholars to devise an acceptable calendar are shown as attempts to match rhythms that exist outside man with the necessary rhythms of a civilised community. The natural rhythms of animal life are demonstrated through cell change, migration, hibernation, digestion and excretion and so on, the rhythm of nature through geological eras, atomic structure and carbon dating, the rhythm of space in discussion of sun cycles and light waves. There is no suggestion that the author has a magic word to open the secrets of time, but his approach is stimulating and makes of time an expanding subject. (pp. 181-82)

> *Margery Fisher, "Foundations: Time," in her* Matters of Fact: Aspects of Non-Fiction for Children, *Thomas Y. Crowell Company, 1972, pp. 165-200.*

[*The following excerpt is from a review of the revised edition published in 1969.*]

First published in 1955, this updated edition again focuses on rhythms found in nature in a far-reaching and thought-provoking manner. From the oldest timepieces (the heavenly bodies) to the atomic clock (rhythms in the atom), man's attempts to create devices to measure time are interestingly discussed and reviewed. Instructions for making star clocks and sundials are explicit; the history of various calendars, including proposed revision of our present one, is also included. Other examples given of physical rhythms are geological (fossils, Grand Canyon rock layers); sound and music vibrations, the wave motion of light and color vibrations; and carbon dating (radioactivity). Equally fascinating are examples found in living organisms: e.g., heartbeat, respiration, metabolism, growth, and motion. Italics are used for technical terms; [Ruth Adler's] illustrations, though lackluster, are pertinent; and school libraries especially will find this a good choice for science project/science fair assignments.

> *Harold F. Desmond, Jr., in a review of "Time in Your Life," in* School Library Journal, *Vol. 16, No. 1, September, 1969, p. 163.*

Fire in Your Life (1955)

An excellent chemical and social survey of fire covers its

history from the cave hearth to the jet engine and explains the whole burning process in rather fascinating and at all times efficient detail. Starting out with primitive days, Mr. Adler speculates wisely on how fire must have been found and used, and sets the stage for early theories about fire from the four elements of the Greek philosophers to the downfall of phlogiston in the light of Lavoisier's experiments. With this advent of modern chemistry and atomic theory came the increasingly profitable use of fire—for comfort, for industry, for propulsion. Each of the ways in which the flames lick directly or indirectly into our lives, and the importance of them, is quite memorably explained.

> *A review of "Fire in Your Life," in* Virginia Kirkus' Service, *Vol. XXIII, No. 17, September 1, 1955, p. 657.*

In much the same style as his *Time in Your Life* and *Tools in Your Life,* the author traces the history of man's use of fire from primitive to modern times. Beginning with some of the mythology that grew out of man's early attempts to understand and explain fire, he traces man's use and control of fire for protection and for improved living; what fire has meant in the development of civilization, and what its potential future uses are. A disproportionate amount of space has been given to the development of the steel industry, only one of the many modern uses of fire, but this is a minor weakness of an otherwise excellent book.

> *A review of "Fire in Your Life," in* Bulletin of the Children's Book Center, *Vol. IX, No. 11, July, 1956, p. 121.*

This survey of the origins of fire and the uses to which mankind has and will put it is comprehensive and well arranged, though the illustrations [by Ruth Adler] are somewhat babyish in tone. Direct and indirect uses of fire are clearly described and known and proposed forms of fuel are assessed. Metallurgy and propulsion naturally figure largely in the story and perhaps such departures from the immediate subject are fair, but an uneasy feeling persists that this is the sort of survey that children of average intelligence ought to be making for themselves with the aid of encyclopaedias and reference books. It seems rather a luxury at the price.

> *A review of "Fire in Your Life," in* The Junior Bookshelf, *Vol. 20, No. 6, December, 1956, p. 332.*

Hurricanes and Twisters   (as Robert Irving, 1955)

In a simpler way this covers much of the material Ivan Ray Tennehill expanded on in *Hurricane Hunters* and sticks more closely to the formation and paths of hurricanes rather than the activities of the weather men. Familiar as Carol, Hazel, Connie, and their many sisters may be to us now, this family history really exposes their personalities and their hurricanologies. Just how twisters are born (over sunny southern seas where water evaporations cause sharp expansions of air) and grow (with a basic pattern of warm and cold pressured up and down drafts caus-

ing swirls) is clearly explained—and in following through on different types of storms and their drastic results, a fascination for the subject is conveyed too. Good basic reference. . . .

> *A review of "Hurricanes and Twisters," in* Virginia Kirkus' Service, *Vol. XXIII, No. 17, September 1, 1955, p. 653.*

How fearfully timely is Robert Irving's *Hurricanes and Twisters.* This excellent book covers its exciting subject in clear, easy-reading style; printed in large type, with subject divisions, it will appeal to many from eleven or twelve to fourteen, at home or in school. Besides excellent line cuts [by Ruth Adler] and diagrams, and maps in the text, there are sixteen pages of dramatic photographs. Parents who share it with their children will be fascinated. (p. 16)

> *"I Have Need of the Sky. . . Business with the Grass," in* New York Herald Tribune Book Review, *November 13, 1955, pp. 16, 28.*

Tools in Your Life   (1956)

Another good socio-scientific survey by the author of *Time in Your Life* and *Fire in Your Life* covers the history of tools from the adz to automation, stresses knowledge as a tool and clearly illustrates how people and their implements react on each other to make society change and grow. Chapter one is a basic definition of a tool, part of which is a comparison of animals' built in tools with the tools man has made for himself. From there, the material is a more or less familiarly patterned history of important tools, the stone ax, fire, and on up to the gasoline engine. But these chapters are supplemented by a healthy look at the effect of tools on tools, and tools on society; how man can use an outmoded tool or a dangerous tool and undermine his life or how he can use good tools to further progress. There is the idea of conquering rather than cooperating with nature, but it is sensibly conveyed and certainly extensively enough to attract older readers.

> *A review of "Tools in Your Life," in* Virginia Kirkus' Service, *Vol. XXIV, No. 4, February 15, 1956, p. 129.*

From early stone tools to present-day automation is a giant's step in man's endeavor to provide, improve, and create the best conditions for living. Adler bridges this span in an interesting and informative fashion with a nontechnical vocabulary, an abundance of clear-cut illustrations [by Ruth Adler], and an invaluable index. Will appeal to any junior or senior high reader who is interested in civilization's development. Pleasing format, attractive binding, and topical paragraphing recommend its purchase for school and public libraries.

> *Frances Lombard, in a review of "Tools in Your Life," in* Junior Libraries, *Vol. 2, No. 7, March 15, 1956, p. 32.*

An interestingly presented account of man's development of tools from the earliest stone-axe to atomic energy. Beginning with the tool-making ability that from earliest times has set man apart from other animals, the development of tools is traced through the sociological effects that have resulted from the introduction of new inventions, or from the clinging to old tools and old ways of doing things. The book will make an excellent companion volume to the Burlingame, *Machines that Built America* (Harcourt, 1953) and the Shippen, *Miracle in Motion* (Harper, 1955).

> *A review of "Tools in Your Life," in* Bulletin of the Children's Book Center, *Vol. IX, No. 10, June, 1956, p. 105.*

Rocks and Minerals and the Stories They Tell (as Robert Irving, 1956)

In a well organized and interesting book, Mr. Irving tells the story of the rocks and minerals of which the Earth consists in a manner that ought to do a lot to satisfy young curiosities. An introductory chapter points to two important things about rocks: they reveal geological history and they are a treasure house. Immediately following is a general account of the four different types of rock—igneous, topsoil, sedimentary and metamorphic. That all the main types are made up of minerals is elaborated in the next sections which expand detail on various kinds from granite to uranium and comment as well on particularly fascinating aspects of mining (coal, diamonds, etc.), the formation of the Earth itself and the uses of important mineral deposits. Recommended.

> *A review of "Rocks and Minerals," in* Virginia Kirkus' Service, *Vol. XXIV, No. 18, September 15, 1956, p. 708.*

A more serious book, much longer and valuable as a supplement to either [*Among the Rocks* by Terry Shannon or *The Story of Rocks* by Dorothy Shuttlesworth], ***Rocks and Minerals*** covers more of the geological history of the earth. How volcanoes, glaciers and earthquakes formed each type of rock, how mountains and oceans came to be, and how to read these stories from specimens collected make a fascinating study for children of eight and up.

> *Dorothy Robertson, "Nature Always Thrills," in* The Christian Science Monitor, *November 15, 1956, p. 15.*

Although an interesting story about the earth and theories as to its origin, this does not measure up to *The Rock Book* by the Fentons, and for usefulness in identification, the *First Book of Stones* is far superior. For the most part, material is accurate, though a few statements are questionable, e.g. the use of vinegar as a test for calcite is not very reliable and the term "conchoidal" is misused. Photographs are excellent and index is good. May serve as supplementary reference for intermediate and junior high grades.

> *H. Seymour Fowler and Lauretta G. McCusker, in a review of "Rocks and Minerals and the Stories They Tell," in* Junior Libraries, *Vol. 3, No. 4, December 15, 1956, p. 27.*

The Stars: Steppingstones into Space (1956, revised edition as The Stars: Decoding Their Messages)

An excellent, detailed account of the nature, structure, and motion of stars. Accurate and up to date. . . . More detailed than most teen-age astronomy books. Text difficult at times and may discourage average reader. Strictly for the scientifically-minded teenager. Highly recommended for libraries wanting a top quality text on modern astronomy.

> *Albert Monheit, in a review of "The Stars: Steppingstones into Space," in* Junior Libraries, *Vol. 3, No. 2, October 15, 1956, p. 135.*

This is a clear introductory explanation for young people and adults of the nature and structure of the stars. The evidence and the reasoning which lead astronomers to reach certain conclusions are given. There are preliminary pages on a few famous constellations, what is meant by directions of the stars; then there is a discussion of the stuff of which stars are made and how we recognize it, scales of brightness, their size, motion and weight. The arrangement of the book is pleasant, subtopics breaking up the text with clear diagrams and photographs when needed. On the theoretical side this is a book to have on your shelf as you begin to study the heavens beside that invaluable "star-finding" guide, *The Stars by Clock and Fist.*

> *H. H. Holmes, "Introductions to the Stars and Mars," in* New York Herald Tribune Book Review, *November 18, 1956, p. 34.*

[*The following excerpts are from reviews of* The Stars: Decoding Their Messages, *published in 1980.*]

Adler takes an unusual approach to astronomy. Beginning with what the layman can see on a clear night, he takes readers step by step through the methods by which scientists accumulate data about the stars. He begins with the location of constellations and progresses to determining a star's composition from its spectrum, then describes calculation of brightness, distance, motion, mass, and density. He concludes with present theories of the evolution of different kinds of stars. All this is comprehensible to those with a background limited to elementary arithmetic. . . . The coverage here is extremely broad at this simple level. While other books may be a little clearer about some aspects of astronomy, Adler has given a coherent picture of how all the knowledge we have gained about stars fits together. So much has occurred in astronomy since 1956 that this revised edition will be an asset to all collections.

> *Carolyn Caywood, in a review of "The Stars: Decoding Their Messages," in* School Library Journal, *Vol. 27, No. 1, September, 1980, p. 79.*

Perhaps the original version of this book made a significant contribution when it came out in 1956. This revision, however, must compete with the numerous, excellent astronomy texts which are now available. Unfortunately, the black and white photographs are too small, and some of the illustrations add nothing to the text. [***The Stars: Decoding Their Messages*** *is designed by Ellen Weiss and illustrated by Ruth Adler and Peggy Adler.*] Young observers of the skies would be much better served by larger illustrations of the constellations, as drawn by H. A. Rey, and countless books present the same technical arguments much more clearly than this one. Occasionally, analogies which are intended to clarify tend only to confuse. For example, the fingerprints which might be detected upon the surface of a letter, and used to detect who touched the letter, are compared in a confusing analogy to spectral analysis: "By comparing the fingerprints on the starlight with the fingerprints of all the elements we know, we find out which ones are on the surface of the star." (pp. 9-10)

> *Clarence C. Truesdell, in a review of "The Stars: Decoding Their Messages," in* Appraisal: Science Books for Young People, *Vol. 14, No. 1, Winter, 1981, pp. 9-10.*

Magic House of Numbers (1957)

The mystery of numbers and their interrelations is compared to a magic house whose stairs may lead you to surprises. Indeed this is proven constantly when curiosities about number sequences are revealed. It is a book that stimulates imagination and would be particularly enjoyable if shared. In addition to facts about numbers, there are puzzles, problems, and games from different parts of the globe, as well as mathematical card tricks devised by the author. These require only a basic elementary knowledge of arithmetic for their solution.

If arithmetic as a subject in the school curriculum were approached as it is here, there would be no doubt that arithmetic could be exciting.

> *Julia Jussim Brody, in a review of "Magic House of Numbers," in* The Saturday Review, *New York, Vol. XL, No. 19, May 11, 1957, p. 60.*

Some years ago high school students (and older people too) interested in arithmetical concepts enjoyed Jerome Meyers' *Fun with Arithmetic.* The problems, the theories, the curiosities he garnered were both illuminating and amusing. Now Irving Adler has written a similar book, which has much the same appeal for younger (or less advanced) students. The introduction to our whole system of numbering may be enlightening to an eleven-year-old whose teacher didn't explain the basic principles or who somehow didn't quite grasp the idea. Important and interesting as this is the young will welcome it for its card tricks, number games and mathematical puzzles (all with answers in the back).

> *Margaret Sherwood Libby, in a review of "Magic House of Numbers," in* New York Herald Tribune Book Review, *May 26, 1957, p. 7.*

Mr. Adler gives us a mixture here, all based on mathematics, of puzzles, games, riddles, card tricks and the intricacies of varied number systems. It is an intriguing and fascinating book especially in the section dealing with number curiosities. Mr. Adler has given us something unusual that stirs the imagination and schools the mind and he shows us new aspects of familiar number symbols. The section

on puzzles without numbers is the least interesting, not very original, and somewhat out of place. But it serves perhaps as a little of the old to temper the new which is in parts something of an exacting study for the young. It is an enlivening book that will appeal to a wide range of age groups who enjoy some mental exercise and agility.

> *A review of "Magic House of Numbers," in* The Junior Bookshelf, *Vol. 22, No. 5, November, 1958, p. 272.*

[*The following excerpts are from reviews of the revised edition published in 1974.*]

If I were twenty or thirty years older, Dr. Adler's book might seem more familiar to me; many of the tricks and procedures he describes were, I understand, part of ordinary math teaching at the turn of the century. If I were twenty or thirty years younger, I might have had some of it—as theory, not technique—in the New Math. As it is, I missed it. For instance, I never learned how to check my work by casting out nines. Dr. Adler explains why this sort of thing works, and with surprising clarity why analogous techniques would work in systems based on numbers other than ten. In addition, he has a fine supply of mathematical tricks and puzzles—some of them new to me and some of them old standbys. I don't think anyone is likely to know all of them, and I doubt even more that anyone can solve all of them unaided.

> *Harry C. Stubbs, in a review of "Magic House of Numbers," in* The Horn Book Magazine, *Vol. LI, No. 2, April, 1975, p. 168.*

Two new chapters have been added to this enjoyable selection of mathematical games and puzzles. Since the additional material—six number games and several fascinations derived from Fibonacci numbers—is negligible, only libraries not having the original edition or needing another copy should consider this revision.

> *Sandra Weir, in a review of "Magic House of Numbers," in* School Library Journal, *Vol. 22, No. 1, September, 1975, p. 94.*

How Life Began (1957)

This book explains the origin of life according to a completely mechanistic theory which is very objectionable to people of certain religious beliefs. The reader must have a rather thorough knowledge of biology and organic chemistry as well as some knowledge of physics and other sciences in order to have a clear understanding of what the authors are saying. This latter fact will limit its usefulness at the high school level. Recommended for purchase only after examination.

> *Viola K. Fitch, in a review of "How Life Began," in* Library Journal, *Vol. 82, No. 13, July, 1957, p. 1804.*

Life's origin and the chemical changes and combinations that have helped to channel the directions evolution has taken, is the theme of this well-written book for the older child. We learn what primitive man believed, and how experiments over the years have changed man's thinking.

Fuller treatment is given to current theories that have resulted from the synthesis of conclusions drawn from research in such fields as biology, geology, physics, and astronomy, with special emphasis on chemistry and the nature of carbon. The author points out that not only does such combined effort in the sciences reveal pieces to this great puzzle, but man may also benefit directly. For example, work done on viruses which are believed to resemble earliest forms of life may lead to cures for some of our most dreaded diseases.

Children interested in the story of evolution will find this a fresh and fascinating approach to the subject.

> *Julia Jussim Brody, in a review of "How Life Begun,"* in The Saturday Review, *New York, Vol. XL, No. 42, October 19, 1957, p. 57.*

[*The following excerpt is from a review of the revised edition published in 1977.*]

In this clear, readable revision of the 1956 edition, Adler expounds evolution theories and supports them well with recent scientific studies, e.g., experiments which have determined that chemicals in the sun, stars, meteorites, etc. are similar to those in the young earth. Considerable updating of the scientific information has been done, though, regrettably, Adler neglects to mention the new theory of quarks, considered by some scientists as the basic building blocks of matter. Still, this well-written account with its interdisciplinary approach drawing together astronomy, geology, chemistry, and biology will be informative and useful to students having some background in basic scientific principles.

> *Cynthia K. Richey, in a review of "How Life Begun,"* in School Library Journal, *Vol. 23, No. 6, February, 1977, p. 70.*

Monkey Business: Hoaxes in the Name of Science   (1957)

This exciting account of frauds and hoaxes in science captures the interest and holds it—often for longer than one wishes. Each of the five chapters is a story in itself; each is devoted to the thesis that "valuable knowledge often makes its first appearance combined with serious errors; science has developed out of superstition, by rescuing the knowledge while it eliminates the errors; and through such process medicine grew out of magic and witchcraft, astronomy grew out of astrology, and chemistry grew out of alchemy." Mr. Adler alerts the young scientist to the importance of challenging sources of information. At the same time he is entertaining, exciting and informative.

> *Glenn O. Blough, "Science's Closet," in* The New York Times Book Review, *November 17, 1957, p. 16.*

Five hoaxes, practical jokes, honest mistakes, and deliberate attempts to deceive are described: a newspaper hoax which claimed proof that the moon was inhabited, the Piltdown man episode, various attempts to manufacture diamonds, mesmerism, and attempts to trisect a triangle. Author shows how scientific knowledge was used to expose these mistakes or hoaxes, and therein lies the chief

value of the book. Some high school students will like it, but it is not an important book. Recommended only where funds and demand permit unlimited purchases. (pp. 37-8)

> *Dorothy Schumacher, in a review of "Monkey Business," in* Junior Libraries, *Vol. 4, No. 6, February 15, 1958, pp. 37-8.*

Energy and Power   (as Robert Irving, 1958)

The precocious student in the first two years of high school, who has not studied physics, will gain insight into the action of energy and power. Older boys and girls now studying physics could also profit from the author's explanation of the transfer of energy, the structure of the atom, heat as motion, and Nature's resistance to man's efforts. The examples chosen to illustrate abstract concepts are drawn from familiar experience. Language is clear: type is large. . . . A scientific book which clearly translates complex ideas.

> *A review of "Energy and Power," in* Virginia Kirkus' Service, *Vol. XXVI, No. 2, January 15, 1958, p. 40.*

Man-Made Moons: The Earth Satellites and What They Will Tell Us   (1958)

Whereas other books have tended to concentrate on the mechanism and launching of satellites, this timely book, after briefly explaining how they are launched, treats thoroughly the types of information which may be relayed to us from earth satellites. Much complex scientific information is treated as simply as possible without sacrificing accuracy. Although it will appeal to some students in upper elementary grades and vocabulary is suited to them, this material will be better understood by junior high students.

> *H. Seymour Fowler and Lauretta G. McCusker, in a review of "Man-Made Moons," in* Junior Libraries, *Vol. 4, No. 7, March 15, 1958, p. 112.*

The Sun and Its Family   (1958)

Accurate, compact, and useful facts about the earth, planets, and sun. Well illustrated [by Ruth Adler] with 45 line drawings which are clearly integrated with the text. Perfect for 8th- and 9th-graders, this historical approach to astronomy covers one of the most popular subjects in junior high science. Companion to **The Stars: Stepping Stones into Space,** both serve as excellent supplementary science reading. Fine format, good print, satisfactory binding. Recommended for all junior high school and public libraries.

> *Anne Jackson, in a review of "The Sun and Its Family," in* Junior Libraries, *Vol. 4, No. 8, April 15, 1958, p. 50.*

Space is close to us now and the Earth is a ball about which Sputniks spin. This book treats the Earth as such a ball, a member of the Sun's family along with other balls, some larger and some smaller. Interesting and with an un-hurried air about it, it is most remarkable for the manner in which it takes up matters which are too often taught students without the trouble of proof—the roundness of the Earth, the fact that it turns, the gravitational force exerted by the Moon—and describes the manner in which scientists have come to these conclusions or obtained these figures.

> *Isaac Asimov, in a review of "The Sun and Its Family," in* The Horn Book Magazine, *Vol. XXXIV, No. 4, August, 1958, p. 274.*

Using the same historical approach so successful in *The Stars: Stepping Stones Into Space,* Irving Adler has now written for young people over eleven a most illuminating book about our star, the sun, and the planets which revolve around it. Beginning with what we see in the sky, he tells how men first theorized from patterns they noticed there, how the Ptolemaic theory arose and the Copernican. Then he gives proofs of the earth's spin and the earth's revolution around the sun, to show why the Copernican theory finally triumphed, and discusses how the size, distance and motion of the sun and planets are measured. In explaining such things Mr. Adler answers some of the most frequently asked questions of young astronomers. Occasionally he oversimplifies so that steps in the proof are missing. For instance, after a fine explanation of what weight is and how we "weigh the sun" mathematically, he jumps a little too fast over the calculations, but the mathematically curious can always find more detailed studies and the beginner needs the simplicity.

> *Margaret Sherwood Libby, in a review of "The Sun and Its Family," in* New York Herald Tribune Book Review, *August 17, 1958, p. 8.*

[*The following excerpt is from a review of the revised edition published in 1969.*]

The author, one of the most competent writers in his field, has updated the original 1958 edition with the latest findings about the planets. The largest addition of information is about the moon, but several paragraphs have been added to the sections on Venus, Mars and Jupiter. Also, one illustration was deleted. If the earlier edition is already in the library collection, this new one is unnecessary since the information added is accessible in any encyclopedia yearbook. For libraries without Adler's book, the new edition would be a worthwhile purchase and a good companion to the newly revised *Exploring the Universe* by Gallant (Doubleday, 1968).

> *Betty B. Douglas, in a review of "The Sun & Its Family," in* School Library Journal, *Vol. 16, No. 3, November, 1969, p. 124.*

Dust (1958)

It is precisely the commonplace nature of Irving Adler's subject which lends fascination to this text. Dust, the lowest observable form of matter, the scourge of the housewife, is presented in a new context and becomes suddenly a formidable part of the universe. In clear, economic language, the young reader is introduced to dust in all its as-

pects and functions—the effect of dust on vision, color, agriculture, adhesion, dead dust, live dust, etc. A helpful and revealing supplement to the study of elementary science.

> *A review of "Dust," in* Virginia Kirkus' Service, *Vol. XXVI, No. 18, September 15, 1958, p. 716.*

Who would have thought that the subject of dust could fill a whole book and be interesting, too? Mr. Adler did and has succeeded admirably in explaining dust, its origin, how it is formed and increases and travels, how important it is, and how very harmful it is. We cannot live without it and often cannot live with it. Recommended for all libraries, 5th grade up.

> *Gladys Conklin, in a review of "Dust," in* Junior Libraries, *Vol. 5, No. 3, November 15, 1958, p. 34.*

The first sentence of the book is, "Dust is a small particle, but it is a big subject." I can't improve on that as a thesis and the author goes on to prove it amply. Beginning with dust as a familiar enemy, he continues to show the number of ways in which dust of various sorts impinges upon our life. Dust can burn, it can explode. It gives us blue sky, twilight, and beautiful sunsets. It brings about rain and conserves our heat. Some dust is alive—bacterial spores—and threatens our health. Mr. Adler forcefully describes the haze of dust that blankets our cities and turns the city-dwellers' lungs black, and finally, cosmic dust, which enters our atmosphere out of disintegrated meteoric remnants and fills the spaces between the stars. After reading this book, a youngster will stare at the dancing motes in a sunbeam with new fascination and respect.

> *Isaac Asimov, in a review of "Dust," in* The Horn Book Magazine, *Vol. XXXV, No. 2, April, 1959, p. 140.*

The Tools of Science: From Yardstick to Cyclotron (1958; revised edition as *The Changing Tools of Science: From Yardstick to Synchrotron*)

A simply and clearly phrased description of a number of scientific instruments, chosen, naturally enough, for their dramatic value. The nature of the subject makes the book episodic and one does not always see the logic of the progression. Why, for instance, are chromatographic devices placed between cameras and radioactive tracers? Nevertheless, the young reader has the chance to view science from a new and practical angle. (pp. 392-93)

> *Isaac Asimov, in a review of "The Tools of Science: From Yardstick to Cyclotron," in* The Horn Book Magazine, *Vol. XXXIV, No. 5, October, 1958, pp. 392-93.*

Knowledge of the tools of science is important in understanding science's methods as well as its subject-matter. Irving Adler has succeeded admirably in describing common and uncommon tools that scientists use to measure mass, distance, time, heat, light and other things. The treatment is interesting and nontechnical—the author assumes no previous knowledge on the reader's part in this

Adler receiving an honorary doctorate from St. Michael's College in 1990.

area of science. He explains the why and how of such instruments as the microscope, the camera, the telescope and seismograph. . . .

This author of a dozen successful science books has provided a book that is not only for the especially interested and talented but also for the many who would be interested, given half a chance. Also, those teachers in elementary schools who sigh and say, "My pupils know more science than I do," will do well to read this book and so will parents who find themselves in the same fix.

> *Glenn O. Blough, "Instruments of Progress,"*
> *in* The New York Times Book Review, *November 23, 1958, p. 48.*

Written to show how man measures, weighs, and analyzes his universe, this gets into exceedingly difficult concepts. Each tool or method is treated briefly so as to convey the general principle, in some cases too briefly for real comprehension. Nevertheless, the book will serve for science-minded 6th-8th-graders as an overview of many delicate, scientific procedures.

> *Agnes Krarup, in a review of "The Tools of Sci-*

ence," in Junior Libraries, *Vol. 5, No. 4, December, 1958, p. 40.*

[*The following excerpt is from a review of* The Changing Tools of Science: From Yardstick to Synchrotron, *published in 1973.*]

Adler's historical survey and explanation of the techniques of measurement, observation, and analysis in physics and chemistry is essentially the same as the 1958 edition, ***Tools of Science.*** The illustrations [originally by Ruth Adler, here by Ruth and Peggy Adler], photographs, and most of the information remain substantially unchanged; however, there is a new chapter on recent developments in scientific apparatus. This material provides adequate explanations of transistors, integrated circuits, lasers, holography, image orthicon and vidicon tubes in television cameras, magnetometers, advanced techniques of spectroscopy, and new methods of detecting and dating archeological finds. Since a basic course in physics and chemistry is needed to understand much of the information here, younger readers will find Goldstein's *Tools of the Scientist* (Prentice-Hall, 1963) more useful.

> *Sandra Weir, in a review of "The Changing Tools of Science: From Yardstick to Synchro-*

tron," in School Library Journal, *Vol. 20, No. 8, April, 1974, p. 62.*

Mathematics: The Story of Numbers, Symbols, and Space (1958)

The beauties of mathematics are invisible to most children who are dragged through it with nose to grindstone, seeing only one step ahead and depending on memory and meaningless rote to get by. For those who have not already acquired a permanent dislike as a result, this little book may be a godsend. It teaches very little mathematics in the formal sense, but it gives quick glances here and there so that whole areas are seen in flashes of a few hundred words apiece. The illustrations [by Lowell Hess] are in sharp, contrasting colors, designed to bring out meanings acutely. The child is introduced to squares and cubes pictorially: he can see the regular polyhedrons in fascinating design; he is shown clearly and graphically how a triangle can give the distance to the moon, and how a simple pattern of numbers can give meaning to the way in which leaves form a spiral up a plant stem. While this will not prepare the reader to pass any tests in elementary algebra or geometry, it will make him wiser, and, perhaps, more interested in learning mathematics, and more patient with the everyday grind of everyday math teaching.

> *Isaac Asimov, in a review of "Mathematics: The Story of Numbers, Symbols, and Space," in The Horn Book Magazine, Vol. XXXV, No. 4, August, 1959, p. 304.*

[*Mathematics*] is bound to appeal even to those for whom arithmetic remains a mystery. The story of the origin of our number system, mathematical puzzles, the theory of primes, of magic squares, of the slide rule and of the most simple form of probability, coin-tossing, are all explained very simply and with very colourful diagrams and charts.

This fascinating introduction by an eminent mathematician illustrates the wonder of mathematical exploration for the average child, in the way we teachers are being encouraged to introduce this important subject, placing less emphasis on calculation and more on understanding. The book is also suitable for the lower forms in the secondary school.

> *Eric Linfield, in a review of "Mathematics," in The School Librarian and School Library Review, Vol. 10, No. 4, March, 1961, p. 379.*

Sound and Ultrasonics   (as Robert Irving, 1959)

Almost before a child can read simple books like Tillie S. Pine's *Sounds All Around* and Franklyn Branley and Eleanor Vaughn's *Timmy and the Tin-can Telephone,* he is ready for more detail which is provided most capably in Mr. Irving's book on the nature of sound, how we hear, how various sound makers are made, the musical scale, how sounds bend and bounce, how certain animal sounds are made. It ends with an excellent explanation of the sound barrier and sound recordings. Many a grownup will be grateful for this when certain deceptively simple ques-

tions are asked and the answers prove difficult to give. Here are the answers for all to read, the eleven- to thirteen-year-olds and their parents. It is one of the best to appear on the subject.

> *Margaret Sherwood Libby, in a review of "Sound and Ultrasonics," in New York Herald Tribune Book Review, May 3, 1959, p. 9.*

Comprehensive coverage of science of sound in language easy to understand. Logical organization of material, from sounds familiar to human experience to areas of ultrasonics and supersonics, makes this a valuable contribution to enrichment of science curriculum. Covers such aspects as nature, origin, and characteristics of sound, human ear, animal sounds, recording and transmission, practical applications of ultrasonics and relationship of air travel to sound. Good diagrams. Index. Juvenile format but recommended for grades 7-12.

> *Alice Ruth, in a review of "Sound and Ultrasonics," in Junior Libraries, Vol. 5, No. 9, May 15, 1959, p. 66.*

This is a most attractive book both in appearance and content. The large, clear type and nicely spaced lines of print make reading a pleasure. The neatly drawn white-on-black illustrations [by Leonard Everett Fisher] are fascinating. Finally, and most important, the author, without any sign of strain, or undue haste, carefully explores the realm of sound. He discusses sound as a wave phenomenon, the various types of vibrations that produce sounds, and the different objects that make sounds, including musical instruments and animal organisms. The last chapters are devoted to the modern science of sound, to telephones, phonographs, and the use of sounds which we cannot hear because their wave frequency is too high. The uses of these ultrasonic frequencies are described interestingly. That these vibrations can be used to clean dirty surfaces was demonstrated some time ago on the Garry Moore show "I've Got a Secret." However, did you know that ultrasonic waves can detect imperfections within metals that are smaller and deeper than can be revealed by X-rays? The book fittingly concludes with comments on jet flights that have broken the sound barrier.

> *Isaac Asimov, in a review of "Sound and Ultrasonics," in The Horn Book Magazine, Vol. XXXV, No. 4, August, 1959, p. 306.*

Hot and Cold   (1959)

Temperature, its manifestations and effects, are throughly scrutinized in this illuminating text. Defining temperature as a continuum, the author discusses the molecular components of heat and cold, their materialization in extreme conditions such as fire and ice, electricity, and the uses to which man-controlled heat may be put. Irving Adler, author of more than a dozen science books, treats this essential subject methodically and in a manner which should both interest and inform.

> *A review of "Hot and Cold," in Virginia Kirkus' Service, Vol. XXVII, No. 12, June 15, 1959, p. 406.*

Mr. Adler is a prolific writer of science books, which is fortunate for there are few who can explain subtle scientific concepts as clearly and deftly as he. Whether it is the picture of heat as rapidly moving molecules or the description of the various devices used to measure temperature, he succeeds at once in being accurate and comprehensible. In his last chapters he takes the reader on two tremendous voyages: first, from the ordinary heat of burning fuel up and up to the unspeakable temperatures within nuclear bombs and at the center of stars (which temperatures we may depend on for hydrogen fusion power in years to come). The other trip goes in the opposite direction—from the temperature of ice down to the eerie world of the approaches to absolute zero (which some day we may use for tiny electronic valves to run our computers).

> *Isaac Asimov, in a review of "Hot and Cold,"* in The Horn Book Magazine, *Vol. XXXV, No. 5, October, 1959, p. 394.*

Seeing the Earth from Space: What the Man-Made Moons Tell Us (1959)

"Based in part on" the author's **Man-Made Moons,** published in 1957, before any satellites had been launched. Both books have the same chapter headings and the same information on what satellites are and how they work, but where the first one could only predict the kind of knowledge that might be obtained from them, this book reports actual results of both Russian and American satellite launchings. Findings in regard to the shape of the earth, gravity, density of electrons, temperature of the upper air, and the Van Allen radiation are described and interpreted. Some of the original illustrations [by Ruth Adler] are retained, but many new diagrams and photographs have been added. A valuable feature is a table showing the date of launching, weight, distance from the earth, length of life, etc., of the first ten successful satellites. As in Adler's other books, material is presented in simple language, without technical detail. Because of the importance of the added material, this book is recommended for purchase, whether or not libraries have the original edition.

> *Dorothy Schumacher, in a review of "Seeing the Earth from Space," in* Junior Libraries, *Vol. 6, No. 5, January 15, 1960, p. 40.*

Electromagnetic Waves (as Robert Irving, 1960)

[*Electromagnetic Waves* and Hy Ruchlis' *The Wonder of Light*], on the same general subject of light and related radiations, are models of their kind. Both are written with admirable directness and simplicity and with the obvious aim of transferring as much real information as possible in clear language.

Ruchlis' book places the larger emphasis of the two on visible light. . . .

Irving's book gives roughly equal weight to light and its six relatives, three of longer wavelength (infrared waves, microwaves, and radio waves) and three of shorter wavelength (ultraviolet waves, X rays, and gamma rays). In

each case, the methods of production and reception are described, and their uses in this modern world of ours.

> *Isaac Asimov, in a review of "Electromagnetic Waves," in* The Horn Book Magazine, *Vol. XXXXI, No. 3, June, 1960, p. 228.*

Brief, clear coverage of electromagnetics: light, radio, infrared, ultraviolet, X-rays, microwaves, gamma radiation, and their interrelationships. . . . Excellent exposition. Despite the clarity of the writing and the relative ease of sentence structure, the nature of the subject matter requires considerable thought and effort from the reader. In this sense, this is not easy reading; in fact, a longer book might have made the same points easier to grasp. Nonetheless, this is quite well done and gives an overall view not previously available. Recommended. (pp. 2487-88)

> *Theodore C. Hines, in a review of "Electromagnetic Waves," in* Library Journal, *Vol. 85, No. 12, June 15, 1960, pp. 2487-88.*

Things That Spin: From Tops to Atoms (with Ruth Adler, 1960)

The Adlers have an unfailing ability to get at the heart of science and express great truths in simple, direct prose. In this little book they begin with six facts about spinning tops and they show how these facts can help us understand a number of phenomena that might otherwise seem very complicated. Gyroscopes, yo-yos and washing machines are considered as everyday examples of spinning objects, but the second half of the book takes up the spinning earth. The seasons and the precession of the equinoxes fall under the six-fact system. At the very end, mention is made of the spinning sun and moon and Milky Way, and even of the spinning electrons and atomic nuclei. A helpful and stimulating book.

> *Isaac Asimov, in a review of "Things That Spin," in* The Horn Book Magazine, *Vol. XXXVI, No. 4, August, 1960, p. 305.*

Numbers Old and New (with Ruth Adler, 1960)

The Adler books of science for children (at various age-levels and on various subjects) are always charming; written simply but without condescension; and carrying a feeling of authority without pedantry. This one is no exception. . . . [The] authors pass lightly over many facts about numbers and number systems. About a third of the book is given over to the various methods that have been employed to write the numbers, and another large part is devoted to more or less amusing facts about numbers: magic squares, numerology, card tricks and so on. In fact, the seven-to-ten-year-old reading this book ought to have enough fun to forget that he is educating himself, too, which is a neat trick when it is managed.

> *Isaac Asimov, in a review of "Numbers Old and New," in* The Horn Book Magazine, *Vol. XXXVI, No. 5, October, 1960, p. 415.*

The Giant Golden Book of Mathematics: Exploring the World of Numbers and Space (1960)

To write about mathematics in a way that young people can understand is not a simple problem. Too often excessive formalism gets in the way of communication. Irving Adler has skillfully avoided this danger. He is not concerned with mathematical skills, but with the ideas of mathematics, and with the basic role of these ideas in our civilization. The text, simply and clearly written, is admirably supplemented by a great wealth of pictures in striking colors, drawn by Lowell Hess. The only flaw in the otherwise excellent exposition is an occasional confusion between number and quantity.

Among other things, *The Giant Golden Book of Mathematics* presents an absorbing account of numbers and number lore—intriguing facts about prime numbers, triangular numbers and square numbers. Then there are stories of number systems with their wonderful properties and their manifold uses.

Word and picture combine to tell about angles, triangles and polygons; about the famous theorem of Pythagoras; about spheres, cones, cylinders and the regular solids. There is much besides. The list looks frightening for young minds, but the writing is always simple and homespun and readable. Ideas are exposed with the aid of everyday examples: notions of coordinate geometry stem from the arrangement of seats in a classroom; probability is related to the tossing of a coin. The reader is taken on short, delightful excursions into recreational mathematics, deductive thinking and the realm of the infinite. Author and artist are particularly successful in underlining the omnipresence of mathematical ideas—in art, in music, in nature, as well as in science and engineering.

> Robert E. K. Rourke, "Sum Total," in The New York Times Book Review, *November 13, 1960, p. 35.*

Adler is well enough known in this field to need no introduction. This book includes the material in the earlier smaller book [*Mathematics: The Story of Numbers, Symbols, and Space*] plus a great deal more. It is a collection or potpourri of examples and explanations of mathematical principles and applications rather than a historical approach like Hogben's. Briefness of the sections and careful linking of good illustrations to text make the book attractive and usable even by those with a fairly low reading level. In only a very few instances does Adler descend to the "Sandy was building a model airplane" level in his examples. Clear introduction to complex ideas is the predominant tendency here. Included are, for example, the sieve of Eratosthenes, construction of regular polygons, the golden section, imaginary numbers, graphing equations, probability theory, and the relations of mathematics to art and music. Not easy stuff but, aside from the rather soppy preface, attractive, interesting, and well done. Can be used to develop a real interest in mathematics.

> Theodore C. Hines, in a review of "The Giant Golden Book of Mathematics: Exploring the World of Numbers and Space," in Junior Libraries, *Vol. 7, No. 5, January 15, 1961, p. 58.*

An oversize book, profusely illustrated by charts and diagrams, that gives brief explanations of many mathematical subjects ranging from the simple to some that are quite complex. Lucid through the explanations are, their usefulness is limited by the brevity of treatment. Only one page is devoted to finite and infinite numbers, for example, and of the two pages that discuss square root, half the space is given to illustration. Some biographical material is included; some of the articles show the application of mathematics in daily life: "Mathematics and Music" or "Calculating Machines", for example. For the young person who is fascinated by mathematics, the book is probably not sufficiently expanded, but it is perhaps most useful to the potential young mathematician with some background but an undeveloped proficiency. Teachers will find the book useful to supplement the curriculum.

> Zena Sutherland, in a review of "Mathematics: Exploring the World of Numbers and Space," in Bulletin of the Center for Children's Books, *Vol. XIV, No. 8, April, 1961, p. 121.*

Electronics (as Robert Irving, 1961)

> [*The following excerpt is from an advance review of* Electronics.]

Mr. Irving deals with difficult scientific concepts in the simplest, most concise manner possible. A general description of the meaning of electronics starts us off, followed by a quick review of electricity and magnetism. "When electronic tubes are in a circuit, they work as part of a team", and the next chapter is devoted to a description of each of the "team members", including resistors, capacitors and transformers. In a chapter on the three main types of electronic tubes and the uses of each, we are enlightened on the operation of radios and broadcasting as we are later on television, when we learn about the phototube. Electronics further refines and improves important inventions and discoveries, exemplified by the electronic microscope, the radar telescope and the accelerators which crack the smaller nuclei of atoms. Clean, uncluttered diagrams and clear, distinct typography match a brisk, forthright text authoritatively presented for the early teens.

> A review of "Electronics," in Virginia Kirkus' Service, *Vol. XXVIII, No. 24, December 15, 1960, p. 1032.*

Fast-growing and fascinating, the allied fields of electricity and electronics are also among the most difficult to understand. Gabriel Reuben conveys all the fascination and avoids being trapped by the difficulties in *Electronics for Children*. This small book is filled with forty-nine experiments, beginning with elementary ones in magnetism and moving smoothly through electricity and electronics. . . .

Electronics, by Robert Irving, is a bigger book, with three attributes: everything is in it; all of its parts are clearly presented, and its index is thorough. But it presents such an overwhelming stream of facts that the reader is apt to be submerged. *Electronics* is good for finding a specific fact but less satisfactory for reading.

> *Henry W. Hubbard, "Current Courses," in* The New York Times Book Review, *August 13, 1961, p. 20.*

The Story of a Nail   (with Ruth Adler, 1961)

The topic has obviously been well researched and facts abound concerning the stories of coal, limestone, coke, wrought and pig irons, and the manufacture of steel, but one seriously wonders how many children really care about nails, as such, whether they are machine-made, handmade, sterilized and finished, have two feet and no head or are double headed. We are impressed with their typology and their roles, but not with their ability to generate interest.

> *A review of "The Story of a Nail," in* Virginia Kirkus' Service, *Vol. XXIX, No. 2, January 15, 1961, p. 56.*

It is to be hoped that librarians and teachers will not let the title of this book blind them to the fact that, while pursuing its title subject, this is also presenting a truly excellent account of the historical development of the steel industry. Clear, well-labelled drawings accompany the simple and meaningful text; recommended.

> *Elizabeth Grave, in a review of "The Story of a Nail," in* Junior Libraries, *Vol. 7, No. 8, April 15, 1961, p. 48.*

Succinctly informative, but rather dry and probably not of great general interest. The first section describes different kinds of nails and their uses; the raw materials from which iron and steel are made are discussed, as are the manufacturing processes. The text is broader than the title indicates; it seems over-extended as a book about nails, and as a book about iron and steel it is not extensive enough. Some historical material is introduced, and a brief word-list is appended.

> *Zena Sutherland, in a review of "The Story of a Nail," in* Bulletin of the Center for Children's Books, *Vol. XV, No. 2, October, 1961, p. 21.*

Shadows   (with Ruth Adler, 1961)

Beginning with personal shadows, this introductory book takes up eclipses, measuring, and judging shape or texture, and telling time by shadows. It mentions also the uses of light and dark in films, art, egg production, and animal life. Excellent for creating awareness of the world around us, especially a kind of universality of scientific observation. Recommended.

> *Agnes Krarup, in a review of "Shadows," in* Junior Libraries, *Vol. 7, No. 8, April 15, 1961, p. 40.*

[*The following excerpt is from a review of the revised edition published in 1968.*]

First published in 1961, this edition contains revisions of such little consequence that there is almost no justification for calling it a revised edition. The pagination and format are the same; there is little new or added material on the subjects covered—personal shadows, measuring devices, light and dark contrasts in art and plant and animal life, eclipses, and so on. On pages 11, 20, and 34, occasional words or phrases have been changed, examples of reediting rather than revising. On page 20, in the description of a sundial used in ancient Egypt, an illustration has been slightly changed, as has a small part of the text. The word list at the end of the book contains one alteration, the definition of "disc." The book is good, a fine title for purchase, but if the 1961 edition is in a library's collection, this one should not be considered for purchase.

> *Beatrice M. Adam, in a review of "Shadows," in* School Library Journal, *Vol. 15, No. 7, March, 1969, p. 147.*

Why? A Book of Reasons   (with Ruth Adler, 1961)

A beginning science book done in a question and answer form with accompanying pictures ties in with the sound factual approach of *Things That Spin* and *Numbers Old and New* but the material is handled differently. There is no central theme. This takes the kinds of questions continually asked by children in 2nd-3rd-4th grades and answers them, so that each topic is complete in itself, within the limitations of the age level and scope. It is a difficult book to evaluate; I'd suggest that it be given to a child with an inquiring mind and acquisitive instinct for collecting unrelated facts.

> *A review of "Why? A Book of Reasons," in* Virginia Kirkus' Service, *Vol. XXIX, No. 15, August 1, 1961, p. 672.*

The Giant Colour Book of Mathematics: Exploring the World of Numbers and Space   (1961)

Stand on a plank floor. Take a thin stick which is exactly as long as the planks are wide. Drop it, and see if it falls on a crack. Keep on doing this and count the times it crosses a crack. When you've had a few hundred shots, sit down and do a simple sum. Double the number of times you dropped the stick, and then divide by the times it fell on a crack. Your answer will be in the region of 3.1415926535897932384 . . . or an approximate value of pi.

Here is a dramatic and illuminating way to stir initial thoughts about pi and the mathematical properties of the circle. An ideal first lesson in school—something to rouse mathematical delight in even the sleepiest corners, and to bring numbers close to life. And yet this was utterly new to me until I reached page 26 of *Mathematics.* Many things here were fresh to me; and yet, in a sense, I'd 'learned' them all at school. Pi, for instance: I knew all about that. I've got a drawer full of parchment certificates somewhere, and the Mathematics one has "Distinction' stamped on it. In other words I was quick at sums and formulae, I knew when to slot pi in, and when to take it out. I got the right answers. And yet I had little understanding of what I was doing (except working for a certificate), no awakened curiosity about the transactions I could so faultlessly handle. Looking through this book I tumbled again and again on comments which illuminated inert mathematical data frozen in my memory, and I became very excited.

Take Fibonacci numbers (1, 1, 2, 3, 5, 8, 13, 21, 34, 55, 89, 144 . . .). I'd 'learned' about those somewhere. But pick any three successive ones. Square the middle one, multiply the other two: the result will always differ by one. I hadn't learned that. I tried it out all along the row, and it works. Why? And why does the spacing of a plant's leaves follow these ratios, and why are the very knuckles of my hand as I write placed according to them? . . . The blood races, and turning page after page I had the old elusive thrill that close ahead would come some sudden clarifying concept to make simple number 'sense' of the universe.

Of course it didn't, but I was in the chase for the first time. The hunt went over very old ground. Page 36 announced that there are exactly five regular solids. Are there indeed? I spent a rewarding time challenging this, attempting to sketch or invent the sixth. But my 'nonahedrons' and 36-sided fantasies all failed the test, and I ended up with octahedrons and icosahedrons like everyone else. I read later that men have been perplexed by this for over 2,000 years, but I left school without ever having sniffed the excitement. This is a fine book for the secondary school child. . . . (p. 702)

> *Brian Jackson, "Thoughts about Pi," in* New Statesman, *Vol. LXII, No. 1600, November 10, 1961, pp. 702, 704.*

Color in Your Life (1962)

By writing accurate, clear, and entertaining books based on recent scientific knowledge and theory, Irving Adler serves both science and young readers. Here he discusses physical, physiological, and psychological color phenomena, touches on aspects of organic chemistry and quantum theory without overwhelming or talking down. He gives abundant examples and a few experiments.

> *Norwood Long, in a review of "Color in Your Life," in* School Library Journal, *Vol. 8, No. 6, February, 1962, p. 46.*

Color is so much a part of life that it is simply taken for granted. Surrounded by colors, people ordinarily give them little thought until, perhaps, an unusual display—a sunset, cherry blossoms in springtime—attracts their attention. Yet the how and why of color has engaged the interest of scientists in many fields for a long time. Their discoveries involve physics, chemistry, biology, physiology and psychology.

On this complex subject Irving Adler writes clearly and imaginatively. He captures and holds interest by answering questions that occur to everyone at one time or another: Why is the sky blue? What makes leaves change from green to yellow and red in the autumn? Why do colors look different in electric and in sun light? Why does a color run? Can color fit a mood? How is color produced on TV? Why are babies born with blue eyes?

Answers are given with short excursions into a variety of sciences and different aspects of the subject are presented so that the reader approaches and sees it in an entirely new way. Scattered throughout the book are graphs and diagrams to show how colors are made and used. Mr. Adler's book is one to awaken curiosity about an everyday experience and increase enjoyment of a familiar wonder.

> *Iris Vinton, in a review of "Color in Your Life," in* The New York Times Book Review, *May 13, 1962, p. 18.*

This is not just another book on colors as the name of Irving Adler should assure us. Not for this author the journalistic approach or that of the merely didactic, elementary school teacher, briskly presenting snippets of information in a more or less pleasing format, information that any informed parent or teacher would have offered a child many times as incidental intelligence. All Mr. Adler's books (and those of his alter ego, Robert Irving) go as deeply into the subject he chooses as the young reader can go unaided, and sometimes, wisely, a little further to stimulate questions and investigations. Moreover, he writes well, presents the scientific facts in a fresh way and constantly suggests novel and interesting relationships. Here he explains in considerable detail for those over eleven the physics of color (the spectrum, reflection, a little about diffraction grating, refraction, etc.), something of their chemistry, and the part our physiological and psychological makeup plays in seeing color. In the course of his lucid exposition he cites everyday experiences to illustrate his points. We are sure that not only young readers but most parents and teachers will learn much from his way of explaining why milk and clouds are white, why a golden cup looks blood red inside, what happens during cooking to turn a lobster red, why a wet sidewalk is darker than a dry one and why astronomers are able to tell the direction of the motion of galaxies and the temperature of particular stars.

> *Margaret Sherwood Libby, in a review of "Color in Your Life," in* New York Herald Tribune Book Review, *May 27, 1962, p. 14.*

Volcanoes and Earthquakes (as Robert Irving, 1962)

A new addition to a competent group of science books, this reflects an excellent job transposing difficult information into comprehensive terms for the curious young scientist. Two separate divisions deal independently with each topic in the title utilizing the same format. The "portraits" of volcanoes and earthquakes describe the step-by-step procedure nature follows in creating them from the time of inception until their climactic eruptions. A rundown on famous volcanoes and earthquakes give the reader some idea of their enormous power. Having outlined how they operate and what they cause the author launches a purely technical discussion on the role of science in defining and in some cases controlling these ancient phenomena. The reader can be assured of accurate information and precise handling—for the author and photographer have proven their abilities in such books as **Rocks and Minerals, Energy and Power, Hurricanes and Twisters** and **Electromagnetic Waves.**

> *A review of "Volcanoes and Earthquakes," in* Virginia Kirkus' Service, *Vol. XXX, No. 4, February 15, 1962, p. 182.*

Histories of famous volcanoes and disastrous quakes, their inner causes and numerous side-effects are all included. If anything, there is too much here, delivered in unyielding, declarative sentences that become boring. Solid and factual as it is, the book fairly trembles for an inverted sentence or two.

> *Henry W. Hubbard, in a review of "Volcanoes and Earthquakes," in* The New York Times Book Review, *August 19, 1962, p. 20.*

The Adler Book of Puzzles and Riddles: Or, Sam Loyd Up to Date   (with Peggy Adler, 1962)

Interesting collection of mathematical and word puzzles, riddles, rebuses, and hidden geography puzzles inspired by the *Cyclopedia of Sam Loyd Puzzles,* (1914). The puzzles are challenging and should provide fun and stimulate thought. The answers are given at the end of the book. Unfortunately, in some cases, the reader is invited to draw lines, trace pieces of a figure, and fill in blank spaces. Therefore, this is recommended for home purchase and for use, under supervision, in a school library. (pp. 116-17)

> *Laura E. Cathon, in a review of "The Adler Book of Puzzles and Riddles: Or Sam Loyd Up-to-Date," in* School Library Journal, *Vol. 9, No. 1, September, 1962, pp. 116-17.*

Air   (with Ruth Adler, 1962)

Facts about the composition of air, its behaviour, its peculiarities, and the uses man has made of its power, are adequately stated, but in a rather condescending and oversimple manner. Certainly children should be helped to pronounce technical terms but not if the text must be interrupted constantly by phonetic directions. 'A fire extinguisher (ex-TING-wish-er) works this way.' Many of these guides to pronunciation are misleading. A child will gather that troposphere should be pronounced TROP-o-sfeer, whereas a far more flexible and usable central syllable, between o and a, can only be given by word of mouth. As a whole, the book needs an attendant adult, preferably a teacher, if it is to be of any use.

> *Margery Fisher, in a review of "Air," in* Growing Point, *Vol. 1, No. 9, April, 1963, p. 142.*

[*The following excerpt is from a review of the revised edition published in 1972.*]

There appears to be little of modern educational value in *Air.* The book is dull, both in typographical layout and in basic writing. It is one of those packed-with-simple-facts types of books that were staples among the supplementary science books written for elementary school children twenty or more years ago. In fact, this book is a 1972 revision of a 1962 edition, but ninety-five percent of the material was commonplace in 1950. The writing consists of elephant-tail sentences strung together in heavy-handed fashion. For example: "Green plants make their own food. They make their food in their leaves. The food they make is sugar. Sugar is the food they need to make them grow." It's simple and it seems clear, but it's deadly boring, and it often isn't clear at all! Saying that the "fire of life burns inside every cell" does not adequately explain metabolism nor does it offer an understandable comparison to a candle flame. Does the book have any value? Yes. Such old-time books have always had some value. For a relatively few dedicated eight-to-eleven year-olds, the book will provide perhaps an hour's worth of bits of information about the atmosphere. But most young readers will probably refuse to read it for more than a few minutes voluntarily. Too many topics are treated in too short a space. There needs to be more and better illustration of many concepts, more dynamic material, and better writing. This kind of book certainly won't help today's average young reader become interested in science.

> *A review of "Air," in* Science Books: A Quarterly Review, *Vol. IX, No. 1, May, 1973, p. 69.*

Storms   (with Ruth Adler, 1963); *Irrigation: Changing Deserts into Gardens*   (with Ruth Adler, 1964)

[Two books] by those two experienced exponents of the art of making scientific facts both comprehensible and interesting. The gift is rare: it lies partly in simple sentence construction, repetition which gives confidence, short chapters, unpretentious illustrations; mostly it comes from the verve of the interpreters.

> *A review of "'The Reason Why' series: 'Storms' and 'Irrigation',' in* The Times Literary Supplement, *No. 3378, November 24, 1966, p. 1097.*

Those most exciting of meteorological phenomena, storms, were once regarded with a superstitious awe. Here they are explained in simple terms so that all can understand them. All sorts of storms are described, many of which like black blizzards, hurricanes and typhoons we do not get over here, fortunately. Enough information is given about warm and cold fronts to explain our weather.

Storms and rain are remote from those areas which need to be irrigated. In **Irrigation** we are brought from ancient Egypt and Babylon to modern Israel, the Aswan High Dam and the U.S.A. Both books are excellent, both have small glossaries . . . and both are well worth their place on the junior library shelves. (pp. 363-64)

> *J. D. Bloom, in a review of "Storms" and "Irrigation," in* The School Librarian and School Library Review, *Vol. 14, No. 3, December, 1966, pp. 363-64.*

Numerals: New Dresses for Old Numbers (with Ruth Adler, 1964)

This comprehensive but rapid overview of systems of numeration other than base ten fills a void in materials for children about this topic. This is a particularly useful book for students who are interested in mathematics but are not studying about other bases in their regular elementary school program. However, reading it requires a background in certain aspects of mathematics such as the use of exponents. The weakness of the book is its rapid treatment which makes it impossible for the reader to discover mathematical principles for himself. It is written to give the student skills in computing in other bases rather than the more important conceptual understanding of other bases. The presentation does not encourage the student to think in terms of another base but rather to think in terms of base ten and then translate to the other base. (pp. 56-7)

> *Rosemarie Blaney, in a review of "Numerals: New Dresses for Old Numbers," in* School Library Journal, *Vol. 10, No. 8, April, 1964, pp. 56-7.*

Houses (with Ruth Adler, 1964)

The history of house building from the cave-man to the urban resident of our time has been compressed with success. It is difficult with such space limitations to avoid over-generalizing and significant omissions. The introduction is good, outlining man's basic shelter needs in simple, succinct terms. The analyses of hunters' houses are clear and cover this area adequately. The portion dealing with ancient farmers' houses is perhaps less effective. Materials and methods of construction in particular periods are described inconsistently in some parts of the book. The illustrations, although reasonably effective, might have provided more indication of human resources and occupancy. However, these criticisms do not detract from the general usefulness of the book.

> *A review of "Houses," in* Science Books: A Quarterly Review, *Vol. 1, No. 2, September, 1965, p. 111.*

With Man as the current popular subject for projects, this book should be a great success. Briefly and competently it traces the development of housing from holes in the ground to new towns and high rise flats. The authors have collected their information and presented it in such a way as to be of interest to a wide range of ability and age. The bright eight-year-old will find it just as useful as the less able fourteen-year-old. To add to its value it has a simple index and bibliography which must prove very helpful when teaching children how to use such aids. I am certain this will be popular in my Secondary Library with many of the less able who are nevertheless very interested in such things. I am also pretty certain many primary teachers will be delighted with most aspects of the book. . . . (pp. 28-9)

> *J. Murphy, in a review of "Houses," in* The Junior Bookshelf, *Vol. 39, No. 1, February, 1975, pp. 28-9.*

Logic for Beginners: Through Games, Jokes, and Puzzles (with Ruth Adler, 1964)

Intended as an introduction to logic, this text seems only partially successful. For one thing, quite a number of the games and puzzles are not really exercises in logic: the reader is, for example, asked on one page to test his memory of details of a drawing on the previous page. In a set labelled "Brain Teasers" the reader is asked if it is a good plan to use a fifteen-year-old encyclopedia article for a report on elementary particles. Answer at the back of the book, "No. Since so many new discoveries are made every year in particle physics, an article that is 15 years old is out of date." The text does include definitions and illustrations of terms and procedures in logic, but they seem appropriate for an older audience than the audience that is addressed in the beginning of the book. An index is appended.

> *Zena Sutherland, in a review of "Logic for Beginners; Through Games, Jokes, and Puzzles," in* Bulletin of the Center for Children's Books, *Vol. 19, No. 2, October, 1965, p. 25.*

Irving Adler's *Logic for Beginners through Games, Jokes, and Puzzles* is longer and more complex [than Vicki Cobb's *Logic*]. He says that knowledge is gained through observation, getting a report from someone who already knows, reasoning from established fact, or a combination of these. Problems with all these are discussed, and the importance of semantics in reasoning is highlighted. Then Adler moves into sets, simple propositions, relations connecting members of a universe of discourse, and syllogisms. The author presents syllogisms using Venn diagrams, as does Cobb. The book's pace, however, is slow, with many examples and invitations to participate, though activities are not as appealing as the title seems to imply. Still, *Logic for Beginners* is clear and logical enough in its progression for anyone who has the interest to follow it through, example by example. It is a book for a highly motivated, bright individual, or for use in a teaching situation. Adults who have not studied formal logic would find both this book and Cobb's *Logic* helpful. (pp. 34-5)

> *Virginia Witucke, "Learning to Think/ Thinking to Learn: A Bibliographic Guide," in* Top of the News, *Vol. 37, No. 1, Fall, 1980, pp. 29-36.*

Heat (with Ruth Adler, 1964)

Short sentences, homely examples and simple explanations lead us gently to an understanding of the nature and function of heat, in the kind of book which we have grown to expect of the Adlers. This is a short, modestly produced information book; it would be wrong to underestimate the achievement of the authors in making a knowledge of science part of our everyday background. The standard of the "Reason Why" series remains at a constant competent level, but the books vary in the demands they make on readers. We should not be misled by the size of this book into thinking it designed for tots; its readership could stretch into the secondary school, and even to adults wanting a short introductory work. (p. 594)

"People, Places, Things," in The Times Literary Supplement, *No. 3458, June 6, 1968, pp. 594-95.*

The Elementary Mathematics of the Atom   (1965)

This book succeeds in illuminating some of the more theoretic aspects of modern physics and chemistry by the use of simple mathematics. The concepts, however, are not simple and understanding requires a great deal of concentrated effort. This effort is worthwhile since it brings down to the level of the bright, interested high school science student, or intelligent layman, areas of science previously available only to the college physics major. It also is a useful adjunct book for high school teachers of advanced science. It develops the molecular theory of matter and the periodic table of the elements, their utilizing principles of motion, electricity, and light, develops the Bohr model of the atom, and then goes on to describe the quantum mechanical model of the atom together with many recent discoveries of atomic physics. This subject matter sounds, and is, complex, but Mr. Adler, who has written a number of simplifications of modern mathematics and science, has accomplished well his objective in this instance. Recommended for any library.

Abraham J. Berman, in a review of "The Elementary Mathematics of the Atom," in Library Journal, *Vol. 90, No. 2, January 15, 1965, p. 260.*

Some years ago an English schoolmaster, Clement Durell, wrote a small book called *Readable Relativity* that achieved the seemingly impossible: a clear, rigorous, simple explanation of the theory, using nothing more than elementary algebra. Durell's book is a gem; in its field it has no equal. Here, however, is an achievement that, if not fully up to Durell's, deserves high praise. Adler, a practiced and versatile explainer of science and mathematics for younger readers, has written an excellent account of modern atomic theory, not merely in general descriptive terms but in mathematical detail, the mathematics being wholly within the grasp of any thoughtful student who has had one year of high school algebra. He describes the fundamentals of the molecular theory of matter, explains the basic relations of motion, electricity and light, develops the Bohr model of the atom with its planetary electronic orbits and as a climax lays before the reader an admirably lucid exposition of quantum and wave mechanics. One has to see this done to appreciate the author's exceptional skill and to enjoy his gift for reducing the most difficult and esoteric concepts of modern physics almost to ABC. Many readers will be grateful to Adler for bringing within their reach matters they could not have hoped to understand— in the sense of actually following the reasoning—without such a book as this. Highly recommended for high school students and any interested adult.

James R. Newman, in a review of "The Elementary Mathematics of the Atom," in Scien-

tific American, *Vol. 213, No. 6, December, 1965, p. 114.*

Electricity in Your Life   (1965)

[This] book provides a serious introduction to the practical aspects of electricity and magnetism. It will be a useful supplement to school instruction in junior physics. The author analyzes the function of many pieces of common electrical appliances, such as the bell, telephone, radio, television and motor. The inventiveness of the young reader will be taxed, perhaps too strenuously, by experimental directions for making a small motor from a tin can.

W. Carey Parker II, "From 'Why Daddy' to 'How Daddy'," in Book Week—New York Herald Tribune, *May 16, 1965, p. 14.*

A clear explanation is presented of the nature of electricity and its relation to the intimate nature of matter. Its relationship to electromagnetism also is explained, along with the uses of electromagnets in common devices and appliances. Activities for the reader are included. . . . Inadequate and misleading phraseology detracts in places: e.g., "One way to tear electrons out of atoms is to rub one object against another," (p. 19); "When electrons are being pushed onto a plate of a capacitor, the more crowded they become the more they push back" (p. 47). While the text attempts to move from very elementary ideas to those more advanced, the presentation tends to be somewhat uneven.

A review of "Electricity in Your Life," in Science Books: A Quarterly Review, *Vol. 1, No. 2, September, 1965, p. 76.*

Evolution   (with Ruth Adler, 1965)

[**Evolution**] is designed to develop a detailed understanding of the meaning of evolution and of how this meaning has been derived. The complexity of structural and functional change is emphasized. This well-written text provides a rare opportunity for the seriously interested young reader to develop a basic understanding of classification, the "timetable of life" recorded in the rocks by fossil remains, structured likenesses and differences among animals, the structure and function of cells, the resemblances of the embryos of vertebrates to each other, natural and artificial selection, heredity, mutations, and the role of the nucleic acids, DNA and RNA, in producing inherited variations. Scientific vocabulary is used throughout but in most instances it is vocabulary with which children are familiar. Aids to pronunciation are included with each scientific term. Detailed diagrams and drawings extend and reinforce the written text and are especially useful in the discussion of DNA and RNA and must be studied closely.

Alphoretta S. Fish, in a review of "Evolution," in School Library Journal, *Vol. 12, No. 4, December 1965, p. 68.*

Irving and Ruth Adler tackle a touchy subject for the seven- to ten-year-old in **Evolution.** Obviously aware of how many schools—even today—will not allow modern biology to be taught, they have trod warily, devoting half their little book to the genetic code, which is not particularly controversial. Even so, the first half of the book manages to make some careful and valid points concerning the interrelationships of life and the development of species.

> *Isaac Asimov, in a review of "Evolution," in* The Horn Book Magazine, *Vol. XLII, No. 2, April, 1966, p. 214.*

The authors undertake a gargantuan task in trying to tell children the "reason why" and all about the many facets of evolution and genetics in 48 small pages of large type. The book discusses likenesses and differences, classification in the animal kingdom, fossils, the chemistry of the cell, embryology, artificial selection, natural selection, heredity, DNA-RNA protein synthesis, the molecular basis of mutation, and fossil man. Too few examples are given, too many areas are touched, and too little background and introduction are given. It would have been far better to expand the material into a series of three or more books and deal with the major topics in greater depth.

> *A review of "Evolution," in* Science Books: A Quarterly Review, *Vol. 2, No. 2, September, 1966, p. 126.*

Coal (with Ruth Adler, 1965)

Described in this interesting, well-written text are the uses, origin, mining processes, and chemistry of coal. Early methods and problems of mining are contrasted with modern methods and problems. Introduction of concepts relating to "chemical bonding," "carbonization," and "hydragenation" take the story of coal to a higher level for the young reader than most books on the topic. Pictures of methods and equipment are particularly useful.

> *Alphoretta S. Fish, in a review of "Coal," in* School Library Journal, *Vol. 12, No. 5, January, 1966, p. 422.*

This is an American importation and a success. The authors know how to arouse interest from the first sentence. The book begins: "Each of us uses about 20 pounds of coal every day. But most of us never see any of the coal we use", and it then proceeds to build on our immediate curiosity. How do we use this coal, why do we never see it, where does it come from? The expected things are here: how coal is formed, how it is mined, what are its byproducts, but the authors go beyond these to deal with safety problems, coal's early history and its effect on industry.

> *A review of "The Reason Why Books: 'Coal',"* in The Times Literary Supplement, *No. 3475, October 3, 1968, p. 1128.*

[The following excerpt is from a review of the revised edition published in 1974.]

Minor corrections in facts and figures are scattered throughout this revision of Adler's highly informative account of coal mining processes and history. The only enlarged and rewritten chapter—on safety in the mines—

reflects today's concern in this area, and the tone is not as optimistic about the future availability of energy resources as was the 1965 edition. Necessary only for libraries not using the previous edition.

> *Shirley A. Smith, in a review of "Coal," in* School Library Journal, *Vol. 21, No. 9, May, 1975, p. 52.*

Atoms and Molecules (with Ruth Adler, 1966)

An important introductory text which should stimulate interest and equip the reader to extend his inquiry into the topics of atoms and molecules. Ideas are presented in a straightforward manner in all but the first few pages where the authors speak of "hidden partners" in compounds, the "stickiness" of molecules, and of the molecule that "stays in place and wiggles like a shaken jelly." In the following pages, however, diagrams and the sequential arrangement of ideas make clear and meaningful a staggering number of ideas about such subjects and qualities as chemical equation, electrostatic, nuclear force, shells, sub-shells, chemically active, chemically inactive, noble gases, alkali metals, halogens, ionic bond, covalent bond, isotopes, and nucleons.

> *Alphoretta S. Fish, in a review of "Atoms and Molecules," in* Library Journal, *Vol. 91, No. 12, June 15, 1966, p. 3254.*

The scope is broad and ambitious for a 48-page children's introduction to the complexities of molecular structure. The explanation begins with analogies involving familiar objects and ideas, and proceeds step-by-step to explain the fundamentals of molecular physics and chemistry. The pace of the text will be too rigorous for many readers. For elementary school children it would have been preferable to include occasional activities or exercises to reinforce learning, for they now are becoming accustomed to involvement in the processes of science in their classrooms, instead of the traditional read-show-tell procedure.

> *Hilary J. Deason, in a review of "Atoms and Molecules," in* Science Books: A Quarterly Review, *Vol. 2, No. 4, March, 1967, p. 267.*

The Wonders of Physics: An Introduction to the Physical World (1966)

Adler may be relied on. He discusses all branches of physics and, in every case, pays particular attention to current developments. Quite properly, he sees nothing wrong in traveling from ordinary light to synchrotron radiation; in going into relativity and nuclear physics in detail; and in delving within the nucleus. Adler believes (and I do, too) that one does not teach only the simple parts of science to young people, but all the parts—each made as clear as necessary. (pp. 454-55)

> *Isaac Asimov, in a review of "The Wonders of Physics: An Introduction to the Physical World," in* The Horn Book Magazine, *Vol. XLII, No. 4, August, 1966, pp. 454-55.*

Irving and Joyce Adler in 1991.

Among the many attempts to popularize science, this book is superior in its breadth, clarity, concern for current research, and for its attactive illustrations [by Cornelius DeWitt]. Dr. Adler begins by asking 25 questions that might occur to a thoughtful observer at the beach. At the end of the book he returns to these same questions and shows the reader that he has now acquired the insight to answer any that may previously have puzzled him. In the intervening 160 pages the reader has been treated to a rapid but meaningful survey of a wide range of physics. Dr. Adler starts with some fundamentals. The concept of a mathematical limit is developed in relation to speed. Mass (the "stubbornness" of matter) is distinguished from weight. Exponential notation is defined. Unity and economy of description is achieved in good discussions of fields (electric and gravitational), and waves (mechanical, sound, and electromagnetic). More exciting to the reader will be the clear qualitative insight he can gain into such topics as electron spin, escape velocity, absolute temperatures, superconductivity, superfluidity, transistors, plasma, shock waves, Cerenkov radiation, de Broglie waves, uncertainty principle, relativity (special and general), Michelson-Morely experiment, clock paradox, fission, fusion, strangeness, and parity. A few of the definitions are vague or oblique. (pp. 185-86)

A review of "The Wonders of Physics: An In-

troduction to the Physical World," in Science Books: A Quarterly Review, *Vol. 2, No. 3, December, 1966, pp. 185-86.*

[Adler's] work is notable for the skill and lucidity with which he makes complicated material comprehensible. In *The Wonders of Physics,* for example, written for older children, the clarity of his prose is such that the book can be given even to a seven-year-old child to explain the difference between the Centigrade and Fahrenheit temperature scales.

The Wonders of Physics bears out Jerome Bruner's assertion that " . . . the foundations of any subject may be taught to anybody at any age in some form." Adler defines the four states of matter (solid, liquid, gaseous, and plasma) succinctly, then discusses them, using subheadings and drawings to make the material easier to understand. The index includes "see also" references. Page numbers in boldface type refer to a page where there is an illustration of the subject. Throughout the text, cross-references are excellent.

> *Zena Sutherland and May Hill Arbuthnot, "Informational Books: 'The Wonders of Physics'," in their* Children and Books, *seventh edition, Scott, Foresman and Company, 1986, p. 488.*

Taste, Touch, and Smell (with Ruth Adler, 1966)

An important, fascinating and comprehensive explanation of the ways in which scientists describe the manner in which man tastes, touches and smells. Included are interesting experiments with touch and answers to the following questions: How is attitude related to pain tolerance? Why does a sore inside the stomach sometimes produce pain in the ear? What is the difference between an analgesic and an anesthetic? What is the advantage of "sniffing" when trying to detect odor? What are the "two-point" touch thresholds for various parts of the body? Why do we see "stars" when receiving a blow in the eyes? The vocabulary is sophisticated, precise, and will expand the language facility of the reader. . . . This is a good companion volume to the Adlers' previous books on the senses, *Your Eyes* and *Your Ears.*

> *Alphoretta Fish, in a review of "Taste, Touch and Smell," in* School Library Journal, *Vol. 13, No. 3, November, 1966, p. 83.*

Magnets (with Ruth Adler, 1966)

The writer of books for primary-school children must be concerned not only with ordinary questions of accuracy but also with the matter of simplification. Has the subject been simplified to the point where something important is lost? It is not always easy to tell, and one is bound to feel more comfortable with an experienced author. I scarcely need worry about a book such as *Magnets* by Irving and Ruth Adler. The Adlers never skimp anything important even in simplifying.

> *Isaac Asimov, in a review of "Magnets," in* The

Horn Book Magazine, *Vol. XLII, No. 6, December, 1966, p. 732.*

What a wonderful book! In every way, it carries on the Adler tradition, giving a clear picture of all the different types of magnets by which we are surrounded. These include our earth, the sun, and the stars, as well as the more familiar bar magnets, horseshoe magnets, and electromagnets. As we delve into the atoms and molecules which make up these materials, it becomes very clear why a magnet acts as it does. An excellent primer for potential scientists and engineers, it should excite the imagination of a wide range of age groups.

> *A review of "Magnets," in* Science Books: A Quarterly Review, *Vol. 2, No. 3, December, 1966, p. 188.*

Sets (with Ruth Adler, 1967)

A book by the Adlers can generally be counted on as an asset to any introduction to the sciences. Set theory, if properly introduced, can give students a much more comprehensive understanding of the whole range of mathematical studies all the way up to advanced levels. The explanations given here manage to simplify without distorting any of the basics. Unfortunately there are very few examples given, and even the best students will require more visual assistance. The approach is somewhat unusual, with major emphasis on the composition of sets rather than on their operations. The short chapters rely heavily on exercises, with answers given at the back of the book. It's a serviceable classroom aid but can't be used alone.

> *A review of "Sets: A Reason Why Book," in* Virginia Kirkus' Service, *Vol. XXXIV, No. 23, December 1, 1966, p. 1223.*

It is difficult to categorize this little book. It is too much of a textbook for any but the most mathematically-avid child to read on his own for pleasure, and it is too limited to be other than a supplement to a text. Since all of the material is included in most new elementary mathematics texts, its best uses would probably be as a review, as a brief introduction for pupils who have attended schools using older texts, and as a lucid second shot at ideas which have probably confused some pupils and teachers using the less well-organized new texts. Among topics covered are sets, subsets, empty set, truth sets, equations, inequalities, intersection and union, least common multiples. Each section is accompanied by problems, for which answers are given at the end of the book. The layout is crowded and unattractive. One wishes that the Adlers had written a supplementary children's book on sets more like their **Logic for Beginners,** which can be read for pleasure. However, as a brief textbook, **Sets** has the clarity, succinctness, and accuracy which characterize most of the Adlers' children's books. (pp. 13-14)

> *A review of "Sets (The 'Reason Why' Books)," in* Science Books: A Quarterly Review, *Vol. 3, No. 1, May, 1967, pp. 13-14.*

Tree Products (with Ruth Adler, 1967)

Trees defined and trees dissected; wood for ancient tools and charcoal for medieval furnaces; trees into logs and logs into lumber; wood pulp into paper and sap into sugar; bark into cork and fruit into . . . mmm. The growing tree has been transformed by technological advances into a myriad of products, several more sophisticated than those cited, and the processes are explained in the slow steps and detailed illustrations suited to the young. Nothing comparable in scope is equally simple.

> *A review of "Tree Products," in* Virginia Kirkus' Service, *Vol. XXXIV, No. 23, December 1, 1966, p. 1223.*

This elementary discussion of the structure and economic uses of trees is marred by over-simplification and botanical inaccuracies; the term "family," for example, is used incorrectly for both "kingdom" and "class." Creosote is not an oil and a cone is not a fruit. Other terms used loosely or erroneously include "pith," "phoeoem," "fruit," and "xylem." Phonetic respellings in parentheses following such words as "elastic" and "resin" appear more difficult to pronounce than the words themselves. The only references other than photograph credits are footnotes recommending several others of the authors' 26 books in the series.

> *Della Thomas, in a review of "Tree Products," in* School Library Journal, *Vol. 13, No. 7, March, 1967, p. 123.*

Communication (with Ruth Adler, 1967)

Communication in the conceptual sense of exchanging ideas and information rather than the technical sense of transmitting messages: a simple survey, one-third on language and writing, one-third on printing, one-third on communicating over distances (from semaphore to satellite), storing information electronically (including motion pictures and computers), and miscellany like specialist languages and translation. The distribution of information indicates the difference from existing studies: both Batchelor and Buehr focus primarily on the *means,* sometimes minor, of sending messages. The combination of drawings and photographs in a varied layout gives this an edge in appearance also. In a clear, concise form that exemplifies the subject, more thought than meets the eye (or ear).

> *A review of "Communication (The Reason Why Books)," in* Kirkus Service, *Vol. XXXV, No. 11, June 1, 1967, p. 646.*

Stressing the meaning and importance of communication, the authors trace very briefly its chronological development from cave paintings to Telstar. Types of communication covered include pictorial, electronic, signals, symbols, and the written word. Less comprehensive and for a younger group than Neal's *Communication From Stone Age to Space Age.* . . . While covering a good deal of the same material as Walter Buehr's *Sending the Word* (Putnam, 1959) and Julie Batchelor's *Communication* (Harcourt, 1953) the Adler book includes Telstar and is more up to date in general.

Dorothy Winch, in a review of "Communication," in School Library Journal, *Vol. 14, No. 1, September, 1967, p. 165.*

[This] book covers much the same material as is in Jupo's *Read All About It!* (Prentice-Hall, 1957) which is written in livelier style but has a different emphasis. The Adlers give good coverage and accurate information, but the writing is dry and the text sprinkled with phonetic explanations of pronunciation; some (but not all) of these words are repeated in a word list at the back of the book, a list that includes such words as "alphabet," which has already been defined when used in the text.

Zena Sutherland, in a review of "Communication," in Bulletin of the Center for Children's Books, *Vol. 21, No. 5, January, 1968, p. 73.*

The Calendar   (with Ruth Adler, 1967)

The concision and simplicity of style characteristic of this series, are somewhat offset in this case by the difficulty of the subject—primarily the arithmetic disparities underlying the evolution of the calendar—making it suitable only for children who can follow the complex figuring. The authors describe the movements of earth and moon which form the basis for measuring days, months and years, explain how "the parts won't fit," and recount the efforts of the Egyptians, the Babylonians, other ancients, and the Romans to reconcile the lunar and solar measurements. The development of the Roman calendar from the legendary first through the Julian and Gregorian calendar is presented in detail with accompanying tables; so is the basis for naming the months and the days. Instructions for making a fifty-year calendar supplement the historical coverage. This has a somewhat limited potential for self-instruction but it could be a useful supplement to a school unit.

A review of "The Calendar (A Reason Why Book)," in Kirkus Service, *Vol. XXXV, No. 22, November 15, 1967, p. 1366.*

Brief, interesting and well done, this may be useful where additional material is needed although it contains much of the same information to be found in Brindze's *The Story of Our Calendar* for the same reading level. Of the two books, the format is more attractive and the presentation more direct and concise in the Adler volume.

Beatrice M. Adam, in a review of "The Calendar," in School Library Journal, *Vol. 14, No. 5, January, 1968, p. 67.*

Sets and Numbers for the Very Young   (with Ruth Adler, 1969)

A workbook of arithmetical fundamentals for the very, *very* young, Conceptually sound but dismayingly reminiscent of Dick, Jane and Sally. "There is a mouse for each cat. There is a cat for each mouse. There are as many mice as there are cats. There are three cats. There are three mice." But look, look, look, it's not all bad because the basic constructs are good, cardinal and ordinal number

meanings communicated through concrete representations—"the meaning of one" to ten, first/second, left/right, more/fewer, as many, one less than, triangle, circle, and square. Each construct is expressed and 'experienced' in variously imaginative participations from tracing the number's outline on a path of arrows to question and answer games, but then illustrated [by Peggy Adler] (per Joan Walsh Anglund) in an abysmal black-and-white way that invites the bored or insulted child to color in all the pictures. The look of the page is so discouragingly crowded that nothing sets up very well, yet it really could be useful as a jumping-off point for parent-teachers' lesson plans.

A review of "Sets and Numbers for the Very Young," in Kirkus Reviews, *Vol. XXXVII, No. 20, October 15, 1969, p. 1114.*

Directions and Angles   (with Ruth Adler, 1969)

No one is likely to get hooked on geometry from reading this volume. It is boring and confusing and despite the interleaved pink-page touch the general effect is old-fashioned and uninspiring. The thin blackboard style line-drawings [by Ellen Viereck] and diagrams which could have been used to give information more vividly than wordy directional prose are mainly relegated to the edges of the pages where they lie like skeletal dodos.

It has been impossible to decide who will need to read, or be able to read, a book which 'will explain the meaning of the directions up, down . . . ' and which has a few basic geometrical facts about angles, directions, planes, Euclidian straight lines, etc. disguised in verbose complications. There is a confusion of practical and theoretical: a child may be happy to 'take two sticks' but what about, 'Comparing angles for size . . . Case I. The side EF falls in the interior of angle ABC. An arrow turning round B like the hand of a clock, starting from the position BA, would reach position EF first. . . . '?

Robert Walker, in a review of "Directions and Angles," in Children's Book Review, *Vol. III, No. 2, April, 1973, p. 57.*

The aim of **Directions and Angles** is to help children towards understanding some basic mathematical concepts, and they try to ease the process with an occasional question, or a little reiteration of important points. But in spite of their efforts, this emerges as a dull book; the authors have failed to relate all their solid information to practical projects, children's interests or the outside world.

A review of "Directions and Angles," in The Times Literary Supplement, *No. 3709, April 6, 1973, p. 390.*

Energy   (1970)

Energy in its many forms is dealt with in this book. Changes from one form of energy to another in order to run different machines are described. Although very simple, it is accurate and not only should serve as excellent collateral reading in science courses but also as preliminary reading for students in upper levels who have never studied science. It is not a textbook, but it is a bridge between everyday events and a good scientific approach to them. There are many excellent practical examples, although in the diagram on page 42, "a compact car = 100 horsepower" should be changed to something else as the equals sign is meaningless. The sentence in the text could be repeated.

A review of "Energy," in Science Books: A Quarterly Review, *Vol. 6, No. 2, September, 1970, p. 115.*

A rather conventional and unimaginative swing through the elementary physics of energy transformations. The writing is stilted and lacks 'zip', there appear to be far too few good activities for children to do, the facts are frequent and very general, and the major generalization: "The original source of . . . energy is the sun" seems rather overdone. It is difficult to avoid gross overgeneralizations in a book of this type, but statements such as "All forces are measured in pounds" (p. 7) should not be allowed to stand. Also, the author does not note the distinction between small calories (p. 16) and large calories *re* food (p. 24)—an alert child might note that according to Mr. Adler it would take the same energy to walk for an hour that it takes to melt less than two grams of ice. In sum, this appears to be an unimaginative attempt to translate a high school physics text to elementary level.

Richard H. Weller, in a review of "Energy," in Appraisal: Children's Science Books, *Vol. 4, No. 2, Spring, 1971, p. 3.*

Language and Man   (with Joyce Adler, 1970)

A cursory overview of language, written and oral, that has a young look inappropriate for the concentrated text. Like Gallant's more thorough *Man Must Speak* (1969), it recognizes several fundamentals—that language is man-made, that it develops and changes. Further, it refers to some crucial areas of language study, language families, infant speech, history of English. However, the information is crammed into 46 pages of unenlivened and sometimes awkward prose. Also, several relevant topics are not included: there is no consideration of the dynamics of communication (tone, body language, sources of interference) and there is no discussion of the difficulties and deficiencies of both historical writing (translation problems, loss of references) or writing in general. Too demanding for a younger child who might be attracted to the format, yet incomplete in coverage. (pp. 1292-93)

A review of "Language and Man," in Kirkus Reviews, *Vol. XXXVIII, No. 23, December 1, 1970, pp. 1292-93.*

A discussion of the importance of speech and of the transmission and diffusion of culture across barriers of time and space, emphasizing the fact that all men are capable of acquiring any language and that infants everywhere make the same sounds, refining their speech to meet approval of the adults with whom they first communicate. There is a competent introduction to the facts that some words re-

semble each other in many languages and that English has been influenced both by proximity and importation of words from other languages. The writing is clear but staid, the book distracting on a few pages because of the difficulty of reading print against a background of pattern in color.

Zena Sutherland, in a review of "Language and Man," in Bulletin of the Center for Children's Books, *Vol. 25, No. 2, October, 1971, p. 21.*

Atomic Energy   (1971)

An elegant, clearly written and accurate little book, it starts with a discussion of fossil fuels and leads into atomic structure, the nucleus, isotopes, nuclear stability, and atomic energy. It would be useful if the student were familiar with the concepts of energy and electric charge. The book keeps up parallel discussions of fission and of fusion and describes clearly some of the nuclear concepts involved, such as chain reactions. There is a clear description of how a nuclear reactor works. Interesting quantitative data are included; e.g., the velocity of neutrons and the temperature in a reactor. There is also a useful discussion of breeder reactors, radioactive wastes and disposal problems, and applications of radioactivity. . . . Dr. Adler also includes a brief history of atomic energy and a discussion of applications of nuclear fuel for production of electricity to meet our future power needs. There is a discussion of pollution problems associated with burning fossil fuels, but the discussion of the pollution problems associated with nuclear reactors is idealized, in this reviewer's opinion. The book ends with a discussion of fusion reactors as a more ultimate means of meeting power needs. (pp. 126-27)

A review of "Atomic Energy," in Science Books: A Quarterly Review, *Vol. 7, No. 2, September, 1971, pp. 126-27.*

Within the context of an ever-increasing need for power and a constantly diminishing supply of fossil fuels, Irving Adler presents a clearly written case for atomic energy as a power source of the future. With short, simplified explanations and strong, clear illustrations, the reader is led through the complexities of the atomic structure, radioactivity, fissionable materials both natural and man-made, the working of an atomic reactor and a brief statement about controlled fusion as a source of energy beyond nuclear fission. The material in this book could be an adequate source of information for the average middle-grade student and should be a stepping stone for the more interested student. Since the subject is beyond the level of the beginning reader, the use of phonetic spelling in the text is disturbing. The illustration [by Ellen Viereck] on page eleven showing a one ton coal truck inside a gallon water jug is extremely misleading. Since the emphasis of the book is on atomic energy for peaceful uses, there is only a brief historical allusion to the use of atomic bombs in World War II and no comments on the hazards of nuclear testing.

Hanna B. Zieger, in a review of "Atomic Ener-

gy,'' *in* Appraisal: Children's Science Books, *Vol. 5, No. 1, Winter, 1972, p. 4.*

The Story of Light   (1971)

The simplicity and clarity of author Irving Adler extends an understanding of light far beyond introductory optics. Actually, the entire electromagnetic spectrum is encompassed and the relation of light to atomic structures is well developed. Fundamentals of the periodic table of elements are brought in by derivation of their brightline spectra and Ritz terms. The relation of light to weather making and stored-energy sources, such as wood and coal is also covered. Relativity is introduced, but in a final flourish, the brain power and creativity of man are billed as the real heroes in conquering and interpreting the vast influences of light. The few small errors detectable by a special scholar in any work are generally sins of omission relating to current forefronts of knowledge; these do not detract from the major usefulness of the volume to the junior high school student. A short glossary of 40 terms reflects the author's capacity for clarity.

> *A review of "The Story of Light," in* Science Books: A Quarterly Review, *Vol. 7, No. 3, December, 1971, p. 220.*

Simplicity need not be either triteness or banality. Comparisons are one means of making concepts clear to the reader, and some writers use comparisons simply and effectively. Irving Adler in ***The Story of Light*** uses a reference to the familiar Aladdin story. Aladdin rubbed a lamp to summon the Jinni. We flick a switch to summon light. Adler goes on to remind us of how difficult it is to get rid of light; it streams in through windows and drapes, or through keyholes. Light cannot be held by force; although we try to grab it, it slides through our fingers. But if we learn about its tricks, we can put to work the energy of light. Referring next to a common experience, bumping into things in the dark, Adler then compares light to a messenger:

> If only the chair could have sent you a message across space, warning you of its presence! Fortunately for you, it can *when there is light in the room,* for the light serves as everybody's messenger. It travels from the table to you and tells you that the table is there.

Frequent comparisons are particularly helpful in the explanations of complex ideas or startling facts.

> *Rebecca J. Lukens, "Nonfiction: 'The Story of Light','' in her* A Critical Handbook of Children's Literature, *second edition, Scott, Foresman and Company, 1982, p. 215.*

Integers: Positive and Negative   (1972)

It is strange that the number line, so obvious and so useful once it is comprehended, is so difficult to teach to the child. We probably introduce it at too late an age, and then usually in connection with beginning algebra. Dr. Adler, in this small book of 46 pages, certainly helps to correct

this state of affairs. The first 24 pages present a series of simple games, beginning with some involving rewards and penalties and showing how one may keep score using positive and negative integers. Addition of integers is introduced in terms of colored directed arrows and then illustrated by games involving displacements. The thermometer scale is explained and then the number line. The rest of the games and illustrations are a little more complicated, but they are still well within the grasp of the child. The book ends with a short explanation of subtraction. The author must be complimented for his skillful treatment of this basic topic. . . .

> *A review of "Integers: Positive and Negative," in* Science Books: A Quarterly Review, *Vol. IX, No. 1, May, 1973, p. 66.*

Petroleum: Gas, Oil, and Asphalt   (1975)

There is much basic information here to start with: we learn that petroleum means rock oil; that it can be a gas, liquid, or solid substance; that it was formed ages ago from living material. A bit of history provides further perspective: petroleum was known in biblical times, and the ancient Chinese drilled as deep as 3,000 feet to find it. Then Adler gets more technical. Diagrams and text explain where oil is found and describe methods of searching it out and pumping it to the surface. But a chapter describing the molecular structure of many petrochemicals seems of limited value to the age group using this book, and final chapters, which appraise U.S. and world petroleum supplies, speak in terms of seeking out new supplies rather than searching for alternatives. Although conservation is advised and pollution is seen as a problem, Adler doesn't discuss the additional environmental problems that loom should industry switch back to coal and the shale oil resources be mined. A practical series with informational strengths in discussions of how things are done today, but without perspective on long-term problems. (pp. 763-64)

> *Denise M. Wilms, in a review of "Petroleum: Gas, Oil and Asphalt," in* The Booklist, *Vol. 72, No. 11, February 1, 1976, pp. 763-64.*

This is an excellent introduction to the discovery, history, technology, and current uses of petroleum. It covers essentially the same material as Shilstone's *The First Book of Oil* (Watts, 1969), with added emphasis on pollution problems and conservation. . . . Twelve pages on the chemical distinctions between petroleum fractionations are of questionable value for use at this age level but should not detract from making this a first choice for updating in this subject area. (pp. 55-6)

> *Shirley A. Smith, in a review of "Petroleum: Gas, Oil and Asphalt," in* School Library Journal, *Vol. 22, No. 9, May, 1976, pp. 55-6.*

This is a very thorough, well-written book about a timely topic. The author speaks intelligently and clearly to children about a topic which is difficult and complex. There is little about petroleum which one would want to know on a basic level that is not included in the text. My only complaint is by now a familiar one to readers of this journal: with a topic so obviously and inextricably involved with important social, economic, political and ethical issues, it is strange and disappointing that there is virtually nothing here to show that the subject of petroleum is an important, complex, and controversial issue in our everyday lives.

> *David E. Newton, in a review of "Petroleum: Gas, Oil and Asphalt," in* Appraisal: Children's Science Books, *Vol. 9, No. 3, Fall, 1976, p. 6.*

The Environment (1976)

Despite the early references to photosynthesis, oxygen and other cycles, and food chains (which Adler doesn't bother to relate to his subsequent points), this is less a scientific description of environmental interdependence than a conventional summary of "what we must do to keep our environment clean and its storehouse full." Citing, in a few simple paragraphs each, such problems as vanishing species, depletion of non-renewable "treasures," and air and water pollution, Adler points out that man's population growth and unique interference with nature's balance have unwanted side effects, and he warns that we need to save and recycle, make laws, and let the developing countries have their share. It sounds like an outline for a 1970 Earth Day program; by now, some of the bland assumptions are questionable and others certainly simplistic. However, you might think of it as an overviewing classroom introduction to more down-to-earth study—or as propaganda in a good cause.

> *A review of "The Environment," in* Kirkus Reviews, *Vol. XLIV, No. 9, May 1, 1976, p. 536.*

In 48 pages, it is difficult if not impossible to cover such a complex topic as the environment! Yet, Adler attempts this and does a remarkable job in covering the basics such as cycles, food chains, air and water pollution, and population control. Due to space limitation, these topics had to be treated very simplistically. . . . An overly simplistic text with a rather high readability level does not make this book the best choice for a school library or science room!

> *Martha T. Kane, in a review of "The Environment," in* Appraisal: Children's Science Books, *Vol. 10, No. 2, Spring, 1977, p. 5.*

Dealing with such topics as cycles in nature, food chains, man's impact on nature, pollution, extinction, resources and conservation, Adler introduces the student to the interrelated aspects of the environmental problem. Because several topics are covered in such a small book, the end result is little more than a series of definitions and comments on the problem. Various aspects of the environmental problem might have been presented in a more inquiry-provoking manner; however, the book would be an interesting addition to an elementary school library.

> *Godfrey Roberts, in a review of "The Environment," in* Science Books & Films, *Vol. XIII, No. 1, May, 1977, p. 41.*

Food (1977)

A thin discussion of the different kinds of food the human body needs for energy and for growth and repair. Because Adler tries to cover too many food-related topics—functions of vitamins, minerals, proteins, and carbohydrates; planning a balanced diet; types of foods eaten around the world and their origins; world hunger; and foods in the future—in too little space, some of the sections are only minimally informative. Terms are italicized when first used but not all are listed in the glossary. . . .

> *Pam Barron, in a review of "Food," in* School Library Journal, *Vol. 24, No. 5, January, 1978, p. 84.*

This is a straightforward account about food—its sources, relation to bodily functions, preservation, historical origins, usual and unusual foods and meal planning. One chapter is devoted to junk foods, the bane of modern people. There may be some nit-picking about ethnological subjects and world hunger, but this is a minor consideration compared to the overall value and scope of this book. The glossary of technical and scientific terms could be more exhaustive.

> *Albert Robinson, Jr., in a review of "Food," in* Science Books & Films, *Vol. XIV, No. 1, May, 1978, p. 42.*

Mathematics (1990)

An excellent book in every way. The mathematical principles are enrichment-level concepts, clearly explained with text and [Ron Miller's] illustration. Adler introduces ancient number theory principles and formulas on the most modern of inventions, the home computer; students will move ahead quickly with his carefully laid computer programming foundation. The illustrations are crucial to the concise text, with flow charts, tables, checker arrangements, and geometric figures. It's a simple book, and that's its beauty. Younger children will enjoy the large format, and those who have access to computers will find their knowledge of them extended with instruction in a little Basic programming while conveying fascinating number facts. Books like this nurture children, and it should be considered in spite of its limited appeal.

> *Kathleen Riley, in a review of "Mathematics," in* School Library Journal, *Vol. 36, No. 12, December, 1990, p. 114.*

Paul Biegel

1925-

Dutch author of fiction and short stories and scriptwriter.

Major works include *The King of the Copper Mountains* (1969), *The Little Captain* (1971), *The Gardens of Dorr* (1975), *The Fattest Dwarfs of Nosegay* (1980), *The Curse of the Werewolf* (1981).

A fantasist praised for his original treatments of traditional fairy tale forms, Biegel is considered an especially versatile and imaginative writer for readers in the primary and middle grades. Acknowledged as the creator of sophisticated works that reflect his understanding of the feelings and emotions of children, he is often lauded for his narrative ability as well as for his distinctive portrayals of characters who are realistic despite their roots in fantasy. "Paul Biegel," writes critic Sylvia Mogg, "is one of today's greatest storytellers," while *The Junior Bookshelf* adds that he has "a touch of genius" and is "a storyteller of the very highest tradition." Biegel is often recognized for using the fairy tale to provide insight into the human condition while retaining a sense of enchantment and a childlike view of reality. His works, fantastic adventures that feature human and animal characters and incorporate action, mystery, and suspense, usually address serious themes and contain socially conscious messages as they explore the nuances of good and evil. Often profiling characters who gain self-knowledge through their searches, Biegel includes such values in his works as altruism, self-acceptance, honesty, sacrifice, and the conquering of greed and sloth. Although his stories are often considered challenging for young readers due to their sophisticated themes and Biegel's use of literary techniques such as flashbacks, subplots, and the interweaving of past history and present events, he is also noted for his playful sense of humor as well as for the inventive wordplay, expressive language, and exuberant read-aloud quality of his books.

An editor and publisher who is highly regarded as a translator of his own works as well as the works of other authors, Biegel is perhaps best known as the creator of *The King of the Copper Mountains,* the first of his books to be translated into English. A collection of short stories reminiscent of the tales of the Arabian Nights, the work revolves around a quest for a magic herb to save the life of King Mansolain, who is dying of heart failure in Copper Castle. While the king's doctor is on his journey, thirteen animals of the kingdom, including a three-headed dragon, come to the castle and tell a story a day to the king to keep him alive. The tales, both serious and comic, reveal the past history of the kingdom and how the animals happened to come to the castle; woven around the stories are the king's biography and the doctor's adventures as he searches for the herb. In addition, Biegel is especially well known for *The Twelve Robbers,* a folktale about how a dozen bandits who decide to make a beggar into a king are transformed by the experience, and *The Gardens of Dorr,*

Biegel's sole work for young adults. In this fantasy, which is noted for its depth and unusual format, he describes a quest by a princess to find the antidote for a spell which has bewitched her city and turned her lover into a flower. Biegel is also the author of several series for younger children; in translation are "The Little Captain" books, fantastic adventure stories about a small boy with incredible freedom who travels to enchanted islands and magical kingdoms with the three young stowaways who board his ship, and the "Virgil Nosegay" stories about a bee-sized but feisty dwarf who lives with the insects. In addition to his fiction, Biegel has written the script for the Dutch television program based on his story *The Curse of the Werewolf* (1981), in which Duke Wildwolf is cured of his lycanthropy and gold fever by the Vergil-quoting Dr. Crock. Biegel is the recipient of several international awards. Among them are the Het Kinderboek van het Jarr, the award for the best book of the year, for *Het sleutelkruid* (*The King of the Copper Mountains*) in 1965, *De kleine kapitein* (*The Little Captain*) in 1972, *De twaalf rovers* (*The Twelve Robbers*) in the same year, and *Het Olifantenfeest* (*The Elephant Party*) in 1974; *The Twelve Robbers* also received the Nienke van Hichtumprijs from the Campert Foundation in 1973. Biegel was awarded the Staatsprijs voor kinder- en jeugdliteratuur, the state prize of the Netherlands, for his body of work in 1973.

(See also *Something about the Author*, Vol. 16; *Contemporary Authors New Revision Series*, Vols. 14, 32; and *Contemporary Authors*, Vols. 77-80.)

GENERAL COMMENTARY

The Junior Bookshelf

Since the award-winning *King of the Copper Mountains* in 1964, Paul Biegel has made a very valuable contribution to our literature for children and young people. Many of his stories have continued to build on the traditional fairy tale foundations. His fantasies are rooted in common human problems, instincts and emotions—common enough to reach every child. The writer does not deliberately address himself to children, but he takes them into account in the shape, style and vocabulary of his books. The reprintings and numerous translations abroad prove that what Paul Biegel has to say finds an echo in very many children. Time after time the reader observes that his novels can be read on many levels; young and old recognise themselves in the mirror that Paul Biegel holds up to them. For Biegel is sharply perceptive, he records a great deal and compassionately gives shape to his observations in his stories. His attitude is completely honest and cannot be better expressed than in his own words:

> The nature of a child is not being small, but growing bigger. It is not for us to go to them but for them to come to us. The more we surround children with things adapted to their size, the more we hold up the natural course of their development. It is not necessary for children to understand all they hear.

A recurrent figure in his work is 'the seeker'. Sometimes he knows what he is seeking, as in *The King of the Copper Mountain;* sometimes he is simply chasing a chimera, as in *Zeven Fabels van Ubim*. Sometimes it seems that as he looks for the thing that is supposed to change him, he is actually changing (*Seven Times Search*). In *The Twelve Robbers* it is only their united greed for gold that can move the robbers to action, but when they are dispatched separately in search of the king's treasure they get stuck, each tangled in the trammels of his own self.

The high point is undoubtedly *The Gardens of Dorr*. Here the theme is fully worked out by the rich princess Melissa, seeking her poor lover, the gardener's boy. The writer's imagination gives an unexpected twist to every obstacle and solution; even the worst of troubles can be eliminated by honesty, self-sacrifice and tenacity.

Not all the stories are on the grand scale, but they are all surprising, especially their plots. Often one story contains various plots subordinate to the main theme. We also find this element of surprise in his choice of words, in the whole of his literary style, sometimes light-footed and playful, then again dramatic and direct. He plays with words, bizarre discoveries and inventions of his own, all in a way that appeals to children and may stimulate them also to have a go at writing something quite different from the usual language of school dictation and composition. Biegel's style is rich but always understandable, so that many young readers can feel and enter into the whole story. This is also why it asks to be read aloud, to be heard.

His sparkling imagination, his probing to the essence of what it means to be human and his skilful writing make Paul Biegel's books a delight for children to read. Moreover, he is well able to convey a child's fears, longings and uncertainties, as illustrated in *The Rag Animal* in which he enters fully into the little girl's grief over the toy animal which has fallen down the well. The grown-ups are almost grotesque in their indifferent and teasing reactions. He paints reality as a small child sees it. (pp. 9-11)

> *"Report of the Jury Awarding the State Prize for Children's and Young People's Literature for 1973," translated by Patricia Crampton, in* The Junior Bookshelf, *Vol. 39, No. 1, February, 1975, pp. 9-11.*

TITLE COMMENTARY

The King of the Copper Mountains   (1969)

The Dutch author of this book has a touch of genius, he is a storyteller of the very highest tradition. This book was awarded the Dutch Children's Book Prize 1965, and as such it is truly outstanding. The publishers will do British children a great service by making more of Paul Biegel's work available for our enjoyment.

Like the stories told by Scheherezade, in the Tales of the Arabian Nights, a human life hangs in the balance. Here it is that of the King Mansolain whose heart is failing. In order to save him the Wonder Doctor sets off on a long journey to search for the precious life giving Golden Speedwell. On his travels he tells all the animals he meets to go to the Copper Castle and tell the King a story to keep his heart active. So it is that the squirrel comes, the three headed dragon, the ten bees, the rabbit-of-the-dunes, and many more. Each tells a story, some of great deeds done; others sad; some amusing; there is even a duet sung by two mice. Interwoven is the King's own story and that of the progress of the Wonder Doctor in his search for the Golden Speedwell.

Each story is a perfect gem, holding the imagination until the last word.

> *A review of "The King of the Copper Mountains," in* The Junior Bookshelf, *Vol. 33, No. 1, February, 1969, p. 22.*

[*The King of the Copper Mountains*] has a threefold structure—the narrative concerning the king's health, the individual stories and occasional snippets telling of the progress of the seeker for the magic herb. This structure is a splendid device for maintaining interest in a long book, always provided the content is worthwhile. Unfortunately, the stories are uneven in quality, for some are trivial and boring—hardly likely to keep the king alive. It is this unevenness of invention which makes this book 'satisfactory' rather than 'outstanding'.

The stories read aloud well, and perhaps this, and the fact

that the balance of good stories over trivial ones is on the right side, make the book recommendable for lower juniors. (pp. 108-09)

> *Colin Field, in a review of "The King of the Copper Mountains," in* The School Librarian and School Library Review, *Vol. 17, No. 1, March, 1969, pp. 108-09.*

[This] exciting, carefully plotted, original fantasy is a series of stories within a story. . . . Suspense builds to a satisfying climax, as each of 13 animals tells his story and the king's faithful hare listens to the faltering heart while waiting for the Wonder Doctor—who does return in time. The book is capped by the stories of a dwarf and the Doctor, who reveal the past history of the kingdom and how the various animals came to the castle; characters and things presented and alluded to throughout the book are linked by these final revelations. Fine for telling or reading aloud. . . .

> *Lillian K. Orsini, in a review of "The King of the Copper Mountains," in* School Library Journal, *Vol. 16, No. 8, April, 1970, p. 114.*

In the great welter of material published each year it sometimes happens that an outstanding book is passed over by the majority of reviewers and compilers of booklists. Just such a book is **The King of the Copper Mountains.** . . .

[Each] story is a little self-contained gem. A family book which will be perfect for reading aloud to a variety of children whatever their age and interests, for it is amusing, serious, simple yet full of detail and complexity, and seemingly all at the same time. NOT to be missed, a delight for any child of 7 up.

> *Jean Russell, in a review of "The King of the Copper Mountains," in* Books for Your Children, *Vol. 6, No. 2, Winter, 1970-71, p. 19.*

The Seven-Times Search (1971)

Many people will already be familiar with the name of Paul Biegel from his enchanting book: **The King of the Copper Mountains,** to my mind an outstanding fantasy for children. This new fantasy from Mr. Biegel is of an altogether different sort. Its title is taken from the theme—the search by a small, unmathematically minded boy, for the system ruling the seven times table. His search takes him into the world of insects and, since magic is an integral part of the story, he finds himself tiny in a world of giants. To me, this is terrifying; he meets large and aggressive caterpillars who imprison him in a cocoon; militant ants attack him for his ignorance of their ways; most appalling of all, a large and extremely hairy spider appears, captured in all its hirsute reality by the illustrator [Babs van Wely]. How Nicky eludes these predators and finds his answers with the help of a fey companion called Feather makes up the plot.

It is perilous to imagine that one knows what will frighten children, but I would hesitate to read this story to a sensitive child.

> *Gabrielle Maunder, in a review of "The Seven Times Search," in* Children's Book Review, *Vol. I, No. 2, April, 1971, p. 50.*

Nicky is fat and wears glasses and he simply can't learn his seven-times table. For this anti-hero an equally unusual heroine; she is under a spell and appears and disappears arbitrarily, sometimes in the form of a feather and occasionally as a nimble little girl. Feather may win back her proper form for ever if she can help Nicky to learn the seven-times without actually telling it to him. Any child, arithmetically minded or not, should enjoy following Nicky through the table, which he learns by a kind of counting-stick method. Turned small for convenience, he spends some time in an ant-hill, where war prisoners are conveniently grouped in sevens. Hugo the bee suggests he should count the stamens in a poppy, and when he is caught by caterpillars and wound into a cocoon he numbers his fellow victims as they hang inside a tree. The sister snails (Sybilla, Priscilla and Drusilla) take their turn in his education and so does an unpleasant spider. The insect characters are presented as human types and the author's artful fancy puts the reader in a mood to accept the moral of the ending—Nicky must be content to be himself, fat and bespectacled and not a handsome athlete as he wishes, and Feather can then be herself too. There is something uniquely appealing about this book. The humour is happy and the story has just the right amount of suspense and excitement. (pp. 1715-16)

> *Margery Fisher, in a review of "The Seven Times Search," in* Growing Point, *Vol. 9, No. 9, April, 1971, pp. 1715-16.*

An ingenious and imaginative fantasy by the Dutch author of the outstanding and charming **King Of The Copper Mountains.** Nicky is plump, clumsy, has poor eyesight and can't learn his seven times table. If he can repeat this table to the Great Magician, he may become a different boy. (pp. 102-03)

[Nicky] is away from home for months, so often hungry, frightened and in danger of his life. He is captured by ants, caterpillars, snails and spiders. It seems an alarming way to learn arithmetic and scarcely calculated to increase a child's love of the insect world! One episode in particular has a nightmare quality for Nicky is wound up in a cocoon, with only his head outside, and is left alone in partial darkness while an emerging butterfly as big as himself crawls damply over his defenceless face.

Nevertheless the story is exciting, has humour and magic, and at the end will touch a child's heart, for Nicky, when at last he meets the Great Magician, asks not for his own wish but Feather's wish to be granted, although he has to part with her. The author has created two children with contrasting personalities who endear themselves to the reader. (p. 103)

> *E. Colwell, in a review of "The Seven Times Search," in* The Junior Bookshelf, *Vol. 35, No. 2, April, 1971, pp. 102-03.*

The Little Captain (1971)

A fine mixture of imagination and humour, events and unusual characters makes this latest translation from the Dutch of another of Paul Biegel's junior books most welcome. The Little Captain gets involved in a series of adventures in his ship, the Neversink. With him in these are adults but, with the true discipline of the sea, they realise who is in command. The island of Evertaller, where the giants are said to live, is as well named as his vessel. . . . And just to give emphasis to the unusual, the last page of the book is headed Contents!

> *H. Budge, in a review of "The Little Captain," in* The Junior Bookshelf, *Vol. 36, No. 2, April, 1972, p. 96.*

[*The following excerpt begins with a comparison between the translations of* The King of the Copper Mountains, *which was translated by the author and Gillian Hume, and* The Little Captain, *which was translated by Patricia Crampton.*]

The Little Captain, though a slighter book, perhaps, than **The King of the Copper Mountains** and different too, in its field of adventure, has the same kind of sustained assurance that marks that notable fairy tale; the translation, indeed, is happier. It is a story told with extreme art, especially in the light yet memorable opening. The little captain is every child's alter ego, dream comrade or ideal; coming from nowhere, busily occupied, living alone, having no ties, held by no outside rules. "He did not have to go to school. The master and the fathers and mothers could not tell him what to do. No one could tell the little captain what to do." A Peter Pan—with differences: for one thing, like a real dream-boy, he says far less. He spends his time patching up his Heath Robinson boat; thus, to make the propeller, he plays his trumpet and melts down the pennies earned in a wood-ash fire on the beach, then pours the stuff into a propeller-shaped hole in the sand. When he does sail out, to the island where, reputedly, one grows up in a night, three of the local children secretly join him: Podgy Plum, Marinka, and timid Thomas. The aged lighthouse-keeper warns them of the stone dragon gate that bars the way; by night the dragons are stone, and crack your boat; by day they warm to life. . . . They get through, none the less.

This episode is not the only peak in the little odyssey, which might have lost in interest after the goal was reached. And left. The strangest, no doubt, is the last—the discovery of a ghost town, made of flotsam, built on towering columns rising out of the sea. All the inhabitants come to see them off:

> They'll reach home safely . . . Podgy Plum, Marinka, and timid Thomas, who had wanted to be grown up overnight, had indeed grown up a bit, because of all their adventures. They still weren't really grown up, and I suppose they will still have to go to school. But as for the little captain . . . he will sail away again one of these days, for the world is full of islands and wonderful adventures.

Everything is seen child-view to the last. No one looks too far below the event. (pp. 475-76)

> *"Fantastic Invention," in* The Times Literary Supplement, *No. 3661, April 28, 1972, pp. 475-76.*

The Little Captain and the Seven Towers (1973)

This translation from the Dutch has many ingredients of the traditional fairy story: the quest, the kingdom under the sea, the enchanted island with trials to be undergone; yet for me, there is something missing. It is not the fault of the down-to-earth humour with which Paul Biegel describes the little Captain and his crew, and the shipwrecked sailors whom they saved in the earlier adventure—they provide, for one thing, a delightful chorus of repeated actions, such as Marinka's pancake-making and timid Thomas' whimpers and deck-swabbing. It is rather the lack of motivation of the adventures (despite the fact that three more sailors are rescued): the children's "trials", for instance, aim to cure sins like greed and sloth which are scarcely relevant to them. (pp. 206-07)

> *M. Hobbs, in a review of "The Little Captain and the Seven Towers," in* The Junior Bookshelf, *Vol. 38, No. 4, August, 1974, pp. 206-07.*

The Twelve Robbers (1974)

Paul Biegel is one of today's greatest storytellers. He uses the old traditional forms, which soon become familiar to the youngest child, but with subtle differences that make his tales very much of today. In this latest story his twelve wild, magnificent robbers are pleased to make a beggar into a king when he appears at the inn where they are carousing. Such is the power of the robbers that their king has a short, but glorious, reign of which the main feature is his ride through the streets throwing gold to the people. Then, suddenly, all the gold vanishes and there is no more for the robbers to steal. All that remain are the gold pieces nailed to the walls of the robbers' 'hour long cave'. Now a robber cannot be a robber if there is no gold to be stolen and, since nobody in all the land has any gold, the robbers conclude that all the gold must be locked up in the real king's castle. This castle is too strong and well-guarded for the robbers to storm it, so they decide to send one of their number to spy out the land. When he doesn't return they send another, and then another and another, until only Jinx the leader is left. Each robber tackles the problem in a different way, according to his character and ability, and each is changed by his experience. But what a marvellous romp of a book this is! The separate adventures make it very good for reading aloud—except that the excitement and pace are so well maintained that it would take a very strong-willed reader to break off, particularly in the face of entreaties from the listener. Private readers can, of course, gorge themselves at one sitting. Richard Kennedy's drawings have the right sort of swashbuckling air and give that extra dimension to the characters, all of whom, even the minor ones, are real and alive. The publishers' recommend ten plus as the age-group, but surely the story should not be denied to younger readers.

> *Sylvia Mogg, in a review of "The Twelve Rob-*

bers," *in* Children's Book Review, *Vol. IV, No. 4, Winter, 1974-75, p. 149.*

The twelve robbers who lived in a cave high up in the mountains stormed out of their hiding-place every day to rob the rich, until one day there was not a gold piece left in the country to seize, except for the king's own treasure. So they set out one by one to try to find the king's treasure. Their names are enough to delight all children who love to roll unusual sounds round their tongues—Trillingburr, Sharpjack, Dapperfleece, Sisal, Prig—but none of them could find any gold. This well-known Dutch author's story will delight many younger readers for the fast action he packs into his stories; their parents will find greater pleasure in the hidden meaning to the tale—the identity of the king's treasure. (pp. 30-1)

B. Clark, in a review of "The Twelve Robbers,"
in The Junior Bookshelf, *Vol. 39, No. 1, February, 1975, pp. 30-1.*

The author describes one robber as 'knowing about words. He could string them together so that you saw the palace before your eyes.' This ability well describes the author's own art, for his stirring, lusty, expressive prose brings the whole tale into sharp focus in the reader's mind. And what a tale! Full of excitement, mystery, fantasy and thrills, it fires the imagination and grips the interest from beginning to end.

E. E. Ashworth, in a review of "The Twelve Robbers," in The School Librarian, *Vol. 23, No. 1, March, 1975, p. 35.*

The Gardens of Dorr (1975)

[Paul Biegel's *The Gardens of Dorr*] suggests a rather older readership than his earlier books, yet the nonsense

Biegel in his home.

in it is as young as ever. Fantasy, after all, deals in ideas, and ideas are open-ended.

The basic structure is a quest: princess and gardener's boy, he bewitched into a flower, she searching through the years for the right place to set the seed to bring him back. Interwoven with this is the story of Dorr, the bewitched city whose fate is bound up with theirs. The images are unforgettable: the crumbling stone city with its blank windows, the black print of hand or lips that is the passport to the city. The characters are not black and white, as in most fairy tales, but mixed and strangely bewildered. Even the dwarf is loyal to his mistress, the witch. Even old Glop, the puff-toad, archetypal Dirty Old Man, is caught up in the people's frenzied whirl towards freedom "because he too was one of them".

Anne Carter, "War over Words," in The Times Literary Supplement, *No. 3813, April 4, 1975, p. 365.*

I find this by far the most satisfying of this very sensitive Dutch author's books. Moreover, the paper and print are attractive, and the wonderful line-drawings [by Eva-Johanna Rubin] from the German edition catch to perfection the mystery, terror and beauty of the story in their fine designs, which at times burst out of their frames in powerful curves and nightmare fantasy scenes. Melinda's search for the lost gardens of Dorr, where she can sow and bring to life again the throbbing seed which is all that is left each year of her lover, turned into a flower by her father's wicked witch-mistress, is a fairy tale with an authentic sense of timelessness and universal truth. Some of the truths are uncomfortable: jealousy, loneliness, and the pathos of the old and silly. The narrative technique is unusual but successful: the story begins near the end (the last chapter begins like the first), and the explanations emerge in a series of apparently unconnected stories, whose details relate gradually to each other. Most are told by the minstrel Jarrick, who follows Melinda to watch over her. Others belong to the hidden inhabitants of Dorr like the old soldier with one boot who keeps the gate, or Miss Jo-Jo and Miss Epsie, whose young men disappeared when the witch placed the city under the petrifying spells of the Silver Ones. The end is no mere "They lived happily ever after": the last struggle is grim and costly, and the last word is with the old King who, with the dwarf ferryman who retires to mourn her, had loved the witch.

M. Hobbs, in a review of "The Gardens of Dorr," in The Junior Bookshelf, *Vol. 39, No. 3, June, 1975, p. 193.*

Paul Biegel's latest fairy tale will delight all his fans and make new ones. It is for older readers than his earlier stories and the pleasure it gives is more subtle. . . .

This is a beautifully-written book, and the author has been partly responsible for the translation so that it represents his intentions exactly. Short stories and flashbacks carry on the narrative, so that the witch's evil power is gradually realised. Is the witch totally evil? Her dwarf is loyal; and the old king prefers her bed to his wife's. There's an ambiguity about this battle for good or evil, life or death, which makes this book a rich experience. However, its

elaborate plot and its high cost—though it is finely produced on good quality paper—would indicate that **The
Gardens of Dorr** is not for every library.

Jessica Kemball-Cook, in a review of "The
Gardens of Dorr," in Children's Book Review,
Vol. V, No. 2, Summer, 1975, p. 59.

Here is another original and highly sophisticated fairy
story by the author of the admired **King of the Copper
Mountains.** Its narrative method is unusually complex, for
one character after another tells, reads or dreams a sub-
story and while the *telling* is an integral part of the whole,
what is told is later seen as a flashback, part of the jigsaw
puzzle which at the end is seen whole. Immediate re-
reading is the natural result. Unusual, too, in a fantasy is
the degree of realism in the characters: the weak, well-
meaning king, infatuated with the witch; his neglected
queen, ineffectually sighing all day in her room; Jarrick,
who clowns as if to give the lie to his unrequited love; Dill,
the hotel-keeper, living by rule when all else has failed;
Glop, the fat old toad, lonely and lascivious; the pitiful,
horrible Epsie, middle-aged and man-mad. The author
and Gillian Hume have done a splendid job of translation—the blunt undecorated prose carries immense conviction. . . .

Iris Wilcox, in a review of "The Gardens of
Dorr," in The School Librarian, Vol. 23, No.
4, December, 1975, p. 335.

Far Beyond and Back Again (1977)

Paul Biegel's new book has much of the same fairytale
mystery and stylised technique of **The Gardens of Dorr,**
but it is a lighter work; the issues are more superficial and
romantic. Two brothers meet before a statue in a wood to
begin a round-the-world quest of whose goal they are ignorant. One goes East, the other West, and their adventures in fact alternate, though we seem at first to have a
series of unconnected fairytale situations. Each is resolved, however, by a silent stranger who at the end goes
East or West. The brothers meet halfway, and thereafter
retrace each other's steps, until they find in the end a
sweetheart and their long-lost father. There are vivid impressions of people and places, and dramatic surprises in
the narrative. The supernatural is interwoven with the
main theme, a witch who knows more of the quest than
the brothers, and phantom ships and their crews who return for the treasure they amassed while alive.

M. Hobbs, in a review of "Far Beyond and
Back Again," in The Junior Bookshelf, Vol.
41, No. 3, June, 1977, p. 173.

Robber Hopsika (1978)

Here, as in his earlier, highly successful books, Paul Biegel
writes an adventure of fantasy and magic which has, running through it, a down-to-earth practical sturdiness. The
two qualities combine to produce stories which enchant
and amuse and which are beautifully readable. Hopsika is
a merry rogue who pursues a highwayman's existence,
constantly apologising to the portrait of his dead mother
for his wicked ways. This simple life is disrupted when he
becomes involved in the rescue of the lovely Josephine
from the clutches of the fearful Master Irongrip. Hopsika's quick wit and ingenuity make for a rollicking story
which fairly burbles on its way.

Eileen A. Archer, in a review of "Robber Hopsika," in Book Window, Vol. 6, No. 1, Winter,
1978, p. 18.

This story of a robber whose mother is dead, but who
takes her portrait with him on all his adventures, gets a
little tedious. The robber's speech is quite amusing, as are
some of the characters, for example the innkeeper's wife
who will put in an aitch where none should be—"Yhes"
or "A caharriage!" There are too many characters altogether, so that the central theme of Hopsika trying to rescue the beautiful Josephine from the wicked Irongrip
tends to be lost in the difficulties of absorbing where the
new characters fit in.

B. Clark, in a review of "Robber Hopsika," in
The Junior Bookshelf, Vol. 43, No. 1, February, 1979, p. 25.

The Dwarfs of Nosegay (1978)

Stories about a hundred bee-sized dwarfs sound incredibly
twee, but in fact **The Dwarfs of Nosegay** by the prize-
winning Dutch writer Paul Biegel is an absolutely enchanting series of short stories for reading aloud to the
very young. Though each can stand by itself, the twenty-
one stories create a year-round saga of the life of the
dwarfs as they live with the bees, butterflies and rabbits
with whom they share their idyllic moor of grasses and
wild flowers. Against the amusing and often touching adventures of the dwarfs as they learn to co-operate with the
bees over the vexed problem of their joint love of honey,
there is the theme of Little Peter Nosegay, the youngest
of the dwarfs, who develops a special relationship with a
butterfly whom he watches emerge from her chrysalis.
After her marriage, which the dwarfs fittingly celebrate,
he promises to look after her children, and indeed as the
year passes and the spring returns he watches the eggs he
found under a nettle leaf become cocoons and then the cocoons in turn become six beautiful butterflies. Thus the
stories, apart from their fantasy, also evoke the marvel of
nature for young children, giving them the sense of the
powerful force of life renewing itself cyclically with the
metamorphosis of winter into spring symbolized by an apparently lifeless cocoon turning into a fragilely beautiful
butterfly. (p. 70)

Lavinia Learmont, "Noah's Ark," in Books
and Bookmen, Vol. 23, No. 273, June, 1978,
pp. 66, 68, 70.

Those of us who have grown up with fairy- and folk-tale
will have for a life-time an assortment of mental pictures—of landscapes wild or serene, of strange dwellings
and fantastic fauna and flora still half believed; and each
writer who re-tells a traditional tale or invents one on a
traditional basis will make a composite world from his

own mental images, from the original source he is using and from his idea of what his readers will enjoy. So, in *The Dwarfs of Nosegay,* the Dutch fantasist Paul Biegel has chosen to present his squat, bearded beings as miniature in size, living on friendly terms with bees and rabbits and using their habitat for their own purposes. In these short, whimsical tales, designed for listening children of four or five, a rabbit burrow provides a holiday lodging (crowded, certainly) for the hundred Nosegay dwarfs, while an old clog serves as a boat by which Little Peter finds a way round the new fence into the farm garden to supply his hungry rabbit friends with lettuce and carrots. Central character of these amiable tales, Little Peter carries the theme of the book, for his concern for the well-being of rabbits and bees extends to the butterflies whose beauty fascinates him and he tends a hatch of caterpillars through the chrysalis stage. In spite of the folk-tale origin of the dwarfs, these are really country tales, depicting small, vulnerable folk ordering their lives in line with the seasons and the weather. The airy, affectionate prose is matched by [Babs van Wely's] drawings in which a sturdy humour in the delineation of dwarfs and animals is softened by delicate glimpses of trees, sky and flowers.

> *Margery Fisher, in a review of "The Dwarfs of Nosegay," in* Growing Point, *Vol. 17, No. 2, July, 1978, p. 3355.*

Letters from the General   (1979)

Paul Biegel is so skillful now with this type of humourous fantasy that he can work successfully at the extreme of the spectrum. Many differing ingredients are presented here, and although they come together sensibly eventually, the mind of the reader is kept alert and questioning throughout the book. Three children stay with an aunt whose first meal for them is apple tart, vanilla custard with whipped cream and ice-cream with hot chocolate sauce. 'Children do only like sweet things?' she asks. With a bit of instruction she does manage shark with butter sauce, rice pudding with cinnamon, baked spinach with pickles, and so the invention goes on. The General, aunt's friend, is on an expedition looking for lost explorers and writes of his adventures along with advice as to how children should be treated . . . a good hiding before breakfast and cold baths to sleep in . . . The reader knows this is all a tease and when the General is reported lost the children are very upset. The other strands of the story (of mice and sparrows and siskins) are interspersed cleverly and the pace of the book never falters, nor does Paul Biegel's imagination cease to sparkle. (pp. 26-7)

> *Eileen A. Archer, in a review of "Letters from the General," in* Book Window, *Vol. 6, No. 3, Summer, 1979, pp. 26-7.*

The bonding together of a number of short tales to create the effect of a longer story is quite frequently attempted: here it is done more successfully than usual.

Oriana, Ben and Keith go to stay with Aunt Matilda who lives in a disorganised house, feeds them a peculiar diet, and tells them instalments from two quite distinct stories: of the sailing mice who venture across the Brollymere and

of the little Siskin bird who wants a wife. In addition Aunt Matilda receives letters from her friend the General, who is lost in the Milesian jungle, and these amount to a third story. Since the author seems in control of all his threads of plot, disbelief can be suspended reasonably easily and the style and wit of the writing enjoyed.

> *R. Baines, in a review of "Letters from the General," in* The Junior Bookshelf, *Vol. 43, No. 4, August, 1979, p. 202.*

[*Letters from the General*] involves four separate narratives under the aegis of a magical aunt and ends with a wedding-feast whose centrepiece is a miniature table for a wedding-party of mice. But it is the sort of book which drops dead if you try to convey its flavour at second-hand. Its pleasure lies in its exuberance and agility and the very thinness of the material over which it dances. (p. 731)

> *Henry Tube, "Cornish Coast to Wild West," in* New Statesman, *Vol. 98, No. 2538, November 9, 1979, pp. 730-31.*

The Looking-Glass Castle   (1979)

The Looking-Glass Castle is very slight, an allegorical fantasy with a moral stated in the last words of the story as "the looking-glass castle ceases to exist as soon as your desires turn into wings". I am afraid that the invention is not strong enough to sustain interest through the complicated, even if brief, story. Jack Prince's closely-detailed line drawings have just that conviction and urgency that the text lacks.

> *M. Crouch, in a review "The Looking-Glass Castle," in* The Junior Bookshelf, *Vol. 43, No. 6, December, 1979, p. 323.*

The Clock Struck Twelve   (1979)

The fact that publishing is in recession cannot be good for education. It may, however, have one beneficial side-effect, if it encourages publishers to cut out some of the dead wood which at present clogs and disfigures their children's lists. At the moment many publishers seem to have abandoned critical judgment in favour of a bland catering to established appetites. . . .

These gloomy thoughts are inspired in general by a recent, and extremely noticeable, lowering of the high standards of the 1960s and 1970s, and in particular by Paul Biegel's *The Clock Struck Twelve.* Biegel is an internationally known and respected author, so his book makes a good example. It is not simply mediocre, but positively bad: fey, trite, laboured, condescending, whimsical.

"Flizz, flizz, flizz, / our wuzzy wings go whizz / and whirl away from thizz" sing Biegel's midges. Gauzy-winged fairies flutter in the company of beetles, caterpillars, lame mice, lovesick frogs and cricket violinists, as if Kipling's Puck had never consigned them to oblivion: "that painty-winged, wand-waving, sugar-and-shake-your-head set of imposters. Butterfly wings, indeed!" Rose Fyleman is alive and well and living in Holland.

Neil Philip, "Apocalyptic Visions," in The Times Educational Supplement, No. 3323, February 15, 1980, p. 28.

In this story of a little boy's dreams, reality and fantasy are merged and blurred, but the characters are clearly and sympathetically drawn.

Ninochka, the exquisite fairy dancer, has her wings torn off accidentally by Yaaling, the ugly love-sick frog. She is cared for by Pots the beetle, Siliacus the caterpillar, Prils the musical grasshopper, and the mice Theodore and crippled Isadore. In the intricate story line, their dangerous and difficult journey, and the quest of the old Elf King, his two sons and his army of Looking Glass Soldiers, are interwoven in an original and exciting way.

The translator Patricia Crampton has interpreted the poetic style of the Dutch author with great delicacy. This is a memorable and moving book which should stimulate the imagination of sensitive children.

A. Thatcher, in a review of "The Clock Struck Twelve," in The Junior Bookshelf, Vol. 44, No. 5, October, 1980, p. 238.

The Little Captain and the Pirate Treasure (1980)

The adventure the Little Captain takes his three young friends through are as amazing, amusing and unexpected as any Paul Biegel has written of before. The steamship 'Neversink', with upturned bath-tub for a boiler, a stovepipe for a furnace and six bottomless buckets for a funnel, sets out with seven treasure chests which are to be returned to their owners, and to reach them the Little Captain sails to the Misty East, the Deep South, the Wild West and the Far North; not that these regions correspond with our understanding of such names. The main characters are as well drawn as ever with plenty of zest and energy, and as they sail the seas there are lots of opportunities for other characters to enter the story. Paul Biegel never fails to open new windows in fantasy and his ideas are unfettered by bonds of convention. Yet as the children cross deserts, sail a Boiling Sea, and climb a mountain of ice, the fantasy is strong but not anarchic.

Eileen A. Archer, in a review of "The Little Captain and the Pirate Treasure," in Book Window, Vol. 7, No. 3, Summer, 1980, p. 13.

A lively creative mind has engineered this coherent and captivating chronicle in which the children, motivated by a commendable altruism, lap up their adventures with a cheerful bravado, suitably tempered by the moans and groans of Timid Thomas. Plenty of action, a strong thread of suspense, a touch of humour and the magic of a skilfully shaped imaginative narrative combine to make this a splendid tale. . . .

G. Bott, in a review of "The Little Captain and the Pirate Treasure," in The Junior Bookshelf, Vol. 44, No. 5, October, 1980, p. 238.

An engaging fantasy, written . . . with great style and humour, this is the third story of the Little Captain and the steamship 'Neversink'. . . . The story is logically told,

with enough characterisation to make the reader care, especially about Timid Thomas for whom one has sympathy. Biegel's imagination is vivid, yet it never runs away with him and the story progresses quite naturally and credibly.

Janet Fisher, in a review of "The Little Captain and the Pirate Treasure," in The School Librarian, Vol. 28, No. 4, December, 1980, p. 374.

The Fattest Dwarf of Nosegay (1980)

Virgil Nosegay is a very fat dwarf about the size of a golf ball. His search for a mirror in which he can see for himself just how fat he really is takes him among animals and human beings. His adventures are never dangerous or frightening but they could well intrigue the small reader as they are recounted in the thirty-one short chapters.

Paul Biegel has won the Dutch Children's Book Prize twice and has two other books translated into English: **The Looking Glass Castle** and **The Dwarfs of Nosegay.** Margery Fisher has called these 'benign, graceful and affectionate', and his latest publication merits the same comments.

D. A. Young, in a review of "The Fattest Dwarf of Nosegay," in The Junior Bookshelf, Vol. 44, No. 4, August, 1986, p. 172.

The Tin Can Beast and Other Stories (1980)

The young heroes in Paul Biegel's collection conquer the elements, slay imaginary dragons, grow wings and altogether prove that the magical expectations of the very young are undashable. Although his inventiveness sometimes gets the better of him, most of these ingenious tales satisfy a deep and universal need in those of us who have remained children: he explores our buried phantasies, illustrates them and brings them to a satisfying resolution. Mr. Biegel somehow always manages to marry these phantasies to a down-to-earth reality. And he concludes his volume with a compendious fairy tale.

Stephen Corrin, "Imaginary Dragons," in The Times Educational Supplement, No. 3369, January 16, 1981, p. 34.

Imagination will be stirred by fantasy in varying degrees but there is one essential common to light fancy and probing vision, an individual inner logic. In the airy pieces in **The Tincan Beast,** the ordinary world is interpenetrated with mystery and nonsense in that effortless way that belongs to childhood; a toy sword will do to kill a dragon, a creature made from an old tin can can be animated by a house-gnome for no particular reason. One or two of these stories seem over-weighted with whimsy—for instance, one in which a wizard mends a television carrying performances from Fairyland. In most cases, though, fancy is firmly directed to a purpose. A dragon with its own part in a story is also reflected in the bullying children who attack the old man who has joined in the traditional fight; a boy frees captive grasshoppers from a box after he has dreamt of hitting his own head against the ceiling. If there is a remote touch of Hans Andersen in the tales, the slightly arch manner and the socially conscious messages suggest far more strongly that this Dutch master of fantasy is suffering from the prevailing puritanical view that children's stories must always do them good. (pp. 3880-81)

> *Margery Fisher, in a review of "The Tincan Beast and Other Stories," in* Growing Point, *Vol. 20, No. 1, May, 1981, pp. 3880-81.*

That there are no less than 28 other stories all equally inventive is a great tribute to Mr. Biegel's versatility. All the ingredients of the traditional children's stories are presented with an eye to the contemporary scene. Who would have thought of a wizard who mended television sets so that they received programmes from Fairyland? Dreams and magic all play their part and there is the essential modicum of common sense which bridges the gap between fact and fantasy.

Seven to eight year olds will get repeated pleasure from this little volume.

> *A. R. Williams, in a review of "The Tin Can Beast and Other Stories," in* The Junior Bookshelf, *Vol. 45, No. 4, August, 1981, p. 149.*

The Curse of the Werewolf (1981)

There is nothing quite like a hoard of magic gold to get a good fairytale under way; and when a whole trunk load of the stuff is deposited at Dr Crock's laboratory accompanied by a mysterious plea for help from the Duke Wildwolf, who claims to be suffering from gold fever, there is no doubt that there is a promising story in the offing. Dr Crock, the impatient seeker after knowledge, determined on a scientific explanation for everything, sets out on his mission of mercy with his enthusiastic servant, who is named with Bunyan-like clarity "Valet", and is a sort of cross between Sancho Panza and Papageno. Their steps are constantly dogged by a pair of incompetent but committed robbers: Onk and Bonk, enticed by the treasure Valet is carrying. Onk is the brains of the outfit, and Bonk, as one might guess, comes in for a lot of blows dealt him by fate—and by Onk.

It proves a most eventful journey. But arriving at last they discover themselves to be two hundred years too late, and the castle in ruins. Legend relates that the embittered, misshapen Duke Wildwolf has sold his soul to his ancestor to learn the secret of making gold, and revenge himself on his two perfectly formed brothers. His chance of release occurs every thirteen years when the castle is restored to its former glory. He must then confront his brothers with his gold in order to be free of the curse. The cycle has come round as Dr Crock arrives; and the story enters a phantasmagorical, hallucinatory phase set between the two brothers' wild carousels upstairs and the Duke's shifting world of gold beneath. At the nub of it all, of course, is the Duke with a bad dose of lycanthropy. In curing him, Dr Crock suffers Faust's dilemma, but as this is a fairy tale, he triumphs and finds his own heart.

Paul Biegel's **The Curse of the Werewolf** has a strong story line using time-honoured features with a judicious mix of the suitably sinister and downright comic, such as when Valet in an excess of zeal emulates the doctor's skill using a chair leg as a splint for the hapless Bonk's leg, ingeniously offering both support and comfort but not, alas, tailored to a quick getaway. . . .

There are, however, uneasy anachronisms and inappropriatenesses of language, though the latter may be imputed to [Patricia Crampton's] translation. It seems strange that the doctor should "disinfect" wounds and subject a revived maiden to a very sophisticated investigation of symptoms, that the lovely maiden herself should be given to uttering "techee", or that the brother's "how much have you got on board?" be followed in the next breath by a "methinks". But it should certainly prove a most enjoyable book, even to those of seven to eleven who do not immediately recognize the constant allusions to the first two lines of the Aeneid.

> *Cara Chanteau, "Gold Fever," in* The Times Literary Supplement, *No. 4069, March 27, 1981, p. 345.*

The persistent legend of the werewolf is an eternally fascinating mystery and the theme has attracted much attention from writers. Paul Biegel adds to the basic tale a rich mixture of re-incarnation, hints of the Midas myth, an enigmatic gipsy woman, two rather obtuse robbers (named somewhat perfunctorily Onk and Bonk), a learned doctor given to quoting Vergil when faced with greater and greater surprises. One is inclined to ask whether the disappearances and re-appearances do not demand too much indulgent ingenuity from the reader. The story line tends to be submerged or lost in the many diversions and by-passes which the reader has to pursue.

> *N. N., in a review of "The Curse of the Werewolf," in* Book Window, *Vol. 8, No. 2, Spring, 1981, p. 25.*

Virgil Nosegay and the Cake Hunt (1981)

Virgil Nosegay, the gnome who lived with 100 others on the moor is an inquisitive, amusing determined little character. When he decides to venture into the world of humans to find a cake for Ianto Gnome's 1000th birthday, just about everything was bound to happen. He stowed away in Andy's mother's picnic bag, and was taken to school as a subject for Nature Study. He made news in print and on T.V. He was studied by 6 learned professors—Chinese, Russian, French, German, American and English, and captured by No. 7 and flown out to the palace of the Curiosity Princess. His attempts to escape back to his moor make hilarious reading. But, he finally succeeds, and with the cake!

Short chapters of three or four pages, lively text, and charming black and white illustrations [by Babs van Wely] combine all the ingredients of a favourite bed-time story book for the younger reader.

> *A. Thatcher, in a review of "Virgil Nosegay*

and the Cake Hunt," in The Junior Bookshelf, *Vol. 45, No. 6, December, 1981, p. 245.*

Crocodile Man (1982)

This is the kind of book likely to wreck the reputation of any reviewer: the sort of book where it is easy to be completely wrong over an author's intentions. The book consists of three tales of Chac, the crocodile man of the Amazon. The stories, in parts at least, have the taste of the traditional folk tale, and yet this taste is obliterated by numerous stylistic oddities—particularly in the dialogue. Whether these oddities are the author's intention or the translator's accident I cannot tell. The opening paragraphs have a memorable oral quality, but the hero's first words are: 'That's not a parrot, nor a monkey. That is a human being.' And 'Do you happen to have a looking glass on you?' is an incongruous form of words from someone who later declares: 'Be off with you! Out of my sight!' For me, stories of this kind must be without blemish if they are to work effectively. Two readings and seven days of thinking leave me baffled and not very amused.

> *Peter Kennerley, in a review of "Crocodile Man," in* The School Librarian, *Vol. 30, No. 3, September, 1982, p. 231.*

[This] imaginative book contains three stories about Chac, a hunter in the River Amazon country, who often wore a crocodile skin to help him with his hunting.

Each story is a clever original adaptation of a well-known South American folk tale. In the first, **"The Stones of the Sun,"** Chac helps seven jungle girls who had been summoned to the mountain plateau of the Andes, where ancient Indian warriors, turned to stone, wait for their revenge on their Spanish conquerors. In **"The Lake of El Dorado"** Chac saves seven mountain gnomes from the high lake of El Hombre Dorado (the golden man) and visits the Queen who lives in a golden palace under the water. In **"The Sleepers of Quatzqualpe"** he rescues people and animals of a native village who were being kidnapped by a giant bat. He thwarts the plan to use the villagers as slaves to clear the remote, overgrown and ruined city of Quatzqualpe, so that the ancient magicians living in suspended animation below it for thousands of years, can come back to life.

The text is easily read, with simple dialogue and plenty of action. The characters, with colourful South American names, move fluently against a well-defined background. (pp. 185-86)

> *A. Thatcher, in a review of "Crocodile Man," in* The Junior Bookshelf, *Vol. 46, No. 5, October, 1982, pp. 185-86.*

Virgil Nosegay and the Hupmobile (1983)

Virgil Nosegay and the Hupmobile is translated from the Dutch [by Patricia Crampton] and it would, I suppose be chauvinistic of me to suggest that as the original title is "Virgilius van Tuil en de oom uit Sweden" ["Virgil Nosegay and the uncle from Sweden"], there may well have

been more laughs in leaving the whole book as it was. All too often, translations, however well done, have a slightly lumpy feel about them. In this book the lumps sometimes become leaden nodules. What about this?

"Then all the voices broke out: 'Uncle from Sweden! Our rich uncle from Sweden is coming to stay! He's coming by road. He may bring us presents. He can sleep with me. No, with me. No, with me!'

Once again Ianto raised his hand."

And well he might. On hearing this I too would have wanted to leave the room.

The story is inventive enough—it concerns a quest by a jolly dwarf in search of his Uncle Frederick, but somehow I could never see past the words.

> *Gerald Haigh, "Smile, Giggle, Laugh, Guffaw," in* The Times Educational Supplement, *No. 3492, June 3, 1983, p. 38.*

The third adventure of the cheery Nosegay dwarfs is built up with a criss-crossing of journeys, the result of one of those good ideas that so often misfires in real life. When the dwarfs' rich uncle writes that he intends to drive from Sweden in his squirrel-car to visit them, impatient Virgil sets out to meet him and is impeded by sundry adventures with thieves, a friendly schoolboy and rather more detached police. For transport Virgil graduates from Shanks's Pony to a battery-powered car from a toy-shop with which the thieves hope he will assist them in their enterprises. The author expertly defers the moment when Virgil and the uncle are re-united with a series of diverting scenes in which oddity and everyday plainness are neatly interwoven.

> *Margery Fisher, in a review of "Virgil Nosegay and the Hupmobile," in* Growing Point, *Vol. 22, No. 2, July, 1983, p. 4114.*

Paul Biegel clearly enjoys making stories for children: there is no sense that the fourth in a series is churned out. There is plenty of adventure in dwarf Virgil Nosegay's journey to meet his Uncle Frederick and the subplot of thieves who try to use him to break into buildings for them. Seven- to nine-year-olds often enjoy stories about 'little people', and journeys are a successful narrative device. Here the two combine apparently epic bravery with a scale (adults seem to be giants) that young children can appreciate.

> *Mary Steele, in a review of "Virgil Nosegay and the Hupmobile," in* The Signal Review of Children's Books, 2, *1983, p. 18.*

Virgil Nosegay and the Wellington Boots (1984)

Leaving Wellingtons out all night is not usually considered a good thing to do but for Jasper it was the start of exciting times when Virgil, fallen into a boot by accident, goes off to live with the boy's unbelieving family. At first enjoying new experiences, the dwarf is not so happy when he ends up in a police station after complaints from snoopy neighbours, but he makes good use of a typewriter in the Lost Property cupboard to send an SOS to Jasper. When he returns to his friends in the spring the enterprising Virgil has stirring tales to tell. The material is stretched a little thin at times in this fourth Virgil tale but the style is as spry as ever and the drawings [by Babs van Wely] emphasise the demure humour of scale and incident proper to these pleasing books for nine-up readers.

> *Margery Fisher, in a review of "Virgil Nosegay and the Wellington Boots," in* Growing Point, *Vol. 23, No. 1, May, 1984, p. 4259.*

This new adventure is as enjoyable as previous ones. The author has a delightful, zany, sense of humour, an imagination that knows no bounds and characters who are instantly attractive be they 'goodies' or 'baddies'. This story will be re-read time and again by enthusiasts.

> *G. L. Hughes, in a review of "Virgil Nosegay and the Wellington Boots," in* The Junior Bookshelf, *Vol. 48, No. 3, June, 1984, p. 124.*

Jan Brett

1949-

(Also illustrates as Jan Brett Bowler) American author and illustrator of picture books and reteller.

Major works include *Fritz and the Beautiful Horses* (1981), *Annie and the Wild Animals* (1985), *The Twelve Days of Christmas* (1986), *Beauty and the Beast* (1989), *The Mitten: A Ukrainian Folktale* (1989).

The creator of original stories and retellings in picture book form for preschoolers and readers in the early elementary grades, Brett is highly regarded for her lavishly illustrated fantasies and adaptations of European folk and fairy tales. Praised for her imagination and artistic skill, she blends her simply told stories, which often feature the relationships of children and animals or update the texts of traditional folktales in a subtle manner, with opulent, heavily detailed paintings in watercolor and line which reflect folk motifs in architecture, artifacts, and clothing. Brett is especially well regarded for her talent as a designer as well as for her portrayals of animals as naturalistic but with personality. She often includes decorative borders around her double-page spreads as integral parts of her works, using them as vehicles to extend her texts, to provide viewers with new information, and to enrich the atmosphere of her stories. Although some observers note that her works may be too elaborate and detailed, Brett is frequently acclaimed for the control of her technique as well as for the stunning quality of her art.

Brett began her career as an illustrator of works by such authors as Seymour Simon, Eve Bunting, Ruth Krauss, and Diana Harding Cross. Her first book, *Fritz and the Beautiful Horses,* describes how a small horse forced to live outside the walls of his medieval city becomes a hero when he carries a group of children to safety. Brett uses the interaction of boys and girls with forest and domestic animals as the theme of such works as *Annie and the Wild Animals* and *The Wild Christmas Reindeer* (1990). In the first story, little Annie lives alone in a cottage except for her cat Taffy. When Taffy disappears, Annie tries to lure a replacement and attracts a bear, a moose, and other woodland animals, none of who are suitable; in the spring, Taffy—whose appearance is previewed in panels around the central story frames—returns with her three new kittens. In *The Wild Christmas Reindeer,* Teeska, asked by Santa Claus to train his reindeer for their Christmas ride, encounters difficulties until she tries patience and kindness. Brett departs from her usual European-influenced settings for *The First Dog* (1988), a work influenced by cave paintings and artifacts which speculates on the beginnings of the bond between people and dogs. In this story, the Paleolithic boy Kip meets a wolf who warns him of danger; the boy offers food to the wolf, which he names Dog, in exchange for protection. Brett is well known for her retellings of such familiar tales as *Goldilocks and the Three Bears* (1987) and *Beauty and the Beast;* she is also

the creator of *The Mitten: A Ukrainian Folktale,* in which Nicki's lost mitten becomes a haven for group of forest animals before it is returned to him, and *The Twelve Days of Christmas,* which uses motifs from eleven European countries to picture the cumulative events of the traditional carol. In 1983, Brett was named Ambassador of Honor, English-Speaking Union of the United States, for her illustrations for *Some Birds Have Funny Names* by Diana Harding Cross; *Some Birds Have Funny Names* was named an Outstanding Science Trade Book for Children in 1984. Brett has also received several parent- and child-selected awards for her works and has held exhibitions of her paintings across the United States.

(See also *Something about the Author,* Vol. 42 and *Contemporary Authors,* Vol. 116.)

TITLE COMMENTARY

Fritz and the Beautiful Horses (1981)

Ostracized from the tall, pompous horses that live within the city walls because he is short-legged and shaggy-haired, the pony Fritz lives a lonely life. He especially longs to be friends with the children who seem frightened of the high-strung mounts they are given to ride. When a bridge cracks and the other horses are too skittish to make the crossing, surefooted and dependable Fritz saves the day. From then on, Fritz is given a special place and recognized as a reliable companion for the children. Though the story is somewhat forced, children will find the simple message comforting and meaningful and the illustrations arresting. Medieval scenes, depicted in subdued earth tones highlighted with deep blues, provide an evocative backdrop for the prancing horses, the rich trappings, and the children's embroidered clothing. Brett captures the movements of the equines well (more effectively than she does the somewhat stiff people), though the pony with flowers entwined in its tail is a bit too lovable for readers to believe its outcast status. One full-page spread is poorly spaced (the rider is lost to the inner margin), but the flaw is minor and doesn't mar the total effect.

> *Barbara Elleman, in a review of "Fritz and the Beautiful Horses," in* Booklist, *Vol. 77, No. 13, March 1, 1981, p. 925.*

This is one of those wishfulfillment fantasies that is so satisfying to readers if it is well done and so misused by pious writers if it isn't. . . . It's the old fairy tale theme of the small and humble succeeding when the big and powerful fail. The story is slight, just adequate for the book. The full-color line and watercolor illustrations, however, are special. The horses are faintly stylized in the Hellenistic manner, with smoothly arched necks and very small heads. The decorative trappings worn by both men and horses feature the intricate floral and geometric designs associated with eastern European needlework. The pictures are so effective that one wishes Jan Brett would trust them a little more and not feel that everything must be said in words. (pp. 109-10)

> *Katharyn Crabbe, in a review of "Fritz and the Beautiful Horses," in* School Library Journal, *Vol. 27, No. 8, April, 1981, pp. 109-10.*

An obvious, dotted-line pseudo-folk tale about Fritz, a kind and gentle pony, also "sure-footed and always willing to work," who is kept outside a certain vaguely medieval walled city because only beautiful horses are allowed within. . . . The story is flat and predictable; the moral far from liberating; and the pictures, though rich in decorative patterns, are static and innocuously pretty.

> *A review of "Fritz and the Beautiful Horses," in* Kirkus Reviews *Vol. XLIX, No. 10, May 15, 1981, p. 631.*

Annie and the Wild Animals (1985)

The meticulous, colorful paintings illustrating this tale are far superior to the thin story line. Annie, a winsome little girl, lives alone at the edge of a forest. When Taffy, her pet cat and only companion, inexplicably disappears, Annie's loneliness spurs her to find a new friend. She places corn cakes in the snow near the woods, hoping to attract a small, furry new pet. Instead, a bear, a wildcat, a moose and other large, frightening woodland inhabitants eagerly

devour Annie's daily offerings. Happily, winter ends, and with the thaw, the wild animals can forage for themselves. Taffy reappears with the spring, and, accompanied by her three kittens, is joyfully reunited with Annie. Each page of art with text is surrounded by an ornamental border, the panels of which visually relate the truth of Taffy's whereabouts while Annie searches unsuccessfully for her replacement. The luminous illustrations create a handsome setting for Annie and the animals, but the quality of the pictures cannot offset the plodding text. This theme has been better served by Jack Gantos' *The Perfect Pal* (Houghton, 1979; o.p.) and in Steven Kellogg's *Can I Keep Him?* (Dial, 1971).

> *Martha Rosen, in a review of "Annie and the Wild Animals," in* School Library Journal, *Vol. 31, April, 1985, p. 75.*

The familiar theme of a cat's puzzling disappearance in **Annie and the Wild Animals** might easily be dismissed with a yawn as just another variation were it not for the author and illustrator Jan Brett's exquisite, tapestry-like watercolor paintings and the way she adds a new graphic dimension to a simple story.

Miss Brett uses colorful borders filled with detail to provide miniature previews of the narrative action and a story around a story, so that the reader instantly becomes an insider. The small glimpses of the world outside Annie's cottage move the tale forward and embellish the pages with grace and skill. It is foretold in the borders, for instance, and therefore no great surprise when it happens, that Taffy will return with three kittens. It *is* a happy ending, and what we expected all along.

The illustrations in **Annie and the Wild Animals** are a veritable treasury of motifs taken from the universal tradition of folk art and crafts, including fanciful ironwork animals, a humorous mosaic cat, carved woodwork on doors and chairs, carved hearts, needleworklike flowers and a merry abundance of patchwork designs.

> *Pat Ross, in a review of "Annie and the Wild Animals," in* The New York Times Book Review, *August 25, 1985, p. 25.*

The simple plot, a child looking for a lost cat, is cleverly extended in illustrations in which every inch of space is used for an extended visual narrative. . . . In fine shading and thick, smooth paint the animals are shown in naturalistic forms, (though often with human expressions in eyes or cocked heads) and decorative details of foliage, small birds or flowers provide a background to scenes whose narrative element is skilfully managed to parallel a brief text. A good example of the give and take of words and pictures in this genre.

> *Margery Fisher, in a review of "Annie and the Wild Animals," in* Growing Point, *Vol. 26, No. 1, May, 1987, p. 4806.*

The Twelve Days of Christmas (1986)

This old folk song has held such perennial fascination for illustrators that it's hard to believe we need another version, but Brett's interpretation is so attractive that it's sure to find a warm welcome.

Using the combination of borders and central pictures employed so effectively in last year's **Annie and the Wild Animals,** Brett crowds each double spread with motifs from one of eleven European countries, in each case repeating "Merry Christmas" in the appropriate language, from Gaelic to Russian. (It may be a challenge to identify some of those Middle European greetings.) The richly colored paintings are full of carefully depicted delights, from soft but realistic foxes and rabbits to geese fancifully dressed as peasant maidens. In a border subplot, a tree is brought home and decorated with ornaments representing all the enumerated gifts—drums, milkpails, etc. Like **Annie,** a trifle busy but full of entrancing detail. Music included.

> *A review of "The Twelve Days of Christmas,"* in Kirkus Reviews, *Vol. LIV, No. 14, July 15, 1986, p. 1117.*

Brett's lavish treatment of the song portrays various levels of meaning; she has illustrated the fantastic gifts in outrageous splendor (seven swans swim in folkloric Russian headdresses), turned them into a border of tree decorations, included a menagerie of animals carrying banners with "Merry Christmas" in different languages, and set into the outer edges of each page an ongoing story about a family's preparations for the big day itself. In the final frame, the decorated tree serves as the centerpiece for their own caroling. The artist demonstrates, once again, that

she will not relinquish a project before every last glorious detail is in place; the clarity of her vision is stunning.

> *A review of "The Twelve Days of Christmas,"* in Publishers Weekly, *Vol. 230, No. 13, September 26, 1986, p. 72.*

A striking and opulent version of the traditional carol. Each verse is set off in a two-page spread, and while the main illustration is boxed, the figures spill over the frames. Each spread has an ethnic theme. For example, the 11 ladies dancing are dressed as Spanish señoritas; the 7 swans a-swimming wear ornate Russian crowns. Small animals appear in frames along the edge, along with the words "Merry Christmas" in the appropriate (but unidentified) foreign language, various Christmas symbols and ornaments that correspond to the main picture, plus a continuing story showing a family choosing and decorating a Christmas tree. Unfortunately, children won't be able to identify most of the symbols or the countries. The final spread, a lackluster formal family grouping, is disappointing. Given the exuberance of the earlier pictures, readers expect a crescendo; they are given a diminuendo.

> *Judith Gloyer, in a review of "The Twelve Days of Christmas," in* School Library Journal, *Vol. 33, No. 2, October, 1986, p. 111.*

Children of a certain age love to count things and Jan Brett's illustrations in [**The Twelve Days of Christmas**] are plump, whimsical and full of the sort of feather-by-feather

From Goldilocks and the Three Bears, *retold and illustrated by Jan Brett.*

detail that makes you want to pat the turtledoves, bite into the pears and bury your nose in the balsam boughs of the Christmas trees that flank the margins. All the ladies are beautiful, the gentlemen noble-looking and the children fur-trimmed and innocent—as we all want to feel at Christmas. This is a warm book to the touch.

> *Phyllis Theroux, in a review of "The Twelve Days of Christmas," in* The New York Times Book Review, *December 14, 1986, p. 29.*

Goldilocks and the Three Bears (1987)

In a charming new edition of a favorite nursery tale, Brett closely follows the traditional text used by Leslie Brooke with only a few updatings (the bears no longer open their bedroom window in the morning), embellishments (nuts and honey in the porridge), and emendations (the bears walk in the woods "while the porridge was cooling," a simplification of "that they might not burn their mouths by beginning too soon to eat it").

Brett's now-familiar use of Eastern European folk motifs and decorative borders is well-suited to the story, and employed very much in Brooke's spirit: the cosy forest home is furnished with belongings decorated with bees, berries, sunflowers, and all manner of things pertaining to bears. The softer-toned borders emulate carved wood and incorporate amplifying vignettes; in addition, they include an enchanting series of mice, who also coexist peaceably with the bears in the brightly colored illustrations and, in fact, are shown on the title page as the diminutive artists who have reproduced themselves in wood. This sumptuously detailed world provides the background for a Goldilocks with flaxen braids and for precisely characterized bears that are large and solid enough to inspire delicious awe.

Perfect to share with individual or group, this belongs on everyone's list.

> *A review of "Goldilocks and the Three Bears," in* Kirkus Reviews, *Vol. VI, No. 22, November 15, 1987, p. 1624.*

Brett's retelling, adapted from Andrew Lang, is strong and smooth. These well-heeled Scandinavian-looking bears live in a house that would put yuppy collectors of country homes and folk art to shame, and the elaborate, imaginative, and richly colored designs bear repeated viewings. Every tuft of beary fur is clear, every item of clothing is ornamented, and every article of furniture is carved, patterned, or decorated. Bear motifs are repeated throughout, including carved bear beds, handmade bear porridge bowls, and a solid bear door. Brett's use of borders continues to expand upon the storyline. Here wide woody borders in the double-page spreads contain elements of the action occuring elsewhere. They alternate with simple narrow borders in the single-page illustrations. Personality emerges nicely. The "little, small, wee" bear bumbles into everything, and the great huge bear is alternately gentle and gruff, but the middle-sized bear attracts little direct attention. Goldilocks is somewhat less successful. At first, her face is finely drawn, but in later pages it's a bit flattened. Overall, some readers might wish

for less decorations and some imaginative space, and may be overwhelmed by the amount of detail, but Brett's fans will be delighted.

> *Leda Schubert, in a review of "Goldilocks and the Three Bears," in* School Library Journal, *Vol. 34, No. 4, December, 1987, p. 70.*

Although the retelling of a favorite nursery tale has some passages that are flat, the text is adequate. The illustrations are stunning in the romantic fairytale tradition: framed pictures that are equally notable for their lavish ornamental detail, their use of space and color, and their textual quality. Architectural details, artifacts, and clothing are ornate, but they escape being obtrusive because they are so deftly balanced and fused.

> *Zena Sutherland, in a review of "Goldilocks and the Three Bears," in* Bulletin of the Center for Children's Books, *Vol. 41, No. 6, February, 1988, p. 112.*

The First Dog (1988)

With her usual skillful technique and loving attention to detail, Brett illustrates a lame, poorly imagined story about how a paleolithic boy (Kip) might have tamed a wolf and named it Dog. Lured by the smell of roast meat, the hungry, full-grown wolf follows the boy—begging for food and warning him of predators, both likely (sabretoothed "cat") and unlikely (mammoth—surely a vegetarian); meanwhile, Kip taunts him. Finally, although this has otherwise been a realistic story, Kip asks the wolf to guard him in exchange for food; we are to believe that a wagging tail signifies acquiescence.

Brett's designs may indeed be inspired by surviving cave paintings and artifacts, but her story is too implausible: Kip's teasing presupposes the wolf's friendliness, and the wolf behaves as if he were already tame; moreover, it seems likely that the first wolves to be domesticated were cubs. For an imaginative fantasy about this subject, go back to Kipling's wonderful "The Cat That Walked by Himself."

> *A review of "The First Dog," in* Kirkus Reviews, *Vol. LVI, No. 13, July 1, 1988, p. 969.*

A simple, imaginative tale of how the first domestication of a wild animal *may* have occurred. . . . The book's glorious watercolor illustrations will attract young prehistory enthusiasts, for amidst the melting ice floes roam the mighty Mammoth, the Wild Horse, the Woolly Rhino and other denizens of the Pleistocene period. Each scene appears on a "canvas" stretched across two pages. Borders show wood and stone carvings, cave paintings, and artifacts. Slide panels on several illustrations show the dangers that Kip avoids by heeding Paleowolf's warnings. This is another of Brett's lavish offerings, intricately designed and filled with eye-catching detail. However, it is a fabricated story told with authority, featuring a modern-looking boy amidst authentic-looking animals and scenery. Children familiar with the ever-growing body of factual material on this period may accept it as the truth, despite its accompanying notes.

*Susan Scheps, in a review of "The First Dog,"
in* School Library Journal, *Vol. 35, No. 3, November, 1988, p. 83.*

Brett's strength is as an artist rather than a storyteller. Her plot is deliberate and slight, and at times seems chiefly a frame in which to hang the illustrations.

The latter, however, are unquestionably spectacular. Towering glaciers, rocky outcroppings, and expansive green plains compose a breathtaking landscape. The creatures that inhabit it are rendered richly and precisely, so that their power and magnificence shine through. And, as in her previous books, Brett's use of decorative borders provides both visual splendor and a wealth of supplementary detail.

*Amy Meeker, "Dogs, Deer, Dragons—and
Flying Umbrellas," in* The Christian Science
Monitor, *November 4, 1988, p. B3.*

Beauty and the Beast (1989)

A single peacock feather, its delicate beauty rendered in meticulous detail, sets the tone for this sumptuous retelling of a classic fairy tale. The story is a familiar one, with true love triumphing over a wicked enchantment in the end (the moral, of course, is "never judge a book by its cover"). But the central attraction is the illustrations. Brett's images glide by in a kaleidoscope of luminous color: iridescent blues and greens flow from page to page, entwined with the radiant shades of Beauty's own symbol, the rose. Brett, whose trademark is her careful detail, leaves hidden clues for sharp-eyed readers that hint at the Beast's secret—such as mottoed tapestries and glimpses of the meddlesome fairy herself, decked out naturally enough as a peacock butterfly. But it's the recurring motif of the peacock, itself a symbol of vanity and surface appearances, that ties the threads of the story together. It's a brilliant marriage of artwork and text; once again Brett proves herself a contemporary illustrator of consummate skill.

A review of "Beauty and the Beast," in Publishers Weekly, *Vol. 236, No. 10, September 8, 1989, p. 69.*

A stately retelling of the classic tale of love and deliverance. Walter Crane, William Morris, and Sir Arthur Quiller-Couch inspired Brett's visual and verbal interpretations. Reading well aloud, this version is economically direct, with a controlled richness that doesn't give way to the distracting excesses of earlier tellings. Following the more modern convention, the merchant here has only three children, all daughters; the role of Beauty's worldly sisters is further reduced, as they neither despise nor deliberately tempt her. This makes Beauty's choices more squarely her own, and helps the story to focus on the central tasks of knowing one's own heart and preparing to shift one's devotion. In the pictures, jeweled borders frame the formal compositions and restrain the sumptious color, costume, and detail filling each page. Tapestries on the walls of Beast's palace echo the pageantry played out before them, revealing the true identities of the boar-headed

Beast and his animal court. A thoughtful, imaginative rendition, in word and in picture, definitely worth having.

*Karen Litton, in a review "Beauty and the
Beast," in* School Library Journal, *Vol. 35,
No. 15, November, 1989, p. 97.*

Brett shows real finesse in drafting various animals as a central motif of the story, but her human faces are awkward except in profile. Perhaps because of this, the characters are frequently profiled, resulting in stiffly arranged compositions that are packed with formal decorative detail. The peacock, which symbolizes vanity in most versions, seems to pop up everywhere here, including the transformation scene, where its feathers, interlaced with willow branches, surround the happy couple and where its appearance is something of a contradiction. Overall, the tone is glamorous to the neglect of the emotional power that has sustained the story for centuries. There are exceptions: a strongly focused opening picture, a Rackham-like silhouette, and a moving double spread dominated by the heads of Beauty and the Beast. In the climactic last page, however, both horse and roses look as if they're made of plastic, and the peacock feathers, gold brocade, and stilted humans add to the artificial sheen. Pretty but problematic.

*Betsy Hearne, in a review of "Beauty and the
Beast," in* Bulletin of the Center for Children's Books, *Vol. 43, No. 4, December, 1989,
p. 79.*

The Mitten: A Ukrainian Folktale (1989)

Using an inventive layout, Brett retells a Ukrainian folktale about a boy's lost mitten that provides refuge for a mélange of forest animals. Double-page spreads feature large central illustrations framed by birch-bark panels. A mitten-shaped window appears on each side of the spread, the one on the left showing the boy's search for his mitten, the one on the right anticipating the action of the following spread. For instance, in the illustration showing a mole approaching the mitten, the borders depict the boy leaping over a snow-covered log and startling a rabbit who then runs from its shelter and, on the next page, finds the mitten. In this way, Brett cleverly foreshadows the upcoming events, which children will quickly catch onto. While some may find the page design overly elaborate, the artwork is nevertheless delightful. The cool, bluish whites of the snowy scenes contrast freshly with the richly colored patterns and details of the Ukrainian clothes. Brett depicts the animals with naturalistic detail, yet conveys their feelings and personalities with subtlety, clarity, and humor. While Alvin Tresselt's *The Mitten* is still in print and a staple of winter-story programs, libraries will want to offer this splendid version as well.

*Carolyn Phelan, in a review of "The Mitten,"
in* Booklist, *Vol. 86, No. 2, September 15,
1989, p. 172.*

In this beautifully illustrated adaptation of the traditional Ukrainian folktale, Nicki begs his grandmother to knit him some snow-white mittens even though she's sure they'll get lost in the snow. Her prediction comes true, and the dropped mitten soon becomes a cozy home for a host of woodland creatures. All the while, although stretched and strained, "Baba's good knitting held fast." But alas, the bear sneezes—sending the mitten and the animals flying through the air and off in all directions. Nicki spies and catches his slightly misshappen mitten as it wafts back to earth, and heads home with both of his mittens. The simple story is told in the third person, and lacks the vitality and lyrical quality of Tresselt's familiar version (Lothrop, 1964). The illustrations and book design, however, are exquisite, perfectly capturing the wintery setting. Brett again makes use of elaborate borders, this time in the way of birch bark and traditional Ukrainian designs to frame her tale. She adds delightful mitten-shaped inserts which give previews of the next page's action. Nicki and his "Baba" are dressed in old style, elaborately embroidered garments and their thatched-roofed cottage is full of simple, decorative handicrafts. As always though, it's Brett's animals that really steal the show. She captures their features and textures in such realistic detail that it almost detracts from the fantasy in the story. An ideal choice for story hours, and a charming lap book to be poured over again and again.

> *Luann Toth, in a review of "The Mitten," in* School Library Journal, *Vol. 35, No. 15, November, 1989, p. 97.*

Although each of the artistic effects is well handled, the overall design is crowded: intricately realistic paintings (some of the faces have the appearance of retouched photographs) are framed in elaborately mottled birch bark upon which is superimposed stylized flowers and the mitten-shaped windows that show action on the side. However, Brett's clever patterning and dominant white tones do work to blend these varied elements at the point when they threaten to become mutually distracting, and young viewers will undeniably enjoy the game aspect of watching the boy and the animals play out their separate dramas. (p. 80)

> *Betsy Hearne, in a review of "The Mitten," in* Bulletin of the Center for Children's Books, *Vol. 43, No. 4, December, 1989, pp. 79-80.*

The Wild Christmas Reindeer (1990)

Little Teeka's attempts to train Santa's reindeer for their Christmas ride meet with disaster until she realizes that she needs to work with the animals in a new way. "Tomor-

row," she says, "no yelling, no screaming, and no bossing, I promise," and with her patient teaching, on Christmas Eve the "wild reindeer [rise] up together and [carry] the sleigh off into the night." Brett's characteristic, richly detailed borders depict the activity at Santa's workshop as each day brings Teeka closer to Christmas. As with *The Mitten,* Brett makes use of Ukrainian motifs—colorful embroidered costumes, festive garlands, carvings and cunning toys decorate every page. The reindeer themselves—sporting names like Lichen, Tundra and Bramble—provide most of the comic action in this sweet Christmas fantasy that shows Brett at her best.

> *A review of "The Wild Christmas Reindeer," in* Publishers Weekly, *Vol. 237, No. 32, August 10, 1990, p. 443.*

Don't look for Dasher or Prancer or even Rudolph in this story. Brett introduces a whole new crew of Santa's reindeer, wild ones, who may be unwilling to come in from the tundra and pull Santa's sleigh. . . . While the story is nothing extraordinary, the artwork surely is. As with her other books, Brett provides ornamental pictures, heavily detailed and decoratively bordered. Brett is at her best drawing animals, and these winsome creatures, though wild at heart, show a streak of gentleness. If there weren't enough going on in the spreads, eye-catching border scenes depict what's happening in Santa's workshop as the big day draws ever closer. Beautifully conceived and finely wrought.

> *Ilene Cooper, "Stars for the Holidays," in* Booklist, *Vol. 89, No. 2, September 15, 1990, p. 168.*

Brett uses side panels to show elves preparing the Christmas goodies before December 24, when Santa loads up. Borders of holiday symbols and a calendar countdown decorate each page. Told in a somewhat colloquial language, this tale with its humorous close-ups of stubborn reindeer and a sharp child protagonist should prove popular at story hours—but children may trample each other in order to see the many details Brett has crammed into her paintings.

> *Susan Hepler, in a review of "The Wild Christmas Reindeer," in* School Library Journal, *Vol. 36, No. 10, October, 1990, p. 34.*

Gwendolyn Brooks

1917-

African American poet and author of fiction and nonfiction.

Major works include *Bronzeville Boys and Girls* (1956), *Aloneness* (1971), *The Tiger Who Wore White Gloves, or What You Are You Are* (1974), *Young Poet's Primer* (1980), *Very Young Poets* (1983).

Regarded as one of the most distinguished American poets of the twentieth century, Brooks fuses the formal structure and language of traditional verse with contemporary black idioms in poetry noted for its objectivity, succinctness, and distinctive use of language. Characteristically depicting working-class blacks who encounter poverty and racism in urban environments, Brooks is acknowledged as one of the few contemporary poets to make children a central part of her poetic vision. Several of her books of adult poetry contain poems about young people who search to find meaning in a world that seeks to deny them; many of these poems chronicle the aspirations and disappointments of the inhabitants of Bronzeville, a black district in Brooks's native Chicago that serves as her microcosm of American life. As a writer for children, Brooks is best known as the creator of her first work of juvenile literature, *Bronzeville Boys and Girls,* a collection of verses about the thoughts, moods, and feelings of the children in the Bronzeville community. Considered a classic for readers in the primary and early middle grades, *Bronzeville Boys and Girls* is often praised for reflecting the same sensitivity and literary skill that Brooks brings to her adult works. In thirty-four closely rhymed poems that are each named for a child, Brooks describes the everyday experiences and emotions of her subjects in forms which rely on simple language, alliteration, assonance, repetition, and meters such as tetrameter and the ballad stanza. Brooks portrays the protagonists of *Bronzeville Boys and Girls* as they interact with their families and friends and engage in make-believe and imaginative play; the children, who have warm relationships with each other and with adults, are especially inspired by the wonders of nature that are part of their urban landscape such as clouds, and the stars. Although many of the poems in the collection are happy ones, Brooks also represents the poignancy of childhood through her inclusion of children who are sad or economically deprived. Neither the poems nor Ronni Solbert's illustrations draw attention to the fact that the children in *Bronzeville Boys and Girls* are black, a point with which some critics find fault; however, most observers celebrate the collection for its beauty, freshness, charm, and universality and acknowledge Brooks for her understanding of the young.

Growing up on Chicago's South Side as a shy child who loved nature and quiet games, Brooks began to write poetry at the age of seven; after reading her early efforts, her mother proclaimed that she would become "the lady Paul

Laurence Dunbar." Inspired by such writers as Emily Dickinson, James Weldon Johnson, Langston Hughes, and the English Romantic poets, Brooks began publishing her poems regularly as a teenager in magazines and newspapers. Her second collection, *Annie Allen* (1949), introduces Brooks's invention of the sonnet-ballad, a form that blends formal language and colloquial speech to outline the growth of her title character from childhood to adulthood in a repressive ghetto environment; for this book, Brooks became the first African American to be awarded the Pulitzer Prize. Although she is noted for writing about the black experience "before being black was beautiful," in the words of critic Martha Liebrum, Brooks's early poems are recognized for transcending race to evoke the universality of her themes. In the late 1960s, her work underwent a radical transformation: after Brooks attended a black writers conference at Nashville's Fisk University in 1967 and was struck by the energy of such young writers as LeRoi Jones (Amiri Baraka), Don L. Lee (Haki R. Madhubuti), and Ron Milner, she began to direct her works to a black audience and to adopt a more forceful tone. Her first children's book to be published in this period, the picture book *Aloneness,* is a single poem in free verse that reveals the need for children to be alone and draws a distinction between loneliness and deep solitude. Like *Aloneness, The Tiger Who Wore White Gloves* is a single poem; in this work, which has self-acceptance as its theme, Brooks describes a tiger who wears white gloves to be fashionable and learns that tigers should be daring, not dainty; the poem is often read as a pointed message to black readers. Brooks is also the author of a manual for high school and college students which gives advice on the writing and reading of poetry and a second volume for young adults that encourages the appreciation of nature and literature and incorporates eight original poems in free verse. Several of Brooks's adult poems have been anthologized in collections read by high school students, notably "We Real Cool," a poem from *The Bean Eaters* (1960) with pool players as its subject which ends "We / Sing Sin. We / Thin Gin. We /Jazz June. We / Die Soon." In addition to her poetry for adults, Brooks is the author of a novel and an autobiography; several of her children's books are dedicated to her children Henry and Nora Blakely. Besides her Pulitzer Prize, which she won in 1950, Brooks is the recipient of many awards for her adult poetry as well as several honorary degrees from universities and colleges; in addition, the Gwendolyn Brooks Center for African American Literature has been established at Western Illinois University. Named Poet Laureate of Illinois, Brooks established the Illinois Poet Laureate Awards to encourage young talent and has conducted many writer's workshops for young people.

(See also *Contemporary Literary Criticism,* Vols. 1, 2, 4, 5, 15, 49; *Something about the Author,* Vol. 6; *Contemporary Authors New Revision Series,* Vols. 1, 27; *Contemporary Authors,* Vol. 1, rev. ed.; and *Dictionary of Literary Biography,* Vols. 5, 76.)

AUTHOR'S COMMENTARY

"Last" Speech to the Court of Two

(For Henry Jr. and for Nora.)

First of all, do not lose faith in yourself or in life. Remember: unhappiness eventually becomes something else—as does everything.

Never believe that doing your best does not matter.

Rejoice in many people. But never let your delight in any one prevent you from doing what you know is right for you.

Be pleased with the things of life that are called little. The talk of birds. The first light of morning. The look of the sky to the west at sunset, (for it has something of softness for a hardened heart, a sick soul, a sluggish mind.) Flowers. A plant growing in a pot. Books. Pictures. Gentle music and music that thunders—any music that *translates* for *you*. The smell of raw coffee in the can. The look of tea in your cup, with a circle of lemon there. The softest green of spring. The developed beauty of autumn. Remember that the autumn of the year and that autumn of living that is middle age are both rich and beautiful "even though" they march with steadiness to winter, to death which, I hope you will be able to concede, is clean, too, because natural.

Good health is a duty to yourself, to your contemporaries, to your inheritors, to the progress of the world.

About Love . . . Little can help you. In this matter you are alone, except for your secret and everlasting unfinished acquaintanceship with your own essential needs. But there is one thing I hope you will do: find out if your "choice" is *kind*—and not to yourself alone.

Mostly keep your head up high. (Sometimes lower it, to cry.)

Scarcely a lesson is Lesson Eight. I need not advise you to *remember that you are black*. The society will see to it that you remember.

"Lastly," little life-lines taped to my closet wall. One—and chief of them: "When handed a lemon, make lemonade." Two: "We close ranks; we adjust ourselves; we carry on." I first heard Reverend Roberts of Coppin Chapel say that, Henry, when you were about nine years old, but I don't know where *he* got it. Three: "Swan *runs* HIS life; he doesn't trot along after it." From "The River People," a TV visit to Bangkok, Thailand. Four: "Go to sleep. You can finish beating yourself in the morning." (Mary Tyler Moore, to herself.) And, however "milkmush," Five: "Brighten the corner where you are."

"Last" and "lastly" are in quotes because, if I "last" longer, I may offer Something More. (pp. 63-4)

There is indeed a new black today. He is different from any the world has known. He's a tall-walker. Almost firm. By many of his own *brothers* he is not understood. And he is understood by *no* white. Not the wise white; not the Schooled white; not the Kind white. Your *least* prerequisite toward an understanding of the new black is an exceptional Doctorate which can be conferred only upon those with the proper properties of bitter birth and intrinsic sorrow. I know this is infuriating, especially to those professional Negro-understanders, some of them so *very* kind, with special portfolio, special savvy. But I cannot say anything other, because nothing other is the truth.

I—who have "gone the gamut" from an almost angry rejection of my dark skin by some of my brainwashed brothers and sisters to a surprised queenhood in the new black sun—am qualified to enter at least the kindergarten of new consciousness now. New consciousness and trudge-toward-progress.

I have hopes for myself. (pp. 85-6)

What are the little black children doing—besides, that is (as reported by Experts) kicking or killing their teachers, collecting Beatle wax and buttons and bubble-gum, trampling lawns and forging new routes to indolence and demoralization? They are writing poetry. Poetry is still in the world, and black children are colliding with some of it. They reach, touch lovely words and strong words with excitement and timid respect. They work hard to merit ownership. Looking at poetry and dealing with it, they realize that in the world there is beauty. That there is horror they know and have always known. New bombs are developed most carefully. Hatreds are here, and multiply. Modern ice and iron marry, and offer presently a frightening progeny. But black children also know that there are flowers. They are not ashamed to speak to daisies and dandelions. Children, of course, commit platitudes a-plenty. Often our grammar school poets address their readers and, more sorrowfully, themselves in a cliche-ridden manner that they assume is "right for poetry." But they are also capable of exaltation and thought and emotion that do them honor. Their nature is not frugal, it is expansive and lifting. It reacts. It reacts to clouds and sunshine. It reacts to dryness, waste, oppression. Some of these very young people have found that poetry is a friend to whom you can say too much. Some of them have found that it is possible, *sometimes,* to reconcile onions and roses. Some of them have found that it is possible to reconcile death and humor. (pp. 207-08)

Little Kathy Henderson of Clayton, Missouri, to the Chamber of Commerce, Topeka, Kansas: "Dear Sir: I am interested in obtaining some information on any monuments in your city to honor the poet and novelist Gwendolyn Brooks who was born in your city. I am studying about her in second year English at St. Joseph's Academy in St. Louis. If you can would you please send me this information." In that request, what a wealth of clean young innocence . . . February 11, 1965. From sixteen year old Placido Tugo of Chicago's Manley Upper Grade Center School on West Polk Street, in reference to my reading of **"We Real Cool:"** "Mrs. Gwendolyn Brooks gave me a good lesson that I hope that I will never forget because I was planning to quit school. But now I know that there is no place like school. I would want to tell her how I feel in side of my heart." And I wrote to Placido. "Dear Placido, What a happiness to know that words of mine could influence one of the largest decisions you will ever make: to stay in school! For this alone, I am most happy that I could come to read to you. Please maintain your decision. Staying in school is overwhelmingly important—even though sometimes it may seem hard to do. I am sure your teachers and principal will do everything possible to help you. They are excited and happy that you are determined to continue. I am very proud of you. BEST wishes!" That poignancy: "I would want to tell her how I feel in side of my heart". . . . (p. 214)

> *Gwendolyn Brooks, in her* Report from Part One, *Broadside Press, 1972, 215 p.*

Virginia Kirkus' Service

These verses for children [*Bronzeville Boys and Girls*], by the author of two other volumes of poetry, **Annie Allen** and **A Street in Bronzeville,** contain the same delicacy of mood and wish that has characterized Gwendolyn Brooks' descriptions of the Negro in his city world. The setting is again Chicago and the technique one of closely rhymed verses embodying an imagery that often provokes a very direct sense of reality. The themes are children's concepts: Timmy and Tawanda love to plot and plan while their elders sit and chat; Robert is a boy who often has that well known feeling of seeing another person when he looks

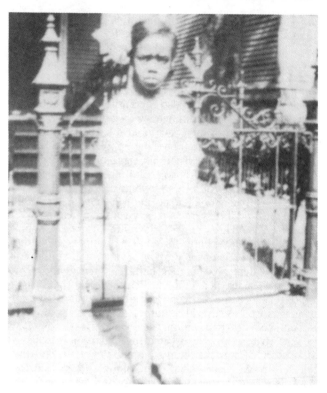

Brooks as a child in front of her home at 4332 Champlain, Chicago.

at himself in the mirror; Maurice feels fine about moving away until he realizes he can't take his friends with him. In all of these there is the attempt to reveal the basic elements of a good life in warm, human terms.

> *A review of "Bronzeville Boys and Girls," in* Virginia Kirkus' Service, *Vol. XXIV, October 15, 1956, p. 788.*

Charlemae Rollins

[Gwendolyn Brooks] has written this charming and thoughtful collection of 36 verses for children [*Bronzeville Boys and Girls*]. Her adult poetry is rich with the reality of everyday experiences, and these poems have it, too, but with the added qualities of gayety and warmth.

The title suggests Chicago's Negro children, but the verses are not limited in their appeal. They reflect the moods and feelings of all kinds of children, describing with amazing accuracy many of childhood's most poignant emotions—how it feels to see a single star; to be afraid of a storm; the tender thoughts of a child in church, "Where it feels good to be good"; or the sobering thought that replaces elation when a boy realizes that he can pack up his ball and bat when he moves but he can't pack his best friend Bill. The poems are gay, carefree, and serious—but none is sad. Adults who enjoy reading poetry aloud to children will welcome these for their fresh viewpoint.

Ronni Solbert's sensitive and expressive drawings reflect and extend the mood and beauty of the poetry.

> *Charlemae Rollins, in a review of "Bronzeville*

Boys and Girls," in Chicago Sunday Tribune Magazine of Books, *November 11, 1956, p. 20.*

Margaret Sherwood Libby

Deep affection for city youngsters is in every line of these poems by Gwendolyn Brooks [*Bronzeville Boys and Girls*]. Some are quite exquisite, others light-hearted comments in verse on childish ideas. Each of the thirty-five poems is named for a child and the reader senses that Miss Brooks has experienced the joys and sorrows, and sudden keen perceptions of each child.

Because Miss Brooks is a Negro poet she has called these "Bronzeville Boys and Girls," but they are universal and will make friends anywhere, among grown-ups or among children from eight to ten.

> *Margaret Sherwood Libby, in a review of "Bronzeville Boys and Girls," in* New York Herald Tribune Book Review, *November 18, 1956, p. 2.*

Beatrice Landeck

In *Bronzeville Boys and Girls* Pulitzer Prize-winning Gwendolyn Brooks gives us slight portrait sketches of children who might live in any city. Only Ronni Solbert's pictures indicate that they are Negroes. Their problems, their pleasures and their moods are universal and some of the poems are really moving, but, in striving to put herself on a child's level, Miss Brooks all too often writes down and so trails off into the commonplace.

> *Beatrice Landeck, "Quartette," in* The New York Times, *December 9, 1956, p. 40.*

The Booklist and Subscription Books Bulletin

[*Bronzeville Boys and Girls* is a] collection of uneven but fresh, pleasing poems about and for children by a Pulitzer Prize winner. Although presumably the children are Negro and the setting Chicago, these sensitive verses expressing the thoughts, emotions, and experiences of childhood will appeal to any children anywhere.

> *A review of "Bronzeville Boys and Girls," in* The Booklist and Subscription Books Bulletin, *Vol. 53, No. 9, January 1, 1957, p. 228.*

August Derleth

[Gwendolyn Brooks] has turned to poems for children of from seven to ten, and offers in *Bronzeville Boys and Girls* a little collection of them. . . . Miss Brooks is not as successful with poems for younger readers as she is in her adult verse, but young readers ought to find much to delight them in this slender book. (p. 46)

> *August Derleth, "A Varied Quartette," in* Voices, *No. 164, September-December, 1957, pp. 44-7.*

Binnie Tate Wilkin

[*Aloneness* is an] extremely perceptive poetic view of the child alone. Simply and effectively, the text reveals one's need to be alone—in contrast to loneliness. In a society where group processes have sometimes become so overwhelming that aloneness is often feared, children find it in-

creasingly hard to view moments alone in a positive way. Independent play and creativity have become more difficult. Books like this one challenge the individual to deal creatively with aloneness.

> *Binnie Tate Wilkin, "The Individual: 'Aloneness'," in her* Survival Themes in Fiction for Children and Young People, *The Scarecrow Press, Inc., 1978, p. 29.*

Virginia Haviland and William Jay Smith

These charming vignettes of boys and girls [in *Bronzeville Boys and Girls*] communicate both the gaiety and sadness of childhood. . . .

Miss Brooks, in her adult poetry, has a highly developed sense of form; and in these poems she catches the attitudes and observations of small children in simple language that is sure to please them.

> *Virginia Haviland and William Jay Smith, "Twentieth-Century Poetry: 'Bronzeville Boys and Girls'," in their* Children & Poetry: A Selective, Annotated Bibliography, *edited by Virginia Haviland and William Jay Smith, second edition, Library of Congress, 1979, p. 31.*

Horace Coleman

The Tiger Who Wore White Gloves is a short children's story in verse. . . . Youngsters who have negative feelings about themselves will gain pleasant insights from reading the story or having it read to them. It's a fun book and a quick reader.

> *Horace Coleman, in a review of "The Tiger Who Wore White Gloves," in* The Black Scholar, *Vol. 12, No. 2, March-April, 1981, p. 92.*

George Kent

In *Bronzeville Boys and Girls* . . . , Brooks' skills effectively work together to comprise a language of poetry that describes for the child his or her experiences. Poems with bouncy rhymes are intermixed with those of more subtle and varied sound patterns. Emphasis upon the monosyllabic word at the end of end-stopped lines and other places, varying lengths of lines, repetition, and other devices sustain an interesting poetics which unpatronizingly presents the childhood world. **"Ella"** reveals something of the magic maintained, even down to a simple use of paradox in the first two lines: "Beauty has a coldness / That keeps you very warm. / 'If I run out to see the clouds, That will be no harm!' " (p. 96)

> *George Kent, "Gwendolyn Brooks' Poetic Realism: A Developmental Survey," in* Black Women Writers (1950-1980): A Critical Evaluation, *edited by Mari Evans, Anchor Press/Doubleday, 1984, pp. 88-105.*

Zena Sutherland and May Hill Arbuthnot

[Gwendolyn Brooks's] poems for and about children, *Bronzeville Boys and Girls,* speak for any child of any race. They show a rare sensitivity to the child's inner life—

the wonderments, hurts, and sense of make-believe and play.

Zena Sutherland and May Hill Arbuthnot, "The Range of Poets for Children: 'Bronzeville Boys and Girls'," in their Children and Books, *seventh edition, Scott, Foresman and Company, 1986, p. 318.*

Gary Smith

One of the enduring paradoxes of Gwendolyn's Brooks's long and prolific writing career is that she is one of America's most honored and popular poets, yet she is also one of its most difficult and demanding. Like the modernist poets T. S. Eliot and Ezra Pound, with whom she is often favorably compared, her poetry is intellectual, urbane, and carefully crafted. However, to the American reading public—especially the rather modest segment that routinely reads poetry—she is chiefly known for a handful of widely anthologized poems, **"kitchenette building," "the mother," "The Lovers of the Poor,"** and **"We Real Cool."** These select poems, however representative they are of her larger body of work, do not challenge the reader with the subtle, complex patterns of her more demanding poetry; at worst, the poems actually create the impression that Brooks is primarily a populist poet in the mold of Langston Hughes or Carl Sandburg. But unlike Hughes's and Sandburg's verse, Brooks's best poetry is not written at a casual level. Although she shares the populist tradition in her thematic concern for the unheralded masses, her poetic techniques—the ways in which she expresses her populism—are not common to the more prosaic approach of populist poetry. As many critics have noted, her poetic techniques are more in line with the elliptical, allusive, and imagistic verse of modernist poetry. Her poetic voice offers a distinct balance between the thematically populist yet technically *belle lettrist*. And, in spite of her often-quoted desire to mediate these extremes in her poetic voice and techniques, to write poetry that would appeal to a tavern as well as classroom audience, Brooks's craftsmanship belongs to a literary tradition that extends itself to seventeenth-century metaphysical poetry.

Another oddity of Brooks's popularity is the bleakness of her poetic vision. To be sure, her bleakness is tempered by an optimism that she inherited, in part, from the New Negro poets of the Harlem Renaissance: Hughes, Countee Cullen, and, to a lesser degree, Claude McKay. But even a casual survey of the subject matter in Brooks's poetry reveals a world fraught with violence and human failure: abortion in **"the mother,"** fratricide in **"the murder,"** prostitution in **"My Little 'Bout-town Gal,"** homicide in **"A Bronzeville Mother Loiters,"** and child abuse in **"In the Mecca."** Long before existentialism became fashionable in American literary circles, Brooks's poetry described a world in which alienated human beings flirt daily with personal and social disasters that edge them close to the abyss of madness.

The paradox here, of course, is not that Brooks's bleakness is without precedent or unexpected of a black woman poet, but rather that it is not consistent with her official title as Poet Laureate of Illinois and her public demeanor as a popular, optimistic poet. For the most part, though,

Brooks's bleakness has not received much critical attention. When her readers have taken notice, they often ignore its darker depths. In the labyrinth corridors of Brooks's poetic vision, most of her characters grope in futile search for some meaning or purpose in their lives. At best, the few who find an escape either through religious intoxication (**"hunchback girl: she thinks of heaven"**) or militant self-belief (**"Negro Hero"**) find themselves alienated from those who do not share their beliefs. Moreover, their confidence is often undercut by the radical strategy of Brooks's poetry: her use of ellipses, metaphysical images, and parodic use of rhyme and meter actually expose her character's confusion and mistaken identity rather than reinforce his or her self-belief (**"The Sundays of Satin-Legs Smith"**). (pp. 128-30)

Brooks's poetry . . . realistically describes the personal pain, frustration, and futility of Afro-American history; in her poetic vision, heroism, self-sacrifice, and brotherhood are articulate ideals, but they remain, for the most part, at the level of idealization, and very infrequently are they realized in concrete terms.

However, if Brooks's poetry about adults is bleak, her poetry about children is even more so. As the most vulnerable members of society, children are the most likely victims in a world plagued by personal and social violence. In Brooks's world view, the suffering of children is irrefutable evidence that the rituals that give meaning and substance to human lives are subordinate to the daily struggle to survive. Hence, two predominant themes in Brooks's poetry, entrapment and the desire to escape, are graphically displayed in the lives of her children. They are born into a labyrinth world of corridors and makeshift apartments, where they soon become trapped by poverty. Quite expectedly, then, the overwhelming desire for many of her children is the need to escape, to flee, the various forms of socioeconomic and psychological oppression that thwart self-fulfillment and threaten to destroy their lives. Because it is to a world free of adults where most of her children wish to escape, their unique ability to imagine this world—albeit on the wings of fantasy—distinguishes them from adults and creates some sense of hope.

Brooks has written poems *about* children and poems *for* children. Of the two groups, the first is the larger and the more meaningful because, in each of Brooks's published works, children are central to its thematic design. *A Street in Bronzeville* contains no less than ten poems written about children, while several others, **"obituary for a living lady," "a song in the front yard,"** and **"of De Witt Williams on his way to Lincoln Cemetery,"** establish a definite link between a character's traumatic childhood and his or her tragic adult life. The first section of *Annie Allen* is titled "Notes from the Childhood and the Girlhood" and, in the third section, "The Womanhood," Brooks includes one of her most distinguished sonnet sequences, **"The Children of the Poor."** *In the Mecca,* the volume that is often cited as the turning point in her career, contains her epic poem, **"In the Mecca,"** that focuses on the senseless murder of an adolescent girl. Finally, in her most recent volume, *To Disembark,* Brooks again dramatizes her concern for the plight of children with two of her longer poems, **"The Life of Lincoln West"** and **"The Boy Died in My Alley."**

Brooks has also published three works for children. The first, ***Bronzeville Boys and Girls,*** is her most sustained effort at portraying children in society from the perspective of the child. Written in vignettes of three or four stanzas, each poem discloses a particular moment in a child's life; each is further individualized by a name or title: **"Beulah at Church," "Mirthine at the Party,"** and **"Eunice in the Evening."** Although few of these children reappear in her other poems, they are of pivotal importance in Brooks's poetry because the crisis that engages their lives is, in a simplified manner, the same crisis that her characters also confront as adults: how to find meaning and purpose in a world that ostensibly denies their very existence. Brooks's two other books for children, ***Aloneness*** and ***The Tiger Who Wore White Gloves,*** are interesting for their prescriptive value. They contain explicit moral themes: aloneness is not loneliness and, in the case of a tiger who mistakenly identifies with something other than his black stripes, be what you are.

In general, though, Brooks's poetry for and about children avoids moral prescription. In theme and design, the poems portray a naturalistic world in which environment dictates the terms by which one lives one's life. And, almost without exception, the environment in Brooks's poetry about children is an enclosed space: alleyways, front and back yards, vacant lots, and back rooms. On a symbolic level, these marginal spaces represent the social restrictions that prevent the mental and physical growth of children; they indicate the margins in which children are expected to live their lives. Although trees, flowers, and grass poke through the concrete blocks of the urban environment, they are only reminders of a forbidden Eden, one that is beyond the reach of Brooks's children. Ironically, elm trees and dandelions become strange exotic life forms, objective correlatives for the children's imaginary flights.

The children in Brooks's poems are unable to escape the perils of their environment. The personae in **"a song in the front yard," "the ballad of chocolate Mabbie,"** and **"The Life of Lincoln West"** are characterized by a willingness to accept the limitations imposed upon their lives and, accordingly, to live perilously close to self-destruction. In **"a song in the front yard"** (*WGB* [*The World of Gwendolyn Brooks*], p. 12), the adolescent girl exists in an enclosed space. She longs for the naturalistic world of the back yard and alley where other children play:

> I've stayed in the front yard all my life.
> I want a peek at the back
> Where it's rough and untended and hungry
>   weed grows.
> A girl gets sick of a rose.
>
> I want to go in the back yard now
> And maybe down the alley,
> To where the charity children play.
> I want a good time today.

The girl desires the untended, hungry weed that symbolizes her need for freedom and growth. Yet her mother stifles her imaginative longings:

> They do some wonderful things.
> They have some wonderful fun.
> My mother sneers, but I say it's fine
> How they don't have to go in at quarter to nine.
> My mother, she tells me that Johnnie Mae
> Will grow up to be a bad woman.
> That George'll be taken to Jail soon or late
> (On account of last winter he sold our back
>   gate.)

The mother's "sneers," although they are intended to protect her child from a *bad* life, do not provide meaningful alternatives to the front and back yard. Nonetheless, it is the girl's lack of imaginative fulfillment that prefigures her ominous fate as a woman. Unable to repudiate or negotiate the perilous limitations of her world, she defies them with naive bravado that will inevitably entrap her:

> But I say it's fine. Honest, I do.
> And I'd like to be a bad woman, too,
> And wear the brave stockings of night-black lace
> And strut down the streets with paint on my
>   face.

In **"the ballad of chocolate Mabbie,"** the immediate barrier to Mabbie's self-fulfillment is intraracial discrimination: black judgment of physical beauty by white standards. For Mabbie, a seven-year-old girl who looks as if she "was cut from a chocolate bar," the divided worlds of the previous poem—front or back yard—are defined by the grammar school gates:

> It was Mabbie without the grammar school
>   gates.
> And Mabbie was all of seven.

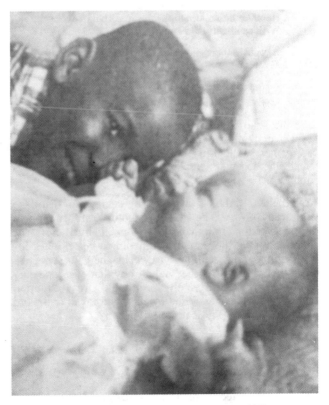

Brooks's two children, Henry and Nora, in 1952.

And Mabbie was cut from a chocolate bar.
And Mabbie thought life was heaven.

The grammar school gates were the pearly gates,
For Willie Boone went to school.
When she sat by him in history class
Was only her eyes were cool.

On one side of the gates is a romantic world with her secret lover, Willie Boone; on the other side is a naturalistic world where the degree of one's blackness determines questions of love and devotion. Mabbie, of course, innocently waits "without the grammar school gates." Like the youthful song of the previous poem, Mabbie's ballad is set apart from the rituals of innocence that give meaning and substance to human life. She is literally trapped in a racial paradox that aggravates the debilitating socioeconomic circumstances of her life. In the next two stanzas, her naiveté is underscored by the dogged persistence of her quest:

It was Mabbie without the grammar school
    gates
Waiting for Willie Boone.
Half hour after the closing bell!
He would surely be coming soon.

Oh, warm is the waiting for joys, my dears!
And it cannot be too long.
Oh, pity the little poor chocolate lips
That carry the bubble of song!

If Mabbie is a victim, her wounds are prefigured in the racial limitations that she cannot imaginatively overcome:

Out came the saucily bold Willie Boone.
It was woe for our Mabbie now.
He wore like a jewel a lemon-hued lynx
With sand-waves loving her brow.

It was Mabbie alone by the grammar school
    gates.
Yet chocolate companions had she:
Mabbie on Mabbie with hush in the heart.
Mabbie on Mabbie to be.

Like the "bad woman" of the previous poem who wears "brave stockings of night-black lace," Mabbie cannot project her self-identity beyond her "chocolate companions." She accepts "with hush in the heart" the obvious choices of her personal world.

Nonetheless, Mabbie's fate pales by comparison with the adolescent boy of **"The Life of Lincoln West."** In a poem that is as prosaic in its voice as it is poetic in its craft, the narrator retells the ordeal of Lincoln as he searches for self-identity and acceptance in a world where his very existence is an affront. As the "ugliest boy that everyone ever saw," he is isolated from any meaningful circle of human relations; his life is enclosed by class and racial caste and by his unnatural physical appearance:

. . . The pendulous lip, the
branching ears, the eyes so wide and wild,
the vague unvibrant brown of the skin,
and, most disturbing, the great head.

Lincoln is rejected by his father who "could not bear the sight of him"; by his relatives who felt "indignant about him"; by his school teacher who "tried to be as pleasant with him as with others"; and finally by his playmates who, although they "enjoyed him because he was / resourceful, made up / games, told stories," reject him "when / their More Acceptable friends came."

However, Lincoln's life is not without meaning and purpose. When he inspects his mirror image, he sees himself as others see him:

He spent much time looking at himself
in mirrors. What could be done?
But there was no
shrinking his head. There was no
binding his ears.

Ironically, this acceptance of his image becomes a triumph of self-identity and racial pride when a white man calls him the "real thing":

One day, while he was yet seven,
a thing happened. In the down-town movies
with his mother a white
man in the seat beside him whispered
loudly to a companion, and pointed at
the little Linc.
"THERE! That's the kind I've been wanting
to show you! One of the best
examples of the specie. Not like
those diluted Negroes you see so much of on
the streets these days, but the
real thing.
Black, ugly, and odd. You
can see the savagery. The blunt
blankness. That is the real
thing."

The "real thing" symbolizes his acceptance of and triumph over his natural conditions:

All the way home he was happy. Of course,
he had not liked the word
"ugly."
But, after all, should he not
be used to that by now? What had
struck him, among words and meanings
he could little understand, was the phrase
"the real thing."
He didn't know quite why,
but he liked that.
He liked that very much.

Lincoln's appearance and his natural inclination to "love Everybody" give Brooks's character a sense of pride in what he is. Lincoln's triumph, therefore, is a victory for racial pride which, when charged with love, transforms harsh realities into hopeful possibilities, a rare achievement in Brooks's poems about children.

Most of the poems Brooks has written for children are similar to those about children. In these poems, poverty and alienation characterize the child's life. The various titles of the poems, **"John, Who Is Poor," "Rudolph Is Tired of the City," "Michael Is Afraid of the Storm,"** and **"Robert, Who Is Often a Stranger to Himself,"** suggest children trapped by socioeconomic circumstances, whose very existence is threatened. However, in other poems for children, there are several important differences. First, the children are more receptive to the imaginative possibilities of their limited lives. Although survival remains the key to their existence, they are able to transcend the socioeconomic limitations of their environment by projecting their identities beyond its harsh realities. For these children, love and friendship are attainable ideals; they exist in spite of the physical and material differences between children. Although adults lurk menacingly on the fringes of the children's world, they do not prevent the children's self-fulfillment. The children readily distinguish between their hopes and the oppressive world of adults. Indeed, in such poems as **"Mexie and Bridie," "Luther and Breck,"** and **"Narcissa,"** the children are able to find self-fulfillment in an imagined world that exists apart from their natural environment; in other poems, such as **"Val," "Timmy and Tawanda,"** and **"Ella,"** the adolescents are able to mediate the differences between their imagined world and actual environment.

The two adolescent girls of **"Mexie and Bridie"** escape from their urban environment by simply moving their fantasy outdoors:

> A tiny tea-party
> Is happening today.
> Pink cakes, and nuts and bon-bons on
> A tiny, shiny tray.
>
> It's out within the weather,
> Beneath the clouds and sun.
> And pausing ants have peeked upon,
> As birds and God have done.
>
> Mexie's in her white dress,
> And Bridie's in her brown.
> There are no finer Ladies
> Tea-ing in the town.

The important feature of the poem is the imaginative similarities of the two girls. As alter egos, they have a common identity that is based not upon shared social disabilities, but rather upon imaginative possibilities. Although Mexie is dressed in white and Bridie in brown—colors that obviously invoke a racial caste system—there is no apparent intraracial discord between them. In their ritual of innocence, they give meaning and substance to what, we infer, is a rather trivial event in their daily lives. Their tea party takes place "out within the weather / Beneath the clouds and sun." In this, the two girls enjoin nature in their youthful ritual. They are, at once, free in their imagination of the enclosed spaces of their environment, yet they realize a place within a projected natural order. Ants, birds, and God partake of their afternoon happening.

In **"Luther and Breck"** (*BBG,* p. 16), two adolescent boys also reject the enclosed spaces of their urban environment and escape to an imagined world of historical England:

> In England, there were castles.
> Here, there never are.
> And anciently were knights so brave
> Off to bold deeds afar,
> And coming back to long high halls
> So stony, so austere!
> These little boys care nothing for
> Their wooden walls of HERE.
> Much rather mount a noble steed
> And speed to save the Queen;

> To chop, in dreadful grottoes,
> Dragons never seen.

The antithetical worlds of the two boys, "there" and "here," are symbolized by the high, stony walls of an English castle and the wooden walls of their apartment building. The important difference, though, is not simply material, stone versus wood, but psychological: The children transpose their identities to a timeless moment in human history. Therefore, they enlarge their identities and become less vulnerable, less given to the emotional paralysis that often afflicts Brooks's children. By prefiguring themselves as knights, they assume social identities as men of action, who are in control of their lives and who are able to act against the forces of evil, "To chop, in dreadful grottoes, / Dragons never seen."

The adolescent girl in the poem **"Narcissa"** (*BBG,* p. 4) uses flowers that grow in her back yard as the vehicle for her imaginative flight:

> Some of the girls are playing jacks.
> Some are playing ball.
> But small Narcissa is not playing
> Anything at all.
>
> Small Narcissa sits upon
> A brick in her back yard
> And looks at tiger-lilies,
> And shakes her pigtails hard.
>
> First she is an ancient queen
> In pomp and purple veil.
> Soon she is a singing wind.
> And, next, a nightingale.
>
> How fine to be Narcissa,
> A-changing like all that!
> While sitting still, as still, as still
> As anyone ever sat!

For Narcissa, the tiger lilies are totems for a complete self-transformation; she identifies herself as "an ancient queen / In pomp and purple veil." She also imagines herself as a "singing wind" and "nightingale," symbols of a creative world in which she projects her identity.

Finally, the boy and girl in **"Timmy and Tawanda"** (*BBG,* p. 3) also realize a measure of self-fulfillment by defying adult taboos and invading forbidden "territory":

> It is a marvelous thing and all
> When aunts and uncles come to call.
>
> For when our kin arrive (all dressed,
> On Sunday, in their Sunday-best)
> We two are almost quite forgot!
> We two are free to plan and plot.
>
> Free to raid Mom's powder jar;
> Free to tackle Dad's cigar
> And scatter ashes near and far;
>
> Free to plunder apple juice;
> Let our leaping Rover loose.
>
> Lots of lovely things we two
> Plot and plan and quickly do
>
> When aunts and uncles come to call,
> And rest their wraps in the outer hall.

Here, unlike the children in the previous poem, Timmy and Tawanda do not escape to a fanciful world of imagination. Instead, they move between antithetical worlds; one is characterized by self-inhibiting social manners; "our kin arrived (all dressed / On Sunday, in their Sunday-best)," and the other is defined by personal freedom, "We two are almost quite forgot! / We two are free to plan and plot." The freedoms in which the children engage are rituals of innocence; but unlike the other children, Narcissa, Luther, and Breck, who imaginatively project their social identities into the timeless world of history, Timmy and Tawanda raid the identities of their parents: "Free to raid Mom's powder jar; / Free to tackle Dad's cigar." The cigar and powder jar are, ironically, totems of the world from which the children seek to escape.

As Brooks's poetry for and about children clearly indicates, she is one of the few modern poets who has made children an organic part of her poetic vision. Her children do not exist in a pastoral world apart from the socioeconomic and psychological problems that beset her adult characters. As the most vulnerable members of society, her children are at the center of her poetic vision; they are the barometers by which we are compelled to judge a world where to be human is achieved only by the fullest exercise of the imagination. Moreover, while the complexity of Brooks's poetic vision prevents her from offering simple solutions to complex moral and socioeconomic problems, her children remain remainders of the value of the imagination. Indeed, in those instances where her children are able to overcome the poverty and racism that ensnare their lives and thwart their self-fulfillment, it is because they are able to imagine a world that is different in detail, if not in substance, from the one they are forced to live in. Finally, Brooks's children are testimony to her belief as a poet: If the harsh realities of an existential world are to be transformed into hopeful possibilities, then imagination or a radical innocence must be an integral part of the effort. (pp. 130-39)

> *Gary Smith, "Paradise Regained: The Children of Gwendolyn Brooks's 'Bronzeville'," in* A Life Distilled: Gwendolyn Brooks, Her Poetry and Fiction, *edited by Maria K. Mootry and Gary Smith, University of Illinois Press, 1987, pp. 128-39.*

D. H. Melhem

Bronzeville Boys and Girls [is] a book of thirty-four poems dedicated to the poet's children, Henry Jr. and Nora. . . . While the charm and warmth of this little gem, illustrated by Ronni Solbert, suggest the virtues of Robert Louis Stevenson's *A Child's Garden of Verses,* its discussion is further warranted.

First, the book extends Bronzeville, the black ghetto that becomes Brooks's microcosm of national life. Second, it deepens the personal and familial context of *Maud Martha,* as if the Brown family and Maud's own life-serving qualities had borne dozens of distinctly rendered and endearing children: fixed in the urban scene but dreaming wider landscapes, immersed in their friends and games and families, and emerging as children anywhere. Maud herself might say with **"Beulah at Church"**: "It feels good

to be good." There is elegance and poverty, the mimicry of a grownup world, and the special terrain of the very young. Like *A Child's Garden,* it encompasses the wonder of growth and the love that encourages it. Brooks is more exemplary, however, than the English poet. She acknowledges no cruel children but implies cruelty, the indifference that sanctions poverty and compels children to be prematurely involved in adult problems. **"Otto,"** who did not get the Christmas presents he had hoped for, insists, "My Dad must never know I care / It's hard enough for him to bear." Sensitivity to needs of grownups also appears in **"Jim"**:

> There never was a nicer boy
> Than Mrs. Jackson's Jim.
> The sun should drop its greatest gold
> On him.

The dropping of "On him" to a separate line reinforces the injunction. Jim sacrifices his baseball game to nurse his mother without permitting her to see his disappointment. In Bronzeville, the gap between the world of children and that of adults narrows toward greater interdependence than in *A Child's Garden.* No nurse mediates between parents and children. The difference is partly one of social class: in Stevenson, upper middle or lower upper; in Brooks, working and modestly middle class.

Stevenson's imagination peoples his near-solitary life with travel and magic, observations of nature and human detail. The first person singular gives a full vision enriched by an extraordinary sensibility. The precocity of Brooks's children is social: they have real identities and relate to friends and family. Names fill the book: in the thirty-four poems, thirty-seven different children are the subjects. Their names, which appear in the fully capped poem titles, typify those in Bronzeville and elsewhere: Mexie and Bridie, Val, Timmie and Towanda, Narcissa, Andre, Keziah, Charles, Cynthia, John, Paulette, Rudolph, Eppie, Ella, Dave, Luther and Breck, Michael, Eldora, Beulah, Skipper, Robert, Lyle, Nora, Mirthine, Maurice, De Koven, Gertrude, Marie Lucille, Cheryl, Jim, Eunice, Vern, Otto, Tommy, and Willie. Others are named in the poems, including a dog (Rover) and a cat (Mootsie). And there is a real-life heroine to dream on. Gertrude says: "When I hear Marian Anderson sing / I am a STUFFless kind of thing." The children themselves have glimmerings of heroic qualities, as do Otto and Mrs. Jackson's Jim, mentioned above. The specificity helps to create a real world that may be entered by many doors. Some of the children speak in their own voices; some poems are narrated in second or third person. Metrical variety, also true of Stevenson, adapts to the content, although in both books tetrameter, ballad stanza, and couplets predominate.

A child's linguistic audacity skips through poems like **"Cynthia in the Snow"**:

> It SUSHES.
> It hushes
> The loudness in the road.
> It flitter-twitters,
> And laughs away from me.
> It laughs a lovely whiteness
> And whitely whirs away,

Brooks at her desk.

To be
Some otherwhere,
Still white as milk or shirts.
So beautiful it hurts.

Here, in little, we find the strengths of Brooks's work. She can feel by way of the child's sensibility. She almost verbalizes the snow. Onomatopoeia can disclose relationships that may become, at their extreme register, animistic. We recognize—unless we have lost all our childlike intuiting—that snow "sushes." Whether or not this is a converging of "slush" (possibly of Scandinavian origin) with "shush" or "hush," the question persists: why these particular sounds?

Brooks is always sensitive to prosodic features of language. "Flitter-twitter" seems nearly tactile and helps define the snow's delicate motion; "whitely" and "otherwhere" are locutions a child might use. "Whitely" follows "whiteness" and precedes "white," identified with milk or shirts, necessities and goodnesses. Their whiteness partakes of the larger reality and value of whiteness, also powerful. The underlying irony: a gentle whiteness that uses its mild power to quell "the loudness in the road." "Loudness" suggests technology and traffic and is not a good in this quiet world. The color white, though racially prob-

lematic, is not spoiled thereby for the child. Often a benign element in Nature, snow covers all and suggests fresh beginnings. The lines themselves flutter down the page in slightly irregular lengths. The basic trimeter line (after initial emphasis by stress and contraction of the first two lines) breaks strategically at the eighth line, indicating a shift, a moving away of the snow to "otherwhere." We hear the alliteration, rhyme, slant rhyme, and assonance.

Other poems describe a tea party; the defensive reactions of a child excluded from an adult party; the freedom (and license) invited by festivities attending the relatives' Sunday visit; **"Narcissa,"** whose solitary world is imaginatively enriched by metamorphoses; **"Andre"** dreaming he can choose his parents and choosing his own; **"Keziah"** hiding in her secret place; **"Charles,"** who goes "inside" himself when he is sick; **"John, Who Is Poor,"** living with his widowed mother, his friends encouraged by the poet to share food with him; **"Paulette"** wanting to run with squirrels and ants, not "To be a lady"; **"Rudolph,"** who is tired of the city, wanting to push away buildings and spread his arms in the country; **"Eppie"** seeking to establish her identity in the form of "something / That's perfectly her own."

Despite or even because of their urban environment, the

children react strongly to natural phenomena: **"Ella"** runs out in winter without her coat to see the clouds, and **"Michael Is Afraid of the Storm." "De Koven"** looks at the "dancy little thing" and concludes, "You are a rascal, star!" because he cannot grasp it and keep it with him to shine always. **"Tommy"** wonders at the seed he has planted which pops out of the ground. Paradoxes of the adult world abound in miniature: **"Beulah at Church,"** clean and sin-free, enjoying her peaceable "goodness"; **"Luther and Breck,"** fighting dragons and playing at being knights, bravely battling to do good. A stranger, such as **"Eldora, Who Is Rich,"** can turn out amiably like the other children, or he/she can be different, like **"Robert, Who Is Often a Stranger to Himself "** when he looks into the mirror. The children love their pets. **"Skipper"** tries to save his goldfish (unlike careless Sally in "the ballad of the light-eyed little girl"); Cheryl admires her cat, Mootsie, "living her lovely little life / With scarcely any sound"; **"Vern"** walks with his comforting puppy after being scolded. Moving is an ever-present tragedy. **"Maurice"** feels important about moving until he realizes he will lose his friends. **"Lyle,"** who has had to move seven times, personifies the enviable tree.

Outside of their warm relationships with one another, the most significant values for the children are familial. For **"Eunice in the Evening,"** the best thing about the dining room is "Everybody's There!" The concluding poem, **"The Admiration of Willie,"** lauds parental capabilities. Their wisdom extends from tying ties and baking cakes to providing medicine, helping at play, and "Kissing children into bed / After their prayers are said." Beauty for the children of Bronzeville chiefly means human relationships. The rare traces of nature inspire appreciation and wonder. Affection—like Tommy watering and caring for the seed—nourishes growth and mutes the harshness of the adult world. The poverty of Bronzeville is economic, never emotional or spiritual. In feelings, the children are indeed rich. Their sturdy qualities, retained in adulthood, will have the heroic capacity to grow and function there. And though parents are not physically present in most of the poems, they are the strength of warmth and closeness from which the marvelous children of Bronzeville have been drawn. (pp. 95-9)

Aloneness is a children's book, less ambitious than *Bronzeville Boys and Girls.* A gently reflective poem of fifty-one lines, it projects a child's experience of solitude. The epigraph quotes Brooks's daughter Nora, who early had distinguished between loneliness and aloneness, enjoying the latter. Black-and-white illustrations accompany verses in blue script, the color absent from the second printing, to Brooks's regret. The pen-and-ink drawings by Leroy Foster present an appealing little black boy.

Feelings and sense impressions define the child's solitude. Brooks employs the indefinite "you" to merge with his narration and the tranquil copulatives of present tense. She posits loneliness as progressive, delicious at first, then decreasingly so, like a small red apple one is eating. The images are child-sized and true. Beginning with a child standing alone, "loneliness means" introduces a list of negative impressions, social and physical, the latter of color, sound, and taste. The imagined color of loneliness, "gray," has been discussed here (e.g., *Maud Martha, The Bean Eaters*) as a recurrent symbol of depression and death. Transition to positive "aloneness" begins with taste, the small apple, "sweet and round and cold and for just you," lexical inversion accentuating the recipient.

An instructive comparison is offered by [William Carlos] Williams's famous poem about the plums in the refrigerator, "so sweet and so cold." His self-imposed Objectivist limits, abandoned in *Paterson,* confine this early piece, where he tries to focus upon the object per se. Brooks's figurative language, on the other hand, relates a concept (aloneness) to a percept (the apple). The psychology summons Ezra Pound's definition of the image as "that which presents an intellectual and emotional complex in an instant of time." Jerome Rothenberg's "deep image" later confronts limitations of the perceptual approach. Clearly, the distance between text and reader is effectively bridged by emotive means, elsewhere called "sympathetic identification."

Let it be noted that citation of Williams at several points in this study does not imply any "influence" by him on Brooks, who objects to any comparisons drawn between her work and his. There are similarities, however, in attitudes toward popular diction and humanist orientation.

From the pivotal apple, Brooks turns to the image of a pond. Aloneness is "like loving a pond in summer," a simile that grasps the experience of a place and time. The water is "a little silver-dark, and kind." The child loves the silver in it and, significantly, the darkness. His world of feeling animistically binds him to what he sees. Just as he can love a "kind" pond, he can love people. In a fine lyric passage, the pond's meaning reaches him:

> Rest is under your eyes
> and above your eyes
> and your brain stops its wrinkles
> and is peaceful as a windless pond.

Aloneness sometimes vanishes into the rhythm of the "pulse and nature." The contemplative act provides a core of sanity, to be reinforced in traveling outward. Giving the child mental space as a basic living space reveals the ground of mental growth.

The poem ends with a dialectical conception of aloneness, "Whose other name is Love." Open to nature, in touch with its own yearnings and impressions, the self respects its reality. There, in the fruition of sensitive maternal listening and the assurance of being heard, even its deepest solitude escapes isolation. (pp. 211-12)

Brooks's first book with Haki Madhubuti's Third World Press [*The Tiger Who Wore White Gloves or What You are You are*] is a work for children, dedicated to Nora, "THE FIRST TIGER," and to Henry Jr., "THE DELINEATOR." While *Bronzeville Boys and Girls* individually surveys the children of a community, *Tiger,* like *Aloneness,* is a single poem. The three differ in tone and style. *Aloneness,* meditative, is basically in free verse; *Tiger,* homiletic, returns to the rhyme of *Bronzeville Boys and Girls* and clips an insistent dimeter and trimeter pattern of rhyming couplets. Visually, *Tiger*'s fully capped letters are often multicolored, tilted, and irregularly sized. Its bold graphics by Timothy Jones include illustrations that highlight the action. The nine-by-twelve-inch format frames the tiger who crouches on the cover. Couplets break and scatter through the drawings, sharing freshness with images and rhymes.

Tiger is a beast fable and represents, like the mock heroic of **"The Anniad,"** Brooks's application of an older literary genre. It may be considered within the rich heritage of animal tales in African American folk literature, their subjects ranging from jungle animals to "Br'er Rabbit." Like beast fables, African tales are usually didactic. They offer a variety of objectives, including "strategies for survival." Brooks's title implies human folly, a subject typical of the genre descended from Aesop, a semilegendary Greek slave, possibly African. (p. 220)

Brooks's tiger wears white gloves to be fashionable; companions shame his egregious behavior. The strength of the tiger accompanies his stripes, emblem of the lash, while his toenails extrude through the gloves. The theme is self-acceptance and pride. Yet a contradiction intervenes. Although the tiger would conform to an impractical, alien style, he is pressured to conform to "natural" group standards. One might argue that the group embodies principles of natural development, an Aristotelian sense of inherent purpose or *telos* or final cause. Just as "All men by nature desire to know," the purpose of a tiger may be determined by its qualities as a field. Brooks writes: "IT'S NA-TURE'S / NICE DECREE / THAT TIGER FOLK / SHOULD BE / NOT DAINTY, / BUT DARING, / AND WISELY WEARING / WHAT'S FIERCE AS THE FACE. / NOT WHITENESS AND LACE!" Living creatures must develop their attributes and esteem them: the tiger qua tiger; the human qua human. As metaphor, the gloves represent phenomena like the return to hair-straightening which, for Brooks, resumes subservience to white values.

White gloves are ascribed to female behavior, "THE WAY IT ALWAYS WAS, AND RIGHTLY SO," a role restriction unpalatable to feminists. The illustrations support the linking of the gloves with white culture. Apart from the ludicrously attired tiger, only doll-like little white girls "WITH MANNERS AND CURLS" are so outfitted. In the group of active girls, one is black, riding on the back of a white child's tricycle, neither wearing gloves. The common association is with decorum and restraint, protection against grimy reality, and disguise (or withholding) of power.

Tiger's lesson in self-valuation will have special import for black children. As part of a minority with a history of repression in this country, they need to resist being overwhelmed by the dominant culture. White children will also find pleasure and profit in reading *Tiger,* even though a feminist might have reservations. Nevertheless, the book effectively serves its modest purposes. (p. 221)

In 1980 Brooks published *Young Poet's Primer,* a useful, concise manual addressed mainly to high school and college students. The first book under her new imprint, Brooks Press, it was followed in 1983 by *Very Young Poets,* "Dedicated to all the children in the world." Twenty "Little Lessons," one to a page, give practical, simply worded advice about writing, reading, and subject matter. "Poems do not have to rhyme!" they begin, and end with "Remember that poetry is your Friend!"

"Eight Poems for Children" reinforce the lessons. The engaging free verse encourages looking at the world and books themselves with love and wonder. **"Books Feed and Cure and Chortle and Collide,"** published as **"A Bookmark"** in 1969, praises the power of books, their "drumbeats on the air." The last poem, **"To Young Readers,"** observes that "Good books . . . are keys and hammers, / ripe redeemers, / dials and bells and / healing hallelujah." Its final stanza announces:

> Good books are good nutrition.
> A reader is a Guest
> nourished, by riches of the Feast,
> to lift, to launch, and to applaud the world.

The Brooks heroic rhythms abide in robust affirmation. The poet routes her appeal outward through a child's basic experience. Mentor and mother, she renders a clear, encouraging guide that would benefit aspiring adults as well as very young poets. (pp. 234-35)

> *D. H. Melham, in his* Gwendolyn Brooks: Poetry & the Heroic Voice, *The University Press of Kentucky, 1987, 270 p.*

George E. Kent

[In 1954, Gwendolyn] stated that she wished to write a good "*solid* book" and "two juveniles." (p. 119)

Ursula Nordstrom of the juvenile department at Harper had responded to twenty-five children's poems Gwendolyn had sent and requested more during early 1955. Encouraged, Gwendolyn maintained a schedule of creating one poem per day until fifteen stood before her. Actually, the children's poetry was a pleasure to work with. **"Mexie and Bridie,"** the first of the collection *Bronzeville Boys and Girls,* was also the first one composed. In it Gwendolyn relived her own experiences as a child playing at having a tea party with a friend. In **"Ella,"** she found that a poem written during her early teens could be worked up to her current standards for publication. It tells of a girl who leaves a meal to run out into the winter to see the clouds. The first stanza reveals the poem's tight economy:

> Beauty has a coldness
> That keeps you very warm.
> "If I run out to see the clouds,
> That will be no harm!"

What emerges from the poems is childhood's sheer drive for joy, beauty, companionship, freedom, and imaginative flights. Mirthine is somewhat envied by the other girls at a party, but it turns out that without her giggles, beads, and bangles, she is no prettier than the others. Materially rich Elnora is a democratized citizen of this universe because of her desire for jolly companionship and play. Luther and Breck play out the old knightly tales and thus transform the limitations of the city setting. But various moods enter the picture and various notes are struck. Rudolph is tired of the city and wishes to escape into the country, and Michael is afraid of storms. Rather interesting language, comporting with the verbal resources of the childhood world, emerges.

> Lightning is angry in the night.
> Thunder spanks our house.
> Rain is hating our old elm—
> It punishes the boughs.

At church, Beulah is surprised by joy while harnessed in by extreme cleanliness and adults.

> only hold your song-book—so!—
> With the big people closing you in,
> And the organ-sound and the sermon
> Washing you clean of sin.
>
> I do not want to stay away.
> I do not think I should.
> Something there surprises me:
> It feels good to be good.

And there is wonder. Robert learns that one may look into a mirror and discover a stranger—"A child you know and do not know." Lyle wishes to escape moving from house to house and to enjoy the permanence of a tree. DeKoven loves the ungraspable stars. But poverty also tinctures in its smears. Otto hides from his father his disappointment in the Christmas presents he receives. And there is John, desperately poor, who lives "so lone and alone" and is not to be bothered with questions concerning the beginning or ending of his hunger.

Gwendolyn's poetic skills are well used in accurately gauging the ways poetry can describe for the very young child the world of his or her experiences. Poems with bouncy rhymes are intermixed with those of more subtle and varied sound patterns. "Ella" is notable for varying its sounds and pacing by use of trochees and iambs. Emphasis on the monosyllabic word at the end of the end-stopped line, variation in the length of the lines, use of repetition, and other devices maintain an interesting poetics that does not patronize the childhood world. (pp. 120-21)

Race is not mentioned in the poems but is clearly represented by the sensitive and lively illustrations of Ronni Solbert, all of which, however, have white faces—a fact that Gwendolyn found disturbing. The responses common to all children, presumably, are placed in the foreground, and there are no conflicts carrying a racial tone or overtone. Obviously, ***Bronzeville Boys and Girls*** represents the more Edenic side of Gwendolyn's own childhood. (p. 122)

> *George E. Kent, in his* A Life of Gwendolyn Brooks, *The University Press of Kentucky, 1990, 287 p.*

Esther Forbes

1891-1967

American author of fiction and nonfiction.

Major works include *Johnny Tremain: A Novel for Old and Young* (1943), *America's Paul Revere* (1946).

The following entry presents criticism of *Johnny Tremain*.

Celebrated as a talented writer and historian who is often praised for her understanding of human nature, Forbes is best known in the field of children's literature for her sole work of juvenile fiction, *Johnny Tremain*, a historical novel for adolescent readers that describes the maturation of a teenage boy in eighteenth-century Massachusetts. Outlining Johnny's development from a talented but abrasive fourteen-year-old apprentice silversmith to a sixteen-year-old man ready to fight for his belief in the American Revolution, *Johnny Tremain* is often considered both a classic example of juvenile historical fiction and an outstanding social document. The story, which spans the years 1773 to 1775, describes how orphaned Johnny comes into contact with the Sons of Liberty after his right hand is severely burned in an accident, destroying his chances for a career as a silversmith. Accepting a position as a dispatch rider for the Committee of Public Safety, Johnny meets such figures as Paul Revere, John Hancock, and Samuel Adams and participates with his friend, the apprentice printer Rab, in the Boston Tea Party. Johnny encounters danger, suffering, and death—Rab, who has become a soldier, is killed in the Battle of Lexington—and overcomes his bitterness to become a confident and courageous patriot ready to stand up for his new nation. Writing in a crisp, economical narrative style that utilizes strong descriptive passages, Forbes addresses both the universal struggles of the adolescent and the actions and reactions of a country preparing for war. She is often lauded for the freshness, liveliness, and moving quality of her treatment, for her strong evocation of time and place, for her historical accuracy, and for her deep understanding of her protagonist and his feelings.

Drawn to write about Colonial America by her ancestry and background, Forbes began her literary career as an author of popular historical and period fiction; she is also the creator of four informational books for adults. While working on her Pulitzer Prize-winning adult biography *Paul Revere and the World He Lived In* (1942), she became interested in the lives of the eighteenth-century Boston apprentices, deciding to tell their stories to show "not merely what was done but why and how people felt." She was inspired to create the character of Johnny Tremain by a historical incident in which a horse boy who, discovering that the British troops were being sent out of Boston on April 18, 1775, informs Paul Revere and sets history in motion. Hoping to bring to her work the level of character development that was usually confined to adult fiction, Forbes originally planned to have Johnny remain neutral during the Revolution but changed her mind when the

Japanese attacked Pearl Harbor. The advent of the Second World War greatly influenced the writing of *Johnny Tremain:* Forbes saw comparisons between the British occupation of Boston and the Nazi occupation of European cities, and she felt that her contemporary audience, forced to grow up quickly during wartime, would understand and relate to the characters and situations in the novel. In addition, she wanted to show her young readers that many of the issues of World War II had parallels in the American Revolution and that her historical characters believed in their cause as much as their modern counterparts. In the late 1970s, Forbes was criticized for presenting a falsification of the past with *Johnny Tremain;* some reviewers argued that her view was one-sided and too reminiscent of the ideology of World War II. However, most observers concur with the *New York Times* statement that "Forbes, a novelist who wrote like a historian and a historian who wrote like a novelist, achieved a reputation as one of the most exciting and knowledgeable authors on the Revolutionary era. . . . With *Johnny Tremain,* she proved her conviction that children can grasp mature writing much better than some writers and publishers believe." Forbes is also the author of *America's Paul Revere,* an informational book for middle graders that highlights both well known and lesser known incidents from Revere's life. *Johnny Tremain* received the Newbery Medal in 1944 and was made into both a Walt Disney film and a television program. Forbes was also awarded the Pulitzer Prize in history for *Paul Revere and the World He Lived In* in 1942, was the first woman member of the American Antiquarian Society, and was the recipient of honorary doctorates in literature and law.

(See also *Contemporary Literary Criticism,* Vol. 12; *Something about the Author,* Vol. 2; *Contemporary Authors Permanent Series,* Vol. 1; *Contemporary Authors,* Vols. 13-14 and Vols. 25-28, rev. ed. [obituary]; and *Dictionary of Literary Biography,* Vol. 22.)

AUTHOR'S COMMENTARY

While I was working on *Paul Revere and the World He Lived In* I became interested in the life of the apprentices in and about the shops and wharves of Boston during the eighteenth century. (p. 261)

I found that whenever these boys (and the much-more-rarely-mentioned girls) appeared in the material I was working on for a nonfiction book, it was hard for me to keep my resolve to make up nothing. As a sort of reward for the Spartan virtue I was practicing, I promised myself that sometime I would write a story and make up anything I wanted as long as I kept it typical of the period. Then I would know not merely what was done but why and how people felt. (p. 262)

[It was a horse boy] who brought word to Paul Revere that the British intended to march out of Boston on the night of the 18th of April in '75. He was employed in a stable near the Province House where General Gage had his headquarters, and he had made friends with the horse boys of the British officers. In fact he encouraged them to believe that he sympathized with their side. On the afternoon of the 18th one of them let slip the information that troops were being sent out that very night, and "there would be hell to pay tomorrow." As soon as he could he ran to Paul Revere's North Square house, that so many of you know, to report what he had found out.

In *Johnny Tremain* the part of the British boy is played by the unspeakable Dove. Johnny himself is the other horse boy who, although sympathizing with the Patriot side, sticks around and keeps his mouth shut for the sake of just such information. I think it is hard for most writers to say exactly when they get an idea for a certain book, but I had this incident in mind long before I had much else. This little incident teased my mind. I would like to have known more about these two boys. Did they really like each other or not? Were they bright boys or stupid boys?—a hundred things. It struck me, as Henry James once said, as "the perfect little workable thing," the germ virus, nucleus from which a story might grow. But I was still busy on *Paul Revere.* That was not the moment to go off on tangents. But once more I said to myself, "Sometime. . . ."

One thing I knew very early I wanted was an obstacle Johnny was to face from the beginning to the end of the book. I thought of Johnny as a brave boy with of course his moments of fear. I wanted to give him a chance to show his courage. This obstacle was to have psychological significance, not purely external such as one may use in an adventure book. I wanted it to be so simple a fairly small child would understand it. So I pitched upon (as people in New England used to say in those days) the burned hand and the ruin of all his plans. Today a boy in his predicament would have proper care and help. Then there was little to help him except his own courage and determination. For children often had to stand up on their own feet and take things like men.

I've several times spoken of my interest in how people felt and thought as being greater than in what they actually did; I suppose one of the most fundamental groupings of novelists is into two classes:—those who primarily want to know *what* is done, and those whose interest is largely in *why.* For better or worse I belong to the second group. I was anxious to show young readers something of the excitement of human nature, never static, always changing, often unpredictable and endlessly fascinating.

In planning the story I wanted to give Johnny room enough to change and grow; not clamp down upon him certain characteristics as unchanging as Little Orphan Annie's optimism. I did not want him to be more consistent than people are in life. If he was courageous, he also felt fear. Affectionate, but he could also hate. Talkative, but sometimes he said the wrong things, or too much, or even too little. Nor were his feelings for the people about him to be unchanging. Take Cilla, for instance. As he starts out she is his best friend, but towards the middle he is even bored by her and her devotion. This of course happens in every high school today. Or Dove. When Johnny realizes Dove is responsible for his burned hand he swears (and he means it) that he is going to get him for that—even if he has to wait ten years. But in less than two years he has Dove completely at his mercy and in the casual way of normal human beings he has really forgotten his oath of vengeance. He even—rather patronizingly—befriends Dove, who has not a friend in the world. Nor are Johnny's relations with the older and much-admired Rab quite as perfect as boys' friendships are apt to be in books. To the very end Rab baffles him, holds him at arm's length. So in other ways I have tried to show human nature is less rigid, more fascinating, than in, say, comic strips. Although, of course, the people in the comics may do more exciting things more constantly.

Yet it seemed to me that the times themselves furnished sufficient narrative excitement. For it is exciting to have your town in the hands of foreign troops. In the papers every day were stories of similar occupation of European cities. The boys and girls of the age I made Johnny Tremain were reading of the treatment Norwegians, Dutchmen, Poles, and Frenchmen were enduring under the Nazis. But look back at the British in Boston. Where were the firing squads, the hostages, the concentration camps? Why didn't General Gage hang, say, a couple of Adamses and Warren and Hancock? These men were certainly involved in high treason. Why, when they caught Paul Revere so busily spreading the alarm to every Middlesex village and farm, didn't they shoot him, instead of merely taking away his horse and telling him to walk home? Why were the women and children of the Patriot leaders never maltreated as a threat against the guilty men? They never were. It seemed to me that too often our schools have held up the British Redcoats as ogres. From everything I could read of the period, it seemed to me their occupation of Boston from 1774 to 1776 was as humane a military rule as any one could possibly imagine. The contrast between the way the British treated the civilian population at that time and what the Nazis are doing today is startling. I'm not of course defending the British point of view—or rather the Tory point of view, for many Englishmen sided with us at that time—but believing as they did, how could they have been more decent? And I really wanted young people today to think of the British in Boston—and the Nazis in, say, Rotterdam.

I have said that the idea of writing such a book as *Johnny Tremain,* I had had in my mind to do "sometime." When I was not thinking of anything else, I thought of Johnny and Dove, Lieutenant Stranger, Cilla, Isannah, Lavinia Lyte. And one thing I knew I wanted to do was to show the boys and girls of today how difficult were those other children's lives by modern standards; how early they were asked to take on the responsibilities of men and women. They were not allowed to be children very long. Then came Pearl Harbor and once again we were at war. In peace times countries are apt to look upon their boys under twenty as mere children and (for better or worse) to treat them as such. When war comes, these boys are suddenly asked to play their part as men. Our young fliers today have much in common with the nineteen-year-old boys who served as captains of armed ships during the Revolution. Their rank did not depend on how old they might be, but how good. It was true then as now. The twentieth-century boys and girls are by the very fact of war closer now spiritually, psychologically, to this earlier generation. Quite suddenly and clearly I saw what I wanted to try to do. Today the boys Johnny's age are not yet in the armed forces, but many of them soon will be and many will lose or have lost older brothers. So I let Johnny lose Rab.

I also wanted to show that these earlier boys were conscious of what they were fighting for and that it was something which they believed was worth more than their own lives. And to show that many of the issues at stake in this war are the same as in the earlier one. We are still fighting for simple things "that a man may stand up." (pp. 264-67)

> *Esther Forbes, "The Newbery Medal Acceptance," in* The Horn Book Magazine, *Vol. XX, No. 4, July-August, 1944, pp. 261-67.*

Alice M. Jordan

The publication of *Johnny Tremain* gives young people an outstanding novel of Revolutionary days in Boston, and may well be counted a red-letter event in children's books. Esther Forbes has now preserved for young people's reading some of the very background of her *Paul Revere,* with its details of domestic life, its penetrating knowledge of co-lonial Boston, its perception of character, its artistry. She tells the story of two years in the life of a boy, apprenticed to a silversmith at Hancock's Wharf, a contemporary of Paul Revere. They were important years for Boston and for the country, they witnessed the Boston Tea Party, the closing of the Port, the Battle of Lexington. Johnny's personal story, however, holds absorbed attention throughout the book. Following an accident to his hand, which barred him from his loved trade, he rode for the patriotic newspaper, *Observer,* and as messenger for the Sons of Liberty. So he came in touch with the Whig leaders, with many of the Tories and the British Army officers. Sam Adams, James Otis, Dr. Warren, General Gage—they are alive and real as they have never been in a children's book. Quick-tongued Johnny is no prodigy, he plays no important rôle in memorable deeds, but he is a true, likable boy, growing up to manhood at sixteen, to understand, as many boys are understanding today, the meaning to all men of the Liberty for which they fight. Miss Forbes ends her rare story with a moving account of the Battle of Lexington where Johnny's best friend lays down his life.

> *Alice M. Jordan, in a review of "Johnny Tremain," in* The Horn Book Magazine, *Vol. XIX, No. 6, November, 1943, p. 413.*

Mary Gould Davis

If Jonathan Lyte Tremain never lived in the flesh, he lives vividly with the men of his time in this book. So we dare to put him among the people of importance.

He is a boy, an apprentice to a silversmith in Boston, when we meet him just before the American Revolution. Casting the handle of a sugar basin for John Hancock, he seriously burns his right hand. He is crippled, the work that he loves must be given up—forever. Johnny goes through some hard and bitter times before he finds his work in the struggle that is to free the Colonies from British rule. The solution comes through a young printer, who likes Johnny and befriends him. Rab, too, is a "person of importance." His death of a mortal wound after the Battle of Lexington affects us. . . . It leaves us with a feeling of futility, an agony of pity for a life that might mean so much if allowed to mature.

This story of Johnny Tremain is almost uncanny in its "aliveness." Esther Forbes's power to create, and to recreate, a face, a voice, a scene takes us as living spectators to the Boston Tea Party, to the Battles of Lexington and of North Creek. It takes us, with Johnny, to the secret meetings of the Sons of Liberty, to the secret training of the Minute Men. We hear and see Samuel Adams and John Hancock and Paul Revere. Over and over again, we share some little incident that makes those days in Boston as exciting and as vital as Washington and London and Moscow are today; the young wife dressing her husband up in a woman's clothes so that he can slip through the British lines, laughing at him, teasing him, and when he has gone giving way to the fears that she has so successfully concealed; Aunt Jenifer calmly sewing on a feather bed while a British officer searches the house and her husband lies, nearly smothered, under it at her feet; Dr. Warren whistling to his mare who "Followed him like a dog" as he goes from house to house in Concord to save what lives he can.

Always the people *live* as people do live under the pressure of great events. Johnny suffers and doubts, grouches and *grows.* (p. 44)

Mary Gould Davis, in a review of "Johnny Tremain: A Novel for Young and Old," in The Saturday Review of Literature, *Vol. XXVI, No. 46, November 13, 1943, pp. 44-5.*

Ellen Lewis Buell

Only a master craftsman, and one who has worked so much in the period that it has become a kind of second home in time, would dare to undertake that most familiar of themes—Boston at the outbreak of the war. Such a novelist is Esther Forbes and to her story she brings so much freshness and vitality that one reads it with the avidity with which one follows today's news, with the extra dividend of pleasurable recognition of half-forgotten episodes thrown in.

The reason, of course, is that Miss Forbes not only knows the wharves, the inns, the very cobblestones of eighteenth-century Boston about as intimately as her own back yard, but because she creates three-dimensional people. Historical figures are clothed in flesh as well as good broadcloth, even casual street figures are endowed for the moment of their appearance with reality, and thus we see the temper of a city and a period. . . .

[Johnny becomes] a man and an American. The proportion between his personal fortunes and the larger theme of the Revolution is so delicately balanced that never for a moment does one forget either. The one is part and parcel of the other, true test of the novelist's skill. Miss Forbes calls this a novel for young and old, and adults will read it for its richness of color, its wit and humor, its illumination of a noble period, but it would be unfair to compare it to her major novels, for basically, in scope and concept, it is a novel for the teen age, and as such the most distinguished one we have had in years.

Ellen Lewis Buell, "A Story of Boston and the Revolution," in The New York Times Book Review, *November 14, 1943, p. 5.*

May Lamberton Becker

Johnny was almost apprenticed to Paul Revere—on whose life and times Miss Forbes is better informed than any one since Revere himself—and the reason why he went no farther has a poignancy to which fiction for the teens is unaccustomed. Johnny's vocation was clear as Cellini's; among the duller boys of the Lapham shop in old Boston he was as arrogant as he was charming. Perhaps he had to be overbearing, to convince himself that having no family did not matter when he knew it did. At any rate, he rode the boys too hard and one of them, scarce realizing what he was doing, brought about the crash of his career. A crucible broke; molten metal coated his hand; it healed with thumb and palm grown together. Art, livelihood, were gone. He kept the poor claw out of sight when he could, but now that he was down, the weak, the cruel and the crafty had their turn.

But at the lowest point of his fortunes his turn came. He was made one of the dispatch riders who did so much to draw insurgents together when the Revolution was drawing on. . . .

The sub-title, "a novel for old or young," will serve if you bear in mind that the young will read for Johnny's sake and the old for the sake of Esther Forbes. Here is history treated with a realism that may be an eye-opener to boys brought up on conventional boys' books. The Revolution goes through the story with a rush and scramble and in its surge men and boys alike are caught up. The inside of people's minds often has as much to do with the story as the outside layer of their actions. This is adult treatment, but the establishment of Johnny's relationship to the Lytes has the curve of a juvenile's plot. The book's chief value is that it brings back Boston and the road to Lexington in a year when boys of sixteen had to be adult.

May Lamberton Becker, in a review of "Johnny Tremain," in New York Herald Tribune Weekly Book Review, *November 21, 1943, p. 8.*

The Junior Bookshelf

Judged purely on its fictional contents [**Johnny Tremain**] is a good piece of writing, with a well-drawn scene and plot and some excellent and unusual characterisation.

Forbes as a young girl.

More than that, however, it is a fascinating picture of Boston city and a genuine and successful attempt to give an un-biassed and well-substantiated account of the early events which culminated in the breakaway of the Colonies from the Mother Country. Though English schools have never, within my memory, defended the British policy of that time, it is unusual for an American novelist to emphasise, as Miss Forbes does, the undoubted fact that many Englishmen sympathised then with the colonists and actively opposed their own government, that the occupying force under Gage behaved well, and that, as James Otis said, "the torch of liberty was first lighted upon the fires of England." Thoughts on continuity and repetition of history are in Miss Forbes mind and her book is a valuable contribution to informal learning and to a true understanding of that freedom for which we still must fight.

A review of "Johnny Tremain," in The Junior Bookshelf, *Vol. 8, No. 3, November, 1944, p. 120.*

Carolyn Horovitz

It should be no surprise, if **Johnny Tremain,** by Esther Forbes, finds its way into the upper "rare" stratosphere of literary excellence. Lauded ever since it first appeared, it continues to be read and regarded as a fine historical novel. It is a book much praised, but it has not, as far as I know, been critically examined. It would be sheer foolishness to pretend that I will now bring to bear a perfected analytical device on this novel. The questions are really simple and seem perfectly obvious. Why did she use time, this particular time for this particular story? Miss Forbes tells in [her Newbery Medal acceptance speech] about how she came to write this book, how it grew in her mind as she was working on another book of the same period. But that is not really the answer to a question which must find its answer in the book itself.

Basically, the story is one of character development, of a boy's struggle with his feelings of inferiority and worth, his attempts to find a place for himself, his problems about establishing relationships with people. It is almost as if he were a symbol of his time: a boy with promise and great natural ability but shackled by a sense of shame and inferiority. Aside from these symbolic values, this boy has the character and attitude of his own time, when men and boys were expected to make their own way. He is forthright, direct, and not unduly alarmed by the necessity of spending a night in the open or missing a meal. Only when he has missed quite a few meals and his hardships are those before which a man would quail does Johnny show signs of suffering. He is not described as showing these traits and qualities of the times; he actively displays them. Although he is a boy of all ages in his teasing and carefully guarded tender feelings, he is a boy of *his* time. In our day and age, such a boy would be sent to juvenile hall.

But in those days, Johnny was needed and soon came to be valued for his courage, just as he came to find values for which to fight and by which to live. In a time of growing, the boy grew in answer to needs greater than his own. The answer to the question, "why *time?*", is apparent in this novel. This boy is of the time, bred, illuminated, and

developed. Although presented in far greater precision than a symbol, he does have symbolic value.

Place comes alive sensuously with the first sentence, the first paragraph:

> On rocky islands gulls woke. Time to be about their business. Silently they floated in on the town, but when their icy eyes sighted the first dead fish, first bits of garbage about the ships and wharves, they began to scream and quarrel.

Miss Forbes brings Boston awake at the same time that the reader plunges into a sense of place—smelling, breathing, hearing, seeing. The novel has base in this way, from start to finish; never is skillful use of place merely a garnish or a layer in a sandwich. Speech and clothes and manner of behavior are all of a piece, but not an undifferentiated piece. Life can be as different in the homes of the Silsbees or the Lytes or the Laphams as it can be in Bel-Air or Aliso Village.

This book does not merely deal with another time and place; it is impregnated with these elements. And the hero, in working out his destiny, is under the same inevitable compulsion that people in the past have always appeared to feel. There was no other way. Yet, during the telling, as during the actual happening, nothing seemed certain, nothing seemed inevitable. To Johnny the events of the day were felt, not as historic events, but as tragedies for his friends:

> Johnny put his hands to his face. It was wet and his hands were shaking. He thought of that blue smock his mother had made him, now torn by bullets. Pumpkin had wanted so little out of life. A farm. Cows. True, Rab had got the musket he craved, but Pumpkin wasn't going to get his farm. Nothing more than a few feet by a few feet at the foot of Boston Common.

There is a sense of the meaning of life, of creed and ethics, of human behavior. Even the meanness of merchant Lyte was finally understood in some measure by Johnny. And Paul Revere's heroism was accepted casually with believability, credibility, coming through the illumination of small detail. One instance is the description of Revere's ride to Portsmouth, before his famous ride. The weather was bad that night:

> From the lowering December sky handfuls of snowflakes were falling, but as soon as they came to earth they turned to ice. It was a bleak, bad, dangerous day for the long ride north.

Revere's wife was in bed, recovering from having borne another child. She rapped on a windowpane at Johnny to come and get a note her husband had almost forgotten, a note about his sick grandmother with which to allay the suspicions of the British soldiers.

In this way, Esther Forbes brings about what Hilaire Belloc calls "the resurrection of the past" by the use of sudden illumination, proportion, and imagination:

> . . . upon the discovery of the essential movements and the essential moments in the action; and upon imagination, the power of seeing the

thing as it was; landscape, the weather, the gestures and the faces of the men; yes, and their
thoughts within.

Wonderful as Miss Forbes' work is, it is not a work which
can be neatly pigeonholed as "suitable for children." It is
"suitable" for anyone who wishes to read a good story of
this period. The excitement of the times is used to its fullest extent in building plot interest; the boy's involvement
in the Revolution is so intrinsic a part of the plot that reading about Johnny Tremain becomes reading about the
American Revolution. If any book can be called a prototype of all that historical fiction should be, this book merits that appellation. (pp. 257-59)

> *Carolyn Horovitz, "Dimensions in Time: A
> Critical View of Historical Fiction for Chil-
> dren," in* The Horn Book Magazine, *Vol.
> XXXVIII, No. 3, June, 1962, pp. 255-67.*

Margery Fisher

[*Johnny Tremain*] was first published in the United States
in 1943 and is now accepted as a classic in both our countries. It deserves the title because the author has so skilfully related personal and national issues, but far more because in Johnny she has created a very real person, a boy
whose faults are first his undoing and then his salvation.
To see a self-satisfied boy become a man, under stress, is
just as exciting as it is to read of how the ideal of freedom
was fought for and died for. Beyond the fascination of
technical and period detail, and the easy narration, there
is in this historical novel a depth of compassion and a lively intelligence that makes it essential and acceptable reading for all young people.

> *Margery Fisher, "An Old Favourite," in*
> Growing Point, *Vol. 4, No. 1, May, 1965, p.
> 516.*

G. Robert Carlsen

A surprising number of adolescent novels attempt to
evoke life in an earlier period of history. One such classic
in this category is *Johnny Tremain*. . . . (p. 46)

Describing the emotions and reactions of Johnny, Miss
Forbes has subtly underscored the idea that human life is
basically the same wherever and whenever it is lived. Paul
Revere and John Adams are presented as men not unlike
people one might know in his own community today. By
reading such a book, the young person has the vicarious
experience of living in an age different from his own and
discovering that the problems of long ago are essentially
like the problems that he may face today. (p. 47)

> *G. Robert Carlsen, "The Adolescent Novel:
> 'Johnny Tremain'," in his* Books and the
> Teen-age Reader: A Guide for Teachers, Li-
> brarians and Parents, *Harper & Row Publish-
> ers, 1971, pp. 46-7.*

Kathy Bird

Since the first colonial settlement, individualism has been
the touchstone of American ideology. Even the most basic
of values, however, must be redefined to fit a constantly
changing environment. Although individualism continues

to be a strong force in governing the lives of the American
people, it is clear that the frontiersman's concept of individualism is quite different from the individualism known
to present day man.

Does American children's literature, past and present, reinforce the value of individualism? Does the present day
literature redefine the concept of individualism to adapt
to existing conditions? The contention of this paper is to
suggest the answer is yes to both questions. (p. 707)

The frontier situation seemed conducive to the fulfillment
of America's concept of individualism. America, with its
vast untouched land, coupled with its virtually untapped
natural resources, provided unlimited opportunity for the
inhabitants. In contrast to crowded and traditional Europe, man possessed an almost overwhelming amount of
freedom to dream, to work, to achieve, and to realize his
true potential. (pp. 707-08)

Although many frontiersmen held the belief that individual man, may, if he strives to do so, make an almost limit-
less advance toward perfect ability, this belief was considerably tempered by the prevailing religious beliefs of the
time. Instead of man being portrayed as the controller of
his destiny, man's achievements were partially credited to
a force greater than they—God. (p. 708)

By the year 1776, predominate values had solidified into
a national philosophy. A common enemy not only unified
a country of great diversity, it caused a group of people
to charter a document defining major American values:
"We hold these truths to be self evident; that all men are
created equal; that they are endowed by their creator with
certain inalienable rights; that among these are life, liberty
and the pursuit of happiness." That each individual
should have the freedom to pursue his own just interests
without hindrance from others is basic to democratic
thought. Social mobility was phenomenal, and correlated
with it could be seen a self-assuredness, almost arrogance,
in the behavior of the common man.

Esther Forbes, in her book *Johnny Tremain,* exalts this
behavior, revealing it as a necessary component for
achievement. Set in Boston in 1776, the story tells of Johnny Tremain, an orphaned boy apprenticed as a silver
smith, and his involvement in prewar activities. In the beginning of the book, Johnny is reprimanded for his excessive pride. His employer strives to dampen his pride
through religion. He reads from the Bible to Johnny:
"When pride cometh, then cometh shame; but with the
lowly is wisdom." Johnny burns his hand while trying to
get an order out on the sabbath. The deformed hand is at-
tributed by Johnny's employer to be God's punishment for
his pride. Handicapped, Johnny can no longer perform the
necessary tasks of a silver smith. This deformity causes
Johnny to lose his self-esteem. Through the help of a small
group of friends that depended on him, however, he slowly
regains his self-confidence.

Esther Forbes, throughout the story, promotes individual
worth. She emphasizes the fact that an individual's self-
concept has a profound effect on behavior and achievement. It was not until Johnny felt wholly accepted that he
could realize his true potential. As in the early colonial

days, religion played an important part in the lives of the American people. Miss Forbes, however, seems to discount religion as having an influence on Johnny's character. . . . Miss Forbes exalts the individual as the instigator of change rather than any religious influence. (p. 709)

> *Kathy Bird, "The Value of Individualism," in* Elementary English, *Vol. 50, No. 5, May, 1973, pp. 707-14.*

Dorothy H. Nelson

Johnny Tremain, the fictional boy immortalized by Esther Forbes in her historical novel as the brash young Yankee who lived through the birthpangs of our country, is a natural for the Bicentennial year.

Students can identify with Johnny, for his was the arrogance of today. He plunged heart and soul into the rebellious spirit of his time. His quick temper and his cocksure air (for he *was* a clever boy) make him so human and alive that Johnny carries with him whole classrooms of youngsters who learn to feel and to experience that Spirit of '76. No other book about early America can cast the spell that *Johnny Tremain* does. By the end of the story, when Johnny at last holds a good gun in his hands, we are ready to fight for him "so a man can stand up!" The thrill, the justice of the Revolutionary War, as felt by those early New Englanders, exudes from these absorbing pages. A sense of pride in the American cause shines through, as Johnny and his brave, inspiring friend, Rab, prepare to meet the enemy. . . .

In this day of sagging patriotism, America's two-hundredth anniversary offers a chance to rekindle the spirits of our young Americans. An indepth study of *Johnny Tremain* will reveal that it's not all speeches and flag waving. The romance of childhood sweethearts, the pathos of a crippling injury, the violence of a tar and feathering, the shock of the firing squad, the humor of a feather-bed disguise, the delight of the silversmith's perfection—they're all there in this Colonial epic to be lived through vicariously by the reader. Esther Forbes' masterpiece contains all the inspiration of the early American patriots. It's a Bicentennial MUST.

> *Dorothy H. Nelson, " 'Johnny Tremain'—A Bicentennial Natural!," in* Language Arts, *Vol. 53, No. 1, January, 1976, p. 45.*

Christopher Collier

For perhaps the tenth time in as many weeks I listened with embarrassment as my host introduced me—on this occasion to about a hundred Connecticut reading specialists—as someone who had at last found something new to say about the American Revolution. Surely, I thought, there are some people in my audience who will think me pretentious and recognize the preposterousness of the statement. If, among the thousands of teachers and librarians I have addressed in the year and a half since the publication of *My Brother Sam Is Dead,* there were those who thought the statement absurd, none have been so rude as to say so. They have left that welcome job to me.

The embarrassment I have felt on these occasions stems from the fact that what is seen as new in the book my brother and I wrote has behind it at least two generations of scholarship among academic historians. The interpretation of the American Revolution that informs *Brother Sam* was thoroughly developed and precisely stated during the first quarter of the twentieth century. Though the historiographic approach is not new, its popularization in juvenile literature apparently is. Indeed, it was largely to fill an historiographic gap that I was moved to persuade my brother, James Lincoln Collier, to collaborate on the work. Historiography—the methodology of historical research and the study of varying historical interpretations—is the great mass of work that lies beneath the tip of the historical iceberg. The method, buried in scholarly apparatus, is concealed from the lay public; and the interpretation is normally so well integrated with description and narration that nonprofessionals are unaware of it. But all written history is interpretation, and novelists present their own historical interpretation whether they are conscious of it or not. Thus, a particular historiographic view is frequently brought unconsciously to readers who are bound to absorb it equally unconsciously.

To state it simply, the historiography of the American Revolution breaks down into three schools of thought—the Whig, the Imperialist, and the Progressive. The range of interpretation is vast, of course, and includes eighteenth-century Patriot and Loyalist presentations as well as Marxist, Stalinist, Freudian, and other off-beat modes. But the main body of secondary literature about the Revolution written over the past century and a half falls into one or the other of these three dominant groups, though some historians combine elements of two of them, and no two interpretations are identical.

The Whig interpretation, which takes its name from the Parliamentary faction opposed to George III's colonial policies, dominated the nineteenth century during the era before the professionalization of the practice of history. Its principal popularizer was George Bancroft (1800-1891), and thus it is frequently referred to as the Bancroftian view. Nineteenth-century Whig historians saw the Revolution as a spontaneous and universal uprising of the colonial yeomanry. Americans, they claimed, had taken up the cause of traditional English liberty in a struggle against the regressive policies of a tyrannical king who was supported by a venal ministry that had, in turn, bought off and corrupted the larger part of Commons. The Whig picture was moralistic and pedantic, depicting simple, freedom-loving farmers marching in a crusade to fulfill God's plan for a rationally ordered society based on principles of liberty and equality. The Whig effort wanted to teach a national patriotism based upon a respectful adoration of the principles of natural rights and social contract and of the men who died to protect them. A much more sophisticated version of the Whig interpretation—the twentieth-century one—shows a great middle-class America fighting to preserve the right to practice self-government under a universally-accepted concept of the British Constitution constructed on Lockean social contract. This viewpoint has dominated professional historiography since World War II, but its nineteenth-century ancestor has never lost its hold over popular and juvenile literature.

The Bancroftian view of the Revolution came under severe attack by the newly-risen class of professional historians during the late nineteenth and early twentieth centuries. The entrance of the United States upon her own imperialist adventures in the 1890's, together with a developing Anglophilia and a host of other changes in the American political and intellectual climate, drew attention to the English side of the conflict. The Imperialist historians sought a much more objective approach to the conflict and looked for research materials in London as well as in the archives of the former colonies. For them, a true view of the war could only be obtained from the center of the empire looking out. They pointed to the fact that there were twenty-four British American colonies, and the reasons for the loyalty of nearly half of them were certainly as worthy of study as the revolt of the others. The Imperialist historians tend to see the American Patriot position as small-minded, short-sighted, and selfish. (pp. 132-34)

Though the Imperialists sharply undermined the nationalism of the old Whigs, there is nothing about their interpretation that necessarily requires a British or a world view. One could approach the study of the Revolution from English sources and still conclude that the Americans had been right in their sense of repression and in their understanding of the rights of man. The same cannot be said about the Progressive interpretation.

Arising contemporaneously with the Imperial view, but developing out of domestic rather than world events, the Progressive concept of the Anglo-American conflict of 1763-1783 was set against a background of internal political strife, economic motivations, and rapid social changes. As young historians looked about them in the 1890's and the years before World War I, they saw an America wracked by a too-rapid industrialization and urbanization with the accompanying tortures of class conflict, the corruption of the political system, and the dominance of economics over ideology. And they read the past through spectacles tinted by the social conditioning of the late nineteenth- and early twentieth-century reform movements known as Progressivism.

The Progressive historians elevated economic impetus—both in its individual and in its collective or class manifestations—above ideological or religious motivations. To them reality was found only in concrete economic fact. They also took the social conflict that engulfed their America—geographically based, class motivated, politically inspired but not, however, generational, sexual, or racial as it might be seen today—to be the normal state of events. They turned to sources that would reveal this reality as it existed in the English colonies of the late eighteenth century. The picture they painted enraged, confused, and ultimately confounded both the old Whigs and the young Imperialists. (pp. 134-35)

The reason, I suspect, that *My Brother Sam Is Dead* appears to say something new is that it stands alone among Revolutionary juvenile literature as an effort to present a view of the war that incorporates elements of both the Whig and Progressive interpretations, with a strong emphasis on the latter. Few children's books on the subject make any attempt to deal with issues at all. For the most part they are merely stories laid in the period and given verisimilitude by incorporating authentic detail. (pp. 135-36)

Johnny Tremain, of course, is the work that must be dealt with. The year before its publication in 1943 Esther Forbes had written *Paul Revere and the World He Lived In.* Though she was not a trained historian, her *Paul Revere* is listed in the prestigious *Harvard Guide to American History,* a selective work which also puts *Johnny Tremain* in a list of historical novels useful for delineating their eras. Miss Forbes, I venture to say, knew what she was talking about.

Diligently as one may search through *Johnny Tremain,* however, one finds no deviation from the standard Whig treatment. Perhaps Johnny's thought as he watches a British officer slap a wounded enlisted man—" 'We are fighting, partly, for just that. Because a man is a private is no reason he should be treated like cordwood' "—is a conscious effort on the author's part to note the equalitarianism that the Progressives tended to emphasize as opposed to the Whig's libertarianism. Or again, she shows her awareness of the Imperial school when she has an English doctor say, " 'You remember that *we* don't like being here in Boston any better than you like having us. . . . We're both in a tight spot. But if we keep our tempers and you keep your tempers, why, we can fix up things between us somehow. We're all one people, you know.' "

Esther Forbes does deal with issues; her story is intrinsically about the American Revolution; a different time and place would make it a different story. She tips her hand early while explaining that the new tea tax would actually reduce the price of tea in the colonies. "Weren't the Americans, after all, human beings?" she has a cynical Parliament ask. "Wouldn't they care more for their pocketbooks than their principles?" The rest of her book demonstrates the reverse. Her treatment is pure nineteenth-century Bancroft. Her spokesman is James Otis—in real life scorned by 1775 by the radical revolutionaries as too conservative and untrustworthy in his divided loyalties. Miss Forbes depicts him as fallen from leadership not because of political events but because of his increasingly frequent periods of insanity—also historically accurate. She brings Otis back to give, in a crowded, smoky, attic meeting place of the Sons of Liberty, a spirited statement of old-fashioned American Lockeanism.

" 'For what will we fight?' " demands Otis.

" 'We will fight for the rights of Americans. England cannot take our money away by taxes,' " is the reply of Sam Adams.

" 'No, no. For something more important than the pocketbooks of our American citizens. . . . For men and women and children all over the world. . . . There shall be no more tyranny. A handful of men cannot seize power over thousands. A man shall choose who it is shall rule over him.' "

Otis then proceeds to demonstrate that John Hancock will give up his property, Joseph Warren sacrifice his family, Paul Revere his business, and John Adams his career—all

Forbes studies an engraving by Paul Revere in the library of the American Antiquarian Society.

to make the world safe for democracy. Sam Adams with his talk of taxes is dismissed: " 'what it is really about . . . you'll never know,' " says Otis. " 'It is all so much simpler than you think,' " the old firebrand announces after downing a second tankard of punch. " 'We give all we have, lives, property, safety, skills . . . we fight, we die, for a simple thing. Only that a man can stand up.' " Esther Forbes leaves no doubt about her meaning, for the final chapter is entitled "A Man Can Stand Up," and at the close of the profoundly touching description of the events after Lexington and Concord and the death of Johnny's closest friend Rab, Johnny thinks again, "True, Rab had died. Hundreds would die, but not the thing they died for.

" 'A man can stand up. . . .' "

Johnny Tremain, with its message of ideologically motivated war, is so much the product of World War II that one who grew up in the 1940's must honor its clear one-sidedness. Younger historians, products of the 1960's who are currently busy reviving the Progressive interpretation of a generation ago, would be less tolerant. But without denying its outstanding literary merit, Miss Forbes' presentation of the American Revolution does not pass muster as serious, professional history. Not so much because it is so sharply biased, but because it is so simplistic. Life is not like that—and we may be sure it was not like that two hundred years ago. Such an event as a war involving the three major European nations, with implications for the western power structure for centuries to come, is

bound to be a complex matter. To present history in simple, one-sided—almost moralistic—terms, is to teach nothing worth learning and to falsify the past in a way that provides worse than no help in understanding the present or in meeting the future. (pp. 136-38)

> *Christopher Collier, "Johnny and Sam: Old and New Approaches to the American Revolution," in* The Horn Book Magazine, *Vol. LII, No. 2, April, 1976, pp. 132-38.*

M. Sarah Smedman

Esther Forbes' tale of Boston during the early days of the American Revolution is by critical standards a fine historical novel. It has been acclaimed as a plum for young and old, as accurate, exciting, witty, rich in color, "almost uncanny in its aliveness." (p. 84)

Adolescents love *Johnny Tremain* for its adventure and, primarily, because the hero, although very much a boy of his own time, is a person who resembles themselves, whose feelings they share, and whom they admire enough to want to emulate. The success of *Johnny,* as of all memorable fiction, derives primarily from the vitality of its protagonist and the authenticity of his development. . . . His arrogance, which springs from youthful vigor and consciousness of his talent, has not yet been tempered with the humility requisite to recognition of other people's right to their place in the world. Derisive of the weaknesses and foibles of those not as quick and capable as he, Johnny has a classic case of hubris; he is full of himself and looks down on the rest of humanity. Projecting from personal recollection, I believe that human beings are never again so sure that they know all there is to know and, consequently, have a right to lord it over the rest of their world, as when they successfully complete the last grade in an upper elementary or junior high school. As W. H. Auden said of Carroll's Alice, Johnny—and readers who recognize themselves in him—"[do] not know, of course, that [their] sense of identity has been too easily won . . . and that [they are] soon going to lose it, first in the *Sturm und Drang* of adolescence . . ."

Johnny's experiences during his next two years adumbrate the maturation of many young readers, for whom, however, the process is likely to be longer and less dramatic, if no less intense. (pp. 84-5)

Johnny Tremain is so real to adolescent readers that they have returned from Boston surprised not to find his mother's grave in the cemetery, disappointed to realize finally that the boy did not actually live, as did Paul Revere, Sam Adams, James Otis, Dr. Warren, and a host of other characters in the book. Not a professional historian, Forbes nonetheless knew and respected historical fact too well to invent non-verifiable thoughts, words, and feelings for actual persons, certainly not for a central character. Consequently, she chose to create a fictional character to live at the center of her novel, a technique theoreticians of the historical novel have advocated since Scott first popularized the genre in the early nineteenth-century.

Johnny, however, is not the kind of fictional character Scott successfully used at the center of so many of his historical fictions. Georg Lukacs' emphasis on Scott's shrewd choice of a passive, somewhat uncommitted hero who can serve as a device to conduct readers through both sides of the historical conflict dramatized in the novel is consistent with his Hegelian view of history as dialectical process. Though Johnny is partisan, Forbes is too thorough an historian to be as guilty of one-sidedness and oversimplification as some critics have charged. As Christopher Collier suggests, Johnny is indeed moved by a national patriotism based upon respect for "the principles of natural rights and social contract and of the men who died to protect them". The events of the novel are seen almost entirely through Johnny's viewpoint. His character is convincing exactly because he does not know more than would any bright, responsive boy of the configuration of all points of view or the interpretation of the total pattern of events of his own times.

Working deftly through Johnny's point of view, however, Forbes, has evoked awareness of points of view other than his own, for example, that of the position and humaneness of the British. This she imparts in several ways: through the camaraderie between Johnny and Lieutenant Stranger, whom the boy almost worshiped for his skill, "though still it was only where horses were concerned they were equals. Indoors [Stranger] was rigidly a British officer and a 'gentleman' and Johnny an inferior. This shifting about puzzled Johnny. It did not seem to puzzle the British officer at all"; through the jolly Pumpkin, who, preferring the smell of manure to gunpowder "had wanted so little out of life. A farm. Cows," and who was to get "nothing more than a few feet by a few feet at the foot of Boston Common. That much Yankee land he'd hold to Judgement Day"; through Johnny's inability to think of Stranger, Sergeant Gale, Major Pitcairn as targets; through the medical officer's explicit address to Rab and Johnny: "You remember that we don't like being here in Boston any better than you like having us. I'd rather be with my wife and children in Bath. We're both in a tight spot. But if we keep our tempers and you keep your tempers, why, we can fix up things between us somehow. We're all one people, you know". Johnny, too, remembers the common heritage of British and Americans, once James Otis has made him aware that "we hold up our torch—and do not forget it was lighted upon the fires of England . . ."

Points of view of Americans other than that of the Whig patriots are also sympathetically conveyed, though always as subsidiary. Forbes makes quite clear that economics played a major role in the War of Independence. As intrusive narrator, the author asks, "Weren't the Americans after all human beings? Wouldn't they care more for their pocketbooks than their principles?" Johnny, of course, agrees with Otis, that revolution is "For something more important than the pocketbooks of our American citizens." However, the principal activator of the Sons of Liberty, Sam Adams, impatient with Otis, maintains that Americans will fight so that "England cannot take our money away by taxes". The book graphically sketches the unemployment and economic paralysis of Boston. The cocky Johnny ridiculed Mrs. Lapham because she scorned "Book larning," which "scalded no pigs" and manipulated her family for economic security; but the wiser youth realizes she "had never been the ogress he thought her a

year ago. . . . Her bartering and bickering had then seemed small-minded to him; now he was enough older to realize how valiantly she had fought for those under her care".

The humanity of other Tories, too, overrides their wrongheaded political stance. When Johnny hears the "Tory, who had been so brave—and foolish—as to follow the Sons of Liberty down a black alley . . . alone now . . . sobbing, not from pain but from humiliation," he is nauseated. Johnny's sympathy for the haughty Tory beauty Lavinia Lyte can be explained by the romantic passion he secretly feels for her from afar, but his compassion for her father, Merchant Lyte, so treacherous to the boy personally, is attributable only to commiseration resulting from mature understanding of the fragility of a man who depended upon health, wealth, and prestige for power over others. In the end, Johnny likes the Lytes' Whig servant, Mrs. Bessie, "all the better" because "she had been unable to see a considerate master, whom she had served for thirty years, a young woman whom she had taken care of since she was a baby, humiliated, tossed about, torn by a mob. Sam Adams might have respected her the less for this weakness. Johnny respected her the more".

Thus, although Forbes' central fictional character is unquestionably partisan and indubitably embodies the author's own vision of the historical period which provides the setting and external conflict of her novel, she does dramatize the character's personal problems, internal struggles, and growth through the interaction of his personal and public lives. Further, she provides ample suggestion that Johnny's—and, therefore, that of the Whig patriots—is not the only view of the American War of Independence. In so doing, she reflects two fundamental concerns of the historical novel which imbue the quite sparse nineteenth and twentieth criticism of that genre. The first, as Rosemary Sutcliff phrases it: "History is People." The historical novel for the young, particularly, must deal with "people with whom children can identify through the fundamental sameness—like calling to like under the changing surfaces". The second: the historical novel must be concerned with public action. In the words of G. R. Stange, "Whatever is particular subject, it is designed to illustrate necessary conditions between the individual life and the social order, to arrive at a coherent interpretation of a significant moment of the past". (pp. 86-8)

[The] historical novelist faces a problem the novelist of contemporary realism does not: thorough research of a time and place. The knowledge, once acquired, must simultaneously infuse the story with historical accuracy and be used selectively and imaginatively. The historical novelist must create a concrete world as authentic as the readers' own, and breathe life into believable, individualized characters, while never overpowering story or reader with extraneous trimmings. Forbes has explained that Johnny Tremain sprouted from her curiosity about the lives of apprentices, whose paths she crossed in research for her Pulitzer-Prize winning *Paul Revere and the World He Lived in.* Determinedly restraining her creative impulse because she was writing "straight" biography, she promised herself that later she "would write a story and make up anything [she] wanted as long as [she] kept it typical of the period. Then [she] would know not merely what was done but why and how people felt".

The historical characters in *Johnny Tremain* are drawn with impeccable accuracy from the research steeping *Paul Revere.* The magnetic but obsessed James Otis who delivers the keynote speech in *Johnny* is depicted in *Paul Revere* as, in 1766, "still the popular idol of Boston, the bold champion of the rights of Englishmen," but as "an infernal nuisance" who had "never lost his magnetism nor [his] rough, masculine charm," "fitter for the madhouse than the house of representatives". The skulking Dr. Church, whom no one in *Johnny* quite trusts, is described in the biography as a "witty, lively fellow" with the "best medical education of any man in Boston," and a flair for "writing Whig poetry"; "high-strung, bombastic, always hard up. . . . There was something queer about Doctor Church. Paul Revere felt it, and so did Joseph Warren". Paul Revere himself is described as a master craftsman, with many "domestic virtues," yet probably "a hard husband for a fragile and ailing girl"; a man with "a good mind, quick and usable, but not a subtle mind", quite suitable for Johnny's hero-worship and the role he plays both in the book and in American myth-history:

> In contrast to the men with whom his name was later to be associated, [Paul Revere] seems to have gone ahead without great ponderings. James Otis' brilliant mind went crazy over questions of empire that never existed for Paul Revere. Paul endured none of the humiliations of repeated failure that mellowed Sam Adams, nor was he ridden with doubts and self-questionings that John Adams . . . was already suffering. John Hancock was proud, touchy, and given to all sorts of lying-downs and headaches, which suggest some psychic block. None of these ailments of the soul, at once so devasting and so educational, as far as we know touched Paul Revere.

Out of her abundance of knowledge of details of the period substantiating such generalizations, Forbes has judiciously selected essential traits to bring characters pointedly alive in her novel.

The inspiration for Johnny himself seems to have been Apollos Rivoire, Paul Revere's father, and Master Johnny Tileston, for eighty years "pupil, usher or master at North Writing School." The former, alone of his family, escaped from persecution of the Huguenots in France to apprenticeship to a goldsmith in Boston. The latter "had a deformed hand, drawn together like a bird's beak. With this loathsome hand, hard as a bone, he used to peck at his pupils, and yet he was one of the most loved men in Boston". Details of the lives of Johnny and the other apprentices are rooted in diaries and other first-hand accounts of actual eighteenth-century Bostonian apprentices. (pp. 89-90)

Since Walter Scott, historical novelists have been interested not only in making the past live, but in the impingement of the past on the present and the degree to which history and character illumine each other. Esther Forbes is no exception. Writing *Johnny Tremain* during World War II, she was, of course, conscious of the Nazi threat to individual and national freedoms. She believed that not only the Americans' struggle for liberty from England, but also the humane British military rule of the Colonies, would incite young readers to think about events of their own day, issues still significant. Critics and novelists have consistently agreed that, as Stange says, "one of the qualities of the serious historical novel is its applicability to the author's own time; the novelist does not recreate the past so that we can escape into it, but so that we can use it to understand the life around us". Hester Burton consciously chooses an event or theme in history for her novels because "it echoes something [she has] experienced in [her] own life". Looking at the past as interpreted and placed in perspective by historians helps clear the fog surrounding the complex present and enables the novelist to explore one's own time. Recent critics, such as Christopher Collier and Joel Taxel, have objected to *Johnny Tremain* because Forbes' presentation of events in Boston in 1773-1775 corresponds entirely to the standard nineteenth-century Whig interpretation of the American Revolution as a spontaneous, universal uprising of colonial yeomanry to preserve traditional English liberties against regressive policies of a tyrannical king; as a crusade of simple, freedom-loving farmers to fulfill God's plan for social justice and equality. But such misreadings of *Johnny Tremain* seem oversimplifications, neglecting aesthetic principles in order to fit the novel into a schematized classification of various views of the Revolution.

Although it may never controvert the facts of history, no single novel, particularly not one for young people, can represent completely the whole of any period in history. An understanding of the whole comes, as Belloc remarked and we are all aware, when "all the books one reads coalesce". *Johnny Tremain* reflects not only Forbes' scholarship, her comprehension of and delight in the period, but also her need to tell of that time and its personal significance to her. The interpretation of historical evidence, whether by historian or novelist, is, as Jill Paton Walsh points out, always "a construct of the mind". When the collective imagination operates upon historical data, history merges with myth. Like that of Scott, Forbes' artistic aim in depicting an historical crisis seems to have been to portray human greatness, liberated in its ordinary as well as its important representatives. As Lukacs interprets Scott, authentic human greatness lies in "the quality of the inner life, the morality, heroism, capacity, sacrifice, steadfastness, etc. peculiar to a given age". *Johnny Tremain* is evidence that Forbes would have agreed with Scott that such human greatness constitutes the very core of historical authenticity. The character Johnny, proud but ultimately tolerant of others' faults and points of view, flawed but at last courageous enough to take measures to compensate for his deficiencies, to heal his wounds, down-to-earth but sufficiently idealistic to believe that individual human freedom and dignity is worth fighting for, is symbolic of Revolutionary Boston as portrayed by Forbes. *Johnny Tremain* keeps alive the American myth that, in Leonard Wibberly's words, "our Revolution established certain inalienable rights for people, which if preserved would protect mankind from tyranny in all the centuries ahead". That ideal may be irreconcilable with conditions wrought by mankind in the past and in the present. Even if never achieved in the future, it is a worthy goal for humans to strive after.

According to T. S. Eliot, the distinguishing mark of a classic is its maturity: maturity of mind, maturity of manners, and maturity of language. *Johnny Tremain* is obviously the work of a mature mind. . . . Certainly Forbes exhibits her awareness of history of peoples other than her own. She does, as Eliot requires, "provide insight into what the conduct of [her] own people might be at its best": through the ideals which sound the motif of the novel, though today, as always, we would hope that "a man can stand up" behind a plowshare rather than behind a gun; through her characters, notably James Otis, Johnny, Rab, and even Pumpkin, for undoubtedly we still agree with Forbes' characters that "men have got the right to risk their lives for things they think worth it".

As a writer for young people, Forbes has not, of course, used language to its full potency. She has, however, used it economically, vividly, often brilliantly. Crisp descriptions quicken a sense of place and fuse place with narrative action in apt metaphors: on Boston Common, where Rab taught Johnny to ride were

> acres upon acres of meadow and cow pasture, hard ground cleared for the drilling of militia. The sun and the wind swept through them. Trees were turned to scarlet, gold, beefy red: blueberry bushes to crimson. Through one patch a white cow was plodding, seemingly up to her belly in blood. The cold, wild air was like wine in the veins. And across the vast, blue sky, white clouds hurried before the wind like sheep before invisible wolves.

The tintinnabulation of Boston's bells reverberates onomatopoetically, thematically, and ironically:

> The town was whist and still, for it was Sunday. As Johnny lay upon his bed, the church bells began to call for afternoon service. They babbled softly as one old friend to another. . . . He had heard them clanging furiously for fire, crying fiercely to call out the Sons of Liberty. He had heard them toll for the dead, rejoice when some unpopular act had been repealed, and shudder with bronze rage at tyranny. . . . but he had never loved them more than on Lord's Days when their golden clamor seemed to open the blue vaults of Heaven itself. You could almost see the angels bending down to earth—even to rowdy old Boston. 'Peace, peace,' the soft bells said. 'We are at peace . . .'

Forbes' technique of conveying strong feelings through description of exterior behavior typifies her preference for understatement, and serves to soften harsh reality, to avoid sentimentality, and to heighten genuine emotion. Her style creates a tension between subject matter and the language restraining it. When Rab is dying, all we are told about Johnny is that he "walked disconsolately about the chamber. He looked out the window. He picked up a pewter candlestick and examined the maker's mark." When Rab called him, "Johnny went to him, sat on the floor beside his chair and put his hands over Rab's thin ones."

Johnny's inexpressible feelings echo through the simple, staccato sentences and the fragments in which he responds to Rab: "I'll take good care of it.' . . . 'Anything.'. . 'I'll go.' "

So while *Johnny Tremain* is not a classic in Eliot's full sense of the term, it does display many of the qualities Eliot enumerates as essential characteristics. Both in its use of history *per se* and in its aesthetic dimension, the novel indicates the greatness, importance, and, I will wager, the permanence of its author in the field of historical fiction for children, particularly that of the American Revolution. Forbes has accomplished what Thackeray was desirous of doing, made history interesting and alive for her readers:

> Why shall History go on kneeling to the end of time? I am for having her rise up off her knees, and take a natural posture: not to be forever performing cringes and congees like a court chamberlain, and shuffling backwards out of doors in the presence of the sovereign. In a word, I would have History familiar rather than heroic . . .

Johnny Tremain offers history familiar rather than heroic; and no other juvenile novel of revolutionary Boston, before or since, has been so widely read nor so well-beloved. (pp. 91-4)

> M. Sarah Smedman, "Esther Forbes' 'Johnny Tremain': Authentic History, Classic Fiction," in Touchstones: Reflections on the Best in Children's Literature, Vol. I, edited by Perry Nodelman, Children's Literature Association, 1985, pp. 83-95.

John Rowe Townsend

[*Johnny Tremain*] is a true historical novel, concerned with actual historical events; and it seems to me (though not for this reason) that it has true classic quality. I have the impression that the author may even have known she was writing a classic; for *Johnny Tremain* has an air of absolute sureness and solidity; like one of its redoubtable New Englanders it knows where it is going and knows it will be treated with respect. (pp. 161-62)

A feature of the book is its strong pictorial quality. The best set pieces not merely are colourful but have a powerful sense of historical occasion, as in the description of the 'great scarlet dragon' of the British brigade, seen first with its head resting on Boston Common, and later marching off on its thousands of feet. The book's main fault is a slight lack of cohesion between its two components: the personal story of Johnny, the smart apprentice whose expectations are dashed by injury, and the broad general subject of the rebellion. The first few chapters might be the start of quite a different kind of book. But the strengths far outweigh this weakness. And there is a fine sense of fair play in the recognition that men of all persuasions are good, bad and indifferent; in the willing acknowledgement that the crowds who sullenly watch the scarlet dragon are all Englishmen, fighting for English liberty. (p. 162)

In the years immediately after the Second World War, American historical fiction for young people stood in the shadow of Esther Forbes's *Johnny Tremain. . . . Johnny*

Tremain was the novel that, above all others, was known and respected by everyone who had even the slightest acquaintance with the field. In 1976, however, it was damned by the historian Christopher Collier for allegedly embodying an old-fashioned interpretation of the American Revolution. . . .

As a British commentator, I have to observe that *Johnny Tremain,* though undoubtedly inspirational, does not seem to me to be one-sided. But a war so complex in its social, political and economic causes will obviously bear more than one interpretation and more than one fictional approach. After thirty years' change in attitudes, something like *My Brother Sam is Dead* (1974), which Christopher Collier wrote in collaboration with his brother James Lincoln Collier, was bound to come. *My Brother Sam* presents, to a generation of young people no longer expected to respond with simple patriotism to the inspirational, an unromantic picture of the war, and counts the cost of victory in terms of individual grief and suffering and the tearing apart of families. (p. 205)

> *John Rowe Townsend, "Past into Present: 'Johnny Tremain'" and "After 'Johnny Tremain',"* in his Written for Children: An Outline of English-Language Children's Literature, *third revised edition, J. B. Lippincott, 1987, pp. 161-62, 205-10.*

Hamida Bosmajian

In Esther Forbes's *Johnny Tremain* the "Sons of Liberty" do not call themselves the "Founding Fathers"; their story, in world or text, begins parthogenetically with an idea, free of biological origin, family ties and dynastic allegiances—an American myth of origin. Only in times to come will that idea be personified in the militant virgin images of Columbia or the Statue of Liberty. It is, therefore, consistent with the values of the novel that Johnny Tremain, too, is a fatherless and motherless child seeking a community of men who declare themselves the champions of Liberty, her freeborn sons who refuse to be enslaved. But Johnny perceives more than heroic postures; he learns that the rebels are political and morally ambiguous men. (p. 53)

The theme of the orphan or abandoned child who becomes a liberator of the oppressed is a familiar archetype, but in *Johnny Tremain* a *group* of people feel themselves collectively abandoned and abused and seek to find the means to liberate themselves by collective efforts rather than through a redeemer-hero. In this the novel is genuinely American, as "we the people" discover discourse and means to define a new community. The mode of the hero and his quest must, therefore, be projected through displacements, not only because of the novel's historical and psychological realism, but also because the traditional concept of the hero goes counter to democratic values. This does not mean that archetypal images and moments, recalling the heroic quest, are absent; they are in disguise, particularly in relation to Johnny, whose youthful process of individuation leaves him at the end on the threshold of possible heroic action so that "a man can stand up".

Forbes's narrative point of view enhances the visibility of

the patterns of myth and romance as subtext to Johnny's "low mimetic mode," as Frye would call it. The novel is not written in the individualistic, a-historical and atomizing first-person point of view so favored in contemporary fictions for young readers. The third-person point of view centers on Johnny's consciousness through the language of an adult observer who is both distant and close to her subject as she tends to his development in the context of the historical-political community. History and the archetypes of tradition shape Johnny's individuation. Moreover, the future that is Forbes's historical present in 1942 is foreshadowed for the young reader through Johnny's situation, as she herself admits in her Newbery Award acceptance speech:

> The twentieth-century boys and girls are by the very fact of war closer now spiritually, psychologically, to this earlier generation. Quite suddenly and clearly I saw what I wanted to try to do. Today the boys Johnny's age are not yet in the armed forces, but many of them will soon be and many will lose or have lost older brothers. So I let Johnny lose Rab. I also wanted to show that these earlier boys were conscious of what they were fighting for and that it was something which they believed was worth more than their own lives. And to show that many of the issues at stake in this war are the same as in the earlier one. We are still fighting for simple things "that a man can stand up."

Today, such intentionality calls for critique. *Johnny Tremain* teaches acceptance of the notion that young men must be prepared to give their lives for causes vaguely understood through simplistically formulated slogans. Yet, as we will see, Forbes is aware of the ambiguity in her intent, for her choice of several important images suggests a language of flaw and fault that implies a critique or at least a problematizing of events and characters. A careful observer of human realities, she knows that the crucible of personal and collective individuation may well be cracked, that the apple of green innocence may contain the worm, and that the artist's hand may be crippled even if the surgeon's knife crudely attempts to set it straight, as in the case of Johnny.

Aside from the censored irony that not only the young hero's friend, but he himself may die, Forbes's well-crafted tale also has unintended fissures, foremost among them the institution of slavery accepted by the Sons of Liberty who call themselves, metaphorically, "enslaved" by the British. Through Forbes's voice, Johnny reflects on the eve of the Revolution: "French slaves to the north of us, Spanish slaves to the south of us. Only English colonies are allowed to taste the forbidden fruit of liberty—we who grew up under England. Johnny thought of James Otis's words. Upholding the torch of liberty—which had been lighted on the fires of England". The real slaves remain marginalized, a crack in the crucible the colonists themselves were conscious of in their fight for liberty and independence.

Since her narrative point of view centers on Johnny, whose experience, knowledge and insight are limited because of his youth, Forbes can background such issues as she devel-

Forbes with her dog Sir Tristam in 1937.

ops her main character. Unlike the heroic quest which moves through the stages of departure, initiation, and return, Johnny's secular, low mimetic growth process follows the Jungian paradigm as Edinger delineates it in *Ego and Archetype.* With no memory of the state of "original wholeness", Johnny individuates from his self-inflation as the gifted silversmith apprentice, to alienation as an unwanted and crippled outcast, to integration as an individual in a new community that is collectively open-ended as it faces the challenges of the future when Johnny will continue to realize his potential, unless he dies in battle. Even though the values of his quest become aligned with those of the Age of Enlightenment, Johnny is surrounded by characters who not only have their own interesting psychologies, but project definite symbolic relations to Johnny as anima or shadow projections.

Shadow, anima, and animus are not exclusive to the modes of myth and romance but are also visible in the low mimetic and ironic modes in literature, art and popular culture. A person's opposite gender is projected through the anima or animus, the woman or man within. Johnny is, therefore, guided or handicapped by young women who at first glance appear to be anima stereotypes such as the elfin sprite, the "dark lady" and the "good girl," but who

reveal in the course of the narrative personalities complicated enough to make each the center of her own story. As anima figures they project and act out problems and desires that Johnny shares. Given the "man's world" of **Johnny Tremain,** Johnny's shadow projections, his potential alter egos, are even more important. How Johnny becomes at least preconsciously aware of his shadow signifies the degree of his maturation at the end. (pp. 53-6)

The anima figures are: Isannah, Master Lapham's granddaughter, a potential coquette whose selfhood is lost; Lavinia, the dark and intelligent beauty who not only beckons Johnny to identify himself with his mother's heritage, but also awakens his first sexual yearnings; Priscilla (Cilla) Lapham, Isannah's sister, the loving, patient and reasonable companion for Johnny's future. His shadow manifests itself through: Jehu, the unindividuated pet slave of John Hancock; Dove, the fellow apprentice who becomes Johnny's nemesis; Rab, the printer rebel, whose seductive personality draws Johnny into the rebels' cause. Lavinia and Rab appear mysterious to Johnny; they arouse his anger and his love beyond what he can understand. But in the end he lets them go.

The process of individuation includes the moment where

the individual experiences "the encounter with the self ", usually at the moment when all seems lost. For Johnny, too, the encounter occurs during the deepest alienation from himself and the world. His hand, scalded and crippled by the molten silver spilling through the cracked crucible, has made him useless as an apprentice. Unemployed and rejected by everyone, he is still too proud to accept the newspaper route of the *Boston Observer*. Filled with self-pity, he goes to his mother's grave, weeping for himself before he falls asleep:

> He sat up suddenly wide awake. The moon had seemingly come close and closer to him. He could see the coats of arms, the winged death's heads, on the slate stones about him. He was so wide awake he felt someone must have called his name. His ears were straining to hear the next words. What was it his mother had said so long ago? If there was nothing left and God Himself had turned away his face, then, and only then, Johnny was to go to Mr. Lyte. In his ears rang his mother's sweet remembered accents. Surely, for one second, between sleeping and waking, he had seen her dear face, loving, gentle, intelligent, floating towards him through the moonlight on Copp's Hill.

The father has averted his face from the boy child, but the future son of liberty is comforted by the transcendent mother who, as we know from folktales and myths, will guide her child from beyond the grave. The approaching moon blends with the floating maternal face and suggests the healing round of the self. But the self does not offer to the alienated ego a road map to self-integration. Therefore, in following the advice of the mother to go to Mr. Lyte, Johnny seems to get into worse trouble when Lyte accuses him of stealing the heirloom silver cup and has him arrested and thrown into jail with the expectation that Johnny will be hung. Ironically, engraved on the cup is the Lyte family crest, "an eye rising from the sea," a half circle promising wholeness. The second half of the round, however, is visualized right after Johnny aligns himself politically: "And the strange sun rising in the west. A sun that was to illumine a world to come". The risen sun is not visualized in the novel, appropriate for the threshold stage of Johnny's development towards being an individual who is both separate from and integrated in the collective history of his time.

John Hancock's slave Jehu and Mrs. Lapham's sickly but seductively beautiful little daughter Isannah survive by surrendering their self-hood for the pleasure of others. Their growth is arrested; they are impersonations rather than persons. Johnny will reject these infantile images of anima and shadow, though he never knows why. The tiny slave comes "mincing in, a glitter of bright colors" who repeats, "like a parrot", what he has been trained to say. Johnny despises him, but does not realize that Jehu's way of physically surviving necessitates a total loss of self by living exclusively for the pleasure of others. That Forbes is aware of this self-destructive defense is evident in her more fully realized portrait of Isannah, whose mother defines her as unfit to live. Isannah is an elfin child with golden hair, amoral, selfish and unpredictable in her affections or revulsions. . . . It comes as no surprise that La-

vinia intends her to be an actress, a profession Lavinia herself seems to have fantasized about.

Jehu and, in more detail, Isannah project the possibility of survival of the ego as pleasing aesthetic object, a temptation acute for those who feel abandoned. Johnny, however, is neither vain nor does he aim to please, especially not persons in authority. His defiant, even unruly attitude maintains for himself at least the appearance of independence and self-reliance, even when he has nothing and compliance might lead to easy acceptability. Jehu and Isannah manifest behavior he rejects. Preconsciously he realizes the consequences when an immature but needy ego becomes subservient to the pleasure of others. (pp. 56-8)

The least likeable young person in the novel is the sixteen-year-old apprentice Dove. Envious of Johnny's privileged position in the shop, Dove hands him the cracked crucible wherein Johnny will melt the silver for John Hancock's sugar basin. While the narrator describes the "swinish Dove" (an oxymoronic combination!) as overweight, "whitish, flaccid and parasitic"—language that does not critique Johnny's verbal abuse of the apprentice—she also tells us that he "was lonely and admired Johnny as well as served him. Johnny preferred to bully him". Johnny, in contrast, is a "rather skinny boy, neither large nor small for fourteen" . . . with "light eyes, a wry mouth, and fair lank hair" who despises the sometimes fawning but usually underhanded Dove, the instrument of his nemesis.

On the day of the accident Master Lapham, no longer at his craft but concerned exclusively with his immortal soul, scolds Johnny for lording it over Dove: " 'We're all poor worms. You are getting above yourself—like I tried to point out to you. God is going to send you a dire punishment for your pride' ". The conventional images and themes of "pride before fall" are portentously clustered for the young reader, but there is also a more subtle statement of Johnny's flaw. The problem is not that he exercises his real talent perhaps prematurely, but that the assignment leads him to excessive self-inflation. His upbringing instilled in him "that working on the Sabbath was against the law as well as against all his religious training. He might very well go to the stocks or to Hell for it". It is significant that Forbes says "training" rather than "faith," for Johnny and the eighteenth century deists seek the secular city, not the community of saints. Yet the Faustian image of selling one's soul for a trivial thing, such as a sugar basin, is underscored by little Isannah who, with the cat in her lap, watches him witchlike and says firmly as he prepares the crucible: "Johnny's going to Hell." While he will not lose his soul, the crippling of the hand will lead him through a temporary and personal hell.

The crucible breaks, the silver scalds his hand. . . . (p. 59)

Instead of sending for Dr. Warren the surgeon, Mrs. Lapham calls the midwife, old Gran' Hopper, and allows Johnny to recover in the birth and death room, where he lies half conscious until the day when his bandages come off and he is born into his new life: "He was utterly unprepared for the sight of his hand when finally it was unwrapped and lay in the midwife's aproned lap". Thumb and palm had grown together. (p. 60)

Now the lowest in the household, Johnny has to accept the mockery of Dove, but vows to Mr. Lapham: " 'If I have to, I'll wait' " " 'ten years to get that Dove' ". Eventually, however, Johnny's treatment of Dove reveals how well he can deal with his shadow. Not only would revenge against the miserable Dove be cowardly, but the impulse must be abandoned for the sake of the larger cause, the collective one that passes through the hybris of rebellion to a future based on law. He meets Dove again during the controlled lawlessness of the Boston Tea Party where Dove loots tea in order to sell it later. Since everyone is disguised as "Indians"—an interesting displacement of blame—Johnny, pointing to Dove, suggests to Rab " 'he swim good,' " whereupon Rab heaves Dove into the harbor for a swim in the tea. Johnny's rage against Dove is now deflected: Dove is violating the rules of the Tea Party, which was not a looter's free-for-all, and the carnival atmosphere allows Johnny to act out his aggressions in a harmless way. Moreover, swimming is a very positive activity for Johnny, for only then does he feel free of his handicap. Finally, Rab, his friend and shadow, carries out the revenge, not just because he is physically stronger than Johnny, but also because "bold Johnny Tremain" displaces his aggressive feelings through Rab.

After he has started his work for the *Boston Observer,* Johnny also works in the British military's stable to gather information from the soldiers and from Dove, now a Tory stable boy. His feelings about Dove have changed: "Dove was garrulous, indolent, complaining, boastful, but it hurt Johnny when the boys bullied him and his masters beat him. He was like a man who owns a dull mean dog. He may punish it himself, but resents it if any one else punishes it. For better or worse, Dove was now his own private property". Dove's low self-esteem, arrogance, self-pity and cowardice are negative qualities that Johnny fights in himself, but he has come far enough not to maintain his ego aggressively against the shadow mediator who inadvertently helps him to his new, exciting, and meaningful life.

Lavinia Lyte, whose seductive dark beauty, coldness, and calculating intelligence are characteristic of the anima as *femme fatale,* stirs Johnny's first romantic longings from the moment she returns from England, though he is always critical of her even when he waits in the Lyte courtyard to catch a glimpse of her. Through Johnny's eyes, we generally get an unfavorable picture of her, but Lavinia carries the burden of her past and is deeply bonded to her father. . . . (pp. 60-1)

For generations the Lyte women were named Lavinia, including Johnny's mother. Symbolically, Lavinia stands for the past, a past Johnny will reject with one definitive gesture. Lavinia's haughty attitude blocks Johnny from realizing his attraction and possible bonding with the Lytes. It is Lavinia who finally clarifies for him the mystery of his father's identity, but by then Johnny has already made his decision. After Lavinia and her father flee from the mob, Johnny and Cilla, the latter wanting to secure the family silver, go into the Lytes' house where Johnny dis-

covers in the family Bible that he is merchant Lyte's grandnephew and that his father's name apparently was Latour. He cuts the family genealogy pages from the Bible and wonders, a few moments later, why he has done so: "Slowly tearing each sheet to ribbons, he fed them to the fire upon the hearth". He even refuses the silver cup of his mother that Cilla offers him and leaves the house with the thought "that the dead should not look at the living—nor the living too long upon the dead".

Just before Lavinia returns to England to marry a lord, she tells Johnny that his father, a naval surgeon, took the name Latour because he was embarrassed to be a prisoner of war: "That's why your name Tremain meant nothing to us". But Johnny's two French names are very meaningful: La-tour implies journey and circle, Tre-main suggests three-handedness—a sound hand, a scarred and twisted hand, a hand set straight. Finally, Lavinia tells him that, technically, she is "Aunt Lavinia" to him, and with that label "the queer hold she had on him for a year snapped". Lavinia, though belonging to the past, liberates him from it and, by labelling herself, breaks the spell of her influence.

The anima figures of Isannah, Lavinia, and Cilla form a cluster as Isannah becomes Lavinia's companion and Cilla her maid. Cilla is Johnny's as yet unripe future; she is loyal and reasonable without surrendering her person. He cannot take her for granted, as is made very clear by the fact that she is wooed by Rab. She, however, decides that Priscilla Silsbee is a poor name, "but Priscilla Tremain is a fine name". Jokingly, she and Johnny talk about names and he hints that she will be one day Priscilla Tremain. "Cilla did not answer, but she reached up through the foliage of the tree and picked a little green apple. She gave it to him. . . . Johnny put the apple in his pocket. He'd keep it forever". Obviously this playful edenic image—the apple as sign of generation and mortality—signifies that both are sexually immature. Johnny puts the apple on his window sill to ripen, but when Rab bites into it and finds that it is wormy, the apple suddenly becomes a symbol of Rab's premature death.

Thus, when Johnny thinks "he had been a fool to think of the apple as a symbol of himself and Cilla," the image becomes even more meaningful. Rab Silsbee, who will fall during the first shots of the revolution, is Johnny's most important peer companion. Rab is rescuer and deceiver, mystery and inspiration, friend, teacher, and trickster.

During his time of alienation, Johnny drifts one day into the printer's shop where the apprentice Rab was "standing at the counter in his leather apron and full white shirt, his thoughtful face framed in hair, black and straight like an Indian's". Here and throughout her portrayal of Rab, Forbes suggests the convention and problematical archetype of the shadow as the hero's dark-skinned companion, a pervasive image in American narratives from *The Leatherstocking Tales* to "Miami Vice." The ethnic stereotype through which the human being is perceived is what makes this symbolization problematical. Here, however, Rab is defined as an Indian only by simile, but he exhibits throughout the story the "instinctual" forces of power, sex, and death characteristic of the type. If such a shadow figure is projected positively, as Rab is here, the "primitive" aspects are displaced and the shadow's energies become meaningful actions. The shadow, as von Franz points out, "becomes hostile only when he is ignored or misunderstood". Rab sees everything and says little. He is the first one to ask Johnny intelligently about his hand, and Johnny talks to him, "able to stand aside from his problems—see himself". Till the end Rab remains a powerful though mysteriously ambiguous role model for Johnny. (pp. 61-2)

Rab is the revolutionary waiting for his event, but he also urges Johnny's growing political alignment, though it will never be as strong as Rab's commitment. For Rab the British are "the enemy," targets of war, but for Johnny, even after he has accepted the cause of the colonists, the British remain human beings with whom the colonists have a disagreement that, unfortunately, will be settled by force. Forbes's psychological accuracy is very convincing as she describes the ambiguity of the moment when a person crystallizes his energies for a cause, when alignment becomes commitment through the spell of political persuasion. The Sons of Liberty meet in the printing shop's attic loft, a loft that does not store memories. Instead, "there was an odd thing about this attic and that was the number of chairs stored there," chairs for the secret club that had "hatched much treason" as the Tories called it. (p. 63)

Johnny hears that the fight is for the eventual liberation of all oppressed—French peasants, Russian serfs, "and all those German states. Are they nothing but soldiers? Will no one show them the rights of good citizens?" This thematic flash forward reveals much of the subtext of the novel, especially in the reference to German militarism, less significant in relation to Frederick the Great of Prussia (1740-86) than to Hitler's soldiers. To defeat them, a new generation of Yankee soldiers must come forth. Rab and Johnny are only precursors in the fight for liberty. They and their successors will need to be educated to give their lives for the cause. When Otis turns directly to Rab and addresses through him the young that will die in war, the tradition of young men being educated for death is affirmed:

> "Some will give their lives. All the years of their maturity. All the children they never live to have. The serenity of old age. To die so young is more than merely dying; it is to lose so large a part of life."

> Rab was looking straight at Otis. His arms were folded across his chest. His head flung back a little. His lips parted as though he would speak, but he did not . . .

> James Otis was on his feet, his head close against the rafters that cut down into the attic, making it the shape of a tent. Otis put out his arms.

> "It is all so much simpler than you think," he said. He lifted his hands and pushed against the rafters.

> "We give all we have, lives, property, safety, skills . . . [W]e fight, we die, for a simple thing. Only that a man can stand up."

With a curt nod, he was gone.

If Johnny is being politically aligned here, Rab becomes ecstatically committed, through the oratory of Otis for whom the house is too small. Rab's face and posture image a heroic *eros* and *thanatos,* but Johnny still is primarily interested in how Otis affects Rab. Yet it is Johnny who, that evening, in response to Rab's questions, repeats Otis's "so that a man can stand up," defining the vague slogan once more. Not the dying, but the standing up is foregrounded.

We never see Johnny holding a musket in the War of Independence, though he is able to get one for Rab, who also never kills anyone. As hostilities are about to begin, Johnny experiences a moment when he is glad that his hand is crippled: "He would never have to face the round eye of death at the end of a musket. For days he felt his own inadequacy. Was the 'bold Johnny Tremain' really a coward at heart?" He had witnessed the execution of a British deserter who preferred the farmer's life to soldiering. Johnny helped him desert by giving him one of the blue farmers' smocks his mother had made for him in exchange for the musket. He sees it riddled with holes and wonders if Rab ever thought that this, too, can be a soldier's death.

Johnny's historical context pressures him to prepare himself to fight heroically, though his youth does not oblige him to do so. Doctor Warren, who will attempt surgically to set his hand straight, tells him that Rab is going to die: "'Rab played a man's part. Look that you do the same'". Johnny's last words to Rab promise to inform the Silsbees of Rab's death, but Johnny's "I'll go" also signifies his commitment. Rab approves: "Then Rab began to smile. Everything he had never put in words was in that smile". Johnny is resolved and without grief at the end. The death of Rab is not personal, it has been displaced for the cause "so that a man can stand up."

At the end, Johnny waits for Dr. Warren's knife, not to become an artist again but to fire a musket. As he waits, a group of battle-weary Yankees march by; "the long horizontal light of the sinking sun struck into their faces and made them seem much alike". They remind him of Rab and in a prayer, expressed and thereby universalized by the narrator, they become an immortal type: "Please God, out of this New England soil such men should forever rise up ready when the need came. The one generation after the other". God does not seem to avert His face now, though this last solar image, the rays of the setting sun striking the community of rebels, suggests the likelihood of death, especially in contrast to the earlier rising sun motifs.

But Johnny the soldier, killing and perhaps dying, is not part of the story. The suffering of war—the wounded and the dead, the widowed and the orphaned—are not included. There is only an illusory conclusive moment as the promise of history lies before Johnny, indeterminable and vague, a theme as old as the promise made to Aeneas, who never found his Rome but who is forever seen plunging his sword into the throat of his enemy at the end of the *Aeneid*. Like his classical predecessors, Johnny is not a blind follower; he made his decision step by step. At the end he "felt free, light, unreal, and utterly alone". He is ready for "today is today." He has now enough courage to face immediate physical pain and then, if his hand can be straightened, join the struggle for a new community. However, tomorrow, as the phrase "today is today" implies, might also be different, might be brighter or darker than today. Leaving Johnny, then, as a son of liberty at the threshold of a new time, unaware yet of the pity and horror of war, Forbes's text empowers the convention of the heroic gesture taken by generations of inexperienced young men resolved in good faith to do battle. (pp. 64-6)

Hamida Bosmajian, "The Cracked Crucible of 'Johnny Tremain'," in The Lion and the Unicorn, *Vol. 13, 1989, pp. 53-66.*

Marie-Louise Gay

1952-

Canadian author and illustrator of picture books.

Major works include *Lizzy's Lion* (written by Dennis Lee, 1984), *Moonbeam on a Cat's Ear* (1986), *Rainy Day Magic* (1987), *Angel and the Polar Bear* (1988).

A creator of picture books in English and French that characteristically portray the daydreams and imaginative play of small children, Gay is often praised for her originality, inventiveness, humor, artistic skill, and understanding of preschoolers and their world. Called "the mistress of 'what if'" by critic Joan McGrath, Gay blends fantasy and reality to describe how her young protagonists, boys and girls alone or with other children, launch themselves into amazing adventures that take them to such places as the sky or under the sea before they return home. These characters, whom Gay usually depicts in a cartoonlike style that stresses their large bodies, broad faces, tiny limbs, and spiked black hair, are often taken from their familiar surroundings into situations that require them to confront—and surmount—surprising transformations. For example, the dauntless five-year-old heroine of *Angel and the Polar Bear* comes face to face with a huge polar bear that emerges from the refrigerator in her kitchen; although terrified at first, Angel eventually befriends him and plays dominoes with him while they eat bananas. Though her characters always return to reality after their exploits, Gay subtly introduces souvenirs of their imaginary journeys; in *Rainy Day Magic*, the story of how the friends Victor and Joey meet a tiger, a snake, and a whale after they are banished to the basement for being too noisy, Joey appears in the final frame with a pink starfish in her hair from the underwater portion of her adventure. Gay writes her stories in verse and prose noted for its simplicity and directness and illustrates her books in watercolor, pen and ink, pencil and colored pencil, pastels, and dyes. Celebrated for the energy, freshness, and expressionistic quality of her art, Gay is acknowledged for the bright colors and attention to detail of her pictures as well as for her distinctive use of perspective and borders; she often extends her drawings beyond their usual confines to provide viewers with parallel stories or additional dimensions.

Gay studied design, drawing, and animation in Canada and the United States, sold cartoon strips and illustrations to magazines, worked as a graphic designer and art director, and contributed pictures to educational books for children before writing and illustrating her first works, picture books in French. She received special acclaim for her art in the popular *Lizzy's Lion,* the first picture book by well known Canadian poet Dennis Lee. In this story in verse, small Lizzy is saved from the robber who attempts to steal her piggybank by the lion she keeps in her bedroom; after the lion eats the robber, Lizzy and the lion go back to bed. Gay illustrates this tongue-in-cheek drama with illustra-

tions noted for capturing the humorous exaggeration of the verses. She departs from her characteristic depiction of youngsters in imaginary worlds with *Fat Charlie's Circus,* a picture book which deals with the emotions and reassurance of children. In this story, a small boy determined to be a circus performer decides to perform a diving act from the tallest tree in his yard and becomes afraid when he reaches the top. His sympathetic grandmother sees his plight and climbs the tree, saying that she will jump with him; in helping his grandmother down, Charlie conquers his fear. In addition to her picture books, Gay is the author of the puppet play *Bonne fête, Willy* (1989), which she adapted in picture book form as *Willy Nilly* (1990), as well as a series of five board books in French which are published under the title of "Drôle d'école"; she is also a sculptor and a designer of clothing and sets for films. In 1985, Gay became the first author and illustrator to win the Canada Council Children's Literature Prize in both the English and French-language categories; she received the prizes for her illustrations for *Lizzy's Lion* as the English-language winner and for the series "Drôle d'école" as the French-language winner. She was also awarded the Amelia Frances-Howard Gibbon Medal from the Canadian Library Association for *Moonbeam on a Cat's Ear* in 1987, an honor she also received for *Rainy Day Magic* in 1988; in addition, *Rainy Day Magic* won the Governor General's Award in the same year. Gay has also received several awards for her fine art and graphic design work.

AUTHOR'S COMMENTARY

[The following excerpt is from an interview by Marie Davis.]

One look at the picture books of Marie-Louise Gay says it all: she sees things differently. The originality of her perspective is expressed in cartoon-like illustrations that have no respect for either the confines of the tidy page or the reserve of the straight line. Daring in form and generous in detail, the illustrations are restless—alive with the irrepressible energy of both their whimsical subjects and their risible creator. (p. 52)

Davis: As a child, were you an habitual scribbler or doodler—did you decorate your pages all the time?

Gay: I started doodling all the time around fifteen or sixteen; before that I think I was just like any child—not more artistic than any other.

Davis: Were you able to take art in college?

Gay: No, I never took art until I was almost nineteen, except for the ordinary art classes you had in school—nothing specialized. I just didn't have an artistic bent. But then I suddenly discovered it around the age of sixteen. From sixteen to eighteen I started drawing a lot—so I wasn't a child prodigy at all. But once I started, I really never stopped. At the time I was going to Jean de Brébeuf, a private college, and I didn't know where I was going, so I was getting really bad marks. But, I was doodling and drawing a lot and, finally, around the end of the year my mother suggested "Well, why don't we try going to an art school?" because there was no hope. I thought of being a history teacher, but I have no memory at all. I didn't know what I was doing; it was a bad part of my life. And then I went to this art school, which was actually not a real art school, it was a graphic design school: *The Institute of Graphic Arts of Montreal.* I really loved it because it was easy for me. But I think I was too restrained because it was graphic arts—really technical stuff.

So a year after I switched to *L'École du Musée des Beaux Arts de Montréal* where I spent two years in animation. There I got my first real art classes, with models and everything. At the same time, I was doing a lot of cartoony things, so I said, well, I'm going to try to sell my cartoons—you know, those cartoon strips with three images. I just went around to magazines until one finally bought some. And after that I just started publishing. I was doing editorial illustration and stuff like that while I was finishing those two years.

So I learnt a lot by myself. I would come back from school and just get into illustration. I'm really self-taught in that sense; I didn't get enough classes.

Davis: But then you went to San Francisco?

Gay: Yes, but I went when I was 26; I had already been publishing for four or five years in magazines and I had been doing a bit of graphic design. I decided to do one year in San Francisco at *The Academy of Art College,* which is a really good illustration school. I just loved it there. At the same time, of course—since I can never stop—I went around looking for work. When I started getting work there I decided I wouldn't leave, so I stayed for three years. I just took classes the first year I was there and then kept on going for three years working at editorial stuff again and educational books for children. Then I finally decided to come back to Montreal.

Davis: It surprises me that you didn't draw or doodle a lot as a child.

Gay: A lot of people are surprised. But I just wasn't interested in art or drawing at all. But one thing I was doing that has a real connection with this is *reading.* I learned to read before I went to school and I am an avid reader—I need a fix; I have to read all the time. And I have been like that since I was five years old. (pp. 53-4)

I just read all the time. I probably wasn't drawing because I was reading. To me, drawing when you're a child or teenager is more like a time of meditation. With me, I think reading took up that time. My parents would bring me to the library every week-end. And I think that's what probably didn't let me draw—I just didn't feel the need to draw. (p. 54)

Davis: What about childhood memories—do you have any ones that, for whatever reason, stand out, or ones that you're particularly fond of ?

Gay: Well, I think a lot of the memories I do have of my childhood—they keep popping up at all sorts of different moments—but what I mostly think of are the trips we used to make, because we travelled all over Canada and the United States by car. That's what I would call the most memorable things of my childhood: those trips and reading books. And what happens is that some of my books are based on ideas that are very close to me, things that I lived in my childhood. But they're not *extraordinary* things. **Rainy day magic,** for example, was a book that came from remembering afternoons in Vancouver in our basement. In Vancouver it was always pouring rain; my sister and I would play in the basement and get bored and always wish something would happen. That just popped up in my mind all of a sudden and I realized, well, I could do that now. I could make something happen. So, I just invented the story from that. It's not a very important childhood incident, really. But the boredom was an important incident, in a certain sense. For children boredom is *very* pressing. So probably it had a bigger impact than I thought. It's just snatches from my childhood that come back to me—little bits.

Davis: Is **Fat Charlie's circus** that way—based on a snippet of memory?

Gay: The first idea for **Fat Charlie's circus** actually was that I wanted to do a book about the circus, because I really love the circus. And then I tied it in with my grandmother ["I think part of the grandmother in **Fat Charlie,**" says Gay, "is how my grandmother would have liked to have been."] and it just came together. Maybe it will happen to me, one day, where I will get the idea for the whole story at once . . .bang! But I don't remember anything really special that I could tell in one complete story—maybe that's why I invent so much. Maybe because I don't remember having something really incredibly exciting happen to me.

Davis: So you're filling up a void?

Gay: Well, yes, maybe that's it. You see, really people's lives are quite *calm*. And it seems to me that the child's imagination wants more than that. I think as adults we want more than that also. We want excitement, we want adventure, we want to *fall in love*. And it *does* happen, but it doesn't happen *all the time*. And I think it's the same thing with kids: they want that difference, that excitement. We all have a need for flying away with our imaginations. I do it on paper.

Davis: What are your drawing habits? Do you carry sketchbooks around with you and doodle in them?

Gay: I always have some paper around and a little pad or something on me. I think I mostly draw at my table now. I used to do a lot of sketching outside, but I just don't seem to have time anymore to do that (which is too bad actually). I'll often take very, very tiny visual notes about things that I'll notice like the edge of a carpet or a little kid who just did something funny, or the position he was in. I just find that kind of thing really intriguing.

Davis: You're very good at that. In **Rainy day magic,** for instance, there's a crayon that has just been squished by a tricycle and it's at that point where it has snapped and has left a drag of colour across the floor—the pages of your books are always crammed with details like that and this has become a hallmark of your work.

Gay: Well, I don't have to take sketches of that—with my kids around, I've got them all over my floors. But I think I have a very strong visual memory, compared to anything else I have in my head. I forget names and I don't know any phone numbers at all—except mine and my boyfriend's office number. But visual memory I have. That I know. It's just snap, snap, snap all the time. I remember once going to do a reading way up north in Kapuskasing or somewhere like that and going for a supper in the parish hall with all the people from the area, and then going to the bathroom and seeing the most *beautiful* bathroom tile I have ever seen in my life. I just adored the pattern. So I took out my pen and stood there doing a drawing of the pattern, just in case, one day, I'd need it somewhere and I'd just look through my book and say, "Oh, that's nice," and I'd use it as a detail in an illustration.

So, I take that type of note, but then I take a lot of written notes for ideas I have all of a sudden for a story. It may not even be a story; it could be just an incident—a tiny little incident. To give you an example, I wrote a puppet play, **Bonne fête, Willy,** last year and it's playing right now at *The National Arts Centre*. I brought Gabriel, my eldest son, to see it, and he was quite excited about it. When he came home, he immediately went upstairs and

got his hand puppets—a rabbit and a wolf—and he crawled under the blanket on the livingroom couch, stuck his two hands out and began doing a little puppet show there. All of a sudden, he lifts the blanket up and says "Bonne fête, Lapin!" An incident like that I'll write down and try to remember. And then maybe in a book it'll just show up in the corner of a story where you'll have one of the kids who crawls underneath a blanket, does a quick puppet show and then crawls back out. Because sometimes when I'm really getting into a story, into the drawing part—the part where for three months I'm really just doing the drawings and where I develop all the outside or inside elements, everything but the story which is there already—that's when I use ideas like that for a sub-story. Because of my involvement with puppets, I was thinking of having puppets behind the scenes for my next story, *Willy Nilly.* So, those are the notes I take.

Davis: What makes a story or an illustration really interesting for you?

Gay: Illustrations that are detailed, that are exciting, that leap off the page, and that you feel are moving. This would probably describe my illustrations a bit because I like them to move, and I like the book to become a receptor, you know, of that movement.

Davis: I often feel with **Angel and the polar bear** that if you tipped it on the diagonal everything would fall out.

Gay: All the water would fall out! That's what I like in illustrations. But I also like really *calm* illustrations; I like Chris Van Allsburg, for example. *Polar express* and *Jumanji* I find very exciting graphically, but when you look at them there's a powerful, serene sense to the illustrations. . . . In the text, I want a story that will make me react to it—I'll find it funny, I'll find it sad: it has to touch me. . . . Something that's exciting and that emotionally touches you: that's what I try to get when I write. . . . I want kids to identify with the kids in the story—even if they don't look like those kids, I want them to identify with the feel, the aura around the kids I draw. Fat Charlie is a fat kid, right. Plump with red hair. There's a lot of fat kids and a lot of kids with red hair, but with that combination there's not that many. Still, what I think is important is what Fat Charlie is living in *his* adventure. The fact that he's just breaking the house apart with his *dream*, and the fact that he gets caught in a corner in his own dream—he's stuck, and he's sad and he's anguished about it and I want kids to identify with that. They'll understand what happened to him. Even if they haven't climbed a tree—that's not important. The fact that once he's up there he's afraid people will laugh at him; and he's afraid period—*that's what's important.*

And his grandmother doesn't say, "Get the heck out of that tree!" She just does the same thing he does; she says, "I'm going to jump and I'm going to be famous"—which makes him realize that notion was pretty stupid.

Davis: It's the limits of the imagination that you're touching on there. I find that one of the interesting themes that you develop in your books. (pp. 55-7)

[Gay:] To me a book is a whole. . . . You can have the

best illustrations in the world and if the text is really nothing it's just not a book and vice versa. You have to have both: you have to be able to read a story and *see* the story. (p. 58)

Davis: One of the things that has been said about your work is that you have a children's drawing style of illustration. I'm not so sure about this. Kids' drawings are exaggerated to some extent—the angles tend to be awkward and the proportions and perspective distorted. Do you think that you have a child's drawing style?

Gay: I wouldn't say that at all.

Davis: Have you ever drawn realistically?

Gay: I can. For example, in the classes I took in San Francisco I had very, very realistic drawings to do, you know, perfect renderings of everything. I can do it. But it doesn't interest me at all. I like going crazy with a drawing. But if you look at my drawings and you say, okay, everything's distorted and the kids are fat, you have to look closer. If you look *underneath* those clothes . . . just try to imagine Fat Charlie *naked.* Have you ever tried to imagine that? He has to look like *something:* he has to fill up those clothes. Well, I draw him naked because I have to find out how his body works underneath his clothes. Just imagine him: skinny, skinny legs, big fat belly! Now, that's important to me because as much as you can distort a drawing there is something there that you would feel is wrong if you didn't *see* the body underneath. This is in general; I'm not saying that I keep on drawing Fat Charlie naked all the time! In a way, when people say everything's distorted, they're missing a lot—all the shadows and all the things are real; everything works. I couldn't *not* make it work. But on a different plane it works. In a different world.

Davis: I've noticed with your pictures of animals, like the tiger and the lion, there's an element of realism there, especially with the tiger in *Rainy day magic.*

Gay: In the case of the tiger—and most of the animals in *Rainy day magic*—I used pictures of different tigers just to get the markings right. So there are elements that are realistic in a way. But in other ways they're not. For example, if you look at the face of the tiger, it's much bigger than it should be. Actually, a tiger has a much smaller head, but I don't like small heads, so I've just enlarged it.

Davis: Small heads and small bodies are out.

Gay: Skinny legs, small feet are in! I just like it like that. That's the way I see things. So I do use information like that from pictures of tigers, but I don't copy, obviously.

Davis: The way you *see* things psychologically also interests me. Your books usually center on one theme, with variations—that's the idea of the discovery or invention of something new. That something new is also potentially dangerous. What are you suggesting about the powers of the imagination there?

Gay: I guess, really, that what I'm getting at here is that children *imagine* a hell of a lot of things—that's just part of their world. The borderline between imagination and reality is very, very *thin.* I'm not suggesting at all that it's dangerous. I'm just getting into it as kids get into it, as kids

want to scare themselves. We've all read books by Maurice Sendak where a kid lies in bed all night with a monster in a closet. I think all kids imagine that. There's a phrase—I don't know it in English—*ils se complaisent dans la peur* (they enjoy being afraid). They're scaring themselves or imagining these terrible scenarios where their parents are going to abandon them at the next street. Kids do this. And kids also have the other type of more positive scenario where they're going to be famous, so they imagine from that. They create *enormous* dramas about—what seem to us—very small events. They imagine that there's something else behind an incident. My little boy just lost one of his brand new gloves and he was crying like he was going to die the next day. I was worried and he wouldn't tell me for the longest time why he was crying. You wonder what's *behind* all that. But you'll never know, of course.

That's the beautiful thing about it: we never *do* know, we just sort of have to guess. That's where I start off from: I guess, I ask, "what does that mean?" I might use that as the subject of a book: the glove. What could a kid be imagining? That it was a magic glove? It just seems that children have such a potential in their imaginations.

Davis: In each and every book, though, what happens is that the child imagines this world, invents it or discovers it, and then it leads into something that is dangerous. It's almost as though the world they create through their imaginations is a fragile one, because it's susceptible to their fears. It can be easily destroyed. What I'm trying to get at, too, is whether or not you see this as a natural thing that children do; in other words, that through the safety of play they can confront their fears.

Gay: Oh, definitely. Exactly, that's it. Look at Fat Charlie who wants to be in the circus—this is a very positive thing, but I think that a child in a way knows that he *won't* become a famous circus person right away. He could. But he *knows* there's a possibility he won't. So, in going up into the tree, he's provoking the bad thing to happen. Actually the child understands a lot more than we think.

Davis: What is peculiar to your vision is that the children in your stories seem almost to be saying, "I know there's something bad out there and I'm going to confront it."

Gay: Probably a lot of that is me. People often ask me: "When you write a book, do you think as a child?" I think we just put our adult feelings in a children's book. So if someone should read my books and decide to analyze them, they would probably find out a lot of things that I don't want to know about. The need for confrontation and all the fears are all there from the moment we're born; and they're still there when I'm writing books 37 years later—the *same fears* are there. The thing is, where are they in your body? Are they on the surface of your body, or are they so deep down that they don't show in your life? I have the peculiarity of being a creator—an illustrator, a writer—and those things come out on the surface. So I have a transparent skin, which is sort of frightening.

Davis: One of the things that is central to your vision is that the action of your books takes place either in the absence of grown-ups or in the imagination—most of the time it's both. Do you ever concern yourself with whether or not a book will prove instructive?

Gay: No, I really don't. I think there are things I really want to say in a book, and I appreciate it when children get the "underidea". But, as you know, there's not much in the way of moral endings in my books or happily-ever-after ones.

Davis: So, your characters are never taught things; they invent them or discover them for themselves? I think of poor Charlie sitting up in the tree while night is falling.

Gay: Yes, that's my favourite image in the book. He's there only with his cat. And with his thoughts, of course. He really has learned something, you see. Did you notice in that image there's no mice or anything around the borders—he's *really, really alone.* That's an unconscious thing I did. I just didn't put them in. The feeling of the illustration was that he was alone, alone. (pp. 58-61)

Davis: Your books usually tell of a journey, an incident or a confrontation that almost inevitably symbolizes some kind of growth in understanding. Now, that's measured, it seems, by changing representations of light, and the depiction of doors and windows and roads as well. My question is whether or not the changing light and the depiction of doors, windows, and roads usually corresponds with different levels of a character's understanding and whether or not the roads are symbolic paths to understanding or wisdom. Think of *Fat Charlie's circus* when Charlie is sitting in the tree by himself, surrounded by darkness; in *Rainy day magic* there's darkness and then the characters move, without knowing it, on to the tiger's back; in *Moonbeam on a cat's ear* there's the darkened doorway with Rosie and Toby Toby just standing there staring out into the night together. So that's the changing light that I'm talking about—does that coincide with different levels of a character's understanding of something?

Gay: That's interesting. I guess it's a bit like breathing for me. You need pauses in a book—dramatic pauses in a book that enable you to change the tempo. The time where you're in between two parts of a story is very important because you have something like a changing room in between, you know, where you're thinking, here we are and now what's going to happen. It's a dramatic highlight in a story. But it happens *inside the mind* of a child, where a child realizes that something has happened, so I try to depict it graphically because I can't show the inside of a child's mind. And so in my drawing, if something is going to happen, I will change the tempo of the story. I will either bring it from reality to fantasy, or in *Fat Charlie's circus,* for example, from complete craziness and happiness and daring to an understanding of, boy, am I ever stupid, what am I doing here.

Davis: So, you represent it as the sun having gone down and the lights having gone out. It's often represented by darkness.

Gay: But it doesn't seem to me that it's darkness in the sense of losing all consciousness. I think the darkness means calm to me. To try to illustrate this point I should talk about *Angel and the polar bear* because there is no moment of darkness in *Angel.* To me the moment that would be the equivalent to that darkness is when the polar bear is waddling down the hallway, where he takes up all the space on the page and you see Angel there, a tiny figure. And that to me is the moment when Oh, oh here we go—something is going to go wrong this time, or something is going to happen. That would be the equivalent of a change in how Angel sees things, and there's no darkness there.

Davis: Yes, it's completely white space.

Gay: Yes, and the white space is taking over. There are actually two points in the story where there's a change, a dramatic pause. The other is when they [Angel and the polar bear] are nose-to-nose.

Davis: There's a visual imbalance in that illustration—so perhaps that provides a jolt.

Gay: I would say the real in-betweener in that story is when the polar bear licks his lips and slowly waddles towards the bedroom. And, of course, since I can't help adding a tiny sub-plot, I put a little cat sort of stuck there on the polar bear with his headband on! Not very many people notice that. That to me is like—this word doesn't work very well in English, but in French it's *un clin d'oeil*—when you wink at someone. It's like an inside joke. There's this cat hanging on to the bear as if saying "it's okay, I've got him, I've got him, I'll stop him!" And you have a whole story going on in this one little spot down there, which a lot of kids, I was really surprised to find, haven't noticed because they're so caught up in that big moment of confrontation. So, that comes at the third or fourth level of reading.

Davis: Are all of those details there to spur the child's imagination?

Gay: Yes. They all come in the last stages of drawing. I don't have all these things going on in the initial stages of drawing—the cats, mice, all the extra things going on are all added afterward. After I've made the pen line of my major drawing—that's when it all starts boiling over. It's after that that I start putting in all the sub-stories and the sub-details because to me that's a really important part of the book. But it just doesn't go with the main story; it has to be done apart from that. If I plan it in advance, it would look contrived to me.

Davis: So you don't start with a coherent whole, you work with bits and pieces up to a coherent whole and you watch it gradually emerge?

Gay: In a way, yes, I start with bits of ideas and bits of drawings and paper scribbles and go back and forth between them until a skeleton story emerges and then I go back to the drawings and flesh them out. The details are my *secret* stories underneath the main story.

Davis: To get to the second part of this question about doors, windows, and roads going up the middle of a page. Are they symbolic paths?

Gay: They are, to me, reminders of the outside. The impression I have is that a book is an object in itself. It is contained. The reason that my drawings try to get out of the

"Hang on," hissed the snake.
"Come slither wis-s-s-s-s-s-s-s me."

But Joey fell off
And splashed into the sea.

From Rainy Day Magic, *written and illustrated by Marie-Louise Gay.*

books is that I want to give the impression that they are part of the real world. My drawings go *out into* the real world. Now, the problem with that is that I have to work with the edges, you see. But if I make a path that goes this way, it suggests that behind the book there's other stuff, and if I open a window over that way, it says there's something else, you see. And then it permits me to create other little worlds.

In *Fat Charlie's circus,* for instance, there are all the borders that go around the different pictures. But just outside of these borders there's some sky and different things happening, and they offer little parallel universes. Like the sub-plots, what's behind the borders just gives more richness to my illustrations—more levels.

For example, in *Rainy day magic* you see the kids on the back of the tiger, and in the background you see the banana trees, which were just plants in an earlier illustration. Every object in the first three pages of *Rainy day magic* is found elsewhere in the book. I have transposed them and, in some cases, have given them a new life. Banana plants become banana trees; you'll find a pair of sunglasses in a little drawer and later they'll be on the cat and then on the starfish; a floppy toy rabbit becomes a real rabbit paddling along in his inner tube. All the objects flow through the book. *Rainy day magic* is really an excessive book in that sense, where I really made a completely different story with those details. And some kids have noticed it. I even met a wonderful librarian out here in Toronto who had actually noticed it and had run a contest with a group of children. They found something like 30 objects that flow and change throughout the book. So, I do that just to give more *outlook* and more *richness* in a

book. I'm not about to tell anyone what a book is about. That's for the kids: let them find out themselves.

Davis: This is all very fitting, too, for stories that are about discovery.

Gay: But I'm not exactly saying, "Hey, you, discover this." I'm saying, "Look, who knows, what's behind this window? Who knows? Maybe we should go look!"

Davis: A lot of the details in your books concern the antics of animals—the cats, mice and fish in your books are given personalities. What's the appeal of humanized animals?

Gay: I just see animals that way; I have the impression they have thoughts and feelings. I talk to my cat as if it were one of my children. With certain animals I don't have that impression, and so I don't draw them. In my next book I have a turtle and a rabbit, and I think I've shown their personalities.

Davis: Would it be fair to say that Nature devoid of human manipulation doesn't interest you that much? I think, of course, of your animals, but also of your trees that have drawings within them.

Gay: Yes, it's all part of that world that I'm creating in my work. You could say the same of the objects in my books which aren't really steady: they have a certain character to them. They are alive. Things that are stuck in cement really don't interest me.

Davis: Yes, you're not interested in vertical lines. Nothing in your work says stability. It says solidity, but not stability.

Gay: Often what happens is that I'll start a drawing and there's something that bothers me, it doesn't move, so I'll just start twisting it. And then, there, now we're set in the right space. If it's too firm, it doesn't work. There's something in that perspective that just doesn't appeal to me.

Davis: One of the distinctive features of your work is the use of the frame. I was wondering if you could say something about the relationship between framing and meaning, between, for instance, visual and emotional constraint.

Gay: I think the relationship is different depending on the perspective in the illustration itself. The frame gives an in and out, an outside and an inside in a drawing. It sometimes will hold things that I judge to be important in the way of dramatic focus. And little things going around the frame give it movement which will make something even *more* dramatic, because you have all these fuzzy things going around the middle which is set.

Davis: Are you speaking about frames *within* an illustration?

Gay: Yes.

Davis: Often a frame *around* a picture can make it seem neat and tidy, less energetic.

Gay: But the frames move and breathe in my pictures. *Fat Charlie's circus* is really the best example of my use of frames, because some of the frames lift off and all of a sudden aren't in the picture anymore. I think of when he's in the tree and there's a crowd around him: there the frame goes off on an angle so that Fat Charlie in the tree is not framed which gives more perspective to the drawing; the tree seems very tall, but it also separates Fat Charlie from the crowd, underlining his aloneness and his daring. A lot of this is intuitive. I just start drawing and feel the need to create different perspectives that focus on things. To me, that example of having the frame open up is like—zoom—all the importance goes to Fat Charlie who's way up there in the tree. There's a lot of camera work in my books.

Now, in *Angel and the polar bear* there are no frames, but throughout the book the water or ice bleeds off the page at the bottom and on the sides, creating a flowing horizontal movement—as if the bottom of the book was floating in the water. The top half of the book is squared off, limited by the white border. So, it's very solid on top and very liquid or icy on the bottom. That's another way of playing with frames, but they're less visible.

Davis: When you think of a framed work of art, you think of the formality and detachment of viewing it from a distance. Are you calling attention to the artificiality of the artwork at all?

Gay: In *Fat Charlie's circus* there is a certain sense of that, of camera movements, of this focussing—it's more conscious of playing with perspective. I'm putting barriers on my work and I'm deliberately breaking them. In other books it was more subtle. But *Fat Charlie's circus* is more of a "normal" story. There is no polar bear coming out of a refrigerator, no tigers in the basement. You might consider that the grandmother climbing that tall tree is far-fetched, but her action is very possible. There was no in-

venting of fierce animals or crazy things, but there was the emotion to zoom in on and, of course, the substory of the two mice which is happening mostly out of the frame.

Davis: You're playing also, then, with the boundaries of art and reality. How art is beyond reality and art is within reality as well. What about the frames of white space, do you use them to create balance? *Moonbeam on a cat's ear* is a quieter book and I'm wondering if part of that stems from there being white space surrounding each page.

Gay: Yes, I would think so. I also think it's the fact that it's a night book, a moon book. It's also a book that I wrote for younger children, as you can see the text is very sparse—if it's there at all. It's very simple. I *love* moon books! I'm actually working on another moon book—which I'm very excited about—but it won't be as serene as *Moonbeam on a cat's ear.* The quietness, the serenity in *Moonbeam* is also due to the contrast between the bluish light and the stark white light. Everything seems to float in space.

Davis: So, the white gives it a more static quality, or quiet quality?

Gay: It's the contrast between the two. It's not just the white, it's the blue compared to the white. The whole book is very blue. And as you've seen, I had tiny little borders in there, but they're not too intrusive. They have little things happening in them, but they're much calmer, like little paintings.

But also that book is done in a different technique. It's on gesso which gives it all the texture, all the lines. That's white paint mixture that I put on the gesso board. I let it dry with the brushstrokes in it and on top of that I put the ink and the watercolour and so the texture comes out, like ridges. If you put your hand on the drawing you would feel the hard ridges. And the way it was printed, you could see that; it was just fabulous.

Davis: The books that focus more centrally on action, *Angel and the polar bear,* for instance, either don't have the frames of white space or you play around with them, or you just don't allow them at all. You've moved away from using frames of white space with each book and in *Fat Charlie's circus* you're moving into using frames *inside* the illustration. Is there progression that you can see here, then, in your artwork?

Gay: No, because in my next book [*Willy Nilly*], there's not one frame! I've enclosed the text in straightforward boxes and all the illustrations are full-colour, double-page spreads that flow freely.

Davis: Do you think of colour as having important narrative implications (as in the predominance of blue in *Moonbeam on a cat's ear*)? Do you have favourite colours for conveying certain emotions?

Gay: If you look at my books you can say *Moonbeam* is a blue book, *Rainy day magic* is a pink book, and not just because of the cover but the effect of it—it's a very cheery book—pinky and bluey and candylike. *Angel and the polar bear* is, of course, an aquatic book with the blues and greens and *Fat Charlie's circus* is a purple book. But when

I sit down to draw, I really can't tell you what I'm going to use as colours. I really don't know.

Davis: And yet I can see patterns in the way you're using colour.

Gay: Yes, for certain moods the colour is just right and I see that after, but at the time I'm drawing it just flows. On my drawing table I have all my bottles of inks and my water colours and pastels and whatever junk there is there, and I'll just sit down when all I've got is a black line on a piece of paper. The whole drawing is there in black line that I've penned in, and then I'll say okay, let's see, and I start just like that. I don't really think about it. Now, the one book where it involved more thought because of the technical difficulties was *Fat Charlie's circus:* what I wanted was to have a different colour for every page of that book. I had thought of that in advance—I just wanted different skies all the time so what I had to do was in advance paint my boards yellow, pink, blue, whatever colour. For example, when he's doing the dishes it's all pink in the background, and I drew on top of that so all the skin had to be reworked with the pink underlay. When it was a blue background it had to be re-worked to give the right tones. That is why this book has a very different colouring; every illustration has layers of colour.

Davis: The colouring has changed, but the shapes haven't. Your shapes happen to be primarily rounded and curved ones—the sort of shapes we associate with softness and yielding. (Even the frames in *Fat Charlie's circus* are rubbery.) Is this one of the reasons why your stories seem comforting and secure?

Gay: When someone uses the expression, "I can't even draw a straight line" they're describing me. I can't draw a straight line; it drives me crazy. So every object that I draw has a thickness, you see. I imagine every object as three-dimensional where the shoe is rounded and could almost be a little person. Everything is *plump* to me. I guess I just don't like straight lines and skinny things. It's not just the comfort and security, it's the texture too—but the texture as in the touching of things.

Davis: You want depth, but you want drawings that are soft too?

Gay: Yes, and that's my way of doing it. It's to show that softness with lines that are shaky and crooked and round and which just follow everything in an object.

Davis: There are also echoing patterns in the same shape family in your work. (For example, in *Moonbeam on a cat's ear,* the shape of the cat's ear appears in the butterfly wings, the tufts of hair, the shape of the billowy curtains.)

Gay: I think that's like a signature. If you look, for example, at some fine artists who do abstract paintings, you'll see there are signature gestures. And I think those are mine in illustration. I can't end a curtain like this [drawing in the air a straight curtain]. It just comes out different for me!

Davis: So, it's not really deliberate.

Gay: Oh, I think it is. It's important that you have a feel-

ing that the curtain *is* moving around, that's it's *being blown,* that it's *living* a bit.

Davis: What media do you use?

Gay: Watercolour, dyes, inks, pen and ink, pencil and coloured pencil, pastels. I sometimes do highlights with pastel. I use bleach to bleach out colours in my drawings, and to bleach out different layers of colours.

Davis: Do you like the definiteness of the line you can draw with pen and ink?

Gay: Yes, but in **Willy Nilly** I've used pencil line for a different effect: a scribbly, flowing, moving effect.

Davis: What about text placement in relation to art work. Do you try to create or disturb visual balance?

Gay: Where it's placed in the illustration is important because, once again, you're directing the eye. That's one thing I always talk about to my students [in illustration classes at L'Université de Québec à Montréal]: you're the one who's telling the people what to look at. So, the illustration will be constructed with the text placed somewhere where it will make you go directly to the action; so, if you've read something on one page, when you turn the page you have to have a visual sense to go with that reading. You're going from looking to reading, looking to reading all the time in a book. So you read and then, when you turn the page, you should automatically, *because of the illustrator,* be brought to a certain thing which echoes what has been written or continues what has been written. You can put the text at the top, bottom, or in the middle of a page—wherever—but it has to be somewhere where it's not forgotten because of the illustration. I'm just like a dictator you know: "You're gonna go look at this and then you'll go down and read this!"

Davis: But the *details* of the illustrations can take the reader off in other directions.

Gay: Yes, those are tangents. But they don't take you completely away from the main story.

Davis: There's also the way in which you use the line that sends the reader off in different directions—there is a horizontal base line but there's also a frenetic underlying diagonal line that jerks attention from one point to another. It takes you right to something and then seems to encourage you to make a U turn.

Gay: That's it. Then you *have* to look at the *whole* picture because your eye is taken *everywhere.*

Davis: Is that why you use the diagonal?

Gay: Oh, of course. I tend to use it really strongly sometimes—too strongly. So one of my most important tools in my studio is a mirror: every time I finish a drawing or a sketch I look at my work in a mirror and then I see if I've gone too far. If everything is *really* weird in the mirror I say, okay, this is a bit too much and I start all over again. And it really works! You have been seeing it through the same eye all day as you worked on it—and all of a sudden you look at it and you see where the faults are right away.

Davis: So you don't end up producing a book that has to be tilted to be read?

Gay: No, it's not only that movement, that *penchant pour la diagonale* that I have. You realize that, because you have titled a lot of stuff too much, you've lost the point of your illustration.

Davis: I've noticed when you've got a diagonal tilt on one side of the spread you'll have a corresponding tilt going in the opposite direction on the other side. That kind of balances things out.

Gay: Certain illustrations are like that; others are not like that at all. Sometimes there'll just be one diagonal or a slash. Once again, I'm not carefully thinking this out, thinking, "Now let's see, how will I get the diagonal from A to B." I draw it, I have my gestures, my way of seeing things, and then I correct it if I see a real problem. So I try different things. Sometimes I do really bad things. With some illustrations in my books (which I won't mention!) I look at them and say, "That's one I shouldn't have done."

Davis: The viewpoint in your books is usually normal audience eye-level. It's not bird's eye or worm's eye. Does this reflect any particular kind of intellectual or emotional stance that you want your audience to take toward the subject matter?

Gay: Are you saying there are no bird's eye views?

Davis: There are a couple, but it's mostly eye level.

Gay: This is true in *Rainy day magic* and *Angel and the polar bear* but not in *Fat Charlie.* It's easier for kids to identify with the story and with the kids in the story than when you have the different views. For example, in *Rainy day magic* there's an exceptionally flat, straight-eyed view in the book. It's funny; when I was doing it I always had the impression of it being like those old movie things you used to crank where the paper with the images on it would go by. And I had the impression that the book is really fast and linear—wooosh—as if they were zooming through the story and just meeting things, meeting things, one after another. And I always had this music going through my head—da da da, da da da, what's going to happen next, what's going to happen next?

Davis: What about the musical energy of rhyming text? Some of the words are expressive rather than referential. That's obvious in *Lizzy's lion. Moonbeam on a cat's ear* has a slight rhyme, a hint of one. In *Rainy day magic* there's a definite ABCD rhyme scheme there, where the rhyming words carry the meaning. Is it more difficult to produce illustrations for rhyming text?

Gay: Well, in some ways because of the movement of rhyme. When I started doing the rhyming in *Rainy day magic* the illustrations were all sketched out, so I knew everything I was going to do. But, I knew that, of course, I would have some trouble with the rhymes because once you've done the illustrations you can't change an elephant into a crocodile, you know, just because it doesn't rhyme anymore. The real problem was the actual rhythm of the book. I found it a bit contrived. As you can see, I didn't

use rhyme in *Angel* and in *Fat Charlie.* I just found it hard to always work the movement of rhyme in with the illustrations. I really like very simple, natural texts where the dialogue sounds like how children talk really. That makes it more difficult than a rhyming book but it also makes for a different type of book. But that's okay, too, you know, because as a creator you have to try to see what happens with different sounds; you have to be open and listen. (pp. 63-72)

> *Marie-Louise Gay and Marie Davis, in an interview in* Canadian Children's Literature, *No. 60, 1990, pp. 52-74.*

GENERAL COMMENTARY

Leacy O'Brien

"I wasn't the kind of child who is always drawing, scribbling in notebooks," says Marie-Louise Gay, but she has grown up to become one of this country's most honoured author/illustrators. (p. 54)

Gay is perfectly at ease in English and French. She was born in Quebec City but her family moved frequently throughout her early childhood, living in centres all across Canada before settling in Montreal when Gay was twelve. While the family spoke French at home, Gay's primary education was completed in English schools and so today she finds it easy to work in either language.

Gay's interest in art grew out of adolescent boredom with high school classes. When she began to fill up notebooks with talented drawings, her mother suggested art school and a career was launched. Gay studied design, drawing and animation in Montreal for three years and was soon amazed to learn that she could earn a living "doing something that was so much fun"—selling cartoon strips and illustrations to local magazines.

Her already considerable talents were further honed by three years of work, research and study in San Francisco: "That's where I really learned to draw." On her return to Canada, she worked as a free-lance art director/production manager for a Montreal publisher, where she picked up valuable technical skills that give her a distinct advantage today as she negotiates the printing and publication details of her own books.

One of Gay's first clients was a children's author from Montreal. As she worked to bring his words to life in pictures, she soon realized that she, too, had important thoughts to share with children. "I felt it was important to talk to children on a level they can appreciate . . . to take children seriously."

Out of this self-discovery grew her first book, *De zéro à minuit.* A dozen books later, it's obvious that Gay still delights in sharing her thoughts and creativity with as many young readers as she can. She reaches out to her audience through the words and pictures of her latest book *Angel and the Polar Bear* and the children respond with rewarding enthusiasm when she visits classrooms and libraries across the country.

Angel and the Polar Bear is the most highly narrative of Gay's English books with just the slightest echo of a Dennis Lee rhyme, and it has generated some of the liveliest classroom discussions yet. "Children are so open," says Gay, "and their link between fantasy and reality is so fragile. I'm always amazed at what they will and won't believe. They have no problem accepting that a polar bear might come out of the refrigerator, but then they tell me that *everyone* knows that you don't keep bananas in the refrigerator!"

To Gay, the classroom visits are energizing. She finds the children's interpretations of her stories wonderful sources of inspiration for future projects. These visits also allow her to share with teachers and librarians an artist's vision of the educator's role in developing a creative process for children. Gay believes a book should be a springboard to the imagination, and she's encouraged by the number of classes that have "gone beyond the book" to create dramas, artwork and other projects inspired by one of her stories.

When she is not on tour with her latest book, Gay draws on "in-house" sources of youthful inspiration. The games of her two active boys often plant seeds that flower into scenarios for new books and drawings. And, she says, motherhood has honed her time-management skills to the point where she can juggle a formidable work-load with amazing ease. (pp. 54-5)

And what lies ahead? More books, of course, plus something new and very exciting. A puppet play called *Bonne Fête Willy,* the culmination of two years' work, premieres this spring. Gay wrote the script and designed and produced the puppets, costumes and sets, and she can't wait to see the show when it plays at the Toronto Harbourfront children's theatre festival in May. Is there a movie in Marie-Louise Gay? She's non-committal BUT . . . "perhaps, perhaps one day." (p. 55)

> *Leacy O'Brien, in an interview with Marie-Louise Gay in* CM: A Reviewing Journal of Canadian Materials for Young People, *Vol. XVII, No. 2, March, 1989, pp. 54-5.*

Joan McGrath

Marie-Louise Gay has both written and illustrated several books for young children. Her *Moonbeam on a cat's ear* won the 1987 Amelia Frances Howard-Gibbon Award to general acclaim. In this delightful fantasy, Rosie and Toby Toby (with the bright red hair) steal out of their beds to the shadow of the apple tree, from which they plan to "reach up and steal the moon right out of the sky".

Moonbeam is a child's drifting-off-to-sleep imaginary adventure, slight in content but superb in its compulsive rhyme scheme and above all in its illustration. Its bright, clear colours, and dazzled, child's-eye view of a world touched by midnight magic as moonlight silvers a sleeping cat's ear must be seen in Gay's delicately luscious colour to be appreciated.

The same holds true for her more recent *Angel and the polar bear.* Angel, almost-six-years-old, is, in time-honoured fashion, rarin' to go while her weary parents still plead that it is too early to get up. Dashed but not defeated, Angel wheels out the small child's heavy artillery: " . . . There's a horrible ugly blue monster under my bed! AND HE IS GOING TO EAT ME UP! There's water all around my bed! Sharks too!!!"

Surprise! This time the imaginative folderol is *true.* There *is* water all around, full of fish and floating toys, and (luckily) a paddle boat to take Angel to the kitchen. When a huge polar bear emerges from the fridge, Angel does the polite and proper thing, and shares her breakfast with him.

It is a child's (dare I say it) gay fantasy come to life, with fish popping out of the toaster, pussy cats in mixing bowls paddling busily over the waves with wooden spoons, or swimming about sporting false shark fins to terrify the unwary. There are clues as to the source of the magic: Angel's headboard is decorated with a fish cut-out, and a framed picture of a polar bear is the first thing she sees as she awakens every morning.

Marie-Louise Gay is the mistress of "what if"; if the sea got into the house; if I could go outdoors at night and play in the moonlight; if I had a pet lion; if I could reach up and touch the moon. Her perfect recall of a child's free-ranging, fresh-eyed delight coupled with the adult artistry to bring joyful fantasy to life on brilliant pages, makes her work a nursery treasure, and an ornament to the growing collection of Canadian picture books. (pp. 68-9)

> *Joan McGrath, in a review of "Moonbeam on a Cat's Ear," in* Canadian Children's Literature, *No. 54, 1989, pp. 67-9.*

TITLE COMMENTARY

Lizzy's Lion (1984)

[*Lizzy's Lion was written by Dennis Lee.*]

As usual with the best of Lee's work, *Lizzy's Lion* is easily learned and remembered: "Lizzy had a lion / With a big bad roar, / And she kept him in the bedroom / By the closet-cupboard door." The rhyming words also convey the meaning and are not merely used for convenience, as is too often the case in children's poetry.

Lizzy's lion isn't a pet, we are warned. Lizzy can handle him because she knows his Secret Lion Name. Not so the burglar who arrives one dark night. He is armed with candies just in case he should run into any lions. But Lizzy's lion doesn't like candies or burglars. The ending is as it should be—horribly funny. Marie-Louise Gay's illustrations match the text in verve, and the robber's ruin is nicely picked out in wintry moonlight.

> *Tim Wynne-Jones, in a review of "Lizzy's Lion," in* Quill and Quire, *Vol. 50, No. 11, November, 1984, p. 11.*

Creating poetry for children and then popularizing it seems to require very special talents, and no other Canadian has had the success in this area that Dennis Lee has enjoyed. He follows last year's very popular *Jelly Belly* with *Lizzy's Lion,* one 56-line poem stretched over a 28-page

Gay in her studio.

book. *Lizzy's Lion* contains the now familiar combination of comedy and violence that marks Lee's children's verse. . . . Lee has always been very fortunate in his illustrators, and Marie-Louise Gay's pictures for *Lizzy's Lion* are great—funny and eccentric, filling up and adding weight to what otherwise seems to be a rather slim volume for the money.

> *Mary Ainslie Smith, in a review of "Lizzy's Lion," in* Books in Canada, *Vol. 13, No. 10, December, 1984, p. 12.*

[*Lizzy's Lion*] seems destined to charm anyone from 2 to 6. But the story may shock parents who are struggling to teach their children the basic ideas of justice. Lizzy keeps a lion in her closet, and the animal attacks a "rotten robber" while she sleeps. Roused by the noise, Lizzy wakes in time to put the robber's "toes & tum & head" in the garbage before going back to bed. Still, Lee's excess in the cause of allaying bedtime fears provides him with an excuse to let his imagination roam. And Marie-Louise Gay's mischievously exaggerated illustrations prevent sober judgment from spoiling the fun. (pp. 62-3)

> *John Bemrose and others, "A Child's Garden of Holiday Books," in* Maclean's Magazine, *Vol. 97, No. 50, December 10, 1984, pp. 62-4.*

Moonbeam on a Cat's Ear   (1986)

Rosie and her cat share a big, fluffy bed with myriad toys. A new moon shines down on them through the window, casting wondrous shadows. They are joined by Rosie's friend Toby Toby, a redhead with a frog on his shoulder. The three pluck the moon from the sky, hop aboard and sail off for adventure. "Was it a dream . . .?" the narrative asks, as the final paintings offer alternative answers, showing Rosie and Toby Toby back in bed, the cat lolling on a slice of moon. The text, told in verse, is masterfully brief. Gay's art is splendid; a little something spills over the border of each picture, adding further dimension. A refreshing and fanciful tale.

> *A review of "Moonbeam on a Cat's Ear," in* Publishers Weekly, *Vol. 229, No. 22, May 30, 1986, p. 62.*

Marie-Louise Gay has produced a lovely jewel of a book. . . . It's a slight tale, charmingly told. . . . This lovely book has all the elements of a classic picturebook, colour overflowing the pages, a few words which resonate and catch the imagination, a distinct personality which will captivate children and adults.

> *A review of "Moonbeam on a Cat's Ear," in* Children's Book News, *Toronto, Vol. 9, No. 1, June, 1986, p. 4.*

Author-illustrator Marie-Louise Gay pulled off a first last year by winning the Canada Council illustration award for children's literature in both the French and the English categories. Her artwork for the series Drôle d'Ecole (board books for which she also wrote the text) won in French, while her illustrations for Dennis Lee's *Lizzy's Lion* won in English.

No newcomer to children's literature, Gay had already produced various French books. But *Lizzy's Lion* marked her first step into the field of English-language children's books.

In view of the success of that first step, it's not surprising that she's now going the distance with **Moonbeam on a Cat's Ear,** a picture-book for which she has done both text and illustrations. . . .

Gay, who teaches illustration at the Université du Québec in Montreal, is first and foremost an artist, which quickly becomes apparent in this book. The text is minimal, a slim bit of rhyme about two children who leave their beds at night to "pull the moon/right out of the sky" and who, using its crescent shape as a boat, sail through the clouds until a thunderstorm drives them back to the safety of home.

But while the text is slight, the illustrations are not. They are a feast for the eyes: rich in colour; busy with tiny, detailed delights; full of the whimsical, scratchy humour that was so much a part of the artist's previous offerings. The drawings seem to burst right off the pages. Borders fail to contain all the elements of the pictures, so Gay has employed inventive graphics to extend her art beyond those confines.

The quirky illustrative style that marked her work in **Lizzy's Lion** is also present here (for example, bodies that feature large heads but tiny hands and limbs). A 10 year old who normally considers himself past the picture-book stage said he thought the story jumped around a bit, but that the pictures were great. Going a step further, he suggested the words were just an excuse for the art, a thought that had also occurred to this reviewer.

> *Bernie Goedhart, "Colourful Books for Kids Illustrate a Fine Range of Talent," in* Quill and Quire, *Vol. 52, No. 6, June, 1986, p. 28.*

Here is the quintessential picture book where words and pictures are united—words sonorous, rhythm lilting, cadence sleepily soothing—pictures iridescent, colours of sea green with the blue of the sky mixed by the hand of a talented artist. The design of the book is unique with marginals which tell and tease the reader to see and look for more in the illustrations and text and whose broken borders help to move the action along towards its comforting and gently teasing ending. Who can forget that sleeping cat with the gentle smile or his tired-looking mouse companion. Tousled-haired Rosie and Toby Toby with the bright red hair seem perfect playmates and friends of the '80s. Was it a dream, was it a fantasy? Was it real? Only the child can tell. Thank you, Marie-Louise Gay, from all the children who will enjoy the sail through the sky and over the blue-green sea and will slumber off to

their own dream world so lovingly introduced to them by you. Their sleep could only be gentle after hearing this tale at bedtime. From caregivers, too, a "THANK-YOU" for providing them with the perfect goodnight book. For me, I don't know whether I would rather be cosily back home after the dream-sail, exhausted from the adventure as Toby Toby and Rosie appear at the book's conclusion, or whether it would be fun to start all over again with the sleeping cat and mouse left on the new moon. No matter, this is a picture book to be read again and again for many years to come to our children and our children's children.

> *Joan Neller, in a review of "Moonbeam on a Cat's Ear," in* CM: A Reviewing Journal of Canadian Materials for Young People, *Vol. XVI, No. 1, January, 1988, p. 8.*

Rainy Day Magic   (1987)

Montreal artist Marie-Louise Gay is a winner who shows no sign of losing her touch. Two years ago, she became the first person to receive *both* the French-language and the English-language Canada Council Children's Literature Prizes for illustration. . . .

Gay decided to try her hand at writing and illustrating her own children's books, and the result in 1986 was **Moonbeam on a Cat's Ear,** which she then adapted into French, calling it **Voyage au clair de lune.** Now she surpasses that effort with **Rainy Day Magic,** which she has written and illustrated—but this time she has given us a far more rewarding text (adapted into French as **Magic d'un jour de pluie**).

In verse, Gay tells the story of young Joey who, dressed in yellow slicker and sou'wester, comes to visit her friend Victor and helps dispel those rainy-day blues. Victor's dad has a headache and begs them to hold down the noise, so "ever so softly" the children cruise through the toys. But their reality is not that of an adult, and their idea of quiet wouldn't soothe anyone's aching head. The accompanying illustration gives a taste of things to come: you can almost feel the room shake as the two roar through on their tricycles, crushing crayons in their wake. Dad blows his stack, the two children barrel downstairs, and fantasy takes over.

An eagle-eyed reader or listener will recognize the giant snake from its portrait on a living-room wall some pages back, the whale as a reincarnation of the fish sloshing about in a bowl on the cupboard in Victor's room, and the tiger as a larger-than-life version of the drawing Victor has taped to his wall.

As usual, Gay's artwork spills out of the borders: only in three cases do the images stay confined within their borders—two of those when the children suddenly find themselves in the dark, and the third when that darkness is pierced by a shaft of light when Mom opens the door to call the children to dinner. The appearance of her familiar, comforting silhouette brings the children back to reality— or does it?

> *Bernie Goedhart, "From Giant Snakes to Punk Pigeons: Escapism at Its Best," in* Books

for Young People, *Vol. 1, No. 3, June, 1987, p. 5.*

[*Rainy-Day Magic*] is told in Marie-Louise Gay's simple rhyming text. . . .

Her pictures are wildly energetic, leading hectically from the familiar to the deliciously scary and back, with amusing detail throughout, and for once the rhyme adds something to a very inventive story.

> *Jan Dalley, "From Titian to Tintin," in* The Observer, *August 2, 1987, p. 20.*

Rainy Day Magic is a delight, a journey through the magical world of a child's daydreams. . . .

The drawings are wonderful. Fresh, vivid colour. Lovely renderings of a jungle, an undersea world, an enormously beautiful blue whale, an appealing pink sea horse ("winning at sea-solitaire") and a mauve starfish wearing sunglasses relaxing in a deck chair amid sea life of yellows and greens.

This enchanting story can be enjoyed by very young children and older ones too. As an adult, I was immediately taken by the charm, wit, rhyming verse, and colour in the story.

I look forward to many more marvellous stories from Ms. Gay.

> *Barbara Egerer, in a review of "Rainy Day Magic," in* CM: A Reviewing Journal of Canadian Materials for Young People, *Vol. XV, No. 5, September, 1987, p. 205.*

The story is simple. It's a rainy day, and a little boy and his girl friend play inside, trying to be quiet because "dad" has a headache. They ride their bikes noisily through into fantasyland, have adventures, and are then called to supper by "mother." Their journey, told in lively rhyme, has the same familiar elements of Sendak's *Where the wild things are*—parental disapproval, a child's banishment, adventure in another world, and a safe return to warm food at home. This classic structure is accompanied by Marie-Louise Gay's extremely original and distinguished illustrations. Her children are unforgettable—their grins and their movements show their overactive imaginations and irrepressible physical vitality. Particularly noteworthy is Gay's skillful use of illustrations which sometimes advance the story ahead of the text's words. As the children in one story crawl up a hump-like surface, they think it's grass, then a bumble-bee; but the child *listening* to the story can move his eyes ahead to the right side of the page and see there that the hump is the back end of a tiger—one whose groggy-red eye has just opened because of the tickling on its back. Until the page turns, the outcome is uncertain. This book is a delight.

> *Mary Rubio, in a review of "Rainy Day Magic," in* Canadian Children's Literature, *No. 46, 1987, p. 107.*

Angel and the Polar Bear   (1988)

"Every single morning when Angel wakes up she yells,

'Mama! Come here!' Angel is almost six years old. She has a very loud voice. And every single morning Angel's mother says, 'It's too early. Go back to sleep.' Angel's mother has a very tired voice. Angel's father sleeps like a log." These opening lines set the tone for another intrepid heroine's tale, one that owes much to the character's lively imagination and to the forbearance of her exhausted mom.

This Angel is far from angelic. With her mischievous eyes, freckled face, and nest of black, spiky hair, she resembles nothing so much as a highly mobile sea urchin—just the sort of thing to cause trouble for the unwitting.

When Angel's mother fails to answer her clarion calls for help in dealing with the ugly blue monster under her bed and the shark-infested waters surrounding it, Angel's powerful imagination comes to her aid. Using the sash of her dressing gown as a tightrope, Angel escapes to her dresser. From the top dresser drawer she pulls out her flippers and her rubber giraffe, and with a splash she paddles off on a voyage around her house.

First stop is her parents' bedroom, where her oblivious mother mumbles that there's cereal in the kitchen. Indeed there is, but what a mess: floating dishes, soggy cereal, and goldfish in the toaster. And that's just the beginning—the refrigerator door opens and suddenly everything freezes, skates replace flippers, and an enormous polar bear appears. After some quite frightening encounters the polar bear and Angel settle into happy companionship, playing dominoes and snacking on bananas.

If all this sounds chaotic and confusing, it probably is. But it will also be very entertaining for anyone Angel's age—6 or so. The combination of slapstick and fantasy, and the droll fun made of the sleepy mom, will certainly tickle funny-bones.

All this activity also gives Marie-Louise Gay ample opportunity to display her talents as an illustrator. Her paintings of Angel on her floating bed and a startled cat on its floating mat are bright and quirky. If Angel is a sea urchin then the polar bear is a great moving mass of Arctic ice—a neat contrast that also makes a very attractive picture. It's probably safe to say that in *Angel and the Polar Bear,* the author/illustrator of *Moonbeam on a Cat's Ear* and *Rainy Day Magic*, among other books, has another success on her hands.

> *Susan Perren, "Feisty Young Heroines' Offbeat Adventures," in* Books for Young People, *Vol. 3, No. 1, February, 1989, p. 9.*

Much of the fun in Gay's books derives from her use of secondary characters—here, for example, Angel's cat. Children following the text and the illustrations will find another, parallel story in the antics of the snorkelling feline. Somehow, the most surprising things make sense. Of course opening a refrigerator can cause rivers to freeze, and of course a polar bear lives on ice, so naturally he comes out of the fridge. And who says Angel and her polar bear can't eat bananas and play dominoes? (p. 36)

> *Linda Granfield, "Wake-up Tales," in* Books in Canada, *Vol. 18, No. 3, April, 1989, pp. 36-7.*

Fat Charlie's Circus (1989)

Fat Charlie knows he's going to be a famous circus performer when he grows up. He practises lion-taming with the cat in his bedroom, he trains his goldfish to jump through a hoop, and he uses the clothes-line as a tightrope. His parents, however, aren't so keen, especially when Charlie smashes a pile of dinner plates.

To show them how great he can be, Charlie decides to do his Daring Diving Act—from the top of the tallest tree in the yard into a small glass of water. Once up in the tree, Charlie realizes he's too scared either to dive or come down. Then Charlie's grandmother climbs the tree and, in helping her down, he too reaches safety on the ground.

This simple plot is told in a spare, direct style. The pacing is tight and the resolution is satisfying and psychologically sound.

Charlie's story is told in Gay's usual rambunctious art style. The pages glow with colour and Gay's child characters, especially Charlie, have warmer and less sinister expressions than those in her earlier books.

Charlie's circus acts are loosely framed to form a picture within a picture in the double-page spreads, effectively linking reality and fantasy. There are interesting details: two small mice acting out their own story on each page, a wheel-chair bound child in the crowd scene.

Fat Charlie's Circus is a well-crafted and imaginative picture book, sure to be a story-hour favorite.

> *Callie Israel, in a review of "Fat Charlie's Circus," in* Quill and Quire, *Vol. 55, No. 12, December, 1989, p. 22.*

Marie-Louise Gay creates another fanciful adventure for children in *Fat Charlie's Circus.* Mischievous Fat Charlie, who juggles china plates and tight-rope-walks the clothes line, embodies perfectly the gay, reckless enthusiasm and ambition of youth. Vivid, colourful illustrations and remarkable attention to detail confirm Gay's talent as an illustrator.

> *A review of "Fat Charlie's Circus," in* Children's Book News, *Toronto, Vol. 12, No. 3, Winter, 1989, p. 13.*

Fat Charlie's Circus is a delightful new book from award-winning author/illustrator Marie-Louise Gay. Fat Charlie is an irrepressible daredevil who is determined to become a circus performer and whose imaginative play includes lion taming, tightrope walking and juggling plates (unsuccessfully). When he defies his parents and attempts a Daring Dive Act, Fat Charlie learns there is more to becoming famous then he had anticipated. With the unexpected help of his grandmother, Fat Charlie manages a satisfactory solution to his dilemma.

Although I had misgivings about the adjective "fat," the story reassured me that Fat Charlie was simply his name rather then a nasty nickname. Indeed, all the cartoonlike characters have a similar build, and there is no emphasis on Fat Charlie's size. In fact, the positive image of the remarkable grandmother, especially with the twist at the end where she participates in the further antics of a thoroughly unchastened little boy, is to be applauded.

As in her other books, Gay's bright and zany illustrations depict the childlike world of the imagination. Her pictures spill out of the stage-like borders with comfortable clutter and invite repeated examination. The action in text and illustration is further extended by two mice who caper around the borders.

The exaggerated humour, familiar from Gay's other books, is also evident throughout—from the plump cat balancing on Fat Charlie's nose on the first page to the last picture of the mice, with tails entwined, perched on two halves of a broken egg. A wonderful story that begs to be shared with children.

> *Alison Mews, in a review of "Fat Charlie's Circus," in* CM: A Reviewing Journal of Canadian Materials for Young People, *Vol. XVIII, No. 2, March, 1990, p. 64.*

The last time Marie-Louise Gay wrote and illustrated a children's picture book, she walked away with both the Governor General's Award and the Amelia Frances Howard-Gibbon Award. She added these coveted prizes to a long and intimidating list that includes the Canada Council Children's Literature Prize, awarded once for her illustration of Dennis Lee's *Lizzy's lion,* and again in the same year, for her creation of the series, *Drôle d'école. Fat Charlie's circus,* Gay's latest picture book, is no less deserving. While the narrative is less fantastic than her previous stories, there is enough of self-styled fantasy in Fat Charlie's vision to support the story, and to make it diverting, without the addition of polar bears that emerge from refrigerators or moons that become magical sailing ships.

The narrative mixes the fantastic and the familiar, improbable incidents and realistic dialogue, into a portrait of a round red-head who is transported by his vision of himself as a budding circus performer. Moving steadily through a series of comic mishaps and adventures, the plot follows Fat Charlie as he makes a determined effort to increase his repertoire of circus acts. Tightrope walking on the clothesline, juggling dinner plates, and lion-taming his devoted companion, a hairy gray cat, do not fully test the limits of Charlie's imagination. It is his Daring Diving Act that, he thinks, will squash the cynicism of his family and bring him well-deserved fame. The light-hearted tone of the story alters when Charlie, sitting atop the tallest tree, looks down upon the "tiny speck" of a water-filled glass—his intended landing point—and realizes that he is too scared to make the dive. He is crestfallen and the illustration—a two-page spread showing Fat Charlie dwarfed by the violet expanse of night sky—heightens his aloneness. His spectators go home to supper, night falls, and Charlie still cannot move. Life is becoming complex. His "rescue" comes eventually, from an unexpected source—his bespectacled grandmother who wears turquoise runners and a look of profound naïvete, she climbs the tree, intending, she claims, to jump with Charlie. That gesture of support is enough to give Charlie the emotional reassurance he needs and the courage to climb down from the tree. The book closes with this eccentric pair practicing their Bicycle Balancing Act, thus sealing our impression that such emotional closeness soothes fears and bolsters dreams. Gay's narrative clearly moves towards insights about the relationship between imagination and reality and, more importantly, about the child's need for uncritical emotional support. And these insights are embedded in the text; like Charlie's grandmother, they are heartwarming and emerge naturally and quietly.

Apart from the thematic interest of the book, much of its lasting appeal derives from characterization and the inventiveness of the illustrations. Except for the opening page, all of the illustrations are full two-page spreads, visually exciting for their intense colours, changes in perspective, and abundance of detail. With these details, Gay suggests the imaginative fullness of Charlie's world and her own appreciation of the importance of setting. She gives impressions of tangible locations, providing minute details that still keep her cartoon-like characters in the foreground at all times, letting them play their roles in appropriate, unmuted settings. The flurries of action and dialogue are reflected in expressionistic drawings that perpetually suggest movement—indeed, that sometimes threaten to escape the page.

This impression is helped by Gay's fondness for the diagonal line and her frequent use of the device of framing, one of her more intriguing experiments with form. Rather than distancing us from the picture enclosed by a frame, the rubbery borders within the larger illustration provide dramatic focus, drawing the reader in to scrutinize its contents. Moreover, the frames can just barely contain their pictures, thus simultaneously echoing Fat Charlie's inability to restrain his imagination, and the story's thematic interest in the imaginative realm's relationship to the outside world. Sometimes the frames suggest the formality of looking at photographs, paintings, or freeze frames. What surrounds the framed picture, then, provides a glimpse into another world (where, among other things, a subplot with impish mice as protagonists is developing), or it suggests the continuity between the two worlds. In either case, the illustrations demand our involvement. Throughout the book, we are asked to focus on the framed event, but to watch what explodes the parameters, to quickly switch our perspective from bird's eye to worm's eye, and to attend to a myriad of details that supply narrative context.

Gay's work is, without question, challenging and innovative. But what is more, *Fat Charlie's circus* has an unusual depth—both in the carefully-shaded illustrations and the subtlety of the text. While Gay has called this latest book a more "normal" story than her previous ones that featured polar bears and moon ships, she is right to insist that in *Fat Charlie's circus* "there was no inventing of fierce animals or crazy things, but there was the emotion there that was very, very important." (pp. 75-7)

Marie Davis, "The Fantastic and the Familiar in 'Fat Charlie's Circus'," in Canadian Children's Literature, *No. 59, 1990, pp. 75-7.*

Willy Nilly (1990)

The picture book world of Marie-Louise Gay is a world in constant flux. In her latest book, *Willy Nilly,* the theme is transformation. Willy receives a magic kit for his birthday and proceeds to turn his sister into the top half of an elephant, the neighbour into a fish, and Aunt Mabel into a rabbit. He eventually finds the antidote to restore them to their true selves. But that's not the whole story. In the frenetic pictures, full of Gay's characteristic dots and squiggles, there are transformations everywhere. A lurid green pit-bull turns into a parrot. An elegant little bat in pink shades appears in odd places. There's a tiger tail—or is it a tiger tie, or a piece of ribbon? The very air, indoors and out, is full of lightning bolts, scudding clouds, and explosions. This could be a disturbing world were it not so good-natured. Somehow we have faith that Willy with his Brillo-pad hair and W.C. Fields grin is at least tenuously in control. *Willy Nilly* began life as a puppet play, and it reflects a puppet show's potential for theatricality, rousing action, and the thrill of being poised on the brink of disaster. Still, this is not Gay's strongest work; though the artwork repays close scrutiny, the plot has an arbitrary feel to it.

Sarah Ellis, in a review of "Willy Nilly," in Quill and Quire, *Vol. 57, No. 1, January, 1991, p. 22.*

Sheila Gordon

1927-

South African-born American author of fiction, nonfiction, and picture books.

Major works include *Waiting for the Rain: A Novel of South Africa* (1987), *3rd September 1929* (1988), *The Middle of Somewhere* (1990).

Recognized as a skillful writer of works for readers in the primary grades through high school, Gordon is best known as the creator of poignant stories with South African settings which are considered among the best books written about the effects of apartheid on the young. She is also highly regarded for writing informational books that reflect the depth of her investigations on world history. In her first book about South Africa, the young adult novel *Waiting for the Rain,* Gordon describes how the conflicts of their culture alter the lives of two friends of different races and backgrounds. *Waiting for the Rain* takes Tengo, who is black, and Frikkie, who is white, from idyllic boyhoods spent on the farm owned by Frikkie's uncle on which Tengo's parents are employed to the confrontation ten years later when the young men meet as protester and soldier in a Johannesburg riot. Underscoring the story is Tengo's desire for education and his developing awareness of the apartheid system; as Frikkie yearns for the day when he can live on the farm he is set to inherit, Tengo becomes increasingly dissatisfied with his own lack of opportunities. At the end of the novel, Tengo, who is debating whether or not to take revolutionary action, is chased by a soldier who turns out to be Frikkie, participating in his year of national service. When Frikkie is wounded, Tengo risks his own life to take his friend to safety before escaping over the border to a place where he can continue his education undisturbed. Noted for depicting the South African situation in a frank yet objective manner, *Waiting for the Rain* is also praised for its superior construction, full characterizations, and evocative setting.

Gordon's next book about South Africa, *The Middle of Somewhere,* has as its background the forced removal of black communities to desolate parts of South Africa to allow for the building of white suburbs. A work of realistic fiction for middle graders, the story describes the devastation of nine-year-old Rebecca, a black child who lives in a village threatened with demolishment, when her best friend Noni leaves the village with her parents after the pronouncement is made. Although Rebecca's father is jailed after making a speech at a demonstration against rehousing, the book ends on an optimistic note when the demonstration succeeds in averting the threat and both Nelson Mandela and her father are released from prison. Gordon is also the author of *A Monster in the Mailbox* (1978), a humorous picture book with a positive consumer message which describes how small Julius, who orders a walking, talking monster from a mail-order house and receives a phony rubber one in return, succeeds in getting

his money back. In her nonfiction for young adults, Gordon provides an introduction to such challenging issues as disease, hunger, violence, and pollution in *World Problems* (1971) and explores the causes of World War II in *3rd September 1939,* a volume named for the day war was declared by Great Britain. Gordon is also the author of an autobiography for adults which details the summer vacations she spent with her husband and three children in rural Scotland as well as an adult novel about a white South African doctor exiled in England for helping a black soldier who returns to find his country filled with racial violence. *Waiting for the Rain* won the Jane Addams Peace Prize in 1988.

(See also *Contemporary Authors,* Vol. 132.)

TITLE COMMENTARY

World Problems (1971)

[The Batsford World Wide Series] is a new series which is apparently aimed at CSE and O-level classes but which is sufficiently lucid and short-winded to be offered to [children] of much younger age-groups. Written by teachers, edited by the chairman of the World Education Fellowship, the books are attractively produced with lots of photos, mostly unhackneyed, and the odd engraving. [**World Problems**] though well written by Sheila Gordon, seems an editorial mistake. It is no fatter than its mates, and inevitably more bitty. It already overlaps with them to some extent (a picture of Boers trekking *again*) and can only, I would think, overlap more with future volumes. (p. 315)

> *Gillian Tindall, "TUC Kid," in* New Statesman, *Vol. 81, No. 2085, March 5, 1971, pp. 315-16.*

[**World Problems**] is a general introduction to the changing problems of disease and industrial development, the continuing problem of hunger and the developing ones of violence and environmental pollution. Particularly effective is the chapter on violence (because it distinguishes between its different causes) and the chapter on disease in which the brief account of progress against malaria is an exciting story well told.

Each problem is neatly set in historical context and carried through to the most up-to-date present. The author succeeds well in her dual aim of introducing some of the fundamental problems in building a more generous, united and peaceful world. The text is illustrated with well-chosen photographs and one or two useful charts. Suggestions at the end of each chapter for follow-up work are imaginative but demanding.

> *"Man as His Own Worst Enemy," in* The Times Literary Supplement, *No. 3605, April 2, 1971, p. 384.*

A Monster in the Mailbox   (1978)

This is the slice-of-life story of a boy named Julius who sends away to a mail order house for a walking, talking monster and, of course, gets only a fake rubber one. The book's strong point, however, lies not in the on-target portrayal of a childhood disappointment but in candid, single-minded Julius himself, a character who brings the spunk of an Encyclopedia Brown to a younger age group. The other characters are one-dimensional, but consistent and well defined. (Who could forget a mother who draws a duckbill platypus?) The ending—Julius takes his hard-earned refund money, buys a used fairy tale book, and becomes engrossed in it—is less than convincing and too tame for so promising a story.

> *Kathryn Meyer, in a review of "A Monster in the Mailbox," in* School Library Journal, *Vol. 25, No. 3, November, 1978, p. 44.*

Although the conclusion is perhaps more an adult wish than one rooted in child-reality, Gordon has created a warm family situation with supportive characters, and she lines her cleverly told, amusing story with a good consumer message that never gets preachy.

> *Barbara Elleman, in a review of "A Monster in the Mailbox," in* Booklist, *Vol. 75, No. 10, January 15, 1979, p. 809.*

As a lesson in bucking the system, this has wit, bounce, and sensitivity dextrously mixed; and the opening chapters lead up to Julius' predicament with some amusing tales of their own (a homeless boa constrictor that would have to be fed "a teeny-weeny little mousie-wousie"—or so brother Buffy teases; a lucky-to-be-alive cat that must be tired, Julius decides, of hearing that it has only eight lives left). The only rub is the ending which has Julius purchase, with his "monster money," *The Monster Book of Fairy Tales*—and find the stories of Hansel and Gretel, Beauty and the Beast, etc., more than compensation for the hoax. In this happy professional family, he must have heard them before—but in any case Charles Addams would have been a more fitting choice.

> *A review of "A Monster in the Mailbox," in* Kirkus Reviews, *Vol. XLVII, No. 3, February 1, 1979, p. 125.*

Waiting for the Rain: A Novel of South Africa   (1987)

Gordon's story walks the fine line between exploration of topical material and riveting narrative.

Tengo, a black child on a South African farm, grows up fairly friendly with Frikkie, the blond Afrikaaner child who will one day inherit the property. The stories of their development are heavily weighted toward Tengo's growing awareness of the rank inequities of the apartheid system; Frikkie's awareness—or lack of it—is described rather than felt. For a time, *Waiting for the Rain* lapses into social history; the stories of the boys seem lost in the earnest effort to fill in important background. The inevitable conflict between the young men, one armed and one considering what sort of revolutionary action to take, restores tension to the narrative; and readers are ultimately gratified by a difficult and genuinely unpredictable conclusion.

One always hopes for a novel in which characters *play* their lives instead of merely representing points of view. Still, of the novels for children published in the last few years on South Africa's difficult and important social crisis, this seems the best so far.

> *A review of "Waiting for the Rain: A Novel of South Africa," in* Kirkus Reviews, *Vol. LV, No. 13, July 1, 1987, p. 991.*

The trouble with this book is that the characters become symbols rather than people. Neither Tengo (who is too good to be true), Frikkie, nor anyone else engages readers' sympathies because each is a vehicle for the sober messages that Gordon wishes to deliver, messages that are terribly important but that make for didacticism rather than compassion. The final coincidence weakens the plot further. Still, young readers *need* every shred of message they can get, and if the book is disappointing as a story, it has its place as a polemic.

> *Marjorie Lewis, in a review of "Waiting for the Rain: A Novel of South Africa," in* School Library Journal, *Vol. 33, No. 11, August, 1987, p. 95.*

A fully realized novel that deserves to be read by adults as well as teens. [It is an] affecting book. . . .

Waiting for the Rain is an honest portrayal of the inhumanity of apartheid. Through the experience of the two young men, readers see some of the influences that led to the 1976 uprising in Soweto, even though no specific dates are mentioned. Young people who have studied or at least heard about apartheid in social studies classes will find an added emotional dimension here.

Gordon is a fine writer whose skill is evident in the way the story builds slowly, without simplistic delineation of right or wrong. She shows an inner struggle as it begins to surface in frustration and finally erupts in revolution. At times her touches of metaphor and imagery are brilliant.

The title of the book comes from the perceptions of Tengo, a sensitive student with a talent for art who can't attend classes because of student demonstrations. He likens himself to crops during a drought, "waiting for the rain." The rain, in this case, comes as a storm, and neither Tengo nor Frikkie is the same ever again.

The novel ends with a dramatic confrontation between the two young men, as Tengo is chased by a soldier who turns out to be Frikkie. This particular ending seems contrived, but it is handled skillfully. The book is a strong one that surmounts even this minor flaw.

> *Stephen Fraser, "Exciting Tales of Challenge and Survival," in* The Christian Science Monitor, *November 6, 1987, p. B5.*

This well-written and carefully constructed novel tells the story of two friends who grow up separate but never equal in an increasingly turbulent South Africa.

The story is balanced nicely. As Frikkie looks forward more and more to the day he can live on the farm, Tengo finds himself increasingly dissatisfied with the future laid out for him.

[Sheila Gordon] has avoided the great pitfalls of such a story—caricature and sentiment. She writes with a determination to be fair and accurate, and, while she includes all the old stereotypes in their proper places—Frikkie's sister grumbling about "a cheeky kaffir," the cheaply salved conscience of the white liberal—she does so in context and without hammering. The reader closes the book in a state of appropriate confusion. This is not a country to be easily understood, nor a situation open to simple solutions.

Despite Ms. Gordon's skill, however, there is something in this story that leaves the reader unconvinced. The characters themselves, and their situations, often feel invented. "A Novel of South Africa" is the subtitle. One could add, "for American Students," so obviously destined is this book for the American market. South African terms give way to American ones: mealies to corn, cross to mad and so forth. Glosses are supplied everywhere. There are, in addition, some serious discrepancies for the knowledgeable reader. How, for instance, does a black child growing

up speaking Afrikaans as his "white" language come so easily to read and speak English from books?

More disturbing is the feeling one has in reading this novel that the story itself serves as a sort of classroom vehicle for information on South Africa. A good book for teenagers should be a good book for anyone. This one—"Ages 12 & up; Grades 7 & up"—seems to suffer in the service of its intended audience.

> *Lynn Freed, in a review of "Waiting for the Rain: A Novel of South Africa" in* The New York Times Book Review, *December 20, 1987, p. 21.*

Sheila Gordon's novel is the story of a friendship doomed to fail because of the circumstances in which it originally blossomed. The apartheid which gnaws at [the young lives of Frikkie and Tengo] is given vivid representation not only in the details of their backgrounds and relationships but also in the landscape in which their story is plotted. Its hovering vultures, crowing roosters, parched fields and grotesque shadows are symbols which, cumulatively, assert the betrayal, expropriation, suspicion and, above all, the threatening violence endemic in a political system of frightening and unmitigated evil. *Waiting for the rain* neither moralises nor pontificates. Instead, it is content to demonstrate, in its totally credible setting and characterisation, the workings of this evil and, perhaps with unusual candour in a children's book, its consequences. If young readers see these most clearly in Tengo's evolution from respectful rural 'kaffir' to his altogether different role in the city's blood-spilling, older ones will be aware of them in the inadequacy of their own 'sympathetic' gestures, impeccably well-intentioned though these may be.

> *Robert Dunbar, in a review of "Waiting for the Rain," in* The School Librarian, *Vol. 36, No. 3, August, 1988, p. 108.*

As a story, [Beverley Naidoo's] *Journey to Jo'Burg* takes us on a short and unsatisfying ride.

In direct contrast, *Waiting for the Rain* demonstrates that books about issues can be good stories. As in *Journey*, the author categorically presents the realities of the South African situation in a story about children. Gordon, however, lifts the aspects of apartheid to an even more universal level through the skillful deployment of structure, logical plot, and character development. The story becomes a classic tale of conflict with sure appeal for children—the dilemma of close friends from different backgrounds who are caught up in forces beyond their control. The novel's action is subsequently constructed around the elements of dual forces—conflict and resolution, black and white, before and after.

Waiting for the Rain is the story of two boys, Tengo, black, and Frikkie, white, who share childhood experiences on a farm and meet years later as protester and soldier. These central characters symbolize personal conflicts and group, national, and even international, relations in South Africa. The characteristics of apartheid are subtly emphasized primarily through the use of the narrative shifts in points of view and descriptions of the contrast in the boys' lives. There is a poignant moment when Tengo observes, with a real sense of loss, the white boys at play while he works in the kitchen. Despite their differences, the relationship between Tengo and Frikkie proves to be deep and binding.

The descriptions of setting and a general sense of emotional foreboding quickly draw the reader into the story. From the beginning, Gordon establishes a portentous atmosphere that provides symbols of the conflicts to come. She maintains this atmosphere with vivid depictions of every aspect of farm life, especially the animals. Dogs, vultures, and roosters are foreshadowing agents and symbolize the undercurrents of human feelings. Gordon utilizes dialogue as an aide in establishing relationships—Frikkie calls the black adults by first names and they answer "yes, little master." The innocent closeness of the boys is indicated indirectly by details such as the sharing of milk from the same cup. Gordon further correlates the personal and situational changes in the story to the forces of nature. This correlation is more sharply defined in the second part of the book when the long drought (hence the book's title) becomes a graphic representation of the effects of apartheid. The struggle mounts to a conclusion as the farmers, and the readers, wait for rain—in a violent storm that we cannot witness but know must come.

The reader gains awareness of the effects of apartheid slowly, along with the main characters as they are painstakingly developed. Frikkie's superficial understanding of Tengo is exemplified by his expressed proprietary feelings, impatience, and disregard for the differences in their relative conditions and needs. His love of the land is evident; he views the farm as a refuge from the pressures of school, and ultimately, as a change in his style of life. Tengo, on the other hand, longs for and wonders about life beyond the farm. He wants books, school, and information to find answers to his questions. Tengo is concerned about universal things such as the stars and sea, and very personal matters that relate to the political situation, such as why his poor family pays school fees that Frikkie's obviously more privileged family does not. Through the two boys, Gordon speaks to us about the individual quests in South Africa which relate to the situations most children can share: want, loss, anger, and pain.

The secondary characters are sharply drawn as well. Joseph, Tengo's cousin, is introduced as a force of change who brings the perspective of the impact of city life. His sensitivity to the need for Tengo to discover his own truths allows the story to progress and blossom without force. Joseph's own growing awareness of the forces of apartheid precedes Tengo's conflict several years later. The women of the story are central in their roles as supporters and instigators of action. They are vibrant, strong, and hardworking in various ways. The city liberal, the farmer's wife, the black mother and grandmother (who speaks for the old world humanist view) form an encapsulated portrait of womanhood in South Africa. For example, Frikkie's younger sister is indicative of how the Afrikaaners view their women, who are protected, spoiled, and able to put the "kaffir" in his place. Frikkie's uncle is the voice of the Boer male, who if not entirely cruel (there are sever-

al illustrations of his kindnesses), must maintain a rigid stance against change. He expresses many of the white man's fears and subsequent justifications for his policies, such as the dangers of education for blacks and the need always to keep them in their place. The reader is given a vivid image of this character as he tells, while cutting a piece of raw bloody meat, the history of the Afrikaaner's triumph over nature and the Africans.

Gordon builds on a series of incidents to convey the frustration and rage that must surely lead to the real life battles of the children in South Africa. One striking example takes place during the uncle's fiftieth birthday party. After Frikkie accidentally breaks some crockery in the kitchen, a visiting cousin disrespectfully commands an elderly black man to clean up the mess. "In a tight, low, terrible voice, Tengo spoke the words that came to him then. 'Don't you call that old man boy.' He took a step toward her. 'You have no respect!' His voice rose as he felt pure anger surge through him. 'Can't you see! He is one of the elders of our tribe—he is older than the oubaas—he is from the chief's family! Who says you can talk to him like that—' He lifted his hand as though to strike her, and his voice dropped as he hissed at her through clenched teeth. 'Don't you ever call an old man boy again'". This incident, at the close of the first part of the book, is a wrenching scene that evokes strong emotion in the characters and readers. The confrontation, which is recognizably symbolic of the greater struggle, marks a decisive point in Tengo's development and a temporary break in the cumulative dramatic tension.

A similar layer of events, settings, and conflicts in the second part of the book leads to a final parallel confrontation between Tengo and Frikkie as young men on opposite sides of the student uprisings. Tengo has gone to Johannesburg in pursuit of an education he feels holds the key to his freedom. He struggles to maintain the impetus to continue studying on his own after the students' boycotts have closed schools. However, Tengo eventually gets swallowed by the turmoil. In a battle between stone throwing students and armed soldiers, he runs from a soldier who is pursuing a sniper. The soldier follows Tengo into a deserted hut where he receives a numbing blow from Tengo. The soldier is Frikkie, who has struggled through school and gained confidence in himself through mandatory army service. In this climactic closing scene Tengo, holding the soldier's gun, is torn by emotions ranging from anger to compassion for the Frikkie he knew as a child. Tengo's final decision to release him is a positive action, but leaves one to wonder what would have happened if roles were reversed. We have by this point come to know and care about the characters' inner turmoils and humiliations.

Although many of the same disturbing elements of the South African issue are treated and included in both novels, there is a striking and significant difference between them. ***Waiting for the Rain*** makes the reader feel the effects of apartheid through strong identification with and caring for the main characters. We are part of the struggle and conflict. The novel, in its veracity, has frequent correlative aspects to the autobiographical *Kaffir Boy* by Mark

Mathabane, a riveting narrative of the hardships of life under apartheid. (pp. 58-9)

Carla Hayden and Helen Kay Raseroka, "The Good and the Bad: Two Novels of South Africa," in Children's Literature Association Quarterly, *Vol. 13, No. 1, Summer, 1988, pp. 57-60.*

3rd September 1939   (1988)

Although this book takes as its theme 'The day war was declared', it actually looks in much detail at the events which led up to that date, so it is perhaps of more use than its title alone would suggest. The first section does concentrate on the actual day, with parliamentary sittings and Cabinet meetings, as well as the more ordinary and mundane doings of the nation. The evacuation of children from the big cities started, and troops were on the move—obviously so to anyone who lived near a main road or railway station. The author quotes from the experiences of many people on that day and brings an immediate feel to the book. The in-depth investigation into the causes of the war, that takes up all the second half, will prove to be of great use to any student studying modern European history. Not only is the rise of Hitler himself catalogued, but the historical reasons are given, from the First World War and before, to show how the climate in which Fascism could flourish gradually developed. The book poses inevitable questions like, 'Why did no one stop him?' and attempts to give the answers. A book for the more able secondary school pupil and also valuable for the teacher dealing with this topic at a variety of levels.

Elizabeth J. King, in a review of "3rd September 1939," in The School Librarian, *Vol. 36, No. 4, November, 1988, p. 149.*

Despite attempts at appeasement in the interests of avoiding war, Hitler's invasion of Poland pushed Great Britain into declaring war on September 3, 1939. Gordon's description of the events of that day and of the factors leading to the formal declaration of World War II are clear, cogent, and interesting. The background factors are discussed in the second section of the book. Beginning with the effects of the Versailles Treaty on the German economy and national morale, Gordon gives a concise recounting of Hitler's rise to power, his increasing encroachment into Eastern Europe, and the reasons why he did not meet with more resistance. Neville Chamberlain's work for appeasement, even to the point of abandoning countries that his government had agreed to defend, becomes understandable as the context for his efforts is made clear. This excellent historical investigation is complemented by numerous black-and-white photographs. Students with an interest in World War II should find this book both informative and rewarding. (pp. 98-9)

Ann Welton, in a review of "3rd September 1939," in School Library Journal, *Vol. 35, No. 5, January, 1989, pp. 98-9.*

The Middle of Somewhere: A Story of South Africa (1990)

For younger readers than is [Beverley] Naidoo's *Chain of Fire*, this is also a story of South Africa's forced removals of black communities to desolate areas of the country. Rebecca and her best friend Noni, both nine, are worried by the talk they've been hearing about a place called Pofadderkloof: "there it will all be new, and clean, and nice." The government makes extravagant promises, but most of the villagers resolve to stay where they are, despite promises and threats. Noni's family is among those who leave, "in the dark, like jackals," and Rebecca feels lonely and deserted. The childlike viewpoint is sometimes artificial but consistently maintained, and Rebecca herself is a rather timid, passive character who does not provide a strong enough center for the story. Because the story is about waiting—for Mama's biweekly visits home, for Papa to be released from prison, for the government to make its next move—it is static, an accurate reflection of reality but less effective as fiction. Characterization is variously subtle but generally idealized. Essentially optimistic, the book ends with Nelson Mandela's (and Papa's) release from prison and the implied promise that "they won't have the nerve to start bulldozing now. The whole world is watching."

Roger Sutton, in a review of "The Middle of Somewhere," in Bulletin of the Center for Children's Books, *Vol. 44, No. 2, October, 1990, p. 29.*

Taking place in the recent past (news of Mandela's freedom comes near the story's end), this is a relatively hopeful book, perhaps unrealistically free of violence (in sharp contrast to Naidoo's *Chain of Fire*). It is, however, appropriate for younger children, and presents a poignant, telling picture of a little girl who can treasure a discarded, blue-eyed doll even as she gets used to having "Feeling sad [become] part of what she did every day" while she longs to have her parents back home. A compassionate book that effectively presents an important part of the truth.

A review of "The Middle of Somewhere: A Story of South Africa," in Kirkus Reviews, *Vol. 58, No. 20, October 15, 1990, p. 1455.*

This, though not a sequel, is related to the author's ***Waiting for the Rain***. The earlier book had as its theme the friendship between a black and a white boy in South Africa and the effect on it of apartheid. By a grim parody Rebecca, the little central character in ***The Middle of Somewhere***, has two dolls, one—to the anger of her brother—white, the other black. In spite of all the grief and humiliation that the system has heaped on her and her family, Rebecca sees no incongruity in the love which she gives equally to both.

Rebecca and her friend Noni live in a village. Mother is a housekeeper in a white town and has time off only rarely for visits home. Father works in a supermarket. The children go to the local school, although there is no room for John who has to do his lessons outside. Now there is a threat to demolish the whole village to make way for a white suburb. Everyone will be forceably rehoused at Pofadderkloof. No one trusts the officials who have painted glowing pictures of fine houses with electricity and water.

At last Noni's parents yield to the pressure and move, and Rebecca is left without her best friend. Anger builds up among the blacks, and this is fuelled when Aunt Miriam returns from Pofadderkloof with news that the promised land is no paradise. The story ends with news of the release of Nelson Mandela and a glimmer of hope for the future.

What one notices most in this strong novel is the absence of anger. The writer maintains throughout a quiet, dispassionate tone which serves to strengthen the impact of her message. The viewpoint is always that of a small girl caught up in great events. 'Feeling sad became part of what she did every day.' It is for the reader to supply the anger as injustice and deception pile up against these simple, honest and hard-working people. There are no villains in the story. Mama's 'madam' is kind in her thoughtless, casual way. Even the prison guard who is in charge of Papa, when he is arrested for sedition, is 'quite nice'. When John reacts violently to this description, Aunt Miriam says that he 'probably has a wife and a lot of hungry children to feed'. It is the system that is on trial here, not individuals caught in its toils.

There is much food for serious thought in this quiet and largely artless tale, all of it a challenge to readers of all ages but within the comprehension of children of Rebecca's and Noni's age. (pp. 111-12)

> *M. Crouch, in a review of "The Middle of Somewhere," in* The Junior Bookshelf, *Vol. 55, No. 3, June, 1991, pp. 111-12.*

X. J. Kennedy

1929-

(Pseudonym of Joseph Charles Kennedy) American poet, author of fiction and nonfiction, and editor.

Major works include *One Winter Night in August and Other Nonsense Jingles* (1975), *Knock at a Star: A Child's Introduction to Poetry* (with Dorothy M. Kennedy, 1982), *The Owlstone Crown* (1983), *The Forgetful Wishing-Well: Poems for Young People* (1985), *Brats* (1986).

The writer of nonsense verse and serious poetry for middle graders that blends traditional forms with experimental variations and contemporary references, Kennedy is considered an especially gifted stylist whose works reflect his love of language and sensitivity to children and their feelings as well as a sense of humor that ranges from wryly affectionate to wickedly pointed. He is also well known as the author of *The Owlstone Crown,* a fantasy novel for children in the middle and upper grades that is his sole work of fiction as well as for *Knock at a Star,* a teaching anthology on which he collaborated with his wife Dorothy that describes the characteristics and pleasures of poetry and includes selections from a variety of sources, most of them contemporary. As a poet, Kennedy addresses a wide range of subjects in verse noted for its precision, fresh imagery, and wordplay. In his nonsense poetry, he reflects the absurdity of contemporary life by describing children, adults, animals, and supernatural beings in familiar domestic situations that he skews with surprising, unexpected twists and turns. Among his most popular poems are those in the collections *Brats* and *Fresh Brats* (1990), cautionary tales that describe how obnoxious children get away with—or pay for—their outrageous behavior; in some of the poems, Kennedy blithely relates how his subjects come to an unfortunate end. In his nonsense verse, Kennedy consistently includes poems that deal with the real world of children. Two of his collections, *The Forgetful Wishing-Well: Poems for Young People* and *The Kite that Braved Old Orchard Beach: Year-Round Poems for Young People* (1991) are comprised mostly of poetry with a realistic base. In these works, which have the personal and family concerns of childhood as their themes, Kennedy provides his usual witty observations while including sensitive portrayals of loss and other feelings. Kennedy often includes simile, metaphor, alliteration, onomatopoeia, and sophisticated language in his works, which are praised for their superior read-aloud quality and appeal to both children and adults. Critic Nancy Willard says of him, "Like the best writers of nonsense, Kennedy turns the ordinary on its head," and reviewer Katherine D. Whalin adds that he "not only knows what good poetry is but what good poetry appeals to children."

Recognized as a national authority on poetry, Kennedy is well respected as a poet for adults as well as children. As with his children's poetry, he writes his adult verse in traditional metrical patterns and is acknowledged for its

amusing and incisive qualities. Kennedy describes himself as "a metrical, rhyming poet, a traditionalist in shape if not in matter. . . ."; he is also an author of textbooks on literature and poetry, a book reviewer, an anthologist, and an editor of books and magazines, and has been a professor of college English. Kennedy created his first juvenile poetry for his own five children and included two of these poems in his adult collection *Nude Descending a Staircase: Poems, Song, A Ballad* (1961); prompted by poet and anthologist Myra Cohn Livingston and editor Margaret McElderry, he began to publish his poetry for children on a regular basis. Kennedy's first books were nonsense poetry; after compiling *Knock at a Star* with his wife, he wrote *Did Adam Name the Vinegarroon?* (1982), a rhyming alphabetical bestiary which depicts real, extinct, and imaginary creatures, as well as *The Owlstone Crown* before publishing his first book of realistic poetry, *The Forgetful Wishing-Well.* In *The Owlstone Crown,* a work inspired by a story Kennedy told to his children and his favorite among his works for the young, Kennedy describes how the orphaned thirteen-year-old twins Timothy and Verity Tibbs enter Owlstonia, a fantastic alternative earth, in their search for their grandparents, who have been imprisoned by the evil dictator Raoul Owlstone. The twins, who are aided in their quest by a bear, a snail, and other creatures, defeat Owlstone and release both their grandparents and their mother, who has been held captive by Owlstone since the twins were infants. Influenced by such works as *The Divine Comedy, The Wizard of Oz,* the plays of Shakespeare, and the detective fiction of Raymond Chandler, *The Owlstone Crown* is perhaps Kennedy's most popular book. *The Forgetful Wishing-Well* was named a Notable Book by the American Library Association in 1985; Kennedy has also received several awards for his adult poetry.

(See also *Contemporary Literary Criticism,* Vols. 8, 42; *Something about the Author,* Vol. 14; *Contemporary Authors New Revision Series,* Vols. 4, 30; *Contemporary Authors,* Vol. 2, rev. ed.; *Contemporary Authors Autobiography Series,* Vol. 9; and *Dictionary of Literary Biography,* Vol. 5.)

TITLE COMMENTARY

One Winter Night in August and Other Nonsense Jingles (1975)

Anyone who knows X. J. Kennedy's King Tut—"Tight as a nut / Keeps his big fat Mummy shut"—will be looking forward to this collection of over fifty bite-sized nonsense rhymes. They won't be disappointed. Not with the munchy perfection of "Look out, here comes Lucky Sukey / Sucking on her mucky-looking cookie" or the wide open exuberance of "With walloping tails, the whales off Wales / Whack waves to wicked whitecaps." The ideas can be as wonderfully wicked as the sounds—**"Waking Up Uncle"** confesses, "My favorite gag / Is filling Uncle's sleeping bag / With prune whip yogurt to the brim." Others are merely intriguing—like the "Instant Storm" cooked up from "frozen French-fried thunder, / Vanilla-flavored lightning bolts, / Fresh-frozen raindrop rattle" or, in a classical vein, "Medusa's looks had what it takes / To knock the rust off boilers. / She had a lovely head of snakes, / She'd put it up in coilers." [Illustrator] David McPhail contributes some leaden imitations of *Juniper Tree* tableaux, but even these can't weigh down this bright and buoyant accomplishment.

> *A review of "One Winter Night in August: And Other Nonsense Jingles," in* Kirkus Reviews, *Vol. XLIII, No. 7, April 1, 1975, p. 380.*

Kennedy possesses a real knack for clever word usage and rhyme and covers a far-flung range of subject matter, but his nonsense verse lacks the outlandish relationship to the real world which makes readers laugh. It sometimes seems to be stream of consciousness rambling, often incoherently silly, and the author has little understanding of children's sense of humor. (It is a rare child indeed who would laugh at " 'Said a census taker to a centaur / 'Pardon me, I'm counting. / Sir, are you man or are you horse? / Please, would you mind dismounting?' "). Moreover, many of the verses are morbid and unpleasant.

> *June B. Cater, in a review of "One Winter Night in August and Other Nonsense Jingles," in* School Library Journal, *Vol. 22, No. 3, November, 1975, p. 79.*

These fifty-odd poems, it is plausible to assume, reflect the tastes of "Katie, Dave, Matthew, Dan, and Josh," to whom they are dedicated and for whom, undoubtedly, they were originally written. They run the gamut from **"Who to Pet and Who Not to"** ("Go pet a kitten, pet a dog, / Go pet a worm for practice, / But don't go pet a porcupine— / You want to be a cactus?"), to six- and eight-liners and other brevities which occasionally sound a faint echo of Carroll or of Lear. And the title-poem recalls the classic mix-up, "It was midnight on the ocean, / Not a streetcar was in sight." Verbally sophisticated children will like the peculiar playfulness. Here and there, the rhymes strain for effect, and the rhythms imitate, to no advantage, those of the so-called young poets Kenneth Koch and Richard Lewis have popularized. Nine times out of ten, however, Kennedy is both skillful and funny.

> *Samuel French Morse, in a review of "One Winter Night in August and Other Nonsense Jingles," in* The Horn Book Magazine, *Vol. LII, No. 1, February, 1976, p. 67.*

A [great] variety of nonsense appears in the books of Bodecker and Kennedy. . . . While [the poems in Bodecker's *Let's Marry Said the Cherry*] are well done, still more finely crafted and more lasting are the poems in *One Winter Night in August.* Among the wacky characters appear a wicked witch, Medusa, a boa who eats bowling balls, a dinosaur, a walking skeleton, and great-great-grandma who sleeps in a treehouse. Here are domestic situations gone awry, with exploding gravy and a monstrous mouse who grabs the birthday cake. Some verses are close to real life, like the one about "baby [who] eats our rugs so clean / He beats a carpet sweeper." These happy, rollicking verses demand to be shared orally. They show a delightful sense of the absurd, love of verbal play, and above all a good awareness of the necessity for restraint in producing nonsense that will wear well and give pleasure for many readings. (pp. 198-99)

> *Alethea K. Helbig, "Trends in Poetry for Children," in* Children's Literature: Annual of the Modern Language Association Seminar on Children's Literature and The Children's Literature Association, *Vol. 6, 1977, pp. 195-202.*

The Phantom Ice Cream Man: More Nonsense Verse (1979)

Writing verse for children seems to require rare delicacy, balancing between adult wit on the one hand, something silly on the other hand, and *on the third hand*—which adds its monstrous brilliance only when the first two are already present—something quite serious, which may also be sad and eccentric: like a dong with a luminous nose, for instance.

Of the new books of poetry for children, one strikes me as approaching this combination. X. J. Kennedy's *The Phantom Ice Cream Man,* makes a worthy sequel to the author's earlier *One Winter Night in August.* There is a joy of rhythm here, a joy of rhyme—as in the title poem, in which "daren't" pairs off with "transparent." One of my favorites is a little exercise in buried metaphor, beginning: "If combs could brush their teeth, / If a needle's eye shed tears, / If bottles craned their necks, / If corn pricked up its ears . . . "

Donald Hall, "On the Third Hand," in The New York Times Book Review, April 29, 1979, p. 25.

X. J. Kennedy runs an abcb rhyme with more literary skill than most nonsense verse manages. In this latest collection of imaginary beasts and far out situations (plus seven limericks), he interests kids in tyrannosaurus rex's teeth, the Nineteenth-Moon-of-Neptune Beasts who devour human rockets like eggs with funny bugs inside, and a vampire bat that attacks the umpire for his call. He reaches out with lively language and upbeat words like "enchilada." The Discontented Cow cries, "Bring on the bratwurst, kid!" Kennedy begins with outrageous statements, "I brush my teeth with ocean sand," and doesn't shield young readers from words like "phosphorus." When he's good, he throws in lines like "All four of my uncle Erics" without making them the punch of the poem. When he's not, he pushes the rhyme and there are fewer surprises, as with the Muddleheaded Messer of drawers or the confusion of squash-eating Bill Bunyan as Sasquatch. . . . A two-scoop cone.

Sharon Elswit, in a review of "The Phantom Ice Cream Man," in School Library Journal, Vol. 25, No. 9, May, 1979, p. 63.

Kaye Starbird's latest, **The Covered Bridge House and Other Poems** is plagued by the same problems which have hindered her work in the past. . . . Momentarily diverting caricatures or observations spiced with occasional verbal ingenuity, her pieces tend to limp as words and lines are forced to serve rhythm and rhyme instead of sense and vision.

Nor is **The Phantom Ice Cream Man: More Nonsense Verse** up to X. J. Kennedy's usual nonsensical stuff. Kennedy is at his best with short four-or six-or eight-liners which connect with contemporary life and deliver a delayed wallop, like **"A Choosy Wolf"**:

"Why won't you eat me, wolf," I asked. / "It wouldn't be much fun to. / Besides, I'm into natural foods / That nothing has been done to."

And **"A Confused Chameleon"**:

"Balls of fire!" cried chameleon Betty, / "I'm so mixed up I'm ready to bust! / I got hit with a bunch of confetti— / Now my color control won't adjust!"

Rollicking rhythms and both subtle and obvious verbal trickery help Kennedy gallop through such absurd tales as that of Mackerel Mack and Halibut Hal, "the two best buddies in the fish corral;" of Tyrannosaurus Rex, whose teeth "Were pearly-white and porous," but now "are total wrecks" that "need a ton of drilling;" and of two ghosts who once traded heads and now have trouble telling "whose body is whose." The verses are inventive, display an infectious delight in words, and get to the point quickly, most of the time. Then, too, Kennedy has the rare ability to appeal to the sense of humor of more than one gener-

ation at the same time, which reminds us that good nonsense, like all good poetry for children, should not be limited in its appeal to a single audience. Even though the verses in **Ice Cream Man** are thinner than Kennedy's verses usually are, they are still better than most of the nonsense being produced for the young these days. X. J. Kennedy at not quite his best is still quite good indeed, but I think his verses in **One Winter Night in August** are sharper. (pp. 140-41)

Alethea Helbig, "The State of Things: A Question of Substance," in Children and Their Literature: A Readings Book, edited by Jill P. May, ChLA Publications, 1983, pp. 138-50.

Did Adam Name the Vinegarroon? (1982)

Kennedy's third gathering of poetry for children, an alphabetical bestiary of creatures actual and fabulous, is worth buying because again [publisher David] Godine has produced a beautiful book—handsome layout, beautiful Electra typeface and a number of truly exciting black-and-white illustrations [by Heidi Johanna Selig]. The sly picture for the Iguana is enough to cause nightmares. Kennedy's verse is uneven: sometimes skilled, never offensive, but hardly memorable. The slapdash forced rhyme of Kennedy's poem on the Eel suggests an occasional condescending slovenliness on the poet's part that doubly disappoints when we see how evocative he can be in a poem such as **"Goshawk."**

Peter Neumayer, in a review of "Did Adam Name the Vinegarroon?" in School Library Journal, Vol. 29, No. 3, November, 1982, p. 86.

X. J. Kennedy's **Did Adam Name the Vinegarroon?** a rhyming alphabetical bestiary, is a lively example of its type. Mr. Kennedy's crocodiles look like "pickles in a barrel," and his xiphosurans (horseshoe crabs to you), found "where low tide sloshes," resemble

some
Old horse's spare galoshes.

Irresistibly drawn to alliteration, he brings us the bulk and tenderness of the woolly mammoth:

A hairy mountain ten feet tall
With peepers moist and misty,
It stood as solid as a wall,
Its twin tusks long and twisty.

[A] punster, he retells the tale of the "bullheaded" Minotaur, while his lion roars "with might and mane." Though Mr. Kennedy's style lacks the finesse and pungency of Mr. Bodecker's and the imagistic precision of Miss Moore's, he rollicks and frolics amiably.

Alicia Ostriker, "Tulip, Julep, Sloshes, Galoshes," in The New York Times Book Review, November 14, 1982, p. 45.

Light verse, like light opera, is a more demanding art than its popularity might imply. Both require a finely tuned ear, an ability to create apt but unexpected images, and a delight in discovering what is uncommon in the common-

Kennedy captions this 1983 photo of his wife Dorothy and himself "The Kennedys at work."

place and what is ordinary in the fabulous. Having met these requirements, the poet has added another challenge: the composition of an alphabetic bestiary in which selections must follow the dictates of sequence yet sustain individuality and variety. The result is an engaging gathering of creatures—some extinct, others imaginary, a few familiar—all presented from a fresh point of view. The collection is notable for alliteration, similes, and unforced rhymes—underscored not only by end-stopped lines but by carefully structured rhythms. Judicious use of homonyms adds an additional fillip of humor to aphorisms which can be extracted like small but perfect gems, as in: "Yet tyrants, under Time's slow hand, / Must one day bow their necks. / Now in museums—bones wired—stand / Tyrannosaurus wrecks." . . . Elegantly and thoughtfully planned, the book is a visual tribute to poetry as art.

> *Mary M. Burns, in a review of "Did Adam Name the Vinegarroon?" in* The Horn Book Magazine, *Vol. LVIII, No. 6, December, 1982, p. 664.*

Knock at a Star: A Child's Introduction to Poetry (with Dorothy M. Kennedy, 1982)

Calculated to appeal directly to young readers, the anthology is stocked with poems chosen from a myriad of varied

poets, ranging from Blake and Herrick to David McCord, Eve Merriam, and Bob Dylan. Carefully divided into four parts further divided into subsections, the book indicates what poems do, how their words create images and musical patterns, and how poetic configurations are formed—such as limericks, haiku, and songs, the music for which is included. One section is particularly concerned with the writing of poetry. Appearing as introductory remarks to the various parts of the anthology or interspersed among the verses, the conversational informal explanations of the authors link and illuminate the evocative offerings, which have been especially chosen for their action, humor, concreteness, and sound effects. The commentaries have avoided both pedantry and prettification by stressing the naturalness of the poetic experience. With an afterword to adults, including a note for people who work with groups of children.

> *Paul Heins, in a review of "Knock at a Star: A Child's Introduction to Poetry," in* The Horn Book Magazine, *Vol. LVIII, No. 6, December, 1982, p. 664.*

Subtly and engagingly, Dorothy and X. J. Kennedy introduce newcomers to poetry by way of relatively light and primarily contemporary poetry and verse. The poems are categorized under headings such as "What Do Poems Do?" ("make you laugh"; "tell stories"; "send messages" and so forth); "What's Inside a Poem?" ("images"; "word music"; "beats that repeat" and so forth). There are sections on limericks, parodies (a splendid one by Koch on Williams' "This Is Just To Say"), Haiku and "found poems." Brief, readable, informative prose sections by the editors gracefully intersperse the poetry. . . . If any book can win young readers to poetry, this one can, for there's not a poem in it that isn't a chuckle, a scare, or an illumination.

> *Peter Neumeyer, in a review of "Knock at a Star: A Child's Introduction to Poetry," in* School Library Journal, *Vol. 29, No. 4, December, 1982, p. 65.*

As a poet teaching in the public schools, I've come to believe that a simple creative writing program, incorporated into the yearly curriculum, can make the difference between a child who groans at the mention of the word "poetry" and one who finds the literary arts exciting and provocative. The formula, not at all surprising, consists of reading poems aloud for enjoyment and writing poetry together for a truly personal involvement. An introduction to poetry must focus on work that's accessible to a young listener, emphasizes the conjuring power of language, and reveals a direct link with the reader's own experience.

If you're searching for books to begin such a program, **Knock at a Star** is an ideal place to start. Mr. Kennedy has written books of poetry for both young and old audiences. He and his wife have created a writing-program and teaching anthology that explores the basic elements and styles of the poet's craft. The selection includes a broad spectrum of modern verse, with a strong emphasis on rhythmic invention, rhyme, and vivid imagery. Moving through each chapter, teacher, parent, or student can read *and* write their way into the pleasure of poetry. The styles presented are wonderfully varied, and described with a genuine sense of wonder. . . . Children from Grade 3 and beyond will find this book a fine tool for poetic explorations.

> *Steven Ratiner, "Rhyme and Imagery to Capture Kids," in* The Christian Science Monitor, *June 29, 1983, p. 9.*

The Owlstone Crown (1983)

When Lew, a ladybug private-eye, tells Tim and Verity Tibbs that their grandparents have been captured by Other Earth's evil dictator Raoul Owlstone, the twins set off to rescue them. First they must escape their cruel foster parents, then find the door between worlds and somehow try to avoid Raoul's marauding army of stone owls. They are aided by two new friends: Fardels, a bear and a prophetic snail called Shelley (after the writers Percy and Mary). However, all are finally captured and brought before Raoul and his consort, the Baroness Ratisha—known for her hypnotic ruby eye. Tim discovers the flaw in Raoul's scheme to take over the Land of Moonflower: the light of the life-giving Moonflower plant (which Raoul is trying to kill) will melt the owlstone which he has used to build his empire. Overcoming all obstacles, Tim and Verity release the plant, destroy the castle, exile Raoul and

Ratisha and are reunited with their grandparents and their mother, who was lost between worlds when the twins were babies. Poet X. J. Kennedy's first work of fiction is a fast-paced fantasy with strong, whimsical characterizations. Full of coincidence and exaggeration, the headlong adventure is reminiscent of Joan Aiken. Rich with amusing detail and poetic imagery, this will make an excellent read aloud.

> *Anne Connor, in a review of "The Owlstone Crown," in* School Library Journal, *Vol. 30, No. 5, January, 1984, p. 78.*

Poet Kennedy makes his debut as a novelist with this heavily symbolic fantasy tale. He traces the adventures of a pair of twins, Timothy and Verity Tibb, who are bent on rescuing their grandparents from an alternative world. . . . A beneficent bear, a prophetic snail, and a pond personified are among the beings Tim and Verity encounter on their rather drawn-out quest, which ends with not only the overthrow of the villain, but also a reunion with their grandparents *and* their mother, long presumed dead. The momentum of the storytelling flags at times, and the fantasy world is neither firmly realized nor well explained. Still, Kennedy's felicitous turns of phrase and his mildly exaggerated characters and situations will hold die-hard fantasy readers to the finish.

> *Karen Stang Hanley, in a review of "The Owlstone Crown," in* Booklist, *Vol. 80, No. 13, March 1, 1984, p. 992.*

The Owlstone Crown is a delightful children's fantasy, written with grace and wit. . . .

The story moves along at a lively pace, with spunky talking animals, and a perky narration by Timothy, occasionally interrupted by Verity for comment or correction. . . .

Without getting allegorical or preachy, Kennedy allows his characters (and his readers) to wrestle with the arbitrariness and nastiness of evil. His story affirms that idealistic individuals can overthrow fascism by individual sabotage and subversion and suggests that an apparently impervious police state is constructed of such flimsy matter that once its collapse has begun, it will rapidly disintegrate. This is a well-written book, highly recommended for younger readers and libraries serving them.

> *Richard Mathews, "Poet's First Novel Written with Grace and Wit," in* Fantasy Review, *Vol. 7, No. 7, August, 1984, p. 48.*

The Forgetful Wishing Well: Poems for Young People (1985)

Kennedy's poetry in this collection is wonderfully terse, controlled and sensitive. Accompanied by a pen-and-ink drawing [by Monica Incisa], each of the seven sections of the book explores a theme of interest to older grade-school children. The drawings are also clean masterpieces of understatement, commenting on the tangle of emotions in the section "Growing Pains" or the clear images in the section "All Around the Year." With these poems that range from the humor of silly rhymes to stark realism. Kennedy again demonstrates, as he did in **Knock at a Star,** that he knows not only what good poetry is but what good poetry appeals to children. His poems sing; they are never forced ("But you can't / Hear an ant / Pant"). **The Forgetful Wishing Well** will long be remembered.

> *Kathleen D. Whalin, in a review of "The Forgetful Wishing Well: Poems for Young People," in* School Library Journal, *Vol. 31, No. 9, May, 1985, p. 90.*

The 70 light, accomplished entries in Kennedy's latest verse collection deal, as his section headings have it, with "Growing Pains" (". . . My wooly bear is packed away, / Why do the nights feel colder?"), "Creatures" (such as "Bats," who ". . . drowse all day in houses' eaves / Like tents collapsed for storage . . . "), "People" ("I don't like Agnes Snagletooth. / How can I ever face her? . . . "), the "Wonders" of simple devices, such as flashlights (their makers "put up light in little cans"), and commonplace "Family Matters" such as the scratchy beard of **"Porcupine Pa,"** a "loving pater" whose kid feels "like cheese / That's up against a grater." Kennedy's musings on such humble objects as **"My Window Screen"** and sour **"Summer Milk"** lack the concentrated transforming vision of Valerie Worth's small poems for children; and it's disappointing that this volume's strongest aural-visual image is **"The Man with the Tan Hands,"** reprinted from Kennedy's very first (1962) collection.

Kennedy's verse is always unassumingly elegant, however, and his easy mastery of form is uncommon in verse for children. (pp. J-38-J-39)

> *A review of "The Forgetful Wishing Well: Poems for Young People," in* Kirkus Reviews, *Vol. LIII, Nos. 5-10, May 15, 1985, pp. J-38-J-39.*

"The discovery of hidden similarities," as Arthur Koestler described the creative process in *The Act of Creation,* is perhaps the critical equivalent of the litmus test with which to separate poetic vision from simple observation. X. J. Kennedy's latest collection of verses passes that test with honors. Grouped into seven audience-directed categories, the seventy selections illuminate familiar concerns and situations so that they become fresh, funny, or poignant. Specific topics range from the agonies of writing thank you letters to a wistful description of an aging pet. The poems about "Creatures" are particularly notable for their imagery and unexpected touches of wit—as in the concluding stanza of **"Owl"**: "And just because he preens like men / Who utter grave advice, / We think him full of wisdom when / He's only full of mice." Diverse verse forms—including a number of remarkably fluid rhymed couplets, varied rhyme schemes, and infectious rhythms, each uniquely suited to content—add depth and dimension to the collection. Characterized by fresh imagery, related to but not restricted by everyday expressions, these are poems to delight the ear and stimulate the imagination.

> *Mary M. Burns, in a review of "The Forgetful Wishing Well: Poems for Young People," in*

The Horn Book Magazine, *Vol. LXI, No. 4, July-August, 1985, p. 460.*

Brats (1986)

These are bright, tight, and inventive, with plenty of playground chanting potential: "On his motorbike Lars stands / Roaring past us—'Look! no hands!' / Soon with vacant handle bars / Back the bike roars. Look, no Lars!" Word choices are simple, with reliance on inventive situations, as when one young brat drenches the T.V. set to find out whether "flash floods / Turn soap opera to suds." Another imp, Sue, sticks a pig to the ceiling with Elmer's Glue. ("Uncle, gawking, spilled his cup. / 'Wow!' he cried. 'Has pork gone up!'"). A few of the selections have a slightly grisly ring (specifically, in the case of Louise, who sneaks up on a snoozing bear), but it's all done in high humor. . . . Neatly crafted poetry that will be highly popular as well.

> *Zena Sutherland, in a review of "Brats," in* Bulletin of the Center for Children's Books, *Vol. 39, No. 11, July-August, 1986, p. 211.*

Kennedy applies his considerable poetic talent to creating a worthy successor to William Cole's *Beastly Boys and Ghastly Girls* (Collins, 1964; o.p.). The 42 poems about horrible children are, for the most part, exactly what is wanted in funny poetry for children. The genuinely humorous characters ("On a bet, foolhardy Sam / Leaps inside a mammoth clam") and inventive situations ("Down the blowhole of a whale / Mal poured ice-cold ginger ale") are presented in fresh, economic language. If two of the poems offer adult rather than childlike humor, the collection is more than redeemed by the other wonderful poems and by [James] Watts' black-and-white drawings that enhance the off-beat humor. **Brats** is a small, well laid-out book that offers many smiles and a few big laughs.

> *Kathleen D. Whalin, in a review of "Brats," in* School Library Journal, *Vol. 32, No. 10, August, 1986, p. 94.*

The poet and anthologist X. J. Kennedy exemplifies the humorous adult empathetically but uncloyingly adapting himself in using adult language to say what happy children may deem outrageously funny.

Brats [is] a collection of short poems of silly children meeting sillier fates. . . . These are neat, lilting verses about hazard-prone rascals who get themselves swallowed by sharks, eaten by bears, transported by hawks and meet other thought-provoking fates.

Mr. Kennedy's humor is sufficiently outrageous to be ribtickling, rather than frightening to the childlike mind. It is a humor that derives in part from the absurdity of the catastrophes; its crux is almost always a pun, and its lightness may derive most interestingly from the poetical form itself.

Mr. Kennedy's iambic tetrameter couplet as a vehicle for humor became entrenched in English by way of a long, satirical 17th-century poem, "Hudibras," mocking Puritan officiousness. And for any native German speaker, the form is synonymous with the 19th-century bad boys Max and Moritz, whose rather more sinister escapades (killing chickens, blowing up the village schoolmaster) are inseparable from the doggerel metre in which those miscreants are rendered. Mr. Kennedy exploits the inherent humor of the form nimbly, demonstrates his technical virtuosity and succeeds in being catastrophic without being mean. (p. 30)

> *Peter Neumeyer, in a review of "Brats," in* The New York Times Book Review, *October 5, 1986, p. 30.*

Ghastlies, Goops and Pincushions: Nonsense Verse (1989)

More genuinely comic verse from the poet and author of **Brats.**

Most of these 62 poems here are new, although some are reprinted from periodicals and other collections. They derive their humor from new views of familiar subjects (16 lines of admonitions begin, "Never stand under an anvil," and conclude: "Stay indoors when your nights have full moons, / And you might have a chance at surviving / In the world of old movie cartoons!"); from the childlike humor of the hilariously disgusting (**"Skunk Cabbage Slaw"**); and from marvelous wordplay, puns, twists of meanings, and juggling with sounds. There's a delicious entry for St. Pat's Day, with the wee folk of Tipperary setting up their own air service near Shannon.

For Shel Silverstein's fans, the deft versifying and wicked humor here should prove equally appealing.

> *A review of "Ghastlies, Goops and Pincushions," in* Kirkus Reviews, *Vol. LVII, No. 3, February 1, 1989, p. 210.*

A child surfeited on similes will welcome **Ghastlies, Goops & Pincushions**. . . . Kennedy achieves, in lilting rhyme and meter, the hilarious blend of the catastrophic and the inane found in the jokes and jingles children make up for each other on the playground. Like the best writers of nonsense, X. J. Kennedy turns the ordinary on its head. A volcano erupts in a living room, a "nibbling sibling" happily snacks on shingles, spare tires and driveway tar; one child is swallowed by a vacuum cleaner, another vanishes into a vat of ice cream. And the neighborhood grocer is anything but friendly:

> By cabbages he's long been dreaded.
> He chops their heads off, sells 'em shredded.
>
> His margarine is seaweed-green.
> Legs poke out of his eggs. Bad scene!
>
> His coffeecakes look twelve years old.
> Nothing he sells has yet been sold
>
> Except to tribes of mangy trolls—
> *They* like his mildewed jellyrolls!
>
> But if *you* meet this real gross grocer,
> Go home and hug your stuffed bear closer.
>
> (p. 21)

> *Nancy Willard, "Rhymes of Our Times," in* Book World—The Washington Post, *May 14, 1989, pp. 15, 21.*

A worthy companion to **Brats,** this compendium of witty, light verse introduces a gallery of most unwanted individuals as well as a variety of absurd antics and—one hopes—unlikely situations. . . . Whether describing Agatha Ghastly who creates enough static electricity to transform Auntie Sue into a light bulb, a snow leopard who becomes invisible after coughing off his spots, or an enterprising baby who manages, while unsupervised, to place a long-distance call, the poet's agile verses, varied in structure, rhythm, and form, not only make the absurd seem real but also reveal the absurdity frequently found in reality. The comic voice is not an easy one to sustain; thus a collection such as this is a demanding test of the poet's skill and imagination. Kennedy once again demonstrates that he possesses both attributes in abundance.

> *Mary M. Burns, in a review of "Ghastlies, Goops & Pincushions: Nonsense Verse," in* The Horn Book Magazine, *Vol. LXV, No. 5, September-October, 1989, p. 633.*

Fresh Brats (1990)

This gallery of poetic mischief-makers features the ghoulish, gross, or catastrophic humor that children love most in the middle grades. It's hard to select favorite examples—students will be popping these poems at each other like spitballs: "To the bottom of his drink / Dad beholds an earthworm sink. / For her bio project, May / Must have used the ice-cube tray." Often the straightforward joke ends with a twist, as in the case of "jealous would-be-actor Jay," who sabotages the Yuletide play with marbles, only to end up in a cast different from the kind he envied. These irrepressibly rhymed verses make an irresistible introduction for reluctant readers as well for enthusiastic listeners.

> *Betsy Hearne, in a review of "Fresh Brats," in* Bulletin of the Center for Children's Books, *Vol. 43, No. 7, March, 1990, p. 165.*

Rare is the sequel that comes up to its predecessor, but Kennedy's new collection of short, snappy poems depicting bratty kids proves just as fresh and funny as the original **Brats.** The double entendre title suggests Kennedy's rejection of the "little pink cakes" school of children's verse: these rhymes promise the bold flavor of bratwurst—with mustard, no doubt. For children who think poetry too sweet and sentimental, Kennedy's acerbic wit is the perfect antidote to their preconceptions, as in this verse: "Tell me, why so pale and wan, / Flattened and deflated, John? / Are you weary? Is maintaining / Your vampire bat a wee bit draining?"

> *Carolyn Phelan, in a review of "Fresh Brats," in* Booklist, *Vol. 86, No. 17, May 1, 1990, p. 1701.*

Like the poems in Myra Cohn Livingston's *Higgledy-Piggledy* (McElderry, 1986), Kennedy's verses are all composed in the same rhyme and rhythmic pattern, making them easy models for young writers to imitate. And like Livingston, Kennedy focuses on the sassy antics of less-than-admirable children, a subject common to the verse of many popular children's poets. Purchase if there is demand for more irreverent comic verses. (pp. 85-6)

> *Barbara Chatton, in a review of "Fresh Brats,"*
> *in* School Library Journal, *Vol. 36, No. 7, July, 1990, pp. 85-6.*

The Kite That Braved Old Orchard Beach: Year-Round Poems for Young People (1991)

Only a few of these deftly phrased poems have appeared before, scattered among topical anthologies; the others are new. Grouped by theme ("Joys," "Family," "Not So Ordinary Things," etc.), they exhibit Kennedy's mastery of his simple verse forms: his word-choices are felicitous, and his expertly honed lines almost never contain forced rhymes or awkward phrases tailored to the meter. Though the insights here are rarely deep, the images are also apt, the descriptions often intriguing. Meanwhile, the tone ranges from wry—or rueful—to neatly concise but straightforward explication. The nine poems about "Birds, Beasts & Fish" rival the hilarity of *Brats;* on the other hand, the seasonal poems are rather ordinary samples of this made-to-order genre, while the "Friends" represent a seemingly overcareful ethnic balance. Still, a solid collection of unusually pleasing poems, from a poet who would make a grand role-model for anyone who cares about the precise use of language.

> *A review of "The Kite That Braved Old Orchard Beach: Year-Round Poems for Young People," in* Kirkus Reviews, *Vol. LIX, No. 3, February 1, 1991, p. 175.*

"Listen, I'm talking in stumbles and bumps," says Kennedy in his casual colloquial voice. A master of family situation comedy, he captures the irritation of a long car trip ("I'm not a good roadmap refolder") and the jealousy of a sibling who wants to try the baby's **"Pacifier"** ("Nights when Robert starts to blubber / Mother plugs his mouth with rubber"). Some of the light verses are preachy; a few reach too hard for rhyme. But kids will love the parody of verses like **"Song for a Valentine"** ("Just the way a baseball needs a mitt to catch it / Just the way an itch needs a hand to scratch it, . . . / That's the way I need you"). Sound, image, and idea come together with physical immediacy in **"Night Fog"** ("The lighthouse light / like a steady power mower / Keeps mowing night"). As in the title poem, some of the best lines combine a wry affection for the mundane and a startling glimpse of flight.

> *Hazel Rochman, in a review of "The Kite That Braved Old Orchard Beach: Year-Round Poems for Young People," in* Booklist, *Vol. 87, No. 12, February 15, 1991, p. 1191.*

Like the **"Poet"** he describes, Kennedy talks "in stumbles and bumps" when "Over a word's back another word jumps / And when it comes down there's a jingle." Although not as consistently successful as his other verse anthologies (*Brats; Ghastlies, Goops & Pincushions*), the 62 poems in this sprightly collection are alternately nostalgic and irreverent. Like James Whitcomb Riley, Kennedy wistfully celebrates family as he tells of having a "cup / Of nice hot milk" at Grandma's house. Reminiscent of Jack Prelutsky's creations, these characters are sometimes impudent and funny, as in **"My Stupid Parakeet Named After You."** Organized in such categories as "Joys" and "Growing & Dreaming," the poems reveal Kennedy's wide-ranging interests, his experimentation with traditional forms and his sensitivity to the wonderings and experiences of young people.

> *A review of "The Kite That Braved Old Orchard Beach: Year-Round Poems for Young People," in* Publishers Weekly, *Vol. 238, No. 9, February 15, 1991, p. 90.*

C(live) S(taples) Lewis

1898-1963

Irish-born English author of fiction.

Major works include the Chronicles of Narnia: *The Lion, the Witch, and the Wardrobe: A Story for Children* (1950), *Prince Caspian: The Return to Narnia* (1951), *The Voyage of the "Dawn Treader"* (1952), *The Silver Chair* (1953), *The Horse and His Boy* (1954), *The Magician's Nephew* (1955), *The Last Battle: A Story for Children* (1956).

The following entry emphasizes general criticism of the Chronicles of Narnia. It also includes a selection of reviews to supplement the general criticism.

One of the most distinguished and influential writers of the twentieth century, Lewis is well known as a Christian apologist, literary scholar, novelist, poet, and critic who informs all of his works with a profound joy in his Christian faith and a strong desire to share this faith with his readers. Although he reflects his respect for children and their clarity of vision throughout his oeuvre, the seven volumes which comprise the Chronicles of Narnia are Lewis's sole contribution to juvenile literature. These fantasies for middle graders, which can be read independently but together form an epic that spans a thousand years, blend the fairy tale and the heroic adventure to describe the history of Narnia—a self-contained world with its own time, landscapes, and culture—from creation to destruction. In addition, the books detail how their association with Narnia transforms the lives of the contemporary English children who are magically transported there whenever the land is beset by evil. The stories, which feature a rich tapestry of real and talking animals and characters from classical mythology, medieval bestiaries, and the supernatural, depict how the young male and female protagonists and the Narnian citizens battle the wicked forces that seek to destroy the goodness of Narnia and the values on which it is built: courage, truth, beauty, loyalty, tolerance, and generosity. Lewis demonstrates the main theme of the series, faith in action, through the exciting and often dangerous adventures of his characters, who encounter war, violence, suffering, and death as they fight for peace in Narnia; in addition, the protagonists experience personal tests of character which are crucial to the preservation of Narnia and bring them closer to maturity. Throughout the Chronicles, Lewis subtly introduces his characters to the essential elements of Christianity, exposing his protagonists—and young readers—to such concepts as sin, redemption, and the mystery of eternity. The pivotal figure in the Narnian saga is Aslan, a real lion who is also the Lion of Judah: Aslan creates the Narnian world with his song, is slain for the redemption of sin, and finally abolishes evil, bringing the just to him in a new creation. Both wonderful and terrible, he appears throughout each volume as a deus ex machina, providing direction for the children and acting as a standard by which to measure their obedience. Lewis ends the series with an apocalypse that

is prompted by the introduction of an antichrist into Narnia. At the end of the final battle, the human children and the virtuous creatures of Narnia pass through a stable door into a joyful afterlife with Aslan; by means of a railway accident in London, child protagonists from throughout the series and adults sympathetic to Narnia are killed and join the rest of the characters in Aslan's country. Although his themes are serious, Lewis includes humor in narrative and dialog as well as in pointed asides that satirize modern British society. He writes the Chronicles in an uncomplicated prose style, blending chivalric language and schoolboy slang with vivid descriptions of the Narnian world while threading familiar childhood thoughts, rituals, and pleasures into his works.

In creating the Chronicles, Lewis drew on his Christian beliefs, his knowledge of world mythology and literature, and his childhood memories. Born in Belfast, he was a quiet, solitary child who learned Irish folktales from his nurse and was swept away by such stories as *Gulliver's Travels* and the tales of Beatrix Potter. Lewis and his brother Warren created the imaginary countries of Animal-Land and Boxen as small boys, peopling their inventions with anthropomorphic animals, knights in armor, and other characters. At the age of twelve, Lewis began reading fairy tales and legends, becoming particularly inspired by the Norse myths; at sixteen, he read *The Iliad* and *The Odyssey* and soon thereafter was introduced to the works of George MacDonald, who along with E. Nesbit was his greatest influence as a writer. At prep school in England, Lewis abandoned his religious faith. In 1925, he was elected as Fellow and Tutor in English at Magdalen College, Oxford, where he would remain for the next thirty years; he later taught Medieval and Renaissance Literature at Cambridge. In 1929, Lewis renounced his atheism, becoming a Christian two years later. From 1930 through the end of his life Lewis resided at "The Kilns," a house near Oxford. In 1939, he opened his home to four schoolgirls who had been evacuated from London due to the Nazi bombing raids; these children served as the models for the Pevensies, the four brothers and sisters who become the kings and queens of Narnia and appear in most of the Narnian adventures. When one of the children showed an interest in a wardrobe in the Kilns and asked if she could go inside it, Lewis was prompted to begin consolidating the pictures he was carrying in his head, such as the one of a faun carrying an umbrella in a snowy wood which he had held since the age of fifteen and which is a central image of *The Lion, the Witch, and the Wardrobe,* the first volume of the Chronicles of Narnia. Writing to utilize the form of the fairy tale and to please himself with the kind of book he would have liked as a child, Lewis began the first volume, which he intended to be only a single work. However, after he had written a large portion of *The Lion, the Witch, and the Wardrobe,* which describes how the Pevensies are drawn into Narnia through an old armoire, Aslan bounded into the story and changed its focus and direction. Lewis then decided to create a series of books that combined fantasy with adventure and pagan myth with the Christian gospel in order to introduce children to the numinous and to prepare them for a personal relationship with Jesus Christ.

Published at a time when realistic stories for older children were more fashionable than fantasies, the Chronicles of Narnia are often noted as exceptional contributions to the fantasy genre which helped to increase its popularity among writers of juvenile literature. However, the series has received a mixed reception since the 1950s: several reviewers complain that Lewis is too obvious in his moral purpose and concentrates more on theology than on narrative. In addition, he is criticized for creating one-dimensional characters, for being too imitative and derivative, and for including instances of violence, suffering, and death in the volumes which make them unsuitable for young readers. Most observers celebrate the Chronicles for Lewis's success in relating his themes to children in a way that is accessible to them and respects both their interests and their range of understanding. He is also praised as a masterful storyteller whose works are colorful, exciting, and moving and whose inventiveness and vision in creating a new mythology with Narnia is an achievement of genius. Critic Humphrey Carpenter has written of Lewis that "no other children's writer can rival the sheer quantity of fantasy-ideas in the seven Narnia books . . . ," while Naomi Lewis adds that "Lewis is perhaps the best-liked post-war 'quality' writer for children."

The Last Battle was awarded the Carnegie Medal in 1956 while *The Horse and His Boy* was commended for the same award in 1954. *The Lion, the Witch, and the Wardrobe* won the Lewis Carroll Shelf Award in 1962. Lewis has also won awards for his adult works and has received many honorary degrees.

(See also *CLR,* Vol. 3; *Contemporary Literary Criticism,* Vols. 1, 3, 6, 14, 27; *Something about the Author,* Vol. 13; *Authors and Artists for Young Adults,* Vol. 3; *Contemporary Authors New Revision Series.* Vol. 33; and *Dictionary of Literary Biography,* Vols. 15, 100.)

AUTHOR'S COMMENTARY

[*The following excerpt is from* C. S. Lewis: Letters to Children, *edited by Lyle W. Dorsett and Marjorie Lamp Mead.*]

[Dorsett and Lamp Mead: One of C. S. Lewis's early fan letters on *The Chronicles of Narnia* came from the United States. Hila was eleven years old when she wrote this letter, complete with a water-color painting that she had done of all of the characters in **The Lion, the Witch and the Wardrobe.** Her first reading of this story was three years earlier when she experienced what she described years later as "an indefinable stirring and longing."

At the time this letter was written, **The Lion, the Witch and the Wardrobe, Prince Caspian,** and **The Voyage of the "Dawn Treader"** were the only books published; **The Silver Chair** would appear later in 1953. However, Lewis had actually finished writing all of the seven volumes a year earlier, in 1952.]

June 3rd. 1953

Dear [Hila]

Thank you so much for your lovely letter and pictures. I realised at once that the coloured one was not a particular scene but a sort of line-up like what you would have at the very end if it was a play instead of stories. **The [Voyage of the] "Dawn Treader"** is *not* to be the last: There are to be 4 more; 7 in all. Didn't you notice that Aslan said nothing about Eustace not going back? I thought the best of your pictures was the one of Mr. Tumnus at the bottom of the letter. As to Aslan's other name, well I want you to guess. Has there never been anyone in *this* world who (1.) Arrived at the same time as Father Christmas. (2.) Said he was the son of the Great Emperor. (3.) Gave himself up for someone else's fault to be jeered at and killed by wicked people. (4.) Came to life again. (5.) Is sometimes spoken of as a Lamb (see the end of the Dawn Treader). Don't you really know His name in this world. Think it over and let me know your answer! (pp. 31-2)

Reepicheep in your coloured picture has just the right perky, cheeky expression. I love real mice. There are lots in my rooms in College but I have never set a trap. When I sit up late working they poke their heads out from behind the curtains just as if they were saying, "Hi! Time for *you* to go to bed. We want to come out and play."

All good wishes,
yours ever

C. S. Lewis
(p. 32)

[Dorsett and Lamp Mead: This letter was written to a fifth grade class in Maryland.]

Magdalen College
Oxford.
May 29th. 1954

Dear Fifth Graders

I am so glad you liked the Narnian books and it was very kind of you to write and tell me. There are to be 7 of them altogether and you are already one behind. No. 4, *The Silver Chair,* is already out.

You are mistaken when you think that everything in the books "represents" something in this world. Things do that in *The Pilgrim's Progress* but I'm not writing in that way. I did not say to myself "Let us represent Jesus as He really is in our world by a Lion in Narnia": I said "Let us *suppose* that there were a land like Narnia and that the Son of God, as He became a Man in our world, became a Lion there, and then imagine what would happen." If you think about it, you will see that it is quite a different thing. So the answer to your first two questions is that Reepicheep and Nick-i-brick don't, in that sense, represent anyone. But of course anyone in our world who devotes his whole life to seeking Heaven will be *like* R[eepicheep], and anyone who wants some worldly thing so badly that he is ready to use wicked means to get it will be likely to behave like N[ick-i-brick]. Yes, Reepicheep did get to Aslan's country. And Caspian did return safely: it says so on the last page of *The [Voyage of the] "Dawn Treader"*. Eustace did get back to Narnia, as you will find when you read *The Silver Chair.* As for who reigns in Narnia to-day, you won't know till you have had the seventh and last book.

I'm tall, fat, rather bald, red-faced, double-chinned, black-haired, have a deep voice, and wear glasses for reading.

The only way for *us* to [get to] Aslan's country is through death, as far as I know: perhaps some very good people get just a tiny glimpse before then.

Best love to you all. When you say your prayers sometimes ask God to bless me,

Yours ever,
C. S. Lewis
(pp. 44-5)

[Dorsett and Lamp Mead: When Laurence, a nine-year-old American boy, became concerned that he loved Aslan more than Jesus, his mother wrote to C. S. Lewis in care of Macmillan Publishing Company. Just ten days later to her surprise and delight, she received this answer to her son's questions.]

[6 May 1955]

Dear Mrs. K . . . ,

Tell Laurence from me, with my love:

1/ Even if he was loving Aslan more than Jesus (I'll explain in a moment why he can't really be doing this) he would not be an idol-worshipper. If he was an idol-worshipper he'd be doing it on purpose, whereas he's now doing it because he can't help doing it, and trying hard not to do it. But God knows quite well how hard we find it to love Him more than anyone or anything else, and He won't be angry with us as long as we are trying. And He will help us.

2/ But Laurence can't *really* love Aslan more than Jesus, even if he feels that's what he is doing. For the things he loves Aslan for doing or saying are simply the things Jesus really did and said. So that when Laurence thinks he is loving Aslan, he is really loving Jesus: and perhaps loving Him more than he ever did before. Of course there is one thing Aslan has that Jesus has not—I mean, the body of a lion. (But remember, if there are other worlds and they need to be saved and Christ were to save them as He would—He may really have taken all sorts of bodies in them which we don't know about.) Now if Laurence is bothered because he finds the lion-body seems nicer to him than the man-body, I don't think he *need* be bothered at all. God knows all about the way a little boy's imagination works (He made it, after all) and knows that at a certain age the idea of talking and friendly animals is very attractive. So I don't think He minds if Laurence likes the Lion-body. And anyway, Laurence will find as he grows older, that feeling (liking the lion-body better) will die away of itself, without his taking any trouble about it. So he needn't bother.

3/ If I were Laurence I'd just say in my prayers something like this: "Dear God, if the things I've been thinking and feeling about those books are things You don't like and are bad for me, please take away those feelings and thoughts. But if they are not bad, then please stop me from worrying about them. And help me every day to love you more in the way that really matters far more than any feelings or imaginations, by doing what you want and growing more like you." That is the sort of thing I think Laurence should say for himself; but it would be kind and Christian-like if he then added, "And if Mr. Lewis has worried any other children by his books or done them any harm, then please forgive him and help him never to do it again."

Will this help? I am terribly sorry to have caused such trouble, and would take it as a great favor if you would write again and tell me how Laurence goes on. I shall of course have him daily in my prayers. He must be a corker of a boy: I hope you are prepared for the possibility he might turn out a saint. I daresay the saints' mothers have, in some ways, a rough time!

Yours sincerely,
C. S. Lewis
(pp. 52-3)

5 Feb[ruary] 1960

Dear Susan . . .

All I can tell you is that pictures come into my head and I write stories about them. I don't know how or why the pictures come. I don't think I could write a *play* to save my life. I am so glad you like the Narnian books. Remember me to David D. . . .

Yours
C. S. Lewis

[Dorsett and Lamp Mead: The oldest in a family of seven girls, Patricia was thirteen and lived in Surrey when she wrote to Lewis.]

8 June 1960

Dear [Patricia]

All your points are in a sense right. But I'm not exactly "representing" the real (Christian) story in symbols. I'm more saying "Suppose there were a world like Narnia and it needed rescuing and the Son of God (or the 'Great Emperor oversea') went to redeem *it,* as He came to redeem ours, what might it, in that world, all have been like?" Perhaps it comes to much the same thing as you thought, but not quite.

1. The creation of Narnia is the Son of God creating *a* world (not specially *our* world).

2. Jadis plucking the apple is, like Adam's sin, an act of disobedience, but it doesn't fill the same place in her life as his plucking did in his. She was *already* fallen (very much so) before she ate it.

3. The stone table *is* meant to remind one of Moses' table.

4. The Passion and Resurrection of Aslan are the Passion and Resurrection Christ might be supposed to have had in *that* world—like those in our world but not exactly like.

5. Edmund is like Judas a sneak and traitor. But unlike Judas he repents and is forgiven (as Judas no doubt w[oul]d. have been if he'd repented).

6. Yes. At the v[ery] *edge* of the Narnian world Aslan begins to appear more like Christ as He is known in *this* world. Hence, the Lamb. Hence, the breakfast—like at the end of St. John's Gospel. Does not He say "You have been allowed to know me in *this* world (Narnia) so that you may know me better when you get back to your own"?

7. And of course the Ape and Puzzle, just before the last Judgement (in the ***Last Battle***) are like the coming of Antichrist before the end of our world.

All clear?

I'm so glad you like the books.

Yours sincerely
C. S. Lewis
(pp. 92-3)

The Kilns, Kiln Lane,
Headington Quarry,
Oxford.
26th October 1963.

Dear Ruth . . . ,

Many thanks for your kind letter, and it was very good of you to write and tell me that you like my books; and what a very good letter you write for your age!

If you continue to love Jesus, nothing much can go wrong with you, and I hope you may always do so. I'm so thankful that you realized [the] "hidden story" in the Narnian

books. It is odd, children nearly *always* do, grown-ups hardly ever.

I'm afraid the Narnian series has come to an end, and am sorry to tell you that you can expect no more.

God bless you.

yours sincerely,
C. S. Lewis
(p. 111)

C. S. Lewis, in his C. S. Lewis Letters to Children, *edited by Lyle W. Dorsett and Marjorie Lamp Mead, Macmillan Publishing Company, 1985, 120 p.*

Eleanor Graham

[***The Lion, the Witch, and the Wardrobe***] is a strange, powerful story; and though open to criticism as reading for children, is likely to remain in the memory because of the simple strength in its writing and the imaginative vigour which brings its scenes so vividly into being.

The opening chapters are quite enchanting as the youngest of four brothers and sisters steps into a wardrobe and out on the other side into a magic land. Candour and reason add strength to the imagination and win the confidence of the reader. Edmund also makes an excursion into the wardrobe. Edmund is not a nice boy; he is mean, spiteful, revengeful. In the end all four go together and learn the true nature of the witch's spell under which the land labours. They hear of the hope of the lion's return and of a legend which concerns themselves and the one chance of doing away with the witch forever. All four are required for it; but Edmund has already made a bargain with the witch, to bring her his brother and sisters.

The story offers much that is lovely before the grim climax is reached, yet all the time the reader is kept curiously and intently aware of the perils that threaten.

I felt the author's magic went all awry from this point on. The tension, the horror and the sheer pain is too great for young readers,—and remember this may well be read by anyone as young as eight or nine. The perception of horror and pain is keen because of a disarming quality which pierces the defences, leaving the young reader vulnerable, soft-hearted, by the time the crisis comes. The worst horror lies in the scene in which the witch prepares to kill Edmund so that, at least, the four children cannot be together for her undoing. Edmund is rescued of course, but there is worse to follow. The witch claims by established right, his blood as a traitor, and his brother and sisters beg the lion to save him. Aslan, King of the Beasts, offers his own life for Edmund's. The witch's crew triumphantly seize him, bind and muzzle him, spit on him, shave off his golden mane, humiliate him, drag him to the altar stone where the witch plunges her knife through the heart and kills him. The description is full and plain and the reactions of the little girls, who have followed the lion right to his death, serve as a window through which the reader is made to feel intimately the whole experience, blood, foam and all. There is a certain beauty even here for minds mature enough to accept it; but for young sensibilities I felt it beyond endurance.

Eleanor Graham, in a review of "The Lion, the Witch, and the Wardrobe," in The Junior Bookshelf, Vol. 14, No. 5, November, 1950, p. 198.

The Times Literary Supplement

Mr. Lewis's [The Lion, the Witch, and the Wardrobe is a] vigorous and fascinating book. . . . [Religion is] its implicit and fundamental theme. He writes of Edmund, Lucy, Susan and Peter, who penetrate by accident through the back of a wardrobe full of fur coats into Narnia; a country strange and familiar and instantly recognized by that remembrance, deeper than conscious memory, which recalls with delight "I have been here before." The forests, the rivers, the springtime glades where kings and queens go hunting a white stag; the castle of Cair Paravel by the sea, with the four thrones waiting in the great hall and the mermen and mermaids singing in the green waves below—all these are part of the mind's hidden landscape. As closely known, as strangely seen, are the fauns and centaurs and giants that live there; the gothic, horrible figure of the witch queen who turns her enemies into statues, and makes the time "always winter but never Christmas"; the wolf Maugrim, head of her secret police; and the magnificent Lion Aslan who allows himself to be killed so that the mean, treacherous Edmund who has tried to betray his brother and sisters into the witch's power may be ransomed from her. The fairy-story is admirable at fairy-story level; but also at the deep, unformulated level of myth. It never loses its vitality, its fantasy, its emotional vividness; it never becomes that tiresome thing, allegory, which can be worked out like a code or a crossword puzzle; but awareness grows that the frozen kingdom thawing with the arrival of the wild and loving Lion, his death in exchange for Edmund's life, his return, his setting the statues free, emblazon in a fabulous and holy heraldry the theme of redemption.

A review of "The Lion, the Witch and the Wardrobe," in The Times Literary Supplement, No. 2546, November 17, 1950, p. vi.

New York Herald Tribune Book Review

[In Prince Caspian: The Return to Narnia,] Mr. Lewis' four English children of last year now reenter their land of magic and help to save his kingdom for a young Prince. It is a wonderfully well written tale for boys who like dwarves, ancient treasures, "sorcery and wickedness," and for those girls who, like Lucy, can remember the time when trees could talk. It hints at the strangely possible magic of time, and tells of the shifts between the worlds of dream and reality, of beasts and people involved in saving good from evil. With all this, it is also colorful and exciting. The author follows his master, George MacDonald, in trying to carry his message to both the young and the old.

This sequel is better than The Lion, the Witch and the Wardrobe, in being easier reading with a simpler plot. It can as well be read before the first book, which those who like this will want at once, for a fuller explanation of the wonderful invention, the lion-king-god Aslan. Here we have style and imagination as seldom met in modern books. The unique sort of excitement and beauty of concepts will overcome, for intelligent children, any extra strangeness of symbolism.

A review of "Prince Caspian: The Return to Narnia," in New York Herald Tribune Book Review, November 11, 1951, p. 5.

New York Herald Tribune Book Review

In [The Voyage of the Dawn Treader,] a puny, mean-minded, bullying sort of boy, Eustace Clarence Scrubb, now joins Lucy and Edmund Pevensie in another adventure to their "secret but real" country, Narnia. Prince Caspian reappears on a marvelous ship whose captain is the Lord Drinian. We plunge into thrilling action, partly reported for us in Eustace's diary. Of course the great lion Aslan appears again, and of course Mr. Lewis's magical symbolism leads up to some chapters on "the very end of the world" in which a Lamb turns into the light-shedding Aslan.

It is a complicated, different sort of fairy tale, exciting and beautiful. It can be read independently of the other Narnia books. Those who like one are apt to read all. They are finding an audience among both boys and girls, and in read-aloud families who have graduated from shorter fairy tales, and even among those who do not generally like fairy tales. The brew is stronger than that of Miss [Elizabeth] Goudge or of George MacDonald. The strange symbolism will not often be understood, but is well worth that place at the back of the child's mind where it will linger until suddenly it is clear.

A review of "The Voyage of the Dawn Treader," in New York Herald Tribune Book Review, November 16, 1952, p. 3.

Naomi Lewis

"Indifferent work," wrote Hugh Kingsmill, "may be assigned to some deficiency in intelligence, but really bad work always illustrates a weakness, usually the chief weakness, in the writer's character." Mr. C. S. Lewis, at least, cannot be accused of not knowing how to write surpassingly well. But his fairy tales have had to serve as a platform for so many small irritabilities, that one could hardly discover his skill as a storyteller for the noise. Kingsley may have carried off this kind of interruptive writing in The Water Babies, but only by an outrageous poetic lunacy that gives to his outbursts the gabbling interest of spells.

The Horse and His Boy, however, must be the best-mannered of all Mr. Lewis's stories: though, perhaps, as a sort of revenge, the least magically wild in its fancy. Even so, in its Arabian Nights setting of sultans and dwarfs and viziers, and of the haunted deserts that keep the cities apart, it is riotously fantastic enough.

Naomi Lewis, in a review of "The Horse and His Boy," in The New Statesman & Nation Vol. XLVIII, No. 1230, October 2, 1954, p. 404.

Amabel Williams-Ellis

The Magician's Nephew has Mr. C. S. Lewis's usual virtues—admirable English, movement, moral, and enough but not too much description. But the present reviewer still cannot swallow Aslan, the *deus ex machina* of all his fairy tales. This personage is a highly moral and decorative lion who not only talks, admonishes and prophesies, but also sings. Surely Mr. Lewis should, all along, have had the courage of his convictions, and given Aslan the shape as well as the nature and functions of an archangel. (p. 52)

> *Amabel Williams-Ellis, in a review of "The Magician's Nephew," in* The Spectator, *Vol. 195, No. 6628, July 8, 1955, pp. 51-2.*

Dorothy L. Sayers

> [*The following excerpt is a letter to the editor of* The Spectator *by Sayers, an English author, playwright, and translator whose detective novels are considered classics of the genre and who is also well known as a commentator on theological subjects. Sayers is responding to the review of* The Magician's Nephew *by Amabel Williams-Ellis excerpted above.*]

May I say, with reference to Mrs. Williams-Ellis's review, that the Lion Aslan in Professor C. S. Lewis's *Chronicles of Narnia* has most emphatically *not* the 'nature and functions' of an archangel, and for that reason has not been given the form of one? In these tales of the Absolutely Elsewhere, Aslan is shown as creating the worlds (*The Magician's Nephew*), slain and risen again for the redemption of sin (*The Lion, the Witch, and the Wardrobe*), incarnate as a Talking Beast among Talking Beasts (*passim*), and obedient to the laws he has made for his own creation (*The Voyage of the Dawn Treader*). His august Archetype—higher than the angels and 'made a little lower' than they—is thus readily identified as the 'Lion of the Tribe of Judah.' Apart from a certain disturbance of the natural hierarchies occasioned by the presence in the story of actual human beings, Professor Lewis's theology and pneumatology are as accurate and logical here as in his other writings.

To introduce the historical 'form' of the Incarnate into a work of pure fantasy would, for various reasons, be unsuitable. Whether, on the other hand, a Talking Beast should be credited with the power of song is a matter for the aesthetics of Fairyland, where cats play the fiddle, horses have the gift of prophecy, and little pigs build houses and boil the pot for dinner. There would seem to be no very valid objection to it.

> *Dorothy L. Sayers, in a review of "Chronicles of Narnia," in* The Spectator, *Vol. 195, No. 6630, July 22, 1955, p. 123.*

G. Taylor

[*The Magician's Nephew*] is a thorough-going fantasy, pointing a moral, which many might consider a poor bet for the nine to eleven-year-old to enjoy. But the writing is so fresh and vivid, the characters, however fantastic, so solid, the adventures so exciting, that I think many children of this age, once started on it, will gallop through it

Lewis as a small boy.

with pleasure, swallowing the sugared pill without realizing its existence and thus absorbing a little of Professor Lewis's wisdom.

> *G. Taylor, in a review of "The Magician's Nephew," in* The School Librarian and School Library Review, *Vol. 7, No. 6, December, 1955, p. 438.*

The Times Literary Supplement

The greatest children's books all have an element of sadness about them—perhaps because they reflect more of life than, currently, writers wish, dare, or have the ability to show. Dr. Lewis's Narnian tales have always dauntlessly cut across contemporary fashion; a great part of their strength derives from this, and from their author's readiness to break into such emotional fields as chivalry, pain, power, fear, worship, Homeric wrath. *The Last Battle* is an impressive book; indeed, it requires to be, for by a ruthless stroke, which it would be fairer not to reveal, Dr. Lewis has made it impossible for himself to continue the Narnian saga. The tale is of power in evil hands. An Ape (called Shift) finds a lion skin and forces an Ass (called Puzzle—a simple fellow) to wear it and pose as the God Aslan. Under this false rule the creatures are persuaded to ways of destruction and ruin, for they do not question the Aslan edict. Tirian, the young king of Narnia, is caught in the horror with his friend, the symbolic and beautiful Unicorn. But at their direst moment two children from the human world (Adam's seed has highest power) come to their aid. The conclusion is striking, and the allegory, for an adult at least, is clear.

Other things may not be so clear. Dr. Lewis's philosophy does not always bear analysis: his attitude, for instance, to "civilization." The Ape desires "roads and big cities and schools and offices and whips and muzzles and saddles and cages and prisons—Oh, everything." Yet for Dr. Lewis anarchy, the back-to-nature life, the rule of no-rule, is even more detestable. Nevertheless, when he writes as a writer and not as a thinker he rises to the nobility and beauty of his theme. The image of the Door is memorable, so is that of Aslan's endless, terrible shadow; so, too, is Aslan's lesson: "All the service thou hast done to Tash, I account as service done to me. . . . "

> *"The End of a Saga," in* The Times Literary Supplement, *No. 2828, May 11, 1956, p. V.*

Chad Walsh

With [*The Last Battle*] the "Narnia" saga comes to an ending as beautiful and satisfying as its beginning, six years ago, in *The Lion, the Witch and the Wardrobe.*

The Narnia books have not been even in quality, but this is one of the best. The Christian symbolism is clear enough, but the book can stand on its own feet as a deeply moving and hauntingly lovely story apart from the doctrinal content.

Now that the seven volumes can be seen in perspective it is evident how vast the achievements of Mr. Lewis as a myth-maker are. The great themes of creation, fall, redemption and final consummation are all contained within the cycle, presented so vividly that child and adult equally find themselves caught up in the spell.

> *Chad Walsh, "War in Narnia," in* The New York Times Book Review *September 30, 1956, p. 46.*

Charles A. Brady

[C. S. Lewis' seven chronicles of Narnia] mark, it seems to me, the greatest addition to the imperishable deposit of children's literature since the *Jungle Books.* Narnia takes its place forever now beside the jasper-lucent landscapes of Carroll, Andersen, MacDonald and Kipling.

Lewis' Aslan, like [T. S.] Eliot's tiger, is also Christ—a totem of the heraldic imagination, however, and not, as in *Gerontion,* a totem of the philosophic mind. It is probably not necessary for the secularized children who are lucky enough to get the Narnia books as presents to know this fact. For, among the many beauties of Dr. Lewis' achievement, are the other facts that the story is self-sufficient and that the echoes attract the mind's ear even when the mind's eye cannot tell for sure the source of the echoes. If the meaning is hidden, it is only because the world, outside of orthodoxy, has temporarily lost the key. Like the adults, the children, too, must be coaxed inside again. Many are, I suspect; and more will be. One of the most trodden, if least acknowledged, roads leading to Damascus is the old imperial high road of the sovereign imagina-

tion. Though Dr. Lewis' Anglican sympathies might prefer to say Canterbury, all roads lead to Rome in the end, including the enchanting one that opens out of the Narnian portal.

But if it is not absolutely necessary for the child-readers to know the explicit correlations of the major symbols, it is still better that they do; and some of them will travel farther down the road for finding out. Dr. Lewis' imagination, while audacious, is audacious after the fashion of the eagle of Revelation, not after that of the heresiarchs. It flies high; it does not depart from orthodoxy.

In an age when lesser men are extrapolating power to achieve Apocalypse, if not Utopia, Dr. Lewis has extrapolated Apocalypse and Ragnarok—always on a child's scale—to achieve Paradise. He extrapolates the theological facts of Christianity and the historic facts of Christendom into a different dimension, a different idiom—not an altogether different one, though—and a different set of images. But the facts do not change. They still add up to Christianity as the medievals knew it in heraldry and as the child mind can treasure it in the context of primal wonder and perennial adventurousness.

The whirligig of time effects strange things. The 1950's may one day be remembered, by recorders of literary anniversaries, not as the decade which saw the death of Mann and the Nobel award to Faulkner, but as the span of time which saw the successive appearances, one each year for seven years, of the seven tales of Narnia. Their literary value is, naturally enough, uneven. It seems to me that the first, the last and the second-last volumes are far and away the best. The installments in between are all good, though; and all should be read, even as one should read all the Cantos of the *Faerie Queene.* (Incidentally, the Narnia stories are like Spenser's masterpiece in more ways than one, even down to being similarly unsynopsizable. And here and now is as good a place as any to note another of their great merits. Besides being a nursery *Faerie Queene,* they are also a child's *Nibelungenlied* and *Divina Commedia,* too.) (pp. 103-04)

[Narnia] is another world, another mode of being, another *place.* The twin poles of the seven stories are the enchanted Narnian lands, where anything can and does happen, and the mellow light of that manmade flower, one of earth's old-fashioned iron lamp posts. Between these two immutable boundaries of all successful fantasy—the soaring unfamiliar and the earthbound familiar—stretch the far marches of world myth: Western, Northern, Arabian, classic, medieval.

Though Lewis' achievement is *sui generis,* it also stands somewhat in debt to the practice of such predecessors as E. Nesbit in the *Bastable* books; and to George MacDonald in both the *Curdie* books and in *At the Back of the North Wind.* It owes even more to the great Northern and Celtic hero tales and to the romances of chivalry. But if the matter is mainly medieval, the manner is opulently Renaissance. In fact, the effect is almost that of a great Masque for children, with music by Purcell and mottos from the Shakespeare of *Midsummer Night* and *Much Ado.* As Peter Quince enjoined his artisans of earth, these chronicles of Narnia bring "the moonlight into a chamber." As Don Pedro said to Hero at the masquerade: "My visor is Philemon's roof; within the house is Jove." Earth's lovely mask is everywhere apparent. The high festivity in this kingdom of the imagination is what the ritualists call *aspectus festivus.*

The child will not respond to these values at once, though they will awaken in his memory when the time comes for full realization. He will respond immediately, however, to the narrative sweep; to the evocation of the heroic mood; to the constant eliciting of the numinous. Very possibly this latter service is the most startling one Lewis renders contemporary childhood, contemporary Catholic childhood not least. He touches the nerve of religious awe on almost every page. He evangelizes through the imagination. It is no accident that in his recent autobiography, **Surprised by Joy,** Dr. Lewis should have paid due tribute to Squirrel Nutkin and Sigurd of the Volsungs as two of the couriers who brought him to the foot of the seven-storey mountain.

One can never afford to be supercilious about the imagination, even in the complicated matter of assent to an intellectual proposition. We know enough now about the unitary nature of the human personality to spare us that particular folly. There is a real sense in which one believes more deeply, and not necessarily less rationally, through the imagination than through the intellect—as students of both John Milton and Thomas Hardy can verify. . . .

Allegory is strong in Narnia, especially in the final chronicle, **The Last Battle,** as befits a tale dealing with Armageddon and the things after Armageddon. . . .

Dr. Lewis' allegory is 17th-century like Bunyan's and Milton's, and 20th-century like G.K.C.'s *Man Who Was Thursday.* It is unabashed and perennial, according to the Chestertonian tenet that every "great literature has always been allegorical—allegorical of some view of the whole universe." The Narnian allegory encompasses Creation, Sin, Time, Eternity, Death, Incarnation and Resurrection. (p. 104)

I should not like to convey the impression that these stories are really difficult. They are profound but pellucid. Their themes are as high as Paradise; but the entrance thereto is as low as Alice's door. If we must stoop our adult heads and become as little children to get through, the children themselves experience no such difficulty. It would do Dr. Lewis no particular service, either, to suggest that his splendid, original fairy tales accomplish more than they actually do. They make children magnificently free of the primal literary things: of epic and lyric. The subtler essences of novel and drama must come later.

But it is much, certainly, to introduce the child personality to such noble and, nowadays, such neglected things as heroism, truth, beauty, duty, the great mystery of our animal kindred, the greater mysteries of time and eternity; to the fact that the earth is the strangest of all the stars and to the reconciling fact of Incarnation; to the numinous, God, death, and the fairy-tale resolution, which is yet so much more than a mere fairy-tale resolution, of life everlasting after death. Even at that, Dr. Lewis is the last person to

wish his inventions over-praised. They are, as he once said of William Morris' romances, nets to catch larger and quite other fish. Things are not quite what they seem. We have known all along that Aslan, the redemptive Lion, is more than a lion.

There are many things one can say against the savage century we live in. But, in its own odd way, it has been peculiarly a century of literary delight. On this plane, where adult literature and literature for children become one, Dr. Lewis' Narnia cycle takes an honored place—this is a high claim, but it measures up—alongside the *Jungle Books, The Wind in the Willows, Sherlock Holmes, Father Brown,* the romances of Buchan, the short stories of Saki, the Tolkien trilogy, the delectable contrivances of Kai Lung, C. S. Lewis' own interplanetary trilogy, and that part of the spacious Wodehouse canon which has to do with the amaranthine Jeeves. What other century, one queries proudly, can offer a bede-roll like this one? (p. 105)

Charles A. Brady, "Finding God in Narnia," in America, *Vol. XCVI, No. 4, October 27, 1956, pp. 103-05.*

M. S. Crouch

The last battle has been fought. Darkness has fallen on the once-lovely land, and Time, called by Aslan from his long sleep beneath the earth, has squeezed the dying sun "as you would squeeze an orange." High King, Kings and Queens, centaurs, unicorns, talking horses and mice, have come to the real Narnia for their reward. After all the inadequacies of expression and of characterisation, one comes to the last page of the last of these seven strange books with deep satisfaction mingled with regret. It has been a memorable experience and a privilege to visit the great magical world of Narnia.

Most writers who come to children's books after achieving distinction in other fields are moved by one of three motives. Many, like Carroll, Grahame, Milne, Tolkien and others, tell a story to delight a particular child. A list of the books which had this origin would include many of the best ever written. Some, like E. Nesbit, turn to children's books as a means of augmenting income. A few find in children's books a particularly satisfactory medium for their ideas. Of this company is C. S. Lewis. (pp. 245-46)

[Professor Lewis] is a Christian apologist. Whether writing of the nature of sin, of an imaginary world, of Milton's Satan, or of the mediaeval romances of the Grail, he is working out his conception of the Christian myth and the Christian philosophy. In the "Narnia" stories, he expounds the same theme in terms of allegory. Sometimes, as in **The Lion, the Witch and the Wardrobe,** the allegory follows closely the pattern of the Gospel story; sometimes, as in **The Horse and His Boy,** its lessons are of a more general character; but the books are all part of a general pattern. One may prefer one book to another; one cannot dispense with any.

This is, necessarily, an adult view. Children will very rightly read the books, if at all, as adventure stories. They will, if they are not very imperceptive, realise that the tales contain clear and acceptable morals, and will like them no less on that account. They will not, unless they are deplorably precocious, see how full and elaborate is the theological and ethical basis of the narrative. That is not to say that the author fails in his aim. The best imaginative books for children are to be read on two planes. The child reads **Prince Caspian** as an exceedingly exciting, imaginative and amusing tale of high adventure. At the same time he absorbs, incidentally and only half consciously, the ideas Professor Lewis has of the nature of good and evil, of loyalty, courage and honour, and of the need for God. The ideas are not grafted on to the story. The action grows out of the ideas.

The chronicles of Narnia are fine heroic tales. In children's books, one may be tempted to think, the almost lost art of narrative is kept alive; certainly Professor Lewis tells a story as few adult romancers can. His timing is excellent. He is inventive, varied. A careless reader might think the books were all battles. Certainly the Holy War is renewed from century to century, and it is the essence of the message that only by continuous striving can the free, wise and holy world of Narnia be preserved. But, among the battle-scenes—and very good battles they are, too—are many quieter memorable episodes. And there are joyous scenes, too, like the Bacchanale in **Prince Caspian** when the wood-folk, filled with the beauty and gaiety of holiness, break the chains that have held them for centuries.

Now that the last story has been told it is possible to see the chronology of Narnia and the genealogy of its reigning house fairly clearly. The series is surprisingly consistent; one is forced to the conclusion that, contrary to the tradition of such cycles, the author had the whole story in his mind when he wrote **The Lion, the Witch and the Wardrobe.** (pp. 246-48)

Professor Lewis has followed tradition in taking the reader immediately *in medias res.* It is a good method. It adds immensely to the excitement of **The Lion, the Witch and the Wardrobe** that so many questions are unanswered and remain so until **The Magician's Nephew** explains how the world began and how evil entered it. It is, I think, important that the books should be read in order of publication (with the possible exception of **The Horse and His Boy,** which stands apart from the main cycle). The author is too conscious an artist to do anything casually or without meaning; he releases information about his strange magical land as cautiously as the War Office releases news. One must accept, therefore, that it is right to see early in the first book that mysterious and homely street lamp burning in the forest, but to wait until the penultimate story to find the marvellous and simple explanation of its presence. (pp. 248-49)

The characterisation of these humans is one of the main weaknesses of the stories. They are lay figures, doing what is required of them but never emerging as individual persons. Lucy is perhaps the most convincing of an unsatisfactory group. In particular, the transition from School-boy to High King is insufficiently realised; the reader finds it hard to swallow that such very ordinary nonentities should become the agents of destiny. Caspian, too, whose reign forms the core of the chronicles, is little more than a stock figure. The minor characters are more fully devel-

oped—or are they merely amusing caricatures? or memorable types? Puddleglum, the Marsh-Wiggle, comes into this category, surely; his gloomy reactions to any situation may be accurately predicted. But, equally surely, Bree, the Talking Horse, is an individual character, and so is Reepicheep the Mouse. Reepicheep is one of the key characters, representing, one must think, an ideal of the author's, because not only does he survive an implied rebuke from Aslan (in **Prince Caspian**), but he alone is permitted to voyage beyond the End of the World, and he stands at the gates of the real Narnia on the last day to welcome home the faithful. Reepicheep, comical in the contrast between his stature and his manner, is not merely infinitely courageous; he alone bears his honour untarnished to the end. Others have moments of doubt. He has a sure touchstone of belief and action.

The Talking Mouse speaks the language of chivalry, and in his mouth it is, if occasionally amusing, always right. The high-flown style of some of the others, particularly the humans, is not always happy, and there seems no satisfactory mean between schoolboy slang and fustian. This is a fault which is sometimes hard to forgive. The less exalted characters have a more homely and infinitely more appealing style, although, as Trufflehunter, the Badger, shows, it can rise to eloquence at the right moment. The 'lofty' style seems to be an occupational disease of the Professor of English Language and Literature (cf. *The Lord of the Rings*).

What makes the "Narnia" stories stand out from the dreary grey mass of much contemporary writing for children is not good style or vivid characterisation or even superb story-telling, but the fact that the author has something to say. His opinions and his faith come out in every page. His mouthpiece may be Aslan (who is God), or the Hermit (in **The Horse and His Boy**), or the Magician of the Island of Voices, or he may speak as the narrator, but he is always worth hearing, and his thoughts come from learning and experience. Moreover, he is not difficult. He has the gift of gnomic utterance: "The truth about trying to make yourself stupider than you really are is that you may often succeed." And he has the rare gift of making his points indirectly, by narrative rather than statement. He does not need to state the difference between real and false heroism. He simply shows us Reepicheep and Rabadash and leaves us to draw unmistakable conclusions.

Below the surface of the stories lie other themes. The theme of **The Voyage of the Dawn Treader,** for example, is very like the theme of the Grail, which Lewis has pondered so deeply. The theme of **The Lion, the Witch and the Wardrobe** is the salvation of the world through Christ's sacrifice. The theme of **The Magician's Nephew** is the entry of sin into the world through fatal curiosity and redemption through courage. Some of the Christian symbolism is very clear, as in the stable in **The Last Battle,** whose "inside is bigger than its outside," and in the "spell for the refreshment of the spirit" which Lucy read and forgot, but which was "about a cup and a sword and a tree and a green hill." Some of the ideas are obscure, thoughts of the author which creep in almost unnoticed. But the main thesis is clear, strong and unchallengeable; the necessity of faith and the necessity for action.

These are universal ideas, which we may perhaps think of as essentially adult ones. Mr. Lewis would not agree. At the heart of the mystery which he propounds is a shining truth which we can comprehend only as little children. To the author the vital ideas of his stories are completely within the child's range. That the ideas are embodied in superb stories, told with fine art, is not a business of "sugaring the pill." The ideas and the action are inseparable.

Ultimately a book is great because it is memorable, because it digs itself deep into the reader's mind, haunts him, becomes part of his personality. The Narnia stories are full of minor irritations; they are sometimes unworthy of their high theme, their language frequently falls short of the demands made of it; but certain episodes, not always the most dramatic, stick deep in the memory. I would trade all the works of Miss X, Mr. Y and Captain Z for the first sight of the frozen world of Narnia, or for Lucy's visit to the Magician's House in the Isle of Voices, or for the moment when the children realise that the ruins in which they stand are the walls of Cair Paravel, where they had reigned as Kings and Queens. Sombre, melancholy, thrilling, gay, the scenes and the events have an actuality, a three-dimensional quality, which marks them as the work of a first-rate inventive genius. Eustace, we are told, "never having read the right books, had no idea how to tell a story straight." Professor Lewis has read all the right books, and flatters them with imitation (the first half of **The Magician's Nephew** is pure Nesbit); but he is more than an imitator. He is a writer in the main stream of English fantasy, and he contributes to it his own clear and original spring. (pp. 250-53)

> *M. S. Crouch, "Chronicles of Narnia," in* The Junior Bookshelf, *Vol. 20, No. 5, November, 1956, pp. 245-53.*

Louise S. Bechtel

[The Narnia series is a] unique contribution to children's literature. The tales have a symbolism which children under twelve may or may not grasp; probably Mr. Lewis is content if their excitement and beauty linger in the mind, until later the symbolism resolves itself. . . .

[*The Last Battle*] opens with a wickedly clever ape imposing his will on an ass, and fitting him with a lion skin to pose as the great god Aslan. The ape seizes power over the talking animals of Narnia, and allies himself with Narnia's enemies. In the weird "last battle," the young prince and two children from the real world fight against great odds. When Aslan finally appears, the good and the evil, animals dwarfs, men, come to a door, are judged by one look at Aslan, and the good pass through to another Narnia. The final chapters make all the meanings clear, with their beautiful interpretation of what may lie beyond death, and what Narnia and our own world may mean in relation to a future life.

This sounds like strong meat for children, but the exciting story is kept on their level. It makes a powerful conclusion to a remarkable series.

> *Louise S. Bechtel, in a review of "The Last Battle," in* New York Herald Tribune Book Review, *November 18, 1956, p. 6.*

John W. Montgomery

The greatest pleasure will undoubtedly be derived from the Narnia Chronicles when they can be appreciated both on the fantasy-adventure and on the allegorical level. Until one reaches early adolescence, the allegory will almost certainly escape him; but if he waits until adulthood to read the tales, the adventure element may not exercise the breathless hold on him which it could at a younger age. (p. 426)

[In his *Developmental Tasks and Education,*] Robert J. Havighurst confirms Dr. Lewis' judgment when he presents as one of ten specific "developmental tasks" of adolescence the problem of "acquiring a set of values and an ethical system as a guide to behavior," and states that "the crowning accomplishment of adolescence is the achieving of a mature set of values and a set of ethical controls that characterize a good man and a good citizen." As the Christian Church has recognized through its age-old rite of Confirmation (normally entered upon during early adolescence), the adolescent years are crucial for decision-making in the matter of a personal *Weltanschauung* or world-view. If this is the case, we are led to ask: Can the Narnia Chronicles in fact aid in providing the adolescent with a meaningful life-orientation?

In his lecture **"On Three Ways of Writing for Children,"** Professor Lewis says, "The two theories [of the fairy tale] which are most often in my mind are those of Tolkien and of Jung," and expresses the opinion that Tolkien's essay "is perhaps the most important contribution to the subject that anyone has yet made." Jung's view (widely accepted both among psychoanalysts and among folklore scholars today) is that the fairy tale presents concepts and images which correspond to the basic universal symbols (or "Archetypes") in man's unconscious mind. Lewis agrees with this, but feels that Jung does not go far enough. "The mystery of primordial images is deeper, their origin more remote, their cave more hid, their fountain less accessible than those suspect who have yet dug deepest, sounded with the longest cord, or journeyed farthest in the wilderness." To Tolkien and to Lewis, tales such as the Narnia Chronicles can, by their very nature, serve as pointers to the great theme of Christian Redemption. Moreover, they will establish in the hearts of the sensitive reader an appreciation of, and a longing for, the Christian Story. If one believes that ethics cannot survive without proper inner motivation; that religion provides the only really effective ethical impetus which men have ever experienced; that Jesus made no mistake when he said, "I am the Way, the Truth, and the Life: no man cometh unto the Father, but by me" (*i.e.,* that Aslan and Tash can never be fused into a Tashlan); and that adolescents in our culture need personal fellowship with the Lord Jesus more than they need anything else;—if we believe these things, then we shall unquestionably find the Chronicles of Narnia of lasting value to the adolescents whom we seek to win for Christ. (pp. 426-28)

> *John W. Montgomery, " 'The Chronicles of*

Narnia and the Adolescent Reader," in Religious Education, *Vol. LIV, No. 5, September-October, 1959, pp. 418-28.*

Margery Fisher

Everything [in the kingdom of Narnia] is the result of character, whether mortal or supernatural, and this makes it perfectly possible to believe in the beasts in **Prince Caspian** who have lost their freedom and power of speech but who recover them when the four children help to overthrow the prince's wicked uncle; to believe in the changing of their cousin Eustace Scrubb, in **The Voyage Of The Dawn Treader,** from a priggish, vegetarian schoolboy to an eager and enterprising traveller in strange lands; to believe in the extraordinary underground kingdom in **The Silver Chair,** where a lost prince, heir to old Caspian, is held underground in slavery to a green lady until certain conditions are fulfilled.

These conditions show the same mingling of magic and mysticism which you find in medieval poems like *Sir Gawain and the Green Knight,* and it is no accident that this story so much resembles the poem, with its magical details. C. S. Lewis is a leading exponent of medieval allegory, and if scholarship sits lightly in these stories, his allegorical purpose gives them meaning that children will not even try to grasp at a first reading.

In these tales he shows a fairy-tale picture of the redemption of man and his right to immortality. The virtues of courage, loyalty and generosity, the faults of greed, conceit and treachery, are familiar in fairy-tale. But Aslan the mysterious Lion, king over all temporal rulers of Narnia, son of the Emperor over the sea, Aslan who comes and goes without warning, who dies to save his subjects, who fills children and beasts alike with awe and love—Aslan is an emblem of Christ.

At the end of **The Last Battle,** Aslan explains to the children that they will not, as in the previous books, return to their own world (pp. 82-3)

I respect C. S. Lewis for coming so unaffectedly to the climax which is obviously, for him, the only possible one; but from a literary point of view the transition from adventure (which has its own ideas and importance) to Christian apologetics seems too abrupt. The history of Narnia, as he presents it, is full of implicit allegory which is enough to carry worlds of meaning to any thoughtful child. The [ending of the story] comes after a long description of the breaking up of Narnia after the last battle with the Calormenes, the forces of unbelief; it is a description of discreation which has the simple intensity of a poem by Blake, and is one of the finest pieces of writing in this kind of story. Like the mythological passages in George MacDonald's stories, it goes behind religious doctrine and speaks to the awe-struck ancestor who survives in all of us. The descriptions in these books tell us more than the sermonizing. They have a literary value as well, for they hold all the stories together.

C. S. Lewis makes us believe in Narnia, rich, fertile, and hospitable; in Archenland, mountainous and mysterious; in Calormen, with its walled cities, its pomegranates and perils, the Eastern feeling which comes out also in the illustrations. Not by the maps which he provides to establish the frontiers, the principal cities and rivers for the seeing eye, but in the words, the evocative names and the finely realized landscapes with which he fills the eye of the imagination, so that you go with the four children to the Stone Table, see the boy Shasta crossing the desert, see the animals dividing at the great Door. In moments of joy, of fear and of poetic vision, this is a very real country. (pp. 83-4)

Margery Fisher, "The Land of Faerie: Traditional Fairy-Tales and Modern Variants," in her Intent Upon Reading: A Critical Appraisal of Modern Fiction for Children, *Brockhampton Press, 1961, pp. 69-96.*

Edmund Fuller

I rate high among Lewis's accomplishments a work generally less well known, as yet, than [his adult space] trilogy, but for which I predict a growing reputation and a long life. This is the series of seven books for children which composes the Chronicles of Narnia. (p. 163)

Dominating the stories is the glowing, golden figure of the Lion, Aslan. He is a real lion but he is also the Second Person of the Trinity, just as in the Nicene Creed Christ is "Very God of very God" who was made man. Aslan is the One "by whom all things were made" and by whom Narnian time is drawn to its close. Lewis shows us that act of creation, Narnia brought into existence and beauty through the song of Aslan; we see, too, the end-that-is-a-beginning as He changes all things, abolishes all evil, and calls His own to Him in new being. But nothing in the chronicles matches for audacity of conception and boldness of invention the analogue of the crucifixion and resurrection. Aslan surrenders himself to cruel death as a substitute for others, in fulfillment of ancient law. He rises again to watch over His creation.

Narnia is peopled with bright, memorable figures: Reepicheep, the valiant mouse; Puddleglum, the marshwiggle; dwarfs, giants, satyrs, beavers, and a wealth of other beasts and creatures. The child who reads of Narnia, while having an enchanting adventure, will see human behavior in its full range; and he will learn the Christian concept of his nature and destiny as a creature. (pp. 164-65)

Edmund Fuller, "The Christian Spaceman: C. S. Lewis," in his Books with Men Behind Them, *Random House, 1962, pp. 143-68.*

Lillian H. Smith

The world called Narnia is the world that C. S. Lewis has created in seven stories for children; each story has a beginning, a middle, and an end, and each may be read independently of the others. Yet in these seven books, taken as a whole, we see a complete story with a beginning, a middle, and an end, in much the same way that we see, first, single stars in the sky, and then see them as a constellation which takes on a pattern our eyes can follow and recognize.

Narnia is not in our world nor in our universe. Narnia has its own sun and moon and stars, its own time. Yet the

Lewis and his brother Warren bought "The Kilns," a home at Headington Quarry, Oxford, in 1930; the four evacuees who helped to inspire the Chronicles of Narnia lived here with Lewis for a period during the Second World War.

landscape is a familiar one, a green and pleasant land of woods and glades, valleys and mountains, rivers and sea. The trees, shrubs, and flowers, many birds and animals, are those we know in our own world. Even the unfamiliar, the strange and fabulous ones, are in old stories we have heard and read. (p. 470)

All our news of Narnia comes from the various human children who find themselves there whenever evil times fall on the land. Centuries of peace and plenty pass unrecorded until four other children, in the story of *The Lion, the Witch and the Wardrobe,* find all of Narnia wrapped in a blanket of snow and ice. Under the witch's spell, it is "always winter and never Christmas." The children and the Narnians are pitted against the witch, who calls to her aid all the "abominations": Ghouls, Boggles, Ogres, Minotaurs, Cruels, Hags, and Spectres. But Aslan, the Lion, has been seen in Narnia, and with his coming the spell of evil over the land weakens, and signs of spring are followed by budding trees and rushing brooks as the children, with the talking beaver as their guide, journey to meet Aslan at the great Stone Table where the battle against the witch will be decided.

Although not the first story in Narnian chronology, *The Lion, the Witch and the Wardrobe* was the first to be pub-

lished, and is, I think, the first for children themselves to read. For, from the moment Lucy opens the wardrobe, steps inside to explore, and is suddenly standing in the middle of a winter forest with snow crunching underfoot, the adventure is a magnet that draws the reader deeper and deeper into the life of Narnia and into concern for all that happens there. At the same time, the reader is aware that there is more to the story than what meets the eye, phrases that set young minds and hearts pondering, overtones that set up rhythms heard not only in this book, but in all the stories as they appeared year after year until the last two, *The Magician's Nephew* and *The Last Battle.* In these the children's questions are answered and the full harmony is heard and intuitively grasped at last.

Each story has its own landscape—or seascape. For C. S. Lewis, the face of nature, its changing moods and seasons whether seen in windswept wastes or in a small mossy glade where hawthorn is in bloom, has its part in his developing theme, in shaping the sequence of events and in giving reality to the reader's imaginings as he accompanies the characters of the story on their adventures in the magical land of Narnia.

The characters themselves, apart from the human children who come there as visitors, reflect the author's mature and scholarly interest in mythology and medieval romances. They reflect and communicate his abiding love for the Old Things which belong, perhaps, to a golden age, backwards in time, when men and birds and beasts spoke to each other in a common language, a fabulous age which, it may be, lived on in myth and fairy tale as a kind of race memory of another, more innocent, world. (pp. 471-72)

We may call these books fairy tales or allegories or parables, but there is no mistake about the significance of what C. S. Lewis has to say to the trusting, believing, seeking heart of childhood. But C. S. Lewis knows well that if children are to hear what it is he has to say to them, they must first find delight in the story he tells. And so the fresh and vigorous winds of his imagination carry his readers exuberantly through strange and wild adventures, adventures that, half consciously, they come to recognize are those of a spiritual journey toward the heart of reality. This is the final quality, I think, of C. S. Lewis' writing about the country of Narnia; that above and beneath and beyond the events of the story itself there is something to which the children can lay hold: belief in the essential truth of their own imaginings. (p. 473)

> Lillian H. Smith, "News From Narnia," in The Horn Book Magazine, Vol. XXXIX, No. 5, October, 1963, pp. 470-73.

Roger Lancelyn Green

[*The following excerpt is from the monograph* C. S. Lewis *originally published in 1963.*]

At the most obvious level [the Chronicles of Narnia] are a series of adventure stories told by a master story-teller with an excellent sense of construction. Except for *The Voyage of the 'Dawn Treader'*, which is a series of adventures as Caspian and his companions voyage from island to island on their quest, each book is a carefully unfolding whole, built up with an instinctive touch from a prosaic beginning and so guided gently and persuasively into the heart of the marvels that coincides with the climax of the adventure. Looking a little deeper, we find that the magic is not only that of the wonders themselves: there is a 'glamour' in the old sense that falls upon us as we enter Narnia, like the softest dew, but growing as we venture deeper and deeper in. This is the subtle creation of atmosphere, of which the sights, the sounds, the smell and taste and feel grow upon us until Narnia becomes a place that we remember or recognise rather than learn about.

Deeper still, and we realise a difference between these stories and most other children's books: though the White Witch or Miraz may represent the evil power, just as there are good powers culminating in Aslan, the real villains as well as the real heroes and heroines are among the children who find their way or are drawn into Narnia. It is Edmund who betrays Peter, Susan and Lucy to the Witch, just as it is Eustace who is the disruptive element on board the *Dawn Treader*. But, to get even nearer to the heart of the matter, although they bring about the peripeties and catastrophes of the plot, a deeper reversal is taking place in them all the time, so that the plot seems suddenly to be concerned with their own internal battles rather than the external adventures. (pp. 135-36)

Deepest of all, and not to be isolated or described, for it is a reflection rather than a substance, is the whole spiritual drama of Narnia, both in the doings of Aslan the great Golden Lion and of all his people and of those whom he has called into Narnia from this other world of Man—of which Narnia is in some sort of a miniature likeness: an echo rather than a reproduction. (pp. 136-37)

The criticism of including in the Narnian stories things 'unsuitable for children' leads to the suggestion made by some critics that Lewis does not understand children and cannot draw them accurately or bring them to life. This is easier to understand, particularly when he is accused of modelling his children on those in E. Nesbit's books. For Lewis undoubtedly draws 'child' in the general from the child he knew best—himself: his extremely retentive memory of the feelings, experiences and thoughts of that childhood is shown in *Surprised by Joy.* For the Narnian stories were not told to actual children; nor had he any but the most superficial acquaintance with the species at the time of writing. All the stories were completed before his brief and intensely happy marriage left him a widower with two stepsons nearing the end of their prep school days. So that the externals of childhood may have been seen to some extent 'through the spectacles of books' (in which naturally E. Nesbit was the most useful), and some of them grafted on to the recollections of his own childhood days, and the child friends and acquaintances of the actual period when Nesbit was writing. This explains why the most completely successful and four dimensional children in his books are Polly and Digory in *The Magician's Nephew*, set (so far as Earthly time is concerned) in the days when 'Mr Sherlock Holmes was still living in Baker Street and the Bastables were looking for treasure in the Lewisham Road'. After them come the completely Narnian children who were never in the human world; Shasta in *The Horse and his Boy* and Prince Caspian (though he is more lightly sketched as he is seldom the centre of the picture). Of Eustace (in *The Voyage of the 'Dawn Treader'* and *The Silver Chair*) it is harder to speak, since as adult readers we are more interested in his spiritual development; but his external characteristics do seem completely credible and true to life. Polly, again, is more shadowy and lightly drawn, as is Susan; but Lucy comes through as a full person in her own right, and would be recognisable at once if we met her.

The adult characters are of much less importance, except in *The Magician's Nephew*, where Uncle Andrew is perhaps slightly caricatured though still acceptable, and Frank the cabby is a beautiful little miniature of simple goodness. The Narnian Kings and Calormenes are much more shadowy: Rilian and Tirian are less distinct than Caspian, and the rest loom a little larger than life in the bewildering mist with its stirring background of music that is our general vision of Narnia.

Out of that mist come character after character for magic moments of their own, gleaming suddenly into life in the midst of an incident and then fading once more into the moving pageant of the background: Mr Tumnus the Faun, a bear or two, the beavers and the badgers, Puzzle the Donkey, the horses Bree and Hwin and, in his own dimensions, Strawberry the cab horse who became Fledge the Hippogryph, and so to the most fully created of them all Puddleglum the Marsh-wiggle and Reepicheep the wonderful Talking Mouse who by the end claims perhaps the highest place in our affections.

The sense of wonder and discovery, the feeling of awakened memory rather than of cunningly drawn mind-pictures, is helped greatly by the descriptions of scenery and of even the smallest facet of nature—always growing naturally out of the narrative and never superimposed. Lewis's long, solitary walks in Ulster and Surrey, and in the country round Oxford have borne good fruit in these vivid composite scenes: the love of all the beauties of scenery and nature, flora and fauna, go to their creation—from the mountains of Donegal—'as near heaven as you can get in Thulcandra'—to the apparently instinctive sympathy with mice or badgers or bears.

In the Narnian stories there is nearly always the curious feeling of the personal experience. Lewis knew ships well from his many crossings over the Irish Sea, and harbours from Belfast and Liverpool: but the *Dawn Treader* is a real galley and not a ferryboat with poop and sails stuck on. Real warfare he knew also, perhaps even hand-to-hand fighting, from the Great War—but hardly with sword and scimitar, longbow and battle-axe: yet there is never a feeling that these have been 'got up' from encyclopedias or reproduced from literary sources.

'I see pictures.' This, on the outer layer at least, is the nearest we can get to explaining the vivid and effective quality of the Narnian books: this, and Lewis's supreme skill in making us see the pictures too. But 'there are gaps. Then at last you have to do some deliberate thinking.' This also explains the occasional weaknesses, the slightly episodic nature of the earlier books, and the brilliant scenes and incidents which occasionally hang together rather than growing out of each other.

There is just a suspicion of this even in *Perelandra.* It is most apparent in *The Lion, the Witch and the Wardrobe,* though the general suspense and the steady heightening of interest and expectancy prevents it from breaking the 'glamour' for the child reader, though the critical adult cannot help feeling from time to time: 'Here are superb incidents, vivid moments, thought-provoking ideas—but they have come separately and been fitted together: oh, so cunningly—but there *is* a trace of the cement.' *Prince Caspian* by the nature of its construction seems less contrived in this way; and *The Voyage of the 'Dawn Treader'* triumphs completely since it is intended to consist of consecutive adventures as the ship sails among unknown islands towards the World's End—and some of the separate incidents in their settings are among the best and most memorable in the whole series.

The Horse and his Boy combines the picaresque with the plot pleasantly and excitingly, but less memorably. Only with *The Silver Chair* does Lewis come fully into his kingdom—or into all the provinces of his kingdom—both constructing a complete and single unity with each incident

growing naturally as part of the whole, and conjuring up the characters, strange or ordinary, against marvellous and unexpected backgrounds, as if the circumstances and not the author had called them into being. *The Magician's Nephew* is just as perfect a unity and as rounded and satisfying an experience, and it is very much a matter of opinion whether it or *The Silver Chair* is the best of the series. . . . (pp. 149-52)

There is no slackening of power in *The Last Battle,* but its nature does not demand an involved plot; the great movement is as of a slowly rising wave or the final surge of the music rising to a solemn climax and fading away into a hushed and awe-filled silence.

Here we come nearest to the deep core of the stories: the moral, or the religious truth which is, in the highest sense, their inspiration. (p. 153)

The truest, the unique strength of the Chronicles of Narnia, the spirit incarnating them, the breath of Aslan which gives them life so that they will, I believe, live to take their permanent place among the great works of children's literature, is 'the whole cast of the author's mind' which has gone into their making. The mind of a true scholar, of one of the best-read men of his age; of a superb craftsman in the art of letters, with a gift for story-telling; of a thinker, logician and theologian who has plumbed the depths of the dark void of atheism and come by the hardest route on his pilgrimage back to God. (p. 154)

> *Roger Lancelyn Green, "Narnia," and "Aslan," in* Henry Treece, C. S. Lewis, and Beatrix Potter *by Margery Fisher, Roger Lancelyn Green, and Marcus Crouch, The Bodley Head, 1969, pp. 131-43, 144-54.*

Russell Kirk

Intelligent children want to know some answers to the ultimate questions; also they love mysteries; and, with a curious quickness, they apprehend allegories. How can one teach a small boy or girl something about the nature of God, the claims of charity, the heroic?

One of the very best instruments for waking imagination and conscience, pleasurably, in children is a series of delightful juvenile allegories by [C. S. Lewis]. This is the series called *The Chronicles of Narnia* (a kind of fairyland, on a time scale quite different from our world)

In his fourth chronicle, *The Silver Chair,* Lewis leads his young readers to understand that this sensate realm of ours, this workaday and highly imperfect world in which we find ourselves, is not the be-all and end-all. His child-characters stray into an underground land governed by a beautiful and malicious witch (who actually is a poisonous serpent). She has deluded and imprisoned a prince from the upper world, through whom she means to extend her dominion. When the children are about to rescue the witch's captive, she cleverly endeavors to convince them that no world exists outside her twilight kingdom.

The "Overworld" of Narnia, she insists sweetly, is merely a child's dream. The children and their friends remind the witch of the sun's existence, in the Overworld. But she replies that they have seen her underground lamps, and have imagined a bigger lamp, in a dream, and have given this impossible, imaginary lamp the name "sun." At last she persuades her victims to repeat, "There never was a sun."

In this children's romance, the symbol of God is a gigantic lion, named Aslan. The children insist that Aslan exists. The witch, however, tells them that they have seen a little cat, and have imagined a bigger cat—which, however, exists only in their disorderly visions. There are no lions, there is no Aslan.

Later in life, children who read the Narnia Chronicles will encounter many people who, like the witch, insist that nothing exists but what is immediately perceived by our five senses. Yet the witch lied; and one of the very practical functions of allegories for children is this: by waking the moral imagination, to teach children that many false spirits are gone forth into the world.

> *Russell Kirk, "The Moral Imagination of Children,"* General Features Corporation, *October 5, 1966.*

Penelope Lively

There is much that is distasteful, or merely absurd, in the content of the [Narnia] books. The very dubious Utopia of Narnia, where the children rule by some kind of Divine Right (defined in *Prince Caspian* as follows: 'Peter, by the gift of Aslan, by election, by prescription, and by conquest, High King over all Kings in Narnia, Emperor of the Lone Islands and Lord of Cair Paravel. . . .'—James I could not have put it better himself!), and their subjects, dwarfs, badgers, moles, etc. are 'decent little chaps' who speak ungrammatically but are unfailingly loyal, have all the cosiness of old family retainers, and make useful cannon-fodder when the time comes for the inevitable battle. There are some very unappealing sentiments expressed: an inherent approval of hierarchy and caste-systems, an unfailing casting of 'dark men' as the Enemy, smelling of garlic and onions, worshippers of alien gods—'Let the vermin be flung into a pit', and no nonsense about Christian tolerance. . . . It may be argued that all this is part of the fairy-story background—just a stiffening of Arabian Nights-cum-Greek mythology and not meant to be taken seriously. But there is much in the books that is clearly meant to be taken very seriously—and I am not at all sure that every child reader will be able to sort out the joke from the message, or even if the message is a desirable one. (p. 129)

> *Penelope Lively, "The Wrath of God: An Opinion of the 'Narnia' Books," in* The Use of English, *Vol. 20, No. 2, Winter, 1968, pp. 126-29.*

Alan Garner

One day last year Thain Dick Plotz arrived unannounced at my door. What he made of the visit I can't guess, but for me it was a sad experience. Thain Plotz is the Founding Thain of the Tolkien Society of America.

Now the reason why Thain Plotz and I couldn't find two words to rub together was that our attitudes were completely opposed. Fantasy has been for me a writer's tool (a crutch, if you like), while for the Tolkien Society of America it is an escape from the reality it is meant to explore. Myth has always been an attempt to come to terms with the world, not to avoid it. Of course we can each have our own ideas about Fantasy, but in order to exercise some control over himself and his material a writer must construct his terms of reference, and pursue them with bigotry—which is one reason for my belief that a writer makes an indifferent critic. You may think, as I do, that Professor Tolkien went over the top years ago, without transatlantic help; that C. S. Lewis's Narnia books are technically inept and morally vile: but we could be wrong. (p. 591)

> *Alan Garner, "Real Mandrakes in Real Gardens," in* New Statesman, *Vol. 76, No. 1964, November 1, 1968, pp. 591-92.*

Brigid Brophy, Michael Levey, and Charles Osborne

[*The following excerpt is from an assessment of* The Silver Chair.]

You can't fake a myth. No amount of donnishly going through the sagas and cycles, noting the runic and riddling speech mannerisms here and the prevalence of Witch-Queen figures there will avail: if your language and your imagination are flat, your repetitive riddling instructions (' "I will tell you, child", said the Lion. "These are the signs by which I will guide you in your quest. First; as soon as . . .But the first step is to remember. Repeat to me, in order, the four signs" ') will read merely like the instructions on a frozen food packet, and your Witch-Queen ('the Lady of the Green Kirtle, the Queen of Underland. She stood dead still in the doorway, and they could see her eyes moving as she took in the whole situation') will no more than similar personages concocted by Walt Disney transcend the *femme fatale* of a suburban tennis club. You cannot fake the ambiguous morality of myths by simply whispering your own prejudices behind your hand ('It was "Co-Educational", a school for both boys and girls, what used to be called a "mixed" school; some said it was not nearly so mixed as the minds of the people who ran it. These people had the idea that boys and girls should be allowed to do what they liked . . . All sorts of things, horrid things, went on which at an ordinary school would have been found out and stopped in half a term . . . the people who did them were not expelled or punished'). You will not buy your child readers' confidence, if you are writing, as C. S. Lewis was, in 1953, by making your narrative address them with a facetiousness and in a slang their fathers would have found old-fashioned ('His name unfortunately was Eustace Scrubb, but he wasn't a bad sort'). And when you attempt a linguistic high-flight for a noble and magical character, you should avoid mixing the vocabulary and cadences of chivalry with those of the boardroom: 'It would not have suited well either with my heart or with my honour', declares the prince at the climactic moment of the plot, 'to have slain a woman'—having begun his previous sentence with 'Yet I am glad, gentlemen'.

Neither, of course, can you fake a classic. Lewis's 'seven Chronicles of Narnia have already taken their place among the great children's classics', the note 'About the Author' at the back of the paperback edition authoritatively informs the children. If so, the sooner they're displaced the better. Back to Underland with them. (And up, as a children's classic, with T. H. White.) (pp. 147-48)

Brigid Brophy, Michael Levey, and Charles Osborne, "The Silver Chair," in their Fifty Works of English and American Literature We Could Do Without, *1967. Reprint by Stein and Day Publishers, 1968, pp. 147-48.*

Eleanor Cameron

[For] Lewis the question of good and evil is of paramount importance, and not because Christianity, as such, is talked about in his children's books. When he puts the battle of good and evil into them, it comes out of his depths and is not simply a device of plotting. And concerning the question of the archaic being related to the civilized and the modern to the barbaric, this too is in Narnia, for it is Old Narnia, the Narnia of the Golden Age, that the children fight to preserve, the world of chivalry, honor, courtesy, "freedom," "gentillesse," all that the idea of the Arthurian legend embodies (an idealization—yes, of course, but therein would seem to lie its power), the world of courage and goodness when the talking beasts and the Black Dwarfs and the Red Dwarfs and the fauns and satyrs could live happily in the open together. Old Narnia is continually assaulted by barbarism, but held always in the hearts of its creatures is the memory of Aslan's song of creation.

At one point Puddleglum says to the witch, "Suppose we *have* only dreamed, or made up, all those things—trees and grass and sun and moon and stars and Aslan himself. Suppose we have. Then all I can say is that, in that case, the made-up things seem a good deal more important than the real ones. . . . I'm on Aslan's side even if there isn't any Aslan to lead it. I'm going to live as like a Narnian as I can even if there isn't any Narnia." It is the ultimate, courageous statement, full of dignity and purpose, which man speaks to the face of the mystery he cannot fathom. And it is a surprising statement, in a way, coming from Lewis, for it reminds us of the existentialist saying that he will live with as much dignity as possible, according to moral principles which he himself must create, in a universe of the Absurd which is not aware of his existence. (pp. 42-3)

Eleanor Cameron, "Fantasy: The Unforgettable Glimpse," in her The Green and Burning Tree: On the Writing and Enjoyment of Children's Books, *Atlantic-Little, Brown, 1969, pp. 3-47.*

Roger Lancelyn Green and Walter Hooper

At present the seven *Chronicles of Narnia,* that unexpected creation of his middle age, seem to be Lewis's greatest claim to immortality, setting him high in that particular branch of literature in which few attain more than a transitory or an esoteric fame—somewhere on the same shelf as Lewis Carroll and E. Nesbit and George MacDonald, as Kipling and Kenneth Grahame and Andrew Lang: a branch of literature in which there are relatively few great classics but in which, as he himself said, 'the good ones last'. (p. 11)

It has often been asked whether Lewis had planned the whole Narnian series from the beginning, or even wrote each book with the next in mind; and whether he set out from the start to 'put across' certain lessons in simple Christianity and then looked about for the most suitable form in which to clothe them. Lewis himself answered the last question in his article **'Sometimes Fairy Stories May Say Best What's To Be Said'** in the *New York Times Book Review* on 18 November 1956 (collected in *Of Other Worlds* (1966), pp. 35-8): 'At first there wasn't even anything Christian [about the pictures which grew together to form *The Lion, the Witch and the Wardrobe*], that element pushed itself in of its own accord.' And again of the first story, 'suddenly Aslan came bounding in . . . '

With regard to *The Chronicles of Narnia* as a whole, there was certainly no idea of more than one book to begin with—though naturally the possibility of a sequel was present in his mind when *The Lion, the Witch and the Wardrobe* was drawing to a close. But it was only a hazy idea—and [series consultant Roger Lancelyn] Green inadvertently held it up for a little while by asking how the lamp-post came to be in Narnia, which led Lewis off on the first abortive attempt which survives as the 'Lefay Fragment'. *Prince Caspian* led on to *The Voyage of the 'Dawn Treader'*, and there the series stopped for the moment—though not the inspiration, for Lewis then paused to tell the purely Narnian tale of *The Horse and his Boy,* before returning to Eustace, who at the end of the *Voyage* had been promised a return to Narnia, which became *The Silver Chair.*

Already Lewis was departing slightly from statements made in the first chronicle: the Pevensies were the only 'Sons of Adam and Daughters of Eve' who had come into Narnia, but in *Prince Caspian* the Telmarines are descended from a boat-load of pirates from earth who got in by way of a magic cave in the South Seas. This incursion was, of course, centuries later than the Pevensies' first visit, and so does not contradict completely; but the introduction of Frank the Cabby and his wife Helen from London, in place of Piers the Plowman and his wife from Charn, in *The Magician's Nephew,* does go contrary to the original statement. Presumably the rather clumsy contrivance of Digory's apprenticeship to the farmer and his wife in a world other than earth shows Lewis's original attempt to conform to his first ideas of Narnia—and it obviously seemed worth assuming that readers would have forgotten a relatively unimportant point in the *Lion* in order to achieve so much better a plot in *The Magician's Nephew.*

It is unfortunate that Lewis recorded so few of the 'pictures' out of which the Narnian stories grew: 'a faun carrying an umbrella, a queen on a sledge, a magnificent lion', almost make up the sum total. The door which Aslan made in the air in *Prince Caspian,* and with it the Stable Door in *The Last Battle,* may owe something to a dream recorded in his diary on 27 April 1923. 'I dreamed first that I was sitting in the dusk on Magdalen Bridge. Then I went up a hill with a party of people. On top of the hill stood a window—no house, a window standing alone. . . . ' The names Caspian and Jadis were remembered from the version of the Cupid and Psyche story which Lewis was writing in verse in 1923: only here their sexes were reversed:

> Now I say there was a prince
> Twin brother to this Psyche, fair as she,
> And prettier than a boy would choose to be,
> His name was Jardis. Older far than these
> Was Caspian who had rocked them on her
> knees,
> The child of the first marriage of the king.

The literary inspirations are even more tenuous. Again and again one can find echoes from legend and literature, ancient and modern—and those of us who have 'read the right books' will find more than those who have not. But such echoes are of little importance, save to suggest what books Lewis had read or to make us marvel at his wide reading and retentive memory. But however much his reading may have suggested to him, Lewis can never be accused of copying another author, save in trifling instances, which were usually subconscious anyway.

Thus Lewis probably came across E. Nesbit's short story 'The Aunt and Amabel' when it appeared in *Blackie's Christmas Annual* for 1909 (published for Christmas 1908, when he was ten) in which Amabel finds her way into her magic world by the same door as the Pevensies—'the station was *Bigwardrobeinspareroom*', which is close to Mr Tumnus's 'far land of Spare Oom . . . bright city of War Drobe'. But Lewis had forgotten the Nesbit story entirely until reminded of it. Occasionally echoes come through from slighter recollections: Queen Jadis's account of her destruction of Charn and its people has a tantalizing ring of Oro's similar description in *When the World Shook,* and the passage under the eaves by which Polly and Digory get into Uncle Andrew's study is surely a continuation of that used by Stalky & Co., in 'An Unsavoury Interlude'—(pp. 248-51)

But it is unsafe to follow such echoes far: how far was the Underland in *The Silver Chair* suggested by [H. Rider] Haggard's underground cities of Mur and Nyo—or by Joseph O'Neill's *Land Under England*? But Lewis might equally well have been thinking of Athanasius Kircher's *Mundus Subterraneus* (1665) or Ludwig Holberg's *Nicolai Klimii Iter Subterraneum* (1741)—or even Jules Verne's *Voyage au Centre de la Terre* (1864) and Bulwer Lytton's *The Coming Race* (1871)! Rider Haggard's remark about Andrew Lang can suitably be applied to Lewis in this context—up to a certain point: 'Whenever he sets to work to create, his wide knowledge and his marvellous memory—and little worth studying in ancient or modern literature has escaped him—prove positive stumbling blocks in his path.' Lewis was at least as widely read and had a similar memory ('the best-read man any of us is ever likely to meet,' said Austin Farrer at his memorial service in Magdalen)—but he was a creator, while Lang was seldom more than an inventor: it could almost be said that Lang used what he had read, but what he had read used Lewis—hence, like Ransom, we feel in Narnia 'a sensation not of following an adventure but of enacting a myth.'

'Were all the things which appeared as mythology on Earth scattered through other worlds as realities?' Ransom asks himself in *Perelandra,* and *The Chronicles of Narnia* seem to be the affirmative answer to this question. For Lewis is making a new mythology that grew out of and embraced the old and gave it a new life in another world: he could no more be accused of plagiarism for introducing fauns and centaurs, dryads and hamadryads, Bacchus and Silenus and satyrs, than Homer could. Homer had the myths and legends, the lays and folk tales of the old Mycenaean world to use in the *Odyssey:* he probably got the Sirens from some lost lay of the Argonauts, the Cyclops from a current folk tale, and so on. But Lewis, besides the literary and legendary legacy of the ancient world, had also all that lies between it and us: he had the plenteous riches of the Arthurian Cycle—it gave him the mystic table on which lay the Stone Knife, with which Aslan was slain by the White Witch, in Ramandu's kingdom, from the Grail Castle of the Fisher King, in the same way as the classical tales gave him the faun and the centaur. There are Talking Animals as in Aesop or Beatrix Potter or Kenneth Grahame; Queen Jadis visits late-Victorian London for one crowded hour rather as the Queen of Babylon does in Nesbit's *The Amulet;* Eustace turns into a dragon rather as Maurice had into a cat or Kenneth into a carp in other Nesbit stories—but all these incidents in *The Chronicles of Narnia* render Lewis's new world no less original than the introduction of playing-cards, chess-pieces, nursery rhyme and proverbial characters does in *Wonderland* and *Through the Looking-Glass.* Indeed the technique is similar, though Lewis Carroll was inventing lands of brilliant and convincing nonsense, and C. S. Lewis lands where fantasy and adventure merge inevitably into the numinous, where vice can be disguised as Turkish Delight and Aslan can be the Narnian Christ with perfect propriety.

For the Bible is, of course, the basic source-book, though most readers, even of mature age, recognize little of it except in Aslan's death and resurrection—and Lewis intended it to be recognized only subconsciously: 'supposing that by casting all these things into an imaginary world, stripping them of their stained-glass and Sunday School associations, one could make them for the first time appear in their real potency? Could one not thus steal past those watchful dragons? I thought one could.'

But *The Chronicles of Narnia* should not be treated as an allegory: they bear no literary relation either to *The Pilgrim's Progress* or to *The Pilgrim's Regress,* and it would spoil their effect to attempt to interpret them allegorically or symbolically—certainly for children. They are and must be read simply as stories.

However, as adults will be analysing, a simple example of how this can be done was given by Walter Hooper in answer to such an attempt (in the *Oxford Times,* 2 Feb. 1968): '*The Last Battle* is modelled pretty closely on Our Lord's apocalyptic prophecy in St Matthew XXIV, but it is the end of Narnia, not of this world, that Lewis is writing about. Aslan (who is Christ) is holding his Last Judgement for that world—the entire Narnian creation. The only people from this world who are present are those who were killed in the railway accident: Digory, Polly, Peter, Edmund, Lucy, Mr and Mrs Pevensie, Eustace and Jill. The last two take an active part in the last battle; the others are reborn in the new Narnia on the other side of the Stable door. Susan was not killed in the railway crash, but even if she were, it is doubtful if she would have been with the others. Her interests are narrowly confined to the Shadowlands (this world) and she is, of her own free will, "no longer a friend of Narnia." Lewis is taking into consideration the fact that many people drift into apostasy. The new Narnia, of which the old was only a "shadow or a copy" is Heaven. Jutting out from the mountains of Aslan are all the *real* countries, one of which is that inner England which, Lewis believed, will never be destroyed. A better understanding of this can be had by reading the chapter on the resurrection in Lewis's **Letters to Malcolm** . . . '—or in Plato's *Phaedo*.

And so the stories can be read and enjoyed on at least two levels: by the child who perhaps knows nothing of the Bible, of classical or Arthurian myth and legend, of any of the authors whose works Lewis knew; and by the reader who knows many at least of these and senses many more. The first has a series of enthralling adventure stories, full of magic and fantasy, and complete in themselves. The second—usually the older reader—finds an added dimension and an additional enjoyment. 'What you see and hear depends a good deal on where you are standing: it also depends on what sort of person you are.'

'People won't write the books I want, so I have to do it for myself: no rot about "self-expression",' wrote Lewis to Chad Walsh in 1948—unconsciously echoing Arthur Ransome's words written ten years earlier: 'You write not

The wardrobe that served as the model for the one in The Lion, the Witch, and the Wardrobe; *it was carved by Lewis's grandfather, Richard Lewis.*

for children but for yourself, and if, by good fortune children enjoy what you enjoy, why then you are a writer of children's books.' The fact that both writers wrote primarily to please themselves, and that neither had children of their own or even a child audience, produces one similarity between their books—however different they are in other respects: there are no private jokes or allusions as, for example, in *Alice* or *Pooh*. There are virtually no personal 'originals' either: Lewis told Walter Hooper that the character of Puddleglum the Marsh-wiggle 'is modelled after his gardener, Paxford—an inwardly optimistic, outwardly pessimistic, dear, frustrating, shrewd countryman of immense integrity. But unlike Paxford, Puddleglum is so much *more* the type of man of which Paxford is typical.' In fact Puddleglum is based on Paxford but no nearer to being a real portrait than MacPhee [in **That Hideous Strength**] is to [Lewis's tutor] William Kirkpatrick: and these seem to be the only originals to whom Lewis admitted.

Nor apparently do the Narnian stories contain any private references, other than those with a literary flavour, such as an occasional submerged quotation or an invention like the pavender, that Narnian fish which is based on a perhaps inaccurate recollection of Warham St Leger's humorous poem 'A False Gallop of Analogies'. Very occasionally a personal prejudice appears a little too strongly, as in the excessive unpleasantness of the school whence Eustace and Jill escape into Narnia in **The Silver Chair,** or the attack on 'civilization' in **The Last Battle** which upset at least one critic when the book was published. (But Lewis added a special footnote to Green's 'Bodley Head Monograph' (1963) which quoted this criticism: 'The critic means by *civilization* things like big cities and offices. I mean things like justice, mercy, free speech, honour and courtesy. It is unfortunate that English uses the word in both senses.')

The critical reception of the seven books was varied and usually guarded. But the readers' reception both in Great Britain and the United States, if slow at first, was enthusiastic and with a mounting and widening enthusiasm that makes them still, nearly 25 years after their publication, among the most popular children's books of the day—and Lewis still the bestseller in the Puffin paperback series, where his nearest rivals include E. Nesbit, Hugh Lofting, Arthur Ransome, Alan Garner and a very few others.

The adverse adult criticism is usually caused by other than purely literary reasons; such critics may be divided roughly into the sceptics and the sentimentalists. The first attack the stories for their Christianity, the second for their presentation of some of the children as unpleasant characters—Edmund for his early treachery, Eustace before his experience as a dragon, and so on. Both are also inclined to object to Lewis's 'cruelty': Aslan's sacrifice, Eustace's sufferings when the dragon's hide is torn from him, Peter's killing of the wolf, and so on. And those who dislike, for either reason, do so very thoroughly and can see few virtues in the series—even condemning them as dull and badly written, condescending, cliché-ridden, devoid of any characterization.

But vast numbers of children read the stories with delight

and live imaginatively in Narnia, even turning into play and acting the events. And very few find anything wrong unless it is pointed out to them by 'watchful dragons' among their elders. Most of the criticisms were answered by Lewis more or less before they were made in his Library Association lecture 'On Three Ways of Writing for Children', which was written at least by March 1952 when he read it to Green. As for the 'cliché' and the 'condescension'—it would be surprising if it were not possible to find any such faults in a collection of seven books by a writer, however skilled, who was venturing into an untried field and then using it to produce work which was, as a whole, new and unique in that kind. Lewis took a little time to escape from the influence of E. Nesbit (a slipshod writer as far as style was concerned, and one who delighted in clichés) and put in certain things which he considered to be part of the literary form with which he was experimenting. Green was able to suggest the quiet excision of most of these—and some of the blame must attach to him for the few which remain—though Lewis would occasionally argue cogently for their retention, and keep them.

The immense popularity of the books is also shown by the change they brought about in what were conceived to be the reading habits, likes and dislikes of children. In the years before **The Lion, the Witch and the Wardrobe,** publishers returned the manuscripts of such books with the almost stereotyped form: 'the modern child is not interested in magic and fantasy.' From 1950 onwards came the swing of the pendulum back to fantasy and fairy tale, the myth and the mythopoeic which has not yet spent itself. There had been no swing so pronounced since the publication of Andrew Lang's first two fairy books in 1889 and 1890 ushered in the re-conquest of Fairyland and the golden age of Nesbit.

In spite of anything that can be said against them, and considering **The Chronicles of Narnia** as dispassionately as possible, it seems safe to say that C. S. Lewis has earned by them a place among the greatest writers of children's books and—surprising as it would have seemed to him—he will probably be remembered as a literary creator for them even more than for **The Screwtape Letters** and **Perelandra.** (pp. 251-56)

> *Roger Lancelyn Green and Walter Hooper, in their* C. S. Lewis: A Biography, *Harcourt Brace Jovanovich, 1974, 320 p.*

Isabelle Jan

Lewis's [Narnia] books are deservedly popular but his imagination tends to run dry and has to resort to German folklore and ancient mythologies to people Narnia with dwarfs and fauns; nevertheless this is done with sufficient spontaneity and assurance to make them unexpected and convincing. Some may prefer Frank Baum's *The Wizard of Oz* to this rather derivative cycle. Its magic is less well integrated into the stories and not so charged with cultural and moral overtones. . . . (p. 72)

> *Isabelle Jan, "Through the Looking Glass," in her* On Children's Literature, *edited and translated by Catherine Storr, 1973, Reprint by Schocken Books, 1974, pp. 56-78.*

Cheryl Forbes

Lewis labeled Narnia "for children." What did he say about the art of writing "juveniles"? How does he accomplish this in Narnia? And what does Narnia offer children? (pp. 7-8)

Lewis wrote for children because he had a story to tell. . . .

Writing for children brings necessary restrictions on vocabulary, reflective passages, digressions, and descriptions of erotic love. And Lewis tried to write chapters of equal length for convenience in reading aloud. Those limitations paradoxically provided Lewis the right amount of freedom to create a world that the reader can see and smell and almost touch. There are no wasted words or chapters or ideas. Form and content meld into a compact, artistic unity. . . .

Lewis did not think it wrong for a story to contain a moral; all his do. But he did think it wrong to put in morals as medicine. If a writer wants a moral in his story, he should include one *he* needs. That gives some immediacy. Even so, Lewis thought starting with didacticism was sure to produce a bad moral as well as a bad story.

In letters and essays Lewis wrote much about the requirements of good writing, no matter what the form. Write for the ear, not the eye. Use simple, straightforward language. Describe a situation or an emotion. Make the reader feel or see what you are presenting; don't rely heavily on adjectives or adverbs. Read as many good books as possible, but avoid nearly all magazines. And always write about what interests you. (p. 8)

Lewis certainly follows his own advice in the Narnia tales. Though the simple vocabulary under less talented hands would sound stilted, he manages to explain situations and describe scenes clearly and vividly. Even when the scene is utterly fantastic—such as entering another country through a wardrobe—touches of what Lewis calls "presentational realism" (a technique he learned from medieval romance) brings the scene immediately before the mind's eye.

The four children are exploring the professor's house on a rainy day when they discover the room with the wardrobe. "There was nothing else in the room at all except a dead blue-bottle on the window-sill," says Lewis. That small detail is a contact point between the reader and the writer. Each of us remembers rainy days and dead bugs, and that simple sentence conveys well how empty the room is. Lewis uses the technique repeatedly. Lucy opens the wardrobe and two mothballs drop out. After a long march the children are tired and "Susan had a slight blister on one heel." Similar touches are found in paragraph after paragraph.

The dialogue, too, flows naturally. The children get tired and cranky, and the older ones lord it over the younger ones. . . . Lewis spends a lot of time talking about such basics as food and drink. Narnians celebrate victories with sumptuous feasts. But during wars, food and water are scarce. Eating and drinking are universals Lewis shares with his readers; they are also part of common grace.

Aslan in creating Narnia provided plenty of good things to be enjoyed as gifts of the Creator and not for themselves alone. (pp. 8-9)

Lewis in different ways throughout all seven books presents the potency of Christianity. . . .

Lewis offers children, then, a vivid story filled with familiar details and extraordinary events. He also presents to them logic, differing concepts of time, loyalty, how to tell whether someone is telling the truth or lying, common sense, love, sacrifice, evil and goodness, war and violence, death, and the importance of the imagination. Children learn what pride is, how difficult obedience can be, and how temptation works. In short, Lewis introduces them to reality, both physical and spiritual. (p. 9)

Narnia demands much of the children who enter there. No one can visit that land without undergoing some change. Edmund finds out he's a traitor and must seek and receive forgiveness. Eustace needs to be converted. Digory must learn to obey. In each tale the children learn that courage, resourcefulness, and sheer hard work are necessary in their adventures. The presence of death is part of the atmosphere that teaches them these things. *The Last Battle* is the only children's story I know of in which everyone and everything dies. But after their deaths the children find light, not darkness; they have escaped from death into life. (But Lewis is not giving us universalism in fancy dress. Susan does not get into the final Narnia.)

Behind all these ideas stands imagination. Lewis constantly appeals to the reader's imaginations: Have you heard it? Can you remember? Can you see it? Here is where he explains spiritual reality. The fact that we cannot see or touch something does not mean that it does not exist; empiricism cannot explain everything. . . .

Shelley in "A Defence of Poetry" says that "a man, to be greatly good, must imagine intensely and comprehensively; he must put himself in the place of another and of many others. . . . The great instrument of moral good is the imagination. . . . Poetry strengthens the faculty which is the organ of the moral nature of man, in the same manner as exercise strengthens a limb." Christ's command to love your neighbor as yourself is an appeal to imagination.

Lewis uses that idea in Narnia. He draws the reader into the tales by imagination, and stretches and exercises that faculty so that children will recognize good and evil (for instance) in the real world because they have with their imaginations experienced it in Narnia. . . . We can say of Lewis what he says of another fantasy writer in "William Morris": "He seems to retire far from the real world and to build a world out of his wishes; but when he has finished the result stands out as a picture of experience ineluctably true. . . . There are many writers greater than [Lewis]. You can go on from him to all sorts of subtleties, delicacies, and sublimities which he lacks. But you can hardly go behind him." (p. 10)

Cheryl Forbes, "Narnia: Fantasy, But . . . ," in Christianity Today, *Vol. XX, No. 15, April 23, 1976, pp. 6-10.*

Susan Cornell Poskanzer

C. S. Lewis' Chronicles of Narnia are strangely powerful fantasies. (p. 523)

The fact is that Lewis' manipulation of fantasy and his readers is so skillful that these works demand a close examination. Just how is Clive Staples Lewis converting us all into devoted Narnians? What devices does he employ to make his fantasies so successful?

A special talent is Lewis' ability to weave childhood thoughts and rituals into his plots. Not only are his children's dialogues convincing but also our own childhoods seem closer and fresher. When poor Eustace, the harmless villain whom Lucy and Edmund are forced to visit, has turned into a dragon, he tears at the bracelet wearing into his swollen arm on hot nights. He scratches, knowing that he shouldn't, just as kids pick at scabs even if they know it won't help matters. Eustace is a magnificent character and through him, Lewis draws numerous images of the stereotyped goodie-goodie kid. In reality almost nothing is too obnoxious for Eustace to attempt. . . . He is all our childhood bullies wrapped into one.

C. S. Lewis' children seem very real in many ways. They have distinct personalities yet they are multi-faceted and dare to misbehave. By Book III of the Chronicles, we can easily characterize their personalities. In most cases when a character speaks, it is clear who it is even if we were not told. Susan is pretty and vain. Peter is scholarly and manly. Edmund is a true adventurer willing to learn from his mistakes. Lucy, who seems to be the favorite (and does, indeed, have C. S. Lewis as a godfather) is tender, compassionate, intelligent, and brave. All the children, on the other hand, show some weaknesses. Edmund allies himself with a possible witch for love of Turkish Delight candy. Lucy does not follow her conscience and walk after Aslan. Caspian considers deserting his crew. Eustace surely must have known his bullying and whining was not right. His transformation into a dragon and ultimately into a tolerable human being, represents one of the great moral stories of the Chronicles. (pp. 523-24)

Adult characters, however, are one-dimensional. They generally enjoy only sketchy descriptions or are caricatures of good or evil. The wise old professor is very understanding of the children's wardrobe adventures. In *The Magician's Nephew* the adults are either good (the warmhearted aunt and mother) or wicked (the incredibly mean uncle). The uncle parallels the sinister Arakeesh and the Tarkaan in *The Horse and His Boy,* evil characters that are overwhelmingly more exciting than the good people. By making these adults less real, they become almost a burlesque of evil and consequently less threatening to young readers.

Children are quickly caught in Lewis' web since they identify so readily with the fantasy's children. Here are everyday kids who become powerful kings and queens of astounding strength and bravery. Kids are represented as being more powerful than kings. . . . What a great ego boost for all children!

Even though Lewis wrote in England over twenty years

ago, the language is surprisingly contemporary. Where English idioms are used, they are readily deciphered from the context of the passage and many children enjoy hearing these foreign phrases in their own language. The child characters are very aware of their own vernacular and when they become kings and queens of Narnia, they embellish their speech with *thys* and *thous*. King Caspian's war declaration [in *Prince Caspian*] shows that they realize that lavish speech presents an aura of power and dignity. . . . (p. 524)

Lewis is constantly poking fun at society's morals and ills. Eustace's parents, "vegetarians, non-smokers, and teetotallers . . . and wore a special kind of underwear," represent a humorous picture of supposedly avant-garde people. The governor (His Sufficiency) who has "no interviews without 'ppointments 'cept 'tween nine 'n ten P.M. second Saturday every month" is a sad reflection of modern bureaucracy. Slavery is rationalized as a necessary economic ill by the Lone Islanders and freedom is the motivating force in *The Horse and His Boy.* Unfortunately Narnia itself is not a province of equal rights. Lewis protects girls from the most violent fights and revolting scenes. The children are all royalty yet Peter is the high ruler, and sadly, only the girls are allowed to be very tender with Aslan.

Much of the violence in the Chronicles is disturbing; there are many gory scenes. Caspian's voyage to seek vengeance for his father's friends' deaths is questionable. And did King Miraz' head really have to roll off? Yet Reepicheep, a hawkish mouse, is the prime advocate of violence and as the mythical two-foot-high mouse, he poses less danger as a model for children than the human characters.

Reepicheep opens the broad topic of Lewis' use of animals in the Chronicles. In employing animals (and especially talking animals) he not only extends the aura of magic but also utilizes them and their talents to act instead of humans where it is more strategic. The animals humble humans and have interdependent relationships with them. Sometimes we would almost forget the characters are animals were it not that Lewis so cleverly uses their particular animal traits and habits to name and describe them. What better name could there be for a mole than Clodsley Shovel? Pattertwig the squirrel and Trufflehunter the badger also illustrate this point. Where a name doesn't actually describe a creature, it seems to fit it onomatopoetically. Thus, Reepicheep mouse, Nikabrick, the bad dwarf, Dufflepuds, the silly mushroom people, and Trumpkin, the good dwarf all sound logical. What's more the creatures, though talking, do follow their own natures. The children are dreadfully afraid that the bulgy bears will fall asleep or suck their paws when they serve as battle marshalls. The squirrels don't understand why everyone can't talk and eat at the same time during a meeting. The beavers use their homes and dams as hiding places for the children in a dangerous crunch. All this is made even more delightful by the fact that Lewis simply cannot help but make his delicious puns constantly: talking mice "armed to the teeth," indeed!

Aslan, the god-like lion, deserves special mention. Through Aslan, Lewis stresses the point that things can

be at once beautiful and terrible, a difficult but interesting concept for children. Aslan protects the children yet insists that they fend for themselves as much as possible. He seems to be omnipotent and omnipresent and exists in Narnia and in our world. He proves in Book I that for him even death is not permanent. The characters speak "in the name of Aslan." . . . In fact, the main structure of the Chronicles is loosely based on the story of Christ. Aslan is, therefore, an important character who gives Lewis an excellent opportunity to preach to his young readers. Yet the religious philosophy and ethics are very subtle and do not interfere with the true fantasy of the stories.

Finally Lewis employs several specific literary devices in his work which are interesting and effective. He frequently speaks directly to the reader in the first person. He continually invades the fantasy to tell us one thing or another from his armchair in England. If Aslan is omnipresent, so is C. S. Lewis, for he constantly offers us morsels of grandfatherly comforting advice in an informal way. He even has the audacity to advertise his other books right in the middle of a muddle. He crashes in with reality yet he is actually twisting reality and fantasy and combining the two more inextricably. He makes Narnia more real since it's so difficult to see where fantasy ends and reality begins.

Lewis also uses foreshadowing skillfully. He manages to warn us ahead of time so that while he is increasing suspense, he is also protecting us from tumultuous shock. Therefore, he slips in such loaded sentences as "If Caspian had been as experienced then as he became later on in his voyage he would not have made this suggestion: but at the moment it seemed an excellent one." He also frequently power packs his last two pages to resolve intricate tales very quickly and to leave a seed to entice us into reading the next volume.

In addition it's interesting how Lewis deals with time which he bends to suit his plots perfectly. Time passage is different in Narnia than on earth: the time relationship is random but time always moves at a quicker rate in Narnia. In this way the children can age very slowly on earth while conditions have completely changed on Narnia, setting the stage for a brand new adventure.

C. S. Lewis' transportation to Narnia and points beyond is stunning. The image of a child exploring in an old armoire, suddenly seeing winter sky and trees beyond the fur coats is delightful. Aslan's doorway in the sky and the magic horn which pulls the children off a grey train platform are marvelous. I especially like the seascape which lures the children to their own sea odyssey because here the author is using another childhood game, for all children know that if you stare at a sea picture for a long time the waves will appear to move. Usually, however, one doesn't also feel a brisk wind and splashes of salt water across the face.

Another virtue of the Chronicles is simply that C. S. Lewis was sufficiently enthusiastic and prolific to continue writing for seven volumes. The result is a wonderfully rich set of fantasies that can be a powerful vehicle in any language arts program. . . . (pp. 524-26)

Susan Cornell Poskanzer, "Thoughts on C. S.

Lewis and the Chronicles of Narnia," in Language Arts, *Vol. 53, No. 5, May, 1976, pp. 523-26.*

Mary Cadogan and Patricia Craig

The author of the Narnia books had a weakening, Christian-allegorical tendency which he failed to contend with: the increasingly overt religious symbolism in the series has made for its overall deterioration. The use of Celtic or Norse mythology in children's books has a validity, a stimulating or enhancing effect of its own which the use of Christian mythology does not, chiefly because the latter is not generally accepted *as* mythological. In the first case it is the reader's imagination which is brought into play, though her moral sense may be indirectly involved; the richness of the reader's response naturally will depend upon the author's powers of suggestion and interpretation. Magic—in the form of legends and superstitions—is a significant part of everyone's experience. When it is used, however, to express a kind of Christianity which it parallels, it is robbed of its imaginative effect: it becomes merely a version of a myth which most children are expected, in the real world, to believe. It is impossible at the present time that a serious children's author could produce a "straight" story of religious conviction, but to dress up the theme in magical clothing can only have an odd, emotionally-strained effect. With C. S. Lewis the subject dictated its own conclusion: the children *had* to be killed in a railway accident so that "Narnia" could be revealed as "heaven"; this is distasteful, a subjective fantasy which has got out of control. (pp. 368-69)

> *Mary Cadogan and Patricia Craig, "Time Present and Time Past . . . ," in their* You're a Brick, Angela! A New Look at Girls' Fiction from 1839-1975, *Victor Gollancz Ltd., 1976, pp. 355-72.*

Bob Dixon

[Lewis has] been the most obvious propagandist of religion in children's fiction in recent times. . . . ***Surprised by Joy,*** his spiritual autobiography, shows a preoccupa-

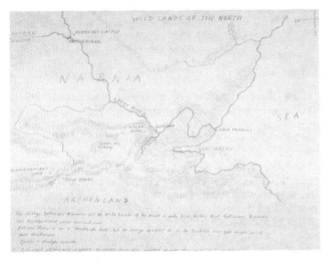

A map of Narnia drawn by Lewis for series illustrator Pauline Baynes.

tion with his own inner life as great as Bunyan's in *Grace Abounding* but without the clarity. This self-absorption excludes consideration of other people and even of the first world war, in which he served and was wounded: 'It is too cut off from the rest of my experience and often seems to have happened to someone else. It is even in a way unimportant.' This strange attitude can be seen again in ***The Screwtape Letters,*** a series of imaginary letters from one devil, Screwtape, to another, Wormwood, who's been given the task of damning someone's soul during the second world war. Screwtape writes, 'The history of the European War, except in so far as it happens now and then to impinge upon the spiritual condition of one human being, was obviously of no interest to Screwtape.' It wasn't of interest to Lewis, either, except in so far as it affected his 'spiritual' state. This is the old, old story—religion as a retreat from great moral and political problems, if not a distraction from them. Another main element of his ideology should be singled out here as it's so important in Lewis's fiction for children. In his book, ***Miracles,*** he states, 'Naturalism gives us a democratic, Supernaturalism a monarchical, picture of reality.' Now, as might be expected, Lewis believes in the supernatural. In fact, in this book, he starts by assuming its existence, then he calls it 'God', then he moves to God as creator of nature (though this cannot, he says, be 'proved as rigorously as God's existence') and lastly to God's power to interfere with nature and create a miracle. Easy. It is, however, with this strange, medieval outlook in mind that we have to approach his work for children. (p. 155)

The first [book dealing with the imaginary land of Narnia], ***The Lion, the Witch and the Wardrobe,*** is still probably the most popular. . . . The mixed mythology which forms the background to the series is mainly Jewish/Christian with certain elements from classical and Teutonic. The first book is an allegory of the story of Christ's death and resurrection with Aslan, the lion, representing Christ. . . . Lewis refers to the whole scene in a letter to Thomas Howard: 'The reason why the Passion of Aslan sometimes moves people more than the real story in the gospels is, I think, that it takes them off their guard. In reading the real story the fatal knowledge that one *ought* to feel in a certain way often inhibits the feeling.' Aslan is resurrected and the four children are crowned kings and queens of Narnia.

In the next book, ***Prince Caspian,*** the only significance, for present purposes, is that the four children are recalled to Narnia to restore a rightful king to the throne with the help of Aslan. This maintains the connection between royalty and godhead.

With ***The Voyage of the 'Dawn Treader',*** however, reactionary views come more to the surface. We meet a new boy, the thoroughly nasty Eustace who, amongst other things, is a republican. Obviously, he doesn't fit very well in royal Narnia and eventually he's turned into a dragon. However, Aslan turns him back again and Eustace gradually starts to become a 'better' boy. . . . Eustace slews two or three of his dragon's skins but then Aslan rips off the remaining ones and throws him into a pool. Here . . .

is the symbol of the husk/shell/skin, the rebirth to a better life and the baptismal water.

In *The Silver Chair,* Lewis's reactionary social views are carried on and are even more apparent. First, he presents a travesty of a progressive school, which he calls 'Experiment House' and then he ridicules it, often in asides like '(girls are not taught how to curtsey at Experiment House)'. Aslan's character is added to in this story. He's terrible, strong, uncompromising and wild and these characteristics continue to be emphasised in the series, especially in *The Last Battle* where it's repeatedly stressed that Aslan is 'not tame'. A powerful god, the believer helpless in his grasp—the picture is familiar from religious writing of all periods. The abandonment of personal responsibility, with religion as an excuse, is another way of looking at it. In *The Silver Chair,* there's still a royal framework. The task this time, carried out by Jill, a girl new to the series, along with Eustace, is to restore a lost prince to the land of Narnia. Eustace, recalling Ransom in *That Hideous Strength* says, 'I'm the King's man'. After the quest, they return from Narnia to begin reforming their school, Experiment House.

Royalty is still very much in the forefront in *The Horse and his Boy,* which is, however, one of the less religious books of the series. Shasta, the 'boy' of the story, is discovered to be Prince Cor of Archenland, a country near Narnia. He speaks, surprisingly, public school English. 'Father's an absolute brick', he says. This underlines another aspect of the series. In spite of the travels far and wide in lands of fancy, we never really leave upper-middle-class England.

The sixth book of the series, *The Magician's Nephew,* is the first in order of time because it tells of the creation of Narnia by Aslan. The lion, heralded by heavenly music, enters singing and another evil witch has to recognise a magic stronger than hers. The story is interesting because it gives good examples of the hints, allusions and partial comparisons that are typical of the series. In the chapter called 'The Founding of Narnia', Aslan takes two of each kind of beast, touches them and makes them talking beasts. The boy in the story, Digory, known as 'son of Adam' has brought an evil witch into a Narnia resembling the garden of Eden. The 'cabby' and his wife, brought from the real world, are made king and queen of Narnia and given dominion over the talking beasts. The witch tempts Digory with an apple, saying it's 'the apple of youth, the apple of life'. After the first book in the series, the allegory is neither particularly close nor ordered. Parallels in material, however, are not so important as the general outlook.

The series ends with *The Last Battle* which is again a mixture with recognisable hints and allusions here and there. For instance, when Shift, the ape, is making use of a stable to deceive people, Lucy remarks, 'In our world . . . a Stable once had something inside it that was bigger than our whole world.' (Lewis often signals points of this kind with capital letters.) Aslan is referred to as 'the good Lion by whose blood all Narnia was saved'. Quotations such as this illustrate how the allegory, especially after the first book, is in certain passages and in details rather than in the overall picture. Other elements, such as the emphasis on royalty, reflect Lewis's personal quirks more than anything else. This emphasis persists in the last book where we have King Tirian, the good beasts and the children pitted against the forces of evil. The end of the story is also the end of the world of Narnia. Aslan presides over the judgement after the trump of doom has been sounded. All the animals, mythical beasts and other creatures stream towards him and look into his face. Those who look in his face and love him go through the 'Door'. The others fall away to the left of the doorway in Aslan's shadow and we don't know what becomes of them. The 'good' ones now find themselves in a kind of heaven though it's referred to as the 'real' Narnia. The Narnia they'd known before, we're told, 'was not the real Narnia. That had a beginning and an end. It was only a shadow or copy of the real Narnia which has always been here and always will be here: just as our own world, England and all, is only a shadow or copy of something in Aslan's real world.' 'The Lord Digory' says this and adds, 'It's all in Plato, all in Plato.' Here, persisting in only a slightly different form, is the religious idea we've been following throughout—the next world is the 'real' one, the one that matters. Correspondingly, our attention is diverted from this world, the scene of so much needless suffering. Of course, it all links up in Lewis. Naturally, it follows that two world wars had no noticeable effect on him. But it doesn't stop there. The effect of this kind of ideology is to resist change. The Narnia books encompass about a thousand years of Narnian history, but they remain, throughout, fixed in an approximation of the Middle Ages, like the author. At the end of the book, the band of the saved meet long-dead friends outside the golden gates and then go through into a beautiful garden. In the centre is a tree with a Phoenix sitting in it and beneath 'were two thrones and in those two thrones a King and Queen so great and beautiful that everyone bowed down before them'. (pp. 157-61)

[In the Narnia books, we see] political quietism, antagonism towards ordinary people, royalism, patriotism, original sin and selfishness—in fact, all the familiar characteristics of religion. (p. 161)

> *Bob Dixon, "The Supernatural: Religion, Magic and Mystification," in his* Catching Them Young 2: Political Ideas in Children's Fiction, *Pluto Press, 1977, pp. 120-64.*

Roger Sale

[Hans Christian Andersen] became so imbued with a faint and faintly self-pitying Romanticism that even his best stories are distorted with authorial self-concern and flecked with satire and moralizing. But Andersen, troubled and vain though he was, was always essentially an oral teller; when we come down yet another century, to something like the fairy tales of C. S. Lewis, we see the damage caused when fairy stories are to be read from books. Lewis had a true and catholic love of older things, and a great longing to be part of their world, but the ear and instinct just weren't there, and the Narnia books, popular though they are with latter-day audiences, are brittle, mechanical, and naggingly preachy in ways older fairy tales never are. (p. 25)

Roger Sale, "Fairy Tales," in his Fairy Tales and After: From Snow White to E. B. White, *Cambridge, Mass.: Harvard University Press, 1978, pp. 23-48.*

Diana Waggoner

Lewis was a true child of Mercury and Philology, an intellect drunk on language, with a facility for metaphor less skillful writers can only envy. At his worst Lewis has the defects of his virtues. His wit becomes glibness, his argument becomes casuistry, his deepest beliefs become debating-points. At his best Lewis is capable of explosions of brilliance and of tender sensitivity. He was that rare thing, a writer with an idiosyncratic style that never palled. The most characteristic things in Lewis are his descriptions of other-worldly landscapes: the trembling silence of the grove of Meldilorn; the fragrant seas and glowing sky of Perelandra; the flowering glades of Narnia. His imagination worked in colors like bright enamel and with the precision of a diamond tool. He was perhaps more capable than [George] MacDonald of capturing the spirit, the mood, of a mystical experience.

But the influence of [Charles] Williams and [G. K.] Chesterton encouraged Lewis to slight his visionary qualities and concentrate on theological argument, with poor results. In ***That Hideous Strength,*** the most Williams-like of all Lewis's novels, the characters are mere caricatures of both the good qualities he approved and the bad ones he abhorred. All his prejudices—against science, against journalism, against vivisection, against sociology—are laid on to the villains, who are eventually dispatched in one of the most savage scenes in modern literature, in which a horde of maddened wild animals invades a dinner party. In ***The Voyage of the "Dawn Treader",*** . . . the three protagonists meet Christ (Aslan) in the form of a Lamb who cooks them a dinner of fish. In ***The Last Battle,*** . . . a girl character loses her entire family at one blow—parents, brothers, sister, cousin, godparents—for the sin of being overly interested in lipstick and stockings. Lewis's emphasis on evangelism led him to condemn modern life wherever he considered it, which naturally spoiled his depiction of modern life in fiction. He simply could not cope with the effects of his arguments in ordinary human society.

His real strength—depicting the supernatural itself—is unsurpassed by any other mythopoeic fantasist, even MacDonald. He created a whole new mythology in his adult fantasies, the Perelandra trilogy, blending the Olympian gods with medieval angelology. In the Narnia books, he successfully combined the lesser Olympians—Bacchus and the Maenads, fauns, dryads, and centaurs—with more homely, English creatures like dwarfs, giants, talking animals, witches, and the inimitable Marsh-wiggles. What Lewis contributed to mythopoeic fantasy was specificity, which it had never had before. The vagueness and moodiness, the misty uncertainty, which most people associate with religious experience, have no place in Lewis's work. He pointed out that a mystical vision, far from being vague and unreal, should be more vivid, more real, more memorable than ordinary life. Williams had seen this, but had been unable to escape the habit of wrapping mystical expe-

rience in an obscuring veil; Chesterton never concerned himself with internal consistency; MacDonald lacked Lewis's lucidity. Lewis alone among mythopoeic fantasists convinces the reader of the vibrant reality of religious experiences, while conveying the mystical, supra-rational, ecstatic, entranced qualities that we think characteristic of them. (pp. 34-5)

Although every story in [the Narnia] series is a reworking in Narnian terms of some aspect of Christian theology, the seven Chronicles of Narnia are among the freshest and most enchanting of fantasies, because they are an utterly satisfying expression of Lewis's imagination. Narnia itself, with its cool green glades, its castles and galleons, its magical blending of English and Mediterranean mythology, its grumpy Marsh-wiggles, gallant Talking Mice, graceful dryads, busy dwarfs, and child Kings and Queens, comes alive despite any flaws in the stories, because Lewis makes it a real place. (p. 255)

Diana Waggoner, "Some Trends in Fantasy" and "A Bibliographic Guide to Fantasy," in her The Hills of Faraway: A Guide to Fantasy, Atheneum, *1978, pp. 28-64, 125-302.*

Gilbert Meilaender

Moral education which interests Lewis does not look much like teaching. One cannot have classes in it. It involves the inculcation of proper emotional responses and is as much a "knowing how" as a "knowing that." It cannot be taught by listening to a lecture or filling out a worksheet. The picture we get when we think of "knowing how" is the apprentice working with the master. And inculcation of right emotional responses will take place only if the youth has around him examples of men and women for whom such responses have become natural—persons whose vision of human nature is shaped in accordance with the *Tao.* The pursuit of the moral life is not an isolated pursuit. Lewis, like Aristotle, believes that moral principles are learned indirectly from others around us, who serve as exemplars. And he, again like Aristotle, suggests that is will be extremely difficult to develop virtuous individuals apart from a virtuous society.

This is also the clue to understanding the place of the Chronicles of Narnia within Lewis' thought. They are not just good stories. Neither are they primarily Christian allegories (in fact, they are not allegories at all). Rather, they serve to enhance moral education, to build character. They teach, albeit indirectly, and provide us with exemplars from whom we learn proper emotional responses. We can think once more of one of the principles of the *Tao,* the law of magnanimity, willingness to expend oneself in a good cause. This is, after all, what that Roman father was appealing to when he tried to teach his son that it was a sweet and seemly thing to die for one's country. It is, Lewis thinks, a message best communicated indirectly: through the father's own example, and also through the stories read to his son. The father's message may well be communicated through a story like ***The Last Battle.*** There, in a passage cited at the outset of this chapter, Roonwit the Centaur, while dying, sends a message to King Tirian telling him "to remember that all worlds draw to an end and that noble death is a treasure which no one is too poor to buy". To overlook the function of the Chronicles of Narnia in communicating images of proper emotional responses is to miss their connection to Lewis' moral thought. (pp. 212-13)

> *Gilbert Meilaender, in his* The Taste for the Other: The Social and Ethical Thought of C. S. Lewis, *William B. Eerdmans Publishing Company, 1978, 245 p.*

Frank Eyre

C. S. Lewis's 'Narnia' books are the most widely read and enjoyed of all the contemporary 'other-world' fantasies. This sustained allegory is unlike most such series in that each book has something new and different to offer and there is no weakening of either inspiration or interest. As every parent who has had the pleasure of reading these aloud to his family will know, every child can find something to his own taste, and pleasure, in one or other of them. For the Narnia tales are, in the very best sense of the word, children's books. They were conceived for children and designed, with great understanding and skill, to appeal to children, in order to say exactly what the author wanted to say—to children. It is ironical, and a curious reflection on the odd state into which the study of children's reading is bringing us, that they should nowadays frequently be criticised for what is, in fact, their strength. It must be admitted that, to adults, the Christian symbolism comes in too easy a guise and that for many of us dear old Aslan becomes rather a bore. But the books were not written for *us,* they were written for children and as stories for children they succeed wonderfully. It will be a sad day if the time ever comes when every book for children has to be intelligent enough to seem admirable in every respect to adult critics. (pp. 132-34)

> *Frank Eyre, "Fiction for Children," in his* British Children's Books in the Twentieth Century, *revised edition, Longman Books, 1979, pp. 76-156.*

Walter Hooper

Aslan is Christ. It is, however, with reluctance that I mention this fact regardless of how well-known it already seems to be. I am reluctant because I do not want in any way to damage Lewis's success in getting "past those watchful dragons" which freeze many people's feelings about Christ and orthodox Christianity. I am sympathetic with those well-intentioned Christians who in Sunday schools, and writing for periodicals, draw attention to the fact that Aslan is meant to be the Son of God; and I know only too well the temptation, when all our evangelistic efforts seem to fail, to hand out to non-Christians the fairy tales with the comment, "Just you read these, and you'll know what I mean." Let us, by all means, give away as many copies of the fairy tales as we can afford: but not, please, with any explanation about who Aslan is. An "explanation" on our part is, I am convinced, very unwise, as it would very likely frustrate Lewis's purpose and blunt the effectiveness of the books. It is often precisely because many readers do *not* know who Aslan is that the Narnian stories have been so successful in getting into the bloodstream of the secular world. Hints about who is what and

so forth have already caused many readers to regard the fairy tales as codes that need deciphering. They were written to give pleasure and (I think) as an unconscious preparation of the imagination. And this—it cannot be denied—they do most effectively without our extra efforts. If the fairy tales succeed in breaking down the partition of prejudices that prevent nonbelievers from even thinking about the Christian tenets (and they appear to be doing this), *then* our efforts will be very much needed. (pp. 99-100)

When I heard that the Narnian tales were, in some places, being taught as a kind of systematic theology, I felt that someone ought to attempt an explanation of why this is impossible: or for those who do think it possible, why they should proceed with the greatest caution. It is my belief that we will not find an exact, geometrically perfect equivalent of Christ's Incarnation, Passion, Crucifixion, and Ascension in the Narnian stories. We are not meant to. This is why we should not press the analogies too closely, or expect to find in the tales the same logic we find in the Christian story. If we do press the analogies too closely, we will, I think, go a long way towards spoiling our receptivity for what the stories have to give us. Here are some examples of what I mean.

1. First, in what way is Aslan the Son of God? I once thought we could say that he is the Son of God *incarnate* as Lion. This may have been because Lewis himself says that Aslan "is an invention giving an imaginary answer to the question, 'What might Christ become like, if there really were a world like Narnia and He chose to be incarnate and die and rise again in *that* world as He actually has done in ours?' " Lewis is, however, using the term "incarnate" rather loosely here, for Aslan is never incarnate as Lion in the same way that Christ was Man. (pp. 100-01)

When Christ became Man, His divine nature was united with that of a natural, human mortal. But Christ as Aslan is never incarnate as a natural, dumb lion; never a cub suckled by a lioness. Indeed, He is not always found in the fashion of a Talking Lion. . . . (p. 101)

Aslan makes it quite clear that he is not a man, not a phantom, but—like Horses, Squirrels, Rabbits, Dogs, and so on—he is a true *Beast.* And *that*—and no more than that—is what Lewis meant when he wrote about Christ being "incarnate" in Narnia.

By taking upon Himself the form of a Man, Christ was (I presume) never free to change His nature into something other than a Man. Aslan is not thus restricted. Quite obviously, it is as a Lion that Lewis thought of Aslan. John the Baptist, after all, thought of Christ as a Lamb ("Behold the Lamb of God"), and in the same Gospel Our Lord speaks of Himself as bread, water, light, a vine—even a door. But of course it is as a Lion that Christ is most often pictured, especially by the Old Testament writers. . . . (pp. 102-03)

Quite apart from the biblical parallels, Narnia is after all predominantly a world of animals, and the Lion, the traditional King of Beasts, seems the most natural and appropriate choice for Lewis to have made. Still, the incarnation of Christ differs in yet another way from Aslan's "incarnation" in Narnia: Aslan does not *always* appear as a Lion.

In *The Voyage of the "Dawn Treader"* Aslan takes the form of an albatross (ch. XII) and a lamb (ch. XVI). In *The Horse and His Boy* he assumes the form of a cat (ch. VI) and on several occasions that of an ordinary dumb lion. And, finally, in the "new Narnia" as envisaged in the last chapter of *The Last Battle,* "He no longer looked to them like a lion." What then? What else but in His resurrected Manhood. It is fortunate, I think, that Lewis does not actually say this, for that fact belongs to all the "chapters" that followed, of which the Narnian Chronicles had been "only the cover and the title page." There would have been no Narnian stories had there not been the great Original, but the stories being what they are, and the readers being what they are, there are undoubtedly others than myself who want to preserve in our memories as long as we can that magnificent leonine form.

2. In order to satisfy God's demand for perfect justice, Christ, the Perfect Man, died upon the Cross for the sins of the whole world. Aslan died on the Stone Table for Edmund Pevensie. We might deduce from this that Aslan would have died for the whole of Narnia, but we are not in fact told that he would or did do so. Try as we might, I simply do not see how we could work out a doctrine of the Atonement from Aslan's vicarious sacrifice for one boy—a boy, not from Narnia, but from this world. I should be very sorry to hear that anyone was attempting to do so, for I think he would have to read into the Narnian stories all sorts of things that are not there, were not meant to be there. What Lewis tells us is that Aslan is obedient to the will of the Emperor-Over-Sea, and that he loves Edmund so much that he is willing to pay his penalty for him. It is moving and beautifully clear, easier for most untrained minds to grasp than the fact that Christ died for all mankind. *And* it gets "past those watchful dragons."

3. The Gospels represent Christ as passing after death into a life that has its own new Nature: He is still corporeal, can eat broiled fish, but finds locked doors no obstacle for Him (John xx: 19) and can ascend bodily into Heaven. He is related to Nature in such a way that Spirit and Nature are fully harmonized. . . . In *The Lion, the Witch and the Wardrobe* we see the Lion undergoing something very like the Passion of Christ: "But how slowly he walked! And his great, royal head drooped so that his nose nearly touched the grass. Presently he stumbled and gave a low moan" (ch. XIV). What does it mean? It means exactly what it says. Nevertheless, I cannot see that any physical change is caused by his resurrection: he was omniscient and omnipotent both before and after the event. It is perhaps pointless to make such heavy weather of a theological problem not even posed, but my worry is—what happens if it *is* posed? In any case, the most reliable hints about the new, resurrected Nature are found, not in *The Lion, the Witch and the Wardrobe,* but in the final chapter of *The Last Battle.* . . . (pp. 103-06)

However, accepting—as I do—that it would be unwise to try and maintain an artificial silence about biblical as well as non-biblical parallels which even Lewis has been accused of having made quite "obvious," I offer the following advice regarding what many others would now wish to open up to closer inspection. (p. 106)

[It is] essential to see . . . that what is in one book or world cannot be the same in another book or world. Put another way, what "Miss T" eats does not remain as it was but *turns into* "Miss T." The instructions Aslan gives Eustace and Jill on how to discover Prince Rilian are meant, I think, to reinforce the importance of following Christ's commandments. On the other hand, if, while reading *The Silver Chair,* we are thinking only of Christ's instructions to the rich young man recounted in St. Mark x: 17-21, we'll have missed what we are meant to be attending to in Narnia. It's afterwards, minutes or hours or perhaps even years afterwards, that the two worlds are to be joined in our minds. . . . But even if that juncture *never* takes place, we will have benefitted enormously from *The Silver Chair,* for it is part of the success of a great author that the sense of his book does not depend on the reader's knowing the original source of its ingredients. (pp. 106-07)

I think we can better appreciate the use Lewis made of biblical parallels when we consider the two opposite dangers into which he could have fallen. Had the parallels been very obvious, he would not, I think, have nearly so many readers. Nonbelievers would have felt they were being "got at" and rejected them at once. On the other hand, our imaginations would not have been attuned to the Everlasting Gospel had he been too subtle—especially as so many people today have never read the Bible. Some middle way was needed. This *via media* came easily to Lewis because he did not begin with morals or the Gospels at all, but wrote stories in which those ingredients pushed themselves in of their own accord. This is understandable to those who spent some time in Lewis's company. He could talk about the saints as naturally and unembarrassedly as you or I could talk about nextdoor neighbours. "Poor Lazarus," I recall him saying, "he had to die all over again!" And because Lewis's primary intention was to tell a story, rather than get a "message" across, the biblical elements blend into the stories. They are more like leaven in dough than raisins in a cake: it is difficult to say where they begin and where they end. Indeed, sometimes the "parallels" elude our discovery by the sheer multiplicity of them, blended into what is a quite simple episode. (pp. 110-11)

I do not think it is specially the identifiable biblical elements which cause us to regard the Narnian stories as Christian books. Almost every page of every book is suffused throughout with moral substance of a quality which I don't believe anyone, whatever his beliefs, could fairly object to. . . . [The] tales are not built around moral themes which were in the author's mind from the beginning: these themes grew out of the telling and are as much a part of the narrative as scent is to a flower. (p. 114)

[The] morality of Lewis's books goes far deeper and touches on levels of human understanding rarely attempted even by those who write for adults. An especially good example occurs in *The Voyage of the "Dawn Treader"* (ch. X). As Lucy searches the Magician's Book for the spell which will make the Dufflepuds visible, she comes across a spell which will let you know what your friends say about you. Not even wishing to avoid this dangerous thing, Lucy says the magical words and hears her good friend, Marjorie, say very unkind things about her to an-other girl. Later, when Aslan discovers what poor, heart-broken Lucy has done, he says, "Spying on people by magic is the same as spying on them in any other way. And you have misjudged your friend. She is weak, but she loves you. She was afraid of the older girl and said what she does not mean." "I don't think I'd ever be able to for-get what I heard her say," answers Lucy. "No, you won't," replies Aslan.

Are there many of us who have not found, like Lucy, that such a dangerous course, once taken, forbids return? I've never seen the enormous difference between what our friends *say,* and what they really *think,* about us so unfor-gettably portrayed.

Finally, before we move onto *The Last Battle,* which de-serves separate and special consideration, it is right that we see how the Narnian stories answer so many of the questions raised by Lewis as he progressed from atheism to Christianity. Paganism, as Lewis came to see, had been only a "prophetic dream" of that which became Fact in the Incarnation. But just as God, by becoming Man, un-derwent a certain humiliation, so the old, richly imagined myths, Lewis believed, must succumb to rational analysis: they must undergo a kind of death before they can be re-born in glory. But "those who attain the glorious resurrec-tion," Lewis wrote in *Miracles,* "will see the dry bones clothed again with flesh, the fact and the myth re-married, the literal and the metaphorical rushing together" (ch. XVI). (pp. 114-15)

[Nowhere] in all of Lewis's fiction are we so likely to forget that there ever has been an estrangement between fact and myth as in the Chronicles of Narnia. This is, I should think, especially true of those young readers who are brought up on the Narnian stories before they know there are such things as "ancient myths"; they will consider the *Longaevi* just as much a part of Aslan's original creation as are the animals. But Lewis had been closing the gap be-tween fact and myth in ways other than his interplanetary novels. A good example is found in his chapter on "Mira-cles of the Old Creation" in which he pointed out that when Our Lord made water into wine at the wedding feast in Cana He was doing "close and small and, as it were, in focus what God at other times does so large that men do not attend to it." This miracle, he said, "proclaims that the God of all wine is present. The vine is one of the blessings sent by Jahweh: *He is the reality behind the false God Bac-chus.* Every year, as part of the Natural order, God makes wine. He does so by creating a vegetable organism that can turn water, soil, and sunlight into a juice which will, under proper conditions, become wine."

But if Christ (Aslan in Narnia) is the *reality* behind the false god, why does Lewis bring into *Prince Caspian* Bac-chus, Silenus, and the Maenads? Because now that we know who the God of wine really is, there is no danger of confusion: Bacchus "can do nothing of himself, but what he seeth the Father do" (John v: 19). Now that we no lon-ger *need* Bacchus, it is *safe* to have him. Besides this, how else could we have a proper romp before the Battle of Beruna Bridge if we forego such a wealth of imaginative experience as we get from Bacchus and his madcap follow-

ers? Although Lewis divested him of his power to cause madness and murder, the god retains his essential wild-ness. In his retinue is his old tutor, Silenus, who "began calling out at once, 'Refreshments! Time for refresh-ments,' and falling off his donkey and being bundled on to it again by the others, while the donkey was under the impression that the whole thing was a circus, and tried to give a display of walking on its hind legs. And all the time there were more and more vine leaves everywhere." After the festivities Susan says to Lucy, "I wouldn't have felt very safe with Bacchus and all his wild girls if we'd met them without Aslan." "I should think not," replies the sensible Lucy (ch. XI).

Thus, without enfeebling his own power, Aslan does through Bacchus that which he did "close and small" cen-turies ago in Cana of Galilee. "Here you are, mother," said Bacchus, dipping a pitcher into the cottage well and hand-ing it to the little old woman. "But what was in it now was not water but the richest wine, red as red-currant jelly, smooth as oil, strong as beef, warming as tea, cool as dew." The same is true of the other mythological creatures in Narnia: all are extensions and expressions of the power and fecundity of their Creator. "Hail, Lord," says the River-god to Aslan (ch. XIV). That gets it just right: there never has been a permanent divorce between fact and myth. (pp. 116-18)

While we know that Lewis wavered occasionally in order-ing some of the events in the first six Chronicles, and that he had to do a little "deliberate inventing" here and there, no one can say that he gave no inklings of the "twist" he was to put into *The Last Battle.* Hint after hint is thrown out in all the other stories that no one may camp forever in Narnia, just as no one may camp forever in this world. If we feel too great a shock at having the old, familiar Narnia crumble beneath our feet, how are we to endure the shock when the real thing happens here? But it would not be fair to suggest that anything remotely like despair is what Lewis was after. Every hint of impending separa-tion from the old Narnia is underpinned by persistent inti-mations of how great a loss it would be to lose the royal and all-loving Aslan, how complete would be our happi-ness to enjoy him forever.

It is difficult to select from the many passages in which Lewis attempts to woo our hearts from all but Aslan the ones that do this best, those which might be called the most typical. I am, thus, obliged to become autobiographi-cal. After numerous readings of the Chronicles the pas-sage which stabs me with the sweetest and sharpest desire comes from the last chapter of *The Lion, the Witch and the Wardrobe.* After the White Witch is dead, Aslan leads the children to Cair Paravel. The castle towered above them and "before them were the sands, with rocks and lit-tle pools of salt water, and seaweed, and the smell of the sea and long miles of bluish-green waves breaking for ever and ever on the beach. And oh, the cry of the sea-gulls! Have you heard it? Can you remember?"

Taken in their context, these words—especially the ques-tions—set me yearning for that "unnameable something" more powerfully than any bluish-green waves and the cry of seagulls in this world have ever done. In this particular instance I do not feel sorry for the children in Narnia (they remain there for five years) but for myself. I can tell from the feel of the book in my hands that for me the adventure is almost at an end. And, forgetting the other stories momentarily, how can *I* live never to meet Aslan again? I am suggesting that for both the reader and those who make it into Narnia, the joys of that world (the place, the inhabitants, the castles, the landscapes) are inseparable from the greater joy of knowing the Lion. We want to be there because *he* is there. We desire the Lion because—well, not only because Aslan is in himself desirable, but because the desire is one of the things he has implanted in us, one of the things of which we are made. (pp. 120-22)

There is a particularly moving example of the children's love for Aslan in *The Voyage of the "Dawn Treader"* (ch. XVI). When they learn that they must return to their own world, the truth dawns upon them that it is not so much the change in *worlds* they dread, but separation from the lion:

> "It isn't Narnia, you know," sobbed Lucy. "It's *you*. We shan't meet *you* there. And how can we live, never meeting you?"
>
> "But you shall meet me, dear one," said Aslan.
>
> "Are—are you there too, Sir?" said Edmund.
>
> "I am," said Aslan. "But there I have another name. You must learn to know me by that name. This was the very reason why you were brought to Narnia, that by knowing me here for a little, you may know me better there."

That, I think, is as frank a statement as Lewis makes anywhere about his evangelistic purpose in writing the Narnian stories.

The English children are, I suppose, from a Narnian point of view, "Gentiles" from an unknown world who become Narnians by adoption. There are, however, native Narnians who, when they see the Lion for the first time, feel a natural and spontaneous devotion to the person of the divine Aslan—as, for instance, Caspian's old nurse in *Prince Caspian*, who when she sees Aslan bending over her sickbed says, "Oh, Aslan! I knew it was true. I've been waiting for this all my life" (ch. XIV). Hwin, the mare in *The Horse and His Boy*, on seeing the Lion, trots up to him and says, "Please, you're so beautiful. You may eat me if you like. I'd sooner be eaten by you than fed by anyone else" (ch. XIV). But from here we move on to the culmination of the triumphant theme of Joy as the "serious business of Heaven."

[*The Last Battle*] is, in my opinion, the best written and the most sublime of all the Narnian stories, the crowning achievement of the whole Narnian creation. Everything else in all the other six stories finds its ultimate meaning in relation to this book. One can read the other stories in any order, but *The Last Battle* must be read last because, as Lewis would say, you cannot possibly understand the "play" until you've seen it through to the end. Lewis insisted on taking us to the end—and beyond.

If *The Last Battle* is re-read less often than the other fairy tales—and I don't know that it is—this is probably be-

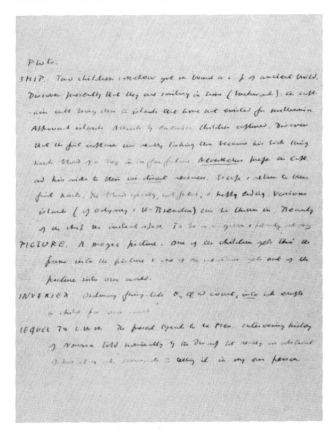

Lewis's plot outline for The Voyage of the "Dawn Treader."

cause the first eleven chapters, which take place in the old, familiar Narnia, are so extremely painful to read. Almost everything we have come to love is, bit by bit, taken from us. Our sense of loss is made more excruciating because we are allowed—even encouraged—to believe that things will eventually get back to "normal." We feel certain that the King, at least, will not be deceived by Shift's trickery: but he is. When Eustace and Jill arrive we know it will only be a matter of time until all is put right. Yet, despite their willingness to help, there is so little they can do without the help of Aslan. And where, by the way, *is* He? Our hearts warm within us as Jewel the Unicorn recounts the centuries of past happiness in which every day and week in Narnia had seemed to be better than the last:

> And as he went on, the picture of all those happy years, all the thousands of them, piled up in Jill's mind till it was rather like looking down from a high hill onto a rich, lovely plain full of woods and waters and cornfields, which spread away and away till it got thin and misty from distance. And she said:
>
> "Oh, I do hope we can soon settle the Ape and get back to those good, ordinary times. And then I hope they'll go on for ever and ever and ever. *Our* world is going to have an end some day. Perhaps this one won't. Oh Jewel—wouldn't it be lovely if Narnia just went on and on—like what you said it has been?"

"Nay, sister," answered Jewel, "all worlds draw to an end; except Aslan's own country."

"Well, at least," said Jill, "I hope the end of this one is millions of millions of millions of years away." (ch. VIII)

So do we all. Yet a few minutes later Farsight the Eagle brings word that Cair Paravel, the high seat of all the Kings of Narnia, has been taken by the Calormenes. And, as he lay dying, Roonwit the Centaur asked the King to remember that "all worlds draw to an end and that noble death is a treasure which no one is too poor to buy" (ch. VIII).

Lewis's didactic purpose ought to be clear to those who are conversant with orthodox Christianity. He uses his own invented world to illustrate what the Church has been teaching since the beginning, but which is becoming more and more neglected or forgotten. Namely, that this world will come to an end; it was never meant to be our real home—that lies elsewhere; we do not know, we cannot possibly know, when the end will come; and the end will come, not from within, but from without.

Most of the events in *The Last Battle* are based on Our Lord's apocalyptic prophecies recorded in St. Matthew xxiv, St. Mark xiii, and St. Luke xxi. The treachery of Shift the Ape was suggested by the Dominical words found in St. Matthew xxiv: 23-24;

> If any man shall say unto you, Lo, here is Christ, or there; believe it not. For there shall arise false Christs, and false prophets, and shall shew great signs and wonders; insomuch that, if it were possible, they shall deceive the very elect.

The Ape almost—so very, very nearly—succeeds in deceiving even the most faithful followers of Aslan, first through trickery and, later, when he becomes the tool of Rishda Tarkaan and Ginger the Cat, in propounding his "new theology": the confusion of Aslan and the devil Tash as "Tashlan." As the monkey Shift is a parody of a man, so his "theology" is a parody of the truth. We are prepared for ordinary wickedness in an adventure story, but with the advent of the "new theology" we move into a new and dreadful dimension where ordinary courage seems helpless.

When it seems quite certain that Eustace and Jill will soon die fighting for Narnia, they speculate as to whether, at the moment of their death in Narnia, they will be found dead in England. Frightened by the idea, Jill begins a confession which she breaks off mid-sentence. "What were you going to say?" asks Eustace. She answers:

> I *was* going to say I wished we'd never come. But I don't. I don't. I don't. Even if we *are* killed. I'd rather be killed fighting for Narnia than grow old and stupid at home and perhaps go about in a bathchair and then die in the end just the same. (ch. IX)

From that point onward Lewis lets go the full power of his imagination, and we are carried relentlessly forward into what is truly the *last* battle of Narnia, in front of the Stable. There King Tirian, the children, and the remnant of faithful Narnians are either slain or make their way in-

side. The Stable has become none other than the way into Aslan's Country and, drawing out this brilliant piece of symbolism, Lewis has Jill say in a moment of selfless appreciation: "In our world too, a Stable once had something inside it that was bigger than our whole world" (ch. XIII).

What is a little confusing, but which is partly explained in chapters IV and V, and fully cleared up in the last chapter, is that all (except one) of the "friends of Narnia"— Digory Kirke, Polly Plummer, Peter, Edmund and Lucy Pevensie, Eustace Scrubb, and Jill Pole—died together in a railway crash in England. They are reborn in glory and, inside the Stable, Eustace and Jill meet all the others. The exception is Susan Pevensie who, "no longer a friend of Narnia" (ch. XII), has drifted of her own free will into apostasy. Liberal clergymen and other "kind" but mistaken people, preferring the temporary passion of Pity to the eternal action of Pity, have found the absence of Susan a reason for calling Lewis "cruel." But they are well answered in *The Great Divorce* where, explaining why those who have chosen Hell shall not be allowed to veto the joys of Heaven, he says: "Every disease that submits to a cure shall be cured: but we will not call blue yellow to please those who insist on still having jaundice, nor make a midden of the world's garden for the sake of some who cannot abide the smell of roses" (ch. XIII). (pp. 122-27)

With a terrible beauty that makes the heart ache, and which is perhaps only matched by Dante's *Paradiso,* Aslan goes to the Stable door and holds His Last Judgement. Those who are worthy pass in, the others turn away into darkness. Inside, the children watch as Aslan, fulfilling the apocalyptic prophecies of the New Testament, destroys Narnia by water and fire and closes the Stable door upon it forever.

After this dazzling feat of the imagination, one might reasonably expect that Lewis could not help but let us down in "unwinding" his story. He knew that the merest slip of the pen could have cast a shadow of incredulity over all that went before, and he proceeded very cautiously in opening the children's eyes to where they are. The question was how do you portray Heaven? How make it *heavenly?* How "unwind" *upwards?*

The answer lay in finding—and then trying to describe— the difference between the earthly and the eternal world. In order to stride the pitfalls into which so many critics of the Narnian stories stumble, it is necessary to do a little demolition work here. First, it's about as natural as sneezing for moderns to call something an "allegory" when it has a meaning slightly different from, or other than, the one the author gives it. In this sense you can "allegorize" practically anything. The reason why Lewis claimed that neither his Narnian stories nor his interplanetary trilogy are allegories is that he was using the traditional definition of the term: by allegory he meant the use of something real and tangible to stand for that which is real but intangible. Love can be allegorized, patience can be allegorized, anything *immaterial* can be allegorized or represented by feigned physical objects. But Aslan, for example, is already a physical object. To try and represent what Christ would be like in Narnia is to turn one physical being into another physical being—and that, of course, does not fall within Lewis's definition of what constitutes an "allegory." On the other hand, there is much in the Narnias, and specially in *The Last Battle,* which would fit Lewis's own description of symbolism. . . .

Symbolism . . . was not for Lewis a fanciful bit of intellectualism. He believed that Heaven is the real thing of which earth is an imperfect copy. His problem was not only of finding some way to illustrate this, but to describe the heavenly life in such a way that it would not seem a place of perpetual negations. (pp. 128-30)

Lewis had a knack of making even the most difficult metaphysical concepts understandable and picturing the otherwise unpicturable. In order that his readers will feel as comfortable in the world beyond the Stable door as the children in the book, he brings in homely details such as the fact that Narnian clothes feel as well as look beautiful and even the very comforting news that "there was no such thing as starch or flannel or elastic to be found from one end of the country to the other" (ch. XII). Then, as the children and many of the animals they have come to love follow Aslan further into the country, their sense of strangeness wears off until it eventually dawns upon them that the reason why everything looks so familiar is because they are seeing for the first time the "real Narnia" of which the old one had been a "copy." As they rejoice in this discovery, Lord Digory, whom we first met as old Professor Kirke in *The Lion, the Witch and the Wardrobe,* explains the difference between the two, adding, "It's all in Plato, all in Plato: bless me, what *do* they teach them at these schools!" (ch. XV). He is referring in the main, perhaps, to Plato's *Republic* and the *Phaedo* in which Plato writes about immortality and the unchanging reality behind the changing forms.

One very important detail, overlooked perhaps by the majority of readers as it is blended so perfectly into the narrative, concerns the manner in which resurrected bodies differ from earthly ones. The children discover that they can scale waterfalls and run faster than an arrow flies. This is meant to be a parallel to the Gospel accounts of Christ's risen body: though still corporeal, He can move through a locked door (John xx: 19) and ascend bodily into Heaven (Mark xvi: 19). But whereas Christ had been the "first fruits" of the Resurrection, *all* now share in this mighty and glorious immortality as prefigured by St. Paul when he wrote, "We shall not all sleep, but we shall all be changed, in a moment, in the twinkling of an eye, at the last trump: for the trumpet shall sound, and the dead shall be raised incorruptible and we shall be changed" (I Corinthians xv: 51-52).

When the children reach the Mountain of Aslan they are joined by all the heroes of the other six books, Reepicheep the Mouse, Puddleglum the Marsh-wiggle, and a host of other old friends. There another surprise awaits them. Lewis had earlier, in his novel *That Hideous Strength,* defined Arthurian "Logres" as the permanent and enduring heart of Britain. So now, without bending any Apostolic teaching so far as I can see, he extends this analogy further by showing the children that "no good thing is destroyed" and that all the countries that were worth saving have be-

come parts of the whole—"spurs jutting out from the great mountains of Aslan" (ch. XVI). Uneasy, nevertheless, that their joy may yet be snatched from them, and that they may be sent back to earth, they turn to Aslan who answers the question in their minds: "Have you not guessed?" he says, "The term is over: the holidays have begun. The dream is ended: this is the morning." (pp. 131-32)

There has never been a book written, I fancy, in which the assumptions of the author were not present, implicitly or explicitly. Even the most blameless stories of child-life have at their base beliefs about something or the other. There is no such thing as not believing *anything.* One who does not agree with the central premises of the Narnian Chronicles must agree with some others. Will they lead to better ends than those of Lewis's books? I have read many modern works of literature about which I am forced to say "I admire the workmanship, but deplore the sentiments"; but only of the Narnian Chronicles can I unhesitatingly say, "This is beautiful, and this is right." (p. 133)

> *Walter Hooper, in his* Past Watchful Dragons: The Narnian Chronicles of C. S. Lewis, *Collier Books, 1979, 140 p.*

Peter J. Schakel

The Chronicles of Narnia are best approached . . . through their narrative art. They are, above all, stories, of interest for their plots, characters, symbols, and structural patterns. They unite the emphasis of the romance on brave knights, courteous behavior, and heroic courage with the imaginary, self-contained world of fantasy, which the reader enters and participates in temporarily for enjoyment and enlightenment, and the magical world of fairy tales and their broad, clear-cut themes contrasting good and evil. The use of myth in the Chronicles, typical of fairy tales, gives them multiple levels of meaning, aimed particularly at the imagination and the emotions; and their use of archetypal plot motifs, character types, and symbols adds depth and universality by relating them to the rest of literature and involving them in matters of ultimate concern to all people. Lewis unifies each story about a distinctive theme or tone and creates in each the flavor of a particular part of the Narnian world. All these varied elements Lewis draws into a unique and appealing combination of adventure, charm, and numinousness in plot, characters, and theme.

The Christian thought of the Chronicles, too, is best approached through their narrative art; it is best accepted as part of the Narnian world rather than interpreted as allegory. The stories do have Christian themes, themes which go deeper than many readers, as they look for biblical parallels, suspect. And it hardly could be otherwise. Lewis claimed that he did not set out to write Christian stories, that the Christian element forced itself in of its own accord. Christianity was so deeply and fully a part of Lewis that his faith would inevitably infuse whatever he wrote. Walter Hooper called Lewis "the most thoroughly *converted* man I ever met." That being the case, it was almost certain that his faith would come through as he created such elementary works as fairy tales. Perhaps without deliberately planning to, Lewis includes in the Chronicles, through images and archetypes, an overview of the faith, an indirect introduction at a children's level to the essential elements of Christianity, similar in scope and many details to **Mere Christianity.** It is one of the greatnesses of the Chronicles, however, that although they do have deeply Christian themes, they are not dependent upon Christianity. A non-Christian reader can approach the stories as fairy stories, be moved by the exciting adventures and the archetypal meanings, and not find the Christian elements obtrusive or offensive.

The Chronicles are not theological or evangelical books. There is no Narnian equivalent for the orthodox Christian belief that salvation is gained by awareness of what Christ has done and "acceptance" of him as savior. Neither Edmund, Eustace, nor Emeth, the three main examples of "salvation" in the Chronicles, knew Aslan before his conversion experience. (pp. 131-32)

The books are, mainly, children's books, and Lewis seems to have intended that they awaken in a child a love for Aslan and for goodness which can grow, as the child matures, into love for and acceptance of Christ. The Chronicles should not be expected to influence readers to "accept" Christ, but they may lead children to love and desire Aslan and, through him, eventually, Christ. (p. 134)

Adults . . . should read the Chronicles like children and share a child's enjoyment of the elements which appeal to the imagination. But adults, out of [in Lewis's words] "interests which children would not share with us," will want to go beyond the imaginative qualities of the stories to their intellectual dimensions. The Chronicles are classics because of the way the intellectual reinforces the imaginative, and there is value for adults in seeing and discussing both aspects together; for them, and for children increasingly as they grow older, a response with the head can and should follow a response of the heart. But to explicate the "meanings" of the books to children would be, in Lewis's words, "patronizing" (**Of Other Worlds,** p. 34), talking down to them out of superior adult interests and perspectives. The Chronicles are not allegories needing interpretation for full effect: they are stories to be enjoyed. Children should be left to enjoy them, imaginatively and emotionally, without being asked to reflect upon their "significance." And because of the archetypal nature of the stories, because their roots reach down to basic human instincts and emotions, out of that enjoyment "meaning" will come, at its own time and in its own way. (pp. 134-35)

> *Peter J. Schakel, in a conclusion to his* Reading with the Heart: The Way into Narnia, *William B. Eerdmans Publishing Company, 1979, pp. 131-35.*

Thomas Howard

We may call Narnia the forgotten country because far from being a wholly new region, like Magellan's Pacific, or Marco Polo's Cathay, or even the astronauts' moon, it is the very homeland which lies at the back of every man's imagination, which we all yearn for (even if we are wholly unaware of such a yearning), and which has long since disappeared from view in the wake of the vessel we call history. (p. 21)

[What] we encounter in the landscape of Narnia is *true*—not in the sense that we will come upon the ruins of Cair Paravel somewhere (there are none), but rather in the sense that Cair Paravel is a castle, and the man from whose imagination castles have disappeared is disastrously deprived, as is the man who has lost the capacity to appreciate how it can be that for a free man to bow in the presence of a great king, far from being demeaning, is ennobling. (p. 23)

The tales of Narnia open up to us a certain kind of world. It is a world which has been made—made by Someone, beautifully made. Its fabric is shot through with glory. There is no peak, no valley, no sea or forest, but bears the weight of this glory, no law of the land that does not mirror the exact pattern of this glory, no spell or incantation or taboo that does not reach through the veil that protects the mundane and the obvious from the great glories and mysteries that press upon them. No creature—no faun, dryad, star, or winged horse—that does not bear about and exhibit in its own form some bit of the shape of that glory. And, alas, there is no evil that does not turn out to be fraud, parody, or counterfeit of that glory. In every case, the appeal of evil in Narnia springs from illusion and leads eventually to sterility, destruction, and anger.

Now, if that is the sort of world which the "fairy" chronicles of Narnia open up to us, it turns out to be a world identical in every significant point with the world that all myths and religions have told us we live in. Taken item for item, at least up to this point, Narnia turns out to be indistinguishable from the world that the sages and seers and saints and druids and prophets have throught they saw. Indeed we could with no difficulty translate these items into the language of Jewish and Christian sacred texts. "It is a world which has been made—made by Someone" becomes Genesis 1. "No peak, no valley . . . but bears the weight of this glory," becomes Psalm 19. "No law of the land that does not mirror the exact pattern of that glory" becomes Psalm 119. The story of evil as fraud and illusion is told in Genesis. And so forth.

The point of all this is that if we find the chronicles of Narnia to be inconsequential in their subject matter, then the world pictured by all myths and religions is inconsequential.

But two cautions arise here. First, the fact that these chronicles speak of that sort of world does not thereby make them good books. You can have terrible books about sublime things. (pp. 24-5)

And second, if we were to claim that there is a significant correspondence between Narnia and the real world, then we have opened up the troublesome topic of allegory, and everyone is off chasing parallels. Aslan equals Christ; the White Witch equals Lilith; Peter equals Saint Peter; and so forth.

Lewis himself dispelled this line of thought. He did not set out to write something like The Pilgrim's Progress, in which we may discover one-for-one correspondences between the characters and images in the story and people or conditions in our own world, so that Christian *equals* you and me on pilgrimage to heaven, and the Giant Despair equals despair, and so forth. That is allegory, but the connection between what we find in Narnia and anything in our own story is closer to analogy, where we say, not "Aslan equals Christ," but rather "As Christ is to this story, so, in a measure, is Aslan to that one." It is at least partly the difference between *symbols* and *cases in point,* which we run into every day. You may see a boy offer to carry a grocery bag for a woman. He is not a symbol of Christ (carrying someone else's burden): rather, he appears in this little act as a case in point of the same thing which was also at work in Christ's act, namely Charity, which always "substitutes" itself for the good of someone else. That is, both the boy with the groceries, and Calvary, are cases in point of this Charity. The boy is not a symbol: he really is enacting and exhibiting Charity, the supreme case in point of which is Calvary. (pp. 25-6)

Thus we make a mistake if we try to chase symbols up and down the landscape of Narnia, or if we try to pin down allegories. It is much better to read these tales for what they are, namely fairy tales. We blunder sadly if we try to read them as anything else—as cryptograms or anagrams or acrostics for Christian theology and morals. (p. 26)

Since the nature of fairy tales is to proceed simply and without apology from one event to the next, it may be that the most useful method of observing what Lewis is up to in these narratives, and the method most faithful to the special technique (if we may give it as cold a name as technique) of fairy tale, is simply to move along the path of the narrative noting what we see and subordinating the "criticism" of fairy tales to the apparently simple pattern of that kind of narrative, rather than to try to force them into the Procrustean bed of, say, the modern novel with the highly structural analysis that is appropriate to that kind of narrative.

There are literally thousands of observations that may be made as one moves along through the landscape of faerie. The following would seem to be at least some of the features worth noting in the land called Narnia, since they not only suggest to us the sort of world in which we find ourselves in these narratives, but also seem to set up resonances with the story, giving us our most important clue as to the nature of Lewis's achievement in these tales.

For one thing, we do not get very far before we discover that it is Lucy who ordinarily seems to see things first. Again and again, whether it is the very first discovery of Narnia beyond the wardrobe, or the first glimpse of Aslan, she has the gift of recognition. If we read far enough in Lewis we will find a theme, hinted at in this small beginning in Narnia, of womanhood as being especially receptive to the approaches of mystery or glory, or the divine, say. We see this in Mrs. Beaver's instant response to the appearance of the four children. " 'So you've come at last!' she said, holding out both her wrinkled old paws. 'At last! To think that ever I should live to see this day!' " (Who can avoid hearing old Anna waiting in the temple with Simeon?) Tinidril, Jane Studdock, Psyche, and Orual herself: they all *see* things.

Then, the image of the "feminine" eldil Perelandra, and indeed the very texture of the landscape in the planet Pere-

landra, warm and fluid, suggest fecundity and nourishment—those qualities brought into play in response to the planting of some seed. Lewis, of course, knew and believed the story in which the figure called upon to respond to the approach of the god was a woman. Her flesh and indeed her very womanhood seemed to be the type and image of all human life as that life stands over against the divine life. What, in that story, is the proper response of that flesh to the approach of the divine? "Be it unto me according to thy word." Either this, or bitterness and desolation.

Again we may note that the narrative returns with more than random recurrence to scenes where we find cups of tea or tankards of beer, and cakes and sandwiches, or a fireside and pipes and hot baths and so forth. Frequently we find this sort of interlude either en route to some great crux in the action or just after some great peril or victory. It is always very commonplace stuff, and that is the whole point. It is a theme right at the center of all of Lewis's vision: simplicity, good fellowship, the goodness of creation, the sheer pleasure of good tastes and smells and textures—fresh bread, raspberries, nuts—even the lowly bean which Lewis lauds in one poem. What are all wars and all economics and all politics about? Do they not all come down in the end to the business of allowing people to return to their hearthsides and to family and friends and good fellowship? What would all exiles and all prisoners and all dying people sell their souls to regain if not these highest pleasures—pleasures mediated to us under the lowly species of tea and cakes and laughter and fondling? In the fairy tale landscape of Narnia we see this recurrently.

And in this connection we may note the place of sheer festivity and merrymaking in Narnia. Here we come upon dancing and drinking and the congregating of many different *sorts* of creatures: dwarfs, fauns, dryads, rabbits, foxes, badgers, centaurs, giants, dogs, and humans. It is clear that the very pattern in the fabric of this world depends on threads of many different colors and materials—very like the pattern in the fabric of the world that stood as the backdrop to Lewis's whole imagination, namely the world in which all things in their varied shapes and colors—*omnia opera domini*— dance and sing: from warriors and seraphim to rabbits and foxes and badgers, with heroes and charwomen and cabbies and all.

With respect to these rabbits and other amiable and harmless-looking small creatures in Narnia we may observe in Lewis's narrative art what he called "good unoriginality." That is, it seems to be fixed in our imaginations that rabbits and bluebirds and deer are not only harmless but good, so that for a storyteller (Lewis commends Disney for this) to assume all these well-worn suppositions on our part is much better than for him to wrench things about and catch us off guard with villainous tomtits or blackguardly lambs. They *look* harmless and trustworthy, so at least for our story let us assume that our imaginations are leading us in the right direction. In Narnia, for example, when the four children find themselves being led along by a robin, Edmund, who it may be recalled is out of sympathy with everything, complains that they have no way of knowing whose side this bird is on. Whereupon Peter, always to be trusted for the right point of view, comments

F. W. Paxford, Lewis's gardener at the Kilns, who served as the model for Puddleglum the Marshwiggle in The Silver Chair.

crisply that every robin in any story *he* knows anything about is good.

The point is that these images are some sort of trustworthy index of something that is real. When Edmund and the Witch see a squirrel with his wife and family, with two satyrs, a dwarf, and a fox, sitting on stools at a table eating a plum pudding that has been decorated with holly, it is quite clear to them and to us that something good is afoot, which of course infuriates the Witch. You don't find things like *that* about without suspecting something good. And when the children hear the jingling bells and see the sledge of Father Christmas, it is abundantly clear that good *is* abroad, since sledges and jingling bells spell joy. (The Witch also had a sledge with bells—but that is the very point: hers was a counterfeit, exactly like the real thing but a cheat. Evil can only parody goodness, it cannot invent new forms of real beauty and joy. That is why in fairy tales you have to beware of attractive disguises—nice old crones selling apples in the forest, say, or angels of light.)

There are variations on the theme of festivity. Sometimes it takes the form of merrymaking and sheer jollity; and at other times it is solemn; equally joyous, but solemn. Festal pomp, with gravity and ceremony presiding over all, seems somehow to be in the cards. When Aslan crowns Peter, or when he sings Narnia into being, or bestows speech on the animals who are to be Talking Beasts, there is hush in the air, and solemnity, that gives us a glimpse of the other face of joy. The expectant motionlessness on the one hand, and the great clamorous rush of all the creatures up into the final Narnia, are the largo and the vivace of joy, we might say.

Once or twice we hear passing tidings of a Milk-white Stag that is seen only at immensely infrequent intervals on the marches of Narnia. It seems to have almost nothing to do with the "plot," but it sounds a note, like old Triton's horn, or like the casements opening on faerie seas forlorn, that haunts us with fugitive beauty. Apparently Narnia is the sort of place where, whatever beauties you may see, there are still more and others, beyond the borders of your ken. Though yours is a story full of joys and terrors, it is not the only story. There are beauties that would burst your heart if you encountered them now, and terrors that would wither you utterly. You may catch hints of them, but they are not part of your story for the moment. Lewis, of course, thought that something like this was true of all possible stories.

The evil which is abroad in Narnia when we first come into the land takes the form of a white witch. We learn from Mr. Beaver that she is of the race of Lilith, Adam's first wife, according to an old and persistent legend. Because of dissatisfaction and disobedience on her part, she was driven into exile, and Eve took her place as the mother of mankind. For this reason, Lilith hates fruitfulness and love and the honest intercourse of man with woman. She is the archetype of all wicked fairies who show up at cradles and christenings, and her particular ploy is illusion. If she can lull you and entice you away from light-of-day reality, and lead you into the sterile limbo of illusion where you will dry up and die, then she has done what she wants to do. She is Lamia, and *la belle dame sans merci,* and the Green Witch of ***The Silver Chair,*** and all others like this. (pp. 39-43)

The greatest fear of these witches is that sons of Adam and daughters of Eve will show up. Human flesh is their greatest hate, as it is Satan's (cf. *Paradise Lost*), for human flesh is the jewel in the crown of the Enemy; human flesh is the heir of the land which the witch holds in her thrall (we find that Narnia is only truly itself, and its denizens truly free and safe if humans are on the Four Thrones at Cair Paravel; apparently some sort of sovereignty is to be borne and exercised for the good of all by *human* flesh, not by fauns or lions or dryads elected by majority vote); and human flesh is the sign of real joy, since it enacts in itself the intelligent dance of Charity, where self-giving equals ecstasy (sex and the marriage sacrament is the great physical metaphor of this); and human flesh is the agent of the final victory over all falsehood and illusion and fraud. In another Story this all follows the sequence: Annunciation-Nativity-Passion-Resurrection-Ascension-Apocalypse. Flesh is the very sign of the *other,* which Lilith hates, but which is the desire and object of Charity. In the image of the Dance we see the one mode of flesh (woman) answering to the other mode (man). Antiphons of joy. Sheer, blissful Fact. It is Fact that stands over against the blandishments and illusions of hell—or of Lilith.

Over against all this dimness stands the wry and merry wisdom of Professor Kirke which in its rare appearances in the narrative furnishes a sort of standard by which we may test what is going on. It is as though he is *there,* like the duke in *Measure for Measure,* or the prince in *Romeo and Juliet,* not as a major character in the action, but as a reference point, the embodiment of order and goodness. It may not be for nothing that Lewis has named him Kirke: We have seen this motif before in the figure of Mother Kirk in **The Pilgrim's Regress.** And Lewis's own mentor MacDonald was a Scot, in whose native land they call the Church the Kirk. Professor Kirke has been to school in Aslan's country (see **The Magician's Nephew:** Kirke is Digory), and has learned the hard lessons of plain obedience, and of trusting against all odds that Aslan knows what he is doing, and of not being too sure what *can't* happen, and of the paradoxes at work in the country of Charity, where every man feeds on the fruit plucked by another's labor, and so forth. So that when the children bring their quarrel about Lucy's absurd report on the wardrobe to him, his question is " 'How do you know that your sister's story is not true?' " And his advice to all of them, learned no doubt from long lessons, is " 'We might all try minding our own business.' " In another place, where everyone asks how on earth these wonders can be, we hear the Professor muttering to himself, "What do they teach schoolchildren these days," since "it's all in Plato."

Here we find a note struck that is important to Lewis's vision, and for which Lewis had venerable precedent in Spenser and Milton, namely the assumption that pagan wisdom and mythology may furnish us with some very significant clues to things. Spenser, in his Christian epic on Charity, *The Faerie Queene,* takes us to such pagan haunts as the Cave of Morpheus and the Garden of Adonis. Milton calls Christ Pan in his hymn for the Nativity. In Narnia we find Silenus and Bacchus themselves, surely the most pagan of all pagan gods, with their vines and wreaths and capering and tippling. And Plato. All of this in a narrative that takes us into a country that we are finally obliged to recognize as *like* the country longed for in the Psalms of the Hebrews and the vision of St. John the Divine.

But is not that country the very antithesis of all pagan countries? No, says Lewis (and Milton, and Spenser, and all Renaissance Christian humanists). Rather, put it this way: that Country is the country hinted at and guessed at and dreamed of and longed for in *all* tales of joy and merriment and homecoming and reunion and harmony. Arcadia and the Garden of the Hesperides and the land of the Hyperboreans and Narnia and all of the other places are like "good dreams." To be sure, often the shafts of light from the real Country fall on the "jungle of filth and imbecility" that is, alas, our imagination, all ridden as it is with cupidity and concupiscence, so that you get chaos and lechery and perfidy romping through the stories. But back of it all shimmers the dream of primaeval and everlasting bliss, and the aching desire for that bliss.

Early in the narrative we come upon a small exchange that opens onto an enormous watershed. The children find that Mr. Tumnus the faun has been taken prisoner by the Witch's police, and it seems that his crime has been his hospitality to Lucy. Lucy protests that they must do something—after all, mere decency would dictate that. Susan and Peter agree, and Edmund objects. As it happens they decide to see what they can do, and on this decision hangs the entire tale. This sort of unobtrusive, even minuscule, juncture in the action, which later turns out to be not only important but crucial, and even, on hindsight, a matter of obedience or disobedience to the voice of Aslan himself—this occurs again and again in these fairy tales.

But what is at work in Narnia that makes this sort of crux plausible is the same sort of judgment that hangs like a canopy over our own story: great things hanging upon apparently insignificant decisions, and the whole weight of responsibility for the great things attaching to those small choices. Abraham pulling up stakes and leaving Ur—and becoming the father of the faithful thereby. The Good Samaritan turning out of his way just for a minute—and becoming for all of history the paradigm of Charity. And all the alarming language about "inasmuch as ye did it unto one of the least of these my brethren . . . ." Good heavens! You mean it was *You?* That time I just stopped by to see old Mrs. Thingummy? And that other time I didn't stop? But what sort of light does that throw on everything I do all day long?

A very frightening light. It seems to work both for good and ill. Edmund's disinclination to bother about Mr. Tumnus, small enough at the moment, is, alas, a deadly accurate index to what Edmund *is:* a selfish and egotistic cad. Emeth's service offered (he thought) to Tash is a deadly accurate index of what Emeth is: a good and right trusty servant. Digory's assumption that he has a right to try out anything (like ringing the little bell) is an accurate index to the character of a boy who lacks the modesty and hesitation that might protect him in the face of the perilous or the forbidden. A scuffle on the edge of a cliff, with Eustace trying to save Jill and then falling over—certainly not Jill's fault: but then, much later, it does seem, unhappily, that some sort of moral weight has been attached to those frantic and half-conscious motions in the struggle. Nothing at all seems to be neutral. It does not seem to matter much whether the incident was worth one talent or ten: the judgment is the same. Faithful custodianship of the small stuff qualifies one for bigger responsibilities. It seems to be true in more stories than one. Or put it another way: it becomes harder and harder to draw exact distinctions between fairy tales and "realistic" tales. Which elements do we wish to write off as implausible? Which oddities about the world of faerie are *not* true of ours?

This question of doing the thing that seems to present itself and that mere decency requires at the moment, appears in an event starker light when it comes to clear duty. Again and again in the chronicles we find someone faced with some daunting task, and the thing which evaporates all theoretical protestings and dodgings, and which quite simply *requires* the thing to be done, is duty. When Peter must undergo his initiation on the way to being named High King, and must kill the wolf, without any assistance from Aslan (or so it appears), we have this: "Peter did not feel very brave; indeed, he felt he was going to be sick. But that made no difference to what he had to do." There seems to be an implacable requirement laid upon everyone to do the right thing, however small or big, at the moment when it presents itself. No other principle will prove of much assistance when the crunch comes. No uncertain emotions will come to your aid then. No visions of glory which you once saw will unfurl themselves and brace you. You've simply got to grit your teeth and do the impossible for no other reason than that it is the clearly right thing to do. Puddleglum is the great exemplar of this. It is not for nothing that Lewis has chosen this damp, gangling, gloomy, unlikely and ungainly marsh-dweller for his brightest hero (even including Reepicheep): heroism does not mean *feeling* brave. There may be a few, a very few, lucky and blithe spirits in the history of heroism who have *felt* like facing the dragon or scaling the walls. But the rest of us, of whom exactly the same tasks are asked, have got to get on with it too. How in heaven and earth can ordeals like this be set for us faint-hearted types? The point is that they *are* set, and the answer has something to do with plain training in obedience, which is itself an early lesson in the course which leads us to discover that Aslan knew what he was doing all along and knew exactly what was required to bring us to the place where we could see and rejoice in and praise that wisdom. But why is the language here getting theological? What we are talking about is fairy tales.

The center of gravity, so to speak, for the whole saga is of course Aslan. It seems to be important that he not appear very much. His comings and goings are infrequent, unpredictable and inexplicable. . . . It seems that [his] name itself radiates sheer, searching truth, so that everything is naked and open before it. (pp. 43-8)

News of Aslan and of his plans for Narnia seems to be found here and there in ancient rhymes and old lore, a motif that recurs in the chronicles. The great thing is to keep repeating the old formulas, and passing them down from generation to generation. The Beavers know the signs of the times for having been familiar with these old rhymes. Dr. Cornelius in *Prince Caspian* instructs the boy prince in the true history of his kingdom by telling him the old tales. In *The Silver Chair,* in an important variation on this theme, Aslan gives the children four things to remember, and their instructions are to keep saying these things over and over, to stamp them on their memories, to repeat them as they walk in the way, to bind them as frontlets between their eyes, and suddenly one finds that one has borrowed language from other ancient stories where the great thing was to remember what had been *said,* come hell or high water.

It is often by ordeal that each of the characters is tested in Narnia. The test is two-fold as are all ordeals in fairy stories: first, to find out what a person is made of; and then to teach that person how to be something that he is not (brave or obedient or merciful or generous). Peter must

fight his wolf, and Lucy must resist the temptations of the Magician's book, and Jill and Eustace must enter the very dwelling of the Green Witch, and Tirian must be lashed to a tree alone and Digory must not eat the apple. But then we discover that there is a third, even more important point to the test: it always seems to be *for the sake of another.* There is no question of mere pointless testing, temptation, or suffering. In every case someone else's good is at stake. The frightening thing is that this good really does seem to depend on the response of the one being tested. There is the possibility of real loss—(though not loss that cannot ultimately be repaired; for example, Edmund, forfeit to the Deep Magic from the Dawn of Time because of his greedy pusillanimity, was saved by the Deeper Magic from Before the Dawn of Time) but Aslan alone knows what price has to be paid for failure in the test.

This oddity—that real things really do depend on what seems to be the frailty of mere creatures (why doesn't Aslan just roar and have done with it?) also appears occasionally in a lighter context. At least four times in the battle in *The Lion, The Witch, and The Wardrobe* we see it. When they have finished the work of freeing the Witch's statues, they find themselves still locked in the courtyard of her castle. " 'Giant Rumblebuffin, just let us out of this, will you?' " Aslan, who could have decimated the entire castle and all Narnia with it with one roar, calls upon the particular gift that Giants bear and must use, namely sheer strength. Shortly after that, Aslan, in organizing the race to the scene of the battle, happens to say just in passing that those with good noses must come in front with "us lions." The other lion cannot get over it. " 'Did you hear what he said? *Us lions.* That means him and me. *Us lions.* That's what I like about Aslan. No side, no stand-off-ishness. *Us lions.* That means him and me.' " Somehow it is not according to the fabric that Narnia is made of that Aslan do it by fiat, alone. And then we see Peter and Edmund fighting as though the entire outcome depends on them, for as it happens it does, at that point. And finally, we see Lucy called upon to bring the phial of cordial, given her by Father Christmas, for the healing of the wounded. It must be she, and she must be quick about it.

Sooner or later, of course, it becomes impossible to carry the discussion of Narnia any further without finding ourselves quite unabashedly head over heels in the language of Christian vision and dogma. The Passion of Aslan; the Witch as Accuser of the brethren; the children made kings and queens; the "no need to talk" any more to Edmund of what is past since his transgressions have been blotted out as a thick cloud; the surly and egocentric nature of evil in Nikabrik, and the Romantic megalomania in pitiable Uncle Andrew and in Jadis; the keeping of the "Hallows" (the Stone Knife) at Aslan's Table; the penitent star renewed day by day with a fire-berry brought from the Sun, and the discovery that what a star is *made of* does not tell the whole story of what a star *is;* the unbearable increase in the atmosphere's sweetness and clarity as the "Dawn Treader" nears the end of the world; the dryads and gnomes and salamanders and mermen who, like the skipping hills and singing morning stars of the Bible, populate the elements in the world that we nowadays see as mere "nature"; the awful sense in which various metamorphoses (Eustace's into a dragon, or Rabadash's into an ass) unveil what that person is; sheer, plain goodness (Frank the cabbie) as fitting one to see and hear splendors that the eyes and ears of egoism (Uncle Andrew) cannot perceive; the tree and the Garden, and the fruit "for others"; the rotten smell of Tash; the Stable whose inside is as big as the universe; and the final great rush up into joy—the joy that for us mortals here can only be pictured in this dazzling imagery of speed and laughter and reunion (especially the reappearance of Reepicheep) and of this *array* of creatures—unicorns, centaurs, dogs, and all— each bearing and exhibiting some unique aspect of the great Glory that flashes through the whole fabric.

Allegory is one way of pressing one thing into the service of another. But, despite many unmistakable, even exact, echoes in Narnia of what appears in our own story, and despite Professor Tolkien's objection that Lewis's Narnia chronicles are too woodenly allegorical, we may, it seems to me, see Lewis's achievement here, not so much in terms of allegory as of genuine fairy tale, which is what he meant to be writing. He tells us in his essay **"Sometimes Fairy Stories May Say Best What's To Be Said,"** that he had fallen in love with the form of the fairy tale itself: "its brevity, its severe restraints on description, its flexible traditionalism, its inflexible hostility to all analysis, digression, reflections, and 'gas'. I was now enamoured of it. Its very limitations of vocabulary became an attraction; as the hardness of the stone pleases the sculptor or the difficulty of the sonnet delights the sonneteer."

We may grant him his case, then: he wanted to write fairy tales. That we discover all sorts of elements in his tales that stir us by their similarity to elements in our own story may be attributable to the same oddity that Merlin came upon when it seemed to him that Ransom was repeating an ancient druidical password, which, it turns out, Ransom did not know about. " 'But . . . but . . . if you knew not the password, how did you come to say it?' 'I said it because it was true.' " (pp. 49-52)

> *Thomas Howard, in his* The Achievement of C. S. Lewis, *Harold Shaw Publishers, 1980, 195 p.*

Gerald Haigh

Narnia, the world of C. S. Lewis's imagination, is considerably more than just an enlivening backdrop to an otherwise commonplace tale. It permeates the action of the stories and reacts with them, creating its own version of reality and bearing the reader confidently into its depths with never a hint of subterfuge or tacked-on excitement.

C. S. Lewis wrote the seven books which comprise *"The Chronicles of Narnia"* over such a brief period of time in the early fifties that they might be seen as one work, a hidden landscape illuminated and left glowing by the restless searchlight beam which had earlier given sharp definition to some of the hidden gardens of Christian understanding in books such as *The Screwtape Letters*. . . .

Not surprisingly, Lewis's didactic and conventionally moral approach, to say nothing of his use of story as a vehicle for his Christian convictions, has aroused criticism.

I have, indeed, heard it suggested that the way the books celebrate heroism, order and authority in a setting which often rings of fjord and saga, raises just a whiff of the jackboot. This, I think, is an illusion; a product of the way that Fascism has borrowed and defiled for ever countless innocent and honest ideals and images.

What Lewis can, surely, be criticized for is the simple stylistic error of sometimes writing down to his audience. I find the opening of *The Magician's Nephew*—which, though written later, is first in the "reading order" of the series to be almost embarrassing:

> In those days if you were a boy you had to wear a stiff Eton collar every day, and schools were usually nastier than now. But meals were nicer, and as for sweets, I won't tell you how cheap and good they were. . . .

Quite apart from the obvious comment that there were plenty of Victorian lads who never clapped eyes on an Eton collar, let alone wore one every day, such a way of addressing the reader was surely already unacceptable in 1955, when it was published. The digs which Lewis makes at such institutions as progressive schools get rather wearing, too.

By contrast, when Lewis is in Narnia, the writing expands and glows. This is where he wants to be; and the scenes and images of that land, although is it not nearly so geographically worked out as Tolkien's world, burn their way undimmed to the reader.

The theological and mythical aspects of the stories do not, I feel, touch the young reader directly—though they do lead to the displaying of the books in church along with the postcards and Good News Bibles; and I know of a curate who has used the ending of *The Last Battle* to help children understand death and bereavement, and the Christian idea of the afterlife. What they do, though, is provide an intellectual backbone which holds the tale together, enabling it to be coherent, confident, and philosophically consistent. The particular achievement of C. S. Lewis lies in the commitment which he brings to this "inner life" in his books, and the strength which the stories derive from it.

> *Gerald Haigh, "Through the Wardrobe," in* The Times Educational Supplement, *No. 3372, February 6, 1981, p. 24.*

Donald E. Glover

The Narnia books are more than simply *in* another world; they create and establish that world as the proving ground for obedience, belief, sacrifice, redemption, and so many more self-transcendent messages that we cannot record all of them or all of the levels at which they affect us as readers: as children, then as adults, as nonbelievers and believers. All readers seem to agree, even if they agree about nothing else to do with Lewis, that here he made his most influential and lasting mark on literature and on his readers.

As he said himself, it is the Lion who draws them all together and brings us up and into his country. We find it easy to become a child again, if we need to in order to enter this world; we slough off our old skin of prejudices and preoccupations and have our vision cleared and renewed for the make-believe we are offered. We weep with Digory and Jill, we lie with Edmund and complain with Eustace. We laugh with Lucy and share both her shame at overhearing her friends and her rapture when she reads the story of refreshment. We feel the pain of Aslan's death and the joy of his return. We move about in Narnia and Calormen and over the ocean to the uttermost East. We become more than we were by letting go of the security of our little, realistic lives and by trying the back of the wardrobe to see if there just might really be another world beyond. (pp. 204-05)

Our chief delight, the moments we would most like to share and save, to safeguard and multiply, are those in the Narnia books. We will probably not agree about all those we would use to show how profoundly Lewis had achieved an art that enchants, but we know that he worked to make his stories simple, his characters accessible, his message oblique, and his plots engaging. Tolkien suggests that there is an elvish craft involved in writing the fairy tale. Lewis never claims that for himself, but we sense as critics that he was a conscious artist as he created these works. We have watched him move from story to story, building the land of Narnia in our imaginations, with its creatures and landscapes, its lands and customs, its dynasties and finally its decline and destruction. The moments which we would preserve are those I have earlier called moments where the style unites organically with the meaning to sanctify that meaning. One example will do for all: when Lucy looks into the book of spells in *The Voyage of the 'Dawn Treader,'* we know that she has seen God, and we feel through her that we have, too, even though neither she nor we actually see anything concrete in Lewis's description of the scene. We feel the truth in his description of her action because the structure of the scene with its magic incantations and book of spells underlines and reinforces the spell which Lucy falls under. From a simple act of *faerie* we get the beatific vision. (p. 208)

> *Donald E. Glover, in his* C. S. Lewis: The Art of Enchantment, *Ohio University Press, 1981, 235p.*

Nicholas Tucker

One of the most successful children's series incorporating an imaginary world was written by C. S. Lewis about the land of Narnia, first discovered when his child characters explore a wardrobe and find that the back of it gives on to an entirely new country. Here, the children meet talking trees, animals and fabulous beasts, all involved in an epic battle between good and evil—the sort of obvious, underlined morality that young readers can readily understand. The author's own heavy-handed humour and prejudices may also be well within a child's grasp, such as all the fun had at the expense of 'very up to date' parents, who are 'vegetarians, non-smokers and teetotallers and wore a special kind of under-clothes'. But the Christian doctrines of atonement and resurrection that Lewis also incorporated into these stories sometimes push the plot into directions that seem cruel and illogical. Even so, this has not affected the popularity with the young of these powerfully-

realised books and it is only later, when the same readers are ready to start trying more complex epic writing, like the novels of Tolkien, that they may then begin to notice some of the flaws in Lewis's fiction. (pp. 99-100)

> *Nicholas Tucker, "Early Fiction (Ages 7-11)," in his* The Child and the Book: A Psychological and Literary Exploration, *Cambridge University Press, 1981, pp. 97-132.*

Brian Murphy

Perhaps of all Lewis' works, the *Chronicles of Narnia* will last longest and be read most deeply. What is most significant and revealing about the fact that even non-Christians want their children to read the Chronicles—an important matter: this giving of the first real books to children!—is not necessarily that they want their children to learn about Christ by analogy with Aslan but rather that the books contain feelings, values, and ways of thought that are so valuable and basic that we want them learned early by children. This may well be Lewis' most profound accomplishment—to transmit to children the things we think are initially, basically, elementally important, interesting, and beautiful. How could any writer ever hope to do more? (p. 81)

> *Brian Murphy, in his* C. S. Lewis, *Starmont House, 1983, 95 p.*

Dennis B. Quinn

I must confess . . . that I have never liked the Narnia stories, even though I had a strong prejudice in their favor because of my admiration for Lewis as a literary scholar and as a Christian apologist. Consequently, although I gave the Narnia books to my children, I never could engage myself in them. When I began to teach children's literature, I compelled myself to read these books. Still not liking them, I tried to understand why. I concluded that they lack high merit simply as fictive art. That is, halfway through volume one, I said to myself, "I'll bet Edgar Rice Burroughs tells a story better than Lewis does." I tested my theory by picking up *Tarzan of the Apes,* a book I had not read since childhood. I found that picking up the book was easy but putting it down was another matter. In fact, after tearing through the first two volumes, I had to force myself to stop for fear of becoming a Tarzan addict. (p. 112)

It is no exaggeration to say that there is more action and suspense in one chapter of Burroughs than there is in a whole volume of Lewis. (pp. 114-15)

In my reading of the Narnia books I was disappointed not only in the story but also in the characters. To be successful, the beings of fiction must live in our imaginations and memories. We use the word *vivid* of such beings, often forgetting that the root meaning of that term is simply "alive," the essential quality of real persons or animals—or, for that matter, real ghosts or gods or angels or fairies or griffins. There are many literary devices for achieving verisimilitude, but behind all of them must lie the conviction of the writer, which is really a kind of testimony. The tellers of the old wonder tales did not need any special literary devices to win belief in their supernatural beings:

they *knew* they were real and that they might actually be encountered on the road or in the forest. In the Narnia books much is made of the importance of believing in Narnia and its inhabitants, but Lewis himself did not believe in them, not as the wife of Bath or Scheherazade believed in things supernatural. Lewis argued that "it is not necessary to believe in them." But Aristotle thought differently. Lewis tried to solve this problem by saying that the dryads and gnomes are symbols of something real, but there is no way that a symbol can be brought to life. The supernatural beings of Narnia are bookish beings of a scholarly rather than of a poetic imagination.

The human beings in Lewis's books are not as symbolic as the mythological beings, but they fail to live, largely because they fail to act. Mere elaboration of character will not bring a fictional person to life. Hansel is the unforgettable boy who dropped breadcrumbs to find the way back home, and Gretel is the remarkable girl who pushed the witch into her own oven. These two children live in our imagination and memory, too, because they have the fears of real children—the fear of being unwanted by parents, the fear of being lost and abandoned. When I remember the plight of these helpless children, my own old pity for them revives. The children in the Narnia books are often alone and lost in the woods, but they never suffer that aching fear of Hansel and Gretel, nor any very strong emotion for that matter, and the memory of them arouses no emotion in me.

Lewis at his desk in 1959.

Are the animal characters in Narnia any more successful as fictional creations? Burroughs, Kipling, and Lewis all write about apes. In **The Last Battle,** there is Shift, one of the principal villains; in *The Jungle Book* a band of monkeys kidnaps Mowgli, and, of course, there are the apes who rear Tarzan. Whereas one can learn something about simians by reading Kipling and Burroughs, one cannot by reading Lewis. In both *The Jungle Book* and *Tarzan,* the apes are presented as tribal creatures. Shift, on the other hand, is solitary. Another feature of the apes that Burroughs and Kipling describe in detail and delight is their arboreal life. Shift has a house in a tree, we are told, but that's the end of it; in Lewis the ape is no more arboreal than is a man. The best of imaginative books for children both stimulate and satisfy the desire for knowledge about such things as animals; and, as Aristotle says, the desire for knowledge is wonder.

In both Kipling and Burroughs the apes are not, however, presented simply because of their inherent interest as beasts; they have significance. In *The Jungle Book* the apes, the Bandar-log, are the enemies of all order and law. They have no leader and are the pariahs of all respectable jungle folk. They are the representatives of all that is anarchic and irresponsible in man. In Burroughs the apes represent almost the opposite. They are the very prototype of the brute law of the jungle, red in tooth and claw. In broader terms they are the savage beast in all men, and Tarzan himself is constantly torn between civilization and the life of the ape. In both Kipling and Burroughs, however, this symbolic meaning arises out of the ape as animal. Lewis's villain, Shift, on the other hand, never does exist as an ape at all. I don't mean that Lewis totally neglects this side of him—Shift does scratch himself as monkeys do, and so forth—but such things in Lewis are always perfunctory or at least incidental. Lewis never lets us forget that Shift is the Ape of God, a diabolical figure who deals in craft and illusion.

I could extend my analysis of the Narnia books into other areas, but the results would be repetitious. The landscape of Narnia, including its buildings and artificial objects, is not memorable. There is nothing in Lewis like the secret garden of Burnett's book or the jungle of Tarzan or Badger's home in *The Wind in the Willows*—all places strange and remote and even magical but places as substantial and familiar as our own back yard: "Marvellous places, yet handy to home."

Dorothy L. Sayers, in praising the storytelling ability of Dante, touches upon a quality that lies at the heart of the matter. She says, "If you want the reader not only to follow but to accept and believe a tale of marvels, you can do it best by the accumulation of precise and even prosaic detail." This "trick of particularity," as she calls it, is well known as the secret of those adult books that became children's classics, such as *Robinson Crusoe* and *Gulliver's Travels.* Those two works contain one of the greatest secrets of the literature of the wonderful. All of the activities of Lilliput, which are nothing but the ordinary activities of life, are observed and described in the most exquisite detail, but we look at them in wonder because they are seen in a strange light of miniature. Mary Norton's Borrowers series borrows from Swift this marvelous trick. In Defoe we read with excitement minute descriptions of the prosaic process of making bread because Crusoe is marooned on an island and must, therefore, learn such elementary things over again. To the Aristotelian imagination, every particular of daily reality is ripe with wonder.

This wonder arises simply because each particular thing *is*. We must recall again that Plato and Aristotle both said that philosophy begins and continues through wonder and that this wonder is something that poets have, too. The primal stuff of philosophy and of poetry is being, the greatest of all mysteries. Beyond this primal fact are others, of course. We may see that things exhibit the marvel of life or of motion or of death. But neoplatonists do not look at the world this way. In *The Allegory of Love* Lewis argued that before the rise of literary allegory there were only two worlds out of which the artist could make his works—the actual world and the world of religion, or nature and supernature—but allegory introduced a third world, the "other world" of pure "fancy." It is clear that for Lewis and his school the actual world and the supernatural world are not enough. Mere reality—mere heaven and earth—is not enough. So be it. But there are consequences. Narnia is a *utopos,* a no place, a shadow-land, and as such, it is unlikely to endure. Dorothy Sayers thought that Spenser managed to induce belief in his world by means of sheer verbal enchantment, as did Keats and Coleridge. Perhaps. Writers of fantasy are themselves often enchanted with words and language, but I don't think anyone will claim for Lewis the verbal gifts of Spenser.

In the meantime, however, the fantasy of Lewis is popular. If his books are as deficient as I claim, how shall I account for this vogue, especially when it exists among highly literate and sensitive readers young and old? It is my view that enchantment with fantasy in general derives in large measure from disenchantment with an all-too-drab modern world. That disenchantment I happen to share with Lewis and his friends, and I share their desire to restore the supernatural dimension of life and literature; but I think the price of fantasy is too high. However besmirched, reality remains full of things enough to make us all happy as kings. Or, to be more theological, how are we to know the reality of God except through the real creation?

Fantasy is harmful to the imagination, and especially to the youthful imagination, because it encourages the reader to turn inward and to distrust if not despise reality. Lewis defended fantasy against the charge of escapism by saying that a child who has read about an enchanted wood may then see enchantment in the actual wood. But fantasy implicitly teaches that there *are* no wonders in the wood; rather, all marvels are in the mind and are of our own making. If we are at liberty to make up marvels, they will no more excite wonder than a surprise party for one's own self excites surprise. Reality is wonderful and surprising precisely because it exists outside of and even beyond our imagination. (pp. 115-19)

> *Dennis B. Quinn, "The Narnia Books of C. S. Lewis: Fantastic or Wonderful?" in* Children's Literature: Annual of the Modern Language Association Seminar on Children's Literature

and The Children's Literature Association, *Vol. 12, 1984, pp. 105-21.*

Ann Swinfen

Although *The Lion, the Witch and the Wardrobe* may have had its very first genesis, as Lewis maintained, in a series of 'pictures' in the mind, yet by the time he came to write it, many years later, he had much more clearly developed intentions. He had already written a number of works of Christian apologetics and his planetary romances with their strongly didactic element. Before embarking on his first Narnian novel, he was very much influenced by reading a manuscript novel by Roger Lancelyn Green. Here, clearly, was an intriguing form, the fantasy novel, in which Lewis could express his views on Christianity. Unfortunately, the element of didacticism is so strong, the events allegorized of such cosmic importance, and Lewis's interest in them so much stronger than his interest in such aspects of his novels as the child heroes and heroines, that the allegorical elements are out of all proportion with the rest of the *Chronicles.* Moreover, the didacticism is too thinly disguised, and sometimes positively distasteful. The result is that the Narnia books are an uneasy and uneven mixture, and the passages of allegory float like stubborn lumps in a rather thin gruel. (p. 115)

The didactic element in the fiction of C. S. Lewis is more overt than in the work of any other recent English author, with the possible exception of the political and social satirists Orwell and Huxley. This is evident not only in his concern to employ the medium of fiction as a vehicle for Christian teaching, but also in the whole cast of his mind as a critic. As he wrote in *A Preface to Paradise Lost* in 1942, 'giants, dragons, paradises, gods and the like are themselves the expression of certain basic elements in man's spiritual experience'. All of Lewis's fictional works are cast in the form of 'theological romance', a genre employed extensively by his predecessors George MacDonald and G. K. Chesterton. The theological romance is a fantasy structured upon elements of myth, legend, folktale or romance, which embodies symbolic theology and a clear ethical code. *The Chronicles of Narnia* are thus fantasies in which all the themes have a religious basis and culminate in a significant 'eucatastrophe'. The climax of each book and the final climax of the *Chronicles* parallel the great eucatastrophes of the Christian faith, and form a *praeceptio evangelica.* (pp. 147-48)

Lewis . . . uses the common European cultural heritage of classical myth, folklore and medieval romance to provide the settings, the narrative structure and the characters of the *Chronicles.* The monsters and demons of folklore 'are themselves the expression of certain basic elements in man's spiritual experience', while the humans or humanized animals provide examples of sin—for example, Edmund (in *The Lion, the Witch and the Wardrobe*) of greed and treachery, Rabadash of worldly vanity, Jadis of spiritual corruption. Edmund is saved, Rabadash punished, Jadis damned. In keeping with Lewis's vision of Hell, Jadis becomes bitter and frozen in her self-imposed torment. In this conception of Jadis as she is transformed into the White Witch, freezing both countryside and hearts by her presence, Lewis is considerably indebted to

Hans Andersen's Snow Queen, another symbol of spiritual death.

In their overall structure, the *Chronicles* form an extended psychomachia, comprehending the creation, fall, moral struggle and last judgment of an entire spiritual world. There are many battle scenes, and an analogy to the Crusader-Saracen wars, with their clash of cultures and religions. This is entirely in keeping with the ethical code which is presented throughout. It is the 'martial virtues' which are constantly stressed—courage, obedience, fellowship. The followers of Aslan are 'soldiers of Christ', and they must exhibit personal courage in the face of danger and despair, whilst remaining unquestioningly obedient to Aslan. Explanations are not necessary for the faithful. All of this is in accord with Lewis's stress on the attainment of virtue through the imitation of a revealed pattern of faith and godliness. Unselfishness, kindness, compassion, pity—the various qualities of 'charity'—are rarely urged, and it is certainly never required of the children to forgive their enemies. Edmund, the repentant traitor, is forgiven, but he is one of the 'fellowship' of children. All other enemies are ruthlessly hunted down and destroyed. It is a code not only militant but vengeful. There are two possible ways of interpreting this attitude towards the 'enemy'. If the whole of the *Chronicles* is intended to be taken as an extended allegory, so that the monsters, the enchantresses, the giants of Harfang, the evil Calormenes and the lapsed Narnians are Vices, then this code of vengeance is perfectly acceptable in conventional Christian terms as an allegory of the suppression of evil within one's own heart. However, Lewis does not seem to intend the characters to be seen in this way—the very fact that some are 'lapsed' Narnians belies their interpretation as Vice figures. This more complex attitude is clearest in *The Last Battle.* One of the traitorous dwarfs is admitted to Aslan's doorway at the Last Judgment. Moreover Emeth, a devout follower of Tash, has fought against the Narnian fellowship in the last battle, but finds himself in Aslan's country. . . . (pp. 153-54)

Certainly, whatever his view of the evil characters in the earlier books, by the time of writing *The Last Battle* Lewis regarded them as capable of salvation. This ambiguous attitude makes the scenes of vengeance and destruction more difficult to accept. The treatment of the non-talking animals of Narnia is another questionable area of Lewis's ethics. Ginger's loss of speech and rational thought is an image of the self-imposed Hell of sin and apostasy. Similarly, in the judgment scene, the creatures who deny Aslan look into his face, and the expression on their faces changes to fear and hatred—except in the case of the Talking Beasts. They cease to be Talking Beasts and become dumb animals. All these, the sinful and the dumb animals, disappear into the black shadow on the left hand of Aslan.

The disturbing aspect of this symbolism is that the non-talking beasts are not simply those damned through sin. Many beasts in the world of Narnia are born without speech, are hunted and eaten by their more fortunate cousins, and have no opportunity for faith and redemption. Except in the Creation scene, no animal in Narnia is seen to earn speech and the chance of salvation. Their position in

Lewis's symbolic theology is never made clear, and the ethics of their treatment by the other Narnians are highly questionable. When Tirian sees the horses being brutally maltreated by the Calormenes in *The Last Battle* he is not really concerned until one of the horses speaks, and he realizes that it is a Talking Beast. This is regarded as 'the really dreadful thing'.

Just as ambiguous as Lewis's treatment of the Vice characters and the non-talking beasts, is the position of Susan in the *Chronicles.* One of the original four children to visit Narnia, Susan becomes a High Queen, and is given the magical horn for summoning help, which plays a notable part in subsequent books. She returns in *Prince Caspian* and is told, like Peter, that she will not visit Narnia again. Similarly Edmund and Lucy, at the end of *The Voyage of the 'Dawn Treader',* learn that they must seek for Aslan now in their own world. The visits to Narnia thus serve as an education for the soul, a preparation for the devout Christian life in the primary world. There is no indication at this stage that Susan has in any way failed in her spiritual training. She never appears again in any of the later episodes (*The Horse and His Boy* being out of chronological sequence). There is perhaps a slight hint that all is not well at the beginning of *The Voyage of the 'Dawn Treader':* 'Grown-ups thought her the pretty one of the family and she was no good at school work (though otherwise very old for her age)'. There is no real evidence in this, which sounds more like sibling jealousy than anything else—an interpretation borne out by Lucy's desire, when looking in Coriakin's book, to become more beautiful than Susan. However, in the final scene of redemption in *The Last Battle,* when all the previous visitors from the primary world return to the 'real Narnia', and even the Pevensie parents are gathered in, Susan is absent, denied entry to the final paradisal scene: 'she's interested in nothing now-a-days except nylons and lipstick and invitations. . . . She wasted all her school time wanting to be the age she is now, and she'll waste all the rest of her life trying to stay that age'. 'All her school time' includes, of course, the period of her visits to Narnia.

In her appearances in Narnia Susan has not been given over to worldly vanity, so that this condemnation comes as a great surprise. Moreover, these small vanities seem hardly comparable with the acts of treachery for which Edmund was forgiven. Did Lewis jettison Susan because he wanted to make a final attack on worldliness, however inconsistent with the earlier portrayal of the character? Or was there no more vital reason than a desire to achieve the mystic number (with its multiple significance in both pagan and Christian belief) of the 'seven friends of Narnia'—to maintain the pattern of the seven books published in seven years, one of which involved a quest for seven lost lords? Such an idea sounds ludicrous, but there seems no more convincing reason. It is in any case further evidence of Lewis's tendency to make his characters into lay-figures, vehicles of his ideas rather than fully realized people in their own right, and an indication of his submerged, but very clear, dislike of women.

The emphasis on the martial virtues, on a stern and unrelenting code of morality, involving much vengeance and little mercy, inevitably has its disturbing aspects. Lewis, like MacDonald, felt that fear had a natural place in religious training. The chain of development should be from fear to awe to joy. However, the stress on punishment, denial, discipline, can lead to definite suggestions of sadism and masochism—the very flaws which Lewis found in Kipling. At times the imagery of violence, as it is associated with the *consuming* love of Aslan, becomes too extreme. The Lion has 'swallowed up' girls and boys, cities and realms. The gentle mare Hwin says, 'I'd sooner be eaten by you than fed by anyone else.' The distasteful episode of the stripping away of the dragon skin from Eustace [is another example]. (pp. 154-56)

Lewis's underlying religious themes are most persuasive when closely related to the structural patterns of the books. The theme of divine love, as embodied in Aslan, is most fully and convincingly presented in the Passion scenes of *The Lion, the Witch and the Wardrobe* and the resurrection of Caspian in *The Silver Chair,* but it recurs constantly whenever Aslan appears as guide or adviser: in the crossing of the ravine in *Prince Caspian;* in his brief appearances at moments of crucial choice or danger in *The Voyage of the 'Dawn Treader';* in the opening and closing episodes of *The Silver Chair* and in the series of 'signs'; in his appearances as both cat and lion in *The Horse and His Boy,* especially when he guides Shasta over the mountain pass. (p. 156)

Every individual eucatastrophe . . . leads up to a final one in each book, and each book leads on to the culminating *Last Battle.* Whether or not Lewis conceived the whole series when he started to write, the pattern is certainly present by the end. In contrast with the general mood of excitement and gaiety of the earlier books, *The Last Battle* is an almost uniformly sombre and tragic story, in which the Holy War takes on its final and explicit form. Many of the characters are archetypal—the apostate, the rational agnostic, the tyrant who manipulates the credulous, the doomed champion of the faith, the Abdiel. The allegorical action is of central importance. The dark and tragic tone remains unrelieved until the violent reversal of the final eucatastrophe, when the Holy War ends in triumph for the righteous, the virtuous souls are united with Aslan-Christ, and the consuming love of the Son of God culminates in the release of Joy for all the redeemed characters.

The central themes in *The Chronicles of Narnia* are quite explicit. C. S. Lewis is not interested in character or individuals, in social relationships or the growth and development of societies, but in Man, and in the soul's constantly threatened struggle towards good. It is therefore the narrative patterns and theological substructure which are most important in an appreciation of his work, the recurrent Christian symbolism and the allegorical action. The effectiveness of these qualities in Lewis's work is enhanced when his imaginative gifts are given free rein, and not restrained by the need to satisfy some didactic purpose. His imaginative power is most evident in many of the descriptive passages which set the Narnian scene, and which make the otherworld of the *Chronicles* so immediately attractive: the wintery landscapes of *The Lion, the Witch*

and the Wardrobe, the Oriental glitter and filth of Tashbaan, the rich banquet on Ramandu's island. It is also evident in the creation of the particular 'flavour' of the individual books. Each book in the *Chronicles* has its own web of sensations: the Spenserian and slightly 'pseudomedieval' quality of *The Silver Chair* combined with elements from very primitive folk-tale and from George MacDonald's *Princess* books; the Arabian Nights and Crusader-Moor atmosphere of *The Horse and His Boy;* Edwardian London in *The Magician's Nephew,* with its gas-lights, steaming cab-horses, and raffish dandy, Uncle Andrew.

These strengths in Lewis's work can be contrasted with the curiously unsubstantiated and bitter attacks on 'modern' education and with the awkward, superficial portrayal of the primary world children. A good index of Lewis's own ease with the imaginative situation in his books is the dialogue. At its best—in the smooth-tongued viciousness of the Calormenes, or the courtly speech in *The Silver Chair*—it is superbly evocative and witty. At its worst, primarily in the unreal slang of the children, it is clumsy and embarrassing. The insincerity of Rilian's exaggeratedly courtly speech is used by Lewis to indicate the falsity of his character under enchantment. Lewis's own failures in dialogue reveal the moments when he too rings imaginatively untrue.

The outstanding qualities of C. S. Lewis, as they appear in *The Chronicles of Narnia,* are thus two: his ability as a picture-maker and the creator of an imaginatively tangible otherworld with its own distinct 'sensations', and his quite definite and avowed moral purpose. Sometimes the two work against each other, as when his moral purpose distorts his artistic integrity, leading to the superficial portrayal of many characters, and perhaps above all in the inexplicable fall and damnation of Susan. However, when the two work in harmony, the finest Narnian scenes emerge: Aslan resurrected to vital power and energy, saving the frozen innocents from the Witch's Hell; the 'Dawn Treader' drifting through silver water-lilies over the sweet waters to the Utter East, where Aslan waits as Lamb and Lion; the Creation of Narnia, with the singing stars and the creatures drawn forth from the rich earth; the final cataclysm, the calling home of the stars, and the crushing of the Narnian sun, followed by the dawn of new hope. The undoubted flaws—the imaginative failures, the occasionally dubious ethics—should not blind us to the outstanding achievement of the Narnian books, and although the most immediately memorable qualities are the nature of the otherworld itself, its vivid life and profuse images, yet the backbone of the whole, providing both themes and structure, is Lewis's religious belief. (pp. 157-59)

Ann Swinfen, "Layers of Meaning" and "Idealisms: Religious and Philosophic," in her In Defence of Fantasy: A Study of the Genre in English and American Literature Since 1945, *Routledge & Kegan Paul, 1984, pp. 100-22, 147-89.*

Humphrey Carpenter

The Lion, the Witch, and the Wardrobe and its sequels, fine as they are (particularly the later books), are governed throughout by a didactic purpose: a determination to convey to children Lewis's own affection for the narrative power of the Christian story, which he has recast in terms of a children's fantasy. He also aims to teach them his particular Muscular Christian ethics, which range from a love of beer and tobacco to a dislike of 'progressive' education and vegetarianism. At its best this didactic voice recalls Kingsley's righteous indignation:

> There was a boy called Eustace Clarence Scrubb, and he almost deserved it . . . He didn't call his Father and Mother 'Father' and 'Mother', but Harold and Alberta. They were very up-to-date and advanced people. They were vegetarians, non-smokers and teetotallers and wore a special kind of underclothes. In their house there was very little furniture and very few clothes on the beds and the windows were always open.

At its worst, Lewis's didacticism is more insidious than this. For example, his character-assassination of Edmund, who goes over to the Witch's side in **The Lion, the Witch, and the Wardrobe,** seems all too near a kind of spiritual Fascism. Edmund is a weak character because he is a weak character: there is no attempt to motivate his unpleasantness, and one has the impression in the early part of the book that he is predestined, quite simply, to damnation.

Moreover, Lewis's personal feeling is almost all for the doctrine, not the narrative. The stories are often marvellously inventive—no other children's writer can rival the sheer quantity of fantasy-ideas in the seven Narnia books, even though many of them are borrowed from recognisable sources. But the invention is always in the end a conscious embodiment of the ideas, not a potent symbol capable of being explored beyond its author's immediate intentions. (pp. 213-14)

> *Humphrey Carpenter, "Epilogue: The Garden Revisited," in his* Secret Gardens: A Study of the Golden Age of Children's Literature, *Houghton Mifflin Company, 1985, pp. 210-23.*

Madeleine L'Engle

My own first encounter with the worlds of fantasy came when I was a solitary only child in New York, and my grandfather, who was living in London, sent me books for my birthday and for Christmas—books by George Mac-Donald and E. Nesbit (that remarkably liberated lady of the nineteenth century), and the *English Children's Annuals,* which were filled with fantasy. Perhaps my own loneliness contributed to the fact that the world of imagination was as real for me as the everyday world—in fact, more real.

I was not aware, until I began to read the MacDonald tales to my children, that he was occasionally preachy during his stories. He was, after all, a Congregational minister, even if he had been asked to leave his church, and preaching came naturally to him. And I would guess that it comes naturally to the child.

I looked at a contemporary copy of *The Water Babies* in a bookshop recently, and saw that it had been radically cut. I am glad that I read it all, sermons as well as story. Again, when I was a child, I didn't even notice that there were sermons in the book, and that I was being taught as

well as amused. Perhaps as children we are more willing to be taught than we are as adults? We are aware that there is an infinite amount to learn, and if we are drawn into a "real" world of fantasy while we are learning, then the learning becomes a pleasure instead of the pain it often is in school.

And here I discover that I am enmeshed in paradox. Being instructed while I was reading seemed perfectly natural to me as a child, and yet I do not, by and large, like didactic stories. *Pilgrim's Progress* never had much attraction for me, and I would guess that this was because it teaches in a different way than the fantasy-spinning of MacDonald, Kingsley, Nesbit—and C. S. Lewis. It is deliberate allegory, whereas the others are inadvertent allegory, and that makes all the difference in the world.

When I took a course in the techniques of fiction with Dr. Caroline Gordon, she taught us that Dante's great work of fantasy, *The Divine Comedy,* could be read on four levels,

> the literal level
> the moral level
> the allegorical level
> the anagogical level [the religious or mystical sense]

and these four levels are to be found in all true fantasy. The literal level is the story itself. The moral level is what the story has to say. It is impossible for a writer of fantasy to say nothing, and if he manages to do so, that in itself says something. But the impulse behind the writing of fantasy is usually an attempt on the part of the writer to express something, a particular personal concern. It is very obvious in MacDonald and Kingsley; they tell us exactly what their concern is at the moment of writing. E. Nesbit is more subtle, perhaps because the world of intuition has, for many centuries, been more available to women than to men, who are taught from early childhood on to live in a restricted, rational world. If they delve into the realms of the intuition it must be apologized for, or explained.

For quite a while I struggled to understand the difference between the allegorical level and the anagogical level. Finally it came to me that allegory is simile; this is *like* this. But an anagoge is metaphor; this *is* this; it contains within it something of that which it is trying to express.

I do not believe that allegory is always conscious, and perhaps it is best when it is not; perhaps I've never much cared for Bunyan because I feel that he is beating me over the head with his allegory. And—despite the sermonizing—MacDonald and Kingsley do not. They are not objective teachers, but subjective ones; the sermon is as much for their own personal benefit as for the reader's.

The anagogical level, I am convinced, is never conscious when it is there, it is sheer gift of grace; the writer cannot strive for it deliberately for that would be to ensure failure.

So I understand Lewis's protestations that he is not writing allegory; of course he isn't. Nevertheless, there is an allegorical level to his stories, and, when he is at his best, an anagogical level. A writer who has grown up on E. Nesbit and Beatrix Potter, who encounters MacDonald as a teenager, in one of the most sensitive periods of life, cannot help having learned from these masters, even if the learning is intuitive and subconscious rather than the rational kind of learning that comes from a struggle with spelling or with the multiplication table or memorizing the imports and exports of Brazil. (pp. xi-xiii)

It doesn't bother me at all that Lewis was convinced that he did not allegorize at all in the *Chronicles of Narnia*. When a writer opens up to a fantasy world, a world which has more depths of reality to it than the daily world, all kinds of things happen in his stories that he does not realize; often the fantasy writer, if he is listening well, writes far more than he knows, and I believe that when Lewis was his best he did exactly that: he listened and he looked and he set down what he heard and what he saw. If grace comes during the writing of fantasy, the writer writes beyond himself, and may not discover all that he has written until long after it is published, if at all. The Narnia stories do instruct, and that is all right, for they are also story, they are also real. If they teach the reader, of any age, what Lewis himself was struggling to learn, that is an added benefit, not a detraction. Probably, as an adult, I am far more aware of the *teaching* in the *Chronicles* than I would have been if I had read them as a child. I don't think that my children noticed it, any more than I, as a child, noticed the teaching in *At the Back of the North Wind* or *The Water Babies*. But I believe that if a writer is writing out of his own truth, then the reader is going to learn from that truth; it need not and should not be didactic, but it is nevertheless teaching, and I am grateful for it. We all have an infinite amount to learn, still, as adults; the learning period should never end; and the best way for me to learn has always been in coming across a writer's shared truth in story. (pp. xiv-xv)

> *Madeleine L'Engle, in a foreword to* Companion to Narnia *by Paul F. Ford, third edition, Collier Books, 1986, pp. xi-xv.*

Paul F. Ford

Each reader brings to the *Chronicles* his or her own story and comes away with expanded horizons and renewed vision. (p. xxiii)

[What] *was* Lewis writing and why? (p. xxvi)

[It] is only partly true, as many have noted, that the *Chronicles of Narnia* have been written to familiarize a body of people, especially children, with certain ideas, namely the Christian faith and the way of life that goes with that faith. Lewis would insist that what he intends to teach is *mere* Christianity, "that which has been believed everywhere, always, by all," in the famous phrase of the fifth-century French theologian, Vincent of Lerins. There were, in fact, two Lewises, the one we might call the Augustine and the other the Aesop. Like Augustine, Lewis came to Christianity in midlife, a man well-trained in the ancient tongues and a philosopher to his fingertips. He changed to become "the most converted man I ever knew," as a friend once wrote of him; and he put the full forces of his intellect and his gifts for communication to do battle for the truth. And like Augustine, Lewis's heart was fired with a sometimes ecstatic love for the world and its Creator. Unlike the North African bishop, however,

Lewis hid his feelings and let his characters reveal in the stories he told the emotions he could not directly share.

The Aesop in Lewis is the older of the two. He learned his Irish folk tales on the knee of his nurse, Lizzie Endicott (who serves as model for Caspian's unnamed nurse in *Prince Caspian*), and was swept away by the newly published Beatrix Potter stories. Soggy Irish days kept him housebound; but this caused him, with his brother, to discover the joys of inventing one's own imaginary worlds. Lewis peopled his worlds with dressed animals and knights in armor: he was nearly born a storyteller. But Aesop was not the pure storyteller. The Greek slave was also a moral educator. And Lewis believed that talking animals and mythological creatures like giants and dwarfs could serve in children's books as picture-writing—hieroglyphs—which could communicate by the very fact of being well-drawn. (pp. xxvii-xxviii)

As a child, Lewis had been told *how* to feel about God and religious realities. And this obligation to feel froze his feelings. Night after night in his school dormitory, he tried to muster all the proper feelings attendant upon saying the Lord's Prayer with devotion. His scrupulosity wearied him and he gladly gave all of this up when he left the practice of his religion in his early teens. There were "watchful dragons" at the Sunday school door. . . . (p. xxix)

A map of Narnia by Pauline Baynes.

Lewis says in an early essay: "Reason is the natural organ of truth; but imagination is the organ of meaning." One can reason about or *look at* another's experience all day and be able only to abstract about it; it is only when we *look along* that person's experience (if not actually, at least in imagination) that we can see, touch, taste what that person is experiencing. In this sense it can be said of theologians and many ordinary people that they contemplate Christianity but they do not enjoy it. In the *Chronicles of Narnia,* Lewis reverses this trend: he allows people, especially children, to look along Christianity without, perhaps, knowing Christ explicitly. He wants people to experience the meaning of the Christian facts first, to have their own feelings spontaneously, and then to become aware that this meaning is fact. But when well-meaning Christians short-circuit this process by decoding the *Chronicles* for their children, the watchful dragons resume their sentry posts outside the Sunday school door. (pp. xxx-xxxi)

Lewis took his storytelling seriously and his audience seriously. In fact, his *Chronicles* have succeeded in restoring storytelling to the sharing of faith from one generation to the next. They reveal a writer at the apex of his art, in which his Christianity naturally effervesces. Yet many people inside and outside the Christian Church suspect him of having concocted his stories as a seven-part, subtle vehicle for converting children. Much as a soft-drink manufacturer adds carbonation to various syrups, so Lewis is accused or praised for selecting the central Christian doctrines and adding allegories to them. This is not the case at all! The stories, in fact the pictures, came first and the effervescence is natural.

Although Tolkien, like Lewis, began his storytelling spontaneously, he polished his stories like gems, revising time and again for inconsistencies. So thorough was his subcreation that he was able to devise whole histories and languages, and to people his novels with characters whose roots went deep into Middle Earth. Lewis, however, was less of a subcreator than he was a storyteller. He let the pictures of Narnia flow from his mind through his pen, and didn't bother about explaining inconsistencies until after the first three books had been published. Thus as pure subcreation, Lewis begins his storytelling at perhaps a less exalted and intricate place than did Tolkien, yet his first three books are alive with inventiveness and fun. (pp. xxxi-xxxiii)

Lewis, like a portraitist finished with his subject, begins [the fourth book] *The Horse and His Boy* to fill in the background by telling a story that takes place in Calormen and Archenland. (p. xxxiii)

The tone has changed when we enter the world of *The Silver Chair.* The scene is Experiment House, the progressive school that Eustace Scrubb attends. In this fifth *Chronicle* (published fourth), Lewis shows how aware he is of the two senses of the word *spell.* Tolkien had written, "Small wonder that *spell* means both a story told, and a formula of power over living men." Since the time he wrote *The Pilgrim's Regress,* Lewis was alive to the paralyzing hold the enchantment of the spirit of the age has on the minds and hearts of living men and women. He often refers in addresses and sermons to his desire to weave a counter-spell. And it is this tone we detect very strongly in *The Silver Chair.* The emphasis is on discipline ("Remember, remember the Signs"), on the power of fear and of the desire for pleasure, and on obstinacy in belief (the very title of an address he gave to the Socratic Club during the same time he was finishing this *Chronicle*).

In *The Magician's Nephew,* Lewis returns to the threads of a story about the creation of Narnia that he had begun and almost immediately abandoned after he had finished *The Lion, the Witch and the Wardrobe.* Less a subcreator than simply alive to his own memories of the turn of the century, he recreates those times as the background for a discussion of the consequences of the unbridled desire for knowledge and power in Andrew Ketterley and his nephew Digory. Lewis's ability to create real characters doesn't fail him, of course, and his Jadis is menacingly real; but she is also the logical outcome of what exists in its beginning stages in the boy and well-advanced in the uncle. A certain balance between the subcreator and the moral educator is re-achieved in the Narnian creation scenes. But the pull is in the direction of the moral educator.

The Last Battle has all the quality of the "twilight of the gods" (one of Lewis's earliest experiences) transformed, though not right away, by the Christian hope of *eucatastrophe,* Tolkien's term for the "joyous sudden turn" of a fairy tale. A sense of invention is lacking, but its absence is scarcely noticed because Lewis is working in the white heat of his artistry within the world he has already created. The story has a life of its own and it moves easily through the eschatological themes of death, judgement, hell, and heaven. It is not only the fitting conclusion to the *Chronicles:* given Lewis's Christian faith, it is their only possible conclusion. (pp. xxxiii-xxxiv)

Many modern Christian theologians, basing their thinking on the best of modern biblical scholarship, have discerned that the Hebrews first knew themselves as a people as the result of their having been miraculously rescued from slavery in Egypt. Their first experience was one of redemption. Only later, when they came into contact with the Babylonian culture in which an elaborate explanation of the creation of the world was given, did they gather their own creation stories together and write, under inspiration, their own origins and the origins of the universe. If, as Charles Huttar suggests, the only adequate literary classification for the *Chronicles* is biblical; if the *Chronicles,* as genre, find their closest analogue in the Judaeo-Christian Scriptures themselves; if the *Chronicles* are a supposal of salvation history (creation, redemption, and completion) in Narnian terms—then reading them in the order of publication has one additional reason to recommend itself. Lewis began by writing a redemption story in *The Lion, the Witch and the Wardrobe.* He then tried to write a Narnian creation story but was unable to complete it at the time. It was only after he had involved himself in the transformation stories of several characters that he was able to tell the story not only of Narnia's beginnings but also of its consummation. I submit that reading the *Chronicles of Narnia* in the order in which they were published enables the reader to experience something truer even than Lewis intended: the primordial necessity of passing first through redemption, then into a reinterpretation of one's own story, and finally allowing the future to take its provident course. (pp. xxxv-xxxvi)

Paul F. Ford, in an introduction to his Companion to Narnia, *third edition, Collier Books, 1986, pp. xxiii-xxxvii.*

C. N. Manlove

In [the Narnia] books it is fair to say that Lewis gave back to children's literature some of the 'high seriousness' that—*pace* Kipling, De La Mare and Masefield—it had been without since the work of George MacDonald, Lewis's literary and spiritual mentor, in the nineteenth century. Certainly, appearing as they did when the vogue for the works of Enid Blyton was still at a peak among British children, the Narnia books came as a welcome relief for parents, librarians and educationalists who had long looked for contemporary works of literature for children which would not pander to the 'baser literary instincts': but of course this would have meant nothing and the books would have gone the way of many a tiresome tract for juveniles in the past, had it not been that they actually delighted children themselves. Lewis's particular skill lay in teaching almost 'without meaning to': he tells a 'straightforward' story of children entering a fairyland and meeting all sorts of delightful creatures and exciting adventures, and before the reader knows what has happened he has traversed the central story of the Gospels—not as a story of someone two thousand years in the past, but as one in the immediate present of school holidays and railway stations, the recurrence of which makes the reader feel not just that the story is being brought up to date but that it is one that is happening again and again and is everlastingly contemporary. (p. 120)

Lewis vowed that he never 'wrote down' to children, or even that his awareness of them as an audience seriously conditioned his writing: 'I was . . .writing "for children" only in the sense that I excluded what I thought they would not like or understand; not in the sense of writing what I intended to be below adult attention. This is typically precise, but it refers to the state of mind in which the material is presented rather than to the material itself. We are still going to find, given Lewis's own 'child' interests, pages devoted to homely beavers, paw-sucking bears and loyal badgers; descriptions (if restrained) of meals; gifts (Father Christmas enters Narnia in *The Lion*); and an element of protection of the children and a general scaling of the narrative to their taste: so that death and violence where they occur are muted, and reality simplified to its basic constituents. There is nothing intrinsically wrong with this, if it does put a bar between the world of the adult and of the child except via condescension or sentimentality. If there is any problem, it is that we feel the 'adult' Lewis behind it writing what he thinks is appropriate for a child: it does not always seem to come quite naturally. More recently, children's writers have tried to get more of 'everyday' and 'dangerous' reality into their books. In Lewis's time and the fifties generally children were no doubt more amenable to moral instruction. But the problem of writing to the real world that children inhabit, and particularly the urge not to treat them as a separate spe-

cies, is a perennial one. Lewis wrote to his idea of the child, but there are many others.

The problem lies not just here but inside some of the works too. Lewis, basically, wants his children to behave like adults. They are to grow up spiritually—yes, certainly from the childish to the child-like—but also they are to learn to manage their world. At the end of *The Lion* the children have literally grown up into Kings and Queens of Narnia. The difference is striking if we compare Lewis's work with that of MacDonald or of E. Nesbit, his other literary model in this area. In *At the Back of the North Wind* (1870) and *The Princess and the Goblin* (1872) MacDonald has his child-characters exist among adults: little Diamond in his family or with the great maternal figure of North Wind, Princess Irene with her nurse Lootie and more importantly her 'grandmother' whom she befriends in the topmost room of the castle in which she lives. In such a context the children can exist naturally as children, and, on occasion, something more: and MacDonald has succeeded in creating wonderful child characters. There are semi-adult figures in *The Lion*—the Beavers, or Aslan—and certainly Aslan could be said to 'protect' Edmund from the evil White Witch: but the children are the sole humans in Narnia, being called Sons and Daughters of Eve and Adam. We have to see them at once as children and as 'grown-up' in relation to Narnia: Edmund's yielding to the Turkish Delight offered by the White Witch and his betrayal of his siblings is seen both as the act of a thoroughly naughty boy and as a piece of primal treachery requiring the ultimate sacrifice on Aslan's part. Of course, for Lewis, mere size is nothing, and 'proportion' alien to the Christian view of reality: the smallest act may be of enormous significance. (His use of Reepicheep the mouse as hero in the Narnia books is almost symbolic of this.) But that is not quite the same as viewing the act two ways at once. Constantly throughout the narrative of this particular Narnian book we feel the uneasy juxtaposition of children and child-adults: quite what are we doing except in wish-fulfilment with a child who leads an army into battle? In the work of E. Nesbit, the children 'bounce off' or are shut away from the adult world: in *Five Children and It* they are granted one wish per day which expires at sunset, and the story portrays their crucial inability as children to do other than get themselves into 'scrapes' with them; in *The Story of the Amulet* the children continue, despite their visits in time to a great number of past civilizations, to behave precisely as their normal and very varied child-selves. In asking us to believe in his children both as children and as adults, Lewis is sometimes in danger of forfeiting our belief in them as either.

But these are hard sayings, and in general the Narnia books are a wonderful success, not least because of Lewis's endless fertility of invention—which is not to say that these books are not strongly rooted in past literature. It may be that the child-characters or the scale of the action are not always easy to take at the level required, or that the 'niceness' of the 'animal' characters becomes on occasion a bit cloying, or that the moralizing, for all its integration, is at times oppressive—but what remains most in the mind is the wealth and purity of Lewis's imagination; his ability to create so consistent a world in Narnia, so potent an image of the heart's desire in *The Voyage of the 'Dawn Treader'*, so beautifully handled an utter transformation of reality in *The Last Battle*, so quietly suggestive a narrative as *The Silver Chair*, so much joy and yearning as comes through *The Magician's Nephew;* and even more than this, his power to capture great primal rhythms, Christian and pagan alike, through the fabric of his stories, and to make the whole series together form a total picture of Christian history from the First Things to the Last. (pp. 122-24)

> *C. N. Manlove, in his* C. S. Lewis: His Literary Achievement, *Macmillan Press, 1987, 242 p.*

George Sayer

[In the following excerpt, Sayer refers to Lewis by his nickname, Jack.]

More than any other stories that I can think of, [the Narnia stories] appeal to all sorts of children. It is easy to find children who are left cold by *Alice in Wonderland* and *The Wind in the Willows;* it is rare to find those who enjoy reading and yet are not delighted by the Narnia stories.

Jack's main object was, of course, to write good stories. He was also concerned with the atmosphere of separate adventures and incidents and with fidelity to the complex world of his imagination. As the series developed, he gained confidence in his imaginative vision and delighted in the rich medley of human, animal, and mythological beings that he was creating. His idea of heaven was of a place where all sorts of people could come together to celebrate, dance, and sing with fauns, giants, centaurs, dwarfs, and innumerable and very different animals. Some of this joyous, festive vision is perceived by many children who read the books. It extends and develops their delight not merely in the real world but in a vision of the created world permeated with the world of myth and imagination.

The natural beauties of Narnia are set against the background of the supernatural and eternal. The apple tree at the beginning of *Prince Caspian* is no ordinary apple tree. The ruined castle in chapter two gives Lucy and Peter a queer feeling; this interpenetration of the natural by the supernatural runs throughout the whole series and has much to do with the characteristic atmosphere. We are in Aslan's country usually without knowing it.

The most precious moments to Jack in his ordinary life were those when he did know it, when he was aware of the spiritual quality of material things, of the infusion of the supernatural in the workaday world. His success in translating these moments into his fairy stories gives the series a haunting appeal; simultaneously it gives its readers "a taste for the other."

Modern children are often thought of as rebellious and anarchistic, yet those who read the Narnia stories accept without opposition a hierarchical society. Aslan is no believer in equality and is of course supreme over all. Below him there may be kings and queens and princes to whom should normally be given our respect and obedience.

After telling Prince Caspian of his true identity, Doctor Cornelius drops down on to one knee and kisses his hand.

People are not equal; among them, some are meant to serve, others to command. Animals are below people and perhaps have their own hierarchy.

The Narnia stories show a complete acceptance of the Tao, of the conventional and traditional moral code. Humanity, courage, loyalty, honesty, kindness and unselfishness are virtues. Children who might perhaps object to the code if they were taught it in churches and schools, accept it easily and naturally when they see it practised by the characters they love. They are learning morality in the best and perhaps only effective way. (pp. 191-92)

[Jack] did not, as is sometimes supposed, begin with a worked out theological scheme in his head and write the stories to exemplify and inculcate it. The actual process was less calculating; he wrote the stories because he enjoyed writing stories and always had. The characters and their actions were of course influenced by his conception of morality and theology. It was in the course of writing, as a result of brooding over the events in the stories, that his ideas developed. They grew less intellectual, more integrated with feeling. Like many of his other books the Narnia stories were important to his own spiritual growth. (pp. 192-93)

[The Narnia stories], along with Tolkien's *The Lord of the Rings,* represent one of the most remarkable phenomena of postwar publishing. The Narnia stories have liberated the children's story from its bondage to realism. Since their publication, magic, myth, fairy tale, and fantasy stories have been written, but none with such inherent theological depth and mythic quality.

The whole series has classic status. The often rather ordinary style and simple characterization to which some of the early reviewers objected are from the children's point of view virtues. They make it all the easier to be swept along by the story. Complex characterization often puzzles and a literary style distracts inexperienced readers. All the evidence suggests that the Narnia stories will be read at least as long as anything else that Jack wrote. (p. 193)

> *George Sayer, in his* Jack: C. S. Lewis and His Times, *Macmillan London Limited, 1988, 304 p.*

A. N. Wilson

[In C. S. Lewis: A Biography, *Wilson begins his chapter on Narnia by describing a debate between Lewis and philosopher Elizabeth Anscombe in early 1948 at the Socratic Club, the Oxford debating society. Centering on a chapter in Lewis's book* Miracles *in which he posits that only Supernaturalists can claim to know the truth, the confrontation is, according to Wilson, "the greatest single factor which drove Lewis into the form of literature for which he is today most popular: children's stories." Wilson continues, "That evening at the Socratic Club was the first in the Society's history that Lewis was thoroughly trounced in argument." Lewis found the debate "emotionally depleting" and after it "was in a state of near-despair." As his friend Hugo Dyson said, he had "lost everything and had come to the foot of the Cross."]*

What had happened at the Socratic Club was no mere intellectual brawl. . . . It awakened all sorts of deeply seated fears in Lewis, not least his fear of women. Once the bullying hero of the hour had been cut down to size, he became a child, a little boy who was being degraded and shaken by a figure who, in his imagination, took on witchlike dimensions. He felt that he was arguing so coherently for the existence of that Other World because he had been there himself. And now here was a grown-up who was not convinced by his explanations of those inner adventures beyond the discernible surface of things. It was all a little like what had happened to his mother when, as a child in Rome, she had believed she saw a statue moving, and none of the grown-ups had credited her tale. Ever since his mother had died, Lewis had been in search of her, and the journey which had begun when he first read George MacDonald's *Phantastes,* and which had continued through his discovery of great Christian literature and wise Christian friends, now chillingly felt as if perhaps it had been a game of make-believe. Unless, unless . . . Unless, that is, Tolkien and Dyson had been right during their great conversation in Addison's Walk in 1931; unless make-believe was really another way of talking about the reality of things; unless the brutal and cerebral way in which grown-ups tried to come to conclusions about the world was not the only way; unless he could explore the way of *Phantastes*—in which another world opens up to the Dreamer through a piece of bedroom furniture. The seeds of the first Narnia story were dawning in his mind. Lewis never attempted to write another work of Christian apologetics after **Miracles.** Even though this book, and the argumentative works which precede it—**The Problem of Pain, Mere Christianity**—remain so vastly popular in the Christian world, and continue to sell in Christian bookshops, he came to feel that their method and manner were spurious. There must be another way 'further up and further in'. (pp. 214-15)

The [Narnia] books were published at more or less annual intervals throughout the 1950s, and they remain hugely popular with the reading public today. . . . Whatever Lewis's future reputation as a theologian or literary critic, he is certain of a place among the classic authors of children's books, together with his own favourites, E. Nesbit, Beatrix Potter and Kenneth Grahame.

The Lion, the Witch and the Wardrobe grew out of Lewis's experience of being stung back into childhood by his defeat at the hands of Elizabeth Anscombe at the Socratic Club. . . . To write an outline of the story, which turns out to be the redemption of Narnia by a great lion called Aslan, who gives himself up for the sins of the children and rises again from the dead, would be to present as an 'idea'—what Lewis himself would have called 'a truth about something'—a story which is felt, in reading, to be reality itself. This story is delightful, a wholly absorbing narrative in its own right. It is as though Lewis, in all his tiredness and despondency in the late 1940s, has managed to get through the wardrobe door himself; to leave behind the world of squabbles and grown-ups and to re-enter the world which with the deepest part of himself he never left, that of childhood reading. In a very few pages, there is a rich concentration of all that he has most intensely felt and enjoyed as a reader—the talking animals

of his own early stories, the fauna of classical mythology, the cold Wagnerian gusts of Northernness brought by the witch, the drama of religious confrontation, when the children witness 'deeper magic from before the dawn of time'. They are E. Nesbit children; they 'jaw' rather than talk; they say 'by gum!' and 'Crikey!' They seem no more to belong to the mid or late twentieth century than Lewis did himself. But generations of children can now testify to the irresistible *readability* of the Narnia stories. This must derive . . . from the fact that Lewis wrote them for the child who was within himself. It is not whimsical to say that Narnia *is* the inside of Lewis's mind, peopled with a rich enjoyment of old books and old stories and the beauties of nature, but always threatened by a terrible sense of loss, of love's frailty. Its method, of a heterodox absorption of so many different influences into one Christian allegory—MacDonald, Malory, Nesbit, Ovid, all have their deliberate echoes here—is one borrowed from Spenser; or perhaps it would be truer to say that it is at one with Lewis's own reading of that poet. The unifying element in *The Faerie Queene* is the place—'Faerie Land itself provides the unity.' Narnia provides a precisely similar unity for all the disparate elements which Lewis chooses to pour into his allegory. . . . The appearance of a familiar figure like Father Christmas among so much that was new and strange is precisely the effect which Spenser achieved by juxtaposing old friends like St George with new monsters of his own invention. (pp. 220-21)

If the Anscombe debate about Supernaturalism had stung Lewis into a quite different sort of writing, the decline of [his friend Janie Moore, whom he called] Minto had also helped to drive him back imaginatively into childhood worlds. There can be little doubt that the energy and passion of the Narnia stories spring from the intensely unhappy and physically depleted state through which he had been passing. With the cooling of male friendships, with the sense that his intellectual defence of himself as a Christian was, at best, flawed, and with the gradual removal of his mother-substitute, he needed more than ever the comradeship which he had only ever found with [his brother] Warnie in the Little End Room [an attic sitting room in their childhood home]. And Warnie, much of the time, was blind drunk. This is what necessitated the escape not merely to the Little End Room, but beyond the wardrobe into imagined lands.

Tolkien's aesthetic objection to the Narnia stories ["He regarded (**The Lion, the Witch and the Wardrobe**)," Wilson writes, "as scrappily put together, and not in his sense a 'sub-creation', that is, a coherently made natural world."] is a perfectly valid one if we attempt to judge Narnia by the standards of *The Silmarillion.* Lewis's books for children show signs of extraordinary haste in composition; they are full of inconsistencies, and by his standards they are not even particularly well written. He frequently repeats epithets, and if the series is read entire by an adult reader the tone of voice can become wearisome. But it is a mistake to judge the Narnia stories as if they were a sort of slapdash *Lord of the Rings.* They are a quite different sort of book, and their readability and fascination stem from wholly individual qualities. The fascination of Tolkien is that his was a finished and enclosed imagination.

His world, with its creatures, gods, angels, languages, lost tales and civilizations, is as complete as the 'real' world; perhaps more so. There is never an intrusive moment in Tolkien of two worlds jarring together; no hint, for example, that the creation story in *The Silmarillion* might relate to anything we have read in the Bible, or that the legendary figures and dynasties might interconnect with other cycles, such as those of the Edda or Homer. Lewis's Narnia books are quite different. Their whole theme is the interpenetration of worlds, and he poured into them a whole jumble of elements, drawn from his reading, and the world he was inhabiting when he wrote the books. (pp. 225-26)

The fact that Lewis threw into the mixture all the things which immediately concerned him certainly makes for a most imperfect 'sub-creation' by Tolkien's strict standards; but it is symptomatic of the much more important fact that in the Narnia stories Lewis is deeply and unselfconsciously engaged in the stories he is creating. He has abandoned here a cerebral and superficial defence of religion of the kind attempted at the Socratic Club. He has launched back deep into the recesses of his own emotional history, his own most deeply felt psychological needs and vulnerabilities. It is this, surely, which gives the books their extraordinary power. They are written white-hot. The time when the comings and goings between our world and Narnia began is not as you might guess remote in history. It was when Sherlock Holmes was still living in Baker Street and the Bastables were looking for treasure in the Lewisham Road; in other words, at the time when a certain Belfast solicitor called Albert Lewis was wooing a girl called Flora Hamilton. The penetration between the worlds began with his parents' marriage, and this is made clear at the end of the series, even if one rejects any Freudian explanation for its beginning. That is to say, we hardly need to dwell on the psychological significance of the wardrobe in the first story; we do not need, though some will be tempted to do so, to see in this tale of a world which is reached through a dark hole surrounded by fur coats any unconscious image of the passage through which Lewis first entered the world from his mother's body. We do not need to be ingenious because, by the end of *The Last Battle,* it is all spelt out for us. If *The Lion, the Witch and the Wardrobe* is a story which hangs on the gospel narrative of the Resurrection, then *The Last Battle* is the Apocalypse in which there is a final conflict with the forces of evil. The old heaven and the old earth pass away, Narnia is destroyed, and then remade for eternity. The children all come together because they and their parents have now entered Narnia for ever, not by the magic of stepping through a wardrobe, but through an actual railway accident, a real death. Only one of the children from the original quartet is excluded from heaven. This is Susan. She has committed the unforgivable sin of growing up. . . .

[What] the children discover when Aslan/Christ has made all things new is that the old things have not passed away at all. They find that not only has the old Narnia been preserved and refashioned, but that England has been too, and some people who are more important even than the many strange characters, fauns, centaurs, talking animals, whom they have met in their imaginative adventures.

> 'Why!' exclaimed Peter. 'It's England. And that's the house itself—Professor Kirk's old home in the country where all our adventures began!'
>
> 'I thought that house had been destroyed,' said Edmund.
>
> 'So it was,' said the Faun. 'But you are now looking at the England within England, the real England just as this is the real Narnia. And in that inner England no good thing is destroyed.'
>
> Suddenly they shifted their eyes to another spot, and then Peter and Edmund and Lucy gasped with amazement and shouted out and began waving: for they saw their own father and mother, waving back at them across the great, deep valley. It was like when you see people waving at you from the deck of a big ship when you are waiting on the quay to meet them.

It was on the quayside that Lewis and Warnie parted from their father only two weeks after their mother had been taken from them. That terrible severance, which took them away from Ireland and childhood and all that had made them comfortable, is here longingly stitched up. *The Last Battle* is the story which Lewis, when he came to write his autobiography for grown-ups, was incapable of telling. It is an exploration on a level which George MacDonald would have understood of the unplumbed psychological depths where regret and longing and unhealed heartbreak find their consolation in old Christian story. (pp. 227-30)

A. N. Wilson, in his C. S. Lewis: A Biography, *W. W. Norton & Company, 1990, 334 p.*

Jon Scieszka

1954-

American author of picture books and fiction.

Major works include *The True Story of the Three Little Pigs: by A. Wolf; as Told to Jon Scieszka* (1989), *The Frog Prince, Continued* (1991), *Knights of the Kitchen Table* (1991).

A fantasist who parodies traditional fairy tales, history, and classic fiction by blending familiar concepts and characters with distinctive twists and contemporary language, Scieszka is regarded as one of the most popular recent writers in the field of children's literature for his inventiveness and wit. He is best known as the author of *The True Story of the Three Little Pigs,* a picture book which retells the famous nursery story from the perspective of the wolf. Telling his woeful tale from prison, Alexander T. ("You can call me Al") Wolf implies that he was framed by the press for blowing down the houses of—and eating—the pigs. Blaming a bad cold for his huffing and puffing, Al, who is pictured by illustrator Lane Smith in conservative glasses and bowtie, claims pure motives for his behavior, including his explanation that he ate the little pigs to avoid their spoiling. Scieszka's next work, the picture book *The Frog Prince, Continued,* offers primary graders another alternative version of a beloved nursery tale. In this story, the prince and his princess are not living happily ever after; he misses his life as a frog and still retains amphibian behavior patterns such as sticking out his tongue and hopping on the furniture. When the prince leaves home to find a witch who can turn him back into a frog, he meets the crones from fairy tales such as "Hansel and Gretel" and "Cinderella" before he changes his mind and returns to his frantic princess; at the end of the book, the prince kisses his bride and they both become frogs. Scieszka's wry and sophisticated perspective in both *The Frog Prince, Continued* and *The True Story of the Three Little Pigs* stresses the satirical aspects of the tales, which are also noted for their accessibility to young readers and superior read-aloud quality.

Scieszka continues his formula of combining classic and modern references in a humorous fashion with the first two volumes of his "Time Warp Trio" series, *Knights of the Kitchen Table* and *The Not-So-Jolly Roger* (1991). Fast-paced adventures for middle graders, the books describe how narrator Joe, who is given a magic wish-granting book by his magician uncle, is transported with his friends Fred and Sam to King Arthur's Britain and Blackbeard's island. The boys confront a fearsome Black Knight, an evil-smelling giant, the dragon Smaug, and Blackbeard and his pirates in stories filled with zany juvenile humor and written in easy-to-read sentences. An elementary school teacher of computers, math, science, and history who also has a master's degree from the writing program at Columbia University, Scieszka was inspired to create *The True Story of the Three Little Pigs* when he re-

wrote fairy tales with his second grade class and realized that they were enjoying the concept of parody. Writing the "Time Warp Trio" books to fill the gap for middle graders between picture books and books with chapters, he intends his stories to act as introductions to other genres of literature for this age group. "I think kids are the greatest audience for a writer," Scieszka has written, adding "no one can believe a story or love one as much as a kid does."

AUTHOR'S COMMENTARY

[The following excerpt is from an interview by Amanda Smith.]

Author Jon Scieszka and illustrator Lane Smith made a splash two years ago with ***The True Story of the Three Little Pigs!*** "by A. Wolf"; in their rendering, the wolf wasn't really out to eat those little piggies—he just had a sneezing fit and blew a house down. He was merely the victim of bad press.

Now there are several more Scieszka and Smith books available or due soon, all from Viking. ***The Knights of the Kitchen Table*** and ***The Not So Jolly Roger,*** the first in the

Time Warp Trio series, in which three boys travel through time, came out this spring, as did Scieszka's *The Frog Prince, Continued,* illustrated by Steven Johnson. Smith's *The Big Pets* appeared in spring as well, and his *Glasses (Who Needs 'Em?*) is due in September; for these Smith did both text and illustration.

Smith, 32, and Scieszka, 37, both live in New York City; they met about six years ago through their respective girlfriend and wife, who had worked together as art directors. Smith is a magazine illustrator freelancing to such publications as the *Atlantic, Rolling Stone* and the *New York Times Magazine.* Scieszka (the name rhymes with Fresca) teaches sixth-grade history and eighth-grade algebra and is the father of a seven-year-old daughter, Casey, and a five-year-old son, Jake.

"Lane and I work so well together because we crack each other up," Scieszka says, and an afternoon spent with the two at Smith's apartment, which also houses his studio, has more than a few minutes of zaniness. "He and I are so different," Scieszka continues. "I loved reading as a kid, science, biology, mathematics. Lane sees how things are put together. Where I liked cartoons because the stories were goofy, Lane would know *why* they were goofy, how the sequence went to make it funny." (p. 220)

Although *The True Story* is Scieszka's first book, his literary career has strong roots. He has a master's degree from the writing program at Columbia, and originally planned to be a college professor and write the Great American Novel. "Then I taught first and second grade and got sidetracked," he claims. "Those are the guys who probably inspired me because I read a lot of stuff to them. Much later it dawned on me, 'Hey, I like to write short stories, and picture books are perfect short stories.' Children's books demand that you pare the story down, and it has to be good—all the rest of the crap is just stripped down to the essentials, like a poem."

Scieszka says that when he was taking his creative writing course, he never imagined writing for children. "Which was kind of stupid of me, because I always liked kids a lot. And I grew up around a lot of kids—like my five brothers. And my dad's an elementary school teacher. I had a riot teaching, too, and [doing a children's book] didn't strike me until after I'd been teaching for about five years."

He took a year off from teaching in 1988 and swapped material with Smith, who tucked it into his portfolio as he made his rounds. Smith says, "I think it helped because we had a complete package to present to them. We put together a book dummy for *The Three Little Pigs.* When Regina Hayes at Viking, who has been our editor throughout, saw them, she said, 'Yeah, they work.' " Scieszka adds, "She became a real champion and protected us"; her initial reaction was, "It's a little weird, but we'll take a chance."

Before finding Hayes, Scieszka says, "Lane and I got turned down in a lot of places, because people thought the manuscript of *The Three Little Pigs* was too sophisticated. That became a curse word—the "S" word. People don't give kids enough credit for knowing the fairy tales and being able to get what parody is. When I taught sec-

ond-graders, that's the age when they first discover parody. They're just getting those reading skills and nothing cracks them up like a joke that turns stuff upside down. Lane and I thought it would be better to push kids and challenge them. If they don't get all the jokes, they'll get some of them."

Smith admits to being "stupefied when *The Three Little Pigs* took off. We would go out on signings, and every other person there was a teacher, and they would talk about how they used the book for point-of-view writing. All of a sudden we were these young educators."

Scieszka comments on the disappearance of the oral tradition in today's world. "With *The Frog Prince, Continued,* some people asked me if I got permission from the author who wrote *The Frog Prince.* 'Yes, I spoke to him directly,' I'd say. 'Fred Grimm, a lost Grimm brother.' I try gently to explain to them that it was out of the oral tradition, and who knows when it was or who wrote it or where it comes from."

Scieszka and Smith consider their Time Warp Trio books an introduction for children to other genres of literature. They have plenty of ideas for new series; the next involves cowboys and Indians and is tentatively titled *The Good, the Bad and the Goofy.* Scieszka says, "I saw a need for something between a picture book and a chapter book. Kids get stuck in that lull there. When I taught third and fourth grades, I couldn't find cool-looking books to hand to boys, who, for the most part, were reluctant readers and didn't want to be seen as dummies. And so we had to pitch it [to Viking] to get Lane to do the covers and make 'em look cool so they'd pick 'em up and not feel bad about walkin' around with 'em. But still make 'em short enough, action-packed enough, disgusting enough."

"Disgusting—key word," Smith adds. Scieszka agrees. "Very key. If disgusting is good once, it's great 10 times." (pp. 220-21)

Scieszka says, "Our audience is hardcore silly kids. And there are a lot of 'em out there."

Smith's palette is unusually dark for children's books. "It's dark," he says, "but it's not really menacing." . . .

Scieszka says the observation about Smith's dark palette "shows up a lot. That's what we had to wrestle against when we were pitching the book. The publishing urge is to lighten things up, make 'em look a little more cheerful. Lane and I would go, 'No, we like them a little more textured.' " . . .

Smith and Scieszka often test new material out on children before it is published. Scieszka says that he gives his "kids out on loan to Lane a lot, just to make sure he develops as a children's author. It's all for his own good, it's not just babysitting—I keep telling him that. 'We'll be back around midnight. See ya. Work on your next book. Try it out on Casey. She's a good critic.' " The two giggle. . . .

Scieszka says he plans to stick with teaching. Does he think about writing adult fiction? "It would be intriguing if a notion came up that just isn't appropriate for kids. I like children as an audience better. But I'm working my way up. This summer I'm thinking about writing for older kids because I've been teaching sixth, seventh and eighth graders. I don't have any urge to go back to adults as an audience, once I've seen the promised land."

Smith adds, "And it is children." (p. 221)

Amanda Smith, "Jon Scieszka and Lane Smith," in Publishers Weekly, *Vol. 238, No. 33, July 26, 1991, pp. 220-21.*

TITLE COMMENTARY

The True Story of the Three Little Pigs: by A. Wolf; as Told to Jon Scieszka (1989)

It turns out that Alexander T. Wolf ("You can call me Al") only wanted to borrow a cup of sugar for a birthday cake for his granny (who looks a bit all-the-better-to-*eat*-you-with herself, and is that a pair of bunny ears poking out of the cake batter?). After knocking politely on the first pig's door, Al's nose started to itch. "I felt a sneeze coming on. Well I huffed. And I snuffed. And I sneezed a great sneeze. And do you know what? That whole darn straw house fell down." And lying in the middle of the straw was the First Little Pig, "dead as a doornail." "Think of it as a big cheeseburger just lying there." And so on. The gruesome humor of the text is kept in the line by the breezy style of Al's narration, a natural (if you dare) read-aloud studded with offbeat rhyme: "I called, 'Mr. Pig, Mr. Pig, are you in?' He yelled back, 'Go away wolf. You can't come in. I'm shaving the hairs on my chinny chin chin.' " With a sensibility akin to Henrik Drescher's but informed with more sophisticated draftsmanship, [Lane] Smith's creepy and witty illustrations get right to the meat of the matter. The Second Little Pig's snuffing leaves his porky bottom posed neatly between a set of fine stick-style tableware; and from our brief glance of the Third (very pink and very mean: "What a pig") we can easily see how A. T. Wolf, "big and bad," soon found himself in Pig Penn. While hardly everyone's cup of tea (or sugar), both read-aloud and read-alone audiences will find a tasty treat.

Roger Sutton, in a review of "The True Story of the 3 Little Pigs," in Bulletin of the Center for Children's Books, *Vol. 43, No. 1, September, 1989, p. 19.*

This exposé of the three little pigs as told to Jon Scieszka by A. Wolf, their arch rival, should be a sensation among the cognoscenti who dote on inside stories. For that's where A. Wolf is—inside the Pig Penn—after being framed by unscrupulous reporters and popular opinion. . . . [His] startling revelations are accompanied by colorfully impressionistic illustrations, integrating elegance of execution with comic timing. Is A. Wolf's story interesting? You bet. Is it true? Hard to say. But don't lend him any sugar!

Mary M. Burns, in a review of "The True Story of the Three Little Pigs," in The Horn Book Magazine, *Vol. LXVI, No. 1, January-February, 1990, p. 58.*

[*The True Story of the Three Little Pigs by A. Wolf*] is even freer and funnier [than Tony Ross's *Mrs. Goat and Her Seven Little Kids*]. . . . The words are beautifully put together, the pictures—by Lane Smith—highly selective, very dramatic. Here is an artist who has got right to the heart of his subject. Tony Ross, I feel, applies a formula, Sciezka and Smith have started from scratch and made their book by pure creativity. (pp. 128-29)

M. Crouch, in a review of "The True Story of the Three Little Pigs,"in The Junior Bookshelf, *Vol. 54, No. 3, June, 1990, pp. 128-29.*

Northrop Frye, in his *Anatomy of Criticism*, states that the satirist "often gives to ordinary life a logical and self-consistent shift of perspective". As Anderson and Apseloff observe in *Nonsense Literature for Children*, children "can appreciate many of the ploys of satire: size and role reversals, exaggerations, irreverence, and scatology". Scieszka has used role reversals in the point of view of the tale, and language reversals in his slight changes of the traditional wording in places such as " 'Little Pig, Little Pig, are you in?' " and "I huffed. And I snuffed" which take on shifts of meaning because of the new approach. His introduction of contemporary language and diction adds to the fun as the much maligned wolf sees that the "whole darn house fell down," and he swears his innocence ("Wolf 's honor") in a delightfully tongue-in-cheek fashion. The juxtaposition of the pseudo-old with contemporary colloquial speech and slang should amuse both child and adult. . . . Any child familiar with the traditional tale cannot help but be entertained by the new point of view and language in this one.

Lane Smith's illustrations also add greatly to the fun. They show the wolf in glasses, bow tie and striped jacket, a perfect innocent. Perspectives vary and borders are not always strong enough to hold in the contents. At one strategic point the letter "N" appears as a string of sausages. After the destruction of their homes, the first two pigs are shown bottom-up in the midst of the rubble; it is hard to tell if they are really dead or are just trying to hide. We have to take the wolf 's word for their demise. (pp. 135-36)

Marilyn Fain Apseloff, "The Big, Bad Wolf: New Approaches to An Old Folk Tale," in Children's Literature Association Quarterly, *Vol. 15, No. 3, Fall, 1990, pp. 135-37.*

Scieszka's hilarious story opens up all kinds of possibilities for response activities. Certainly, many older children may choose to do some background research on trials and then read other versions of this familiar tale in order to gather the evidence needed to script and conduct the trial of Mr. Wolf. The story might also motivate children to retell other favorite folktales from new perspectives.

M. G. Gillis, in a review of "The True Story of the 3 Little Pigs!" in Language Arts, *Vol. 68, No. 2, February, 1991, p. 143.*

The Frog Prince, Continued (1991)

As in *The True Story of the Three Little Pigs*, Scieszka offers another tongue-in-cheek "rest of the story," telling what happens *after* the Princess kissed the frog. Readers won't be surprised to learn that they *do not* live "happily ever after." In fact, they're downright miserable. He misses the pond; she's tired of him sticking out his tongue and hopping on the furniture. In desperation, the bug-eyed hero decides to find a witch who can turn him back into the happy frog he once was. Successfully surviving encounters with several sinister but dimwitted witches from other tales, he finally meets Cinderella's Fairy Godmother who tries to help, but the transformation is definitely NOT what he had in mind. As the clock strikes midnight, he returns to human form and hurries home to his beloved Princess where the tale ends unexpectedly, but indeed happily. Johnson's surreal illustrations are right on target for the offbeat story. Painted in deep, shadowy colors and expertly composed, they are filled with subtle and surprising humor that continually rewards viewers with laugh-out-loud visual treats. The overall design is clean and spacious, with figures and objects moving past the ragged borders of the pictures and across the pages, matching the verbal movement perfectly. Readers will relish the pleasure inherent in combining traditional fairy tale motifs with modern, everyday objects and actions. A winner. (pp. 83-4)

> *Linda Boyles, in a review of "The Frog Prince Continued," in* School Library Journal, *Vol. 37, No. 5, May, 1991, pp. 83-4.*

Once upon a time in the land of children's books there resided certain conventions: fairy tales would be relatively simple stories, and the lessons they provided would be both practical (cry wolf too often and no one will listen when the real wolf comes) and moral (virtue is, in the end, rewarded). There were some unfortunate stereotypes (the kind tend to be beautiful, women with sharp noses tend to be witches), and some heroes were dolts, which you know if you've ever had a 3-year-old look up and ask you, "*Why* does she think the wolf is her grandma?"

Now, possibly because children are more sophisticated—if that is the word to describe the condition produced when a toddler up late with an earache can pick up the channel switcher and wind up on Channel 35, where an adult male is masturbating to disco music—there is something new: the anti-fairy tale, a mordant treatment of the form's conventions in a manner that might be called not Grimm but somewhat grim.

The Frog Prince, Continued by Jon Scieszka begins where "The Frog Prince" left off. He's already been kissed by the Princess and is now a nice yuppie-looking man in a suit and tie, but, alas, he is not happy. His wife, the Princess, who looks like Sydney Biddle Barrows, is always nagging him to stop sticking out his tongue as if he's catching flies. He wants to know how come she never wants to go down to the pond anymore; she says she'd probably be in a better mood if he'd stop hopping around on the furniture.

You know what happens next: she finds a lily pad in his pants pocket and declares she wishes she'd never kissed his slimy frog lips, and the Frog Prince packs his bag and leaves. Then he goes on a great adventure where he tries to get a witch in the forest to turn him back into a frog so he can be happy again. But the witches he meets are ap-

parently heavily influenced by Stephen Sondheim. The first one threatens to cast a wicked spell on him because she thinks he's there to wake up Sleeping Beauty before the 100 years are up. (This witch zaps people into spells with a television channel switcher.) The next one, whom he finds at a beauty parlor having her hair done and reading Hague magazine, fears he's come to rescue Snow White and offers him a poison apple.

The Prince is terrorized by more witches who don't understand what story they're in, and at the end, tired and bedraggled and ready to re-count his old blessings, he returns home to a by now anxious and rueful Princess, who is eager to kiss his moist amphibian mouth. The moral being, in a harsh and confusing world it's sometimes best to trust what you have and to fight boredom not by changing your outer world but your inner one.

Steve Johnson's illustrations are artistically interesting—witty and spooky at the same time. But at bedtime most parents prefer benign and sunny, because children have nightmares and the day-to-day world yields more than enough fodder for an imaginative child's bad dreams. So I'm not sure spooky is a good thing. But it *is* good if you wrote and illustrated the book in part to make your grown-up friends laugh. Mr. Scieszka's first book, **The True Story of the Three Little Pigs,** for example, has been a huge hit with adults. My friends laughed at this book too, but they have three decades on the nursery school set.

To fully appreciate **The Frog Prince, Continued,** you have to have a highly developed sense of irony and a sharp sense of the absurd, which most children don't develop before they can read, despite exposure to random television programming. The jacket says **The Frog Prince, Continued** is for ages 5 and up, and it's definitely up because those under 6 or maybe 7 will inevitably be confused by it. And that's all right. There's time ahead for ironic humor. People who sell things for children are always claiming too broad an age group, probably so they'll have a bigger pool of potential buyers. This is not only unhelpful to the consumer, it's counterproductive to the seller: hit a 3-year-old with, say, the "Peanuts" characters too soon and they'll be bored, refuse to listen and turn against Charlie Brown and Lucy forever. Although appearances are sometimes deceiving, little children are not sophisticated and they don't know it all. So it's worth waiting a few years before introducing them to Jon Scieszka's sense of humor. My guess is that the rest of the family will still be laughing at **The Frog Prince, Continued.**

> *Peggy Noonan, "Those Moist Amphibian Lips," in* The New York Times Book Review, *May 19, 1991, p. 25.*

The co-author (with A. Wolf) of **The True Story of the Three Little Pigs** assays another humorous embroidery of a traditional tale with somewhat less notable success. The picture of the erstwhile frog and his princess bickering ("Stop sticking your tongue out like that"; "How come you never want to go down to the pond anymore?") is genuinely funny, and the prince's quest for a witch to turn him back into a frog—during which he runs into witches from several other tales—is amusing. But the conclusion—glad to get back to his princess, he kisses her and they *both* become happy frogs—seems limp and unmotivated. Meanwhile, Johnson's paintings, though he adopts some of Lane Smith's fey menace and induces tension by canting his perspectives, lack Smith's wit, imagination, and masterful sense of design. Still, the situation and dialogue are irreverently comical and Johnson's caricatures are adroitly satirical. It's an entertaining effort—just not up to that superlative first book. (pp. 732-33)

> *A review of "The Frog Prince, Continued," in* Kirkus Reviews, *Vol. LIX, No. 11, June 1, 1991, pp. 732-33.*

Mr. Scieszka offers an alternative view of "happily ever after" in this iconoclastic look at the prince who was once a frog and the princess bride who kissed away his amphibious appearance. Like Sondheim's *Into the Woods,* Scieszka's tale is a sophisticated variant on traditional themes; it has a wry, adult perspective and yet is accessible to younger readers who enjoy—and understand—the art of parody and lampoon. . . . The dialogue is witty; the plot, as logical as it is offbeat. Steve Johnson's paintings, executed in a rich and somber palette, are like stage settings; his depiction of the various characters is inspired, overlaying the eighteenth-century ambiance with deliberate and delicious anachronistic touches. The contrast between the elegance of the book design and the absurdity of the plot is particularly notable, underscoring the concept that well-conceived comedy can be very high art indeed. (pp. 451-52)

> *Mary M. Burns, in a review of "The Frog Prince, Continued," in* The Horn Book Magazine, *Vol. LXVII, No. 4, July-August, 1991, pp. 451-52.*

Knights of the Kitchen Table; The Not-So-Jolly Roger (1991)

The author of the hilarious *The True Story of the Three Little Pigs* comes up with an entertaining formula in this first "Time Warp Trio" story [*Knights of the Kitchen Table*]: Narrator Joe is given a magic book ("*The Book*") that transports him and two friends to King Arthur's Britain, where they find themselves confronted by a fearsome Black Knight—who's easy to defeat with some quick dodging when he's in mid-charge. Then Lancelot, Gawain, et al. happen by and take the boys for heroes—a reputation they sustain by tricking the loathsome giant who's menacing the castle into fighting the terrible dragon (Smaug) that has also just turned up.

Scieszka unobtrusively slips in several classic references and defines some chivalric jargon by having the boys comically paraphrase it; there is some daring juvenile humor on the subject of the giant's various atrocious smells, and the contrast between the boys' breezy manner and the knights' pseudo-formality is also good for several laughs. A little forced, but this should serve its purpose. [Lane] Smith's drawings deftly reflect the blend of everyday kid with zany, mock-gruesome adventure.

> *A review of "Knights of the Kitchen Table," in*

> Kirkus Reviews, *Vol. LIX, No. 9, May 1, 1991, p. 609.*

Following the success of their debut collaboration, *The True Story of the Three Little Pigs,* [in *Knights of the Kitchen Table* and *The Not-So-Jolly Roger*] Scieszka and Smith introduce the Time Warp Trio: Joe, Fred and Sam. With the aid of a magic book that Joe receives from his uncle, a circus magician, the threesome catapults through history as unlikely adventurers. The first and more entertaining stop is King Arthur's court, where they do battle against an evil knight, a giant and a dragon as Sir Joe the Magnificent, Sir Fred the Awesome and Sir Sam the Unusual. The second story brings the trio face to face with the ruthless Blackbeard and his band of treasure-seeking pirates. Once again, the boys' artfulness helps them narrowly to escape death by pistol, cutlass and a walk on the plank. Both books demonstrate Scieszka's perfect ear for schoolyard dialogue and humor—most notably of the bodily function variety. The subtle personality distinctions among the protagonists are nicely drawn, and Smith's amusing illustrations invigorate the text.

> *A review of "Knights of the Kitchen Table" and "The Not-So-Jolly Roger," in* Publishers Weekly, *Vol. 238, No. 22, May 17, 1991, p. 64.*

The "Time Warp Trio" consists of three friends, one of whom has received a wish-granting magic book as a birthday present from an uncle. The book sends them back in time to Camelot (*Knights*) and a desert island (*Roger*). The device is tired, the puns are weak, and the tone is too knowing. The jokes are dumb, mostly based upon the boys' anachronistic attitudes and slang: "Your mother was a sardine can," says Fred to the armored Black Knight. There are lots of sound effects, lots of explosions, and lots of disgusting emissions ("Ten brave knights fell like bowling pins, victims of gas warfare"); while it all adds up to standard fourth-grade chucklebait, the three boys are indistinguishable and the plots predictable. Smith's pen sketches have more personality than the text, but their new-wave weirdness only underlines the staleness of the stories. Scieszka's picture-book texts have proven him capable of tight, funny prose . . . ; books for newly independent readers deserve no less.

> *Roger Sutton, in a review of "Knights of the Kitchen Table" and "The Not-So-Jolly Roger," in* Bulletin of the Center for Children's Books, *Vol. 44, No. 11, July-August, 1991, p. 274.*

A book from his magician uncle transports Joe and his friends, Fred and Sam, back in time to swashbuckling adventures fraught with dangers at every turn. In the first story, quick thinking and derring-do save them from a fire-breathing dragon and a foul-smelling giant; in the second, an encounter with the dreaded Blackbeard almost causes their demise. Tongue-in-cheek humor, laced with understatement and word play, makes for laugh-out-loud reading, as verbal insults are hurled, and the boys outwit their foes. Villains and heroes clash, as do modern and archaic language and dress, causing misunderstandings and mayhem. Short, easy-to-read sentences and lots of zany dialogue perfectly suit the breathless pace. Smith brings new dimension to black-and-white drawings, as looming villains tower over the trio, brandishing swords or lances, and the boys escape their captors. A true melding of word and pictures, and jolly good fun.

> *Trev Jones, in a review of "Knights of the Kitchen Table" and "The Not-So-Jolly Roger," in* School Library Journal, *Vol. 37, No. 8, August, 1991, p. 169.*

Margery Sharp

1905-1991

English author of fiction.

Major works include *The Rescuers* (1962), *Miss Bianca* (1962), *The Turret* (1963), *Bernard the Brave* (1976).

A writer considered an especially original and witty fantasist who is often praised for her sophisticated literary style and talent for characterization, Sharp is best known as the creator of Miss Bianca, the dainty, pampered anthropomorphic mouse whose gentility is matched by her courage and resourcefulness. Miss Bianca, a poet who is the beloved pet of the son of a diplomat, appears as either the protagonist or a supporting character in nine humorous fantasies for middle graders about the Mouse Prisoners Aid Society (MPAS), an association dedicated to helping or freeing human beings confined against their will. Both as president of the MPAS (Ladies' Section) and in retirement, Miss Bianca becomes involved in a variety of cliffhanging adventures that take her to the Orient and the Antarctic as well as to settings closer to home, such as castles, palaces, and salt mines, that are fraught with danger. Miss Bianca is accompanied on her exploits by her faithful admirer Bernard, a humble pantry mouse whose relationship with Miss Bianca—who is attracted to him but remains uncommitted due to their difference in class status—provides a subplot to the stories; Bernard, who proves himself an intrepid adventurer, is the featured character in two of the books in the series. Throughout their adventures, which often center on the freeing of children, the mice are spurred on by their concern for human life, risking personal safety to thwart human and animal villains and restore justice. Sharp contrasts the nobility of the mice with the inhumanity of her adult human characters, and her stories are noted for satirizing behavior and convention while entertaining young readers. Acknowledged as distinctively elegant parodies of romantic adult adventure stories, the "Miss Bianca" books are often considered challenging for their audience due to the elaborate language, mature humor, and light, mannered style with which Sharp invests them; critic Marcus Crouch writes that "nowhere in children's literature are the words themselves of more significance." However, Sharp is often lauded for the charm and convincing quality of her works as well as for her portrayal of Miss Bianca, whom critics Sam Leaton Sebesta and William J. Iverson call "of all mouse characters, . . . the most distinguished."

Sharp wrote her first "Miss Bianca" novel, *The Rescuers,* after thirty years of writing adult fiction and plays. Well known for creating popular romances that reflect her dry wit and creation of unconventional, appealing heroines, she turned to children's books for, as she says, "complete release of the imagination." In *The Rescuers,* which is often noted as a classic, Miss Bianca and Bernard rescue a Norwegian poet imprisoned in the terrible Black Castle with the help of Nils, a seafaring Norwegian mouse who

has been enlisted as a translator; in *Miss Bianca in the Antarctic* (1970), Miss Bianca and Bernard, who are retired from active duty in the MPAS, are again called upon to rescue the Norwegian poet. Later in the series, which takes Miss Bianca to a position as Perpetual Madam President of the MPAS, Sharp introduces Algernon, a lisping, poorly stuffed teddy bear who courageously helps Bernard in the adventures in which he is the protagonist. The series is illustrated by a number of artists, such as Garth Williams, Erik Blegvad, Faith Jacques, and Leslie Morrill, whose pictures are noted for adding to the success of the books. In addition to her stories about Miss Bianca, Sharp is the author of fantasies and realistic fiction for readers in the early primary grades, notably *The Magical Cockatoo* (1974), a tale set in Edwardian London in which Lally, a small girl who lives with her grandmother, is taken on adventures by a porcelain cockatoo who comes alive when struck by moonlight. *The Rescuers* was commended for the Carnegie Medal in 1959 and has been adapted to film by the Walt Disney Studios, which also used the "Miss Bianca" characters in a film set in Australia; three of Sharp's adult novels have also been made into films.

(See also *Something about the Author,* Vols. 1, 29; *Contem-*

porary *Authors New Revision Series,* Vols. 18, 134 [obituary]; and *Contemporary Authors,* Vols. 21-22, revised edition.)

AUTHOR'S COMMENTARY

[The following excerpt is from an interview by Roy Newquist.]

[Roy Newquist]. "Her style is impeccable, her taste sublime, her humanity infinite." Thus did a Midwest reviewer recently sum up an appraisal of Margery Sharp which sweeps from *The Nutmeg Tree* to *Martha In Paris,* from *Britannia Mews* to *The Turret.* On both sides of the Atlantic, Miss Sharp commands a growing legion of fans which will never miss a word she writes. Her rare gift for fantasy that is never a step removed from life or the significance of life is apt to grant immortality to heroines named Julia, Martha, and—yes, Miss Bianca. (p. 538)

N. How did your series of children's books enter the picture?

Sharp: I enjoy writing them immensely because they are a complete release of the imagination. The first of the Miss Bianca series was called *The Rescuers.* It was about the Prisoners Aid Association of Mice—mice are traditionally the prisoner's friend, you know—so I describe how the organization works with all its branches in various countries, the basic idea being the cheering of prisoners in their cells. You might say that it's national service stuff all mice go through. But then there are adventures when they feel prisoners have been wrongly imprisoned and should be released. It's fascinating to me, and I hope to the people who read the books.

I think a great deal of the success has been due to Garth Williams' illustrations. His technique is marvelous, but he shows the most wonderfully sympathetic imagination. For example, in one place I describe the chairman's chair as being made from walnut shells, so Garth Williams carpentered a walnut shell into a chair and then drew it.

N. The stories have gone into a number of translations, haven't they?

Sharp: I'm delighted about this. For one thing, the foreign companies have told me that the stories are written in such good English they are a pleasure to translate. Then it's fascinating to see the questionnaires at the end of chapters, like the Dutch edition, for schools, where one question reads, "Why did they put Nils in the pocket closest to the poet's heart?" Answer: "Because they were both Norwegians." It's all very fascinating. (p. 539)

> *Margery Sharp and Roy Newquist, in an interview in* Counterpoint, *Rand McNally & Company, 1964, pp. 537-42.*

GENERAL COMMENTARY

Marcus Crouch

Walter R. Brooks's curiously appealing stories . . . are no more about pigs than is *Animal Farm,* but they make use of the piggishness in man and the manliness in pigs to make valid points. This is true, also, of Margery Sharp's charming stories about Miss Bianca, the brave and talented mouse . . . Miss Bianca and the members of the Prisoners Aid Society over which she presides are all mouse, and Miss Sharp is meticulously consistent in keeping them to scale. The mechanics of their daily lives and their journeys—Miss Bianca habitually travels on duty by Diplomatic Bag or in a Rolls, but for the great adventure of the Diamond Palace she goes with the rank and file by public transport, the municipal dust-cart—is worked out as carefully and honestly as the economy of Mary Norton's *The Borrowers.* But the mouse society is a miniature of the everyday world, and the author makes gentle fun of convention by presenting it in mouse-guise. The stories have all the authority that a highly skilled novelist can give them. The touch is perfect, light as a feather—or a mouse's whisker. (pp. 105-06)

> *Marcus Crouch, "Laughter," in his* The Nesbit Tradition: The Children's Novel in England 1945-1970, *Ernest Benn Limited, 1972, pp. 101-11.*

Margaret Blount

The two most notable mouse fantasies [are Michael Bond's stories about Thursday] and [the] *Miss Bianca* books. . . . (p. 160)

Most of the best mouse stories have been written by women, and heroines are the rule. Margery Sharp's Miss Bianca is a female Pimpernel in a minute, mock-heroic saga of imprisonments, escapes, the rewarding of virtue and overcoming of villains by nimble wits, resource, courage and patience—all the traditional weapons of the weak against the strong. Miss Bianca adds to these something unique in animal stories and unfashionable as a virtue; the integrity bestowed by breeding and the discipline of perfect manners and strict adherence to etiquette. Of course, it is human etiquette; it always is, even in *The Jungle Books.* Only, interestingly, is it Animal in that most human story *The Wind in the Willows* where etiquette is shown to mean non-reference to death, pain, unpleasantness, or even yesterday.

But these are things which Miss Bianca would never mention if she thought they would distress her listeners. The *Miss Bianca* stories . . . are adult fantasy, springing from an original idea, that of a Mouse Prisoners Aid Society, or MPAS, formed to comfort and cheer humans in dungeons and perhaps help them to escape; one of those self-proliferating ideas capable of infinite development that gets better and better as it goes on. The character and exploits of the heroine, the inventive wit of the narrative, involve one very strongly in such issues as whether Miss Bianca will ever condescend to marry her humble admirer, Bernard; whether she will retain her office as Madam Chairwoman of the MPAS; the ethics of helping to rescue an unworthy prisoner who may, or may not, have reformed; how Miss Bianca will manage to deal with the two outrageous professors who insist on joining her in the Salt Mines rescue. The likeliness of these adventures on a human level would probably be acceptable in a comic fairy tale; the small size of the mice place them in an almost-real world and compel one to take them seriously. If mice had human brains and lacked a great measure of human original sin, this is how they might behave. One could say the same of Michael Bond's Peck family who behave much as humans do, in miniature; but Miss Sharp's mice are intensely concerned with human lives. They seem to know everything that is going on and are determined to right wrongs, restore orphans, release prisoners and bring happy endings at great personal peril; without human life, on the usual giant scale, their fields of endeavour would be limited, to their detriment. They are in the position of a healthy young society coping with odds rather than a settled group devoted to in-fighting.

There are two elements in these fantasies that appear at first to cancel each other—but perhaps they succeed in giving them a sort of equilibrium. The mice are very like Borrowers in that their miniature living is full of expedients and the pleasant vandalism (or agreeable use of common objects for extraordinary purposes) that every doll's house owner knows; their chairs are matchboxes, their committee room an old carriage lamp, carpets and pictures are postage stamps and the platform in the moot-hall is a chocolate box, the moot-hall itself is an old wine cask. The mice do not appear to have made anything for themselves (apart from the furnishings of Miss Bianca's exquisite porcelain pagoda which is part of the high life at the Embassy where she lives, rather than part of day-to-day existence). It is all Borrowing, shelf, pantry and cupboard living. But the human world into which they venture from these rather prosaic surroundings is the oddest, unreal, fairy-tale place: long railways and waggon routes lead into barren wastes, the enemies are the Black Castle, the Salt Mine, the Diamond Palace, and their rulers or gaolers—Ruritanian or Bohemian dukes and tyrants, including the most unpleasant cat ever invented, Mamelouk the iron tummed.

In this setting the mice, in delicate human parody, have much play with committee procedure and mouse rivalries—even a dash of university politics. The mixture is enchantingly real and unreal—if only mice did behave like this, the world would be a happier place. In fact, the humanity of the mice is contrasted with the inhuman people; few pleasant humans are shown, apart from the victims—children and poets regarded as friends to mice—who are rescued. The mice are cultivated and educated—the Chairwoman can quote Suckling—and appear to have read *Jane Eyre* and to understand the seriousness of parental deprivation. Miss Bianca's poem 'O flitting form, half-house half-bird' owes much to Wordsworth. Miss Bianca herself, Lady and Poetess, is a rounded character who grows with each story. She is described as silver-white with brown eyes (anyone who has owned a mouse of this colouring will agree that it represents the ultimate in mouse-beauty) but, in her porcelain pagoda in the Embassy, she is the pampered pet of the Ambassador's son. She is a Marie Antoinette who announces, with happy unconcern, that she 'dotes on cats' and seems quite ignorant of the outside world and its dangers; indeed, she faints with shock when asked to participate in the dangerous adventure of travelling in a diplomatic bag to permit a Norwegian mouse to rescue a poet. She sets out uncertainly

with her companions, Bernard (loyal but plebeian, 'a short sturdy young mouse . . . he looked rough but decent: no one was surprised to learn that he worked in the pantry') and Norwegian Nils (' "Not a family man, or anything of that sort?" "Not me," said Nils. Several of his friends round the bar roared with laughter'). But breeding tells, or Manners Makyth Mouse. Miss Bianca proves to have nerves and courage enough to inspire the rescue, save the lives of her companions and bring the poet home at last. Her courage and resource develop during the course of the stories. At first she makes mistakes: drawing a picture of a garden party hat instead of a chart, carrying 'only toilet articles and a fan' with her to the Black Castle, worrying about the class differences between herself and Bernard—she is attracted, but could she marry a pantry mouse? Her courage, like human courage, is often mixed with vanity. She does not mix with the fieldmice they meet on the journey, excusing their lack of manners by their evident lack of opportunity to observe the best models, which the fieldmice overhear and resent: ' "No manners indeed!" they chorused. "The lady says we never learnt no manners! Hands up who goes to dancing class!" '

Though Miss Bianca braves the cat with courage amounting to foolhardiness she is not indifferent to discomfort and thunderstorms. Her poem 'Black as the Castle press my mournful thoughts' is as romantic as *Childe Harold*. Bernard's greatest feat is scaling the body and face of a sleeping gaoler; he functions on a lower plane. Miss Bianca never manages to bridge the class gulf. 'Fond as she was of Bernard and much as she admired him, their backgrounds were too different for them ever to be more to each other than they were now.' Her relationship with Bernard remains platonic and is a strong theme in later books: for ever will he love, and she be fair. Miss Bianca becomes, in fact, a kind of Virgin Queen, exquisite and unattainable. (Afterwards, Bernard graduates from the pantry to a bachelor flat in a cigar cabinet, but it is no use; he is one of nature's doormats. Even Miss Sharp admits that, though of sterling worth, he lacks personality.)

Miss Bianca's courage and achievements grow with each book; in the second, she thinks nothing of attempting the conquest of the Diamond Castle alone, save for the doubtful help of the Ladies' Guild, who are soon routed. She is often in desperate straits and always the faithful Bernard is there to help. On later journeys—to the Salt Mines for instance—she is better prepared for travelling. Daring and fearless, she is also the mistress of perfect tact and diplomacy, never saying a hurtful word or permitting her feelings to overcome her. She restrains tears lest their effect should give her an unfair advantage, her exquisite manners enabling her to enlist the services of a colony of bats, a pair of bloodhounds and a racehorse. She is always careful of her appearance, grooming her fur and polishing her silver chain (her only adornment, apart from a lace fascinator worn on a river outing), knowing in her feminine heart that to look beautiful is a help towards feeling courageous. In short, Miss Bianca is a perfect gentlewoman. Her handling of the famous—and perhaps touchy and sensitive racehorse Sir Hector, in *The Turret*—is a model of polite conversation. Conquering her doubts about the etiquette of visiting a single horse in his quarters, Miss Bianca—offering her almost invisible visiting card—talks about fame. Sir Hector replies, and they continue with delicately Japanese self-deprecation, apologising for the inability of each to offer a chair to the other with the perfect good manners of natural, and trained, courtesy. They end with quotations from Cervantes and Bacon.

The French Ambassador was heard to say of Miss Bianca, as she bowed gracefully among the wine glasses on the dinner table: '*Je n'ai jamais rien vu de plus joli.*' She is a Queen among mice, as unforgettable as [C. S. Lewis's] Reepicheep (perhaps the only mouse worthy of her hand? But Reepicheep is somehow as celibate as she is virginal; and that is part of the charm of both.)

Garth Williams—the Rembrandt of animal portrait artists—shows very mouselike mice, quite different from his portrayal of Stuart Little, or Templeton from *Charlotte's Web*. The character of each individual is beautifully evident. . . . He draws no clothes, apart from occasional hats. They are not necessary—neither author nor artist needs them for characterising—not mice like humans, but intelligent mice. (pp. 163-69)

> Margaret Blount, "Lilliputian Life: The Mouse Story," in her Animal Land: The Creatures of Children's Fiction, William Morrow & Company, Inc., 1975, pp. 152-69.

Sam Leaton Sebesta and William J. Iverson

Of all mouse characters, Margery Sharp's Miss Bianca is the most distinguished. . . . [This] white-furred, brown-eyed pet of the ambassador's son earns immortality as Perpetual Madam President of the Mouse Prisoners' Aid Society. Accompanied by the gallant but very ordinary mouse Bernard, she saves human prisoners—a poet, a little girl, Teddy-Age-Eight—from horribly dangerous villains and captivities. Her remarkable physical courage is matched by her refinement, her ability to speak with conviction to mouse and human worlds alike, and her talent as a poet. The writing style in these books is complex. The sentences include many subordinate clauses and parenthetical statements. Some good readers are able to manage them, but others will enjoy the stories only if they are read aloud. (p. 203)

> Sam Leaton Sebesta and William J. Iverson, "Fanciful Fiction," in their Literature for Thursday's Child, Science Research Associates, Inc., 1975, pp. 177-214.

Zena Sutherland and May Hill Arbuthnot

Most of the fantasy tales about animals are humorous, as are Margery Sharp's **Miss Bianca** stories. Miss Bianca is the most genteel of mice, but her courage is unbounded. With her faithful (but quite ordinary) admirer, Bernard, she embarks on adventures as lurid and melodramatic as those of any detective story, but she is always calm, always completely in charge of the situation. (p. 248)

> Zena Sutherland and May Hill Arbuthnot, "Modern Stories of Talking Beasts," in their Children and Books, seventh edition, Scott, Foresman and Company, 1986, pp. 244-48.

TITLE COMMENTARY

The Rescuers   (1959)

This is Margery Sharp's first book for children and it is a highly successful one. She has chosen a fresh and original theme and handles this rich imaginative picture with both delicacy, spontaneity and boldness. "The Prisoner's Aid Society"—an association of mice dedicated to the helping and freeing of prisoners—delegates the difficult and dangerous task of freeing a Norwegian poet imprisoned in the Black Castle, a notorious and terrible prison, to three mice, Miss Bianca a refined pet mouse, Bernard a humble pantry mouse, and Nils a Norwegian seafaring mouse. These three contrasting types, after initial meetings, negotiations and preparations, set out on their hazardous assignment and all three return as heroes and heroine of the hour and winners of special orders of merit. Miss Sharp has lavished individual attention upon each of these main characters so that each is a highly individual and very real person. At times the precociousness and refinement of the aristocratic Miss Bianca threaten to swamp the other two and colour the whole book but her affectation is a good natured one and is soon tempered by the outside world into which she ventures and by the rough but kindly natures of the other two animals. Thus the three make a varied but well balanced picture. There is gaiety and good humour here in spite of grim adventure and hazards. Miss Sharp has something of the poet in her—the poet of the traditional animal or fairy story, and here gives us a tale that has that classical quality. (pp. 295-96)

> A review of "The Rescuers," in The Junior Bookshelf, Vol. 33, No. 5, November, 1959, pp. 295-96.

Readers of Grimm know that Well-Begun is Half-Done, and readers of Margery Sharp are fully aware that, once she has begun to spin a yarn, there is no stopping her or pausing for sober reflection until a triumphant ending is reached, to the satisfaction of all concerned. How she does it is very often nobody's business, but the fact remains that unless you are completely immune to charm and unwilling to go along with care-free fantasy, you will find this little book as beguiling as any she has written.

Possibly the story has some hidden meanings, less savagely satirical than are found in Gulliver's adventures in Lilliput, less starkly mysterious than those suggested by *The Wind in the Willows,* but it is equally likely to be seized by any member of the family who reads, wants to be read to or be shown Garth Williams' drawings of these intrepid mice.

There is quite a considerable body of mouse literature for the serious student of comparative anatomy, and this work should take an honorable place on the shelves. But do not be surprised if it is seldom to be found where you last saw it. Miss Bianca is a veritable minx of a mouse, and there is very little hope of keeping her where she does not wish to be. I predict that any household she invades is likely to echo to the cry, "Where is my copy of **The Rescuers** now?"

> Aileen Pippett, "A Veritable Minx of a

Mouse," in The New York Times Book Review, *November 29, 1959, p. 60.*

The Rescuers is an entertaining fantasy by an expert writer of popular *adult* fiction; she now transfers her brisk romantic skills to eight or nine-year-old level. This is neatly done: the characters are principally mice. . . . Mindful of her audience, the author does not fall into sentimental traps; comedy prevails throughout.

> *"The Wisher and the Wish," in* The Times Literary Supplement, *No. 3014, December 4, 1959, p. xv.*

The hand that Margery Sharp has now turned to fantasy is notably deft, as might be expected from the author of a long line of expert and entertaining novels.

[The] little band that eventually sets out to penetrate the Black Castle is suitably resolute. Miss Bianca, a beautiful and hitherto pampered young white mouse, feels a special sympathy for the prisoner because she herself is given to scribbling verses; Bernard, a sturdy pantry mouse, has already been decorated for gallantry in face of cats; and Nils, a seafaring, diamond-in-the-rough mouse from Norway, will of course be able to address the poet in his own tongue. In the end, these three accomplish their mission, though not before they have encountered a number of almost insurmountable obstacles and had several close brushes with death, notably at the paws and jaws of Mamelouk, the Black Castle cat, who has a coat like a thundercloud and eyes like dirty emeralds.

Perils beset the writing of such a work, but Miss Sharp accomplishes her mission, too. She has no trouble in persuading us to suspend belief; her mice, despite their human characteristics, remain intrinsically mouselike, and are engaging individuals as well; the pitfalls of archness on the one hand or pretentious symbolism on the other are nimbly avoided. We read with delight, and even with excitement, a good tale told for its own sake.

It should be added that in Garth Williams **The Rescuers** is blessed with a perfect illustrator. Pictures and text combine to make one of those very special books, not specifically for adults or for children either, that should appeal to the imaginative of almost any age.

> *Dan Wickenden, "A Fantasy by Margery Sharp," in* New York Herald Tribune Book Review, *December 27, 1959, p. 9.*

A fantasy that may prove as enduring as it is endearing, with gentle satire that can be enjoyed by adult readers and with pace and humor for younger readers or listeners. . . . [The mice's] heroic venture is delightfully detailed. . . .

> *A review of "The Rescuers," in* Bulletin of the Center for Children's Books, *Vol. XIII, No. 6, February, 1960, p. 105.*

Miss Bianca (1962)

Miss Sharp should have resisted the temptation to write a sequel to **The Rescuers** for that was a *tour de force* which

had a very special quality of absurdity and satire which **Miss Bianca** fails to duplicate. One can scale down the extravagances of a super adventure story to mouse size and make it a vehicle of commentary on human foibles—and get away with it once. But when Miss Bianca, as chairman of the Mouse Prisoners' Aid Society, organizes the women members to rescue an orphan girl from the diamond castle of the great duchess—and gets left alone there—the analogies seem to break down of their own weight. Of course the rescue is ultimately achieved, a home found for the orphan child, Miss Bianca reunited with her rather dull gallant, and the deserting members allowed to get away with it all. But it is strictly on child level this time. A poor second. (pp. 712-13)

> *A review of "Miss Bianca," in* Virginia Kirkus' Service, *Vol. XXX, No. 15, August 1, 1962, pp. 712-13.*

[Miss Bianca] is not the kind of *femme fatale* to be easily forgotten—nor to have only one exploit to her credit. Here she is again, with her valiant friends and faithful adorer, Bernard, once more demonstrating what her biographer, Margery Sharp, so rightly calls her "taste for flamboyance in welfare work."

This time, the object of her solicitude is an orphan girl of 8 named Patience who has been kidnapped and is held in cruel bondage within the Diamond Palace of the ugliest of all Ugly Duchesses. . . .

How the valiant and resourceful creature got herself and Patience out of [a] jam and the subsequent dangers they encountered you must read for yourself, for only Margery Sharp has the secret of how to tell this kind of tale. She spreads the fantasy thick but does not let it cloy. Her invention never flags; her wit is neat, and her feeling for children and animals is genuine. She has the courage of her gaiety. Her book is a trifle, but it is delicious.

> *Aileen Pippett, "Lion-Hearted Rodent," in* The New York Times Book Review, *October 21, 1962, p. 56.*

The story has an ingenious and exciting fairy-tale plot, although the Grand Duchess' treatment of the child seems unnecessarily sadistic and unpleasant and the pursuit by two bloodhounds and their inhuman master, could be horrific for sensitive children. There are amusing episodes, but surely at times the humour is too sophisticated and satirical for children.

> *A review of "Miss Bianca," in* The Junior Bookshelf, *Vol. 26, No. 6, December, 1962, p. 313.*

[Margery Sharp] has the artistry to describe the world of the Prisoners' Aid Society so that the reader feels himself mouse-size and looks up to see men like trees walking. . . . The cross-country journey, the bloodhounds (so enormous and clumsy to our mouse-eyes), the farmer's sons in the Happy Valley, their faces full of coarse good-humour, are all described in a witty, high-spirited style, and brought to life also in drawings which emphasise the question of scale. With such intelligence and attention to detail, the story cannot but delight and convince.

Margery Fisher, in a review of "Miss Bianca,"
in Growing Point, *Vol. 1, No. 7, January,*
1963, p. 106.

The Turret (1963)

[Again] a chanson de geste extolling the virtue, charm, intelligence and guile of the incomparable white mouse, Miss Bianca. As are the preceding books, this is illustrated with delightful drawings [by Garth Williams]; as are the preceding books, this is written with a charm that is compounded of whimsy, humor, sentiment, sentimentality, and satire. The story-line is good enough, but it is of small import; it is the author's style that is enjoyable.

Zena Sutherland, in a review of "The Turret,"
in Bulletin of the Center for Children's Books,
Vol. XVII, No. 9, May, 1964, p. 146.

[*The Turret* is a] story that depends on style for its success—this and the fact that Margery Sharp has always been a compulsive story-teller. Miss Bianca the white mouse has just resigned the Presidency of the Prisoners' Aid Society (Ladies' Section), and partly to signalise this, partly from softness of heart, she undertakes to rescue the prisoner in the turret, who is no other than her old enemy Mandrake. The story is exciting as ever, beautifully told, and full of a humour essentially adult but limpid and gay.

Margery Fisher, in a review of "The Turret,"
in Growing Point, *Vol. 3, No. 4, October,*
1964, p. 379.

This is Miss Sharp's third book about that endearing mouse, Miss Bianca, and the activities of the Mouse Prisoners' Aid Society. Like its forerunners it is a charming book. To retain such a high standard is in itself an achievement, but the author seems to develop the characters of her principals with each story. (pp. 236-37)

The prose is so delicate and economical one could almost imagine this to be how Jane Austen would have written about mice.

Again it is suitable for a wide age group, though perhaps it is best read as the finale of a trilogy fully to appreciate its charm and delicacy. (p. 237)

A review of "The Turret," in The Junior Bookshelf, *Vol. 28, No. 4, October, 1964, pp. 236-37.*

Lost at the Fair (1965)

A boy goes to the fair with his smaller sister in tow; he describes the sights of the fair, he loses his sister and finds her in the tent of the wizard of whom they are both frightened. That night the boy gets praise and cake from Mother, because he looked after his sister and the dog. There is some interest in the gay background, but the busy illustrations [by Rosalind Fry] lessen this appeal; the writing style in this easy-to-read book is dull and stilted: "Let's ask the Fat Lady. Maybe she saw Sue. She was a kind Fat Lady, a very kind Fat Lady. She was very sad to hear I had lost my sister Sue." (pp. 169-70)

Zena Sutherland, in a review of "Lost at the Fair," in Bulletin of the Center for Children's Books, *Vol. XVIII, No. 11, July-August, 1965, pp. 169-70.*

The idea of this story is appealing, but much is lost in the telling. Vocabulary is on first-grade level, but poorly constructed sentences, e.g. "I and my sister, my sister Sue, and our good dog Danny, all went to the Fair," and sentences which continue from one page to another are confusing to beginning readers. Also, the idea of the wizard changing a child or a dog into a rabbit (expressed both in words and pictures) may prove frightening to young readers. Not recommended.

Hope H. McGrady, in a review of "Lost at the Fair," in School Library Journal, *Vol. 12, No. 1, September, 1965, p. 2881.*

Lovers of this author's "Miss Bianca" stories might well be disappointed in this story. It is for younger readers and has very little plot or originality in it. One child gets lost at the fair. her brother looks for her, and finds her. The wording is very repetitive which would be alright if this book were suitable for children to read for themselves but the vocabulary is too complicated for the youngest do-it-yourself-readers, and the plot much too slight for the slightly older ones. The characters are dull and one gets no atmosphere of the fair. (pp. 40-1)

A review of "Lost at the Fair," in The Junior Bookshelf, *Vol. 32, No. 1, February, 1968, pp. 40-1.*

Miss Bianca in the Salt Mines (1966)

Miss Bianca in the Salt Mines carries on the great tradition of its predecessors; it is well constructed, daintily pieced together, devastatingly satirical and totally diverting for readers of a wide variety of ages. The rescue of Teddy-Age-Eight from the salt mines is a desperate adventure which takes all the heroine's inflexible feminine drive ("You men are altogether too clever for me"), since two new characters, obstructionist old mouse professors, are added to the team of rescuers.

"One Foot on the Ground," in The Times Literary Supplement, *No. 3378, November 24, 1966, p. 1087.*

While the present story is more adult in tone and, possibly, in interest than **The rescuers** and its two sequels, Miss Bianca has lost none of her charm as an elegant, intrepid mouse heroine and Garth Williams' drawings are as delightfully right as ever. May be most enjoyed when read aloud.

A review of "Miss Bianca in the Salt Mines," in The Booklist and Subscription Books Bulletin, *Vol. 63, No. 8, December 15, 1966, p. 453.*

You really have to write awfully well not to be cloying about a dainty little white mouse who writes poetry, chairs meetings, inspires love in every murine breast, and courageously leads an expedition to a salt mine to rescue an eight-year-old boy who is being held prisoner. Margery Sharp writes with charm, verve, just enough whimsy to be beguiling and just enough acerbity to be funny. Bianca and her three escorts effect the release of the prisoner through no miracles, but a series of determined or intelligent decisions. Our old friend Bernard is a stalwart, but the two elderly professors who have insisted on coming along have about the same function as stage comedians. They are fun, they give the author a chance to take pokes at academic life, and they double the opportunities for Garth Williams to be funny and enchanting at the same time.

> *Zena Sutherland, in a review of "Miss Bianca in the Salt Mines," in* Bulletin of the Center for Children's Books, *Vol. 20, No. 9, May, 1967, p. 146.*

Miss Bianca in the Orient (1970)

The toughest Tom cat has been known to melt into a puddle of delight when faced with one of Margery Sharp's endearing little tales about Miss Bianca, beautiful and brave white mouse. . . . [This] latest in the adventures of the Mouse Prisoners' Aid Society is a charmer, with just the right amount of wit and whimsy. . . .

> *A review of "Miss Bianca in the Orient," in* Publishers Weekly, *Vol. 197, No. 22, June 1, 1970, p. 63.*

When last seen Miss Bianca, that dear little mouse, was in the *Salt Mines* from which she should never have emerged. Now, her whiskers pomaded and her tail coiffured, she flies to the Orient to the court of a Ranee; gives recitals (consisting of "Le Camembert") on the harp; and teaches courage by confronting and rebuking the elephants. . . . Micro-droppings of beneficent whimsy in a flowered chamberpot.

> *A review of "Miss Bianca in the Orient," in* Kirkus Reviews, *Vol. XXXVIII, No. 11, July 1, 1970, p. 623.*

Miss Bianca in the Orient describes the fifth rescue undertaken by the beautiful President of the Mouse Prisoners' Aid Society, who once more has the help of devoted Bernard. The problem is to snatch away an orphaned page-boy from the Ranee's palace before by her orders he is trampled by one of the royal elephants. With a witty side-glance at the long association of elephant and mouse in fable, the author provides a splendidly logical climax to a story which abounds in decorative detail and some lively subordinate characters; the vain peacock is perhaps the most entertaining, the deluded elephant Hathi the most congenial and the Ranee makes a fine traditional villain. Sophistication and pure fun meet in a unique combination in these books and the new addition to the series is as fresh, spry and witty as the rest. (pp. 1638-39)

> *Margery Fisher, in a review of "Miss Bianca in the Orient," in* Growing Point, *Vol. 9, No. 6, December, 1970, pp. 1638-39.*

Book number five in the Miss Bianca series will delight her fans. They will discover that Miss Bianca is quite at home in a romantic world of luxurious costumes, lush tropical surroundings, and mysterious occult events. (p. 666)

This whimsical adventure concerns an imperious Ranee who holds the power of life and death over her subjects, two of whom Miss Bianca is determined to rescue from death. Of course the rescue is accomplished, but the method of rescue is the excitement of **Miss Bianca in the Orient.**

Readers who enjoy this form of whimsy will be delighted by Margery Sharp's new novel. Miss Bianca is as charming as ever. . . . **Miss Bianca in the Orient** is a particularly pleasant escape from the real world and its ever-present pressures. (p. 667)

> *John W. Conner, in a review of "Miss Bianca in the Orient," in* English Journal, *Vol. 60, No. 5, May, 1971, pp. 666-67.*

Miss Bianca in the Antarctic (1970)

The indomitable little white mouse, Miss Bianca, and her ever-faithful friend, Bernard, have retired from active duty with the Mouse Prisoners' Aid Society. Far from sliding gently into old age, however, they are almost immediately plunged into a new adventure that requires their own desperate rescue from the freezing Antarctic. Margery Sharp continues to tell these whimsical little animal tales with imagination, wit and genuine charm. She never slides over the narrow line between acceptable fantasy and the embarrassingly icky. . . .

> *A review of "Miss Bianca in the Antarctic," in* Publishers Weekly, *Vol. 200, No. 6, August 9, 1971, p. 39.*

Miss Bianca, an ever resourceful character, retires from the Mouse Prisoners Aid Society (M.P.A.S.) at the start of this book but needless to say her retirement is short-lived. Together with Bernard, with whom I felt a certain empathy in that his achievements are doomed for ever to be overshadowed by those of Miss Bianca herself, she goes to the Antarctic to rescue a stranded person. (p. 192)

The characters all exist in their own right and the world created is an extremely credible one, assisted by the delightful minutiae which the author supplies concerning the more humdrum problems of life.

I can never help but admire Miss Bianca's own lack of modesty and the numerous occasions on which she quietly finds it necessary to correct other people's *faux pas.*

Margery Sharp has created a fantasy society whose problems and pleasures are an excellent comment on our own, the lively style and satirical wit that she employs to do this make this a story that may be read and enjoyed by both children and adults alike at different levels. (pp. 192-93)

> *Vivien Jennings, in a review of "Miss Bianca in the Antarctic," in* Children's Book Review, *Vol. I, No. 6, December, 1971, pp. 192-93.*

Margery Sharp's enterprising mice adapt cheerfully to the most unpromising habitats. **Miss Bianca in the Antarctic** shows the author's customary joyous disregard of fact; she even introduces a polar bear and her cub in the interests of her fiction, explaining that they are on an exchange visit with seals. Miss Bianca and Bernard have in fact retired from active participation in the Mouse Rescue Society when they learn that the poet they once extricated from the Black Tower has now carelessly allowed himself to be left behind on the Antarctic ice-cap. Memorial wreaths and a volume of Shakespeare's plays provide the means of retrieval and survival for the heroic mice, and a mischievous polar bear cub and an Emperor penguin with delusions of grandeur constitute danger. Once more Margery Sharp has concocted an ingenious cliff-hanger that wittily parodies many an adult adventure story. I hope this book indicates that real retirement is far from Miss Bianca's mind.

> *Margery Fisher, in a review of "Miss Bianca in the Antarctic," in* Growing Point, *Vol. 10, No. 8, March, 1972, p. 1890.*

Miss Bianca and the Bridesmaid (1972)

At the Embassy the niece of the Ambassadress is preparing for her wedding when suddenly the bridesmaid, little Susan, vanishes completely. A conversation with the dolls in the Embassy collection leads Miss Bianca to believe that Susan has been kidnapped by Dowdy the wooden doll in revenge for her life of hard knocks, and the courageous poetess, with faithful Bernard, sets out along the Main Sewer in search of the child. Margery Sharp's inventiveness is endless and she has done nothing more spontaneously and wryly comic than the meeting of the mice with a group of angels demoted from churchyard to crypt and consoling themselves with sacred music. As always, fun and feeling judiciously mixed. . . . (p. 2042)

> *Margery Fisher, in a review of "Miss Bianca and the Bridesmaid," in* Growing Point, *Vol. 11, No. 5, November, 1972, pp. 2041-42.*

In what she describes as the "last"—can she really mean this?—of her tales of Bernard and Miss Bianca, Margery Sharp tells of another adventure of the Mouse Prisoners' Aid Society. Not in fact the most successful of Miss Bianca's enterprises. She and the faithful—if not quite top-drawer—Bernard pursue a wild mouse chase along the Main Drain, exhibiting their customary courage, persistence and—at least on Miss Bianca's part—sang froid; but the missing Susan, lost or stolen on the even of the wedding in which she is due to play a vital if secondary part, really finds herself.

Highly as Miss Sharp regards her exquisite small heroine, these stories are a delightful by-product of her talents. She tells the tales with elegance and formality, savouring the fine incongruity of such balanced periods proceeding from the tongue of a house-mouse, but the reader, while surrendering willingly to the enchantment, can never be quite unaware of an artifice of a kind which does not belong to the finest writing for children. Miss Sharp pleases herself, as all the best writers do, but in her delight in her own invention there is, perhaps, a touch of self-indulgence.

It is unnecessary, not to say ungenerous, to use the sledge-hammer of criticism to crack so elegant and fragile a nut of a mouse. Whatever flaws of judgment or interpretation the Miss Bianca tales may reveal, they show also the precious quality of style, a quality shared richly by Erik Blegvad's illustrations which so happily blend tenderness and satire.

> *"Of Mice and Rats," in* The Times Literary Supplement, *No. 3687, November 3, 1972, p. 1317.*

The author has a rare gift for creating truly funny, highly improbable situations in the most ordinary of places. She ennobles her heroine with such great character that even when she is committing the most outrageous deeds (from which the faithful Bernard will surely rescue her) one cannot fail to love her. There is great style and gaiety in the writings, and they have an elan and finesse that makes the book one not to be missed, not least for the line drawings by Erik Blegvad.

> *J. Russell, in a review of "Miss Bianca and the Bridesmaid," in* The Junior Bookshelf, *Vol. 36, No. 6, December, 1972, p. 389.*

The Magical Cockatoo (1974)

Margery Sharp has such a reputation that it seems sad to diminish it by **The Magical Cockatoo**. A turn-of-the-century little girl lives dully in an elderly household until she makes friends with her grandmother's porcelain cockatoo. Animated by moonlight, he suggests adventures to her, which end in her nobly assisting in a counter-revolutionary plot in the Buchan style. The elegance of the writing and of the production cannot disguise final failure.

> *A review of "The Magical Cockatoo," in* The Times Literary Supplement, *No. 3774, July 5, 1974, p. 715.*

The cockatoo was of Limoges porcelain (1760), and it hung on a gold hoop in Lally's grandmother's drawing-room in Edwardian London. Lally had dared herself to come downstairs at midnight—life was dull while her brother, who used to exchange dares with her, was away at school. On moonlight nights, however, the cockatoo could both speak and fly (though the uncertain English weather led to difficulties in this matter). It was a haughty bird, who spent much time meditating on the causes and consequences of the French Revolution, and it suggested to Lally a new type of dare, such as getting herself accepted for the adult First Aid classes and befriending the lame retired ambassador next door. The old man educates her taste by his wonderful collection of curios and her palate with gourmet food, and precipitates her into a dangerous Ruritanian venture to restore a rightful heir, because a child could pass unsuspected through London back-streets. She has been enabled to explore these through the uncongenial visits to the First Aid class, which also allow her to become the heroine of what, but for her, might have been a fatal accident. The cockatoo is unimpressed by her adventures (he has heard them already from the gossiping sparrows), but her brother, despite his now lofty position, is full of admiration. Margery Sharp's style, as one would expect, is delightfully readable and rhythmical, full of sly comments on adult behaviour. There are plenty of jokes for young readers or listeners too, of course, and Faith Jaques' line-drawings will give deep pleasure to all ages.

M. Hobbs, in a review of "The Magical Cocka-
too," in The Junior Bookshelf, *Vol. 38, No. 4,*
August, 1974, p. 238.

The Children Next Door   (1974)

[*The Children Next Door*] is a story hung on one peg—understanding. Colin and Janet, lonely in a tower block after living in a village where there are plenty of playmates, invent friends picturesquely named Gloria and Ronald, while Thomas, their six-year-old brother, imagines for himself a twin who keeps hamsters. By the time they have thoroughly confused Cousin Agnes, who housekeeps for their widower father, and have disposed of the health foods that she sends from her shop to entertain their "friends" at tea, they are glad to abandon these elusive children for the sake of a boy and girl from Australia who come to live with their grandmother in the next flat. The point is a nice one but the story, with its fairy-tale dénouement, has a flimsy grasp on the reality of either character or circumstance, and the usual effervescence of Margery Sharp's humour is unhappily missing.

Margery Fisher, in a review of "The Children
Next Door," in Growing Point, *Vol. 13, No. 6,*
December, 1974, p. 2522.

Bernard the Brave   (1976)

Miss Bianca's part is small in **Bernard the Brave** but to him her admiration when she learns of his solo enterprise in rescuing Miss Thomasina from bandits is the only reward he values. Even then he resists the temptation to accept her impetuous and uncharacteristic invitation to share the Porcelain Pagoda with her "though we can never be more than best, best friends"; no doubt even Bernard's devotion would not survive the loss of his simple bachelor life in the cigar-cabinet. In this new adventure, in which he gets the kidnapped heiress back to the law courts just in time to foil the plot of her wicked uncle, he has a new ally, Algernon the teddy bear. This endearing toy seems at first, with his lisp and inadequate stuffing, a somewhat poor substitute for Miss Bianca, but events prove that his courage equals hers, if his looks do not. Light-hearted parody of some of the stock situations of melodrama keeps this balloon of a tale in the air, and Bernard, so often eclipsed by Miss Bianca, comes into his own as a hero. There seem endless possibilities for the intrepid mice who are so racily drawn in Margery Sharp's incisive words and (in this latest story) in Faith Jaques's composed and expressive line.

Margery Fisher, in a review of "Bernard the
Brave," in Growing Point, *Vol. 15, No. 4, Oc-*
tober, 1976, p. 2967.

Devoted readers of the Miss Bianca stories—of whom there must now be a large number—may be disappointed

to find that their heroine does not play the leading part in this latest story, but, nevertheless, this account of the fabulous bravery of Bernard is a worthy successor to all the others, and Miss Bianca quietly, but very influentially, helps to bring about the rescue of Miss Thomasina which Bernard and his friend Algernon the teddy-bear are trying so hard to do. Those who appreciate the humour and witty phrase which we have come to expect from this author will find that these qualities are here in full measure.

B. Clark, in a review of "Bernard the Brave,"
in The Junior Bookshelf, *Vol. 40, No. 5, Octo-*
ber, 1976, p. 271.

Bernard the Brave is called "a Miss Bianca story", but in fact the elegant president (retired) of the Mouse Prisoners' Aid Society is offstage for most of the time. This is the tale of Bernard alone, doggedly furthering the good work of the MPAS while Miss Bianca is on holiday with the Boy.

The rescue which he carries out in her absence involves a missing heiress, a wicked guardian, and an eleventh-hour appearance to claim an inheritance, the very stuff of the adventure stories which Miss Sharp so wittily parodied earlier in the series.

The enormity of Bernard's undertaking is placed in perspective by his mouse-size difficulties—for example, how to get down to the ground floor without having to cope with stairs. But Bernard alone seems to me not quite as endearing as Bernard the faithful support of his adored Madam Chairwoman. He is a plodder, a bit dull out of his natural role of foil to Miss Bianca's sparkling wit and delicate perceptions. . . .

Like the other **"Miss Bianca"** adventures, it is full of adult humour and makes no concessions. The reader must not only not baulk at words such as nefarious, rebarbative, and midinette, but be able to relish them—they are a great part of the fun.

For the joke—and it is one that Faith Jaques has caught better than the previous illustrators, Erik Blegvad and Garth Williams—is that these large, genteelly conducted and stylishly carried off affairs are, after all, the affairs only of mice.

Jennifer Chandler, "Of Mice and Guinea-
pigs," in The Times Literary Supplement, *No.*
3890, October 1, 1976, p. 1248.

Bernard into Battle   (1979)

Like earlier stories about Miss Bianca, the beautiful white mouse who led so many of the death-defying forays of the Mouse Prisoners' Aid Society, and her stalwart admirer Bernard, this has a deliberately nonsensical plot (rats invade the ambassadorial premises while the family and staff are on holiday, and it is the loyal mice who—with help—repel them) told in a wonderfully suave and witty style. As always, the derring-do could be appreciated by younger readers were they able to appreciate the light and polished style that mocks the romantic adventure tale; while it's lightweight, the story can be enjoyed for the mock raptures and heroics that make it as elegant a spoof as feathery fiction can be.

Zena Sutherland, in a review of "Bernard into Battle: A Miss Bianca Story," in Bulletin of the Center for Children's Books, *Vol. 32, No. 7, March, 1979, p. 127.*

Miss Sharp tells the heroic story with her customary mannered elegance and strength. Miss Bianca plays a minor part this time, although she heartens her followers with a number of characteristic poems. This is Bernard's tale, and he shows that he can reinforce his undoubted reliability with a touch of panache. But, excellent as the narrative is, the important thing here, as always, is style. Nowhere in children's literature are the words themselves of more significance. The typography too is stylish and so are the decorations, by [Leslie Morrill,] an artist new to this series and one who stands up well to comparison with such formidable predecessors as Garth Williams and Erik Blegvad. (p. 330)

M. Crouch, in a review of "Bernard into Battle," in The Junior Bookshelf, *Vol. 43, No. 6, December, 1979, pp. 329-30.*

There seems little doubt that Margery Sharp enjoys the opportunities which her mouse-saga has given her, for satire, parody and sly comment. **Bernard into Battle** is estab-lished as mock-heroic long before the reference to Waterloo and reinforcements—by the poems with which Miss Bianca compensates for being kept out of the action, by the judicious grandiloquence of the language in which war is described. . . . The mock-epic strain is as entertaining as ever in this, the ninth instalment of the saga, and the circumstantial detail is as ingenious and appealing, from the lances and daggers contrived from the Ambassador's box of pen-nibs to the ancient Gorgonzola which temporarily routs the invaders and the disguise in which Bernard penetrates the enemy council to learn their plans:

> Uncommonly large for a mouse as he was—he weighed four and a half ounces—he could very well pass for a juvenile rat, except that his teeth weren't long and pointed enough. In the Scouts' dressing-up box however were a set of false ones made out of orange-peel for the use of the Demon King in their pantomimes, and these Miss Bianca carefully affixed over his own with the aid of chewing-gum.

Sequels can be dangerous but as regards Michael Bond and Margery Sharp, at least, there seems little cause for concern.

Margery Fisher, in a review of "Bernard into Battle," in Growing Point, *Vol. 18, No. 6, March, 1980, p. 3659.*

Ernest H(oward) Shepard

1879-1976

(Also worked as E. H. Shepard) English illustrator and author of nonfiction and fiction.

Major works include the illustrations for A. A. Milne's *When We Were Very Young* (1924), *Winnie-the-Pooh* (1926), *Now We Are Six* (1927), and *The House at Pooh Corner* (1928); Kenneth Grahame's *The Wind in the Willows* (1931); and the self-composed *Drawn from Memory* (1957) and *Drawn from Life* (1961).

The following entry emphasizes general criticism of Shepard's career. It also includes a selection of reviews to supplement the general commentary.

Called "the perfect illustrator" by critic Bevis Hillier, Shepard is considered among the greatest illustrators of the twentieth century as well as a major figure in the field of literature for children. Lauded as an especially gifted artist whose intimate, economical black-and-white line drawings, decorations, and silhouettes blend so completely with their texts that they become inseparable from one another, he is respected for his interpretive characterizations and sensitive understanding of children and childhood as well as for the technical skill, charm, expressiveness, vitality, accessibility, and humor of his art. Shepard is regarded as a prolific, consummately professional illustrator whose career ranged from the end of the Victorian age of illustration to the late twentieth century. Often compared to Sir John Tenniel, the illustrator of Lewis Carroll's "Alice" stories, Shepard is usually acknowledged as the most beloved English children's artist to have emerged since Tenniel. As an illustrator, Shepard contributed drawings to works by some of the most familiar names in both juvenile and adult literature, such as Frances Hodgson Burnett, Charles Dickens, Eleanor Farjeon, Laurence Houseman, Thomas Hughes, George MacDonald, Mary Louisa Molesworth, Samuel Pepys, and William Makepeace Thackeray. He is best known, however, for the illustrations he provided for the verses about Christopher Robin and the fantasies about Winnie-the-Pooh by A. A. Milne as well as for Kenneth Grahame's animal epic *The Wind in the Willows;* he is also highly regarded for his work in Richard Jefferies' *Bevis* (1932) and Hans Christian Andersen's *Fairy Tales* (1961). Reflecting superior draftsmanship, attention to detail, and a use of line that was clear and precise without being heavy, Shepard's pictures are praised for capturing the features, personalities, and moods of both children and anthropomorphic animals. Later in his career, Shepard added watercolor paintings to the Milne books and to *The Wind in the Willows,* but these are generally considered less successful than his original work in black and white; he also contributed illustrations in black and white and color to the many adaptations of and spinoffs from the four titles by Milne.

The son of architect Henry Donkin Shepard and Jessie Harriet Shepard, the daughter of watercolor painter Wil-

liam Lee, Shepard drew and painted since early childhood. By the age of twenty, he had won two major art scholarships for his work in oils, a medium in which he worked regularly after art school, and was contributing drawings to periodicals. By 1914, he had become a regular contributor to *Punch* magazine and was elected to its editorial board in 1921; Shepard's association with *Punch* lasted fifty years, a time during which he attained the positions of second cartoonist and principal cartoonist. In 1924, he became a regular exhibitor at London's Royal Academy and began his collaboration with A. A. Milne, who was also a member of the *Punch* round table. Shepard and Milne were introduced through E. V. Lucas, the *Punch* editor who was also an author and chairman of the book publisher Methuen; later, Shepard provided the illustrations for two of Lucas's works. Although Milne initially disliked Shepard's art, he realized that Shepard was the perfect illustrator for the verses and stories about his small son and his toys. Working from the original models, from his son Graham and his teddy bear Growler, and from the settings around Milne's homes in London and Sussex, Shepard created illustrations that are acknowledged as essential to the success of Milne's works for children; the *New York Times Book Review* notes that "Mr. Milne should go down on his knees every night and thank God for having sent him an illustrator so perfectly attuned to the spirit of his task as Mr. Shepard has proved himself to be." A verse written by Milne confirms this statement: "When I am gone / Let Shepard decorate my tomb / And put (if there is room) / Two pictures on the stone: / Piglet, from page a hundred and eleven / And Pooh and Piglet walking (157) . . . / And Peter, thinking that they are my own / Will welcome me to heaven." Shepard also had a positive professional relationship with Kenneth Grahame. Shepard had already successfully illustrated Grahame's autobiographical family stories *The Golden Age* (1928) and *Dream Days* (1930) when he met with the author to discuss his approach for Grahame's greatest work *The Wind in the Willows.* At Grahame's direction, Shepard explored the countryside and riverbanks around Grahame's home near Pangbourne; Shepard's illustrations not only pleased the author but are often considered definitive, the yardstick by which all subsequent art for *The Wind in the Willows* is measured. Shepard also illustrated Grahame's short stories *The Reluctant Dragon* (1938) and *Bertie's Escapade* (1945).

In 1957, Shepard began a new career as an author with the publication of the first of his two books of self-illustrated autobiographical reminiscence, *Drawn from Memory.* Describing his happy seventh year as well as the sights and sounds of Victorian London in smooth, affectionate prose, the profusely illustrated *Drawn from Memory* was followed four years later by *Drawn from Life,* which takes Shepard from the death of his mother at the age of ten through his marriage at the age of twenty-four. Shepard is also the author and illustrator of the fantasies *Ben and Brock* (1965) and *Betsy and Joe* (1966), works for primary graders which draw on the relationships between children, adults, and talking animals and are noted for their influences from the works Shepard illustrated by Grahame and Milne. Shepard received the University of Southern Mississippi Medallion in 1970 for his contributions to children's literature and the Order of the British Empire in 1972 for his contributions to art. On his ninetieth birthday, Shepard was honored with an exhibition by London's Victoria and Albert Museum, which currently houses his drawings and sketches for the Milne books.

(See also *Something about the Author,* Vols. 3, 24, 33; *Contemporary Authors New Revision Series,* Vol. 23; and *Contemporary Authors,* Vols. 9-10, rev. ed., and Vols. 65-68 [obituary]).

ILLUSTRATOR'S COMMENTARY

"There are certain books that should never be illustrated" is true in many senses, and I had felt that **The Wind in the Willows** was one of these. Perhaps if it had not already been done, I should not have given way to the desire to do it myself, but it so happened that when the opportunity was offered me, I seized upon it gladly.

The characters that Kenneth Grahame chose for his story—the little animals from the woods, the fields, and the waters of England—and which he portrayed with such sympathy and understanding showed, to me, how clearly he had seen into the mind of a child. Indeed, they had grown from the letters and stories he used to write from time to time to amuse his own child.

Mother Earth has a lot to offer to those who try to understand her and to know the ways of the little people who live, who burrow, who scratch, and store, and who climb and swim; whose short lives are spent in the hunt for a livelihood, be it worms or beetles, nuts or fish. Like us human folk they are forever busy—Mole, the field worker, the digger; Rat, the perfect waterman, wise about currents, eddies and what not; Badger, big and stout, uncouth but oh! how dependable, a champion of the smaller folk; and Toad, the impossible and lovable, never out of a scrape and never ceasing to boast. These are not caricatures, they are the real thing, brought to life by a man who loved them and all that they stand for, and it was he who told me where they lived and where to find them.

Kenneth Grahame was an old man when I went to see him. Not sure about this new illustrator of his book, he listened patiently while I told him what I hoped to do. Then he said, "I love these little people, be kind to them." Just that; but sitting forward in his chair, resting upon the arms, his fine handsome head turned aside, looking like some ancient Viking, warming, he told me of the river near by, of the meadows where Mole broke ground that spring morning, of the banks where Rat had his house, of the pools where Otter hid, and of Wild Wood way up on the hill above the river, a fearsome place but for the sanctuary of Badger's home and of Toad Hall. He would like, he said, to go with me to show me the river bank that he knew so well, " . . . but now I cannot walk so far and you must find your way alone."

So I left him and, guided by his instructions, I spent a happy autumn afternoon with my sketch book. It was easy to imagine it all, sitting by the river bank or following the wake of little bubbles that told me that Rat was not far away. Across the water lay the flat meadows and somewhere there I knew that Mole was, even now, making ready his bed for the winter, to wait for the first breath of spring—and again beyond, on the rising ground, the great expanse of Wild Wood with Badger laying in his winter stores. Toad, I imagined, would be snoring in postprandial ease in his armchair away down stream at Toad Hall. I poked and pried along the river bank to find where was Rat's boat house, and where Mole had crossed the water to join him, and, as I listened to the river noises, the little plops and ripples that mean so much to the small people, I could almost fancy that I could see a tiny boat pulled up among the reeds.

Dusk was settling, down on the water, with a rising mist, but, above, the late sun was shining on the wood—a faint afterglow of autumn glory, when I turned homewards, treading carefully just in case something was underfoot.

I was to meet Kenneth Grahame once again. I went to his home and was able to show him some of the results of my work. Though critical, he seemed pleased and, chuckling, said, "I'm glad you've made them real." We seemed to share a secret pleasure in knowing that the pictures were of the river spots where the little people lived.

This is the story that I can tell of how it came about that I was to play my part in helping to bring **The Wind in the Willows** a little nearer to the reader. If I had not met Kenneth Grahame I should never have had the temerity to embark on the work, but he gave me encouragement that no one else could have given me, and I wish that he could have lived to see the finished work, whatever his verdict would have been. (pp. 273-75)

> *Ernest H. Shepard, "Illustrating 'The Wind in the Willows',"* in Horn Book Reflections on Children's Books and Reading: Selected from Eighteen Years of the Horn Book Magazine, 1949-1966, *edited by Elinor Whitney Field, The Horn Book, 1969, pp. 273-75.*

The Bookman, London

We have only one fault to find with [**When We Were Very Young**], and that is that its pages are not so large as the pages of *Punch,* in which the poems and pictures originally appeared. Mr. Shepard's pictures are as much part of the fun as Mr. Milne's poems, and the present small size hardly does justice to the setting; for the pictures are not mere illustrations, but a sort of pictorial meadow through which the verses meander delightfully.

> *A review of "When We Were Very Young,"* in The Bookman, *London, Vol. 67, No. 399, December, 1924, p. 132.*

Helen Cady Forbes

[In **When We Were Very Young,** Ernest Shepard] looks at children with the understanding sympathy and sense of humor and a recollection of his own childhood that make it possible for him to take a fair share in making this book. Ernest Shepard, as well as Mr. Milne, shows that he loves the absurdities and extravagances so dear to children—

> . . . Sillies, I went and saw the Queen.
> She says my hands are purfickly clean!

> *Helen Cady Forbes, "Delicious Sillies,"* in New York Herald Tribune Books, *December 14, 1924, p. 6.*

Marcia Dalphin

[Those who have known and loved E. V. Lucas's] *A Book of Verses for Children, Anne's Terrible Good Nature,* and *The Slowcoach,* that fascinating story of a whole family of children who traveled around England in a caravan, will be delighted to find that in **Playtime and Company** Mr. Lucas has collected the verses he has written for children and that the inimitable Ernest Shepard has done scores and scores of delightful drawings for it. Mr. Lucas's children are very British. Their talk is of tuck and ices, of sweeps and poulterers, bullfinches and dormice. But Mr. Shepard's children, the picture children of **Playtime and Company** and **When We Were Very Young,** have nothing so limiting as a native country, they are at home anywhere. (p. 459)

> *Marcia Dalphin, "Christmas Cargoes by Rein-*

deer, Ltd.," in The Bookman, *New York, Vol. LXII, No. 4, December, 1925, pp. 457-63.*

The New York Times Book Review

[The poems in E. V. Lucas's **Playtime and Company**] are rollicking and genial rhymes about people and things in many lands, but mainly, of course, about those that touch the lives and thoughts of little English boys and girls. Mr. Shepard's drawings have the same qualities of charm, characterization and skill in the use of line that mark his illustrations of the Milne books. (p. 6)

> *"Children's Books in Christmas Array,"* in The New York Times Book Review, *December 6, 1925, pp. 6, 28.*

Anne Carroll Moore

Winnie-the-Pooh is full of drawings by the same clever pen that illustrated **When We Were Very Young,** and though it is ingratitude to bite the hand that has fed us so many quaint and lovable conceits, yet we venture the opinion that both books suffer from over-illustration. Still, how hard it would be to choose any to leave out! Certainly not that one of Pooh swarming up a huge tree, his proportions all inadequate, one short, plump leg braced against the trunk and all the rest of his stoutness flung desperately abroad over the limb, nor yet any of those delectable tree houses, in which for the first time we see realized to our satisfaction the dreams we got reading *Swiss Family Robinson.*

You have only to look at the picture of Pooh living "in the forest all by himself under the name of Sanders" to know that Mr. Shepard is in the authentic line of the good English illustrators of children's books. In childish script over the door is printed "Mr. Sanders," and true to the immemorial custom of all young letterers *the S turned backward.* By the bell-rope you read the inscription, "Rnig Also." As Pooh says to Owl in another connection, "It's good spelling, but it wobbles, and the letters get in the wrong places." It is only the real artists who, playing around in their own nice minds, take these infinite pains.

> *Anne Carroll Moore, "Mr. Shepard's Pictures,"* in New York Herald Tribune Books, *October 17, 1926, p. 8.*

The Bookman, London

Told in Mr. [A. A.] Milne's own particular way the story [of **Winnie-the-Pooh**] is delicious. The illustrations are by Ernest H. Shepard, who catches perfectly the author's whimsical fancies and expresses them in his pictures. "Winnie-the-Pooh" should be sure of a great welcome from every child and grown-up to whom he is introduced this Christmas.

> *A review of "Winnie-the-Pooh,"* in The Bookman, *London, Vol. 71, No. 423, December, 1926, p. 166.*

The New York Times Book Review

A. A. Milne's **Winnie-the-Pooh** is a wholly charming little tale written for and about and partly by that same small Christopher Robin who inspired the verses of **When We**

Were Very Young. . . . Ernest H. Shepard, who enhanced so much the charm of the previous book, does equal service for this with pictures and decorations that are alive with expression, vitality and humor. (p. 6)

> *"Christmas Books for Youthful Eyes," in* The New York Times Book Review, *December 5, 1926, pp. 6, 20.*

The New York Times Book Review

Not in many years had a volume of children's verse been welcomed as **When We Were Very Young** was welcomed; its buoyancy, its spontaneity, its rhyming that came as easily as breathing, its never self-conscious playfulness; quickly won for it a place among the books of its kind that really matter. **Now We Are Six,** though it may not—indeed, how could it?—have the same pristine freshness, is in every sense a worthy successor. The drawings by Mr. Shepard are as droll and as fetching as ever, and Mr. Milne should go down on his knees every night and thank God for having sent him an illustrator so perfectly attuned to the spirit of his task as Mr. Shepard has proved himself to be.

> *"Now That Christopher Robin Is Six," in* The New York Times Book Review, *October 23, 1927, p. 5.*

A. A. Milne

Mr. E. H. Shepard, of all people, needs no introduction at my hands. Anybody who has heard of me has certainly heard of Shepard. Indeed, our names have been associated on so many title pages that I am beginning to wonder which of us is which. Years ago when I used to write for the paper of whose staff he is now such a decorative member I was continually being asked by strangers if I also drew the cartoons. Sometimes I said "Yes." No doubt Mr. Shepard is often asked if he wrote **"The King's Breakfast."** I should be proud if he admitted now and then that he did.

I must confess that I am writing this Introduction a little self-consciously; feeling, no doubt, much as Mr. Elliott feels when asked to photograph Mr. Fry. We have a perfectly true story in our family that one of us was approached by an earnest woman at some special function with the words, "Oh, are you the brother of A. J. Milne—or am I thinking of Shepperson?" E. H. Shepard, though surely he owes something to that beautiful draughtsman, is not to be mistaken for Claude Shepperson, nor am I that other, to me unknown, from whom I have so lamentably failed to profit; but you see what she meant. You see also what I mean; and how I am hampered by the fear that somebody may read this Introduction, and feel that Mr. Shepard is not being very modest about himself. For if I let myself go, I could make him seem very immodest indeed.

Perhaps this will be a good place in which to tell the story of how I discovered him. It is short, but interesting. In

From The House at Pooh Corner, *written by A. A. Milne. Illustrated by Ernest H. Shepard.*

those early days before the war, when he was making his first tentative pictures for *Punch,* I used to say to F. H. Townsend, the Art Editor, on the occasion of each new Shepard drawing, "What on earth do you see in this man? He's perfectly hopeless," and Townsend would say complacently, "You wait." So I waited. That is the end of the story, which is shorter and less interesting than I thought it was going to be. For it looks now as if the discovery had been somebody else's. Were those early drawings included in this book, we should know definitely whether Townsend was a man of remarkable insight, or whether I was just an ordinary fool. In their absence we may assume fairly safely that he was something of the one, and I more than a little of the other. The Shepard you see here is the one for whom I waited; whom, in the end, even I could not fail to recognize.

Art is not life, but an exaggeration of it; life reinforced by the personality of the artist. A work of art is literally "too good to be true." That is why we shall never see Turner's sunsets in this world, nor meet Mr. Micawber. We only wish we could. But Life does its best to keep the artist in sight. Whether sunsets tried to be more Turneresque in the 'fifties I do not remember, but the du Maurier women came in stately procession well behind du Maurier, and banting youth toils after Shepperson in vain. Kensington Garden children are said to be the most beautiful in the world, but in a little while Shepard will make them more beautiful than ever. Bachelors remain bachelors because they are always just a little too late for the fair, their adoration having shifted with the years from the du Maurier girl to the Gibson girl, and from the Gibson girl to the Baumer girl, until bachelordom was a habit. But every mother prays simply for a little Shepard child, and leaves it to Mr. Shepard whether it is a boy or a girl. . . .

Which reminds me that, whether anybody else or not is liking this introduction, Mr. Shepard himself is beginning to feel anxious about it. However modest we are in public, in private we are never too modest for praise; but we do like to be praised for the right thing. Mr. Arnold Bennett will remain unmoved if you tell him that he knows all about the Five Towns, but he will blush delicately if you assure him that he knows all about Town. So with the rest of us. No artist but hates to be pinned in a groove like a dead and labelled butterfly, and none of the secular but loves so to pin him, feeling that thus, and only thus, is he safe. Not many of the pictures here are pictures of children, but I can imagine Mr. Shepard saying wearily, when their legends were sent to him for illustration, "Children again! But I can *do* children! Give me something I'm not so sure about, like the inside of a battleship or a Bargee's Saturday Night." (pp. 33-6)

My one regret is that there are still no bargees. Not because, as some dull people seem to think, only the slow, the insensitive and the unimaginative are proper subjects for a work of art, but because a Shepard bargee would so plainly be anything but slow, insensitive and unimaginative. He would not be tied to the heavy lorry-wheels of the realist, but would soar over the Tower Bridge on wings; and we should say sadly to ourselves, "If only bargees were really like that!"

And in a little while they would become more like that. (pp. 36-7)

A. A. Milne, "Introducing Shepard," in his By Way of Introduction, E. P. Dutton & Co., Inc., 1929, pp. 33-7.

Mary Ethel Nesmith

As one reads one after another of Mr. Milne's little poems, all teeming with cleverness and humor, one is fascinated with Mr. Shepard's interpretation of them through his irresistible little drawings. Certainly Mr. Milne has been fortunate in finding Mr. Shepard who seems to understand child life quite as well as does Mr. Milne himself. (p. 173)

Mary Ethel Nesmith, "The Children's Milne," in The Elementary English Review, Vol. IX, No. 7, September, 1932, pp. 172-73, 192.

May Hill Arbuthnot

Never was an author more happily paired with an artist than A. A. Milne with Ernest Shepard. The tiny pen-and-ink sketches capture the mood of every poem—Christopher Robin going hoppity, hoppity, hop; the banister-sliding King; and Mary Jane sulking over her rice pudding after kicking a disdainful shoe into the air. Indeed, you have only to glance at one of these tiny figures to know exactly what is happening inwardly as well as outwardly. In **"Halfway Down,"** the small figure is planted in a dreamy, meditative but solid pose that makes you feel just how hard it's going to be to dislodge him. **"Puppy and I"** skip joyously; and Christopher Robin, looking pained and surprised at the absence of rabbits, catechizes the men in **"Market Square."** Pooh is there, too, the same solid, jaunty teddy bear we shall meet later on in the Pooh stories. These are pen-and-ink sketches with a liveliness and a swift characterization that match the clever verses. There is action, too, of course, but it is the interpretative quality of these pictures that makes them illustrations in the best sense of the word. (pp. 94-5)

May Hill Arbuthnot, "Verses in the Gay Tradition: Ernest H. Shepard," in her Children and Books, Scott, Foresman and Company, 1947, pp. 94-5.

May Massee

Ernest Shepard has that same charming quality and gaiety and humor in his drawings for **When We Were Very Young** and the other Milne books [as W. Heath Robinson and Charles Robinson]. It is no wonder that the children love the Shepard drawings, for without being flattering they do show children with their best foot forward. And children like straightforward small drawings that have something to say and say it quietly but with real humor.

May Massee, "Developments of the Twentieth Century: 'When We Were Very Young',' in Illustrators of Children's Books 1744-1945, Bertha E. Mahony, Louise Payson Latimer, Beulah Folmsbee, eds., The Horn Book, Inc., 1947, p. 226.

Louise S. Bechtel

[We] are fortunate indeed to have [Kenneth Grahame's *Bertie's Escapade*] printed as a most delightful little separate children's book, with thirty-seven inimitable drawings by Mr. Shepard, every one of which we treasure. . . .

With the rarely amusing pictures, it becomes a "must" for the Christmas stockings of all who love this author and artist. This great company by now includes many ages. Age has nothing to do with the privilege of peeping in on a funny bad dream of Kenneth Grahame's, or loving a pig and two rabbits as drawn by Ernest Shepard.

Bertie's feast in the inner pigsty, his face as he proposes a toast to Mr. Grahame, Mrs. Mole waiting up with a candle for Mr. Mole—we didn't know how much we needed this at Christmas of 1949.

> *Louise S. Bechtel, "By Four Favorite Authors," in* New York Herald Tribune Book Review, *November 13, 1949, p. 7.*

Anne Carroll Moore

[*Bertie's Escapade*] is a lovely story of Bertie the Pig and his Christmas Eve adventure. Bertie's motto is "deeds not grunts" and the Shepard drawings live up to all his actions.

> *Anne Carroll Moore, in a review of "Bertie's Escapade," in* The Horn Book Magazine, *Vol. XXV, No. 6, November-December, 1949, p. 522.*

Louis Slobodkin

The chaos that whirls through contemporary art has even now fluttered a few pages in children's books. In the 1949-50 season there were drawings by the students of the great modern masters. Others were done in the styles (imitative and diluted) of the great modern masters. But there were no drawings by the modern masters themselves. Fortunately, we do have one book by a master draughtsman, Kenneth Grahame's *Bertie's Escapade* with its sparkling drawings by Ernest H. Shepard.

To my way of thinking (and I claim no originality for these thoughts) an illustration in a children's book should open windows in the pages of a book; it should serve to let in light. It should get beyond the surface of the paper and dig deep to create space—boundless space. It should raise (or suggest) full-bodied, luminous form. It should extend the lyric flow and unify the mood and emotional concept of the script. If it does not do these things, it is not an illustration for a children's book. It belongs in a book for adults.

I do not claim Shepard's drawings in *Bertie's Escapade* have all the elements I hope to see in illustrations. Rather he tends to achieve them. His style is built on years of solid development; it is completely woven into his consciousness. And although his style is built on long tradition, it is his own.

Shepard is a communicative artist. His drawing is not for the precious few; it is for the many. There is no attempt to distill line or form or space to its very essence. Pure gold needs some gross earthy alloy to give it body and substance. Perhaps it's because of this earthy alloy ever present in Shepard's art that I turn to his drawings with so much pleasure.

Is Shepard modern or old-fashioned? (Not that the children who love his work care—but just for argument's sake, "Is he?") The newest and very dewiest quality a piece of modern art should have, I have been told, must be a "humanistic quality."

Is there anything warmer or more "humanistic" than the drawing [of Bertie, Peter, and Benjie finding themselves propelled suddenly into Spring Lane in front of Mr. Stone's lodge]? . . . (p. 293)

Have you ever seen Donatello's large-bottomed infants tottering and rocking on their tiny feet? Or the dancing cherubs on the pulpit in Florence or the angels making music in Padua or that Cupid wearing pants in the Florence Museum?

This drawing of Bertie, Peter and Benjie made me think of them when I first saw it. It may seem pretty far-fetched to find the elements of Donatello in this little drawing. But aside from his handling of the masses of the main figures, look at the whirling indications on the wall that have so good a tone relation to the rest of the drawing. Mr. Donatello often used such devices in his reliefs. And another relation—there's nothing soft or sweety-sweet in Shepard's drawings of these stout-bottomed little beasts—there's nothing cuddlesome. Donatello rarely produced cuddlesome babies—even those who sat on the Madonnas' laps were real infants.

Donatello and Shepard in his own way preach crisp forminess. Now that we've already taken up Bertie and his friends and the way they stand in space on the snow,—what of the snow, the snow-sprinkled bushes, the knobby wall? Everything takes its place and function.

Getting all that to happen with only a pen is quite a performance. Do children appreciate such a technical feat? I believe they do, for I believe they will marvel as I do on how the snow can be so white and lie down on the ground the way it does. How can the air be so clear and cold, and the night so still, and how did Shepard do it all with just a few scratches and specks of black ink? (p. 295)

> *Louis Slobodkin, "Artist's Choice," in* The Horn Book Magazine, *Vol. XXVI, No. 4, July-August, 1950, pp. 293-95.*

Frank Eyre

The [contemporary] period has been notable for a general raising of the standard of illustration rather than for outstanding individual work (with the possible exception of Mervyn Peake). The illustrator who has given most pleasure is undoubtedly Ernest H. Shepard, whose delightful line drawings for *The Wind in the Willows* and A. A. Milne's books are as inimitable as the work of Tenniel. It is lamentable that in many recent editions of his work the reproduction is so poor that much of their delicacy is lost. (pp. 37-8)

> *Frank Eyre, "Books with Pictures: 'The Wind in the Willows'," in his* 20th Century Chil-

dren's Books, *Longmans, Green and Co.,
1952, pp. 37-8.*

Polly Goodwin

In [Eleanor Farjeon's **The Silver Curlew,**] a new version
of the old story of Rumpelstiltskin, a well loved English
story teller and poet spins a fanciful fairy tale about the
beautiful but lazy miller's daughter who married the king
of Norfolk under false pretenses, fell under the evil spell
of a black imp, and was magically saved for the traditional
happy ending. The Shepard drawings, in perfect tune with
the book's rich drollery, are all one could wish for.

> *Polly Goodwin, in a review of "The Silver Cur-
> lew," in* Chicago Tribune—Books, *September
> 5, 1954, p. 6.*

Sir John Squire

Men frequently give us reminiscences of their boyhood,
and sometimes they are mistaken in their belief that prolonged descriptions of governesses, gardeners and prepa-
ratory school masters will prove as interesting to their
readers as they are to themselves. Memories of early childhood are much rarer, especially very vivid ones. For that
reason alone Mr. Shepard's happily-named book [**Drawn
from Memory**] would be one of the most notable of its
kind since Mr. Siegfried Sassoon's "The Old Century" and
Sir Laurence Jones's "A Victorian Childhood"—both of
which, however, carried their narrators into riper years
than Mr. Shepard's, who, born in or about 1880, confines
himself to the 'eighties of the last century.

Mr. Shepard has the rare advantage of being able to illustrate his own book, with the accompanying certainty that
the illustrations will fit the text as the hand fits the glove.
That the illustrations . . . would be found delightful, even
were they not embedded in a text at all, needs scarcely to
be said in a country where multitudes of children have
loved his illustrations to books by Kenneth Grahame and
A. A. Milne, and their elders have, for fifty years, encountered his drawings weekly in *Punch,* with never-failing
pleasure. As it is, the book is all of a piece in quality and
mood. Mr. Shepard, throughout his life, seems to have
been all of a piece too.

Mr. Shepard has retained the finest attributes of childhood
into his late seventies: he has never lost touch with his
early sensibilities and responses. The man retains the
child: the child also foreshadowed the man. There was environment, of course, and heredity. His father was an architect, his mother's father was a water-colour painter,
their circle of friends was drawn from the extremely cultivated society of St. John's Wood in those days. But this
child was a genius in the way of draughtsmanship. . . .
[When] barely of age he was exhibiting at the Royal Academy.

This is a difficult book to write about, simply because the
pictures are as important as the text, and because the days
of which Mr. Shepard writes are "far away and long ago."
Readers of different generations are bound to view it from
different angles. Septuagenarians and young octogenari-
ans will exclaim to themselves throughout their perusal:
"Oh, yes, I remember the lamplighters, the muffin-men

with their bells, the hansom-cabs, the linkboys in the fogs
and the ladies' bustles: how it all comes back to me!" Their
juniors will probably think: "How odd! I can hardly imagine what it must have been like. It's as remote as the Regency!"

Not so remote to me. I can remember Queen Victoria's
first Jubilee, but not in such detail as Mr. Shepard. . . .

Amongst many reasons why I am glad to have survived
is that I have lived to read this enchanting book of recollections. . . .

Although I may have shared childhood with Mr. Shepard,
I never shared his talent with pen and pencil. He can make
a receding line of simple Georgian railings exciting and
lovable: he does it often and often again in this delicious
book.

> *Sir John Squire, "The Childhood of an Artist,"
> in* The Illustrated London News, *Vol. 231,
> No. 6177, October 26, 1957, p. 714.*

Gwen Morgan

[**Drawn from Memory,** Shepard says], tells of the happiest
period of his childhood—his seventh year. Mr. Shepard
also gives his readers—and viewers—a feeling for settled,
secure late Victorian London with characters mostly now
lost into the past—the messenger man, the milk woman,
and the lamplighter. Then there is Septimus, the cock-
horse so real to the little boy who tethered the steed to the
Georgian lamppost outside his front door.

The tale takes on added interest because the artist lived in
a house on one of the classic-inspired terraces built more
than 120 years ago.

Best of all, the book gives people more of his fresh and
gentle drawings to warm the spirit. Shepard has the power
of delicately stirring one's own imagination, of kindling it
and refreshing it.

He drew scores of illustrations from memory during this
last year especially for the book. But four or five drawings
are included that he did when he was 7 years old. These
childhood sketches are amazingly powerful in action and
character.

"Whenever I used to see something that impressed me
greatly," he said, "I came home and drew it."

His father, an architect, and his mother, daughter of a
painter, saved his scraps of drawings and, only a year or
so ago, Shepard came upon them in a small wooden box
which once held French writing paper. He resolved to include several in his book.

One day recently, after the book was finished, he and I visited his boyhood home on the regency terrace. The house
was empty and workmen were making ready to renovate
the interior.

"Come on," he said, "let's burgle the place."

So we slipped inside. Shepard stood still in the center of
the hall. This was the first time he had been here in 70
years. We tramped up the stairs, its balustrade shredding
old velvet, into what had been his small bedroom. We

From The Wind in the Willows, *written by Kenneth Grahame. Illustrated by Ernest H. Shepard.*

looked out the window where the classical plaster statues still could be seen standing on the roof of the nearby terrace. Here, at 7, he had lain sick with scarletina and thru the window came a jumbled vision which showed one of the plaster ladies serenely sailing over a runaway horse-drawn street car.

"I didn't remember that she had on so many draperies," Shepard said, smiling.

Outside, the tall black lamppost with "G IV" for George the Fourth on its base still was standing. This had been Septimus' hitching post. Shepard looked at it and said slowly: "I really didn't realize I had remembered it all so well."

I wasn't surprised. He had been a boy of great perception to so provide himself with impressions that were strong enough to re-create this memorable period of his life. How did I know? I had seen the contents of the small wooden French box.

> *Gwen Morgan, "The Man Who Drew Pooh," in* Chicago Sunday Tribune Magazine of Books, *November 3, 1957, p. 2.*

Rumer Godden

We are so familiar with the illustrations to *The Wind in the Willows* and to A. A. Milne's *When We Were Very Young* and the "Winnie-the-Pooh" stories, and the drawings seem so much an integral part of the books, that we forget they had, in fact, to be drawn, created. We take for granted Ernest Shepard's quite extraordinary gift for making characters real people. Look at Rat or Toad, Pooh Bear himself, or my favorite, Piglet.

In *Drawn From Memory,* . . . this gift makes a new impact, for each of the book's exquisite drawings is vivid, alive: the dear tricycle horse, Septimus, tethered to a lamppost; the array of Aunts—Fanny, Emily, Annie and Alicia; the shopwalker with wings in Mr. James Shoolbred's store. And the drawings can speak—they hardly need their captions. Turn, for instance, to the small Ernest in his new cap on Page 67: "I was doubtful about the peak," or, again, on Page 162: "Too shy to kiss her."

The true artist cannot be separated from the man—or from the child. Many eminent people have written their childhood memories but none that I can think of has literally "drawn from memory" as the title tells. Not only can Mr. Shepard write vividly of the days of the Eighteen Eighties, of his London home in Kent Terrace, of his mother, father, brother, sister and all manner of friends, such as the milk-woman with her cans of milk slung on a wooden yoke across her shoulders and over her plaid shawl. On almost every page he draws them. That he is a born artist is shown by the remarkable drawing he did at the age of 7 of the fire-engine with horses racing to the great fire at Whiteley's Stores. This little sketch already shows the draughtsmanship and care that was in every line he made.

It is not only the drawings that make this short autobiographical sketch rare; the whole is beautifully blended. Its mildness may lead some readers to dismiss it as too slow and temperate to be interesting. Yet mildness in its best meaning is very likable: gentle, calm, pleasantly affecting the senses—qualities not common in our times. The book gives something else, too, a feeling of home such as I have met in few childhood memoirs. It is a small boy's world but it has sound values, is stable and kind. It gave us what one can only call the vintage men and women of Mr. Shepard's generation and it is good to be reminded that these values are still part of us, just as that London of the Eighteen Eighties is part of London now, of its flavor, its pulse. . . .

I wish we could give our children the secure, if haphazard, certainty of the days of *Drawn From Memory.*

> *Rumer Godden, "The Artist as a Boy," in* The New York Times Book Review, *November 17, 1957, p. 44.*

Louis S. Bechtel

The Tenniel among illustrators of the past thirty years surely is Ernest H. Shepard. Both drew for "Punch" for three decades: both created visually immortal characters in children's books. Probably Christopher Robin, Pooh and Piglet and Mr. Toad are even more widely loved than Alice. Mr. Shepard's familiar charm and great skill are at their peak in [*Drawn from Memory,* this] new book about himself as a boy in over a hundred pictures, with his own text.

There are vividly factual memories of one already an artist at seven to eight years old, a remarkably good one as we see in a surprising sketch made at this time. (Note the face of Queen Elizabeth, and the handling of a crowd.) The prose style is quiet and modest—no Freudian analyses, no jocose comparisons with life today, no false notes of adult emotion read into the past. So the whole illumines a happy, middle-class Victorian childhood with unique and memorable clarity.

The scenes range from the great Jubilee celebration to a funny vicarage tennis tea, from the excitement of one's first pantomime to the thrill of vacations on a farm and by the sea. In the London of seventy years ago, the boy races his superb hobby-horse-tricycle against horse-drawn buses. He is terrified by "Jack o' the Green" men, sick after watching a slum fight, absorbed in the paintings at Hampton Court and in the big gun on a man o' war. He shows discriminating interest in a great variety of adults—an uncle who fought in the Boer War, characterful servants. He gives short shrift to the only two celebrities he glimpsed, Beerbohm Tree and Mr. Gladstone, "a scruffy old gentleman."

The boy is beginning to draw almost continuously, and is always comparing life with remembered pictures. Drawing is seen as just one of many activities, some childish, some manly, all centered on a very happy home, in which the children are not so separated from the family by the nursery as they would have been in a richer home.

We know only from the foreword that the beautiful, adored young mother died the year after these happenings. This lends the last pages a poignance of which the boy himself is unaware. One night, he lies in bed planning how to draw the marvels of the pantomime. Downstairs, his mother is at the piano, singing "Robin, Lend Me Thy Bow." The man of today says only this, to end his book: "I think she knew it was my favorite song."

Irresistibly we turn back for a second look at all the enchanting pictures, to fortify our friendship with that lovable boy who grew into our Mr. Shepard. As we turn, with so much to smile at, we read again the one moment from the boy's future, when as a young soldier he stands behind a battlefield in France, hearing soldiers sing a song of his childhood. Some of us will remember that page longer than all the happy ones.

Louise S. Bechtel, "An Artist's Happy Victorian Childhood," in New York Herald Tribune Book Review, *December 22, 1957, p. 5.*

Margaret Sherwood Libby

E. H. Shepard has . . . done six pages of new drawings in full color [for *The World of Pooh*] which are charming and which we are almost sure we would have loved if we had not grown to know the animals and Christopher Robin precisely as they are drawn in his black and white sketches. We do like the "enchanted place on the very top of the forest," the stoutness exercises and the bridge, but even in these Pooh is less individual. Moreover, we find it disturbing not to have these pictures near the text they illustrate. And while we are being very Eeyorish, let us add that we'd prefer all the black and white sketches to be as dark as in the original books. Some of the new ones are and some lose character in the enlargement. Nice as it is, therefore, to have this extra volume with its pleasing

print and wide margins, we do hope the small ones will still be available.

Margaret Sherwood Libby, in a review of "The World of Pooh," in New York Herald Tribune Book Review, *February 2, 1958, p. 9.*

Margaret Sherwood Libby

One glance at the jacket of *The World of Christopher Robin* . . . , and we knew we would treasure it right along with the older edition. The King (who was not a fussy man but only liked a little bit of butter on his bread) is delightful in color, pink striped pajamas showing off the blue ribbon of his Order of the Garter very nicely; and the Queen's ribbon is pink! There they are (and again on the end papers) prancing around joyously with the Cow and Christopher Robin and two turtles (from the "Old Sailor") doing a wonderful hornpipe. We like the simplicity of these figures against a white background better than complete scenes in color. Uniform with *The World of Pooh,* which came out last year, this book also has generous margins, and it contains all the beloved poems and all the famous black and white Shepard pictures slightly enlarged, as well as eight new full-page color illustrations. Our favorites of these are King Hilary and the one where Pooh and Christopher are doing sums with a "Hunny"-powered sputnik orbiting on the nursery wall.

Margaret Sherwood Libby, "Wit, Wisdom and Gayety in Original Picture Books for the Youngest," in New York Herald Tribune Book Review, *November 2, 1958, p. 2.*

Peter Green

[Kenneth Grahame's] highest gift was for characterization; and in *The Golden Age* he made children live as they were, not as their elders would wish them to be. This was a completely new achievement; and it soon caught on. . . .

[*The Golden Age* and *Dream Days*] must stand or fall, in the last resort, by the childish family quartet round whom they are built: Charlotte, Harold, Edward, Selina, with the personality of the narrator omnipresent in the background. [Grahame's] success may be gauged from the fact that these prototypes have left their mark on almost every subsequent fictional family of the kind, from E. Nesbit's *The Railway Children* to Arthur Ransome's *Swallows and Amazons.* This is all the odder since we know practically nothing about them in the way of external detail: they are never physically described, and their background is of the sketchiest. Our visual impression of them is almost entirely derived from E. H. Shepard's evocative drawings and silhouettes. (p. 191)

Just as in his earlier books Grahame had achieved a convincing fluidity of viewpoint, which shifted without effort from child to adult, so with *The Wind in the Willows* he takes the process one step further. All the animal characters veer constantly between human and non-human behaviour. (pp. 284-85)

This fluidity explains why it has always been so difficult to illustrate *The Wind in the Willows* convincingly. Like Harold or Selina, the animals are not conceived in visual terms—or rather, they are never the same for two minutes running: both their size and their nature are constantly changing. Grahame himself was well aware of this problem, and dealt very prettily with queries about it. When asked specifically (apropos the escape on the railway train) whether Toad was life-size or train-size, he answered that he was both and neither: the Toad was train-size, the train was Toad-size, and therefore there could be no illustrations. He later capitulated, and Mr. E. H. Shepard came as near as possible to capturing the essence of Rat, Mole, and Toad; but the point remains that the inner eye sees no incongruity in these metamorphoses (and in fact hardly notices them), while visual representation at once pins down Grahame's imagination to a single static concept. (p. 285)

[Grahame] was delighted (as countless children and adults have been) by the drawings Mr. Shepard produced; but it is curious to note that by now the scene of *The Wind in the Willows* had been transferred in his mind to the country and riverside surrounding his new home. So potent, in fact, have the Shepard illustrations been that many people remain convinced to this day not only that Rat and Mole lived near Pangbourne, but that *The Wind in the Willows* was actually written there. (p. 346)

> *Peter Green, in his* Kenneth Grahame, 1859-1932: A Study of His Life, Work and Times, *John Murray (Publishers) Ltd., 1959, 400 p.*

The Times Literary Supplement

The tales [in Brenda and Reidar Romskaug's *Norwegian Fairy Tales*] are short and abrupt: they seem like fragments of coloured glass from the kaleidoscope, beautiful in themselves, but seldom fitted together to form a complete shape. This sparseness is not helped by the style, which is too simple and matter-of-fact to produce much feeling of magic or wonder—or by the illustrations, which insist on the commonplace to the point of ugliness.

This makes the more pleasurable an escape from pure folklore into a more literary Fairyland: our guide [in *Hans Andersen's Fairy Tales*] is Hans Christian Andersen and his scenes and characters are pictured by none other than Ernest H. Shepard. "To speak of Andersen is superfluous", as Andrew Lang said, "of Andersen so akin in imagination to the primeval fancy, so near the secret of the heart of childhood." But of Mr. Shepard it is a joy to speak in this context—for he has produced the first illustrations that are wholly worthy of their text. And he remembers that it is children who will be looking at his pictures, and that the pictures themselves are no more than an interpretation of the text: they must be accurate, they must be clear—and above all they must reflect what Andersen says. The beautiful Princess must be beautiful; the Witch must look "like nothing but herself"; the Snow Queen must be superhuman, a person from another world.

> *"Simply Fabulous: Old Tales in a Modern Dress," in* The Times Literary Supplement, *No. 3118, December 1, 1961, p. xii.*

The Times Literary Supplement

At Heatherley's, his first art school, Mr. Shepard found too much attention paid to stippled finish, and he learnt nothing of construction or design. There is not much construction about *Drawn from Life,* his second book of recollections, but the finish is prettily stippled. Drawings by the author decorate the text, the layout is admirable and the book is a pleasure to look at and to handle.

Mr. Shepard's *Drawn from Memory* covered roughly a year of his childhood and now *Drawn from Life* takes him from the death of his mother in 1890, when he was ten years old, up to his marriage at the age of twenty-four. Whereas the first book was like a series of drawings for a single picture, this one is a random sketchbook in which figures and landscape are continually changing. Childhood is perhaps an easier subject that adolescence because the adolescent never likes to hold a pose for very long. But this is no self-portrait. Mr. Shepard is essentially the eye behind the pencil and his main interest is not himself. The "Giddy Kipper" of the 1890s is perhaps most alive in his own sketches of the period and it is interesting to compare today's drawings of Normandy as he remembers it with what he drew in 1897.

Drawn from Life is like a photograph album, a series of stills and not a moving picture. A face or a piece of furniture will recur on another page—Lizzie the cook first with and then without her cherished cat; and surely we saw that book case at Theresa Terrace?—but characters appear and disappear without much explanation. Florence Chaplin, the author's future wife, is introduced as casually as the girl with the pigtails at Llandrindod Wells and it is only at the end of the chapter entitled "In Love" that "I sat there long after it was dark, thinking, thinking of Florence and hardly daring to own to myself how much I cared for her". There are slightly blurred groups of students, various military subjects and Baden Powell taking up more space than Henry Irving.

Turning the pages, we come to the Golden Jubilee, the Queen in her open carriage which seemed to rock a little, and the jostling crowds in Oxford Street that evening. The girl on a bicycle smiling under her boater must be Florence, and there she is again in front of her newly finished mural. There is no picture of the wedding but there are several of the cottage, plain rather than *orné,* small and square with a rickety front gate, where to live on twenty-one shillings a week was no great hardship.

> *"Life Lines," in* The Times Literary Supplement, *No. 3124, January 12, 1962, p. 27.*

Marcus Crouch

Among illustrators of the 'twenties Ernest H. Shepard was the most characteristic of his age. Rackham and Kay Nielsen and other 'colour-plate' artists did work of much the kind and quality that had been done for a decade or more. Shepard drew for line-blocks of an economical sort. His methods and his style were of his time, and he matched the humorous homely fantasy of the 'twenties admirably. In addition to the Milne books he did much good work, notably in Grahame's *Dream Days* and *The Golden Age,* although it was not until 1931 that he reached his best in a new edition of *The Wind in the Willows.* (p. 52)

Marcus Crouch, *"The Years Between," in his* Treasure Seekers and Borrowers: Children's Books in Britain 1900-1960, *The Library Association, 1962, pp. 38-54.*

Pamela Marsh

We may never have eaten seedcake and buttered toast by the nursery fire, ridden a horse-tram, worn an Eton collar, but, all the same, most of us have a Victorian childhood in our background. It doesn't matter how far we were born from the Round Pond, Christmas pantomimes, and summer bathing machines, there are always writers eager to take us back there. Long secure summer days and cozy fogbound nights seem to act as a preservative so that writers like Ernest Shepard need only break the seal to find their youth still intact.

But it is not only in the volumes of his autobiography, **Drawn From Memory, Drawn From Life,** that Mr. Shepard has added to our childhood-by-proxy. His illustrations are so much a part of our actual childhood that it is as hard to imagine Christopher Robin or Toad of Toad's Hall without Shepard as it is to imagine Alice without Tenniel.

There is a quality of uncomplicated Victorianism about his memories and the way he relates them. . . .

Mr. Shepard writes simply and affectionately about those oh-so-long-ago, secure, complacent days, and what his words don't tell us his delightful sketches do.

Pamela Marsh, "Seedcake and Buttered Toast," in The Christian Science Monitor, *March 21, 1963, p. 7.*

From Drawn from Memory, *written and illustrated by Ernest H. Shepard.*

Marchal E. Landgren

Shepard is not the least self-conscious [in **Drawn From Life**]. His account has all the characteristics of a personal exhibition of the family photograph album. Persons and places are identified as the pages are turned, and anecdotes are given as they come to mind. . . . This book will be read by his many admirers and is recommended for public libraries.

Marchal E. Landgren, in a review of "Drawn from Life," in Library Journal, *Vol. 88, No. 10, May 15, 1963, p. 1995.*

The Times Literary Supplement

Ernest Shepard's talent for drawing wild animals in domestic situations is as strong in **Ben and Brock** as it was when he illustrated **The Wind in the Willows** more than half a century ago. Badgers always were, and still are, his forte and if a rather weak story is the excuse for bringing to his admirers delicious new pictures of this toffee-nosed animal, it must be accepted in a spirit of gratitude by the three generations whose childhood has been enriched by this artist's vision of Winnie-the-Pooh, Piglet, Eeyore, Ratty, Mole, Badger and Toad.

"Drawn to Scale," in The Times Literary Supplement, *No. 3303, June 17, 1965, p. 503.*

Alice Dalgliesh

One marvels at the durability of Christopher Robin and his animals and at the ability of E. H. Shepard to make fresh pictures in color [for **The Pooh Story Book**]. . . . So closely have his illustrations become identified with the Milne stories that one cannot easily imagine them with any others. . . .

Alice Dalgliesh, in a review of "The Pooh Story Book," in Saturday Review, *Vol. 49, No. 4, January 22, 1966, p. 45.*

Virginia Kirkus' Service

Ernest Shepard is the distinguished illustrator of A. A. Milne and Kenneth Grahame. [**Ben and Brock**] is his first venture into writing for children and in both the dialogue and the anthropomorphizations, the Grahame influence is complete. However, the combination of Ben, a boy, and Mr. and Mrs. Brock, two domestic and articulate badgers, is not a happy one. The story is a series of accidents. Ben meets Brock. The underground castle of Brock is blown up. New arrangements for the Brocks are made after the marauding smuggler crabs are taken in custody by a human policeman. Very British in dialect and designations, this is like a lesser draught from the wake of **Wind in the Willows** with illustrations in Shepard's familiar style.

A review of "Ben and Brock," in Virginia Kirkus' Service, *Vol. XXXIV, No. 3, February 1, 1966, p. 105.*

Selma G. Lanes

Few books, of course, have been as happy in their artistic associations as the A. A. Milne foursome (**When We Were Very Young, Now We Are Six, Winnie-the-Pooh** and **The**

House at Pooh Corner) with the drawings of Ernest H. Shepard. There were, to be sure, *Alice* and John Tenniel, as well as *Mary Poppins* and Shepard's own daughter, Mary. But, in the case of the elder Shepard, it is really unthinkable to entertain seriously the idea of anyone else's appropriating Milne, even after his work falls into the public domain here some 15 years hence. So completely has Shepard distilled the essence of Milne with his small miracles of spirited line drawing that the work of any other illustrator could only diminish our experience of Milne by comparison.

Few illustrators, of course, come to their task under so happy circumstances. Only three years apart in age, both Milne and Shepard were products of similar, comfortable, late Victorian upbringings. Sharing similar backgrounds and temperaments, they also shared, to a notable degree, nostalgia for a common childhood. Recalling his reaction to Shepard's first drawing for Pooh, Milne had said: "I remembered all that Reynard the Fox and Uncle Remus and the animal stories in Aunt Judy's Magazine had meant to us. Even if none of their magic had descended on me, at least it had inspired my collaborator; and I had the happy feeling that here was a magic which children from generation to generation have been unable to resist." How right Milne was we can judge anew in this spring's reissue of *The Christopher Robin Story Book,* that gourmet's sampling from all four works. The advertised "new format" is little different from the old, except that new plates give the drawings a freshness they often lacked in prior printings. The new, full-color jacket illustration by Shepard is peopled by old friends, but somehow less incisively depicted than of yore. Aside from this, it is the same, which is no cause for grumbling.

From Milne, Shepard went on to illustrate more than 30 books for adults and children. Never, however, was he to match the triumph of the Milne tetralogy. This judgment will not be altered by *Ben and Brock* which Shepard, young in heart at 86, offers as the first children's book he has both written and illustrated. A pleasantly rambling tale of contemporary adventure, it has buried treasure, ghosts, an atom-bomb scare, a beetle who plays the euphonium, five smuggler-crab villains and last, but assuredly most, an engaging badger couple named Brock and a boy hero, Ben. The drawing has much of Shepard's old charm and his story holds us to the end. But once there, we are left with no resonant echoes in the corridors of the imagination. Perhaps this is, in part, the fault of our age. What is an author to make of a modern badger-heroine who can think of nothing better to do with treasure than "buy a washing machine, and a fridge and a telly as well." A man who has known intimately Mole, Rat, Badger, and even Toad must sigh for those heroic protagonists of a golden age.

Shepard's role as artist for Kenneth Grahame's *The Wind in the Willows* was very likely the most elaborate effort of his career as a children's illustrator. The work, while charming in its own right, has little of the verve and spontaneity of the Milne drawings. Unquestionably it was a far more difficult undertaking to enter Grahame's concentrated world of the imagination than it was to accompany

Milne on a light-hearted ramble through the familiar byways of an English childhood. "There are certain books that should never be illustrated," Shepard agrees in the preface to his own illustrated edition of *The Wind in the Willows.* He had felt the Grahame work was one of these, and history, in a sense, bore him out. Published in 1908, the book was in its eighth edition and was a classic on both sides of the Atlantic when it was first illustrated in 1913. "Perhaps if it had not already been done," said Shepard, "I should not have given way to the desire to do it myself."

So overshadowed have the earlier artists been by Shepard's monumental effort for the 38th edition in 1933 that we tend to think of him as Grahame's first illustrator. He did, indeed, create the Mole, Rat, Toad and Badger we know today. (p. 29)

It was Shepard who finally placed Mole, Rat, Toad, Otter, Badger, etc. in the locale Grahame had always intended. . . . His hundred-plus small illustrations make living presences of all the animals and bring *The Wind in the Willows* considerably closer, particularly to the young listener who may occasionally grow impatient with the longer lyrical passages. We might argue that Shepard's Mole looks too much like an earless and upright Eeyore (with a dash of Piglet thrown in); but, still, if Grahame had had no other illustrator, he would have been well served. In 1959, Shepard added eight full-page color illustrations, but large-scale work was not his forte and the water colors are simply diluted variations on the black-and-white drawings. . . .

[Shepard] cultivated new ground with as green a thumb as children's literature is likely to behold. (p. 30)

> *Selma G. Lanes, "The Graphic History of Piglet and Toad," in* Book Week—The Washington Post, *May 8, 1966, pp. 29, 30.*

E. Louise Davis

Though reminiscent of the whimsical children and animals of Milne and Kenneth Grahame, [the] story of the boy Ben who caught Brock the badger eating his bulbs, shot him with his slingshot, and then helped him home [in *Ben and Brock*] is a disappointment. Ben's capture by some smuggler crabs in Brock's cellar and his rescue seem dragged into the story. Too many fortuitous happenings keep the plot limping along. Line drawings in Mr. Shepard's usual charming style are the best part of this book.

> *E. Louise Davis, in a review of "Ben and Brock," in* School Library Journal, *Vol. 12, No. 9, May 15, 1966, p. 158.*

Margaret F. O'Connell

[*Betsy and Joe*] is a loosely knotted string of episodes about an old man and a talking squirrel. If some important details are remembered too late, it hardly matters. The engaging naturalness of Mr. Shepard's line drawings put his modest book just on the border of that pleasant world known to friends of Pooh.

> *Margaret F. O'Connell, in a review of "Betsy and Joe," in* The New York Times Book Review, *May 7, 1967, p. 51.*

Marian Herr Scott

[*Betsy and Joe* is the] story of a friendship between Joe, a tramp, and Betsy, a talking squirrel whose adventurous spirit leads her into a series of difficulties from which Joe rescues her. Joe is not a fortunate choice as a main character nor as a subject for illustration, for he totally lacks appeal and personality. While some of the drawings are reminiscent of the Pooh books, on the whole, this is disappointing in both story and illustrations.

> *Marian Herr Scott, in a review of "Betsy and Joe," in* School Library Journal, *Vol. 14, No. 1, September, 1967, p. 122.*

Kirkus Service

The newest addition to the Pooh complex is a selection of the verses (from *When . . .* and *Now . . .*) most popular with young children [*The Christopher Robin Books of Verse*] illustrated with some of the incomparable black and white vignettes and with handsome new watercolors. Now children can be properly impressed with the bearing of the guards at Buckingham Palace and see the antics of the three little foxes against a panorama of the Fair; especially nice is the arrival of Pooh and Piglet **"In the Dark"**. All of this is attractively laid out on large pages and the best thing we can say about it is that it looks as if it had always been.

> *A review of "The Christopher Robin Book of Verse," in* Kirkus Service, *Vol. XXXV, No. 20, October 15, 1967, p. 1267.*

The Junior Bookshelf

[*The Pooh Story Book*] is presumably a blast of the authentic Pooh against the Disney heresy. One sympathises. Yet it rarely pays to meddle with perfection and most lilies are best ungilded. The small scale of the original Shepard pictures matched that of the text. Blown up, they lose their intimacy. Coloured, they lose their touch of mystery. Pooh in line is more than Bear. In colour he seems just a teddy-bear. Christopher Robin, not the most successful of Shepard's interpretations, is now sentimentalised still further. The new pictures do not amount to much, although there are small and pleasing touches in the sketching in of landscape. Some of the redrawn pictures are definitely less good than the originals, notably the favourite one of Pooh and Christopher Robin playing Pooh-sticks, the altogether pleasing frontispiece of *The House at Pooh Corner,* now provided with a technicolour sunset and with the fine balance of the original lost. (pp. 379-80)

> *A review of "The Pooh Story Book," in* The Junior Bookshelf, *Vol. 31, No. 6, December, 1967, pp. 379-80.*

David Fletcher

Of such illustrations as I have seen [for *The Wind in the Willows*] Ernest Shepard's come nearest to negotiating waters far more tricky than ever were those of the River itself; yet even these have not entirely succeeded. Toad is the rock on which they are finally wrecked. Amusing (delightful when dressed as a washerwoman) though Shepard's Toad is, never for an instance is it other than a make-believe figure of the Mickey Mouse breed, never a proper toad and so never a toad-become-country-squire. Can it ever be other than so? For what can one do with a creature that one moment seems to be almost as large as a man, the next has so shrunk that the woman on the barge picks him up without trouble and pitches him into the water, then a few minutes later has re-expanded in size so much as to be able to mount on a horse and ride off on its back?

Of course, from a visual point of view there can be no solution. Compromise is the best one can hope for. While I am glad to have known Shepard's very amusing little figures and have delighted in the settings, so peaceful, so typically rural, in which he has placed them, for me the best edition of *The Wind in the Willows* is the first, the one without pictures. Here indeed is one of those books (I can think of others) that cannot be perfectly illustrated—save by myself! (p. 90)

> *David Fletcher, "The Book That Cannot Be Illustrated," in* The Horn Book Magazine, *Vol. XLIV, No. 1, February, 1968, pp. 87-90.*

Charlotte S. Huck and Doris Young Kuhn

Perhaps the best-loved of children's poets is A. A. Milne. . . . The illustrations by Ernest Shepard seem as much a part of A. A. Milne's poetry as Pooh belongs to Christopher Robin; it is hard to imagine one without the other. (p. 417)

> *Charlotte S. Huck and Doris Young Kuhn, "Poetry," in their* Children's Literature in the Elementary School, *second edition, Holt, Rinehart and Winston, Inc., 1968, pp. 385-444.*

Nicholas Tucker

There are two main editions of *The Wind in the Willows*. . . . Both have colour and line illustrations by E. H. Shepard . . . and by Arthur Rackham. . . . Perhaps the Shepard edition just wins, with its abundant line illustrations brilliantly characterizing the different animals, although Rackham is far better at capturing the actual atmosphere of the river and surrounding countryside.

> *Nicholas Tucker, "The Children's Falstaff," in* The Times Literary Supplement, *No. 3513, June 26, 1969, p. 685.*

William Trevor

After long years of black and white, colour has come to the world of the River Bank too [in the Methuen edition of *The Wind in the Willows*]. Ratty and Moly gleam now in pretty tints, the latter gaily in blue, the former, as befits him, more sombre in his choice. The lengthy dressing-gown of Mr Badger is seen to be a reddish brown and the cotton print gown that the washerwoman so immodestly shed in a dungeon is pink flecked with crimson, as indeed is the mid-calf dress of the gaoler's daughter. The Squire of Toad Hall bounces in and out of a yellow-green skin, and the Hall itself—as we've always guessed—is of honest English brick, once red, now weathered.

With great delicacy, E. H. Shepard has coloured his original interpretations, but otherwise there's thankfully nothing new in this nicely-produced edition. The harvest-mice still hunt through the estate agents' advertisements for winter flats, the swallows dream of violet seas and lizard-haunted walls. In the gardens of Mole End the statues of Garibaldi and the infant Samuel and Queen Victoria continue to share a general dignity, the beer in the cellar is still Old Burton. The world is alive and well on the River Bank, which is all, in one way, that need be said. (p. 659)

> *William Trevor, "Immodest Proposals," in* New Statesman, *Vol. 82, No. 2121, November 12, 1971, pp. 659-60.*

Thomas Burnett Swann

When Pooh appeared in his own book, not only did he enjoy a multiplicity of names, but he reveled in illustrations by Ernest Shepard which have become inseparable from him and his friends and which have reappeared in all subsequent editions. Before Shepard made his sketches, he visited the animals in Christopher Robin's nursery and found his prototypes for Piglet, Tigger, Kanga, Roo, and Eeyore as well as Pooh (though not for Owl and Rabbit). Being an artist and not a photographer, he skillfully altered—and thereby improved—his models. He reduced Piglet's head and elongated his snout. He broadened Eeyore's rear and Kanga's pouch. Most important, he plumpened Pooh's stomach, shortened his arms, and lent to his button-eyes the vacancy of an inveterate and none-too-intelligent dreamer or, when a honey jar is in sight, the amiable calculation of a none-too-intelligent schemer. Shepard's animals are simple drawings in black and white, but their simplicity is that of Milne's writing, the simplicity of genius, of capturing essentials in a few unerring strokes, in the way of Thurber with his woeful hounds and puzzled hippopotamuses. (p. 90)

> *Thomas Burnett Swann, in his* A. A. Milne, *Twayne Publishers, Inc., 1971, 153 p.*

Margaret Blount

At first [in **Ben and Brock**] it seems that Mr Badger [from **The Wind in the Willows**] has risen again, but when one reads instead of looking, it is not so. Mr Brock, marauding, pushing through into the garden and digging up tulip bulbs, is at first much more of an animal than the Toad's guardian and friend. But then comes the clever size equation (used to such effect in the illustrations of **The Wind in the Willows**) and the boy Ben, of about equal height, is following Mr Brock to his underground house and meeting Mrs Brock and learning the family history in one of those cosy burrows that we know so well. The smaller, working-class Victorian kitchen or parlour would appear, to a modern child, to have all the warm, dark earthiness of rabbit hole or badger sett. Sharing this dwelling is the lodger, too, one of the most engaging insect creations; the musical black beetle Mr Pipe, of few words, long hair and glasses. His extra arms help him while playing the organ and other instruments, especially percussion and tympani, and also with composing, as he writes up to four instrumental parts simultaneously—all this while never looking very different from the beetle that got away from Christopher Robin's Nanny. A full-size human policeman does not think any of these characters odd. When his luck

From Drawn from Life, *written and illustrated by Ernest H. Shepard.*

turns, Mr Brock ends up in the Royal Enclosure at Ascot, with his wife appropriately dressed. Strangeness and magic have no part in [this fantasy]; visual pleasure is strong.

Ernest Shepard's drawings [in **The Wind in the Willows**] admit one into the small world of river bank growth, hedgerow, wood and burrow, and yet make the purely human action credible. Toad's imprisonment in the Tower of London, his washerwoman adventures and escape by train and horse, where his creator is himself carried away and forgetful of the nature of his hero, are made believable, if charadelike, by a growth in the size of the animals and a lessening of the humans. (p. 150)

All the personages in the Pooh stories have houses or burrows or the corner of a thistly field and Pooh makes up verses as he 'stumps along' which remain unappreciated by everyone except author and reader. The appearance of each animal—as in all toys—gives its character, and in contrast to the human world, things are always what they seem. Brisk motherly Kanga, mournful, sarcastic Eeyore, timid Piglet who needs reinforcement from his friend Pooh even to make a decision, bright optimistic Tigger, pedantic Owl and efficient Rabbit are all what their faces and bodies have made them. Shepard's drawings underline this; and character dominates toy. Even Piglet—who starts out in preliminary sketches as fat and happy looking with short ears and a pig's face—grows small and wistful with ears that can blow in the wind and turn pink with emotion. (p. 178)

> *Margaret Blount, "Dressed Animals and Oth-*

ers" and "Only Toys," in her Animal Land: The Creatures of Children's Fiction, *William Morrow & Company, Inc., 1975, pp. 131-51, pp. 170-90.*

Brian Alderson

The simplicity of Shepard's life and his undeviating sense of purpose as a graphic artist must have made the drafting of his biography an easy enough task for the editor of [*The Work of E. H. Shepard*], Rawle Knox. . . .

E. H. Shepard has won his claim to household renown through his book illustrations and a close study of his approach to the craft over some 70 years could have done nothing but good for our better appreciation of its demands and difficulties. How did Shepard read the texts that he chose, or was chosen, to illustrate? How did he set about organizing his responses on paper?

These questions may well be unanswerable in biographical terms, but they are nonetheless important because of a certain reticence, or lack of enthusiasm, that mars much of his book illustration. Certainly Rawle Knox's book confirms that Shepard was a perfectionist in everything he undertook, that he early appreciated the need to draw and to go on drawing in order to master an exactness of pose and movement in the fleeting lines of pen or pencil. Certainly one learns something of the character of his work by reading the few remarks on his quest to gain air and space in his drawings. But why, with this generally acknowledged mastery of technique, does he so rarely seem to get to the heart of a book?

No better example of this strange uncertainty of sympathy could be found than in the two recently reissued editions of Kenneth Grahame's *The Golden Age* and *Dream Days,* which Shepard first illustrated in 1928 and 1930. . . .

Whatever the publisher may say about these illustrations being "unsurpassed", and whatever evidence there is for their popularity, they seem to me to belittle the irony and nostalgia in Grahame's texts. Part of the reason for this is the disconcerting way in which Shepard veers from linear representation to silhouette, sometimes combining both in one drawing, and this is symptomatic of his ambiguous stance towards the stories. One is never quite sure how far he is out to caricature, how far reflect the self-absorbed quality of the prose. A similar mis-match occurs in *Bevis,* where the craftsmanship is never in doubt but where a dimension is lacking in the portrayal of that book's ruthless hero. (It also appears that at least two of Shepard's drawings in these books—**"Savage Maltreatment"** and **"The New Sea!"**—do not correspond with the setting given by the authors.)

But most disappointing of all is the book's erratic treatment of the masterpieces: the four books by A. A. Milne and *The Wind in the Willows.* Here, within the limits of his texts, Shepard is acknowledged as irreplaceable, but this surely raises the question of what is irreplaceable about him. It will not do for the editor to say that discussion of these pictures is an "insult to artist and author (let alone the reader)"—or even for Mr. Hillier to tell us that he "cannot—forgive the pun—bear Pooh", while going on

to say that nothing can "satisfactorily replace Shepard's pictures".

If Shepard caught the perfect note for these books (and some comparative illustrations from other illustrated editions of *Wind in the Willows* might have helped here) why did it so often elude him in his other illustrated books? And if—master of line that he was—he caught the perfect note in the black and white illustrations, what justification is there for their systematic modification through the addition of colour and for their being carved up to suit various commercial ploys?

> Brian Alderson, "Where to Draw the Line," in The Times Educational Supplement, *No. 3311, November 23, 1979, p. 30.*

William Feaver

[Shepard] had illustrated *The Golden Age* in 1928 and its sequel *Dream Days* in 1930. These . . . represent Shepard in his liveliest vein, combining silhouette and plein-airy line drawing, shadow play and black-and-white reportage. *The Wind in the Willows* was an even greater triumph. For the artist not only succeeded in preserving the author's peculiar twists of scale and anthropomorphics, the mixture of Thames Valley and Gilbert and Sullivan, the bestial, the human and the Runnymede lyrical, he also added precision. Rat wore the right trousers. Toad's waistcoat and shirtfront were well chosen. The Wild Wood was both natural and spooky, not overdone as in the Arthur Rackham illustrations that came a few years later.

Late in life Shepard took to providing coloured versions of his original drawings. These were a disaster: the atmosphere vanished, the places became banal, the creatures trite. . . .

A. A. Milne, we are told, was touchy about the way his verses and whimsicalities were upstaged by the Shepard interpretations. But if ever there was an author given the kiss of life by his illustrator, Milne was the one. Shepard made Christopher Robin almost bearable. He transformed Eeyore from a shambling depressive into the only truly artistic soul in the Forest.

No one has succeeded (I do not know if anyone has even tried) to supplant Shepard's Christopher Robin and friends. The Disney studios had a go at animating one or two episodes and succeeded in losing everything but the tweeness. Methuen Children's Books have now, regrettably, brought out two episodes from *The Wind in the Willows* illustrated in deplorable style. Adrienne Adams gives *The River Bank* a faintly Alison Uttley Little Grey Rabbit look. Beverley Gooding in *The Open Road* owes something to Racie Helps. The pictures get in the way of the words. The story is made to look both over-written and dim-witted. E. H. Shepard died three years ago, so he is not to know of this challenge to his authority. He was born a century ago this week. On the one hand his publishers have done him proud; on the other they have mishandled his achievements.

> William Feaver, "The Master of the Wild Wood," *in* The Times Literary Supplement, *No. 4004, December 14, 1979, p. 121.*

Rawle Knox

In June 1921 Sir Owen Seaman invited Kipper to join the *Punch* table, which in fact meant an appointment to the regular staff. (p. 100)

Kipper settled in well at the table, most of whose members he knew casually already. . . . E. V. Lucas was there, very much the grand man of letters, but soon responding to Kipper's natural friendliness. Lucas was also a director of Methuen, the publishers, and it was he who first suggested Kipper should illustrate some children's verses A. A. Milne was writing, some of which would be used in *Punch* before appearing in book form. (p. 104)

Milne's new verses were **When We Were Very Young.** At first the author was not at all enthusiastic about Kipper; he was probably looking for the owner of a name as well-known as his to be illustrator. But Lucas was influential and persuasive. Kipper did the drawings for eleven of the verses that were to appear in *Punch,* and Milne was convinced. For *Punch* they were something quite new, new even as Shepards. They had the immediate charm and fresh precision of so many of his sketches, attributes that sometimes seemed to get lost in the elaboration of the finished work. . . . The size of the *Punch* page made the illustrations even more effective than they were in the book published later that year (1924), as can be seen here in **"The King's Breakfast;"** and even more so in **"Lines and Squares,"** for which the book had to omit the bear which has just finished breakfasting on a business man unwary enough to step on a line. E. V. Lucas took good note of the effect of his own advice, and within a year Kipper was illustrating a book of his verses, **Playtime and Company.** (p. 106)

After the success of **When We Were Very Young,** Milne had definitely accepted Kipper's work. When he started to plan **Winnie-the-Pooh** he told him that he must draw the pictures for the book. Yet the two men were never close. 'I always had to start again at the beginning with Milne,' said Kipper, 'every time I met him'. Milne's letters were always friendly but nonetheless formal, considering the involvement of the collaboration. Milne's instructions were detailed, far more so than any Kipper had received from other authors. And Kipper went to immense trouble, going down to visit Milne at his Cotchford Farm home, in Hartfield, Sussex, and wandering round Ashdown Forest, to get the feel of the countryside that Milne hardly ever described in print. He drew sketches and had photographs taken of Christopher Robin and the toys. Later, when publishers' returns had reconfirmed the success of their partnership, Milne was almost honeyed in public. There was the verse:

> When I am gone
> Let Shepard decorate my tomb
> And put (if there is room)
> Two pictures on the stone:
> Piglet, from page a hundred and eleven
> And Pooh and Piglet walking (157) . . .
> And Peter, thinking that they are my own
> Will welcome me to heaven.

Those who knew Milne will not miss the sarcasm in the penultimate line. But in fact Shepard *had* appropriated

Christopher Robin's companions and made them his own creations, largely because he could see into the mind of a child, any child, better than the father, in this case, could see into the mind of his own. Christopher Robin was a late and only son. . . . Milne obviously doted on him, but looked at him and reported on him with that literary mind of his. Kipper understood Christopher Robin's loneliness as Milne did not. When the Shepards went to visit at Cotchford Farm, [Shepard's daughter] Mary recalls, [Shepard's son] Graham, more than ten years C.R.'s senior, went to play with him down by the stream—with an old log floating there that became a battleship, an alligator, anything that might take to the water. C.R. reacted with the delight of one who had never known anyone older than himself actually *playing* games with him. Kipper's mind could always play, but it is hardly surprising he never became intimate with Milne, and indeed Milne may not have wished it. Those literati of the 'twenties could be a strange breed, masters of the prickly hand in the velvet glove. (pp. 112-13)

In the early 'thirties Kipper was greatly praised for his work on the Victorian boys' adventure book **Bevis,** by Richard Jefferies. It was a story that took hold of Kipper's always ready imagination, written 'when Swindon was a country town, and Coate Farm, where the boys lived, was surrounded by meadows, with Coate Water, the big lake, on the far side. The lake was the boys' unexplored sea. . . . I went there one day that year, and found farm and lake much the same as it must have been when Bevis lived there.' Kipper was none too soon, for with the rapid expansion of Swindon the lake shortly became an 'ornamental water' for the town. Even more satisfying for him, though, had been his collaboration with Kenneth Grahame on **The Wind in the Willows** the year before. In earlier editions the book had already been illustrated by three different artists, none of whom satisfied Grahame. Nor had Kipper, who of course knew the book well, thought much of them; indeed he believed that **The Wind in the Willows** was one of the books—he had a mental list of them, he said—that should *not* be illustrated. When he was offered the work he took it on simply because others had tried and he was sure he could do better. Grahame was not at all so certain; he had always thought Arthur Rackham to be the man, but Rackham had already once turned down the idea. (Grahame died in 1932, after which Rackham did illustrate yet another edition; but his drawings did not have the popular appeal of Kipper's.) (p. 181)

When he took Grahame his sketches the old man was happy. He had told Kipper: 'I love these little people; be kind to them' and Kipper was more than that, for as he said he was more excited at the prospect of that work than of any other he had undertaken, in spite of its immense difficulty. It is amusing to find Milne, in the introduction to *Toad of Toad Hall,* the play he beautifully fashioned from **The Wind in the Willows,** remarking that Grahame's story 'is not worked out logically. In reading the book it is necessary to think of Mole, for instance, sometimes as an actual mole, sometimes as such a mole in human clothes, sometimes as a mole grown to human size, sometimes as walking on two legs, sometimes on four . . . ' He was writing of course of the difficulty in putting Grahame's animals on to the stage, but it was just as hard for the illustrator, and, logical or not, Milne had mixed two real animals with a lot of toys in **Winnie-the-Pooh,** and Kipper had overcome that one. Kipper never forgot the excitement of the river by Pangbourne, and when Grahame died his widow Elspeth replied to Kipper's letter of sympathy: 'He liked you so much, and was looking forward to your coming here during these summer days when the river and garden are so beautiful . . . I wish I could see you sometimes—for I do feel there was a bond between you besides that of your united work.' (pp. 181-82)

Drawn From Memory appeared in '57, and also in that year eight new full colour plates for an edition of *The World of Christopher Robin,* one of the many 'combination' books of the Milne-Shepard fantasy now to be produced to keep up with the demand for Pooh and all about Pooh. . . .

Drawn From Memory was a fair success, which was later to go into several paperback editions. Kipper was immensely pleased at this public acceptance of stories which he had told again and again to his children since the time when they were interested enough to listen, and he was encouraged to prepare a sequel. He was now, at the age of eighty, launching out on a new career as a writer and he took, if possible, more care over *Drawn From Life* than he had over the earlier work. (p. 222)

[In] 1958 Kipper turned down an earnest request from an American publisher that he illustrate a new edition of *Peter Pan,* a plea that was repeated but Kipper said he was too busy on his second book of reminiscences, which in fact did not reach print until 1961. Many would have thought *Peter Pan* the ideal subject for him, but it seems possible that Barrie's play was one of the subjects Kipper had registered as impossible to illustrate, perhaps on the grounds that anyone who had been exposed to that make-believe world in youth would have a very fixed idea in mind as to how it should look. Kipper's refusal is the more interesting in that soon afterwards he accepted an offer to do new pictures for Hans Andersen's *Fairy Tales* which—bearing in mind all those that had gone before—was indeed a challenge. The new Hans Andersen came out in the same year as *Drawn From Life* and contained some of the most charming later work of a rejuvenated Kipper.

It is hard to say how and when the public devotion to Pooh developed, as it did, almost into a fetish. The books had remained steadily popular, with parents as well as children, since they were first published in the 'twenties. Milne died in 1956, and the many tributes to him then revived interest in the works, but the publishers did not make any extra special advertising effort. Yet quite outside the book world, demand for reproduction of Pooh and his companions in the Wood grew and grew. . . . (p. 226)

On rolled and tumbled Winnie-the-Pooh, with Kipper doing new colour, colouring old drawing, producing fresh dust-jackets and even new line. There were a Pooh Cook Book, a Pooh Party Book and a Pooh Song Book. Kipper did confess in private (but only in private, for he was too honest and too sensible to deny the value of his bread and butter) that he was getting rather tired of that 'silly bear'.

But by the mid 'sixties he was doing better out of Pooh than ever before. (p. 230)

After finishing two books of reminiscences Kipper now well into his eighties, launched out into the tumbled seas of authorship for children. In 1965 came **Ben and Brock,** the story of a ten year-old country boy and a badger—that badger again!—whose ancestral underground home is discovered to be partly occupied as a smuggler's cave. In the next year Kipper followed it with **Betsy and Joe,** which tells of a tramp who befriends a squirrel. The tramp is an old soldier of the first World War, and in its original form the book was mainly concerned with reminiscences of war. But when his publishers suggested that a little more action was needed in a children's book, Kipper was quite happy to take advice. So Betsy, kidnapped to do a high wire act, is rescued by the friendly circus boy, Dan. The two books are not the most magnetic of children's tales, but their publication gave Kipper great pleasure, and of course they got off to a good start with his own drawings. (pp. 236-38)

Kipper was over ninety when he did his last work for publication, colouring his original line drawings for **Winnie-the-Pooh** and **The House at Pooh Corner,** which then went into further editions. . . . He died in 1976, when preparations were being made to celebrate the 50th anniversary of the publication of **Winnie-the-Pooh,** festivities in which, I am sure, he would have indomitably joined. . . .

He never really changed—until, perhaps he grew too old to care very much; and if he ceased to care at the end, that was only because he was unable to work, and work—art—had meant more to him than anything else in life. He might not have chosen to be remembered as the visual creator of Winnie-the-Pooh and Toad of Toad Hall; but it must have given him many wry smiles in later years when he found that the demand for his original drawings of these animals, up to their various antics, grew so insistent that it drove up the prices of 'Shepard' oil and water colour paintings he had done largely for pleasure. (p. 238)

Rawle Knox, "1920-1940: Success, Tragedy and Professionalism" and "1955-1976: The Unfading Old Soldier," in The Work of E. H. Shepard, *edited by Rawle Knox, 1979. Reprint by Schocken Books, 1980, pp. 99-182, 221-44.*

Bevis Hillier

I had known Shepard's work since the year of my birth, as I was named from Richard Jefferies' **Bevis: the Story of a Boy,** of which I received the Shepard-illustrated edition of 1932 at Christmas 1940, when I was nine months old. When you and the hero of a children's book are, to the best of your limited knowledge, the only two in the world bearing a certain name, you inevitably tend to identify with him. The name starts out of the page at you. The fictional Bevis—raft-building, tree-climbing, handy with an axe—could hardly have been more different from the pallid swot I became; yet I liked his imperiousness, his readiness to assume the lead, and the uninhibitedly selfish way he lorded it over his friend Mark.

So I grew up with Shepard's illustrations to **Bevis,** and

Shepard with a piece of his art.

loved them. Often one finds that the things one admired as a child look trumpery to the adult; but a more tutored eye has only given me a deeper appreciation of Shepard's mastery. My favourite drawing always was, and still is, the one on page 33, **'The Willow was obstinate'**.

If I try to analyse its appeal (which seems as offensively clinical as analysing why one likes one's family) I first observe how well it represents the passage it illustrates:

> The raft came to another bend, and Bevis with his pole guided it round, and then, looking up, stamped his foot with vexation, for there was an ancient, hollow willow right in front, so bowed down that its head obstructed the fair way of the stream. He had quite hoped to get down to the Peninsula . . . But the willow was obstinate.

Next, consider the power of the composition. The main line of Bevis's body, which is continued in a leaning tree faintly suggested at the top of the drawing, forms a diametric cross with the willow bole. You can sense the push of his left arm against the old tree—just as you can feel the weight of the mast against his shoulder in 'The mast fitted', a later illustration.

Only a few artists have been able to petrify movement so as to convey a still continuing force. Lautrec—who, we should remember, was only fifteen when Shepard was

born—is among them: Merete Bodelsen has written of his 1893 Jane Avril poster: 'In the photograph, Jane Avril is a woman who lifts one of her legs; in Lautrec's drawing she acts and dances.' In a drawing, this tension of suspended movement is like the conflict between characters which sustains our interest in a novel or play. It is the aspect of Shepard's work which his followers have most often tried, and most often failed, to achieve.

What else typifies a Shepard drawing? A fastidious clarity of line. A Vermeer-like consciousness of light direction. A nice judgment of where to set the boundaries of a vignette, with a fuzz of foliage, a white rock, densely cross-hatched night sky or a line of stunted pollards. And a genius for pointing up a telling detail—for example the garden sieve hanging on the wall in the second **Bevis** illustration, its sides splitting and springing apart, and, in the same drawing, the mess of curly wood-shavings under the workbench vice.

As with Tenniel's illustrations to the *Alice* books, one feels no illustrations could ever replace Shepard's for **Bevis**. With **The Wind in the Willows** he had a formidable rival in Arthur Rackham, whose gnarled drawings have been described as 'the evil of all roots'; but to me Shepard's drawings are still the canonical ones. Nobody else's Mr Toad could ever be so egregiously conceited, no one else's

Mole so velvetly self-effacing. With the Milne illustrations, I am in a difficulty. I cannot—forgive the pun—bear Pooh, or any of his twee retinue, with the possible exception of the misanthropic Eeyore. But, I can see that nothing could ever satisfactorily replace Shepard's pictures.

The endearing modesty which shines from Shepard's two volumes of autobiography (and makes one wonder how he ever steeled himself to write them) made him the perfect illustrator. Like Gerald Moore, the accompanist, who called his memoirs *Am I Too Loud?,* Shepard never allows his own personality to obtrude in what is also, after all, a form of accompaniment. He translates, never transmutes.

What, finally, is Shepard's place in the history of English illustration? I see him as the end of a tradition, not the beginning of one. He is the last of the great Victorian 'black and white' men. He has more in common with his beloved Charles Keene than with any other artist, and the debt he owed him is obvious; but there are also strong affinities with [George] du Maurier, F. H. Townsend, the first art editor of *Punch,* and the *Punch* illustrator H. M. Brock. . . . Caran d'Ache, the marvellously deft French cartoonist, was an influence on all that generation, and had Shepard's power to suspend animation as well as disbelief. Phil May was the nearest English equivalent to Caran d'Ache, but his ruthlessness in eliminating lines went far beyond Shepard's: 'Fougasse' (Kenneth Bird) was a more obvious inheritor of May's style.

The European illustrator of children's books whose work most resembles Shepard's is the Swedish artist Carl Larsson, whose delightful works *Our Home* and *Our Farm* have become popular in England in the version by Olive Jones published by Methuen Children's Books. The similarity between the two men's styles is extraordinary: at times they are almost interchangeable. Yet there is no evidence that either knew the other's work, and certainly *Our Home,* published in Sweden in 1899, must have been illustrated in ignorance of Shepard. Both men's draughtsmanship shows a flawless underlying awareness of human anatomy. Such is their sureness that neither needs to scribble in a preliminary imbroglio of lines from which the final design is to be teased out, as in a Topolski or even an Augustus John drawing. Their line takes an unerring, seemingly pre-ordained course, like that of Holbein or Ingres. But quite apart from the similarities of draughtsmanship, which extend even to certain recurrent postures of figures, the two artists have an unsentimental understanding of children which recalls the 'Eustace and Hilda' novels of L. P. Hartley—in which the creator so completely manages to put himself inside the child's skin that one suspects a case of 'arrested development'. Richard Jefferies had the same gift, which is one reason why Shepard was so ideal an interpreter of *Bevis.* (pp. 246-50)

Bevis Hillier, "A Master of Line," in The Work of E. H. Shepard, *edited by Rawle Knox, 1979. Reprint by Schocken Books, 1980, pp. 245-51.*

Nancy Larrick

The poetry books of A. A. Milne—*When We Were Very Young* and *Now We Are Six*—came out in the 1920s with small pages, no color, and many tiny pen-and-ink drawings by Ernest H. Shepard. The illustrations are a delightful complement to the poems, catching the mood, the personality of children and even their toys to a remarkable degree. The poems became tremendously popular, but the book is quiet and understated in appearance. . . .

In 1967, E. P. Dutton brought out *The Christopher Robin Book of Verse,* consisting of selections from the first two A. A. Milne poetry books with full-color illustrations by E. H. Shepard on alternate pages. The new color illustrations are so similar to the original black-and-white drawings in style and detail that it is easy to assume that Shepard merely added color to the originals: A closer look shows that these are fresh new paintings with all the charming detail and whimsy of the originals. (p. 116)

Nancy Larrick, "The Changing Picture of Poetry Books for Children," in Wilson Library Bulletin, *Vol. 55, No. 2, October, 1980, pp. 113-17.*

Quentin Bell

Conscientious lovers of Literature and Art suffer acutely in our society if they happen also to be the parents of young children. They are assailed from all sides by commercial artists, skillful people but without taste or talent, and these purvey hideous rubbish on cereal packets, in comic books, on the screen, in newspapers, and in the form of toys and packaging of all kinds. The stuff is carefully designed to appeal to the young and to debauch their sensibilities. Horrible to relate, our children, who when they wield a brush seem capable of exquisitely tasteful audacities, love the poisonous fare that is provided for them and lap it up as though it were nectar and ambrosia. . . .

[When] a children's book *does* emerge which seems to us both wholesome and palatable we rush for it enthusiastically. It becomes a Christmas or birthday present which, we hope, will be not only acceptable to the child but an antidote to the poisons with which it has perforce been fed. In the Twenties the great cultural panacea was Edy Legrand's *Macao et Cosmage.* That in itself should make us pause in our search for educational and artistic productions, for, unless the jaundiced eye of age be mistaken, this seems very much a period piece of Art Deco and, like so much Art Deco, distinctly third-rate.

A little later, and perhaps with equal wisdom, cultured parents fell with avidity upon *Winnie-the-Pooh,* the result of a harmonious collaboration between Ernest Shepard and A. A. Milne. This achieved a success that went far beyond the narrow cultural domain in which M. Legrand had exerted so strong an appeal; the book was received with rapturous gratitude not only in cultured homes but in homes which in some measure aspired to culture. Winnie was canonized and adored even in our ancient seats of learning, which indeed are rather fond of an occasion to unbend and relax, so that Winnie was actually clothed in the dignity of a learned tongue. Few of us have actually read *Domus apud Pooh,* but I imagine that it is a model of jocular Latinity and puts Winnie almost on a par—in academic circles—with Alice.

A time came when people began to tire of the winsome

charm of Christopher Robin, and it was then *Tim to the Rescue,* written and illustrated by Edward Ardizzone, that claimed our admiration and saved the always precarious aesthetic aspect of our nurseries. Since then I do not think that any other artist has dominated this particular field of literature as much as did Shepard and Ardizzone. Neither of them was simply an illustrator of children's books. Indeed both of them worked in a great variety of forms and media; both were serious and gifted artists and the one may be seen as the natural successor of the other. . . .

[Shepard] was a student at the Royal Academy Schools and certainly a very gifted student to judge by the few examples of his early work [in *The Art of E. H. Shepard*]; it is clear also that he was an exceptionally gifted child. Then, after he had left the Academy, something happened: he went on making some very good drawings but he also made some very bad ones. Looking through the illustrations to the book edited by Rawle Knox, and remembering what one can of *Punch* and other publications, one gets the impression, not that Shepard was an artist who failed in early life, as has been the case with so many British painters (in fact Shepard seems to have done good work at almost every period of his career), but that he was consistently and continually unequal. "Unequal" is indeed a wild understatement.

Shepard never loses his visual curiosity, although he frequently mislays it. Again and again we are attracted by some sensitive piece of drawing from which we perceive that he has seen and been moved by nature and has recorded his sensations with delicate sincerity. In such drawings there are a kind of tidy description of contour and a very sure understanding of intervals which are hard to describe but delightful to observe. One can only say that we are intensely aware of the artist's pleasure in his work, and we ourselves are pleased by it. In such drawings he is not dramatic or even imaginative; their strength lies in the artist's ability very beautifully to state facts. If about 70 percent of the illustrations to this book were torn out we should have the record not of a great but of a very sensitive and workmanlike draftsman.

The trouble comes when we have to consider that awkward 70 percent. Some of the worst are intended to be funny, and we have to remember that Shepard was working for a humorous magazine for much of his life, and here the delicacy of his vision is replaced by bold and would-be effective linear generalizations. Then there are a great number of coy, winsome inventions in which truth is sacrificed in the interests of a dubious sentiment. There are a few unlucky attempts at more heroic themes for which Shepard had no aptitude at all. Here and there Dr. Jekyll gets confused with Mr. Hyde; there are, for instance, some competent-looking nude studies and children's heads where a slick black pencil has added those few accents which can make a perfectly decent drawing look vulgar and, as they say, "effective," and it is here, so I believe, that we come to the root of the trouble.

Shepard I believe was bothered by beauty. One of the great influences of his youth was Frank Dicksee, later Sir Frank Dicksee, president of the Royal Academy, one of the most ardent of the late Victorian devotees of Beauty. He painted Shepard's mother, who certainly appears to have been immensely good-looking, and something of his agreeable flattery seems to reappear in Shepard's self-portrait made while he was a student. The same influence may be discerned in other early works by Shepard, including a rather inept study of his wife in fancy dress and other drawings of her and of their children in which Shepard's gift for factual statement is overwhelmed by an unmanageable load of sweetness.

Beauty, as those who know Sir Frank's later work may perhaps agree, is a dangerous goddess; for one thing she lives on such very poor terms with truth, and truth was always Shepard's strong suit. For another thing she is deceptive, and that which we believe to be the genuine and eternal article turns out, as the years elapse, to have been no more than an evanescent and fugitive semblance of the real thing, a mere creature of fashion. Finally there is the awkward fact that if we accept beauty in the sense in which Sir Frank conceived her, one hardly knows what to do when the circumstances make her presence inappropriate.

The devotee of beauty is very much at the mercy of his subject, and I think that Shepard was at his best when his theme was sufficiently agreeable not to put him out and yet not so obviously romantic as to encourage him positively to wallow in beauty. He draws best in front of landscapes or of models who are not too obviously charming; when he has a pretty girl or a sweet child to portray he gets into trouble. The funny, the grotesque, the obviously ugly leaves him ill at ease and all too likely to fall back upon the easiest kind of cliché; and when the subject demands something like a serious or even a sublime treatment he wanders into an inept prettiness. (p. 50)

[In] the late Thirties Shepard took over [as cartoonist for *Punch*]. . . .

Shepard was a disastrous choice: it is astonishing that he accepted the post. Shepard was by this time celebrated, he had made a reputation for himself as a master of dainty art. But daintiness might be suitable enough for *Winnie-the-Pooh* or even for *The Wind in the Willows,* but for a political cartoon it was entirely out of place, and it was inevitable, when finally the paper decided that it must somehow drag itself into the twentieth century, that Shepard should go.

Competent, tasteful, pretty, and sometimes much better than pretty, such are the comments which come to mind when we consider the work of Shepard. The affectionate tributes of his friends do much to convince us that he was an agreeable human being whom one would have liked to have known. Only the contribution by Mr. Bevis Hillier, who compares Shepard to the Swedish watercolorist Carl Larsson, in which he may be right, and to Vermeer, in which I am pretty sure that he is wrong, attempts to place Shepard as an artist. Mr. Hillier also compares Shepard to Keene, in which I think he is more subtly wrong, for although there are line drawings by Keene which Shepard might very reasonably have admired, Keene is an excellent example of an artist who avoided just that sweetness, that cloying passion for beauty which so bedevilled the work of Shepard. In fact, in a sense, Ardizzone owes more to Keene than did his predecessor. (p. 51)

Quentin Bell, "Fine Art for Kids," in The New York Review of Books, *Vol. 27, No. 20, December 18, 1980, pp. 50-1.*

American Book Collector

We remember [Shepard] as the creator of the way in which we see Pooh, Piglet, Eeyore, and all the rest of Milne's characters; he may be more responsible for their survival than Milne's text, which is a little heavy on the patronizing side. He is, too, my own entryway to the world of Toad, Ratty, Mole, and Badger, Arthur Rackham's competing illustrations having somehow failed to impress themselves upon my memory, while Michael Hague's wonderful new ones are *too* new for any estimate of their staying power to be made. . . . (p. 66)

[In *The Art of E. H. Shepard,* editor Rawle Knox is] good at indicating one essential respect in which Shepard can be regarded as "Victorian," that is, in his devotion to the work with which he filled the leisure that regular employment by *Punch* afforded him. Indeed, work seems to have been Shepard's true constant throughout his long life, and an anodyne against the more than ordinary run of afflictions that he endured—from the unexpected death of his mother when the boy was but ten, to the death of his brother, to whom he was apparently very close, during the slaughter on the first day of the Somme (Shepard was himself with the Royal Artillery that day, a thirty-six year-old wearing one pip; he emerged from the war a major with the Military Cross), to the death of his first wife, also suddenly, in early middle age, to the sinking of his only son's ship during the second war. The vision which conveys the sheer joy with which Mole pops out into the sun-filled springtime fields at the opening of *The Wind in the Willows* was hoarded at some cost; the man's friendliness, which Knox constantly refers to, must have concealed—one supposes—a rigorously disciplined privacy and steadiness which nothing would be allowed to disrupt. Indeed, Knox speaks constantly, too, of his "professionalism"; and what his book portrays very well is precisely the professionalism with which Shepard approached his work, meeting deadlines, consulting with editors and authors, always observing, sketching much more detailed and many more versions than his final product "required." [Bevis] Hillier writes of his "modesty," adding: "Shepard never allows his own personality to obtrude in what is . . . , after all, a form of accompaniment. He translates, never transmutes." In the same place he calls him "the perfect illustrator"; and by these sorts of professional standards, he certainly was just that. (p. 67)

A review of "The Work of E. H. Shepard," in American Book Collector, *Vol. 2, No. 2, March-April, 1981, pp. 60, 66-7.*

Louisa Smith

One of the dangers of being a children's book illustrator is that, like an actor in a situation comedy series, one becomes known only by the illustrations for one particular book or author. Names such as John Tenniel, W. W. Denslow, Wesley Dennis come quickly to mind. The other danger is, of course, not being known at all. Illustrators comparatively seldom receive the critical attention that authors do. E. H. Shepard, however, belongs to the first category. As the editor/author of *The Work of E. H. Shepard,* Rawle Knox points out, the American fetish for Pooh books in the sixties thrust Shepard into the spotlight complete with dolls, coloring books and soap products. . . . It was an unusual position for a rather retiring, inconspicuous artist. (p. 41)

Knox borrows from Shepard's two autobiographical books, **Drawn from Memory** and **Drawn from Life,** a debt he acknowledges. These books would be well worth the reader's consideration as a complement to *The Work of E. H. Shepard.* . . . The writing in the books recalls the light touch of his drawing style. [Penelope] Fitzgerald refers to his style at one point as "lost and found line." and Knox comments that "he spurred in me the quick hop-skip of an inner smile." These comments probably come the closest to capturing the quality of Shepard's style. The line is more suggestive than tight or heavy, an ephemeral quality that belies the years of practice, lessons and struggle. (p. 42)

Louisa Smith, in a review of "The Work of E. H. Shepard," in Children's Literature Association Quarterly, *Vol. 6, No. 4, Winter, 1981-82, pp. 41-2.*

Patrick Skene Catling

Obviously one cannot help retaining favourite books from one's own childhood. I was reminded of innocent perfection when I referred to *The Work of E. H. Shepard,* in which some of his best illustrations are reproduced, many in colour. Though Christopher Robin could make me feel faintly queasy on the wrong day, Shepard, like Quentin Blake, with his fine draughtsmanship repeatedly compensated for A. A. Milne's tendency to sprinkle a bit too much sugar on his characters. And Shepard's illustrations for Kenneth Grahame's **Wind in The Willows** are classically authoritative, if not definitive to the exclusion of all who would offer their own interpretations. (p. 25)

Patrick Skene Catling, "Wild Things," in The Spectator, *Vol. 249, No. 8056, December 4, 1982, pp. 24-5.*

Brian Alderson

The Wind in the Willows, by its very density, is strongly resistant to hacking and chopping. . . .

Indeed, illustrating **The Wind in the Willows** is as problematic a job as abridging it. In absolute terms it can be argued that pictures are just not necessary, the words "so thoroughly illustrate themselves" as Maxfield Parrish once remarked. In practical terms the book's sudden shifts in scale pose sharp difficulties. . . .

The difficulty was overcome with inspired ease by E H Shepard (who at one time also regarded the book as unillustrable)—but the success of his line-drawings resides ultimately not in their craftsmanship but in their complete identification with the author's own vision. "I love these little people, be kind to them" Grahame had said to Shepard when he was preparing the illustrations, and Shepard's affectionate response is the measure against which all other illustrations must be judged. (p. 29)

Brian Alderson, "Be Kind to Them," in The Times Educational Supplement, *No. 3472, January 14, 1983, pp. 29-30.*

Susan E. Meyer

"Ernest Shepard was a professional," his colleagues agreed. Drawing from the time he could first hold a pencil nearly to the day he died at ninety-six, Shepard's output of illustrations was constant and consistent. Although he suffered the untimely loss of four close family members—his mother, brother, wife, and son—Shepard's work continued uninterrupted, perhaps even *accelerated* by his sorrow, a steady pulse beat of drawing, drawing, drawing. Over the years he illustrated nearly 100 books and was a regular contributor to *Punch* and other periodicals, but he is still celebrated primarily for his little black-and-white drawings that appeared in four slender volumes about Christopher Robin and Winnie-the-Pooh. . . . Shepard was, by nature, a moderate man, and his success never blinded him to what he knew to be his most enduring reward: a job well done. Ernest Shepard was, indeed, a professional, first and foremost. (p. 143)

Susan E. Meyer, "Ernest H. Shepard," in her A Treasury of the Great Children's Book Illustrators, *Harry N. Abrams, Inc., 1983, pp. 143-56.*

Ethel L. Heins

Just as Beatrix Potter's animals were created with absolute fidelity to the natural world, so Ernest Shepard made his creatures in the A. A. Milne books look uncannily like "stuffed toys on the nursery shelf." Shepard's drawings, deceptively relaxed and informal, completely match the author's rambling literary style; but the artist was actually a genius at accuracy of mood and detail and at precision of draftsmanship—an engaging exactitude that surely helped to make the Christopher Robin books into children's classics.

Ethel L. Heins, in a review of "The Pooh Sketchbook," in The Horn Book Magazine, *Vol. LX, No. 4, August, 1984, p. 488.*

Zena Sutherland and May Hill Arbuthnot

[The] pen-and-ink sketches of Christopher Robin, Pooh, and their companions show mood, character, and situation. Shepard's interpretative ability is shown again in illustrations for Kenneth Grahame's ***The Reluctant Dragon*** and ***The Wind in the Willows.*** Even Rackham's illustrations for this latter book cannot surpass some of Shepard's sketches. Mole "jumping off all four legs at once, in the joy of living," or Toad picnicking grandly or waddling off disguised as a washerwoman—these pictures and many others are sheer perfection. In 1957 Shepard made eight color plates for ***The World of Pooh*** and followed, when he was eighty, with eight more for the Golden Anniversary Edition of ***The Wind in the Willows.*** His color plates are beautiful but add nothing to the virtuosity of his pen-and-ink sketches.

Zena Sutherland and May Hill Arbuthnot, "Artists and Children's Books: Ernest H. Shepard," in their Children and Books, *seventh edition, Scott, Foresman and Company, 1986, p. 142.*

Ann Thwaite

[The partnership between Milne and Ernest Shepard seems] as apt and inevitable as Gilbert and Sullivan. (pp. 251-52)

As soon as [*Punch* editor E.V.] Lucas saw the children's poems, he realized that they would make a splendid book when there were enough of them, and that, in the meantime, some of them should appear in *Punch*. It was obviously important to find the right illustrator. . . . Lucas was sitting next to Shepard at the *Punch* Table when he suggested (so Shepard remembered) doing some drawings and seeing what Milne thought of them.

Milne knew Shepard's work well, though Shepard had not actually joined the Table until 1921, after Milne had left *Punch*. Before the war, when Shepard was contributing his first cartoons, Milne had actually said more than once to the art editor, F. H. Townsend, 'What on earth do you see in this man? He's perfectly hopeless.' And Townsend had replied complacently, 'You wait.' Shepard had always had difficulty with the jokes.

The Shepard who illustrated Milne's first collection of children's poems, and who would go on to illustrate the other children's books, was the one for whom Milne had waited. As men, they had very little in common and were never friends. . . . [They were also] of very different temperament. Milne found Shepard's attitude to the war particularly hard to take. 'For him,' Rawle Knox would write, ' "The Great War" was a natural extension of his life, practically all activity interested him and this was more exciting than most . . . He had always been fascinated with guns.' Shepard ended up 'a pillar of Sussex society', as Milne would never be. Shepard thought him 'a rather cagey man, Milne. It was difficult to get beyond the façade, as it were.' (p. 252)

[Milne] was delighted from the moment he saw the first drawings Shepard did—the ones for **'Puppy and I'**, the poem that recalls that long-ago Gordon Setter, Brownie, who appeared out of nowhere just as the puppy does in the poem. The child and the puppy demonstrate admirably Shepard's particular pleasure in what Penelope Fitzgerald has called 'the characteristic movement of the design from right to left'. It was the feeling of life, 'the tension of suspended movement', in Shepard's drawings that made him so outstanding when he was doing his best work.

One critic would say that Shepard's illustrations belong to the verses 'as intimately as the echo does to the voice'. Certainly the extraordinary success Milne would enjoy owed a good deal to Shepard, but any suggestion that it was because of Shepard can be easily dismissed when one looks at the long-forgotten books of children's verse Shepard would also illustrate delightfully in the next few years, such as Georgette Agnew's ***Let's Pretend*** and Jan Struther's ***Sycamore Square***. A lot of people would try to jump on the merry-go-round. One can't help wondering what

Milne felt as he read E. V. Lucas's own contribution *Play-time and Company* (published a year after Milne's first poems), complete with Shepard's Pooh-like bear on a bed, a Christopher Robin look-alike and even a poem about rice pudding, with these strange lines addressed to the reluctant nursery eater:

> . . . When you next the pudding view,
> Suppress the customary 'Pooh!'
> And imitate the mild Hindu. . . .

Shepard without Milne nearly always sank without trace, unless he were illustrating, as he would, books that were already established, such as (to Milne's great pleasure) new editions of *The Wind in the Willows* and *Bevis.* (p. 253)

'Milne's instructions [for the illustrations for *Winnie-the-Pooh*] were detailed, far more so than any Kipper had received from other authors,' said Rawle Knox. 'Kipper' was Shepard's nickname, but Milne never used it. They were still not at all close. 'I always had to start again at the beginning with Milne every time I met him, I think he retired into himself—very often and for long periods,' Shepard said much later, but the letters suggest Milne was not at all withdrawn at this point. He often pressed Shepard for meetings.

Shepard had always worked from models—'The idea of working without models never occurred to him.' Milne knew this and was anxious, in March 1926, that the artist should come to Mallord Street and meet the toys. 'I think you must come here on Thursday, if only to get Pooh's and Piglet's likeness.' But he wanted Piglet small 'as you will see when you read the sixth story'—that is the one where Piglet is too small to reach the knocker. In the original sketch, in the *Royal Magazine,* Piglet is shown in mid-air, jumping up and down. For the book, Shepard provided a convenient flowerpot. In fact it was even more important that Piglet should be small for the seventh story—the rather disquieting story where Kanga and Roo are not welcomed to the Forest, and Piglet impersonates the kidnapped joey and jumps into Kanga's pocket in his place. (p. 294)

The trouble was that, in 'real life', Christopher Robin's original Piglet was almost as big as Pooh; he came up to his shoulder anyway. Not at all the right shape or size for that adventure. As for Pooh, Milne wrote (sending four of the stories 'so that you can get an idea of them at once'): 'I want you to see Billy's Bear. He has such a nice expression.' But Shepard had been drawing teddy bears for years, based on his son Graham's Growler, that magnificent bear, and he was really not inclined to change now. Growler was there already, anyway, in *When We Were Very Young,* not only as himself in 'Teddy Bear', but clearly identified as Christopher Robin's own bear, on his bed in the last picture in the book.

Shepard would even go so far as to say (after Milne's death and, indeed, after the death of his own son) that he used Graham as the model for the child: 'Christopher Robin's legs were too skinny. So I decided to draw my own son, Graham, who was a sturdy little boy. Otherwise I was a stickler for accuracy. All the illustrations of Christopher

Robin and Pooh and Piglet and the other animals were drawn exactly where Milne had visualized them—usually in Ashdown Forest.' It was a natural enough claim for Shepard to make in his extreme old age. But Graham was eighteen at the time of *Winnie-the-Pooh,* and indeed anyone who has seen the juxtaposition in Christopher Milne's own memoirs of the 'butterfly photo' and one of Shepard's drawings would find it difficult to give much credence to Shepard's claim. Christopher's real legs look quite as sturdy as in the drawings, and Christopher himself would say, 'It is true that he used his imagination when he drew the animals but me he drew from life. I did indeed look just like that.' The clothes, the hairstyle—that was just how they were, his mother's ideas carried out by Nanny, who made the smocks and shorts and cut (rather rarely) his hair.

John Macrae of Dutton's, Milne's American publisher, claimed to have been in the room, presumably in March 1926, when the partnership was in action.

> During the process of bringing *Winnie-the-Pooh* into existence, I happened to be present at one of the meetings of Milne and Shepard—Milne sitting on the sofa reading the story, Christopher Robin sitting on the floor playing with the characters, which are now famous in *Winnie-the-Pooh,* and, by his side, on the floor, sat E. H. Shepard making sketches for the illustrations which finally went into the book . . . Christopher Robin, the true inspiration of these four books to both the author and the artist, was entirely unconscious of his part in the drama.

This sounds a little too neat, a little too good to be true, but it is accurate enough to what we know (Shepard did sketch the animals in pencil from what Milne called 'the living model') and was written only nine years after the event. (pp. 294-95)

[In 1924,] the whole Shepard family went down to Cotchford for the day to give the artist a chance to sketch and explore the actual setting of the book, 'all the spots where the things happened'. If Milne seemed reticent and rather stiff in Mallord Street, it was not so in Sussex that spring. 'He was a different man,' Shepard remembered many years later. 'He was quite different, going over the ground and showing me the places.' Milne had, in fact, had only just a year to get to know Ashdown Forest, but he already loved it, and as he wrote the stories, though the landscape is hardly mentioned, they are set firmly in a real place under a real sky. (pp. 297-98)

[The] illustrations are still recognizably of the Sussex background Milne showed to Shepard more than sixty years ago. (p. 298)

Part of the strength and charm of the stories comes from the juxtaposition of toy animal and forest. Milne writes something simple, such as Pooh was 'walking through the forest one day, humming proudly to himself ', and Shepard shows a jaunty toy bear walking through real Ashdown Forest over real rough grass with real trees in the background; or Milne writes: 'One fine winter's day when Piglet was brushing away the snow in front of his house', and Shepard shows a diminutive toy piglet making a tiny path with a tiny broom away from the trunk of a fine beech tree. (p. 299)

> *Ann Thwaite, in her* A. A. Milne: The Man Behind Winnie-the-Pooh, *Random House, 1990, 554 p.*

Colin Thiele

1920-

Australian author of fiction, nonfiction, and short stories; poet; and editor.

Major works include *The Sun on the Stubble* (1961), *Storm Boy* (1963), *Blue Fin* (1969), *The Fire in the Stone* (1973), *The Shadow on the Hills* (1977), *The Valley Between* (1981).

One of the most distinguished Australian writers for children and young adults, Thiele is a prolific and versatile author who is often lauded for his skill as a storyteller and stylist, his distinctive treatment of character and theme, and his evocative rendering of setting and community life. He is also recognized for contributing several classic works to Australian juvenile literature as well as for the range of his literary oeuvre, from fast-paced contemporary adventure novels to nostalgic historical stories and picture books with Australian backgrounds. Considered perhaps the most regional of all contemporary Australian writers for profiling a wide variety of Southern Australian landscapes and seascapes, he is noted as a passionate environmentalist whose works often include messages about conservation and are acknowledged for their universality despite their nationalistic flavor. Thiele is also praised for creating perceptive, moving stories which reflect his thorough understanding of human nature, especially that of the young. He usually depicts how his quiet, sensitive adolescent protagonists discover themselves and their self-worth by confronting the forces of nature; these young men and women, who often become attached to wild animals or have relationships with Aborigines and older adults, prove their courage or learn about the workings of the natural world at transitional points in their lives, experiences which bring the characters from innocence to a greater awareness of reality. Although Thiele includes such concepts as loss, tragedy, and death in his novels and stories, he invests the books with humor and underscores them with a philosophy that reflects his belief in the human spirit and in the peaceable coexistence of people and nature. As a literary stylist, Thiele is often acknowledged for the clarity and vigor of his prose as well as for his joyful wordplay, authentic dialect, and lyrical images and descriptions.

Thiele's works are greatly influenced by his personal background. Born to German immigrant parents on a Southern Australian farm, Thiele developed a love for reading and nature before he was sent away from home to complete his elementary education. After becoming a teacher, he taught at the grade school, junior high, and high school levels as well as at a teacher's college before becoming its principal. Thiele began his literary career as a poet for adults and later wrote scripts for radio. His first book, *The Sun on the Stubble,* is a collection of humorous short stories based on his boyhood experiences that is so popular that it is reprinted nearly every year in Australia; Thiele

also draws on his German-Australian background for his story collections *The Shadow on the Hills* and *The Valley Between,* among other works. Although *The Sun on the Stubble* is often considered a children's book, *Storm Boy* is the first book that Thiele directs to young people. In this novel, Storm Boy, who lives on the Australian coast with his beachcomber father, makes a pelican his pet. When the bird is killed thoughtlessly by duck hunters, the boy is left with new insights into human cruelty and the rights of animals to live in peace. Another of Thiele's most acclaimed novels for adolescents is *Blue Fin,* a work which was prompted by his teaching experience in a tuna fishing community. The story of how fourteen-year-old Steve "Snook" Pascoe, an accident-prone misfit, discovers his hidden potential when he saves his father and himself from a shipwreck, *Blue Fin* is often regarded as Thiele's most important book. In addition to his novels for teenagers, Thiele has written realistic stories and fantasies for primary and middle graders, picture books, nonfiction, and a volume of poetry for children; he is also the editor of several collections of plays for young people and short stories for adults as well as the creator of poetry, novels, plays, and nonfiction for this audience. Thiele won the Australian Book of the Year Award for *Blue Fin* in 1970 and *The Valley Between* in 1982; *Shatterbelt* was shortlisted for the same award in 1988. *Blue Fin* was also placed on the International Board on Books for Young People (IBBY) Honour List in 1972. In 1977, Thiele was made a Companion of the Order of Australia for his services to literature and education. He has also received awards for his adult poetry and has had several of his children's books adapted to film.

(See also *Contemporary Literary Criticism,* Vol. 17; *Something about the Author,* Vol. 14; *Something about the Author Autobiography Series,* Vol. 2; *Contemporary Authors New Revision Series,* Vols. 12, 28; and *Contemporary Authors,* Vols. 29-32, revised edition.)

AUTHOR'S COMMENTARY

It is not always easy to analyse directions and developments in our own lives. When people ask me why I began writing for children more than twenty years ago I have to answer, 'I'm not quite sure', although in my heart I am aware of a network of intermeshing influences that helped to push me that way.

Very early in my life I came to enjoy language, perhaps because I was a bilingual child. I also liked listening to stories in school and at home and even found the nightly Bible readings in our house interesting enough—at least in the narrative parts. I read whatever I could lay my hands on, which wasn't very much, and I read in both German and English. I enjoyed 'composition' lessons, and usually gained good marks and a word of encouragement written in red ink at the end of my stories. But I hesitate to say that any of these things turned me into a would-be writer.

My later studies at secondary and tertiary level confirmed my literary leanings. Adelaide just before World War 2 seemed to be an exciting place. Rex Ingamells and Max Harris were raising the flags of the Jindyworobaks and Angry Penguins, and other young writers—Ian Mudie, Flexmore Hudson, Paul Pfeiffer, Geoffrey Dutton—were emerging vigorously. Most of these people were poets. I have since speculated on the reasons for the fact that poetry has always been my first love, and that for the fact that poetry has always been my first love, and that for the first twenty years of my writing life I wrote little else but verse. Almost all of this, of course, was for adult audiences; as far as I can recall very little of it was written for children. Even today people are sometimes surprised to hear that fewer than half of my publications are children's books.

Where, I therefore ask myself, did the impulse towards children's literature come from? I think some of it came from teaching, from education. I had already completed my teaching qualifications, as well as graduating from the university, before being swallowed up by the war. I had also experienced the pleasure and pain of teaching quite young children—five to eight-year-olds—for a year. I like to think that this, coupled with more than a decade spent in high schools immediately after the war, gave me a good many insights into the lives of children and young adults. And as we battled with prescribed texts for external English examinations I think I saw more clearly the relationship between life and literature, and developed a yen for revealing and interpreting the nature of the world as I saw it, and in my own way.

Other things undoubtedly influenced what I finally did. My boyhood on my father's farm and my love of the natural environment that sprang from it, my conviction that stories should be entertaining especially when surrounded by official requirements in education that were often dull, my observation that the world and the people in it could be happy and sad, cruel and kindly, stupid and wise, all at the same time, and my belief that our daily experiences often educated us more profoundly than formal lessons whether we thought so at the time or not—all these and more were part of the general background which I carried forward into my writing.

The influence of the emotions on human response also interested me from an early stage. It seemed that while we taught with the intellect we learnt with the heart. As a teacher and writer I was therefore very conscious of the fact that children had feelings, and that these often dominated their days, buoying them up or weighing them down. There was little point in trying to hammer principles of mathematics or science into them when their hearts were breaking over the death of a pet or violence at home or a sense of personal failure.

Yet, while it was easy enough to see issues of this kind among living people it was quite another matter to make them come to life in a story. This was a question of art, the author's art, that teased and beckoned and remained imperfectly realised, as it has been with authors everywhere for thousands of years. For in what exactly does the 'spirit' of a place and its people reside—the texture of sand or stone or pavement underfoot, the touch of the air under heaven, the tone of a voice, the tremor of an eyelid? How does one arrange words on paper to recreate the most tremulous moments of human experience, or to reveal truths about our existence without platitude or sentimentality—and to do all this in the context of a readable and entertaining story? I am not suggesting at all that I have been able to achieve these things, but rather indicating the kinds of goals I thought it reasonable for children's authors to set themselves.

Another comment I might make relates to working methods. Because I have worked fulltime in a very demanding profession all my life I have had to relegate my writing to 'spare moments', and these have tended to be very spare indeed because of the evening and weekend commitments I have to meet. Writing under these conditions demands intense self-discipline. Opportunities must be taken when they occur. There are no second chances. Procrastination is impossible. Perhaps I should thank my pragmatic and dedicated forebears for the ability to write under circumstances such as these. In any case, I don't think that writers can afford to sit and wait for shafts of divine inspiration to fall upon them like rays of pentecostal light. They need to rely on their own creative energy. They need, simply, to get on with it.

To end where I began. I suppose the real origin of my children's books is my interest in children. I have worked with them all my life. I can't abide seeing them short-changed. I like to think that authors can contribute something worthwhile to their lives. (pp. 227-29)

> Colin Thiele, "Notes by Colin Thiele," in In-nocence and Experience: Essays on Contem-porary Australian Children's Writers *by Wal-ter McVitty, Thomas Nelson, 1981, pp. 227-29.*

GENERAL COMMENTARY

Frank Eyre

[Realism] is well served in Australian children's writing; some of the best contemporary realistic writing is by Aus-tralian authors, and it seems possible that if a serious work of the 'social realism' kind now being so strongly advocat-ed *can* at the same time be made a book that will appeal to children, it may well come from an Australian author. Colin Thiele's books about South Australian country life have not yet achieved the international reputation of some other Australian books, but they are sensitive and moving stories which reveal a deep understanding of boys and their nature and contain vivid descriptions of lovingly ob-served birds, animals and natural surroundings that de-serve to be known more widely. (p. 166)

> Frank Eyre, "Regional Writing," in his British Children's Books in the Twentieth Century, *revised edition, Longman Books, 1979, pp. 161-76.*

Walter McVitty

Colin Thiele is probably the most beloved of contempo-rary Australian children's writers: he is held in a generally high regard which approaches reverence. Those who know the man only through his writing will have dis-cerned the personal qualities for which he is so fondly ad-mired and respected, for they permeate his books, which are not only widely read but universally enjoyed.

The willing reader finds it easy to respond to Colin Thiele's sure sense of story—a certain instinct for an abun-dance of good yarns told from the heart, often with full recall of his own childhood experiences, in language en-riched with the freshness and clarity of a poet's imagina-tion and a respect for words. The books reflect a benign interest in ordinary people depicted faithfully in their own everyday environment in particular places and periods which have special significance for the author. They have an admirably child-like sense of wonder at the order and beauty of the natural world, overlaid by concern for its precarious future in the face of man's insensitivity and his potential to destroy it all.

No other modern Australian children's author has made his readers laugh so much, so readily and so often. Yet it is real life and not escapist trivia which Colin Thiele pres-ents to his readers. He never distorts ultimate truths or compromises his professional integrity for the sake of fac-ile popularity by resorting to cheap jokes, by evasively fan-ciful solutions to problems or by indulging in sentiment for its own sake. His stories frequently end in pathos rath-er than joy and his knockabout farce and jocular pranks sometimes lead directly to tragedy. Only a hard heart would be unmoved by the emotional force of some epi-sodes in his books and, just as whole groups of children respond with happy abandon to hilarious moments, so too are they brought to tears by the sudden intervention of outrageous fortune (especially, of course, when this in-volves the death of an adored animal).

Colin Thiele is, by profession, a teacher, and has been since 1946. His knowledge of things which will most inter-est children comes from the considerable contact he has had with the young, in one way or another, and perhaps from the child in himself. The factor which most shapes the writing of Colin Thiele, the dedicated teacher, is an ir-repressible desire to educate. We meet didacticism in the work of so many Australian children's writers that it seems to be something of a national characteristic. Colin Thiele's didacticism is different. It is not an element of, but rather the *raison d'être* of, some of his work for children. Instead of over-zealous encyclopaedic instruction or the mere interpolation of statistics, it is revealed through a de-sire to help *mould* the young reader in some way, to shape his sensibilities and attitudes—indeed, to make him *better* as a person—or perhaps help him see ways of overcoming personal problems through vicarious experiences. Colin Thiele has often expressed the view that all children's writ-ers, whether by intention or not, are educators:

> One of the functions of literature for a reader of any age is the revelation of mankind to man—to comment on the variousness of the human con-dition, to heighten his awareness of the miracu-lous diversity of life. But the writer for young people has a different, perhaps far greater, re-sponsibility: he must lead his young followers with what humanity and compassion he can compass to travel a worthwhile road to adult-hood, avoiding brutality on the one hand and sentimentality on the other.

This kind of respectful didacticism can be seen as a predis-position of the educator but in Thiele's case it is usually kept in proper check, so that, for instance, in telling the story of **Blue Fin,** the details of the tuna fishing industry are taken for granted, because the central concern of the whole book is really human relationships and the growth of individual worth and self-respect on the part of its hero. The didacticism is not always under such control, howev-er: **Albatross Two,** for instance, is a less absorbing book, in terms of human drama, because its hero is not really in-volved in any deep inner struggle and hardly perceives basic problems, being so attracted by the technology of offshore oil drilling that the reader is asked to share some lengthy lecture sessions on the subject rather than an ex-amination of questions of opposing loyalties or conflict of interests.

In common with most other Australian children's writers, Colin Thiele is concerned about the despoliation and de-struction of the natural environment (he speaks of 'man's gigantic World Mess approaching its climax more and more rapidly') and it is on this point that another type of didacticism intrudes into some of his books. Even granted that the environmental problem is a most serious one, and so much of the damage already irreversible, the resulting messages about conservation are potentially tedious, and this possibly explains why some of Colin Thiele's books are less popular than others.

Colin Thiele is the most truly regional of Australian children's writers. His books are set fair and square in that part of the world he most knows—South Australia. They range over its vineyards, its old German farming communities, harsh opal fields, the wind-swept beauty of the Coorong and the coastal fishing towns. . . . But although his work is distinctly regional—and perhaps even because of it—its concerns are clearly universal. He has commented on this matter with typical eloquence:

> Whether [the writer] sets his story within the horizons of a family of potato growers or fishermen or gold miners or city businessmen does not matter in the least. For the edges of life may be as blunt or as sharp there as anywhere else. Love and bitterness, stupidity, excitement, envy and gratitude—the enjoyment and understanding of one's fellow man and of the earth and all its creatures—these may be dealt with as tellingly in Sleepy Hollow as in the most cosmopolitan crossroads of the world. Illumination is in the individual rather than the mass: the universal lies in the heart of man, not in any façade of streets, or hills, or houses.

Colin Thiele's 'sleepy hollow' was the Barossa Valley locality of Eudunda, which he called Gonunda in *The Sun on the Stubble,* his first children's book (and one of the most popular in this *genre* in modern times, having been reprinted almost annually ever since). It is a collection of twelve self-contained stories arising from boyhood experience, redolent, in its 'night-frights', of James Thurber's *My Life and Hard Times* but more particularly of Steele Rudd's 'Dad and Dave' stories from *On Our Selection.* . . . What gives Colin Thiele's material its special flavour is that it depicts childhood life in what would now be called an 'ethnic' community, for the Barossa Valley was, and still is, a region settled by hard-working, rural, religious Germans. As presented by the author, these gregarious farmers and storekeepers were rather dour, stolid, literal-minded rustics whose normally phlegmatic ways often turned to blustering overreaction when faced with the unexpected or unfamiliar. The vagaries of such a homogeneous group of people, especially given their stubborn tendency to impose conventional German syntax onto ordinary English make for plenty of ludicrous situations, although the comedy depends much upon Colin Thiele's ability to produce the outlandish from the ordinary. The humour is basic and simple depending on nothing more sophisticated than being unexpectedly discovered while smoking illicitly, or Dad's ingenuous insistence on draining the oil from his first motor car, as directed, when it reaches its first 500 miles, even though at the time he is far out in the country on a lonely road—and unaware that the oil has to be replaced!

What gives shape to *The Sun on the Stubble,* uniting its episodes into a whole, is that the telling covers a time of transition in the life of its young hero Bruno Geister. It is his last year of primary schooling at Gonunda, and this

marks not only the end of childhood innocence but, finally, his exile to the city of Adelaide for secondary schooling. . . . This realisation of irrevocable change—an awareness of turning points and crucial moments after which things will never be the same again—is the unifying theme of *The Sun on the Stubble,* stated explicitly by the author in a very brief prologue and returned to in a final coda, but never far away at any time in between. The same wistful realisation concludes Colin Thiele's next children's book, the highly successful *Storm Boy,* and in fact appears as a dominant *motif* in most of the books which follow.

The central character in *Storm Boy* is a young lad who lives a hermit's existence with his father Hide-Away Tom in a beachcomber's shack between the long stretch of water known as the Coorong and the open sea, which is evoked in vivid, active imagery typical of the whole:

> From thousands of miles round the cold, wet underbelly of the world the waves come sweeping in towards the shore and pitch down in a terrible ruin of white water and spray. All day and all night they tumble and thunder. And when the wind rises it whips the sand up the beach and the white spray darts and writhes in the air like snakes of salt.

Storm Boy raises an orphaned pelican, which becomes a most willing helpmeet, learning the trick of carrying a fishing line, complete with hook and sinkers, from Hide-Away Tom to Storm Boy, fishing out in the water. During a severe storm a tugboat is wrecked offshore and the line-carrying pelican is used as the rescuer of the six stranded crew. The grateful mariners offer to pay to send Storm Boy away to school in Adelaide. As with Bruno Geister, formal education will be undertaken unwillingly, for it will entail estrangement. Meanwhile, tragedy strikes, for the pelican is in turn shot, like his parents before him, by duck-hunters. Invariably, the young reader shares Storm Boy's grief at this point and there is no need for angry sermonising.

The effectiveness of *Storm Boy,* as an engaging and moving piece of literature, is largely due to the spare, vigorous prose which, having such limited compass, cannot afford to be self-indulgent. The surge of the brief narrative adds to the emotional force—there can be no waste of sentiment in a statement as brusque as: 'And at nine o'clock Mr Percival died'. Furthermore, the whole notion of Storm Boy's unfettered life and his pet bird is a strongly romantic one, and the setting has its own undeniable appeal. The certain success and longevity of this most popular book is easy to understand.

February Dragon is Colin Thiele's 'bushfire' novel. Like *Storm Boy* it is designed to produce in the reader an awareness of a tragic and largely man-made problem. It is a cautionary tale, intentionally didactic—the publisher's blurb states that it was written 'with the encouragement of the Bushfire Research Council of South Australia [and] contains a message for all Australians, young and old alike'. Rather than hammer away at propagandist messages, Colin Thiele does just the opposite—apart from a short ominous lecture which comprises the third chapter, there is little mention of bushfire, its arrival being postponed until the end, with devastating literary effect. Colin Thiele's novel is quite unlike everyone else's. He is not as interested in the fire itself, as an entity, as he is in the way of life it destroys. By presenting, at leisurely pace, a composite picture of an appealing rural existence, he is able to produce in the reader a sympathetic reaction of hurt and deprivation when the final disaster comes. (pp. 199-205)

The setting for *February Dragon* is actually just over the South Australian state border, inside Victoria. Since the author wants the message of this book to be widely applicable, he has abandoned the peculiarly Teutonic environment of his childhood in favour of a more distant setting. This makes it more generalised than it otherwise might have been. At the same time, one notes that the author has taken some aspects from *The Sun on the Stubble* and worked them in to *February Dragon* (foreshadowing a refining which was to be continued in *The Shadow on the Hills*). There's the bedlam caused by a possum inside a house, the children's amused interest in the romantic affairs and courtship of their teachers, and being caught while enjoying a smoke ('drawing at the pipe stems until the tobacco in the bowls glowed like gentle volcanoes . . . they might have been a couple of old philosophers or drovers yarning in the sun'), although this particular incident is used to show how the carelessness of the smokers might easily have started a bushfire, so it does not exist solely as an amusing incident.

The Sun on the Stubble and *February Dragon* are collections of separate anecdotes but *Blue Fin* is a fully sustained novel, with only one interpolated incident—the attempt by the boys to ensconce a large, dead tuna on the Mayor's chair, although this also serves to illustrate the hero's penchant for landing in trouble. . . . For some, *Blue Fin* remains Colin Thiele's 'big' work, to be regarded as his most distinguished contribution to Australian children's (or adolescent) literature, but then serious 'problem' novels—and this is one—are always more likely to generate such a response. There's something Conradean about the nature and scope of *Blue Fin* which tells of man's struggle with the sea but, more particularly, of its role in initiating into manhood awkward, gangly (yet perceptive and sensitive) fourteen-year-old 'Snook' Pascoe, who has been convinced by his tuna-boat-captain father, and also by an unfeeling schoolteacher, that he is a failure, a misfit, a no-hoper. His father is reluctantly forced to take him on as a temporary crew-replacement on the 'Blue Fin', a fishing boat which has had such a long run of bad luck that it is regarded as jinxed. (pp. 205-06)

On Snook's trip 'Blue Fin' seems to have a change of luck, for it encounters a large school of tuna, but the polers are working so much 'at fever pitch, their hopes simmering and their concentration stretched' that they do not notice, in the midst of the calm, the arrival above them of thunderhead clouds and a terrifying waterspout:

> Gigantic updrafts and downdrafts of air swept through the vortex above them. A spiralling funnel of black air spun like a maelstrom, faster and faster, its downward tip hanging from the sky like an enormous nozzle, a dark cornucopia of death and destruction. It was as soft as gossamer and as hard as iron. As if suspended by some ma-

licious practical-joker it gradually came lower and lower; but still the five people on the boat, engrossed in their noisy battle with the fish, saw and heard nothing.

Such a passage shows the power of Thiele's writing, and the poet's precise and illuminating imagery; few other writers would have been equal to the task. Thiele leaves the reader in no doubt as to what this almost unimaginable phenomenon would be like. . . . (pp. 207-08)

Colin Thiele's work is given conviction through the fact that he always writes directly from his own experience. This is as true of *Blue Fin* as of the stories of his own childhood. Its origins spring from the years between 1946 and 1955 when he was a teacher at Port Lincoln and many of his pupils were sons of fishermen. *Blue Fin* objectifies his concern for young people growing up in that particular environment—their possibilities for growth, the factors influencing them, their own future battles with the sea, and his own experiences fishing with them sometimes.

Apart from the heroic human drama, the achievement of *Blue Fin* is in its unromanticised view of the lives of those who go down to the sea in ships, and the potential of Thiele's prose for arousing feelings of dread, as this remarkable passage shows, terrifying in what it implies—speaking directly to one's primeval fear of the unknown, it produces a sort of nautical vertigo:

> Yet they sailed far out of sight of land to the edge of the Continental Shelf where the ocean floor plunged down in a great glissade from its shallow coastal bench to the cold deeps beyond. Here an echo-sounder strumming gently to the tune of a hundred fathoms suddenly seemed to slip down a hillside two miles deep, and the crew, pressing their ears into the pillows on their bunks at night dreamt bad dreams of the chasms beneath them on the other side of the thin hull.

In spite of its aspects of darkness, *Blue Fin* remains an encouraging affirmation of life, but Colin Thiele's next novel *The Fire in the Stone* seems uncharacteristically pessimistic. It ends with the conventional Thiele notion of finality and change, with its hero Ernie, a gentle, timid boy, turning his back on his father and the opal mining community which has served as 'home' for five years of his sad life of yearning for security, stability and acceptance. But this time the mood is depressingly sombre, marking this author's transition from innocence to experience, at least in his children's novels. . . . (pp. 209-10)

The Fire in the Stone sees Colin Thiele recognising the growing incidence of family breakdown in contemporary society. Ernie's mother having 'cleared out' when he was only nine, his father has taken Ernie away from Adelaide to start a new sort of life, hundreds of miles north:

> Those years had been hard for Ernie. Five years of dirty sweat-marked books at school, five years of heat and cold and wind and dust. Five years of loneliness. The teachers said he was a loner. It was probably true . . . Only with Willie Winowie, a thin little Aboriginal . . . did he seem to have some real affinity; but even that

was a strange friendship of silence and few words.

Because his father is often away, Ernie spends much free time gouging for opal and one day his pick breaks through to 'the fire in the stone'. Since from the narrative point of view this book is an adventure story, with local colour, one almost automatically predicts that Ernie's new-found wealth will soon be stolen from him and that the interest will be in the tracking down and apprehending of the thief. The difference is in the ending, for ultimate financial reward brings no contentment, and indeed leads to the death of the Aboriginal boy.

Albatross Two tells of the changes made to the 'age old calm' and settled lives of the inhabitants of the fishing village of Ripple Bay by the arrival of a giant offshore oil-drilling platform. (pp. 210-11)

Albatross Two is a heavy-handed book after the excellence of Colin Thiele's earlier work. The feeling of anguish over man's idiotic and heedless onrush to exploit his vulnerable planet is understandable, but literature gives way too often to sermonising in *Albatross Two*. There are other faults—the attempts at reproducing the sound of spoken American ('It's a mighty carmplicated arperation. And mighty carstly, yes sir.') are both unnecessary and irritating; the characters are stereotyped, with little scope for development, and the usually precise and evocative language of the poet is here conspicuously absent.

Magpie Island is a short variation on the *Blue Fin* theme but a bird is used as a metaphor for the achievement of people like Snook, those who defiantly remain alive in a hostile environment. It tells of a lone magpie blown off course and stranded on an icy, wind-swept island off the South Australian coast, at the western edge of the fishing grounds. Like Snook's, his story is summed up by the author as one of dogged endurance: 'The everlasting picture of one against the world. Something for people to get their inspiration from.' Humans play little part in *Magpie Island*—it is Thiele's 'anthropomorphic' story, written to express his feeling for the 'fine nuggety bird with solid shoulders and strong businesslike beak', the white-backed magpie which was his childhood companion. The focus of attention is always on the lonely bird itself, rather than on the response of humans (as in *Storm Boy*) and, although a fisherman's son brings a female magpie to the island to be a mate for the stranded bird, it is also a human who causes its death. *Magpie Island* is perhaps too much of a metaphor—too objective a correlative—to evoke emotional response in the way that *Storm Boy* does so effectively.

The richness of the author's Eudunda boyhood is returned to with great gusto in *Uncle Gustav's Ghosts,* a book to scare most young readers gently as well as amuse them. Although the events in which various apparitions appear before Uncle Gustav are described with sufficiently convincing eeriness, each phenomenon has a quite logical explanation, made obvious to the alert reader. *Uncle Gustav's Ghosts* is a return to the episodic, short-story form, in which self-contained parts are linked by common characters, setting and a final resolution of the cumulative mystery—which has to do with the disappearance of a

Thiele as a student at the University of Adelaide, 1938.

bride and groom on their wedding night half a century earlier.

Uncle Gustav's Ghosts, having no serious themes, personal problems and conservationist issues, allows Colin Thiele to enjoy his role as a storyteller. Apart from the fun in spinning spooky-comical yarns, he indulges himself in reproducing the fractured English of his forebears, revelling in juicy words such as 'quatsch' (which sounds 'as if Uncle Gus had landed someone in the face with a handful of mashed potatoes') and sentences which are as engagingly ludicrous as the people who utter them: 'I vill tonight dis cheeky beggar a lesson learn; he vill t'ink a t'underclap has him by d' t'roat got'. The action sometimes stops for the recording of some diverting absurdity or other, carefully observed from the point of view of the young boy:

> Benny was in the kitchen having breakfast, and goggling in amazement at the discussion going on between his mother and old Mutter Eisenstein. Mutter was dunking wheat biscuits into hot milk and trying to pop them into her mouth before they bent over like plasticine and plopped down on the table in soggy dollops. Whenever she succeeded in getting one up to her mouth her teeth clicked out a little tune of triumph and delight like castanets.

One feels that this is an actual image remembered from childhood, and the *idea* of recording it, as well as the *way* of recording it, reminds one that Colin Thiele is writing for children and helps explain why they respond to him so readily, on equal terms. (pp. 211-13)

The most comical writing describes Uncle Gustav's reaction to what he perceives as *another* spectre (actually an uprooted scarecrow) sitting beside him in his jinker and holding the reins. Gus is on his drunken way home and the author extracts the most from his inebriated state, in writing enlivened by irony:

> . . . instead of leaping bodily from the jinker and rushing off through the vines yelling, 'ghoul! ghoul!' he slid uncertainly to the far end of the seat and looked his fellow passenger over. What with the furious jolting of the jinker, the effects

of the wine, and the whipping and lashing of the tendrils about his legs and body he found it hard to focus his gaze clearly. But he had little doubt that his colleague was a woman in a white dress who was driving recklessly.

For a second Uncle Gus was in a quandary. If his travelling companion had been a man he would have been inclined to abuse the stuffing out of him for imbecile carelessness, but with a woman certain courtesies had to be observed. Since she continued to lean over the reins in stony silence Uncle Gus decided that it was up to him to make the opening move.

'Guten Abend (Good evening)', he said thickly and politely.

No answer. The folds of the driver's dress flapped in the wind of their movement; there was a clothes-line floppiness about the sound. Gus was not deterred.

'Reisen Sie weit (Are you travelling far)?' he asked in a tone so full of honey that he sounded drunk instead of gallant.

It has been said that Colin Thiele's books seem to be written as much for performing as for reading and the drollery of scenes such as this shows why. (pp. 214-15)

Uncle Gustav's Ghosts contains some ingredients found in Colin Thiele's other Germanic farming-community stories, such as the rural ritual of the 'surprise party' for newlyweds, the famous bush 'tin-kettling', which Uncle Gus launches by conducting his awful orchestra (redolent of the Bremen Town Band) made up of tubas, drums, violins, old tins, milk buckets, sheets of roofing iron, cowbells and shotguns. (p. 215)

To the child reader, each novel is of course a completely self-contained experience, needing no reference to other books, but Colin Thiele's work is a homogeneous entity. One novel seems to grow out of another (not necessarily in any onward sequence), incorporating variations on previously examined themes, presenting different perspectives of the same characters, even retelling salient events but in different ways. Colin Thiele seems to be constantly revising, enriching and refining his core of ideas. The tuna to be propped on the mayor's chair in **Blue Fin** becomes a goanna placed beside the sleeping Nick in the cabin of a truck in **The Fire in the Stone** and then an octopus furtively placed in a gift-wrapped sewing basket in **Albatross Two**—each one a practical joke with more or less unfortunate consequences. Thiele's young heroes commonly have only one true parent and tend to be rather quiet, mild, unimposing and gentle people, conscious of the need (and even responsibility) to take into account the feelings of others. Nevertheless, they are given to landing in trouble with adult authorities (teachers especially) without ever agonising about unjust treatment or regarding themselves as martyrs. Events such as country 'tin-kettlings' and places such as general stores in country towns are described in similar fashion in more than one book; children predictably become attached to particular wild birds; there's usually an old 'character' who owns a blunderbuss; identical pairs of young rogue males intrude with rifles

and shoot at anything with wings; external forces, whether from Adelaide or from the United States, impose their view on progress on formerly serene fishing communities—and so on. The interested observer therefore sees each new Colin Thiele book always in the light of what has come before, knowing that it is unlikely to be radically different.

Tessa Noble does mark a change in that, in **The Hammerhead Light,** she is Colin Thiele's first attempt at depicting a young heroine. Yet even so, she is really an expansion of the tentative portrait of Tina Banks, Link's young sister from **Albatross Two.** Both girls live by the sea and spend much time with an elderly man who shares with them the love of a tamed bird. In both books are matching passages describing these fresh and vital young girls running unfettered and joyously birdlike along beaches, at one with nature—in a kind of free and ecstatic ballet, a celebration of life and innocence. Since Colin Thiele's previous novels had been told from the viewpoint of boys, the switch to an attempt to project into the manner and mind of a girl can be seen as something of an experiment—a not fully successful one. Tessa, like Tina, is too idealised to be convincing—it is as though she has been imagined in the same sort of romantic sentiment which gave rise to Little Nell. Her emotional responses to situations are the projections of an adult fancy: she is given to pathos, compassion, pity and universal suffering. Generally, Tessa's frequent crying for the woes of the world seems overstated for someone of an age given more to self-interest than philanthropy. . . . (pp. 216-17)

The notion of a friendship based on mutual respect between a child and an old man living a hermit life in a humpy is also pursued in Colin Thiele's next book **The Shadow on the Hills,** in which he moves back yet again from his seaside milieu to that of his original German farming community. Given the suggestion that Thiele's development as a writer seems to be one of redefining ideas and revisiting familiar ground, it should not be surprising that **The Shadow on the Hills** is probably the finest achievement of them all, combining as it does the best features of its precursors but refining them through experience. Here, for the first time, the setting of the author's own childhood is the inspiration for a complete novel rather than a series of linked episodes. His boyish alter ego is now called Bodo Schneider instead of Bruno Geister, but it is, of course, the same character, just as old Axel, who was described in **The Hammerhead Light** as 'looking like a prophet from the Bible', is clearly the prototype of Ebenezer Blitz who, in **The Shadow on the Hills,** is similarly described. But Ebenezer lives the role, striding the rocky wilderness with his wild dog Elijah, shouting, proclaiming and preaching. Bodo first encounters this bearded Old Testament thunderer while lost in a fog; both are rabbit trappers (as were Bodo's counterparts, Bruno and Benny, earlier). During subsequent encounters, the boy's original awe turns to respect and affection. . . . The last pages are a reworking of the end of **The Hammerhead Light**—the old hermit is to move away from his humpy and the environment of which he had seemed so much a part to live in an institution. Alone up on the hills Bodo surveys the landscape below, just as Bruno had done. He realises that everything is changing and his childhood has run its course (but this is no more than an emotional moment—he's no Tessa Noble, with all her sobbing and weeping). He comes down from the heights, but not to go away to school or elsewhere, for these are the days of the great Depression. At the age of twelve he must put away childish things and start the first day of his life as a working man: 'He stepped off the knoll, leaving the rocky outcrop clear and empty, and walked down to take over the waggon from his father'.

The transition in Colin Thiele's works from a state of innocence to an older, wiser but sadder one of experience is most clearly shown in a comparison of *The Sun on the Stubble* and *The Shadow on the Hills.* The titles themselves, from *Sun* to *Shadow,* suggest the change wrought over two decades. The nostalgic fun of a colourful boyhood certainly survives in *The Shadow on the Hills* but it incorporates darker moments and sometimes terrible passions—there are undercurrents of malevolence, spite and revenge. Real poverty is confronting the Schneiders too, and Bodo's father could well end up like Ebenezer. Even the natural world is no longer so benign—for example, prized turkeys are killed by a nocturnal marauder, and the reader is not spared the grisly scene. (pp. 218-20)

There is so much richness in *The Shadow on the Hills* that *The Sun on the Stubble* and various books which followed seem a sort of preparation for it. Typically, *The Shadow on the Hills* covers its young hero's final year of basic schooling and follows an established pattern of starting and ending with the long school holidays, which allow for free-ranging activities and mark points of significant change. Bodo and Ossie are constantly in trouble with the miserly storekeeper or their teacher who, we note again, is being courted by one of the local lads. In one familiar scene the boys are spying on the lovers, who are entwined high in a haystack, and they decide to jump on them from a platform above, armed with a great flashlight, and yelling:

> The result was galvanic. The two lovers, who were intricately interlocked in one another's arms, flew apart like a bursting pod. The attack was a complete surprise, and the combined shock of noise and brilliant light was shattering. The woman gave a scream that put Bodo's shriek to shame, and the man recoiled against the wall of bags with a yell.

> (pp. 220-21)

That simile of rudely interrupted lovers flying apart like a bursting pod sounds casual enough to be part of any bush-storyteller's yarn—at least, that's its style. The effect is, of course, deliberate and calculated. Not only does it have the freshness and originality of precise poetic language, it is arresting, appropriate and humorous and is exactly the sort of easily visualised imagery most likely to appeal to children. Colin Thiele indulges in spontaneous word-play far more readily and successfully than any of his Australian contemporaries. He even *invents* words when it suits the sense he wants to convey and nothing else will do: Tessa Noble goes 'larruping' along the beach to visit Axel and the dog Woppit in *February Dragon* 'grampuses' about furiously in Heaslip's dam. Thiele's imagery

is always a delight: the driver of *February Dragon*'s school bus, Mr Harvey (always called Miss Strarvy because 'people never seemed to have time to pause between the "Mr" and the "Harvey"'), used to whistle as he drove—'so loudly that his lips looked like the underside of a mushroom'. *The Shadow on the Hills* is full of pleasurable inventiveness, and verbal ingenuity, from the simple analogy of gobbling turkeys 'parading proudly like puffed-up galleons' to the amused irreverence of a description of a photograph of Bodo's ancestors: 'Grandfather Schneider, looking like an angry walrus, Grandma in a long black dress with a high white collar, and Bodo's father and mother on their wedding day, imprisoned for ever in an oval frame of polished wood like a rather superior dunny seat'.

A further observation to be made about the above is that it is one of many references made by the author, no matter how obliquely, to aspects of basic bodily functions, selected parts of the anatomy, and related furnishings, which children designate as *rude* because they know that such references are often offensive to adults. Although playground language is commonly peppered with a whole range of associated terminology, used among peers with abandon, children tend to avoid such language when in the company of adults, out of regard for their more sensitive ears. Oddly enough, authors mistakenly reciprocate when writing for children. Colin Thiele doesn't though. Although he can be stylishly bawdy, he addresses his audience on equal terms. (pp. 221-22)

Reading lists for teenagers commonly include books by Colin Thiele and even in the United States he is regarded as a novelist whose work is 'chiefly directed at the adolescent reader'. His involvement in writing for young people has certainly coincided with the remarkable growth of the adolescent and 'young adult' novel in the United States but the view of life he presents is so markedly different from the one generally assumed as a basis for the teenage *genre* that to include him as part of it is misleading. At one stage in *The Shadow on the Hills,* during a sharp verbal exchange with a girl, Bodo asks a question about himself ('What am I? Infected or something?') and it comes as something of a surprise because it is rare for Thiele's characters to refer to themselves in any way at all (whereas, for instance, Ivan Southall's characters talk like this *all* the time). The lonely, bored, frustrated, maladjusted, misunderstood heroes and heroines of the contemporary American Young Adult Problem Novel generally have an all-consuming egocentric view of the world, but even in falling overboard and getting involved in pranks, 'Snook' Pascoe of *Blue Fin* is at least out and about and doing things. He is always involved in life, no matter how unlucky it might be for him, instead of negatively agonising over the world's refusal to revolve around him. Certainly, Thiele's children are younger than those found in Young Adult fiction from the United States but one feels that at any age Bruno, Link, Craypot, Ossie and all the rest will remain eternally boyish—one can't imagine them faced with the dilemmas of drugs, homosexuality, pregnancy, abortion and the rest of the preoccupations of this *genre*. This is probably a cultural difference: perhaps Australian males don't really grow up while Americans aspire to mature as early as possible.

Furthermore, Colin Thiele's children have too many obligations to be constantly worrying about themselves. They are all involved in some kind of work or another, whether it be for their own part-time earnings (for example, Bruno, Bennie and Bodo are all rabbit-trappers, selling the skins to merchants; Ernie gouges for opal, and so on) or in carrying out daily chores necessary for the shared well-being of their family (for example, routine farmyard tasks, expected of the girls as well as boys). All this is real work, as an obligation, in which these children are involved at an age *before* the self-indulgent years of misery even begin for their affluent, indolent 'young adult' literary counterparts. (pp. 223-24)

Yet again, one notices that Thiele's children, being more in touch with the feelings of others, become aware that *adults* are sometimes the lonely, alienated ones. (p. 224)

The notion of a self-contained but problematical state of adolescence is perhaps an indulgent luxury which not all societies can afford. That might have been the case in Colin Thiele's youth. The syndrome of agonised adolescence doesn't exist in the milieu presented by his books. For one thing, his child characters are responsible members of what we would now call an extended family. The fourteen-year-olds are not hived off to share their imagined miseries with other fourteen-year-olds—Bodo's peer group is really his whole family, including assorted uncles, and old Ebenezer too. More than this, Thiele's children grow up as part of a secure, ordered, homogeneous and supportive wider community. The German farming settlements are obviously of this kind but so too are the others; the children in **The Hammerhead Light** or **Albatross Two** are part of the 'soft gentleness of an old fishing village' in which each person fulfils himself in roles which are of mutual benefit. If there is a dance, or a local show or a tin-kettling or a spotlight fox-hunt, it is a community affair and, children being part of the community, they participate accordingly. Any other modern novelist concentrating on the relationship between an adolescent and an old man would have been more likely to exploit some inherent sexual peculiarity of the situation or would present it from the standpoint of what's in it for the child protagonist. The former consideration never arises in Thiele's work, while the latter proposition would be reversed.

Perhaps the opportunities to live the innocent sort of life evoked by Colin Thiele in these books have gone forever, along with the erosion of the concept of family and the abandoning of the values of an older morality which, while undoubtedly more restrictive than the comparative hedonism which has replaced it, at least seemed to offer some degree of stability and contentment. If other writers are 'telling it like it is' for today's young readers, perhaps Colin Thiele has been merely letting them know how it once was in certain times and places. Thiele is not trying to promote some sort of puritanical work ethic and general morality; nor is his view of the real world of today's children a blinkered one, for in his appealing particular milieu lie universal truths. Yet one shares, with Bruno and Bodo, regret for the loss of a time and place that are no more. (pp. 225-26)

I am content to leave the last word about this most admirable writer to his colleague Max Fatchen:

> Colin Thiele is a quiet man and a gentle one. It's the gentleness of great strength and the quietness of an enormous well of peace and conviction that the man has inside of him. He has, without noise or sensation, reached out and with his warm genius touched the hearts and minds of countless people throughout the English-speaking world and beyond. He offers us, without bombast, the proposition that the human spirit is alive and well, that we can all co-exist, that issues can be discussed and examined with friendliness, and that we do not have to pound each other to pieces to impress society.

(p. 226)

Walter McVitty, "Colin Thiele: Universality in the Heart of Man," in his Innocence and Experience: Essays on Contemporary Australian Children's Writers, *Thomas Nelson, 1981, pp. 197-232.*

Margaret Carmody

[To] ask Thiele a question is to set a flood in motion. It is a flood of childhood memories, of names and places; a flood of ideas and principles; a flood of information and feelings about why he writes, how he writes and what it is like to be a children's writer. (p. 7)

Thiele loves to speak of his own childhood, spent in the German community in the Barossa Valley in South Australia:

> It was a society where honesty and hard work were of the utmost importance.

But he holds no illusions about that society. Thiele was part of the generation which emerged from the Valley, from its safety and familiarity, and from its conservatism and religious bigotry.

It was a life of family prayer twice a day, of the Bible in German, of German spoken at home and English at school. His own mother, who still wore old-fashioned black dresses that buttoned right up to the throat even in the 1950's, always preferred to speak in German. And his elder sister still refers to his wife as "That girl from outside the Valley".

Life in the Barossa Valley, with all its conservatism, insularity and factionalism clearly fascinates Thiele who has a very strong sense of place and of history. It is to him utterly unbelievable that a debate on the millennium should split a pioneer society—yet it did just that. What was even more surprising for Thiele, however, was that when he wrote a book which dealt in part with these features of Valley Life—*Labourers in the Vineyard*—he received letters from people living in the Barossa who called this book "blasphemous" and listed all the instances of what they regarded as blasphemy from the book.

A love of nature and the workings of the natural world are a legacy of his Barossa childhood. His father, who went to school for only two years was not unlike many of the fathers in his books: he was tremendously kind, he was a great innovator, especially where farm machinery was concerned and, as well, he was a "self-taught naturalist". Thiele marvels at the skill of the early explorers and settlers: men like Goyder who contributed so much to the pioneer life. Independence, facing crises and coming to a mature understanding of the world around the emerging adolescent are pervasive themes in the children's fiction of Colin Thiele. Thiele possesses an intense curiosity about the manifestations and laws of the physical world, both natural and man-made:

> When children say 'I'm bored' I say, 'How CAN you be bored? Look at the world around you! How is rain made? Why do we have rain and hail [in Adelaide] but not snow? What is the difference between hail and snow?'

Thiele's energy and enthusiasm as he poses these questions have a challenging impact on me and must similarly affect any children he speaks to.

In his writing, he challenges the modern child to find answers to the questions of how the physical world works. He depicts his child hero engaged in asking these questions, seeking answers, synthesising information and drawing conclusions of his own, often under the guidance of an adult friend.

From Thiele's love of nature springs a desire for absolute accuracy in dealing with the natural world. He believes historical and technical accuracy are of primary importance in his writing for children. He talked about the dilemma he faced at the end of *Fire in the Stone:*

> I asked some explosives experts up at Coober Pedy, I said to them 'What would happen to some children in that size hole, with that much explosive, could anyone possibly survive?' And they all said 'No, not unless they were outside the room or lying down.' So I thought about that and I realized that, if Willie was going to be in the gallery at the time of the explosion, then he would have to die—otherwise it wouldn't be accurate. In the film he was in the tunnel, and so he didn't die.

The film loses the significant symbolism of Ernie's pick trapping Willie's foot, and Willie's warning leap which sends Ernie flying, thus saving his life.

More on the accuracy of *Fire in the Stone:*

> There were no girls in *Fire in the Stone* because there WERE no women at Coober Pedy.

Thiele admits he has romanticised the landscape of the opal fields:

> I LIKE Coober Pedy because of its boundless landscape, and no fences. But it is a very dangerous, violent society.

Thiele makes no apology for writing about his own childhood and tells me how he once tried to write a story set in Lapland. A friend had been there for a year and provided him with photos, tapes, and so on:

> I was very enthusiastic and I started to write and then I realized that I didn't know the sound that a snow shoe makes on snow. I just didn't know.

I had never heard it. So I decided I couldn't write it and I packed up all the material and gave it back.

He attributes the success of *Blue Fin* to his intimate knowledge of the tuna industry, gained while he was a teacher at Port Lincoln. He compared the success of *Blue Fin* as a novel, with *Albatross Two.* He had written it in a hurry and he hadn't internalized the information sufficiently, so that while it was certainly accurate, it lacked the subtlety of *Blue Fin:*

> There is a difference between didacticism and preaching. The bad thing about *Albatross Two* was the preaching.

When I asked him why he wrote almost entirely about boys, he said:

> I can only write about what I know and have experienced. Life in the Valley was very different for girls than boys. . . . I write about boys because I was one, once.

He feels he actually knows very little of what it was like to be a girl in the Barossa. Girls had far less freedom than boys. This was easing for his sisters; whereas for his mother's generation there had been no question of dances, his sisters were allowed to go to dances and have evening dresses, "which they made themselves, of course". Thiele feels that girls really are different from boys: that girls have intuition, that they have a sensitivity to people and situations which he as a man would never have or fully understand.

Though many years have passed since Thiele lived in the Barossa Valley, his own childhood spent there provides a flood of reminiscences:

> If a child of five's job is to bring in the wood, and he does not do it, then when he comes in cold and wet, there will be no warm fire to greet him. Everyone had a job to do, from three year olds to old grandfathers. Parents worked from dawn till dusk: every moment of the day was spent working. The women actually worked harder than the men because, on top of all the haymaking and milking and chooks and so on, they also ran the house and nurtured the children. . . .

The work which the child performed was important because it demanded a sense of responsibility from the child: responsibility to himself, to others, and to the animals and their shared environment. This sense of responsibility is a major theme in Thiele's writing.

Life in the Barossa in the 1930's was not much different from the late 1800's:

> Life in 1925 in the Barossa was very like life in Western New South Wales in the 1890's, as Lawson described.

Thiele goes on to compare the milking in Lawson's 'A Day on a Selection' with that in *The Valley Between:*

> It was a PIONEERING life.

Childhood as a time of freedom and innocence is a major

theme of Thiele's and springs from his own childhood experience:

> We were allowed enormous freedom to range as far and wide as we liked even 20km from the house. The reason we were allowed to do that was because it was a small community and therefore our parents felt we were safe. Our parents were so busy they hardly noticed [us]. It was a pioneering society and to us 'exploring' was quite appropriate. We *could* have got into all sorts of dangers; we could have fallen down a well, had a shooting accident or been gored by a bull . . . but we didn't!

Thiele feels that Man and Nature have been put here for a purpose and we should be able to live peacefully together. It is when man breaks the rules that trouble starts. From his love of nature, especially birds, springs his hatred of firearms. He loathes sporting shooters and one theme of his writing is the destructiveness of firearms: yet they were a positive part of life in his own childhood:

> The rules for the use of firearms were strictly adhered to in the Valley. There were never any accidents. The shooting of foxes is alright because there is a REASON for the shooting. I can remember the malicious, wanton killing of 80 turkeys which brought my mother to tears . . .

Thiele believes that the modern suburban child is very restricted:

> It is just not possible to duplicate the freedom of Barossa life for kids in the suburbs, because the safety of a small community, the open areas, and the rules about firearms and so on are not present in suburban society. Once we had completed our jobs we took our leave and sometimes didn't come back all day. But of course we had to be back by a certain time.

Thiele is not keen to discuss influences on his work, but he does admit to his own upbringing within the pioneering German Community in the Barossa, his reading of the entire works of Thomas Hardy on his train journeys to and from school in years eleven and twelve, and his own lifetime spent teaching children.

From his own experience as a teacher, Thiele holds that children are interested in understanding the technical world and the issues raised therein. I asked him why he hadn't ever included a detailed character of a teacher in any of his books and he replied that he had never done a character of a teacher because he's afraid people would accuse him of using people he knew. (pp. 7-11)

Colin Thiele genuinely believes that there is in most people's lives a critical event which constitutes a turning point from childhood to adolescence, and that this crisis which sets new limits on the strengths and abilities of that young person is a positive event. He said that he was thinking of the crisis through which an individual must pass, and the positive effect it has, when he 'concocted' the quote at the beginning of the *Rim of the Morning:*

> The Boy and the Man went up the hill of the world together. But the Man grew old and stayed behind to rest. Then the Boy went on

> until he reached the rim of the morning, and there in magic and pain and wonder, he looked out alone . . .

Thiele does not address the problem of prolonged adolescent transition as is often the case today when so many young people remain at school, dependent on their parents, or are unemployed and largely directionless. He writes, rather, from his own experience and sticks to his theory of a critical event. This allows him as a writer to combine all the forces which besiege the individual into one horrifying event where pressures from family, from society, from within himself and from a hostile nature can be combined so that the individual must deal with them all in one fell swoop.

The setting is an integral part in the development of the individual, especially in the Barossa books where the circumstances of the Great Depression make the concept of a crisis highly relevant. However, the setting is really only the vehicle by which Thiele presents his main theme of the child emerging from his innocent world into the world of adolescence.

Colin Thiele believes in the universality of experience. Greed and malice have existed always and always will. And so too honesty and kindness. He recounts the story of the Good Samaritan or that of an Australian rescuing a mugged person in New York in 1982 as examples of these aspects of human nature. He believes that while society has changed a great deal over the last two and a half thousand years, man has remained essentially the same. (p. 12)

> Margaret Carmody, *"An Interview with Colin Thiele,"* in The Lu Rees Archives, Notes, Books and Authors, *Vol. 8, 1987, pp. 7-13.*

TITLE COMMENTARY

Storm Boy (1963)

The setting of *Storm Boy* will be [unfamiliar to English readers] . . . but by the end of the book it will be surprising if they do not feel they know the part of the South Australian coast celebrated in this remarkable story, even if they have not seen the equally remarkable documentary film based upon it. Here a boy lives with his widower father, free of the ninety-mile beach with its wreck-treasures, the sandhills and marshes of the wild-life sanctuary, and enjoying the friendship of Fingerbone, a solitary Aboriginal living nearby. A new relationship with the pelicans named Mr. Proud, Mr. Ponder and Mr. Percival begins when the boy finds them as deserted fledglings and rears them himself. Two are released in the sanctuary later, but Mr. Percival, who had needed special care, becomes the boy's inseparable companion, until he too falls victim to holiday gunmen. Here is yet another lesson in conservation, conveyed through the burning indignation of Storm Boy against hunters, the indignation of a boy used to freedom and accepting the right of his fellow animals to enjoy it also. The narrative is openly, warmly emotional, with a sense of place developed within the framework of a boy's experience. (pp. 3361-62)

*Margery Fisher, in a review of "Storm Boy,"
in* Growing Point, *Vol. 17, No. 2, July, 1978,
pp. 3361-62.*

Thiele creates, as usual, a vivid picture of the wild South
Australian coast, but in so few pages even he can't develop
characters and plot to match. Boy finds three birds, shel-
ters and trains one, and finally loses it. The relationship
between the boy and the animal he raises isn't as detailed
as in, say, North's *Rascal* (Dutton, 1963) or Maxwell's
Ring of Bright Water (Dutton, 1961), though the bird's behavior is certainly entertaining. Young readers who would
appreciate the length might find unfamiliar words and expressions difficult, but this would be a pleasant enough
short book for middle graders.

Sue Sprague, in a review of "Storm Boy," in
School Library Journal, *Vol. 25, No. 6, February, 1979, p. 60.*

Sometimes in a similar spirit to the black-and-white social
realists, a writer for children starts out to show children
the fact of death (or of copulation) but because he is dealing with facts, however socially mediated and shaped, his
intention and its creative realization stand in an easier relation than when we speak, in abstract terms, of 'practices
and structures'. The most familiar device is for the novelist
to take hero or heroine through the experience of loving
and caring for a pet, and having it die. Steinbeck's *The Red
Pony,* Marjorie Rawlings's *The Yearling,* the lovely Australian tale *Storm-Boy* by Colin Thiele which tells of a
boy's friendship with a pelican pointlessly shot at the end
by a hunter, are all examples of such a framework. Each
book maintains the simple, two-way movement of child
and creature, and restores their relationship to a paradise
in which the inevitable innocence of both creates a mutual
trust which has no need of speech nor of society. Adults
only break into the charmed circle of loving, speechless
understanding when death and danger threaten. Before
then, the child returns to a natural state which has no need
of grace, and to which he is not so much tutored as *recalled* by the animal: the pony, the deer, the pelican.
(*Charlotte's Web* has something of the same quality.) The
beauty of these tales is their paradisal quality—and it is
important to say that paradises may come true in any
life. . . . Each novel celebrates the beauty of natural loyalty and unpossessive love. Death threatens, and then appears as loss. Loss cuts both ways. It is experienced partly
as bitter, intolerable anguish for oneself ('How shall I
manage without him?') and partly as some larger groping
into the dark unknown sea for an explanation, a yearning
outwards to know what has happened to the lost being,
how he fares in the lost world, what can be made *im*personally of this broken connection, this for the moment in-
escapable feeling of incompleteness.

Loss is, we say, like something being cut off. It is an ampu-
tation. This is not true for children (and for the essential
childishness of all good men and women) who relish
fiercely present joy because they know it will soon be lost:
this afternoon on a summery beach, this birthday picnic,
this Christmas Day. The loss by death in these novels is
abrupt and arbitrary. In our times, perhaps this is the best
a novelist can do. (pp. 284-85)

*Fred Inglis, "Love and Death in Children's
Novels," in his* The Promise of Happiness:
Value and Meaning in Children's Fiction,
Cambridge University Press, 1981, pp. 271-91.

February Dragon (1965)

The author of this interesting story of life in the Bush has
obviously an intimate knowledge of the Australian countryside and the daily life on a Bush Homestead.

Resin, Turps and Columbine are the three happy-go-lucky
children of the Pine family, and the book is concerned
with their everyday happenings, and their one great family
disaster.

Although an imaginative fictional story the book has that
rare quality of imparting knowledge whilst telling an exciting and interesting tale. All too often informative books
written in narrative form are stilted and forced. Children
cannot be fooled and soon see through this thin disguise
to make them learn. The facts and figures blend easily into
the text which is well written with needle sharp descriptions of the village characters and of the animal personalities.

The "February Dragon" of the title is the dread bushfire.
There is no sentimental glossing over the harsh truth and
nature is soon at her most cruel. The sheep are burnt alive
in the field; Turps's pony screams to death unheard in the
stable; dozens of families lose their homes and all that they
possess, and a terrible death comes to Old Barnacle Bill,
who ran the village shop and was just too old to run from
the fire.

This book will make a deep impression on all who read it,
and will, we hope, not be the last from the pen of this excellent Australian author.

A review of "February Dragon," in The Junior
Bookshelf, *Vol. 30, No. 4, August, 1966, p.
256.*

Bushfire is the February Dragon that rears its head in so
many Australian juveniles. Here it writes a jarringly tragic
finish to the otherwise unremarkable goings on at Bottle-
brush Farm in Upper Gumbowie where, in assorted episodes, Pinch the pet possum attacks snobbish Aunt
Hester, Turps gets a pony for her eleventh birthday, Woppit the dog runs amok after a medicinal application of tur-
pentine to his mangy backside, and Aunt Hester (again!)
is served a live crayfish with her Christmas Eve crackers.
Rather too much of the humor hangs on names: one incident concerns the wedding of the town schoolteachers,
Miss Lemon and Miss Strarvy (Mr. Harvey); and the children themselves are known as Turps, Resin, and Columbine Pine. Nor do these goings on really prepare us for the
wholesale destruction of pets, livestock, and homestead
that ensues from Aunt Hester's pigheaded decision to hold
a pork chop picnic on a day when the scrub is tinder dry;
though, admittedly, the fire and its aftermath bring Thiele
to the top of his accustomed form.

A review of "February Dragon," in Kirkus Reviews, *Vol. XLIV, No. 13, July 1, 1976, p. 733.*

The Thiele family circa 1970. From right: daughter Sandy, Colin, wife Rhonnie, daughter Jan, son-in-law Jeff Minge.

The . . . *Dragon* is the dormant but ever-present threat of brushfire waiting only for a spark to awaken it. Unfortunately, the rambling story itself lacks the requisite spark. Built around the daily adventures of the three Pine children, it's pleasant and sometimes fun but not continuously involving, and the excessive use of cute nicknames, e.g., "Miss Strarvy" for the male teacher Mr. Harvey, is plain annoying. Thiele's characters are better drawn than those in Mavis Clark's *Wildfire* (Macmillan, 1974), which also has as its theme brush fire in Australia, but the Clark book is more exciting.

> *Karin K. Bricker, in a review of "February Dragon," in* School Library Journal, *Vol. 23, No. 5, January, 1977, p. 98.*

Blue Fin **(1969)**

[Snook Pascoe] is an anti-hero in tune with the present day . . .—gangling, accident-prone, noisy and confused with the course of life. The picture of Snook that remains in my mind is of the boy slithering down the ceremonial stairs of the civic building in Port Lincoln and narrowly escaping collision with the Governor, after he and his

chums have propped a tuna, duly robed, in the Mayoral chair.

This is a gloriously unconventional adventure story, full of the classic qualities of heroism, speed and drama but shot with irreverent guffaws of laughter and the uncompromising acceptance of life's grotesque accidents and frustrations. The plot follows *Victorious Troy* pretty closely. Snook, in disgrace all round and with no apparent future, is taken on as a crew member for the long school holidays when his father's ship *Blue Fin* goes out from South Australia for the tuna catch. . . . Then a typhoon overtakes the ship, the crew are lost, father is hurt, and the boy is left to deal with a damaged engine and a tank full of fish, their livelihood, rapidly thawing for failed electricity. Snook copes—but without a complete triumph and in the hit and miss way his temperament dictates. Courage and guts are seen to be his but he is still accident-prone. The character is beautifully drawn and shrewdly so; the story depends on character and action in proper balance and earns high praise for this. And it is a very good story. (pp. 1439-40)

> *Margery Fisher, in a review of "Blue Fin," in* Growing Point, *Vol. 8, No. 6, December, 1969, pp. 1439-40.*

No-one thinks of deep sea fishing as being an easy job, but it might be natural to gravitate towards this sort of work if a boy had enjoyed fishing along river banks. Colin Thiele makes boys realize that there is no comparison. This is not a story which has been soft-pedalled for children, it is about the dangers deep sea fishermen meet, the fierce competition, the difficulty in making money, and the dangers which have to be faced. It is a tale of courage and heroism and yet the chief character is nobody's idea of a teenage fictional hero, he is quite the reverse until the end of the story. This is a book which will be enjoyed by any boy who finds ordinary living a bit dull and uneventful.

A review of "Blue Fin," in The Junior Bookshelf, *Vol. 34, No. 1, February, 1970, p. 43.*

Snook Pascoe is as unprepossessing as his name and, what's worse, the butt of his father's frustration when his tuna boat, *Blue Fin,* has a run of bad luck. Then Snook goes along on an Easter weekend fishing trip to help out his shorthanded father, and when *Blue Fin* is hit by a tornado, seriously wounding his father and killing the rest of the crew, Snook proves his worth by keeping the boat afloat and repairing the motor to bring them back to port. The pattern is a familiar one, but seldom this well executed, and Snook's emotions are carefully calibrated and taut—as he forces himself to do the backbreaking work of pumping out the hold, feels helpless fear in the face of his father's deteriorating condition, and grows more and more confident as the boat nears home. Thiele's view of the relationship between the sea and its disabled victims— "Light swaddled in darkness. Life rocked by death"—is unabashedly poetic but never maudlin. And just as Snook is giving in to the elation of having brought *Blue Fin* safely home—the boat is struck by another disaster and crashes onto the rocks, destroying itself and the valuable tuna catch that would have given the family a new start. A grim but thoroughly believable ending, and a full-bodied sea adventure for all hands.

A review of "Blue Fin," in Kirkus Reviews, *Vol. XLII, No. 9, May 1, 1974, p. 490.*

Flash Flood (1970)

The Stevens family are on a caravan holiday in the Australian Bush. One night they camp in a dried out creek and the next morning Even-Stevens takes his dog Bullet for a walk. There is a terrible thunderstorm, Bullet bolts after a rabbit and the boy is finally found by the local ranger. His family, too, suffer from the flood, losing their caravan. They return home without the dog, but two days later he is found by the ranger and the story ends happily. This is a simple tale for six to eight-year-olds, but Colin Thiele is a poet as well as an excellent prose writer and what is so important about this book for the young reader is his economical use of adjectives. . . . This is a book to be recommended, for children will read and re-read it and perhaps subconsciously absorb some of the author's skills.

J. Murphy, in a review of "Flash Flood," in The Junior Bookshelf, *Vol. 35, No. 2, April, 1971, p. 106.*

Flip-Flop and Tiger Snake (1970)

Colin Thiele's naturalistic tale, ***Flip-flop and Tiger Snake,*** which rather distantly evokes *Rikki-tikki-tavi,* takes the form of a picture-book with an extended story decked in green and black; the illustrations [by Jean Elder] lightly suggest "people in a story" while at the same time providing the proper backing for an accurate piece of natural history. Flip-flop is a frog whose life cycle from spawn to metamorphosis is watched by Peter Martin, whose farmhouse home is near a water-hole. The foolhardy frog (his character conveniently borrowed from nursery rhyme) ignores the advice of old Boomer the bullfrog to look out for snakes, and eventually has to flee into the farmhouse, where the snake follows and is driven out by Mr. Martin with a pogo-stick. After panting in a drain pipe, the frog at last gets back to the pond a sadder and wiser animal. Both moral and facts are delivered in direct prose in which a modicum of animal chat fits quite naturally. English as well as Australian children should learn from, and enjoy, this instructive tale.

Margery Fisher, in a review of "Flip-Flop and Tiger Snake," in Growing Point, *Vol. 10, No. 1, May, 1971, p. 1742.*

The interest of very young children would be hard to sustain throughout the rather long narrative, though the large format and pictures would certainly appeal to them. Older children may require a more factual natural history approach to the creatures and the Australian countryside in which they live.

The author uses the story framework to trace the life story of the frog, but the approach is always educational and as such it does not fill in the details and clarity required by the subject. The book is neither a good story nor a clear life history of the frog. . . .

J. Russell, in a review of "Flip-Flop and Tiger Snake," in The Junior Bookshelf, *Vol. 35, No. 3, June, 1971, p. 172.*

The Fire in the Stone (1973)

This solid, tense, realistic adventure is set vividly in Australian opal mining country where fourteen-year-old Ernie, seemingly a middling kind of kid, lives with his shiftless father in a crude dugout. Early on Ernie makes a valuable find in an abandoned mine but loses all to an unknown thief except the few stones he's stuffed into his pockets—and his father takes off with the $1500 he gets from selling those. Later there's a much larger opal theft and Ernie and two friends, one of them Willie, an Aborigine from the Reserve, secretly track the culprit and the cache in the same underground mine. The thief is caught, but not before setting a trap that explodes on the unsuspecting boys; Ernie, blind to the "sea of red" (the gleaming treasure that is the fire in the stone) which he unearths in the process, desperately digs their way out from the resulting cavein . . . but Willie never recovers consciousness. In the end Ernie, restless in the limited mining community and unaware that his friend has just died, sets out with his reward money to look Willie up in the hospital in Adelaide; "after that he would see about himself." Ernie's relationships and encounters with his father, with Willie, with the motley townsmen and the Aborigines on the Reserve are observed with unsentimental clarity, and the unique, strongly realized locale gives further weight to the breathless moments of danger and impressive feats of endurance. (pp. 1066-67)

A review of "Fire in the Stone," in Kirkus Reviews, *Vol. XLII, No. 19, October 1, 1974, pp. 1066-67.*

Here with a vengeance is the real world: the world of Ernie, who lives alone with his wastrel father in a house dug out of sandstone, in the strange lovely-desolate part of Central Australia where men seek their fortunes in the opal fields. . . .

[Ernie] learns about greed and prejudice and stupidity, but he also learns about friendship, from his "cobbers" Nick Andropoulos and Willie Winowie—an Aborigine boy through whom the parallel between American Indians and the uprooted "boongs" of Australia is tellingly drawn.

This is a marvelous novel, not only bringing Australia to vivid life but giving the young reader an uncompromising, provocative picture of the situation of man.

Susan Cooper, "Chair-gluers for the 8-14's," in The Christian Science Monitor, *November 6, 1974, p. 12.*

A story that has elements of suspense and romantic adventure is set in the Australian opal fields. . . . Thiele creates the setting with harsh realism, constructs his tale deftly, and creates believable characters in a fast-paced story that is just as evocative as Mavis Clark's *Spark of Opal* . . . setting. (pp. 123-24)

Zena Sutherland, in a review of "Fire in the Stone," in Bulletin of the Center for Children's Books, *Vol. 28, No. 7, March, 1975, pp. 123-24.*

What is so fascinating and rare is the picture painted by this skillful author, in the dry, dun colors of an arid landscape, of an Australia no one who has only seen Melbourne and "Sinny" and gleaming Canberra could even guess at. Inland Australia seems to have much in common with the raw new lands opening up in this country at the turn of the century. Men struggling with a harsh, intractable landscape, emotions centered desperately on greed and luck.

The opal diggers of Australia's Badlands are a sorry lot, fossicking with crazy hope in the underground potch, noodling on the mullock heaps thrown up by past gougers, as a wino noodles over trash heaps for a drain of booze in the bottom of a bottle.

Any land where they talk about noodling and boongs and humpies and walkabout can't be that hopeless. Mines peter out. Men are crooked and cruel. Fathers are no damn good. Grandmothers are drunk. But Ernie and boong Willie Winowie know about the value of human life

and love on the inarticulate levels where friendships are cemented slower, but firmer.

The writing, unlike too many 12 and up books, is perceptive, evocative, funny, lyrical. If kids—or whoever buys books for kids—can overcome the insular reserve of "Who wants to read about Australia?" it's marvelously well worthwhile.

Monica Dickens, in a review of "Fire in the Stone," in The New York Times Book Review, *February 23, 1985, p. 8.*

Magpie Island (1974)

This is an unashamedly emotional portrait of an animal and a habitat, in which author and artist alike show a strong response to the strange beauty and changing scenes on a small offshore island in South Australia. The book centres round the fortunes of a magpie which is blown on to the island after venturing too far from land in the excitement of mobbing an eagle. Magpie adapts to a new food-cycle and new competitors (shag, tern and fairy penguin) and a boy on a fishing trip with his father instigates the finding and transporting of a mate from the mainland. A nest is built, eggs are laid, but a sideslipping aeroplane kills the female and Magpie is left alone as "Endurance carved into a silhouette. The everlasting picture of the one against the world", as the fisherman puts it as they sail away from the island. The verbal message, sincere though it is, strikes less deep in the end than the paintings [by Roger Haldane], which focus on a shell, a feather, a dead branch, a bird preening, with a controlled intensity and a superb selection of shape and colour to make a series of evocative studies.

Margery Fisher, in a review of "Magpie Island," in Growing Point, *Vol. 14, No. 1, May, 1975, p. 2651.*

Here is a nature story of real quality. It is of the calibre of those experts of the past, C. G. D. Roberts and Ernest Thompson Seton. . . .

The tale is told in gloriously vigorous prose. The illustrations are vivid and splendidly reproduced. This little book is a classic in its way. It particularly lends itself to being read aloud—to a class, to a gaggle of kids by the fireside, or to a small boy at bedtime. Mr Thiele avoids the obvious sentimental ending which the sardonic adult reader expects. Full marks to him! Let him not rest on his laurels! For this is a real heart-pleaser which deserves further successors.

James Falkner, in a review of "Magpie Island," in The School Librarian, *Vol. 23, No. 4, December, 1975, p. 330.*

An impressively produced book. In spite of a weak beginning the story of a magpie surviving on an island far out to sea grows in intensity as the problems implicit in the situation are developed. In this Colin Thiele demonstrates a sincere concern for the environment and for ecological truth. The often excellent prose is marred by an unevenness and a variation in tone which a competent editor might have expurgated. Although many of the illustrations, especially those in colour, are interesting and contribute to the success of the book, some of the others accentuate an intrinsic uncertainty which finds occasional expression in sentimentality. (pp. 43-4)

> *Ena Noel, in a review of "Magpie Island," in* Bookbird, *Vol. XII, No. 4, December 15, 1975, pp. 43-4.*

Albatross Two   (1974; U.S. edition as *Fight against Albatross Two*)

Albatross Two is sensational and occasionally sentimental but it is a vigorous book, giving a panoramic view of a small township on the South Australian coast altered and upset by the arrival off its shores of an oil rig. Colin Thiele has set his scene firmly, stated his theme and studied it from every angle. In the centre of the story are the villagers—fishermen, storekeepers and the like—and their families. . . . The plot is exciting enough for anyone, ending with a dangerous eruption under water and the removal of the rig. The dramatic solution to the village's problem is so obviously authentic in details, the story is so well told, the characters play their parts so naturally, that one hardly feels like complaining that the happy ending belongs too obviously to fiction rather than to reality.

> *Margery Fisher, in a review of "Albatross Two," in* Growing Point, *Vol. 14, No. 2, July, 1975, p. 2668.*

Conservation and pollution could be the signposts of the seventies. Colin Thiele has written a carefully documented book about the effects of an off-shore oil rig on a remote bay in south Australia. Everything is black and white and the oil men are condemned before they take to sea. Luddites is the word that springs to my mind. One knows the dangers of oil pollution but nowhere in this book is there any attempt to evaluate. The characters are stereotypes—Tina is the girl who loves birds—one realises from the opening chapter the fate that lies in store for her tame penguin Piglet, and her brother Link who goes to work on the rig and has a secret sympathy for the oil men. Many of the characters have impossible nicknames and speak in almost unreadable dialect, both of which factors irritated me enormously. I am sure the technicalities are correct but the book lacked a soul and was therefore for me a failure.

> *Joan Murphy, in a review of "Albatross Two," in* The School Librarian, *Vol. 23, No. 3, September, 1975, p. 252.*

With the arrival of *Explorer King*, a giant oil rig set up over an offshore well called Albatross Two, life changes for Link and his sister Tina in the southern Australian fishing town of Ripple Bay. An early confrontation over an accidentally damaged fishing boat precipitates feelings of anger and mistrust between villagers and oilmen. When Link accepts a job as substitute cook's helper and goes to live on the rig, he begins to enjoy the men's comradery, to understand the technical intricacies, and to respect the workers' expertise and dedication. He is there when Albatross Two blows out and, upon returning home, swiftly re-

alizes the hostilities of the fishermen as they fearfully and helplessly watch the oil spill move toward shore. Tina, whose pet penguin is only one of many birds caught in the mire of the oil leak, is livid and even blames her brother for taking the rig job. She and Mr. Hackett, a retired zoology professor, fight diligently to save the creatures as turmoil and dissension crowd around them. Just as there is no easy answer to the contemporary world's battle between environmentalists and energy seekers, so Thiele ends his suspenseful story on a realistic note of inevitable change, for good and for bad. Although readers may feel overfed on offshore well lingo, the careful plot development, the tense escalation of opposing forces, and Link's inner conflicts as he finds himself sympathetic with both sides make this a relevant novel for today. (pp. 1598-99)

> *Barbara Elleman, in a review of "Fight against Albatross Two," in* The Booklist, *Vol. 72, No. 22, July 15, 1976, pp. 1598-99.*

The Hammerhead Light   (1976)

Thiele returns to a fishing village in Southern Australia, where this time the locals of Snapper Bay are threatened not by an oil rig (*Fight Against Albatross Two*), but by the Marine and Harbor Department, which wants to blow up their beloved Hammerhead Light. Twelve-year-old Tessa Noble and ancient "Uncle" Axel work together to save the lighthouse, in the process rescuing and caring for a whimbrel when the sea bird loses a leg, and resurrecting the lighthouse to guide Tessa's parents out of a storm and into harbor. For all their effort, the Hammerhead Light collapses anyway, as Axel falls into the ruin of old age. If the plot moves predictably, it moves smoothly, and the unsentimental look at aging, along with Tessa's gradual change from the role of ward to guardian in her relationship with the old man, adds ballast.

> *A review of "The Hammerhead Light," in* Kirkus Reviews, *Vol. XLV, No. 6, March 15, 1977, p. 286.*

Thiele is adept at creating a convincing, dramatic setting for his stories of Australia; here the characters move against a background of a small town intent on preserving the old, abandoned lighthouse that is on a spit of land dangerously battered by winter storms. . . . There's no pat ending: the lighthouse collapses and old Alex, much to Tessa's anguish, is sent from the hospital to a residential home. The structure is taut, the characterization percipient, but the two strong points of the story are the evocation of atmosphere and the deep friendship between the girl and the old man. (pp. 151-52)

> *Zena Sutherland, in a review of "The Hammerhead Light," in* Bulletin of the Center for Children's Books, *Vol. 30, No. 9, May, 1977, pp. 151-52.*

The Shadow on the Hills   (1977)

Once again Thiele projects a vivid panorama of life "down under," this time focusing on the small, south Australian community of Gonunda, circa 1930, which is hometown to twelve-year-old Bodo Schneider. In his last year of school and soon to join the ranks of "horny-handed" German farmers who have settled the area, upfront and uncomplicated Bodo dips schoolgirls' pigtails into inkwells, spies on his teacher "spooning" in the haystacks at the Harvest Ball, and lets loose the prize bull of local power-broker Moses Mibus in the hopes that "Herr Von Ribentropp" will knock up the Schneider heifers. Counterpointing all this standard Peck's-bad-boyishness is Bodo's involvement with half-crazed hermit Ebenezer Blitz who delivers wild sermons in the neighboring hills, vowing to destroy Moses Mibus for dirty-dealing him out of his farm years back. Bodo finds himself squarely in the middle of an increasingly vicious feud which, through a complicated pileup of events, lands Mibus in jail, his empire literally in ashes, and Blitz in a nursing home. Thiele leaves a convincing ragged edge to his plot and avoids the trap of dispensing justice too neatly. Unfortunately, the heated rivalry between Moses and Ebenezer never moves us as it's meant to because there are no fleshed out portraits here, only quick profiles of all the characters, even Bodo. It's the background—the texture and feel of life in Gonunda—that is most keenly present; and, rather ironically, it's a remote and unconnected happening, the Depression, which ultimately has the greatest impact on Bodo and the rest of the townfolk. Thus the novel adds up to more than the sum of its parts, due to Thiele's unfailing knack for catching a simpler, bygone world and pinning it down with tack-sharp observations.

> *A review of "The Shadow on the Hills," in* Kirkus Reviews, *Vol. XLVI, No. 5, March 1, 1978, p. 248.*

Wheat prices, sheep, and local gossip are the main concerns of life in small town, Depression-era Southern Australia. For impish Bodo Schneider and his cronies the steady, slow passage of days is relieved only by hard work and harmless fun. . . . As usual, Thiele ably conveys the ambience of his native land, and the character of Bodo does much to enliven the otherwise snail-paced plot which follows the author's formula of blending family, friends, and small town doings down-under.

> *Barbara C. Campbell, in a review of "The Shadow on the Hills," in* School Library Journal, *Vol. 24, No. 8, April, 1978, p. 89.*

This has, despite some incidents rife with action and drama, less story line than most of Thiele's fiction, but the lack of sustained plot is compensated for more than adequately by the vivid evocation of place—a small town in Australia—and of time—a depression year in which financial stress creates a tension that is a catalyst for dramatic events. Yet the chief appeal of the book is probably in the immediacy of a boy's involvement in the pattern of rural life, the mores of a German-Australian community, the humorous predicaments like being treed by a bull or the more serious ones like being an eye-witness to a crime committed by a miserly man who has had a long-standing feud with an old hermit who thunders Biblical quotations when he encounters anyone.

> *Zena Sutherland, in a review of "The Shadow*

on the Hills," in Bulletin of the Center for Children's Books, *Vol. 31, No. 11, July-August, 1978, p. 186.*

The Sknuks (1977)

[*The following excerpt is from a review of the Austrian edition which was published as* Die Ttupak.]

Unlike many of the other politically "hot topics" of our times, the issue of nuclear power has long-term and very crucial implications for the quality of life that coming generations, including young readers of children's literature, can hope to experience as adults. For this reason, works for children and young people are making an especially significant contribution to the heated debate among Germans about nuclear concerns. Indeed, it appears that the education of Germany's youth about the issue of nuclear power has become a veritable mission for several authors of children's books. (p. 31)

Among the most striking modern works to treat the issue of nuclear power is *Die Ttupak* ("Die Kaputt"—"The Wrecked" reversed). It was not originally a German book, but rather the Austrian translation of an Australian work. The wholesale adoption via translation of appropriate foreign children's works is a common phenomenon among publishers of German children's literature. While *Die Ttupak* is the result of just such a translation, its young German readers are largely unaware of its origins and regard it as a German-language work.

Ostensibly *Die Ttupak* focuses on the visionary creatures who are described in the forward as:

> . . . the most terrible living beings the world has ever known. They are even worse than those creatures called "human beings" who once destroyed the beautiful planet Earth.

The actual theme of the work, however, is a retrospective look at the destruction of the human race by human beings, about whom the author reports:

> They produced the most awful weapons, in order to force their enemies into submission.
> Their enemies were to be blinded or die.
> That's the way they behaved.
> FOR THEY HAD NO CONSCIENCE.
> They built factories for firearms and cannons and bombs.
> They invented horrible poisons and lethal rays and guided missiles. . . .

While the war-mongering of the now-extinct human community hardly merits author Colin Thiele's praise, he singles out one of their deeds as especially contemptible: their use of atomic energy. Thiele intones: "They even tried to smash the very smallest particles—and that is [as if you tried] to lead a cobra with a piece of thread."

The startling juxtaposition of a single filament and a deadly viper creates a most memorable image of Thiele's abhorrence of the generation of nuclear energy. Accompanying this, a simple, but forceful illustration of the exploding atom emphasizes well the criticism of the human race for its wanton behavior.

The message of the Thiele book is not a happy one. Most unsettling is the presentation of the earth's destruction as an accomplished fact, as the documentation of bygone human events by strange creatures who will have survived us. Even the youngest readers of this work feel compelled to identify themselves as members of that scurrilous race which has not yet moved beyond turning Thiele's apocalyptic vision into a reality. (pp. 35-7)

> *Ruth R. Kath, "Nuclear Education in Contemporary German Children's Literature," in* The Lion and the Unicorn, *Vol. 10, 1986, pp. 31-9.*

Chadwick's Chimney (1979)

This adventure is set in South Australia where underground caves abound. The hero is fourteen-year-old Ket, whose father trained divers in the Navy and from whom Ket has learned of the perils of pot-holing. Mysterious occurrences around his home town tempt Ket, his sister and two friends to investigate.

The plot is skilfully constructed, with tension created on the first page by a 'phantom motor bike'. Each chapter ends with a cliff-hanger, or by posing a question, so that one is compelled to read on. The descriptions of the underground caverns and the dangers of exploring them are naturally incorporated into the narrative, so that the reader is able to appreciate the climax without distracting, technical explanations. And although the climax *is* predictable, this does not lessen the suspense. Emotional moments are saved from sentimentality by Thiele's dry wit. . . .

My main criticism is that the characters are more like caricatures than real people. Ket is too much the level-headed, knowledgeable hero; his father too aloof and stern. However, as pure adventure, the book holds one's attention, and its unusual setting is a bonus.

> *Anna Kopytynska, in a review of "Chadwick's Chimney," in* The School Librarian, *Vol. 28, No. 2, June, 1980, p. 183.*

The Valley Between (1981)

[*The Valley Between*] is an episodic novel documenting the family relationships, feuding, and response to social change that typified a German-speaking district of South Australia 30-40 years ago. The 13-year-old protagonist has just left school to help on the farm, taking first steps toward manhood. All of the characters are convincing and unforgettable and the interaction of personalities and incidents shows astute understanding of people. Many humorous incidents and a definite sense of place add up to excellent fiction for 12 to 16 year olds.

> *A review of "The Valley Between," in* The Reading Teacher, *Vol. 36, No. 9, May, 1983, p. 943.*

Pinquo (1983)

A warmhearted story about the reciprocal relationship between man and animal. Two children, with the help of an ornithologist, save the life of a penguin who as a result becomes very devoted to them. The bird proves the truth of a somewhat mythical Aboriginal saga and, after an earthquake, successfully warns not only the members of his own species but also the town inhabitants of a coming spring tide. It becomes its paradoxic fate, however, to die together with many other penguins when the shores become contaminated with oil.

In the development of Pinquo's and the children's life together, both the human and the animal worlds emerge in all their complexity and stratification: the social order of the animals as well as the sub-society in the village seem to be intact, but they are both threatened by "modern" trends such as huge oil tankers, mass tourism, etc. (pp. 36-7)

> *A review of "Pinquo," in* Bookbird, *No. 2, March 20, 1986, pp. 36-7.*

Seashores and Shadows (1985; U.S. edition as Shadow Shark; British edition as Sharks in the Shadows)

Despite the title . . . , this is not just a shark-hunt adventure—although it includes some terrifying scenes of one. Twelve-year-old Joe has come from Melbourne to live in a small coastal town with his uncle's hard-pressed family that includes his cousin Meg, who is his age but taller and handier than he. When Scarface, a 20-foot rogue white shark reappears, Uncle Harry interests a shark hunter in hiring his boat, and the cousins go along to cook. The preparations and attempts at hooking the shark are grippingly described. Their second attempt ends in disaster when the boat catches on fire; Meg, Joe, and Meg's badly burned and injured father land on an island without any means of getting help. How the cousins cope under stress and improvise their survival and rescue—the shark and other shadows fading to the background—is the focus of the last four chapters. The resolutions are almost a letdown after the melodramatic piling up of calamities, but this Australian author has written a real page-turner that might even be considered for reluctant readers. (pp. 200-01)

> *Ruth M. McConnell, in a review of "Shadow Shark," in* School Library Journal, *Vol. 34, No. 7, March, 1988, pp. 200-01.*

Colin Thiele's story of hard-pressed fishermen and farmers in South Australia may strike some as a little too violent for the over-ten readers but the violence fortunately is not so much between humans as between men and environment. 'Scarface', the shark, becomes a minor Moby Dick but does not entirely dominate the lives of people at Cockle Bay. Pastoral and maritime affairs play a large part and provide interest enough without the more spectacular incidents such as the shark's attack on the fishing boat and the explosion aboard the *Seahorse* which results in shipwreck for Joe, Meg and the badly burned Uncle Harry on the uninhabited Wayward Island. A fine gallery of minor characters gives a sense of reality and life to the whole tale.

> *A. R. Williams, in a review of "Sharks in the Shadows," in* The Junior Bookshelf, *Vol. 52, No. 3, June 3, 1988, p. 154.*

Inevitably, readers will be reminded of *Jaws,* as the young hero in a lively new adventure story also contends with a huge shark, known as Scarface. Luckily for young readers, the author concentrates on fishing know-how and is not diverted by adult escapades. . . . The tense battle of fisherman and fish is knowledgeably and excitingly described as the craft and experience of each is drawn into an endurance contest and war of wills. . . . Good characterization, an interesting setting, the excitement of the struggle between Lane and Scarface and the saga of island survival combine in an absorbing adventure tale wherein both reader and protagonists are pleased that old Scarface survives the encounter. (pp. 629-30)

> *Ethel R. Twichell, in a review of "Shadow Shark," in* The Horn Book Magazine, *Vol. LXIV, No. 5, September-October, 1988, pp. 629-30.*

Farmer Schulz's Ducks   (1986)

Colin Thiele's tale of the troubles of Farmer Schulz's ducks in crossing the main road to reach "the pools of the peaceful, weedy Onkaparinga River"; and the safe access which was at last constructed for them, is lively, interesting, logical, credible and aptly told. It will appeal to many readers for its humanity, its sly digs at officialdom and its nicely chosen words (except for the description of the cows in the paddock "with udders as full as back packs"

Thiele with students and books.

which I thought an ugly, jarring and incongruous metaphor, disturbing the restful pastoral scene). *Farmer Schulz's Ducks* will be read aloud, for sharing, with the young ones and enjoyed later by many of them when they can read for themselves.

Mary Milton has painted a wonderful set of duck portraits. She defines differences and shows their quirks, parading them for the reader's delight, in subtle, skilfully executed watercolours. . . . (p. 42)

Acknowledging that this well-designed book is clearly the work of an accomplished author and a talented artist, it grieves me to say that I do not believe that their combined effort succeeds. The components have not welded into an artistic whole. I agree with the editorial statement that "Colin Thiele has produced his best ever picture story book text". However this text has not been illustrated and therefore the book fails to fulfil its promise.

The disappointment begins at the first double-page opening when, instead of finding the lovely Onkaparinga valley, "full of apple trees and cabbage patches, pastures and gardens", we see a tranquil river scene of anywhere. There is no hint of the ordered farmland which has been described. Children are literal. They will seek the cabbages! Next the narrow road crossed over bridges, went past trees and "ran right past the front gate of Farmer Schulz's farm". An excellent portrait of a polled hereford cow completes the page, but there is no hint of road nor tree nor gate behind it. Three geese appear later, on cue, but without a backdrop of the farm's "pear trees and apples, pastures and goats on the hillside, carrots and cucumbers, berries and bacon". Beatrix Potter would be devastated that her lessons have been overlooked.

Where the farm produce in cellar and pantry is so vividly described, credibility requires that we see it. I could not believe that the chance had been missed to picture the cellar full of hanging sausages, butter, cheeses and preserves, vegetables and fruit, no doubt, with dishes of scalded cream set in the pantry near by.

Towards the end of the story comes the report of the Bridge of Ducks which was famous throughout the land. Busloads of tourists came to view, police had to control the crowds at weekends, and television reporters and photographers recorded it all. These joyous riots are illustrated by a static half portrait of Mr and Mrs Average gazing straight at the reader, with their cameras focused on nothing. What a wasted opportunity! And the last straw is that there is no picture of the ducks spilling out of the duck pipe which was the ultimate solution to their problem.

I have given samples of the mismatches of text and illustrations, a letdown, for the story is so vital and visual that readers must look forward to comparing the artist's interpretations with their own. It is successful only in the actual pages about ducks. Since the story is, in total, much more than that, the book does not meet the prime criterion for a successful picture story—that the text and the illustrations are in true union, not, as this appears, a marriage of convenience. In spite of my criticisms, however, I would buy the book for libraries and some homes, where its separate elements will appeal to a variety of readers from all age groups. (p. 43)

Beatrice Fincher, in a review of "Farmer Schulz's Ducks," in Reading Time, Vol. XXXI, No. I, 1987, pp. 42-3.

A lively story richly told, this relates the dilemma of a farmer in changing times. His ducks have always crossed the road to the river in the morning and returned at night. With the city expanding, cars rush headlong in a collision course with the birds despite warning signs. Even a bridge over the road crashes, with ducks aboard, before the onslaught of a speeding truck. Finally, the farmer's youngest daughter, who has suggested several sensible solutions, conceives of a duck pipe under the road, through which the ducks waddle safely through the year. "In winter, when the rain poured down and the water swept out of the pipe in a torrent, they came skidding and skiing, swimming and splashing in a wild, rollicking rush—a waterfall of ducks." The descriptions of the birds (like jewels in a fairy tale), the stylistic rhythm and repetition invoking the seasonal landscapes, the humorous commentary on hurried and harried humans (sentences describing the Germanic Mr. Schulz occasionally invert verbs to the end of the sentence) all make this a fitting companion to *Make Way For Ducklings*. . . . An unforgettable visit to the Onkaparinga River in South Australia.

Betsy Hearn, in a review of "Farmer Schulz's Ducks," in Bulletin of the Center for Children's Books, Vol. 41, No. 9, May, 1988, p. 190.

Thiele is a gifted stylist, and, fortunately, he doesn't restrain his colorful language even when writing, as here, for young children; his dialogue and descriptions are delightful. An inspired combination of realistic family story, fable, pungent social commentary, and constructive problem-solving, this is a fine story to share.

A review of "Farmer Schulz's Ducks," in Kirkus Reviews, Vol. LVI, No. 12, June 15, 1988, p. 905.

Shatterbelt (1987)

Colin Thiele has written some of the very best Australian children's books. **Storm boy** has a special place in our literature and **The fire in the stone** was one of the most challenging and compassionate novels written in the 1970s. Since **Sun on the stubble,** Thiele has provided a wise and benign voice for children and young people to listen to and enjoy. His latest work does not have the tautness of **Blue fin** or the emotional strength of **Storm boy,** but it does have the strong characterisation we have come to expect.

Tracy has forebodings of a fearful disaster but no one will take any notice of her. Even her girl friend Sally thinks she is peculiar. Tracy is not sure just how the disaster will happen until all the clues come together at a local fete. In a tense conclusion, she is able to save everyone from being trapped in either a mine or a collapsing building when the earthquake strikes. The problems Tracy has with her unsympathetic mother and the relationship she develops with the elderly neighbour and mine owner, Mr. Bailey, are the main concerns of the book and they are convincingly realized. Readers of upper primary age will enjoy this pleasant adventure.

Stella Lees, in a review of "Shatterbelt," in Reading Time, Vol. XXXI, No. IV, 1987, p. 47.

Colin Thiele's reputation as an author of children's books is such that to review his latest offering, **Shatterbelt,** is almost superfluous. It is the sort of book which will be bought automatically on the strength of the author's name, and rightly so, because it is an enjoyable story, competently crafted. **Shatterbelt** is not, perhaps, up to the standard of Thiele's best work, but it is still well worth reading, and will undoubtedly satisfy Thiele's many admirers.

Tracy, the young heroine of the novel, is plagued by prescient visions of disaster. Not, perhaps, the most original of premises for a book to work from, and predictably her mother (with whom she enjoys a less than satisfactory relationship) is disinterested and dubious about her daughter's apparent "gift".

Tracy is, naturally, vindicated in the final chapter when she is able to save fifty people, including the Premier of South Australia from an earthquake, to which the Mount Lofty Ranges (like most of Thiele's work the book is set in his home state of South Australia) are apparently prone. (pp. 29-30)

Natalie Jane Prior, in a review of "Shatterbelt," in Magpies, Vol. 3, No. 1, March, 1988, pp. 29-30.

Jodie's Journey (1988)

Jodie's journey is another fine example of Colin Thiele's skill. Over many years his books have portrayed a thorough knowledge of the material and setting of each tale. However, none can be closer to Thiele than when he tells the story of champion rider, Jodie, whose dreams dissolve when she is stricken with juvenile arthritis. Thiele has suffered acutely from the disease for some forty years, so writes with both knowledge and a deep understanding of the feelings of young victims. More importantly, the story will encourage many young people to understand how they can emulate Jodie in her resolute struggle to overcome her handicap and live a reasonably normal life. This is a novel of bravery, determination and just a touch of humour. . . .

Once again, Thiele has succeeded in giving young readers an uncomplicated, true to life story, to which many can relate, enjoy and find a degree of self identity.

Laurie Copping, in a review of "Jodie's Journey," in Reading Time, Vol. XXXIII, No. II, 1989, p. 29.

This fine story of Jodie's battle to cope with the extreme pain and limitations imposed on her by [juvenile arthritis], as well as the ignorance and misunderstanding of other people, is told with compassion and humour. There is no happy ending for teenage Jodie other than the prospect of operations to replace her diseased joints artificially, and the triumph of her own will to adapt to the disease. The story reaches a powerful climax when Jodie and Monarch are trapped at home in the Adelaide Hills on the morning of the horrific Ash Wednesday bushfires.

An inspiring book written by a master storyteller who knows all about the cruel effects of rheumatoid arthritis, having suffered from it himself for 40 years.

> *Mandy Cheetham, in a review of "Jodie's Journey," in* Magpies, *Vol. 4, No. 2, April, 1989, p. 30.*

Poems in My Luggage (1990)

This is a book of humorous, naively wise, wondering, and yarning poems that are full of Australian images: bunyips, snakes, sheepdogs, possums, goannas, opal miners, and sparrows. Thiele is keeping alive a set of rural images and characters that have come to be associated with Australia, with the tall yarn and the dry wit of an unpretentious nation. Though some might see this vision as dated, these poems convince us that humanity and nature can still be revealed to us through such a world. Like many poets he enjoys word-plays, and one of the most entertaining in the book is **"Plurals."**

It is a book that can show children how much poetry there is in ordinary events, as encouragement to writing poems themselves.

> *Kevin Brophy, in a review of "Poems in My*
> *Luggage," in* Reading Time, *Vol. XXXIV, No. I, 1990, p. 31.*

Farmer Pelz's Pumpkins (1991)

Farmer Pelz is no doubt Farmer Schulz's brother-in-law. Instead of keeping ducks he grows pumpkins—the best and biggest in the world. But the three town toughs are jealous of dear old Pelz. First they paint a big face with a drooping moustache on his prize-winning pumpkin and label it, "Hermann the Hermit". Then they cause a truck load of Pelz's pumpkins to turn into a waterfall—with four tonnes of melons "leaping and bouncing down the middle of the main street". After all the flapdoodle the young men get their deserts and Hermann becomes a local hero.

Thiele's tale is told with great gusto in highly elaborate and ornate language that reads aloud wonderfully well, and trips off the storyteller's tongue. The farming community is well portrayed and behind the facade of caricature there are real and recognisable people. The bubbling fun of the text is captured in the illustrations [by Lucinda Hunnam] which have the embellished detail of a Shirley Hughes and the dramatic action of a Quentin Hole. The final picture of the Annual Pumpkin Festival sets the feet tapping and Thiele's last sentence becomes a benediction. (pp. 29-30)

> *Maurice Saxby, in a review of "Farmer Pelz's Pumpkins," in* Magpies, *Vol. 6, No. 4, September, 1991, pp. 29-30.*

Ed Young

1931-

Chinese-born American author and illustrator of picture books and reteller.

Major works include *The Emperor and the Kite* (written by Jane Yolen, 1967), *The Terrible Nung Gwama: A Chinese Folktale* (1978), *Yeh Shen: A Cinderella Story from China* (retold by Ai-Ling Louie, 1982), *Lon Po Po: A Red Riding-Hood Story from China* (1989).

Respected as a writer and artist of original works and re-tellings in textual and wordless forms as well as an illustrator of over forty titles by other authors, Young creates books which characteristically reflect his Chinese heritage in subject and style. He is highly regarded as a brilliant illustrator whose impressionistic watercolor paintings and pencil drawings incorporating Oriental motifs and other cultural elements are acknowledged for their originality, stunning beauty, and evocative quality. Noted for his extensive research as well as for the authenticity of his books, Young is also praised for investing all of the elements of his works—text, illustration, and design—with equal care as well as for the distinctive use of light, shadow, and perspective in his illustrations. Critic Ethel L. Heins says of him, "Young is never stereotypical in his art; he is utterly versatile, meeting the challenge of each text with imaginative vision and consummate skill." Young is perhaps best known for his interpretations of Oriental folktales with a universal flavor that he writes in a succinct, matter-of-fact style; *Lon Po Po: A Red-Riding Hood Story from China*, a retelling of the favorite nursery tale, is often considered his most popular book. In this version of Red-Riding Hood, the story revolves around three sisters who unwittingly admit a wolf masquerading as their grandmother into their home when their mother is away. Rather than being rescued by a hunter as in the Western version of the tale, the girls kill the wolf by enticing him into a high tree in a basket and letting go of the rope. Young illustrates the story in shaded pastels that weave dark lupine shapes throughout the narrative, dividing his pictures into vertical sections that resemble Chinese screens or panel paintings. Young is also the illustrator of the folktale *Yeh-Shen: A Cinderella Story from China*, a retelling by Ai-Ling Louie is which a magic fish transforms the heroine and the slipper that confirms her status is gold instead of silver or glass. In this work, Young is again noted for his unusual layouts and for the way his pictures flow out of their frames.

Raised in Shanghai and Hong Kong, Young came to the United States at twenty to study architecture, a course supplanted by his interest in art. After working in advertising design and as a magazine illustrator, he began providing pictures for children's books by such authors as Janice May Udry and Elizabeth F. Lewis; he has since illustrated fiction, retellings, and nonfiction by such writers as Aesop, Oscar Wilde, Robert Frost, Jean Fritz, Diane

Wolkstein, James Howe, Nancy Larrick, and Jane Yolen. His artistic collaboration with Yolen on *The Emperor and the Kite* is especially well received. A retelling from an old Chinese tale, the story describes how Princess Djeow Seow, the smallest and least loved of the children of an emperor imprisoned in a tower when his reign is overthrown, helps her father escape by sending him a rope tied on her kite; Young uses the technique of Oriental paper cutouts to create his pictures, which are cut from single pieces of paper and incorporate the kite and its string as a motif. For *Chinese Mother Goose Rhymes: Ju tzu ko t'u* (1968), a collection selected and edited by Robert Wyndham which includes translations of rhymes from the Peking area, Young designs his illustrations to be read vertically like a Chinese scroll; in *High on a Hill: A Book of Chinese Riddles* (1980), Young collects twenty-seven riddles he heard as a child in Shanghai, providing the riddles in verse and their answers pictured on the following pages in black and white drawings surrounded by thin red borders, a format which he uses frequently in his works. Two of Young's books, *The Rooster's Horns: A Chinese Puppet Play to Make and Perform* (1978) and *The Terrible Nung Gwama*, were published in cooperation with the U. S. Committee for UNICEF; in *The Rooster's Horns*, Young and collaborator Hilary Beckett tell the story of how a rooster is tricked out of his beautiful horns by a wily dragon and then demonstrate how to make puppets from the characters and put on a show with them, while in *The Terrible Nung Gwama* Young retells the Chinese folktale of how a poor young woman outwits the monster who has vowed to devour her by using items left for her by sympathetic passers-by. Young is also the creator of two wordless books, companion volumes about the adventures of a cat and a dog that he illustrates in his characteristic style, and the illustrator of folktales from countries such as Thailand, Persia, Arabia, and Africa. *The Emperor and the Kite* received the Lewis Carroll Shelf Award in 1968 and was named a Caldecott honor book in the same year. *Yeh-Shen* was named a *Boston Globe/Horn Book* honor book in 1983. Young received the Caldecott Medal for *Lon Po Po* in 1990 and has also been frequently exhibited by the American Institute of Graphic Arts.

(See also *Something about the Author,* Vol. 10 and *Contemporary Authors,* Vols. 116, 130.)

AUTHOR'S COMMENTARY

[The Following excerpt is from an interview by Dulcy Brainard.]

[Ed Young] carefully chooses his words in speaking about his career and the stories he's illustrated, many of which are Oriental in origin or approach. Nevertheless, the source he seems so close to is less a matter of race or culture than of essential humanity.

"I have never lost the child in me," he says when asked about creating art for children. "I think anybody who's alive has a child in him that responds to anything that has true meaning." (p. 208)

Challenge and growth are central to Young's perception of his role as artist and illustrator. "I feel the story has to be exciting for a child," he insists. "When I'm involved with a children's book, I have to grow first in order to create something exciting. On *In the Night, Still Dark* [Atheneum, 1988] I spent a tremendous amount of time discovering new tools and seeing what worked." The book retells an ancient Hawaiian creation myth; its illustrations are dramatic, with sweeping, strong colors rising from a black page. "*Foolish Rabbit's Big Mistake* [Putnam, 1985] took a long time too. When the type was already set, I changed its style completely—it was the first time I used big images across the pages."

Of the 40 books he's illustrated for more than 10 different publishers, many, such as *Yeh-Shen, A Cinderella Story from China* are folk tales retold; others, like Jane Yolen's *The Emperor and the Kite,* a Caldecott Honor Book in 1968, and *Eyes of the Dragon* by Margaret Leaf (Lothrop, Lee & Shepard, 1987) have the timeless quality of fairy tales. Two recent projects include Oscar Wilde's *The Happy Prince* and *The Voice of the Great Bell,* a Chinese ghost story by Lafcadio Hearn, retold by Margaret Leaf (Little, Brown, 1989). Young has also illustrated historically based stories, such as *The Double Life of Pocahontas* by Jean Fritz (Putnam, 1985).

Whether illustrating fantasy, folk tale or fact, he feels accuracy is essential. "I just did a Chinese Red Riding Hood for Putnam and drew a whole series on how wolves communicate with each other, using their ears, their tails and the way they hold themselves," says Young of **Lon Po Po,** scheduled for release this fall. "That had to be right because the wolf talks to the children in the story, so he has to be alive to them. Then I had to know how the children talked to each other, how they lived in the compound, how the trees would grow. Once you know everything about the story, you can express it in fresh ways."

Of course, research can't supply the whole picture. Inspiration and significance—elements he found missing [when he worked] in advertising—are what Young says he thrives on now. "If I like a story, I sit down and do a picture about this size." His fingers frame a small, perhaps two-inch, square in the air. "This has no research, it just comes out of my head. Then the editor and I talk about deadlines and decide if it will be worthwhile for us to collaborate. Then I go and read up on the culture and do another round." His hands spread, maybe a foot's worth of space. "Then I can tell what I don't know about the story, what I had to find out."

His next step is determining the appropriate medium, use of color and style as detail. He reaches a decision only after considerable experimentation. Acknowledging his good fortune in working with publishers who often leave deadlines open, he's quick to add, "I'm always ahead of time—I have my own deadline in my stomach."

Young's meticulous attention to detail is balanced by his flexibility, both of which are rooted in his deep respect for the story—and he expects the same balance from a story's author. Words and illustrations often are reworked several times. "In the end it is two people finding a place where each one is strong. Then the book thrives." . . .

In a deeper way, balance and enhancement belong to the process of his work. He talks about **Birches,** the Robert Frost poem he illustrated. Far from being merely pictorial renderings of the poet's words, Young's evocative watercolors offer a clear example of how he believes text and illustration work together. "When I first read it, I thought, 'Gosh, Robert Frost! You can't do enough pictures to express any better what the words say already.'"

His Chinese upbringing supplied him with the clues, Young says. "A Chinese painting would be at a loss without the words; they are complementary. There are things that words can do that pictures never can, and likewise you have pictures that words can never describe. They both want to encompass a whole experience. If one repeats the other, it limits that experience. You need to be able to go back and forth so the words and the pictures become a composite, doing something together that neither one can do alone."

The house he shares with his wife Filomena is being renovated, a work-in-progress, like the three projects laid out on the raw wood of the ground floor, which is one large room. One, for Orchard Books, illustrates an Ojibway Indian tale about protecting papooses from creatures that come in nightmares. With collages of beige and dark-blue paper, Young explains, "I'm playing with the possibilities of light and dark, the day and nighttime." Another Indian tale, an Aztec legend he is illustrating for Atheneum, is also done with collage, but with colors ranging from muted to brilliant, in papers with many patterns and textures.

Spreading half the depth of the house are series of pencil drawings on unlined index cards, the frames for a film of *Sadako and the Thousand Paper Cranes,* based on the story by Eleanor Coerr about a Japanese girl who died of leukemia after the bombing of Hiroshima. To be narrated by Liv Ullman, the half-hour film will require 700 frames, developed from at least 200 pictures. That's equivalent to 10 to 20 books, Young points out, but film is an area he's always wanted to explore. As he displays his sketchbook filled with studies of Japanese children, clothing, landscapes and buildings, it's clear he finds in the story his requisite for involvement in any project: the opportunity for growth.

"That's why I'm in this," says Young with a smile. (p. 209)

> *Dulcy Brainard, "Ed Young," in* Publishers
> Weekly, *Vol. 235, No. 8, February 24, 1989,*
> *pp. 208-09.*

GENERAL COMMENTARY

Publishers Weekly

When an illustrator with a strong philosophy of total involvement works only on books he enjoys, the product conveys his joy to the reader.

Such a viewpoint was expressed to *PW* recently, in an interview at World Publishing Co. offices, New York, with Ed Young, a newcomer to illustration, who enjoys a rapidly growing reputation. (p. 92)

Mr. Young's work has exceptional beauty. For his books, he combines oriental motifs and folk art to appeal to American children. With delicate paper cutouts, as in [*The Emperor and the Kite*], and stylized drawings, in *Chinese Mother Goose,* and an extraordinary use of color in both, he does communicate joy to the reader.

His personal philosophy stems in part from his interest in Tai-chi-chun which he teaches. It is a discipline of both mental and physical awareness, and a spiritual way of life demanding total involvement. Mr. Young thinks people become divided if they do what they are not interested in doing. He says he tries to do only what he feels is meaningful, and as an illustrator he is concerned with making a meaningful statement for his immediate society.

What attracts him in accepting a manuscript is the quality and content of a story and the possibility of exciting pictures. For some stories he illustrates the exciting parts, for others, the general impressions. To begin work on *The Emperor* he picked the 12 or 15 most exciting parts and paced the sketches throughout the manuscript. In working with poems, such as *Poetry for Young Scientists,* he illustrated general impressions. He thinks there is one approach which lends itself to a subject and it's up to the artist to find it. . . . Overall design is important to him. He works on materials the same size as the book planning the art in relation to the page and type units.

The verses in *Chinese Mother Goose* are translations of authentic rhymes from the vicinity of Peking. Feeling particular empathy for the content, he designed the book as an oriental scroll, with the book turned the long way, and spreads reading from top to bottom. He has written the poems in Chinese calligraphy which forms decorative borders running down both sides of each page. His illustrations are units contained by outlines, which give the effect of cutouts, but are not. Internal lines describe the stylized forms and objects and carry the color and design. The colors are marvelous blends of inks and dyes.

The nature of Ed Young's art, its delicacy, subtle, unusual colors, and designs for two-page spreads presented several production problems for Jack Jaget, art director for juvenile books at World; happily both the illustrator and art director were pleased with *The Emperor.* . . . (pp. 92-3)

To reproduce the paper cutouts most effectively, they were mounted on glass. By lighting them front and back, the platemaker captured their luminosity. Light was also angled in the shooting to cast a slight shadow. The shadow added dimension to the cutouts and made them distinguishable from flat drawings after reproduction. Testing the skill of the bindery were the thin kite lines running across spreads, which had to meet in the gutters. . . .

Ed Young's creative talents and American printing craftsmanship have joined to make important contributions to children's literature and to visual education through quality color and design. (p. 93)

> *"Illustrations Reflect a Philosophy of Joy," in*
> Publishers Weekly, *Vol. 194, No. 10, Septem-*
> *ber 2, 1968, pp. 92-3.*

Patricia Jean Cianciolo

With the proliferation of adaptations of folktales published each year, one will often find that the artists have included in their illustrations many of the characteristics found in the art of that particular folk culture whose variant of a folktale they are illustrating. In several of the books illustrated by Ed Young, are to be found thoroughly authentic graphic interpretations of Persian folk art and Chinese art. For example, one will find exotic Persian miniatures in *The Girl Who Loved the Wind,* an original tale written in the style of a folktale by Jane Yolen and in *The Red Lion,* an old Persian story retold by Diane Wolkstein. Typical of the Persian miniatures—and of Ed Young's collage pictures—the reader will encounter the perfected draftsmanship that has much in common with children's drawings. They contain a wealth of interesting detail, but the kinds of things that are detailed and the perspective and sense of proportion given to them are reminiscent of the way children portray things—with figures that are placed in different planes, in the "high horizon" convention, so that each is seen separately, and human figures, animals, and natural objects are portrayed as idealized symbols. In other words, they are presented in an elabo-

From The Emperor and the Kite, *written by Jane Yolen. Illustrated by Ed Young.*

rate but uncomplicated way. That beauty of line, the rich, warm tones in the colors used, and, most of all, a perfectionism typical of Persian art are seen in Ed Young's illustrations, too.

Young's illustrations for **Cricket Boy,** an adaptation of a Chinese fable by Feenie Ziner, depict many of the symbols and traditions of long-ago China. His miniature paintings appear within moon-shaped spaces, which are suggestive of the moon-shaped fans carried by members of the Chinese court on informal and romantic occasions. Young's moon-shaped canvases are brush paintings, emulating the impressionistic style that was used by the Chinese artists of antiquity to decorate such fans. The full moon to the Chinese represents happiness in being together—a very appropriate symbol to use in this story of how the cricket boy would bring honor to his father and the name of Hu. For the reader, the hair styles of the men contrasting with that worn by the cricket boy, the presence of flags symbolizing the power of the soldiers and the authority of the emperor, the inclusion of Chinese characters simulating the captions commenting on the theme or contents of each painting, even the artist's stamp bearing his name, so often found on Chinese art—all these and many more details add to the feeling of authenticity that Ed Young's illustra-

tions convey. (pp. 12-13)

> *Patricia Jean Cianciolo, "Folk Art," in her* Picture Books for Children, *revised edition, American Library Association, 1981, pp. 12-13.*

TITLE COMMENTARY

The Emperor and the Kite (1967)

[The Emperor and the Kite *was written by Jane Yolen.*]

Using the authentic and intricate Oriental papercut technique, Mr. Young enhances and complements this delightful version of the Chinese legend of Djeow Seow, smallest daughter of the Emperor, who rescues her father from his imprisonment in a high tower by weaving a rope of grass and vines and strands of her own hair, then sending the rope to her father with her kite. The illustrations are superb; the detail and color capture the essence of the story; the pictures in continuity from page to page add to the drama of the situation.

> *Barbara H. Gibson, in a review of "The Em-*

peror and the Kite," in School Library Journal, *Vol. 14, No. 3, November, 1967, p. 64.*

Ed Young has illustrated Jane Yolen's delightful story using a Chinese technique. Each picture is cut from a single piece of paper. The effect is one of great delicacy and lightness. The princess's splendid kite flutters across the page and every picture has a fluid look.

> *Pamela Marsh, "Where Taste Begins: The Critical Eye," in* The Christian Science Monitor, *November 2, 1967, p. B3.*

The stark white pages of this Honor Book provide a background which allows the striking hues and mottled outlines to stand out clearly and distinctly. The stylized patterns of robes, grass, vines, leaves, and flowers form bold outlines much like the clear, rigid lines of a woodcut. On pages lacking much illustration, the simple line of the kite string continuing off the page is enough to move the eye across the spread to the action beyond. At times only the small figure of Djeow Seow skillfully balances the stark, empty compositions.

Young concentrates and synthesizes his illustrations down to the bare minimum. There is no superfluous detail, often no background at all; only the events of importance to the theme find expression in the illustrations. This economy reinforces the simple, honest efforts of a heroine who accomplishes a task much larger, literally and symbolically, than her small stature. Just as the black shapes of the evil intruders visually reflect their character, so the innocence of the small, humble child is reflected in this tiny figure juxtaposed with and counterbalancing the enormous shapes of tower, rope, and kite. (p. 339)

> *Linda Kauffman Peterson, "The Caldecott Medal and Honor Books, 1938-1981: 'The Emperor and the Kite'," in* Newbery and Caldecott Medal and Honor Books: An Annotated Bibliography, *by Linda Kauffman Peterson and Marilyn Leathers Solt, G. K. Hall & Co., 1982, pp. 338-39.*

Chinese Mother Goose Rhymes (1968)

[*The poems in* Chinese Mother Goose Rhymes *were selected and edited by Robert Wyndham.*]

Lullabies, nonsense rhymes, game songs and riddles in lilting translation reflect universal childhood concerns and experiences—for example, a toe-counting rhyme: "This little cow eats grass, / This little cow eats hay, / This little cow drinks water, / This little cow runs away, / And *this* little cow does nothing / But lie down all the day." The 10⅝″ × 8¼″ format is designed to be read vertically, like a Chinese scroll bound at the top. Ed Young's paintings charm the eye and resemble the paper-cut illustrations which made **The Emperor and His Kite** a runner-up for the 1968 Caldecott Medal, but are softer in outline, freer in detail, to make a gentle, almost luminous visual accompaniment. Mr. Young has also provided calligraphy for the original verses in striking borders for each page. The art work captures the essence of a foreign culture which might otherwise be overlooked—so polished are the

verses, so certain to delight young American readers or listeners today.

> *Margaret A. Dorsey, in a review of "Chinese Mother Goose Rhymes," in* School Library Journal, *Vol. 15, No. 4, December, 1968, p. 42.*

There's always room for one more collection of Mother Goose, especially if it's as new as this gathering of over 40 traditional rhymes, riddles, lullabies and games which have amused Chinese children since before the time of the emperors. . . .

Pictorially, the book is a visual delight. Ed Young's illustrations, inspired by classic Chinese art, show soaring dragon kites, prancing ponies and pig-tailed children with a master's use of line, color and pattern. Bordering them is Chinese calligraphy for each verse. The oblong format, "designed to be read vertically like an oriental scroll," is an intriguing gimmick, yet makes the book awkward to handle.

> *Margaret F. O'Connell, in a review of "Chinese Mother Goose Rhymes," in* The New York Times Book Review, *December 8, 1968, p. 52.*

The Rooster's Horns: A Chinese Puppet Play to Make and Perform (with Hilary Beckett, 1978)

In an attractive combination picture story and how-to book, readers are told the brief tale of the way rooster was tricked forever out of his beautiful horns and then are shown just how to put the story on as a puppet play. Rich pastel drawings in salmons, oranges, and smudged gray-black lines are substantial and avoid the vacuous look that too often plagues Oriental poster-style art. A second section following the story offers supportive step-by-step directions for making the puppets and developing good performance techniques. The tracing patterns—labeled as such—may still require a cautionary reminder from librarians not to cut them out. Practical and simple.

> *Denise M. Wilms, in a review of "The Rooster's Horns: A Chinese Puppet Play to Make and Perform," in* Booklist, *Vol. 75, No. 6, November 15, 1978, p. 551.*

Young and Beckett combine a play and a project in a book that is handsomely illustrated with drawings in rich but subdued colors. The play, based on an amusing Chinese folktale, tells the story of how Rooster, who long ago had beautiful horns, is tricked into losing them to Dragon, abetted by the wily worm—and that's why worms are afraid of roosters, and why the rooster crows each dawn, calling for his lost horns. The story is followed by instructions for making the puppets and mounting a shadow puppet performance; instructions are clear and sequential, and the final pages have actual-size drawings from which to trace puppet parts.

> *Zena Sutherland, in a review of "The Rooster's Horns: A Chinese Puppet Play to Make and Perform," in* Bulletin of the Center for Chil-

dren's Books, *Vol. 32, No. 9, May, 1979, p. 167.*

The Terrible Nung Gwama: A Chinese Folktale (1978)

A delicate, decorative presentation of a graphic, amusingly indelicate story. First, though, one has to accept the illogic of a poor young woman who, taking some cakes to her "venerable" parents, refuses to give them up to a dread, all-devouring Nung Gwama, despite his warning that he'll eat her later instead, "a painful and also an undignified death." Then, weeping, she stays put (venerable parents notwithstanding) while one after another passerby offers her something to hold off the monster—needles to stick in the door and prick him, manure to dirty his hands, a snake to put in the washing pot (and bite him if he wants to wash his hands), and so on to the seller of millstones who leaves one ("It is very, very heavy") for her to hang over her bed, with the (innocent) thought that she can lure him under it. (How she will hang it unaided we never do know.) All comes to pass as they hope, and with some lively, ear-splitting action—which the pictures interpret as shadowy blobs—the Nung Gwama meets his end, the woman is rewarded for his destruction, and everyone lives "happily ever after." In the hands of a more exuberant artist, this might have been rousing entertainment; here it's venerated into a vaporous never-never land.

> *A review of "The Terrible Nung Gwama: A Chinese Folktale," in* Kirkus Reviews, *Vol. XLVI, No. 23, December 1, 1978, p. 1306.*

In Ed Young's retelling of an old Chinese folktale, a young woman meets the terrible monster The Nung Gwama. She refuses to give it the cakes she is carrying, and it threatens to come back that night and eat her. How she outwits the monster forms the rest of the book. The tale itself is interesting in its telling and has a marvelous Chinese atmosphere. Still, the story is too quickly told and could use more fleshing out. Also, the illustrations could have been more crisply done. All in all, it is not a bad book, but it needed a bit more work.

> *Ruth Hooten, in a review of "The Terrible Nung Gwama: A Chinese Folktale," in* Children's Book Review Service, *Vol. 7, No. 7, February, 1979, p. 66.*

The plot pattern here is a familiar one, last seen in Betsy Bang's *The Little Old Woman and the Rice Thief.* . . . The telling is vigorous and modern, though a slightly coy tone artificializes the drama. Young's illustrations rely on composition for effect: excepting the Nung Gwama, figures are small scale against an expansive earth-toned background, with the young woman's chalk-pink robes offering the focal point for each bordered page.

> *Denise M. Wilms, in a review of "The Terrible Nung Gwama: A Chinese Folktale," in* Booklist, *Vol. 75, No. 12, February 15, 1979, p. 937.*

The Lion and the Mouse: An Aesop Fable (1979)

Aesop's fable of the mighty lion captured, the tiny mouse

to-the-rescue, is here rendered as a phrase by phrase . . . frame by frame . . . opening by opening . . . cliffhanger. Throughout, the action is fragmented ("A mouse / ran / over / the body of / a sleeping lion" takes seven pages); and when the drama escalates, we see only its constituents (when the lion roars, his open mouth; when the mouse begs to be released, the dangling mouse). Children must first compose the whole from the parts, which some find it difficult to do, and then link these assorted fragments one to another—without ever a full sentence or a complete picture. The suspense becomes, in effect, the story—and the moral, archaically phrased ("A change in circumstance can make the strong weak and the weak strong"), appears as an afterthought.

> *A review of "The Lion and the Mouse," in* Kirkus Reviews, *Vol. XLVIII, No. 7, April 1, 1980, p. 434.*

Ed Young can draw. For his version of the Aesop **The Lion and the Mouse** he has a rather good mouse and some first-rate rope for the mouse to gnaw at. But here he is, trying to make 30 pages out of a tale that could easily be told in one, and so Mr. Young strains, invents, distracts himself from lion and mouse with odd angles, lots of blank space, portions of anatomy. It is as though someone asked Mr. Young: "Can you do it?" Yes indeed, he can, but it seems a waste of good talent to try.

> *Roger Sale, in a review of "The Lion and the Mouse," in* The New York Times Book Review, *May 11, 1980, p. 24.*

The familiar fable of the small mouse who rescues his former captor from entrapment is given an elegant, fresh interpretation through a series of meticulously shaded pencil drawings, remarkable for their originality. Framed by a thin red border and set against generous expanses of off-white pages, the sequence of the illustrations suggests the pacing which a storyteller might use to create suspense. The effect is heightened by the perspective presenting, in effect, a mouse's-eye view of the events, an approach which not only captures the imagination but is a logical complement to the theme articulated at the story's end by the vindicated pontificating mouse: "A change in circumstance can make the strong weak and the weak, strong." Because of the size and subtlety of the illustrations, the book could not be successfully presented to a large audience; but it is wonderfully suitable for the individual reader or for a small group.

> *Mary M. Burns, in a review of "The Lion and the Mouse: An Aesop Fable," in* The Horn Book Magazine, *Vol. LVI, No. 3, June, 1980, p. 283.*

High on a Hill: A Book of Chinese Riddles (1980)

Short rhyming verses fashioned into imaginative riddles are repeated in exquisite Chinese characters and pictured in delicate, soft gray pencil sketches, forming together an unusually well designed riddle book. Young, who heard these witticisms as a child in Shanghai, has chosen 27 selections to stimulate and amuse. Subjects are mostly from the animal kingdom—monkey, cat, silkworm, swallow, mouse, firefly—and an especially clever arrangement features the various parts of the human head. Text, art, and bilingual approach ensure that this will be a triply savored experience.

> *Barbara Elleman, in a review of "A Book of Chinese Riddles," in* Booklist, *Vol. 76, No. 20, June 15, 1980, p. 1540.*

A small, subtle, artfully designed book of riddles from the Chinese—mainly describing animals. For example, " 'Twixt two curved tiles he makes his home / I'm sure from there he'll never roam" characterizes a clam. Each riddle is written first in verse; overleaf the riddle appears again in Chinese characters with the answer printed in red in tiny letters. Shadowy illustrations drift across the pages, slowly changing from the animal previously described into the shape of the answer to the next riddle. The red fine-line border on each page adds a further touch of color to the restrained appearance. The riddles will not be easy for some children to grasp, but the book is distinguished for the beauty of its illustrations as well as for the Oriental elegance of its design. (pp. 400-01)

> *Ann A. Flowers, in a review of "High on a Hill: A Book of Chinese Riddles," in* The Horn Book Magazine, *Vol. LVI, No. 4, August, 1980, pp. 400-01.*

Riddles, most of them written in rhyming couplets, have circulated orally in all parts of China from generation to generation and from time immemorial. But it was only in the 1920s after the language reform movement that the rich repertoire of folk songs, stories, rhymes, riddles and tongue-twisters in the everyday language of the people began to be systematically collected and written down. Ed Young, with the help of his family, has made an intriguing collection of riddles, all about insects and animals except for the last few involving parts of the human physiognomy, and has drawn pictorial answers for each one. Some of the English is a little contrived but the succinctness of the original Chinese always causes problems. The riddle in translation appears first, with the Chinese text in characters and picture answer appearing as the page is turned. The soft-toned pencil drawings are admirably suited to the good quality white paper of the book, each page being framed with a fine vermillion line. The layout, design, printing and binding have a rare unity and the whole makes a most attractive book.

> *Dorothea Scott, in a review of "High on a Hill: A Book of Chinese Riddles," in* School Library Journal, *Vol. 26, No. 10, August, 1980, p. 59.*

Yeh-Shen: A Cinderella Story from China   (1982)

[Yeh-Shen: A Cinderella Story from China *was retold by Ai-Ling Louie.*]

Here may well be the original of the story we know as "Cinderella" (or "The Juniper Tree"). All of the essentials are already in place: the wicked stepmother, jealous stepsister, helping hand from a magical source, slipper dropped in flight and marriage to the king as a happy result. There are differences in detail: It is a fish, befriended by the heroine, who transforms her dress so that she, too, can go to the festival; the symbolic slipper is golden, and there is more of an emphasis on its smallness and on the tiny feet of Yeh-Shen. Despite these details and the authenticity of the regional costumes, the illustrations, by focusing on the characters and eschewing exotic scenery or interiors, remind us that the tale belongs to the realm of the universal rather than of the particular. Ed Young's luminous pastels and watercolors shimmer against the white background. The layout is unusual: each spread is divided into four screenlike panels by narrow red borders, within which the type is confined. Some of the illustrations are placed within the panels too, but often they flow across the page diagonally, interrupted, but not broken up by, the screenlike layout. It is not so much Ed Young's style as his treatment of the page space, forcing the eye towards the corners and away from the center, that seems Oriental. Through all the illustrations, subtle enough to be apparent only in subsequent readings, swims the unobtrusive motif of the ancillary fish, the curves of whose body define most of the picture areas. A note on the provenance of the story adds to the interest of the book. Every library will be enriched by it.

> *Patricia Dooley, in a review of "Yeh-Shen: A Cinderella Story from China," in* School Library Journal, *Vol. 29, No. 4, December, 1982, p. 57.*

The story is interesting as a folklore variant, but it's also smoothly and simply retold, and the illustrations are stunning: the artist's use of space and mass in composition is restrained and effective, the lines are soft, the colors melting, often trailing off across the page with faintly-seen details of design that echo the stronger use of design at the focus of the painting.

> *Zena Sutherland, in a review of "Yeh-Shen: A Cinderella Story from China," in* Bulletin of the Center for Children's Books, *Vol. 36, No. 7, March, 1983, p. 129.*

The reteller has cast the tale in well-cadenced prose, fleshing out the spare account with elegance and grace. In a manner reminiscent of Chinese scrolls and of decorated folding screens, the text is chiefly set within vertical panels, while the luminescent illustrations—less narrative than emotional—often increase their impact by overspreading the narrow framework or appearing on pages of their own. In the Chinese tale a magical fish assumes the function of the fairy in the familiar version; and in many of the pictures the fish subtly serves as both background and unifying symbol. Preceding the artist's work was undoubtedly a crystallization of a total concept, which has been executed with chromatic splendor—a unique combination of brilliance and restraint. (pp. 160-61)

> *Ethel L. Heins, in a review of "Yeh-Shen: A Cinderella Story from China," in* The Horn Book Magazine, *Vol. LIX, No. 2, April, 1983, pp. 160-61.*

The luminous paintings glow across pages arranged to evoke an old Chinese book, although Ed Young's style in pastels and watercolor is richer than it is spare. The text is based on a Ch'ing edition of an encyclopedic work that retains the T'ang story by Tuan Ch'eng-Shih, more than 1,000 years old; two printed pages of the Chinese text are reproduced. Cinderella is found first written down in Europe in an Italian tale of the 17th century. The sense of the storyteller's unity across the world is strong here, in a very attractive book delightful on its own terms, even if you had never heard of Cinderella.

> *Philip Morrison and Phylis Morrison, in a review of "Yeh-Shen: A Cinderella Story from China," in* Scientific American, *Vol. 249, No. 6, December, 1983, p. 46.*

Up a Tree   (1983)

A wordless picture book of the original, action-narrative sort—like *What Whiskers Did* or *A Boy, a Dog and a Frog*—except that, instead of a sequence of actions, there's just a single, lame incident. A cat, chasing a butterfly, starts up a tree and gets stuck; by the time some (Asian) Indians come with a ladder, it's reached a branch and won't come down (when the cat bristles, the lead Indian falls off the ladder); but the sight of a man carrying fish brings it down pronto. The cat is somewhat caricatured, making this less than ideal even for cat-lovers. A negligible idea occupying a very few pages—to be no sooner seen than forgotten.

> *A review of "Up a Tree," in* Kirkus Reviews, *Vol. LI, No. 3, February 1, 1983, p. 119.*

This wordless book features attractive and intriguing pencil illustrations set in narrow red frames—often two or three illustrations in a series to a page. The frame may become part of the scene, as when the cat hangs from it. Subtle details in the illustrations make this book more suitable to art-loving adults rather than children, who may not understand the action. On one page, we see the barking dog only as it is reflected in the cat's two eyes. It is only when people arrive to help the cat that we learn (from their clothing) that this story is set in the Middle East. This is an interesting addition to wordless picture book collections.

> *Margaret Montgomery, in a review of "Up a Tree," in* School Library Journal, *Vol. 29, No. 9, May, 1983, p. 68.*

Exceptionally fine illustrations give substance to a wordless book about the plight of a cat caught in a tree. Starting on the title page with the whimsical transformation of the form of a butterfly into the face of a cat, we then see the little animal chasing the butterfly up a tree trunk, the cat's astonished indignation at being stuck, the complications caused by a barking dog, and the useless attempt at rescue by a man with a ladder. Only the thought of fish for dinner brings the cat down, and it insouciantly trots off. Fine red lines frame most of the drawings, setting off the soft gray-and-white illustrations of the cat and of the helpful bystanders. An elegantly designed book, superb in its depiction of feline expressions, both fierce and wistful. (pp. 296-97)

> *Ann A. Flowers, in a review of "Up a Tree," in* The Horn Book Magazine, *Vol. LIX, No. 3, June, 1983, pp. 296-97.*

The Other Bone   (1984)

Still another wordless, essentially vacuous incident—as a dog dreams of a bone, wakes to find itself boneless, rummages for one in a garbage can, makes off with it . . . and, looking at its reflection in a pool (you can guess what's coming), drops the bone it has to seize the reflected one. Does it get back its own bone? Young stretches that out, like everything else (or there'd be no book), but the answer is no—although some children may be puzzled by the last-page sight of the bone, resting by what is presumably meant to be seaweed. Hardly worth a single skip-through, the dog's exaggerated antics notwithstanding. (Rendered in Young's usual velvety shadings, they look incongruous, and more-than-necessarily absurd.)

> *A review of "The Other Bone," in* Kirkus Service, *Vol. LII, Nos. 1-5, March 1, 1984, pp. J12.*

Muted gray tones portray the adventures of a beguiling hound and his short-lived ownership of a large, promising bone. With restrained humor the artist captures the dog's anticipation, pride, bewilderment, and disappointment as he first sniffs out the bone and then loses it in a pond when he snaps at a second one he sees clamped in his reflected jaws. Although the book is wordless, small children should be able to follow the simple story line, empathizing with the animal's loss through his own foolishness and greed—a situation not uncommon at any age—and rejoicing in the jaunty personality of the dog. Surrounding each of the pictures is a fine green line, which becomes doubly effective when the drawing strays over its boundary; for example, an illustration splendidly captures the dog's boisterous head-to-tail shaking, which sends drops flying beyond the picture's tidy green frame. (pp. 191-92)

> *Ethel R. Twichell, in a review of "The Other Bone," in* The Horn Book Magazine, *Vol. LX, No. 2, April, 1984, pp. 191-92.*

Simple pencil drawings (nicely framed with thin green line) clearly tell the action-filled story with fluid grace. Emotional content is expressed through the dog's eyes: a cocky sideways glance after stealing the bone from a garbage can, "what's *this*?" to the reflected image in the pool, and a look of utter pathos, bewilderment, and desolation after losing the bone to the depths. (pp. 197-98)

> *Zena Sutherland, in a review of "The Other Bone," in* Bulletin of the Center for Children's Books, *Vol. 37, No. 10, June, 1984, pp. 197-98.*

Birches   (1988)

[Birches *was written by Robert Frost.*]

Frost's spare phrases conjure up vividly concrete mental pictures which are not reflected in Young's lovely, but often abstracted and incongruent, watercolors. In double-

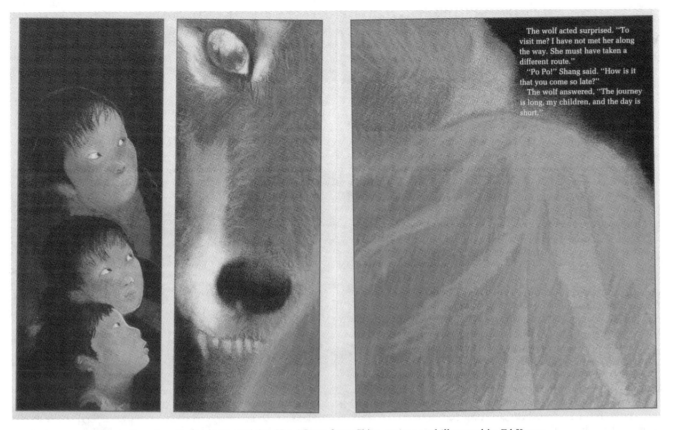

From Lon Po Po: A Red-Riding Hood Story from China, *written and illustrated by Ed Young.*

page spreads above the cream band that contains the few lines of text per page, Young's flowing atmospheric washes catch the New England landscape in all seasons and moods, but neither their sweeps and splotches nor their impressionistic shapes that blur into precision get across that crucial central image of the bend of those trees toward earth. Their perspective is sophisticated and does convey something of the climb and descent imagery, but as a whole, the paintings provide a musical background rather than illumination of the poem. A literal interpretation isn't necessary, or perhaps even desirable, but there should be some congruence between art and text; and these softly frenzied abstractions tend to be disconcerting and dissonant. The full-color (but with an autumnal cast) pictures stand back; while adults may appreciate the non-interference with the text, children will find it distancing. The complete poem is reprinted at the end of the book, offering an intriguing contrast to seeing it page by page and illustrated. *A Swinger of Birches* (Stemmer House, 1982), a collection of 38 Frost poems for young people, illustrated by Peter Koeppen, is much less dramatic artistically, but a better straightforward introduction to the poetry. Susan Jeffers' illustrations for the picture book edition of "Stopping by Woods on a Snowy Evening" (Dutton, 1978) offer a better example of expansion of the text without contradiction or confusion.

> *Nancy Palmer, in a review of "Birches," in* School Library Journal, *Vol. 35, No. 2, October, 1988, p. 152.*

"Birches" is not as easily accessible a poem for young readers, but it contains an ample supply of powerful images and provocative questions, anchored by Frost's rich and distinctive voice. Rather than attempt a literal interpretation of the poem, Young traveled through the poet's New England countryside and captured its simple elegance and darker mysteries. We are presented with a walk through the autumn and winter woods as Frost's poem slowly unfolds. A well-deserved B-plus for this one.

> *Steven Ratiner, "Poetry Report Card: Grades from A to C," in* The Christian Science Monitor, *November 4, 1988, p. B7.*

Illustrating poetry can be a highly contentious artistic enterprise. Narrative verse by its very nature lends itself perfectly to the picture book form; but the reader's imagination may be constrained when the haunting ambiguity of a brief lyric poem, like "Stopping by Woods on a Snowy Evening," is subjected to explicit pictorial representation. The artist has not illustrated "Birches" with literal images. Just as a composer or a choreographer can be inspired by a work of literature, Ed Young has made elegant, graceful paintings that are subtly analogous to the text. Descriptive and reflective, the poem speaks of the natural beauty of the birch tree and of the exuberant young "swinger of birches"—and ultimately of the poet's own heavenly aspirations while contentedly remaining earthbound. "I'd like to get away from earth awhile / And then come back to it and begin over . . . I'd like to go by climbing a birch tree, / And climb black branches up a snow-white trunk / *Toward* heaven, till the tree could bear no more, / But dipped its top and set me down again." Ed Young has never stereotyped his art; he is utterly versatile, meeting the challenge of each text with imaginative vision and consummate skill. Visually suggesting, rather than interpreting, the moods and nuances of meaning in the lines of poetry, the beautifully composed illustrations, with their muted seasonal colors and arresting, almost impressionistic variations in pattern and design, neither overwhelm nor attempt to explicate the superbly stated text; in their own way the paintings parallel the poetic experience. (pp. 85-6)

Ethel L. Heins, in a review of "Birches," in The Horn Book Magazine, *Vol. LXV, No. 1, January-February, 1989, pp. 85-6.*

Lon Po Po: A Red-Riding Hood Story from China (1989)

As he did in A-Ling Louie's **Yeh Shen: A Cinderella Story from China,** Young illustrates an intriguing Asian variant of a favorite folktale, in this case one in which a young girl saves herself and her sisters instead of waiting around in the wolf's stomach for rescue by a hunter. Said to be more than a thousand years old, "Lon Po Po" is definitely the most liberated version of Little Red Riding Hood, including an early French version in which LRRH manages to save herself but not to dispense with the wolf. Here, three girls have been tricked into opening the door for a wolf disguised as their grandmother. When the oldest realizes the truth ("Po Po, Po Po, your hand has thorns on it"), she convinces him to try the nuts of the ginko tree, after she and her sisters have climbed safely, by letting them haul him up in a basket. Once, twice, three times they drop the basket ("I am so small and weak, Po Po, I could not hold the rope alone"), bumping the wolf's head and breaking "his heart to pieces." The wolf makes an eerie appearance in Young's art, with white staring eyes, a long sinister muzzle, and shadowy textured fur. Rendered in watercolor and pastel, impressionistic images in each panel offer the kind of illustrative suggestion best suited to symbols from oral narrative. A must for folklore and storytelling collections.

Betsy Hearne, in a review of "Lon Po Po: A Red-Riding Hood Story from China," in Bulletin of the Center for Children's Books, *Vol. 43, No. 3, November, 1989, p. 74.*

Not for the faint-hearted, **Lon Po Po** (Grandmother Wolf), is a tale of menacing danger and courage. The similarities to Red Riding Hood are many: a visit to grandmother, a mother's warning disregarded, a villainous wolf who dresses as Granny, a series of questions the heroine poses to the wolf, and, of course, a happy ending. On the other hand, there is no woodcutter conveniently strolling by the door. In this version, the children must rely on their wits to save themselves. They triumph, yet even after the wolf's death, a threatening aura of evil remains.

The sense of foreboding arises from the illustrations more than the text. Dark, lupine shapes are subtly woven through every piece of artwork. The opening scene that

shows mother waving goodbye as her children stand at the cabin door is portrayed against a brooding backdrop that is recognizably the elongated head of the wolf. When the frightened children gaze down between the branches at the beast, the angle of the tree trunk and limb form a shadowy but unmistakable wolf's open jaw, jagged teeth at the ready, just as they begin to hope that he is dead. Even the ending holds little triumph or comfort; the last scene is no cozy reunion, but a double-page spread showing their house surrounded and all but engulfed by dim, enigmatic forms—the inscrutable forces of nature and our fears—with, again, the wolf's body forming an integral part of the landscape.

Young creates a series of powerful illustrations in pastels and watercolors. Contrasting broad areas of subtly shaded darkness with incandescent candle- and moon-lit scenes, he underscores the innocence of the children and the malevolence of the wolf. The separation of some of the spreads into three or four vertical panels, as in Chinese screen or panel paintings, recalls the story's roots as well as the artist's own. His command of page composition and his sensitive use of color give the book a visual force that matches the strength of the story and stands as one of the illustrator's best efforts. The dust-jacket illustration, featuring a white-eyed wolf staring over his shoulder against a mottled Chinese red background, foreshadows the emotional power within.

Recalling an Indian prayer to the spirit of a deer before releasing the arrow to kill it, Young dedicates the book "To all the wolves of the world for lending their good name as a tangible symbol for our darkness." The simple blue-and-peach pastel sketch that accompanies this tribute involves the viewer in a Gestalt shift: the bent figure is that of grandmother and wolf. Is Young saying that evil is within us all, or in our perception of the world? In this compelling book, he offers much to ponder.

Carolyn Phelan, " 'Lon Po Po: A Red-Riding Hood Story from China,' by Ed Young," in Booklist, *Vol. 86, No. 6, November 15, 1989, p. 672.*

This compelling tale, translated from a "collection of Chinese folktales," may be the finest book yet from this excellent illustrator—and is certainly among the most beautiful books this year. . . .

Another suspenseful version of this tale appeared in Yep's *The Rainbow People.* Young's graceful translation is both mellower and nobler in tone, while the story is still satisfyingly frightening as the children contend in the dark with the invader. Young's dramatic illustrations, in watercolor and pastel, appear in vertical panels—one or two per page—with some double-spread vistas extending across two or three panels, a device he uses effectively in his wonderfully harmonious designs. The story's terror is both mitigated and enhanced by the artist's suggestive, soft-edged style: there's none of Hollywood's ghoulish precision, but plenty of the mists and shadows where creatures of the imagination thrive—highlighted by the sisters' expressive eyes. A symphony of lovely color progresses from page to page, always related yet fascinating in its variety and contrasts. Even Young's eloquent dedication—"To all the wolves of the world for lending their good name as a tangible symbol for our darkness"—is perfect. Absolutely splendid.

> *A review of "Lon Po Po: A Red-Riding Hood Story from China," in* Kirkus Reviews, *Vol. LVII, No. 22, November 15, 1989, p. 1679.*

A gripping variation on Red Riding Hood. . . . The text possesses that matter-of-fact veracity that characterizes the best fairy tales. The watercolor and pastel pictures are remarkable: mystically beautiful in their depiction of the Chinese countryside, menacing in the exchanges with the wolf, and positively chilling in the scenes inside the house. Overall, this is an outstanding achievement that will be pored over again and again.

> *John Philbrook, in a review of "Lon Po Po: A Red-Riding Hood Story from China," in* School Library Journal, *Vol. 35, No. 16, December, 1989, p. 97.*

By dividing the illustrations into three and sometimes four longitudinal sections, Young has given his fine retelling the look of old Chinese decorative panels. What is in the panels is quite another matter; a wolf, long of tooth and mean intent, inveigles his way into a house by pretending to be the grandmother of three little girls who have been left alone. The power of the wolf's threatening presence bursts out of the narrow panels as a fearsome eye peering through the narrow doorway slit or a huge shadow leaping across the wall. . . . The slightly blurred illustrations are subdued in color but seem to throb with the mystery and terror of the wolf and the round-eyed fright of the children. Although the placement of the text on colored backgrounds is sometimes a disadvantage, the wonderfully fine illustrations more than compensate.

> *Ethel R. Twichell, in a review of "Lon Po Po: A Red-Riding Hood Story From China," in* The Horn Book Magazine, *Vol. LXVI, No. 1, January-February, 1990, p. 79.*

Oscar Wilde's The Happy Prince   (1989)

[Oscar Wilde's The Happy Prince *was written by Oscar Wilde.*]

A lush new edition of Wilde's familiar story of the statue prince who gives his riches to the poor with the help of a little swallow—which is gradually converted from self-importance to love by the prince's generosity. Young has created a series of misty, richly hued double-spreads that capture all the story's dignity and sweetness, though not its underlying irony. Wilde's language itself certainly doesn't require such amplification, and fortunately it is Young's style to suggest rather than to define, leaving the reader's imagination free to extend the story as it will. A very beautiful book.

> *A review of "The Happy Prince," in* Kirkus Reviews, *Vol. LVII, No. 11, June 1, 1989, p. 842.*

Wilde's beautiful fairy tale concerns the prince-statue who sacrifices all he has to help others and the swallow who gives his life for the love of the Happy Prince. Although several illustrated versions of the classic tale are available, Young's impressionistic artwork speaks directly to the heart. Focusing mainly on the statue and swallow rather than on external events, the artist never shies away from the story's essential, exquisite pathos. Reflecting shifting moods in the text, the softly shaded pastels vary from vibrant yellows to dusky blues and greens. Skilled use of light and shadow give the double-page spreads drama and depth. A handsome new edition of Wilde's timeless story.

> *Carolyn Phelan, in a review of "The Happy Prince," in* Booklist, *Vol. 85, No. 20, June 15, 1989, p. 1830.*

Young has created stunning illustrations for Wilde's fairy tale. He uses an impressionistic style which evokes rather than defines the characters. His illustrations are predominantly sweeping two-page spreads with large swathes of color. Cool blues, blacks, and greens for the statue's surroundings provide a strong contrast with the warm yellows and oranges of the Swallow's tales and thoughts of Egypt. Dusky reds are used in the scenes in which the Swallow delivers the Prince's charity to the poor seamstress, playwright, and matchgirl. For all of the visual beauty of this version, however, Wilde's story today seems blatantly sentimental and will appeal primarily to adults wanting to share a warmly remembered story with their children. The depiction of the old Jews in the Ghetto bargaining and weighing money, although merely mentioned in passing, is the kind of stereotype common in Wilde's time but offensive nowadays. As **The Happy Prince** is part of the "Great Books" discussion program, schools using the program may find this a priority purchase but for others, despite its beauty, it is likely to be a shelf sitter.

> *Louise L. Sherman, in a review of "The Happy Prince," in* School Library Journal, *Vol. 35, No. 11, July, 1989, p. 78.*

CUMULATIVE INDEX TO AUTHORS

This index lists all author entries in *Children's Literature Review* and includes cross-references to them in other Gale sources. References in the index are identified as follows:

AAYA: *Authors & Artists for Young Adults* Volumes 1-7
CA: *Contemporary Authors* (original series), Volumes 1-135
CAAS: *Contemporary Authors Autobiography Series,* Volumes 1-14
CABS: *Contemporary Authors Bibliographical Series,* Volumes 1-3
CANR: *Contemporary Authors New Revision Series,* Volumes 1-35
CAP: *Contemporary Authors Permanent Series,* Volumes 1-2
CA-R: *Contemporary Authors* (first revision), Volumes 1-44
CDALB: *Concise Dictionary of American Literary Biography,* Volumes 1-6
CLC: *Contemporary Literary Criticism,* Volumes 1-69
CLR: *Children's Literature Review,* Volumes 1-27
CMLC: *Classical and Medieval Literature Criticism,* Volumes 1-8
DC: *Drama Criticism,* Volumes 1-2
DLB: *Dictionary of Literary Biography,* Volumes 1-112
DLB-DS: *Dictionary of Literary Biography Documentary Series,* Volumes 1-9
DLB-Y: *Dictionary of Literary Biography Yearbook,* Volumes 1980-1990
LC: *Literature Criticism from 1400 to 1800,* Volumes 1-18
NCLC: *Nineteenth-Century Literature Criticism,* Volumes 1-34
PC: *Poetry Criticism,* Volumes 1-3
SAAS: *Something about the Author Autobiography Series,* Volumes 1-13
SATA: *Something about the Author,* Volumes 1-66
SSC: *Short Story Criticism,* Volumes 1-9
TCLC: *Twentieth-Century Literary Criticism,* Volumes 1-44
YABC: *Yesterday's Authors of Books for Children,* Volumes 1-2

Aardema (Vugteveen), Verna (Norberg)
1911- 17
See Vugteveen, Verna Aardema
See also SATA 4

Achebe (Albert) Chinua(lumagu) 1930-.... 20
See also CANR 6; CA 1-4R; SATA 38, 40

Adams, Richard 1930- 20
See also CANR 3; CA 49-52; SATA 7

Adkins, Jan 1944-..................... 7
See also CA 33-36R; SATA 8

Adler, Irving 1913-.................... 27
See also CANR 2; CA 7-8R; SATA 1, 29

Adoff, Arnold 1935- 7
See also CANR 20; CA 41-44R; SATA 5

Aesop 620(?)-564(?)BC 14

Ahlberg, Allan 1938- 18
See also CA 111, 114; SATA 35

Ahlberg, Janet 1944- 18
See also CA 111, 114; SATA 32

Aiken, Joan (Delano) 1924-........... 1, 19
See also CANR 4, 23; CA 9-12R; SAAS 1;
SATA 2, 30; AAYA 1

Alcock, Vivien 1924- 26
See also CA 110; SATA 38, 45

Alcott, Louisa May 1832-1888 1
See also YABC 1; DLB 1, 42;
CDALB 1865-1917

Alexander, Lloyd (Chudley) 1924- 1, 5
See also CANR 1, 24; CA 1-4R; SATA 3,
49; DLB 52

Aliki (Liacouras Brandenberg) 1929-......9
See Brandenberg, Aliki (Liacouras)

Andersen, Hans Christian 1805-1875 6
See also YABC 1

Anglund, Joan Walsh 1926-............. 1
See also CANR 15; CA 5-8R; SATA 2

Anno, Mitsumasa 1926-............. 2, 14
See also CANR 4; CA 49-52; SATA 5, 38

Ardizzone, Edward (Jeffrey Irving)
1900-1979 3
See also CANR 8; CA 5-8R;
obituary CA 89-92; SATA 1, 28;
obituary SATA 21

Armstrong, William H(oward) 1914- 1
See also CANR 9; CA 17-20R; SATA 4

Arnosky, Jim 1946- 15
See also CANR 12; CA 69-72; SATA 22

Aruego, Jose 1932-..................... 5
See also CA 37-40R; SATA 6

Ashley, Bernard 1935-.................. 4
See also CANR 25; CA 93-96; SATA 39, 47

Asimov, Isaac 1920-................... 12
See also CANR 2, 19; CA 1-4R; SATA 1,
26; DLB 8

Atwater, Florence (Hasseltine Carroll)
19??-........................... 19
See also SATA 16

Atwater, Richard (Tupper) 1892-1948..... 19
See also CA 111; SATA 7, 54

Avi 1937-............................ 24
See Wortis, Avi
See also CANR 12; CA 69-72; SATA 14

Awdry, W(ilbert) V(ere) 1911-.......... 23

Aylesworth, Thomas G(ibbons) 1927-......6
See also CANR 10; CA 25-28R; SATA 4

Ayme, Marcel 1902-1967............... 25
See also CA 89-92; DLB 72

Babbitt, Natalie 1932-................... 2
See also CANR 2, 19; CA 49-52; SAAS 5;
SATA 6; DLB 52

Bacon, Martha (Sherman) 1917-1981......3
See also CA 85-88; obituary CA 104;
SATA 18; obituary SATA 27

Bang, Garrett 1943-
See Bang, Molly (Garrett)

Author Index

CUMULATIVE INDEX TO NATIONALITIES

Nationality Index

CUMULATIVE INDEX TO TITLES

Big Little Davy (Lenski) **26**:120
Big Ones, Little Ones (Hoban) **13**:104
The Big Orange Splot (Pinkwater) **4**:166
Big Red Barn (Brown) **10**:66
Big Sister Tells Me That I'm Black (Adoff) **7**:33
The Big Six (Ransome) **8**:180
Big Tracks, Little Tracks (Branley) **13**:29
Bigfoot Makes a Movie (Nixon) **24**:138
The Biggest House in the World (Lionni) **7**:132
The Bike Lesson (Aiken) **19**:24
Bilgewater (Gardam) **12**:167
Bill and Pete (de Paola) **4**:61
Bill and Pete Go Down the Nile (dePaola) **24**:98
Bill and Stanley (Oxenbury) **22**:142
Bill Bergson and the White Rose Rescue (Lindgren) **1**:135
Bill Bergson Lives Dangerously (Lindgren) **1**:135
Bill Bergson, Master Detective (Lindgren) **1**:135
A Billion for Boris (Rodgers) **20**:191
Bill's Garage (Spier) **5**:228
Bill's New Frock (Fine) **25**:23
Bill's Service Station (Spier) **5**:228
Billy Goat and His Well-Fed Friends (Hogrogian) **2**:87
Billy's Balloon Ride (Zimnik) **3**:242
Billy's Picture (Rey) **5**:196
Bimwili and the Zimwi: A Tale from Zanzibar (Aardema) **17**:7
Binary Numbers (Watson) **3**:211
Birches (Young) **27**:220
The Bird and the Stars (Showers) **6**:246
The Bird Began to Sing (Field) **21**:77
The Bird Smugglers (Phipson) **5**:184
Birds at Home (Henry) **4**:109
Birds, Frogs, and Moonlight (Cassedy and Suetake) **26**:12
Birds on Your Street (Simon) **9**:208
Birds: Poems (Adoff) **7**:37
Birdsong (Haley) **21**:146
Birk the Berserker (Klein) **21**:164
Birkin (Phipson) **5**:180
Birth of a Forest (Selsam) **1**:160
Birth of an Island (Selsam) **1**:160
Birth of the Firebringer (Pierce) **20**:184
Birth of the Republic (Carter) **22**:22
The Birth of the United States (Asimov) **12**:50
Birthday (Steptoe) **2**:162
The Birthday Door (Merriam) **14**:203
The Birthday Party (Oxenbury) **22**:144
The Birthday Present (Munari) **9**:125
Birthday Presents (Rylant) **15**:174
The Birthday Tree (Fleischman) **20**:63
The Birthday Visitor (Uchida) **6**:257
A Birthday Wish (Emberley) **5**:100
The Birthday Wish (Iwasaki) **18**:154
Birthdays of Freedom: America's Heritage from the Ancient World (Foster) **7**:95
Birthdays of Freedom: From the Fall of Rome to July 4, 1776, Book Two (Foster) **7**:97
The Bishop and the Devil (Serraillier) **2**:136
Bitter Rivals (Pascal) **25**:186
Bizou (Klein) **19**:95
The Black Americans: A History in Their Own Words, 1619-1983 (Meltzer) **13**:145
Black and White (Brown) **10**:52
The Black BC's (Clifton) **5**:53

Black Beauty: His Grooms and Companions. The Autobiography of a Horse (Sewell) **17**:130-47
Black Beauty: His Grooms and Companions. The Uncle Tom's Cabin of the Horse (Sewell) **17**:130-47
The Black Cauldron (Alexander) **1**:11; **5**:18
The Black Death, 1347-1351 (Cohen) **3**:39
Black Dog (Mattingley) **24**:125
Black Folktales (Lester) **2**:112
Black Gold (Henry) **4**:113
Black Hearts in Battersea (Aiken) **1**:2
Black Holes, White Dwarfs, and Superstars (Branley) **13**:43
Black Is Brown Is Tan (Adoff) **7**:32
The Black Island (Hergé) **6**:148
Black Jack (Garfield) **21**:98
Black Jack: Last of the Big Alligators (McClung) **11**:185
The Black Joke (Mowat) **20**:172
Black Magic: A Pictorial History of the Negro in American Entertainment (Meltzer and Hughes) **13**:125; **17**:44
Black Misery (Hughes) **17**:45
The Black Pearl (O'Dell) **1**:145
The Black Pearl and the Ghost; or, One Mystery after Another (Myers) **16**:138
Black Pilgrimage (Feelings) **5**:106
Blackberry Ink: Poems (Merriam) **14**:202
The Blanket (Burningham) **9**:47
Blaze: The Story of a Striped Skunk (McClung) **11**:186
Blewcoat Boy (Garfield) **21**:122
The Blonk from Beneath the Sea (Bendick) **5**:38
Blood (Zim) **2**:225
The Bloodhound Gang in the Case of Princess Tomorrow (Fleischman) **15**:111
The Bloodhound Gang in the Case of the 264-Pound Burglar (Fleischman) **15**:111
The Bloodhound Gang in the Case of the Cackling Ghost (Fleischman) **15**:111
The Bloodhound Gang in the Case of the Flying Clock (Fleischman) **15**:111
The Bloodhound Gang in the Case of the Secret Message (Fleischman) **15**:111
The Bloody Country (Collier and Collier) **3**:44
Blossom Culp and the Sleep of Death (Peck) **15**:165
A Blossom Promise (Byars) **16**:65
The Blossoms and the Green Phantom (Byars) **16**:65
The Blossoms Meet the Vulture Lady (Byars) **16**:64
Blowfish Live in the Sea (Fox) **1**:76
Blubber (Blume) **2**:16
Blue Canyon Horse (Clark) **16**:80
The Blue Day (Guillot) **22**:60
A Blue-Eyed Daisy (Rylant) **15**:170
Blue Fin (Thiele) **27**:204
The Blue Jackal (illus. Brown) **12**:106
Blue Moose (Pinkwater) **4**:163
Blue Mystery (Benary-Isbert) **12**:73
The Blue Sword (McKinley) **10**:123
The Blue Thing (Pinkwater) **4**:166
Blue Trees, Red Sky (Klein) **2**:97
Blueberries for Sal (McCloskey) **7**:205
Blueberry Corners (Lenski) **26**:105
Bluebirds Over Pit Row (Cresswell) **18**:104
Bo the Constrictor That Couldn't (Stren) **5**:231
Boat Book (Gibbons) **8**:95

Bob and Jilly (Schmidt) **22**:221
Bob and Jilly Are Friends (Schmidt) **22**:222
Bob and Jilly in Trouble (Schmidt) **22**:223
The Bodach (Hunter) **25**:78
The Bodies in the Bessledorf Hotel (Naylor) **17**:60
Body Sense/Body Nonsense (Simon) **9**:217
The Body Snatchers (Cohen) **3**:39
Boek zonder woorden (Bruna) **7**:51
Bold John Henebry (Dillon) **26**:25
Bollerbam (Janosch) **26**:74
Bones (Zim) **2**:226
The Bongleweed (Cresswell) **18**:105
Bonhomme and the Huge Beast (Brunhoff) **4**:39
Boo, the Boy Who Didn't Like the Dark (Leaf) **25**:130
Boo, Who Used to Be Scared of the Dark (Leaf) **25**:130
A Book about Names: In Which Custom, Tradition, Law, Myth, History, Folklore, Foolery, Legend, Fashion, Nonsense, Symbol, Taboo Help Explain How We Got Our Names and What They Mean (Meltzer) **13**:146
A Book of Astronauts for You (Branley) **13**:31
A Book of Christmas (Tudor) **13**:201
The Book of Dragons (Nesbit) **3**:162
The Book of Eagles (Sattler) **24**:224
A Book of Flying Saucers for You (Branley) **13**:39
A Book of Goblins (Garner) **20**:108
A Book of Mars for You (Branley) **13**:34
A Book of Moon Rockets for You (Branley) **13**:28
The Book of Nursery and Mother Goose Rhymes (de Angeli) **1**:52
A Book of Outer Space for You (Branley) **13**:37
A Book of Planet Earth for You (Branley) **13**:42
A Book of Planets for You (Branley) **13**:29
A Book of Satellites for You (Branley) **13**:27
A Book of Scary Things (Showers) **6**:247
A Book of Seasons (Provensen and Provensen) **11**:212
A Book of Stars for You (Branley) **13**:33
The Book of the Goat (Scott) **20**:198
A Book of the Milky Way Galaxy for You (Branley) **13**:32
The Book of the Pig (Scott) **20**:199
The Book of Three (Alexander) **1**:12; **5**:18
A Book of Venus for You (Branley) **13**:36
Border Hawk: August Bondi (Alexander) **5**:17
Bored—Nothing to Do! (Spier) **5**:226
Boris (ter Haar) **15**:115
Borka: The Adventures of a Goose with No Feathers (Burningham) **9**:38
Born to Trot (Henry) **4**:111
The Borrowers (Norton) **6**:220
The Borrowers Afield (Norton) **6**:221
The Borrowers Afloat (Norton) **6**:222
The Borrowers Aloft (Norton) **6**:223
The Borrowers Avenged (Norton) **6**:226
Boss Cat (Hunter) **3**:97
Boss of the Pool (Klein) **21**:164
Bostock and Harris: Or, the Night of the Comet (Garfield) **21**:114
Bound for the Rio Grande: The Mexican Struggle, 1845-1850 (Meltzer) **13**:131
Bound Girl of Cobble Hill (Lenski) **26**:104
The Boundary Riders (Phipson) **5**:178

Title Index

Title Index

Title Index

Title Index

Title Index

Title Index

Title Index

Title Index

Title Index

Title Index

Title Index